The
International Critical Commentary
on the Holy Scriptures of the Old and
New Testaments.

UNDER THE PRESENT EDITORSHIP OF

THE REV. ALFRED PLUMMER, M.A., D.D.
Sometime Master of University College, Durham

PLANNED AND FOR YEARS EDITED BY

THE LATE REV. PROFESSOR SAMUEL ROLLES DRIVER, D.D., D.LITT.
THE REV. ALFRED PLUMMER, M.A., D.D.
THE LATE REV. PROFESSOR CHARLES AUGUSTUS BRIGGS, D.D., D.LITT.

THE INTERNATIONAL CRITICAL COMMENTARY

A CRITICAL AND EXEGETICAL COMMENTARY

ON THE

EPISTLE TO THE HEBREWS

BY

JAMES MOFFATT
D.D., D.Litt., Hon. M.A. (Oxon.)

Edinburgh: T. & T. CLARK, 38 George Street

PRINTED IN GREAT BRITAIN BY
MORRISON AND GIBB LIMITED
FOR
T & T. CLARK, EDINBURGH
NEW YORK: CHARLES SCRIBNER'S SONS

FIRST EDITION . . . 1924
LATEST REPRINT . . 1968

TO THE MEMORY OF

THREE SCOTTISH EXPOSITORS OF ΠΡΟΣ ΕΒΡΑΙΟΥΣ :

A. B. BRUCE,

A. B. DAVIDSON,

AND

MARCUS DODS.

PREFACE.

———◆———

IT is ten years since this edition was first drafted. Various interruptions, of war and peace, have prevented me from finishing it till now, and I am bound to acknowledge the courtesy and patience of the editor and the publishers. During the ten years a number of valuable contributions to the subject have appeared. Of these as well as of their predecessors I have endeavoured to take account; if I have not referred to them often, this has been due to no lack of appreciation, but simply because, in order to be concise and readable, I have found it necessary to abstain from offering any catena of opinions in this edition. The one justification for issuing another edition of Πρὸς Ἐβραίους seemed to me to lie in a fresh point of view, expounded in the notes—fresh, that is, in an English edition. I am more convinced than ever that the criticism of this writing cannot hope to make any positive advance except from two negative conclusions. One is, that the identity of the author and of his readers must be left in the mist where they already lay at the beginning of the second century when the guess-work, which is honoured as " tradition," began. The other is, that the situation which called forth this remarkable piece of primitive Christian thought had nothing to do with any movement in contemporary Judaism. The writer of Πρὸς Ἐβραίους knew no Hebrew, and his readers were in no sense Ἐβραῖοι. These may sound paradoxes. I agree with those who think they are axioms. At any rate such is the point of view from which the present edition has been written ; it will explain why, for example, in the Introduction there is so comparatively small space devoted to the stock questions about authorship and date.

One special reason for the delay in issuing the book has been the need of working through the materials supplied for the criticism of the text by von Soden's *Schriften des Neuen Testaments* (1913) and by some subsequent discoveries, and also the need of making a first-hand study of the Wisdom literature of Hellenistic Judaism as well as of Philo. Further, I did not feel justified in annotating Πρὸς Ἐβραίους without reading through the scattered ethical and philosophical tracts and treatises of the general period, like the *De Mundo* and the remains of Teles and Musonius Rufus.

"A commentary," as Dr. Johnson observed, "must arise from the fortuitous discoveries of many men in devious walks of literature." No one can leave the criticism of a work like Πρὸς Ἐβραίους after twelve years spent upon it, without feeling deeply indebted to such writers as Chrysostom, Calvin, Bleek, Riehm, and Riggenbach, who have directly handled it. But I owe much to some eighteenth-century writings, like L. C. Valckenaer's *Scholia* and G. D. Kypke's *Observationes Sacrae*, as well as to other scholars who have lit up special points of interpretation indirectly. Where the critical data had been already gathered in fairly complete form, I have tried to exercise an independent judgment ; also I hope some fresh ground has been broken here and there in ascertaining and illustrating the text of this early Christian masterpiece.

JAMES MOFFATT.

GLASGOW, 15*th February* 1924.

CONTENTS.

INTRODUCTION.

—♦—

§ 1. ORIGIN AND AIM.

(i.)

DURING the last quarter of the first century A.D. a little master-piece of religious thought began to circulate among some of the Christian communities. The earliest trace of it appears towards the end of the century, in a pastoral letter sent by the church of Rome to the church of Corinth. The authorship of this letter is traditionally assigned to a certain Clement, who probably composed it about the last decade of the century. Evidently he knew Πρὸς Ἑβραίους (as we may, for the sake of convenience, call our writing); there are several almost verbal reminiscences (cp. Dr. A. J. Carlyle in *The New Testament in the Apostolic Fathers*, pp. 44 f., where the evidence is sifted). This is beyond dispute, and proves that our writing was known at Rome during the last quarter of the first century. A fair speci-men of the indebtedness of Clement to our epistle may be seen in a passage like the following, where I have underlined the allusions :

36[2-5] ὃς ὢν ἀπαύγασμα τῆς μεγαλωσύνης αὐτοῦ, τοσούτῳ μείζων
ἐστὶν ἀγγέλων, ὅσῳ διαφορώτερον ὄνομα κεκληρονό-
μηκεν· γέγραπται γὰρ οὕτως·

ὁ ποιῶν τοὺς ἀγγέλους αὐτοῦ πνεύματα
καὶ τοὺς λειτουργοὺς αὐτοῦ πυρὸς φλόγα.

ἐπὶ δὲ τῷ υἱῷ αὐτοῦ οὕτως εἶπεν ὁ δεσπότης·

υἱός μου εἶ σύ,
ἐγὼ σήμερον γεγέννηκά σε·

αἴτησαι παρ᾽ ἐμοῦ, καὶ δώσω σοι ἔθνη τὴν κληρονομίαν
σου καὶ τὴν κατάσχεσίν σου τὰ πέρατα τῆς γῆς.
καὶ πάλιν λέγει πρὸς αὐτόν·

κάθου ἐκ δεξιῶν μου,

ἕως ἂν θῶ τοὺς ἐχθρούς σου ὑποπόδιον τῶν ποδῶν σου.

τίνες οὖν οἱ ἐχθροί; οἱ φαῦλοι καὶ ἀντιτασσόμενοι τῷ θελήματι αὐτοῦ.

To this we may add a sentence from what precedes :

36¹ Ἰησοῦν Χριστὸν τὸν ἀρχιερέα τῶν προσφορῶν ἡμῶν, τὸν προστάτην καὶ βοηθὸν τῆς ἀσθενείας ἡμῶν.

2¹⁸ δύναται τοῖς πειραζομένοις βοηθῆσαι. . . . 3¹ κατανοήσατε τὸν ἀπόστολον καὶ ἀρχιερέα τῆς ὁμολογίας ἡμῶν Ἰησοῦν.

The same phrase occurs twice in later doxologies, διὰ τοῦ ἀρχιερέως καὶ προστάτου (τῶν ψυχῶν ἡμῶν, 61³) (ἡμῶν, 64¹) Ἰησοῦ Χριστοῦ. There is no convincing proof that Ignatius or Polykarp used Πρὸς Ἑβραίους, but the so-called Epistle of Barnabas contains some traces of it (e.g. in 4⁹ᶠ· 5⁵·⁶ and 6¹⁷⁻¹⁹). Barnabas is a second-rate interpretation of the OT ceremonial system, partly on allegorical lines, to warn Christians against having anything to do with Judaism ; its motto might be taken from 3⁶ ἵνα μὴ προσρησσώμεθα ὡς προσήλυτοι (v.l. ἐπήλυτοι) τῷ ἐκείνων νόμῳ. In the homily called 2 Clement our writing is freely employed, e.g. in

11⁶ ὥστε, ἀδελφοί μου, μὴ διψυχῶμεν, ἀλλὰ ἐλπίσαντες ὑπομείνωμεν, ἵνα καὶ τὸν μισθὸν κομισώμεθα. πιστὸς γὰρ ἐστιν ὁ ἐπαγγειλάμενος τὰς ἀντιμισθίας ἀποδιδόναι ἑκάστῳ ἔργων αὐτοῦ.

1⁶ ἀποθέμενοι ἐκεῖνο ὃ περικείμεθα νέφος τῇ αὐτοῦ θελήσει.

16⁴ προσευχὴ δὲ ἐκ καλῆς συνειδήσεως.

10²³ κατέχωμεν τὴν ὁμολογίαν τῆς ἐλπίδος ἀκλινῆ, πιστὸς γὰρ ὁ ἐπαγγειλάμενος.

12¹ τοσοῦτον ἔχοντες περικείμενον ἡμῖν νέφος μαρτύρων, ὄγκον ἀποθέμενοι πάντα.

13¹⁸ προσεύχεσθε περὶ ἡμῶν· πειθόμεθα γὰρ ὅτι καλὴν συνείδησιν ἔχομεν.

"It seems difficult, in view of the verbal coincidences, to resist the conclusion that the language of 2 Clement is unconsciously influenced by that of Hebrews" (Dr. A. J. Carlyle in *The New Testament in the Apostolic Fathers*, p. 126). As 2 Clement is, in all likelihood, a product either of the Roman or of the Alexandrian church, where Πρὸς Ἑβραίους was early appreciated, this becomes doubly probable.

There is no reason why Justin Martyr, who had lived at Rome, should not have known it ; but the evidence for his use of it (see on 3¹ 11⁴ etc.) is barely beyond dispute. Hermas, however, knew it ; the *Shepherd* shows repeated traces of it (cf. Zahn's edition, pp. 439 f.). It was read in the North African church, as Tertullian's allusion proves (see p. xvii), and with particular interest in the Alexandrian church, even before Clement wrote (cp. p. xviii). Clement's use of it is unmistakable, though he does not show any sympathy with its ideas about sacrifice.[1] Naturally a thinker like Marcion ignored it, though why it shared with First Peter the fate of exclusion from the Muratorian canon is inexplicable. However, the evidence of the second century upon the whole is sufficient to show that it was being widely circulated and appreciated as an edifying religious treatise, canonical or not.

(ii.)

By this time it had received the title of Πρὸς Ἑβραίους. Whatever doubts there were about the authorship, the writing never went under any title except this in the later church; which proves that, though not original, the title must be early. Ἑβραῖοι[2] was intended to mean Jewish Christians. Those who affixed this title had no idea of its original destination; otherwise they would have chosen a local term, for the writing is obviously intended for a special community. They were struck by the interest of the writing in the OT sacrifices and priests, however, and imagined in a superficial way that it must have been addressed to Jewish Christians. Ἑβραῖοι was still an archaic equivalent for Ἰουδαῖοι; and those who called our writing Πρὸς Ἑβραίους must have imagined that it had been originally meant for Jewish (*i.e.* Hebrew-speaking) Christians in Palestine, or, in a broader sense, for Christians who had been born in Judaism. The latter is more probable. Where the title originated we cannot say; the corresponding description of 1 Peter as *ad gentes* originated in the Western church, but Πρὸς Ἑβραίους is common both to the Western and the Eastern churches. The very fact that so vague and misleading a title was added, proves that by the second century all traces of the original destination of the writing had been lost. It is, like the *Ad Familiares* of Cicero's correspondence, one of the erroneous titles in ancient literature, "hardly more than a reflection of the impression produced on an early copyist" (W. Robertson Smith). The reason why the original destination had been lost sight of, was probably the fact that it was a small household church—not one of the great churches, but a more limited circle, which may have become merged in the larger local church as time went on. Had it been sent, for example, to any large church like that at Rome or Alexandria, there would have been neither the need

[1] Cp. R. B. Tollington's *Clement of Alexandria*, vol. ii. pp. 225 f.

[2] It is quite impossible to regard it as original, in an allegorical sense, as though the writer, like Philo, regarded ὁ Ἑβραῖος as the typical believer who, a second Abraham, migrated or crossed from the sensuous to the spiritual world. The writer never alludes to Abraham in this connexion; indeed he never uses Ἑβραῖος at all.

nor the opportunity for changing the title to Πρὸς Ἑβραίους. Our writing is not a manifesto to Jewish Christians in general, or to Palestinian Jewish Christians, as πρὸς Ἑβραίους would imply; indeed it is not addressed to Jewish Christians at all. Whoever were its original readers, they belonged to a definite, local group or circle. That is the first inference from the writing itself; the second is, that they were not specifically Jewish Christians. The canonical title has had an unfortunate influence upon the interpretation of the writing (an influence which is still felt in some quarters). It has been responsible for the idea, expressed in a variety of forms, that the writer is addressing Jewish Christians in Palestine or elsewhere who were tempted, *e.g.*, by the war of A.D. 66–70, to fall back into Judaism; and even those who cannot share this view sometimes regard the readers as swayed by some hereditary associations with their old faith, tempted by the fascinations of a ritual, outward system of religion, to give up the spiritual messianism of the church. All such interpretations are beside the point. The writer never mentions Jews or Christians. He views his readers without any distinction of this kind; to him they are in danger of relapsing, but there is not a suggestion that the relapse is into Judaism, or that he is trying to wean them from a preoccupation with Jewish religion. He never refers to the temple, any more than to circumcision. It is the tabernacle of the pentateuch which interests him, and all his knowledge of the Jewish ritual is gained from the LXX and later tradition. The LXX is for him and his readers the codex of their religion, the appeal to which was cogent, for Gentile Christians, in the early church. As Christians, his readers accepted the LXX as their bible. It was superfluous to argue for it; he could argue from it, as Paul had done, as a writer like Clement of Rome did afterwards. How much the LXX meant to Gentile Christians, may be seen in the case of a man like Tatian, for example, who explicitly declares that he owed to reading of the OT his conversion to Christianity (*Ad Graecos*, 29). It is true that our author, in arguing that Christ had to suffer, does not appeal to the LXX. But this is an idiosyncrasy, which does not affect the vital significance of the LXX prophecies. The Christians to whom he was writing had learned to appreciate their LXX as an authority, by their membership in the church. Their danger was not an undervaluing of the LXX as authoritative; it was a moral and mental danger, which the writer seeks to meet by showing how great their religion was intrinsically. This he could only do ultimately by assuming that they admitted the appeal to their bible, just as they admitted the divine Sonship of Jesus. There may have been Christians of Jewish birth among his readers; but he addresses his circle, irrespective of their origin, as all members of the People of God, who accept the Book of God. The writing, in short, might have been called *ad gentes* as aptly as First Peter, which also describes Gentile Christians as ὁ λαός, the People (cp. on 2¹⁷). The readers were not in doubt of their religion. Its basis was unquestioned. What the trouble was, in their case, was no theoretical doubt about the codex or the contents of Christianity, but a practical failure to be loyal to their principles, which the writer seeks to meet by recalling them to the full meaning and responsibility of their faith; naturally he takes them to the common ground of the sacred LXX.

We touch here the question of the writer's aim. But, before discussing this, a word must be said about the authorship.

Had Πρὸς Ἑβραίους been addressed to Jews, the title would have been intelligible. Not only was there a [συνα]γωγὴ Ἑβρ[αίων] at Corinth (cp. Deissmann's *Light from the East*, pp. 13, 14), but a συναγωγὴ Αἰβρέων at Rome (cp. Schürer's *Geschichte des Jüd. Volkes*³, iii. 46). Among the Jewish συναγωγαί mentioned in the Roman epitaphs (cp. N. Müller's *Die jüdische Katakombe am Monteverde zu Rom* . . ., Leipzig, 1912, pp. 110 f.), there is one of Ἑβρέοι, which Müller explains as in contrast to the synagogue of "vernaclorum" (Βερνάκλοι, βερνακλήσιοι), *i.e.* resident Jews as opposed to immigrants; though it seems truer, with E. Bormann (*Wiener Studien*, 1912, pp. 383 f.), to think of some Kultgemeinde which adhered to the use of Hebrew, or which, at any rate, was of Palestinian origin or connexion.

(iii.)

The knowledge of who the author was must have disappeared as soon as the knowledge of what the church was, for whom he wrote. Who wrote Πρὸς Ἑβραίους? We know as little of this as we do of the authorship of *The Whole Duty of Man*, that seventeenth-century classic of English piety. Conjectures sprang up, early in the second century, but by that time men were no wiser than we are. The mere fact that some said Barnabas, some Paul, proves that the writing had been circulating among the *adespota*. It was perhaps natural that our writing should be assigned to Barnabas, who, as a Levite, might be supposed to take a special interest in the ritual of the temple— the very reason which led to his association with the later Epistle of Barnabas. Also, he was called υἱὸς παρακλήσεως (Ac 4³⁶), which seemed to tally with He 13²² (τοῦ λόγου τῆς παρακλήσεως), just as the allusion to "beloved" in Ps 127² (= 2 S 12²⁴ᶠ·) was made to justify the attribution of the psalm to king Solomon. The difficulty about applying 2³ to a man like Barnabas was overlooked, and in North Africa, at any rate, the (Roman?) tradition of his authorship prevailed, as Tertullian's words in *de pudicitia* 20 show: "volo ex redundantia alicuius etiam comitis apostolorum testimonium superinducere, idoneum

b

confirmandi de proximo jure disciplinam magistrorum. Extat
enim et Barnabae titulus ad Hebraeos, adeo satis auctoritati
viri, ut quem Paulus juxta se constituerit in abstinentiae tenore :
'aut ego solus et Barnabas non habemus hoc operandi potestatem ?' (1 Co 9⁶). Et utique receptior apud ecclesias epistola
Barnabae illo apocrypho Pastore moechorum. Monens itaque
discipulos, omissis omnibus initiis, ad perfectionem magis tendere,"
etc. (quoting He 6⁴ᶠ·). What appeals to Tertullian in Πρὸς
Ἑβραίους is its uncompromising denial of any second repentance.
His increasing sympathy with the Montanists had led him to
take a much less favourable view of the *Shepherd* of Hermas
than he had once entertained ; he now contrasts its lax tone
with the rigour of Πρὸς Ἑβραίους, and seeks to buttress his
argument on this point by insisting as much as he can on the
authority of Πρὸς Ἑβραίους as a production of the apostolic
Barnabas.   Where this tradition originated we cannot tell.
Tertullian refers to it as a fact, not as an oral tradition ; he
may have known some MS of the writing with the title Βαρνάβα
πρὸς Ἑβραίους (ἐπιστολή), and this may have come from Montanist
circles in Asia Minor, as Zahn suggests.   But all this is guessing
in the dark about a guess in the dark.

Since Paul was the most considerable letter-writer of the
primitive church, it was natural that in some quarters this
anonymous writing should be assigned to him, as was done
apparently in the Alexandrian church, although even there
scholarly readers felt qualms at an early period, and endeavoured
to explain the idiosyncrasies of style by supposing that some
disciple of Paul, like Luke, translated it from Hebrew into
Greek. This Alexandrian tradition of Paul's authorship was
evidently criticized in other quarters, and the controversy drew
from Origen the one piece of enlightened literary criticism which
the early discussions produced. Ὅτι ὁ χαρακτὴρ τῆς λέξεως τῆς
πρὸς Ἑβραίους ἐπιγεγραμμένης ἐπιστολῆς οὐκ ἔχει τὸ ἐν λόγῳ
ἰδιωτικὸν τοῦ ἀποστόλου, ὁμολογήσαντος ἑαυτὸν ἰδιώτην εἶναι τῷ
λόγῳ (2 Co 11⁶), τουτέστι τῇ φράσει, ἀλλὰ ἐστὶν ἡ ἐπιστολὴ
συνθέσει τῆς λέξεως Ἑλληνικωτέρα, πᾶς ὁ ἐπιστάμενος κρίνειν
φράσεων διαφορὰς ὁμολογήσαι ἄν. πάλιν τε αὖ ὅτι τὰ νοήματα
τῆς ἐπιστολῆς θαυμάσιά ἐστι, καὶ οὐ δεύτερα τῶν ἀποστολικῶν
ὁμολογουμένων γραμμάτων, καὶ τοῦτο ἂν συμφήσαι εἶναι ἀληθὲς πᾶς
ὁ προσέχων τῇ ἀναγνώσει τῇ ἀποστολικῇ. . . . Ἐγὼ δὲ ἀποφαινό-
μενος εἴποιμ' ἂν ὅτι τὰ μὲν νοήματα τοῦ ἀποστόλου ἐστίν, ἡ δὲ
φράσις καὶ ἡ σύνθεσις ἀπομνημονεύσαντός τινος τὰ ἀποστολικά, καὶ
ὡσπερεὶ σχολιογραφήσαντός τινος τὰ εἰρημένα ὑπὸ τοῦ διδασκάλου.
εἴ τις οὖν ἐκκλησία ἔχει ταύτην τὴν ἐπιστολὴν ὡς Παύλου, αὐτη
εὐδοκιμείτω καὶ ἐπὶ τούτῳ. οὐ γὰρ εἰκῇ οἱ ἀρχαῖοι ἄνδρες ὡς Παύλου
αὐτὴν παραδεδώκασι. τίς δὲ ὁ γράψας τὴν ἐπιστολὴν, τὸ μὲν ἀληθὲς

θεὸς οἶδεν (quoted by Eusebius, *H.E.* vi. 25. 11–14).[1] Origen is too good a scholar to notice the guess that it was a translation from Hebrew, but he adds, ἡ δὲ εἰς ἡμᾶς φθάσασα ἱστορία, ὑπό τινων μὲν λεγόντων, ὅτι Κλήμης ὁ γενόμενος ἐπίσκοπος Ῥωμαίων ἔγραψε τὴν ἐπιστολήν, ὑπό τινων δὲ ὅτι Λουκᾶς ὁ γράψας τὸ εὐαγγέλιον καὶ τὰς Πράξεις. The idea that Clement of Rome wrote it was, of course, an erroneous deduction from the echoes of it in his pages, almost as unfounded as the notion that Luke wrote it, either independently or as an amanuensis of Paul—a view probably due ultimately to the explanation of how his gospel came to be an apostolic, canonical work. Origen yields more to the "Pauline" interpretation of Πρὸς Ἑβραίους than is legitimate; but, like Erasmus at a later day,[2] he was living in an environment where the "Pauline" tradition was almost a note of orthodoxy. Even his slight scruples failed to keep the question open. In the Eastern church, any hesitation soon passed away, and the scholarly scruples of men like Clement of Alexandria and Origen made no impression on the church at large. It is significant, for example, that when even Eusebius comes to give his own opinion (*H.E.* iii. 38. 2), he alters the hypothesis about Clement of Rome, and makes him merely the translator of a Pauline Hebrew original, not the author of a Greek original. As a rule, however, Πρὸς Ἑβραίους was accepted as fully Pauline, and passed into the NT canon of the Asiatic, the Egyptian, and the Syriac churches without question. In the Syriac canon of A.D. 400 (text as in Souter's *Text and Canon of NT,* p. 226), indeed, it stands next to Romans in the list of Paul's epistles (see below, § 4). Euthalius, it is true, about the middle of the fifth century, argues for it in a way that indicates a current of opposition still flowing in certain quarters, but ecclesiastically Πρὸς Ἑβραίους in the East as a Pauline document could defy doubts. The firm conviction of the Eastern church as a whole comes out in a remark like that of Apollinarius the bishop of Laodicea, towards the close of the fourth century: ποῦ γέγραπται ὅτι χαρακτήρ ἐστι τῆς ὑποστάσεως ὁ υἱός; παρὰ τῷ ἀποστόλῳ Παύλῳ ἐν τῇ πρὸς Ἑβραίους. Οὐκ ἐκκλησιάζεται. Ἀφ᾽ οὗ κατηγγέλη τὸ εὐαγγέλιον Χριστοῦ, Παύλου εἶναι πεπίστευται ἡ ἐπιστολή (*Dial. de sancta Trin.* 922).

It was otherwise in the Western church, where Πρὸς Ἑβραίους was for long either read simply as an edifying treatise, or, if regarded as canonical, assigned to some anonymous apostolic

---

[1] There is a parallel to the last words in the scoffing close of an epigram in the Greek Anthology (ix. 135): γράψε τις; οἶδε θεός· τίνος εἵνεκεν; οἶδε καὶ αὐτός.

[2] "Ut a stilo Pauli, quod ad phrasin attinet, longe lateque discrepat, ita ad spiritum ac pectus Paulinum vehementer accedit."

writer rather than to Paul. Possibly the use made of Πρὸς Ἑβραίους by the Montanists and the Novatians, who welcomed its denial of a second repentance, compromised it in certain quarters. Besides, the Roman church had never accepted the Alexandrian tradition of Paul's authorship. Hence, even when, on its merits, it was admitted to the canon, there was a strong tendency to treat it as anonymous, as may be seen, for example, in Augustine's references. Once in the canon, however, it gradually acquired a Pauline prestige, and, as Greek scholarship faded, any scruples to the contrary became less and less intelligible. It was not till the study of Greek revived again, at the dawn of the Reformation, that the question was reopened.

The data in connexion with the early fortunes of Πρὸς Ἑβραίους in church history belong to text-books on the Canon, like Zahn's *Geschichte d. NT Kanons*, i. 283 f., 577 f., ii. 160 f., 358 f. ; Leipoldt's *Geschichte d. NT Kanons*, i. pp. 188 f., 219 f. ; and Jacquier's *Le Nouveau Testament dans L'Église Chrétienne*, i. (1911).

Few characters mentioned in the NT have escaped the attention of those who have desired in later days to identify the author of Πρὸς Ἑβραίους. Apollos, Peter, Philip, Silvanus, and even Prisca have been suggested, besides Aristion, the alleged author of Mk 16⁹⁻²⁰. I have summarized these views elsewhere (*Introd. to Lit. of NT.*³, pp. 438–442), and it is superfluous here to discuss hypotheses which are in the main due to an irrepressible desire to construct NT romances. Perhaps our modern pride resents being baffled by an ancient document, but it is better to admit that we are not yet wiser on this matter than Origen was, seventeen centuries ago. The author of Πρὸς Ἑβραίους cannot be identified with any figure known to us in the primitive Christian tradition. He left great prose to some little clan of early Christians, but who they were and who he was, τὸ μὲν ἀληθὲς θεὸς οἶδεν. To us he is a voice and no more. The theory which alone explains the conflicting traditions is that for a time the writing was circulated as an anonymous tract. Only on this hypothesis can the simultaneous emergence of the Barnabas and the Paul traditions in different quarters be explained, as well as the persistent tradition in the Roman church that it was anonymous. As Zahn sensibly concludes, "those into whose hands Πρὸς Ἑβραίους came either looked upon it as an anonymous writing from ancient apostolic times, or else resorted to conjecture. If Paul did not write it, they thought, then it must have been composed by some other prominent teacher of the apostolic church. Barnabas was such a man." In one sense, it was fortunate that the Pauline hypothesis prevailed so early and so extensively, for apart from this help it might have been difficult for Πρὸς ʽΕβραίους to win or to retain its place in the canon. But even when it had been lodged securely inside the canon, some Western churchmen still clung for a while to the old tradition of its anonymity,[1] although they could do no more than hold this as a pious opinion. The later church was right in assigning Πρὸς ʽΕβραίους a canonical position. The original reasons might be erroneous or doubtful, but even in the Western church, where they continued to be questioned, there was an increasing indisposition to challenge their canonical result.

(iv.)

Thrown back, in the absence of any reliable tradition, upon the internal evidence, we can only conclude that the writer was one of those personalities in whom the primitive church was more rich than we sometimes realize. "Si l'on a pu comparer saint Paul à Luther," says Ménégoz, "nous comparerions volontiers l'auteur de l'Épître aux Hébreux à Mélanchthon." He was a highly trained διδάσκαλος, perhaps a Jewish Christian, who had imbibed the philosophy of Alexandrian Judaism before his conversion, a man of literary culture and deep religious feeling. He writes to what is apparently a small community or circle of Christians, possibly one of the household-churches, to which he was attached. For some reason or another he was absent from them, and, although he hopes to rejoin them before long, he feels moved to send them this letter (13[28f.]) to rally them. It is possible to infer from 13[24] (see note) that they belonged to Italy; in any case, Πρὸς ʽΕβραίους was written either to or from some church in Italy. Beyond the fact that the writer and his readers had been evangelized by some of the disciples of Jesus (2[3, 4]), we know nothing more about them. The words in 2[3, 4] do not mean that they belonged to the second generation, of course, in a chronological sense, for such words would have applied to the converts of any mission during the first thirty years or so after the crucifixion, and the only other inference to be drawn, as to the date, is from passages like 10[32f.]. and 13[7], viz. that the first readers of Πρὸς ʽΕβραίους were not neophytes; they had lived through some rough experiences, and indeed their friend expects from them a maturity of experience and intelligence which he is disappointed to miss (5[11f.]); also,

---

[1] According to Professor Souter (*Text and Canon of NT*, p. 190) the epistle is ignored by the African Canon (*c.* 360), Optatus of Mileue in Numidia (370–385), the Acts of the Donatist Controversy, Zeno of Verona, an African by birth, and Foebadius of Agen (*ob. post* 392), while " Ambrosiaster" (fourth century?) "uses the work as canonical, but always as an anonymous work."

their original leaders have died, probably as martyrs (cp. on 13⁷).
For these and other reasons, a certain sense of disillusionment
had begun to creep over them. Πρὸς Ἑβραίους is a λόγος
παρακλήσεως, to steady and rally people who are πειραζόμενοι,
their temptation being to renounce God, or at least to hesitate
and retreat, to relax the fibre of loyal faith, as if God were too
difficult to follow in the new, hard situation. Once, at the
outset of their Christian career, they had been exposed to mob-
rioting (10³²ᶠ·), when they had suffered losses of property, for the
sake of the gospel, and also the loud jeers and sneers which
pagans and Jews alike heaped sometimes upon the disciples.
This they had borne manfully, in the first glow of their enthusiasm. Now, the more violent forms of persecution had
apparently passed; what was left was the dragging experience
of contempt at the hand of outsiders, the social ostracism and
shame, which were threatening to take the heart out of them.
Such was their rough, disconcerting environment. Unless an
illegitimate amount of imagination is applied to the internal data,
they cannot be identified with what is known of any community
in the primitive church, so scanty is our information. Least of
all is it feasible to connect them with the supposed effects of the
Jewish rebellion which culminated in A.D. 70. Πρὸς Ἑβραίους
cannot be later than about A.D. 85, as the use of it in Clement
of Rome's epistle proves; how much earlier it is, we cannot
say, but the controversy over the Law, which marked the Pauline
phase, is evidently over.

It is perhaps not yet quite superfluous to point out that the use of the
present tense (e.g. in 7⁸· ²⁰ 8³ᵗ· 9⁶ᶠ· 13¹⁰) is no clue to the date, as though this
implied that the Jewish temple was still standing. The writer is simply
using the historic present of actions described in scripture. It is a literary
method which is common in writings long after A.D. 70, e.g. in Josephus,
who observes (c. Apion, i. 7) that any priest who violates a Mosaic regulation
ἀπηγόρευται μήτε τοῖς βωμοῖς παρίστασθαι μήτε μετέχειν τῆς ἄλλης ἁγιστείας
(so Ant. iii. 6. 7-12, xiv. 2. 2, etc.). Clement of Rome similarly writes as
though the Mosaic ritual were still in existence (40-41, τῷ γὰρ ἀρχιερεῖ ἴδιαι
λειτουργίαι δεδομέναι εἰσίν . . . καὶ Λευίταις ἴδιαι διακονίαι ἐπίκεινται . . .
προσφέρονται θυσίαι ἐν Ἱερουσαλὴμ μόνῃ), and the author of the Ep. ad
Diognet. 3 writes that οἱ δέ γε θυσίαις αὐτῷ δι' αἵματος καὶ κνίσης καὶ ὁλοκαυτω-
μάτων ἐπιτελεῖν οἰόμενοι καὶ ταύταις ταῖς τιμαῖς αὐτὸν γεραίρειν, οὐδέν μοι
δοκοῦσι διαφέρειν τῶν εἰς τὰ κωφὰ τὴν αὐτὴν ἐνδεικνυμένων φιλοτιμίαν. The
idea that the situation of the readers was in any way connected with the crisis
of A.D. 66-70 in Palestine is unfounded. Πρὸς Ἑβραίους has nothing to do
with the Jewish temple, nor with Palestinian Christians. There is not a
syllable in the writing which suggests that either the author or his readers
had any connexion with or interest in the contemporary temple and ritual of
Judaism; their existence mattered as little to his idealist method of argument as their abolition. When he observes (8¹³) that the old διαθήκη was
ἐγγὺς ἀφανισμοῦ, all he means is that the old régime, superseded now by
Jesus, was decaying even in Jeremiah's age.

(v.)

The object of Πρὸς Ἑβραίους may be seen from a brief analysis of its contents. The writer opens with a stately paragraph, introducing the argument that Jesus Christ as the Son of God is superior (κρείττων) to angels, in the order of revelation (1^1–2^{18}), and this, not in spite of but because of his incarnation and sufferings. He is also superior (κρείττων) even to Moses (3^{1-6a}), as a Son is superior to a servant. Instead of pursuing the argument further, the writer then gives an impressive bible reading on the 95th psalm, to prove that the People of God have still assured to them, if they will only have faith, the divine Rest in the world to come (3^{6b}–4^{13}). Resuming his argument, the writer now begins to show how Jesus as God's Son is superior to the Aaronic high priest (4^{14}–5^{10}). This is the heart of his subject, and he stops for a moment to rouse the attention of his readers (5^{11}–6^{20}) before entering upon the high theme. By a series of skilful transitions he has passed on from the Person of the Son, which is uppermost in chs. 1–4, to the Priesthood of the Son, which dominates chs. 7–8. Jesus as High Priest mediates a superior (κρείττων) order of religion or διαθήκη than that under which Aaron and his successors did their work for the People of God, and access to God, which is the supreme need of men, is now secured fully and finally by the relation of Jesus to God, in virtue of his sacrifice (6^{20}–8^{13}). The validity of this sacrifice is then proved (9^1–10^{18}); it is absolutely efficacious, as no earlier sacrifice of victims could be, in securing forgiveness and fellowship for man. The remainder of the writing (10^{19}–13^{24}) is a series of impressive appeals for constancy. The first (10^{19-31}) is a skilful blend of encouragement and warning. He then appeals to the fine record of his readers ($10^{32f.}$), bidding them be worthy of their own past, and inciting them to faith in God by reciting a great roll-call of heroes and heroines belonging to God's People in the past, from Abel to the Maccabean martyrs (11^{1-40}). He further kindles their imagination and conscience by holding up Jesus as the Supreme Leader of all the faithful (12^{1-3}), even along the path of suffering; besides, he adds (12^{4-11}), suffering is God's discipline for those who belong to his household. To prefer the world (12^{12-17}) is to incur a fearful penalty; the one duty for us is to accept the position of fellowship with God, in a due spirit of awe and grateful confidence (12^{18-29}). A brief note of some ethical duties follows (13^{1-7}), with a sudden warning against some current tendencies to compromise their spiritual religion (13^{8-16}). A postscript (13^{17-24}), with some *personalia*, ends the epistle.

It is artificial to divide up a writing of this kind, which is not a treatise on theology, and I have therefore deliberately abstained from introducing any formal divisions and subdivisions in the commentary. The flow of thought, with its turns and windings, is best followed from point to point. So far as the general plan goes, it is determined by the idea of the finality of the Christian revelation in Jesus the Son of God. This is brought out (A) by a proof that he is superior to angels (1^1–2^{18}) and Moses (3^{1-6a}), followed by the special exhortation of 3^{6b}–4^{13}. Thus far it is what may be termed the Personality of the Son which is discussed. Next (B) comes the Son as High Priest (4^{14}–7^{28}), including the parenthetical exhortation of 5^{11}–6^{20}. The (C) Sacrifice of this High Priest in his Sanctuary then (8^1–10^{18}) is discussed, each of the three arguments, which are vitally connected, laying stress from one side or another upon the absolute efficacy of the revelation. This is the dominant idea of the writing, and it explains the particular line which the writer strikes out. He takes a very serious view of the position of his friends and readers. They are disheartened and discouraged for various reasons, some of which are noted in the course of the epistle. There is the strain of hardship, the unpleasant experience of being scoffed at, and the ordinary temptations of immorality, which may bring them, if they are not careful, to the verge of actual apostasy. The writer appears to feel that the only way to save them from ruining themselves is to put before them the fearful and unsuspected consequences of their failure. Hence three times over the writer draws a moving picture of the fate which awaits apostates and renegades ($6^{4f.}$ $10^{26f.}$ $12^{15f.}$). But the special line of argument which he adopts in 5–10^{18} must be connected somehow with the danger in which he felt his friends involved, and this is only to be explained if we assume that their relaxed interest in Christianity arose out of an imperfect conception of what Jesus meant for their faith. He offers no theoretical disquisition ; it is to reinforce and deepen their conviction of the place of Jesus in religion, that he argues, pleads, and warns, dwelling on the privileges and responsibilities of the relationship in which Jesus had placed them. All the help they needed, all the hope they required, lay in the access to God mediated by Jesus, if they would only realize it.

This is what makes the writing of special interest. In the first place (a) the author is urged by a practical necessity to think out his faith, or rather to state the full content of his faith, for the benefit of his readers. Their need puts him on his mettle. " Une chose surtant," says Anatole France, " donne le l'attrait à la pensée des hommes : c'est l'inquiétude. Un esprit qui n'est point anxieux m'irrite ou m'ennuie." In a sense all the NT writers are spurred by this anxiety, but the author of Πρὸς Ἑβραίους pre-eminently. It is not anxiety about his personal faith, nor about the prospects of Christianity, but about the loyalty of those for whom he feels himself responsible; his very certainty of the absolute value of Christianity makes him anxious when he sees his friends ready to give it up, anxious on their behalf, and anxious to bring out as lucidly and persuasively as possible the full meaning of the revelation of God in Jesus. What he writes is not a theological treatise in cold blood, but a statement of the faith, alive with practical interest. The situation of his readers has stirred his own mind, and he bends all his powers of thought and emotion to rally them. There is a vital urgency behind what he writes for his circle. But (*b*), more than this, the form into which he throws his appeal answers to the situation of his readers. He feels that the word for them is the absolute worth of Jesus as the Son of God; it is to bring this out that he argues, in the middle part of his epistle, so elaborately and anxiously about the priesthood and sacrifice of Jesus. The idealistic conception of the two spheres, the real and eternal, and the phenomenal (which is the mere σκιά and ὑπόδειγμα, a παραβολή, an ἀντίτυπον of the former), is applied to the sacrifice of Jesus Christ, which inaugurates and realizes the eternal διαθήκη between God and man. In a series of contrasts, he brings out the superiority of this revelation to the OT διαθήκη with its cultus. But not because the contemporary form of the latter had any attractions for his readers. It is with the archaic σκηνή described in the OT that he deals, in order to elucidate the final value of Jesus and his sacrifice under the new διαθήκη, which was indeed the real and eternal one. To readers like his friends, with an imperfect sense of all that was contained in their faith, he says, "Come back to your bible, and see how fully it suggests the positive value of Jesus." Christians were finding Christ in the LXX, especially his sufferings in the prophetic scriptures, but our author falls back on the pentateuch and the psalter especially to illustrate the commanding position of Jesus as the Son of God in the eternal διαθήκη, and the duties as well as the privileges of living under such a final revelation, where the purpose and the promises of God for his People are realized as they could not be under the OT διαθήκη. Why the writer concentrates upon the priesthood and sacrifice of Jesus in this eternal order of things, is due in part to his general conception of religion (see pp. xliii f.). For him there could be no religion without a priest. But this idea is of direct service to his readers, as he believes. Hence the first mention of Jesus as ἀρχιερεύς occurs as a reason for loyalty and confidence ($2^{14f.}$). Nothing is more practical in religion than an idea, a relevant idea powerfully urged. When the writer concentrates for a while upon this cardinal idea of Jesus as ἀρχιερεύς, therefore, it is because nothing can be more vital, he thinks, for his friends than to show them the claims and resources of their faith, disclosing the rich and real nature of God's revelation to them in his Son. Access to God, confidence in God, pardon for sins of the past, and hope for the future—all this is bound up with the διαθήκη of Christ, and the writer reveals it between the lines of the LXX, to which as members of the People of God his friends naturally turned for instruction and revelation.   This διαθήκη, he argues, is far superior to the earlier one, as the Son of God is superior to angels and to Moses himself; nay more, it is superior in efficacy, as the real is superior to its shadowy outline, for the sacrifice which underlies any διαθήκη is fulfilled in Christ as it could not be under the levitical cultus.   The function of Christ as high priest is to mediate the direct access of the People to God, and all this has been done so fully and finally that Christians have simply to avail themselves of its provisions for their faith and need.

What the writer feels called upon to deal with, therefore, is not any sense of disappointment in his readers that they had not an impressive ritual or an outward priesthood, nor any hankering after such in contemporary Judaism; it is a failure to see that Christianity is the absolute religion, a failure which is really responsible for the unsatisfactory and even the critical situation of the readers.   To meet this need, the writer argues as well as exhorts.   He seeks to show from the LXX how the Christian faith alone fulfils the conditions of real religion, and as he knows no other religion than the earlier phase in Israel, he takes common ground with his readers on the LXX record of the first διαθήκη, in order to let them see even there the implications and anticipations of the higher.

But while the author never contemplates any fusion of Christianity with Jewish legalism, and while the argument betrays no trace of Jewish religion as a competing attraction for the readers, it might be argued that some speculative Judaism had affected the mind of the readers.   No basis for this can be found in 13[9f.].   Yet if there were any proselytes among the readers, they may have felt the fascination of the Jewish system, as those did afterwards who are warned by Ignatius (*ad Philad.* 6, etc.), "Better listen to Christianity from a circumcised Christian than to Judaism from one uncircumcised."   "It is monstrous to talk of Jesus Christ and ἰουδαΐζειν" (*ad Magnes.* 10). This interpretation was put forward by Häring (*Studien und Kritiken*, 1891, pp. 589 f.), and it has been most ingeniously argued by Professor Purdy (*Expositor*[8], xix. pp. 123–139), who thinks that the emphasis upon "Jesus" means that the readers

were exposed to the seductions of a liberal Judaism which offered
an escape from persecution and other difficulties by presenting
a Christ who was spiritual, divorced from history; that this
liberal, speculative Judaism came forward as "a more developed
and perfected type of religion than Christianity"; and that,
without being legalistic, it claimed to be a traditional, ritualistic
faith, which was at once inward and ceremonial. The objection
to such interpretations,[1] however, is that they explain *ignotum
per ignotius*. We know little or nothing of such liberal Judaism
in the first century, any more than of a tendency on the part of
Jewish Christians to abandon Christianity about A.D. 70 for their
ancestral faith. Indeed any influence of Jewish propaganda,
ritualistic or latitudinarian, must be regarded as secondary, at
the most, in the situation of the readers as that is to be inferred
from Πρὸς Ἑβραίους itself. When we recognize the real method
and aim of the writer, it becomes clear that he was dealing with
a situation which did not require any such influence to account
for it. The form taken by his argument is determined by the
conception, or rather the misconception, of the faith entertained
by his friends; and this in turn is due not to any political or
racial factors, but to social and mental causes, such as are
sufficiently indicated in Πρὸς Ἑβραίους itself. Had the danger
been a relapse into Judaism of any kind, it would have implied
a repudiation of Jesus Christ as messiah and divine—the very
truth which the writer can assume! What he needs to do is not
to defend this, but to develop it.

The writing, therefore, for all its elaborate structure, has a
spontaneous aim. It is not a homily written at large, to which
by some afterthought, on the part of the writer or of some editor,
a few *personalia* have been appended in ch. 13. The argumentative sections bear directly and definitely upon the situation of the readers, whom the writer has in view throughout,
even when he seems to be far from their situation. Which brings
us to the problem of the literary structure of Πρὸς Ἑβραίους.

(vi.)

See especially W. Wrede's monograph, *Das literarische Rätsel d. Hebräerbriefs* (1906), with the essays of E. Burggaller and R. Perdelwitz in *Zeitschrift
für Neutest. Wissenschaft* (1908, pp. 110 f.; 1910, pp. 59 f., 105 f.); V.
Monod's *De titulo epistulae vulgo ad Hebraeos inscriptae* (1910); C. C.

---

[1] Cp., further, Professor Dickie's article in *Expositor*[8], v. pp. 371 f. The
notion that the writer is controverting an external view of Christ's person,
which shrank, *e.g.*, from admitting his humiliation and real humanity, had
been urged by Julius Kögel in *Die Verborgenheit Jesu als des Messias*
(Greifenswald, 1909) and in *Der Sohn und die Söhne, ein exegetische Studie
zu Heb.* 2[5-18] (1904).

Torrey's article in the *Journal of Biblical Literature* (1911), pp. 137–156; J. W. Slot's *De letterkundige vorm v. d. Brief aan de Hebräer* (1912), with J. Quentel's essay in *Revue Biblique* (1912, pp. 50 f.) and M. Jones' paper in *Expositor*[8], xii. 426 f.

The literary problem of Πρὸς Ἑβραίους is raised by the absence of any address and the presence of personal matter in ch. 13. Why (*a*) has it no introductory greeting? And why (*b*) has it a postscript? As for the former point (*a*), there may have been, in the original, an introductory title. Πρὸς Ἑβραίους opens with a great sentence (1[1f.]), but Eph 1[8f.] is just such another, and there is no reason why the one should not have followed a title-address any more than the other.[1] It may have been lost by accident, in the tear and wear of the manuscript, for such accidents are not unknown in ancient literature. This is, at any rate, more probable than the idea that it was suppressed because the author (Barnabas, Apollos?) was not of sufficiently apostolic rank for the canon. Had this interest been operative, it would have been perfectly easy to alter a word or two in the address itself. Besides, Πρὸς Ἑβραίους was circulating long before it was admitted to the canon, and it circulated even afterwards as non-canonical; yet not a trace of any address, Pauline or non-Pauline, has ever survived. Which, in turn, tells against the hypothesis that such ever existed—at least, against the theory that it was deleted when the writing was canonized. If the elision of the address ever took place, it must have been very early, and rather as the result of accident than deliberately. Yet there is no decisive reason why the writing should not have begun originally as it does in its present form. Nor does this imply (*b*) that the personal data in ch. 13 are irrelevant. Πρὸς Ἑβραίους has a certain originality in form as well as in content; it is neither an epistle nor a homily, pure and simple. True, down to 12[29] (or 13[17]) there is little or nothing that might not have been spoken by a preacher to his audience, and Valckenaer (on 4[3]) is right, so far, in saying, "haec magnifica ad Hebraeos missa dissertatio oratio potius dicenda est quam epistola." Yet the writer is not addressing an ideal public; he is not composing a treatise for Christendom at large. It is really unreal to explain away passages like 5[11f.] 10[32f.] 12[4f.] and 13[1-9] as rhetorical abstractions.

Πρὸς Ἑβραίους was the work of a διδάσκαλος, who knew how to deliver a λόγος παρακλήσεως. Parts of it probably represent what he had used in preaching already (*e.g.* 3[7]). But, while it has sometimes the tone of sermon notes written out, it is not a

---

[1] Ep. Barnabas begins with ἀδελφοί, οὕτως δεῖ ἡμᾶς φρονεῖν περὶ Ἰησοῦ Χριστοῦ ὡς περὶ θεοῦ, etc.; 2 Clement starts with a greeting, χαίρετε, υἱοὶ καὶ θυγατέρες, ἐν ὀνόματι κυρίου τοῦ ἀγαπήσαντος ἡμᾶς ἐν εἰρήνῃ.

sermon in the air.   To strike out $13^{19.\ 22\text{-}24}$ or $13^{1\text{-}7.\ 16\text{-}19.\ 22f.}$
(Torrey) [1] does not reduce it from a letter or epistle to a sermon
like 2 Clement.   Thus, *e.g.*, a phrase like 11^{32} (see note) is as
intelligible in a written work as in a spoken address.   It is only
by emptying passages like $5^{11f.}$ and $10^{32f.}$ of their full meaning
that anyone can speak of the writer as composing a sermon at
large or for an ideal public.   Part of the force of $5^{11f.}$, *e.g.*, is due
to the fact that the writer is dealing with a real situation, pleading
that in what he is going to say he is not writing simply to display
his own talent or to please himself, but for the serious, urgent
need of his readers.   They do not deserve what he is going to
give them.   But he will give it!   A thoroughly pastoral touch,
which is lost by being turned into a rhetorical excuse for de-
ploying some favourite ideas of his own.   According to Wrede,
the author wrote in $13^{18.\ 19}$ on the basis of (Philem ^{22}) 2 Co
$1^{11.\ 12}$ to make it appear as though Paul was the author, and then
added 13^{23} on the basis of Ph $2^{19.\ 23.\ 24}$; but why he should mix
up these reminiscences, which, according to Wrede, are contra-
dictory, it is difficult to see.   Had he wished to put a Pauline
colour into the closing paragraphs, he would surely have done
it in a lucid, coherent fashion, instead of leaving the supposed
allusions to Paul's Roman imprisonment so enigmatic.   But, though
Wrede thinks that the hypothesis of a pseudonymous conclusion
is the only way of explaining the phenomena of ch. 13, he agrees
that to excise it entirely is out of the question.   Neither the
style nor the contents justify such a radical theory,[2] except on
the untenable hypothesis that 1–12 is a pure treatise.   The
analogies of a doxology being followed by personal matter (*e.g.*
2 Ti 4^{18}, 1 P 4^{11} etc.) tell against the idea that Πρὸς Ἑβραίους
must have ended with 13^{21}, and much less could it have ended
with 13^{17}.   To assume that the writer suddenly bethought him,
at the end, of giving a Pauline appearance to what he had
written, and that he therefore added $13^{22f.}$, is to credit him with
too little ability.   Had he wished to convey this impression, he
would certainly have gone further and made changes in the
earlier part.   Nor is it likely that anyone added the closing
verses in order to facilitate its entrance into the NT canon by
bringing it into line with the other epistles.   The canon was
drawn up for worship, and if Πρὸς Ἑβραίους was originally a
discourse, it seems very unlikely that anyone would have gone

[1] To excise $13^{1\text{-}7}$ as a "formless jumble of rather commonplace admonitions" is a singular misjudgment.

[2] The linguistic proof is cogently led by C. R. Williams in the *Journal
of Biblical Literature* (1911), pp. 129–136, who shows that the alleged
special parallels between He 13 and Paul are neither so numerous nor so
significant as is commonly supposed, and that the only fair explanation of
He 13 as a whole is that it was written to accompany 1–12.

out of his way, on this occasion, to add some enigmatic personal references. In short, while Πρὸς ʿΕβραίους betrays here and there the interests and methods of an effective preacher, the epistolary form is not a piece of literary fiction; still less is it due (in ch. 13) to some later hand. It is hardly too much to say that the various theories about the retouching of the 13th chapter of Πρὸς ʿΕβραίους are as valuable, from the standpoint of literary criticism, as Macaulay's unhesitating belief that Dr. Johnson had revised and retouched *Cecilia*.

§ 2. The Religious Ideas.

In addition to the text-books on NT theology, consult Riehm's *Lehrbegriff des Hebräerbriefs*[2] (1867), W. Milligan's *Ascension and Heavenly Priesthood of our Lord* (1891), Ménégoz's *La Théologie de l'Épître aux Hébreux* (1894), A. Seeberg's *Der Tod Christi* (1895), A. B. Bruce's *The Epistle to the Hebrews* (1899), G. Milligan's *The Theology of the Epistle to the Hebrews* (1899), G. Vos on "The Priesthood of Christ in Hebrews" (*Princeton Theological Review*, 1907, pp. 423 f., 579 f.), Du Bose's *Highpriesthood and Sacrifice* (1908), A. Nairne's *The Epistle of Priesthood* (1913), H. L. MacNeill's *Christology of the Epistle to the Hebrews* (1914), H. A. A. Kennedy's *Theology of the Epistles* (1919, pp. 182–221), and E. F. Scott's *The Epistle to the Hebrews* (1922).

Many readers who are not children will understand what Mr Edmund Gosse in *Father and Son* (pp. 89 f.) describes, in telling how his father read aloud to him the epistle. " The extraordinary beauty of the language—for instance, the matchless cadences and images of the first chapter—made a certain impression upon my imagination, and were (I think) my earliest initiation into the magic of literature. I was incapable of defining what I felt, but I certainly had a grip in the throat, which was in its essence a purely aesthetic emotion, when my father read, in his pure, large, ringing voice, such passages as ʻThe heavens are the work of Thy hands. They shall perish, but Thou remainest, and they shall all wax old as doth a garment, and as a vesture shalt Thou fold them up, and they shall be changed; but Thou art the same, and Thy years shall not fail.' But the dialectic parts of the epistle puzzled and confused me. Such metaphysical ideas as ʻlaying again the foundation of repentance from dead works' and ʻcrucifying the Son of God afresh' were not successfully brought down to the level of my understanding. . . . The melodious language, the divine forensic audacities, the magnificent ebb and flow of argument which make the Epistle to the Hebrews such a miracle, were far beyond my reach, and they only bewildered me." They become less bewildering when they are viewed in the right perspective. The clue to them lies in the philosophical idea which dominates the outlook of the writer, and in the symbolism which, linked to this idea, embodied his characteristic conceptions of religion. We might almost say that, next to the deflecting influence of the tradition which identified our epistle with the Pauline scheme of thought and thereby missed its original and independent contribution to early Christianity, nothing has so handicapped its appeal as the later use of it in dogmatic theology. While the author of Πρὸς ʽΕβραίους often turned the literal into the figurative, his theological interpreters have been as often engaged in turning the figurative expressions of the epistle into what was literal. A due appreciation of the symbolism has been the slow gain of the historical method as applied to the classics of primitive Christianity. There is no consistent symbolism, indeed, not even in the case of the ἀρχιερεύς; in the nature of the case, there could not be. But symbolism there is, and symbolism of a unique kind.

(i.)

The author writes from a religious philosophy of his own—that is, of his own among the NT writers. The philosophical element in his view of the world and God is fundamentally Platonic. Like Philo and the author of Wisdom, he interprets the past and the present alike in terms of the old theory (cp. on 8^5 10^1) that the phenomenal is but an imperfect, shadowy transcript of what is eternal and real. He applies this principle to the past. What was all the Levitical cultus in bygone days but a faint copy of the celestial archetype, a copy that suggested by its very imperfections the future and final realization? In such arguments (chs. 7–10) he means to declare "that Christianity is eternal, just as it shall be everlasting, and that all else is only this, that the true heavenly things of which it consists thrust themselves forward on to this bank and shoal of time, and took cosmical embodiment, in order to suggest their coming everlasting manifestation."[1] The idea that the seen and material is but a poor, provisional replica of the unseen and real order of things (τὰ ἐπουράνια, τὰ ἐν τοῖς οὐρανοῖς, τὰ μὴ σαλευόμενα), pervades Πρὸς ʽΕβραίους. Thus faith ($11^{1f.}$) means the conviction, the practical realization, of this world of realities, not only the belief that the universe does not arise out of mere φαινόμενα, but the conviction that life must be ordered, at all costs, by a vision of the unseen, or by obedience to a Voice unheard by any outward ear. Similarly the outward priest, sanctuary, and sacrifices of the ancient cultus were merely the shadowy copy of the real, as manifested in Jesus with his self-sacrifice, his death being, as

[1] A. B. Davidson, *Biblical and Literary Essays* (p. 317).

xxxiiTHE EPISTLE TO THE HEBREWS

Sabatier says, "une fonction sacerdotale, un acte transcendant de purification rituelle, accompli hors de l'humanité" (*La Doctrine de l'Expiation*, p. 37). Such is the philosophical strain which permeates Πρὸς Ἑβραίους. The idea of heavenly counterparts is not, of course, confined to Platonism; it is Sumerian, in one of its roots (cp. on 8⁵), and it had already entered apocalyptic. But our author derives it from his Alexandrian religious philosophy (transmuting the κόσμος νοητός into the more vivid and devotional figures of an οἶκος or πόλις θεοῦ, a πάτρις or even a σκηνὴ ἀληθινή), just as elsewhere he freely uses Aristotelian ideas like that of the τέλος or final end, with its τελείωσις or sequence of growth, and shows familiarity with the idea of the ἕξις (5¹⁴). The τελείωσις (see on 5⁹) idea is of special importance, as it denotes for men the work of Christ in putting them into their proper status towards God (see on 2¹⁰). "By a single offering he has made the sanctified perfect for all time" (τετελείωκεν, 10¹⁴), the offering or προσφορά being himself, and the "perfecting" being the act of putting the People into their true and final relation towards God. This the Law, with its outward organization of priests and animal sacrifices, could never do; "as the Law has a mere shadow of the bliss that is to be, instead of representing the reality of that bliss (viz. the 'perfect' relationship between God and men), it can never perfect those who draw near" (10¹).

This gives us the focus for viewing the detailed comparison between the levitical sacrifices and priests on the one hand and the κρείττων Jesus. "You see in your bible," the writer argues, "the elaborate system of ritual which was once organized for the forgiveness of sins and the access of the people to God. All this was merely provisional and ineffective, a shadow of the Reality which already existed in the mind of God, and which is now ours in the sacrifice of Jesus." Even the fanciful argument from the priesthood of Melchizedek (6²⁰-7¹⁷)—fanciful to us, but forcible then—swings from this conception. What the author seeks to do is not to prove that there had been from the first a natural or real priesthood, superior to the levitical, a priesthood fulfilled in Christ. His aim primarily is to discredit the levitical priesthood of bygone days; it was anticipated in the divine order by that of Melchizedek, he shows, using a chronological argument resembling that of Paul in Gal 3⁸ᶠ·, on the principle that what is prior is superior. But what leads him to elaborate specially the Melchizedek priesthood is that it had already played an important rôle in Jewish speculation in connexion with the messianic hope. Philo had already identified Melchizedek outright with the Logos or possibly even with the messiah. Whether the author of Πρὸς Ἑβραίους intends to contradict Philo or not, he takes a different line, falling back upon his favourite psalm,

the 110th, which in the Greek version, the only one known to
him, had put forward not only the belief that messiah was ἱερεὺς εἰς
τὸν αἰῶνα κατὰ τὴν τάξιν Μελχισέδεκ, but the Alexandrian belief
in the pre-existence of messiah (v.[3] ἐκ γαστρὸς πρὸ ἑωσφόρου
ἐξεγέννησά σε). Here then, by Alexandrian methods of exegesis,
in the pentateuch text combined with the psalm, he found
scripture proof of an original priesthood which was not levitical,
not transferable, and permanent. This priesthood of Melchizedek was, of course, not quite a perfect type of Christ's, for it
did not include any sacrifice, but, as resting on personality,
not on heredity,[1] it did typify, he held, that eternal priesthood of
the Christ which was to supersede the levitical, for all the ancient
prestige of the latter. As this prestige was wholly biblical for
the writer and his readers, so it was essential that the disproof of
its validity should be biblical also. Though he never uses either
the idea of Melchizedek offering bread and wine to typify the
elements in the eucharist, in spite of the fact that Philo once
allegorized this trait (*de Leg. Alleg.* iii. 25), or the idea of
Melchizedek being uncircumcised (as he would have done, had
he been seriously arguing with people who were in danger of
relapsing into contemporary Judaism), he does seem to glance
at the combination of the sacerdotal and the royal functions.
Like Philo, though more fully, he notices the religious significance of the etymology "king of righteousness" and "king of
peace," the reason being that throughout his argument he
endeavours repeatedly to preserve something of the primitive
view of Jesus as messianic king, particularly because the idea of
the divine βασιλεία plays next to no part in his scheme of
thought. Sometimes the combination of the sacerdotal and
royal metaphors is incongruous enough, although it is not
unimpressive (*e.g.* 10[12. 13]). Primarily it is a survival of the
older militant messianic category which is relevant in the first
chapter (see 1[8f.]), but out of place in the argument from the
priesthood ; the reference is really due to the desire to reaffirm
the absolute significance of Christ's work, and by way of anticipation he sounds this note even in 7[1. 2]. Later on, it opens up
into an interesting instance of his relation to the primitive
eschatology. To his mind, trained in the Alexandrian philosophy of religion, the present world of sense and time stands
over against the world of reality, the former being merely
the shadow and copy of the latter. There is an archetypal

---

[1] The writer is trying to express an idea which, as Prof. E. F. Scott
argues (pp. 207 f.), "underlies all our modern thought—social and political
as well as religious," viz. that true authority is not prescriptive but personal ;
"the priesthood which can bring us nearer God must be one of inherent
character and personality."

order of things, eternal and divine, to which the mundane order
but dimly corresponds, and only within this higher order, eternal
and invisible, is access to God possible for man. On such a
view as this, which ultimately (see pp. xxxi–xxxii) goes back to
Platonic idealism, and which had been worked out by Philo, the
real world is the transcendent order of things, which is the
pattern for the phenomenal universe, so that to attain God man
must pass from the lower and outward world of the senses to the
inner. But how? Philo employed the Logos or Reason as
the medium. Our author similarly holds that men must attain
this higher world, but for him it is a σκηνή, a sanctuary, the real
Presence of God, and it is entered not through ecstasy or mystic
rapture, but through connexion with Jesus Christ, who has not
only revealed that world but opened the way into it. The
Presence of God is now attainable as it could not be under the
outward cultus of the σκηνή in the OT, for the complete sacrifice
has been offered " in the realm of the spirit," thus providing for
the direct access of the people to their God. The full bliss of the
fellowship is still in the future, indeed; it is not to be realized
finally until Jesus returns for his people, for he is as yet only their
πρόδρομος (6[20]). The primitive eschatology required and received
this admission from the writer, though it is hardly consonant
with his deeper thought. And this is why he quotes for example
the old words about Jesus waiting in heaven till his foes are
crushed (10[12, 13]). He is still near enough to the primitive period to
share the forward look (see, e.g., 2[2f.] 9[28] 10[37]), and unlike Philo, he
does not allow his religious idealism to evaporate his eschatology.
But while this note of expectation is sounded now and then, it
is held that Christians already experience the powers of the
world to come. The new and final order has dawned ever since
the sacrifice of Jesus was made, and the position of believers is
guaranteed. "You have come to mount Sion, the city of the
living God." The entrance of Jesus has made a fresh, living
way for us, which is here and now open. " For all time he is
able to save those who approach God through him, as he is
always living to intercede on their behalf." Christians enjoy the
final status of relationship to God in the world of spirit and
reality, in virtue of the final sacrifice offered by Jesus the Son.

(ii.)

What was this sacrifice ? How did the writer understand it ?
(a) The first thing to be said is that in his interpretation of the
sacrifice of Jesus, he takes the piacular view. Calvin (*Instit.* ii.
15. 6) maintains that, as for the priesthood of Christ, "finem et
usum eius esse ut sit mediator purus omni macula, qui sanctitate

sua Deum nobis conciliet. Sed quia aditum occupat justa
maledictio, et Deus pro judicis officio nobis infensus est, ut nobis
favorem comparet sacerdos ad placandam iram ipsius Dei, piacu-
lum intervenire necesse est. . . . Qua de re prolixe apostolus
disputat in epistola ad Hebraeos a septimo capite fere ad finem
usque decimi." Matthew Arnold is not often found beside
Calvin, but he shares this error. "Turn it which way we will,
the notion of appeasement of an offended God by vicarious
sacrifice, which the Epistle to the Hebrews apparently sanctions,
will never truly speak to the religious sense, or bear fruit for
true religion " (*St. Paul and Protestantism*, p. 72). Arnold saves
himself by the word "apparently," but the truth is that this
idea is not sanctioned by Πρὸς Ἑβραίους at all. The interpretation of Calvin confuses Paul's doctrine of expiation with the
piacular view of our author. The entire group of ideas about
the law, the curse, and the wrath of God is alien to Πρὸς
Ἑβραίους. The conception of God is indeed charged with
wholesome awe (cp. on 12$^{28.\ 29}$); but although God is never
called directly the Father of Christians, his attitude to men is
one of grace, and the entire process of man's approach is
initiated by him (2^9 13^{20}). God's wrath is reserved for the
apostates (10$^{29-31}$); it does not brood over unregenerate men, to
be removed by Christ. Such a notion could hardly have occurred
to a man with predilections for the typical significance of the OT
ritual, in which the sacrifices were not intended to avert the
wrath of God so much as to reassure the people from time to
time that their relations with their God had not been interrupted.
The function of Christ, according to our author, is not to appease
the divine wrath (see on 2$^{9f.\ 17}$), but to establish once and for all
the direct fellowship of God with his people, and a picturesque
archaic phrase like that in 12^{24} about the αἷμα ῥαντισμοῦ cannot
be pressed into the doctrine that Jesus by his sacrifice averted or
averts the just anger of God. On the other hand, while the
author knows the primitive Christian idea of God's fatherhood,
it is not in such terms that he expresses his own conception of
God. Philo (*De Exsecrationibus*, 9) describes how the Jews in
the diaspora will be encouraged to return to Israel and Israel's
God, particularly by his forgiving character (ἑνὶ μὲν εἰπεικείᾳ καὶ
χρηστότητι τοῦ παρακαλουμένου συγγνώμην πρὸ τιμωρίας ἀεὶ τιθέντος); the end of their approach to God, he adds, οὐδὲν ἕτερον ἢ
εὐαρεστεῖν τῷ θεῷ καθάπερ υἱοὺς πατρί. But the author of Πρὸς
Ἑβραίους lays no stress upon the Fatherhood of God for men;
except in connexion with the discipline of suffering, he never
alludes to the goodness of God as paternal, even for Christians,
and indeed it is only in OT quotations that God is called even
the Father of the Son (1^5 5^5). He avoids, even more strictly

than Jesus, the use of love-language. The verb ἀγαπᾶν only occurs twice, both times in an OT citation; ἀγάπη is also used only twice, and never of man's attitude towards God. There is significance in such linguistic data; they corroborate the impression that the author takes a deep view (see on 12²³) of the homage and awe due to God. Godly reverence, εὐλάβεια (see on 5⁷), characterized Jesus in his human life, and it is to characterize Christians towards God, *i.e.* an awe which is devoid of anything like nervous fear, an ennobling sense of the greatness of God, but still a reverential awe. This is not incompatible with humble confidence or with a serious joy, with παρρησία (cp. on 3¹⁶). Indeed "all deep joy has something of the awful in it," as Carlyle says. Ἔχωμεν χάριν is the word of our author (12²⁸); the standing attitude of Christians towards their God is one of profound thankfulness for his goodness to them. Only, it is to be accompanied μετὰ εὐλαβείας καὶ δέους. We are to feel absolutely secure under God's will, whatever crises or catastrophes befall the universe, and the security is at once to thrill (see on 2¹²) and to subdue our minds. Hence, while God's graciousness overcomes any anxiety in man, his sublimity is intended to elevate and purify human life by purging it of easy emotion and thin sentimentalism. This is not the primitive awe of religion before the terrors of the unknown supernatural; the author believes in the gracious, kindly nature of God (see on 2¹⁰, also 6¹⁰ 13¹⁶ etc.), but he has an instinctive horror of anything like a shallow levity. The tone of Πρὸς Ἑβραίους resembles, indeed, that of 1 P 1¹⁷ (εἰ πατέρα ἐπικαλεῖσθε τὸν ἀπροσωπολήπτως κρίνοντα κατὰ τὸ ἑκάστου ἔργον, ἐν φόβῳ τὸν τῆς παροικίας ὑμῶν χρόνον ἀναστράφητε); there may be irreverence in religion, not only in formal religion but for other reasons in spiritual religion. Yet the special aspect of our epistle is reflected in what Jesus once said to men tempted to hesitate and draw back in fear of suffering : "I will show you whom to fear—fear Him who after He has killed has power to cast you into Gehenna. Yes, I tell you, fear Him" (Lk 12⁵). This illustrates the spirit and situation of Πρὸς Ἑβραίους, where the writer warns his friends against apostasy by reminding them of ὁ θεὸς ζῶν and of the judgment. We might almost infer that in his mind the dominant conception is God regarded as transcendental, not with regard to creation but with regard to frail, faulty human nature. What engrosses the writer is the need not so much of a medium between God and the material universe, as of a medium between his holiness and human sin (see on 12²³).

(*b*) As for the essence and idea of the sacrifice, while he refers to a number of OT sacrifices by way of illustration, his main analogy comes from the ritual of atonement-day in the levitical code (Lv 16), where it was prescribed that once a year the highpriest was to enter the inner shrine by himself, the shrine within which stood the sacred box or ark symbolizing the divine Presence. The elaborate sacrifices of the day are only glanced at by our author. Thus he never alludes to the famous scapegoat, which bore away the sins of the people into the desert. All he mentions is the sacrifice of certain animals, as propitiation for the highpriest's own sins and also for those of the nation. Carrying some blood of these animals, the priest was to smear the ἱλαστήριον or cover of the ark. This had a twofold object. (i) Blood was used to reconsecrate the sanctuary (Lv 16¹⁶). This was a relic of the archaic idea that the life-bond between the god and his worshippers required to be renewed by sacred blood; "the holiness of the altar is liable to be impaired, and requires to be refreshed by an application of holy blood."[1] Our author refers to this crude practice in 9²³. But his dominant interest is in (ii) the action of the highpriest as he enters the inner shrine; it is not the reconsecration of the sanctuary with its altar, but the general atonement there made for the sins of the People, which engrosses him. The application of the victim's blood to the ἱλαστήριον by the divinely appointed highpriest was believed to propitiate Yahweh by cleansing the People from the sins which might prevent him from dwelling any longer in the land or among the People. The annual ceremony was designed to ensure his Presence among them, "to enable the close relationship between Deity and man to continue undisturbed. The logical circle—that the atoning ceremonies were ordered by God to produce their effect upon himself—was necessarily unperceived by the priestly mind" (Montefiore, *Hibbert Lectures*, p. 337). What the rite, as laid down in the bible, was intended to accomplish was simply, for the author of Πρὸς Ἑβραίους, to renew the life-bond between God and the People. This sacrifice offered by the highpriest on atonement-day was the supreme, piacular action of the levitical cultus. Once a year it availed to wipe out the guilt of all sins, whatever their nature, ritual or moral, which interrupted the relationship between God and his People.[2] For it was a sacrifice designed for the entire People as the community of God. The blood of the victims was carried into the inner shrine, on behalf of the People outside the sanctuary; this the highpriest did for them, as he passed inside the curtain which shrouded the inner shrine. Also, in contrast to the usual custom, the flesh of the victims, instead of any part being eaten as a meal, was carried out and burned up. In all this the writer finds a richly symbolic

[1] W. Robertson Smith, *The Religion of the Semites* (1907), pp. 408 f.
[2] Cp. Montefiore, *op. cit.*, pp. 334 f.

meaning ($9^{1f.}$). Jesus was both highpriest and victim, as he died and passed inside the heavenly Presence of God to establish the life-bond between God and his People. Jesus did not need to sacrifice for himself. Jesus did not need to sacrifice himself more than once for the People. Jesus secured a forgiveness which the older animal sacrifices never won. And Jesus did not leave his People outside; he opened the way for them to enter God's own presence after him, and in virtue of his self-sacrifice. So the author, from time to time, works out the details of the symbolism. He even uses the treatment of the victim's remains to prove that Christians must be unworldly ($13^{11f.}$); but this is an after-thought, for his fundamental interest lies in the sacrificial suggestiveness of the atonement-day which, external and imperfect as its ritual was, adumbrated the reality which had been manifested in the sacrifice and ascension of Jesus.

Yet this figurative category had its obvious drawbacks, two of which may be noted here. One (a) is, that it does not allow him to show how the sacrificial death of Jesus is connected with the inner renewal of the heart and the consequent access of man to God. He uses phrases like ἁγιάζειν (see on 2^{11}) and καθαρίζειν and τελειοῦν (this term emphasizing more than the others the idea of completeness), but we can only deduce from occasional hints like 9^{14} what he meant by the efficacy of the sacrificial death. His ritualistic category assumed that such a sacrifice availed to reinstate the People before God (cp. on 9^{22}), and this axiom sufficed for his Christian conviction that every-thing depended upon what Jesus is to God and to us—what he is, he is in virtue of what he did, of the sacrificial offering of himself. But the symbol or parable in the levitical cultus went no further. And it even tended to confuse the conception of what is symbolized, by its inadequacy; it necessarily separated priest and victim, and it suggested by its series of actions a time-element which is out of keeping with the eternal order. Hence the literal tendency in the interpretation of the sacrifice has led to confusion, as attempts have been made to express the con-tinuous, timeless efficacy of the sacrifice. That the death was a sacrifice, complete and final, is assumed (*e.g.* 7^{27} 9^{14} $10^{10.\ 12.\ 14}$). Yet language is used which has suggested that in the heavenly σκηνή this sacrifice is continually presented or offered (*e.g.* 7^{25} and the vg. mistranslation of 10^{12} "hic autem unam pro peccatis offerens hostiam in sempiternum sedit"). The other drawback (b) is, that the idea of Jesus passing like the highpriest at once from the sacrifice into the inner sanctuary (*i.e.* through the heavens into the Presence, 4^{14}) has prevented him from making use of the Resurrection (cp. also on 13^{12}). The heavenly sphere

of Jesus is so closely linked with his previous existence on earth,
under the category of the sacrifice, that the author could not
suggest an experience like the resurrection, which would not
have tallied with this idea of continuity.

On the other hand, the concentration of interest in the
symbol on the sole personality of the priest and of the single
sacrifice enabled him to voice what was his predominant belief
about Jesus.   How profoundly he was engrossed by the idea of
Christ's adequacy as mediator may be judged from his avoidance
of some current religious beliefs about intercession.   Over and
again he comes to a point where contemporary opinions (with
which he was quite familiar) suggested, *e.g.*, the intercession of
angels in heaven, or of departed saints on behalf of men on
earth, ideas like the merits of the fathers or the atoning efficacy
of martyrdom in the past, to facilitate the approach of sinful
men to God (cp. on 11⁴⁰ 12¹⁷·²³·²⁴ etc.).   These he deliberately
ignores.   In view of the single, sufficient sacrifice of Jesus, in
the light of his eternally valid intercession, no supplementary
aid was required.   It is not accidental that such beliefs are left
out of our author's scheme of thought.   It is a fresh proof of
his genuinely primitive faith in Jesus as the one mediator.   The
ideas of the perfect Priest and the perfect Sacrifice are a theological expression, in symbolic language, of what was vital to the
classical piety of the early church; and apart from Paul no
one set this out so cogently and clearly as the writer of Πρὸς
Ἑβραίους.

(iii.)

Our modern symbolism does no sort of justice to the ancient
idea of priesthood.   Matthew Arnold says of Wordsworth:

> "He was a priest to us all,
>   Of the wonder and bloom of the world,
>   Which we saw with his eyes, and were glad."

That is, "priest" means interpreter, one who introduces us to a
deeper vision, one who, as we might put it, opens up to us a
new world of ideas.   Such is not the ultimate function of Christ
as ἱερεύς in our epistle.   Dogmatic theology would prefer to
call this the prophetic function of Christ, but the priestly office
means mediation, not interpretation.   The function of the highpriest is to enter and to offer: εἰσέρχεσθαι and προσφέρειν forming
the complete action, and no distinction being drawn between the
two, any more than between the terms "priest" and "highpriest."

The fundamental importance of this may be illustrated from
the recourse made by Paul and by our author respectively to the

Jeremianic oracle of the new covenant or διαθήκη. Paul's main interest in it lies in its prediction of the Spirit, as opposed to the Law. What appeals to Paul is the inward and direct intuition of God, which forms the burden of the oracle. But to our author ($8^{7\text{-}13}$ $10^{15\text{-}18}$) it is the last sentence of the oracle which is supreme, *i.e.* the remission of sins; "I will be merciful to their iniquities, and remember their sins no more." He seizes the name and fact of a "new" covenant, as implying that the old was inadequate. But he continues: "If the blood of goats and bulls, and the ashes of a heifer, sprinkled on defiled persons, give them a holiness that bears on bodily purity, how much more will the blood of Christ, who in the spirit of the eternal offered himself as an unblemished sacrifice to God, cleanse your conscience from dead works to serve a living God? He mediates a new covenant for this reason, that those who have been called may obtain the eternal deliverance they have been promised, now that a death has occurred which redeems them from the transgressions involved in the first covenant" ($9^{13\text{-}15}$). That is, the conclusion of Jeremiah's oracle—that God will forgive and forget—is the real reason why our author quotes it. There can be no access without an amnesty for the past; the religious communion of the immediate future must be guaranteed by a sacrifice ratifying the pardon of God.

This difference between Paul and our author is, of course, owing to the fact that for the latter the covenant[1] or law is subordinated to the priesthood. Change the priesthood, says the writer, and *ipso facto* the law has to be changed too. The covenant is a relationship of God and men, arising out of grace, and inaugurated by some historic act; since its efficiency as an institution for forgiveness and fellowship depends on the personality and standing of the priesthood, the appearance of Jesus as the absolute Priest does away with the inferior law.

This brings us to the heart of the Christology, the sacrifice and priestly service of Christ as the mediator of this new covenant with its eternal fellowship.

Men are sons of God, and their relation of confidence and access is based upon the function of the Son κατ᾽ ἐξόχην. The author shares with Paul the view that the Son is the Son before and during his incarnate life, and yet perhaps Son in a special sense in consequence of the resurrection—or rather, as our author would have preferred to say, in consequence of the ascension. This may be the idea underneath the compressed clauses at the opening of the epistle ($1^{1\text{-}5}$). "God has spoken to us by

---

[1] As Professor Kennedy points out, with real insight: "all the terms of the contrast which he works out are selected because of their relation to the covenant-conception" (p. 201).

a Son—a Son whom he appointed heir of the universe, as it
was by him that he had created the world. He, reflecting God's
bright glory and stamped with God's own character, sustains the
universe by his word of power; when he had secured our
purification from sins, he sat down at the right hand of the
Majesty on high; and thus he is superior to the angels, as he
has inherited a Name superior to theirs. For to what angel did
God ever say—

'Thou art my Son,
To-day have I become thy Father'?"

(referring to the ancient notion that the king first became conscious of his latent divine sonship at his accession to the throne).
The name or dignity which Christ inherits, as the result of his
redemptive work, is probably that of Son; as the following
quotation from the OT psalm suggests, the resurrection or
exaltation may mark, as it does for Paul, the fully operative
sonship of Christ, the only way to inherit or possess the
universe being to endure the suffering and death which purified
human sin and led to the enthronement of Christ. Our author
holds that this divine being was sent into the world because he
was God's Son, and that he freely undertook his mission for
God's other sons on earth.

The mission was a will of God which involved sacrifice.
That is the point of the quotation ($10^{5f.}$) from the 40th psalm
—not to prove that obedience to God was better than sacrifice,
but to bring out the truth that God's will required a higher kind
of sacrifice than the levitical, namely, the personal, free self-
sacrifice of Christ in the body. Even this is more than self-
sacrifice in our modern sense of the term. It is "by this will,"
the writer argues, that "we are consecrated, because Jesus Christ
once for all has offered up his body." No doubt the offering is
eternal, it is not confined to the historical act on Calvary. "He
has entered heaven itself, now to appear in the presence of God
on our behalf" (9^{24}): "he is always living to make intercession
for us" (7^{25}). Still, the author is more realistic in expression than
the tradition of the *Testament of Levi* (3), which makes the
angel of the Presence in the third heaven offer a spiritual and
bloodless sacrifice to God in propitiation for the sins of ignorance
committed by the righteous. Our author assigns entirely to Christ
the intercessory functions which the piety of the later Judaism
had already begun to divide among angels and departed saints,
but he also makes the sacrifice of Jesus one of blood—a realism
which was essential to his scheme of argument from the
entrance of the OT high priest into the inner shrine.

The superior or rather the absolute efficacy of the blood of

Christ depends in turn on his absolute significance as the
Son of God; it is his person and work which render his self-
sacrifice valid and supreme.   But this is asserted rather than
explained.   Indeed, it is asserted on the ground of a presupposition which was assumed as axiomatic, namely, the impossibility
of communion with God apart from blood shed in sacrifice
(9²²).   For example, when the writer encourages his readers by
reminding them of their position (12²⁴), that they "have come
to Jesus the mediator of the new covenant and to the sprinkled
blood whose message is nobler than Abel's," he does not mean
to draw an antithesis between Abel's blood as a cry for vengeance
and Christ's blood as a cry for intercession.   The fundamental
antithesis lies between exclusion and inclusion.   Abel's blood
demanded the excommunication of the sinner, as an outcast
from God's presence; Christ's blood draws the sinner near and
ratifies the covenant.   The author denies to the OT cultus of
sacrifice any such atoning value, but at the same time he reaffirms
its basal principle, that blood in sacrifice is essential to communion
with the deity.   Blood offered in sacrifice does possess a religious
efficacy, to expiate and purify.   Without shedding of blood there
is no remission.   We ask, why?   But the ancient world never
dreamt of asking, why?   What puzzles a modern was an axiom
to the ancient.   The argument of our epistle is pivoted on this
postulate, and no attempt is made to rationalize it.

In the Law of Holiness, incorporated in Leviticus, there is
indeed one incidental allusion to the rationalê of sacrifice or
blood-expiation, when, in prohibiting the use of blood as a food,
the taboo proceeds: "the life of the body is in the blood, and
I have given it to you for the altar to make propitiation for
yourselves, for the blood makes propitiation by means of the
life" (i.e. the life inherent in it).   This is reflection on the
meaning of sacrifice, but it does not carry us very far, for it only
explains the piacular efficacy of blood by its mysterious potency
of life.   Semitic scholars warn us against finding in these words
(Lv 17¹¹) either the popular idea of the substitution of the victim
for the sinner, or even the theory that the essential thing in
sacrifice is the offering of a life to God.   As far as the Hebrew
text goes, this may be correct.   But the former idea soon became
attached to the verse, as we see from the LXX—τὸ γὰρ αἷμα
αὐτοῦ ἀντὶ τῆς ψυχῆς ἐξιλάσεται.   This view does not seem to be
common in later Jewish thought, though it was corroborated by
the expiatory value attached to the death of the martyrs (e.g.
4 Mac 17²²).   It is in this later world, however, rather than in
the primitive world of Leviticus, that the atmosphere of the idea
of Πρὸς ʽΕβραίους is to be sought, the idea that because Jesus
was what he was, his death has such an atoning significance as

to inaugurate a new and final relation between God and men, the idea that his blood purifies the conscience because it is *his* blood, the blood of the sinless Christ, who is both the priest and the sacrifice. When the author writes that Christ "in the spirit of the eternal" (9^{14}) offered himself as an unblemished sacrifice to God, he has in mind the contrast between the annual sacrifice on the day of atonement and the sacrifice of Christ which never needed to be repeated, because it had been offered in the spirit and—as we might say—in the eternal order of things. It was a sacrifice bound up with his death in history, but it belonged essentially to the higher order of absolute reality. The writer breathed the Philonic atmosphere in which the eternal Now over-shadowed the things of space and time (see on 1^5), but he knew this sacrifice had taken place on the cross, and his problem was one which never confronted Philo, the problem which we moderns have to face in the question : How can a single historical fact possess a timeless significance? How can Christianity claim to be final, on the basis of a specific revelation in history? Our author answered this problem in his own way for his own day.

(iv.)

For him religion is specially fellowship with God on the basis of forgiveness. He never uses the ordinary term κοινωνία, however, in this sense. It is access to God on the part of worshippers that is central to his mind ; that is, he conceives religion as worship, as the approach of the human soul to the divine Presence, and Christianity is the religion which is religion since it mediates this access and thereby secures the immediate consciousness of God for man. Or, as he would prefer to say, the revelation of God in Jesus has won this right for man as it could not be won before. For, from the first, there has been a People of God seeking, and to a certain extent enjoying, this access. God has ever been revealing himself to them, so far as was possible. But now in Jesus the final revelation has come which supersedes all that went before in Israel. The writer never contemplates any other line of revelation ; outside Israel of old he never looks. It is enough for him that the worship of the OT implied a revelation which was meant to elicit faith, especially through the sacrificial cultus, and that the imperfections of that revelation have now been disclosed and superseded by the revelation in Jesus the Son. Faith in this revelation is in one aspect belief ($4^{2f.}$). Indeed he describes faith simply as the conviction of the unseen world, the assurance that God has spoken and that he will make his word good, if men rely upon it ; he who draws near to God must believe that he exists and that he does reward those who seek him (11⁶). Faith of this noble kind, in spite of appearances to the contrary, has always characterized the People. Our author rejoices to trace it at work long before Jesus came, and he insists that it is the saving power still, a faith which in some aspects is indistinguishable from hope, since it inspires the soul to act and suffer in the conviction that God is real and sure to reward loyalty in the next world, if not in the present. Such faith characterized Jesus himself (2¹³ 12²). It is belief in God as trustworthy, amid all the shows and changes of life, an inward conviction that, when he has spoken, the one thing for a man to do is to hold to that word and to obey it at all costs. This is the conception of faith in the early and the later sections of the writing (3⁷ᶠ· 10³⁸–12²). The difference that Jesus has made—for the writer seems to realize that there is a difference between the primitive faith and the faith of those who are living after the revelation in Jesus—is this, that the assurance of faith has now become far more real than it was. Though even now believers have to await the full measure of their reward, though faith still is hope to some extent, yet the full realization of the fellowship with God which is the supreme object of faith has been now made through Jesus. In two ways. (i) For faith Jesus is the inspiring example ; he is the great Believer who has shown in his own life on earth the possibilities of faith.[1] In order to understand what faith is, we must look to Jesus above all, to see how faith begins and continues and ends. But (ii) Jesus has not only preceded us on the line of faith ; he has by his sacrifice made our access to God direct and real, as it never could be before. Hence the writer can say, "let us draw near with a full assurance of faith and a true heart, in absolute assurance of faith" since "we have a great Priest over the house of God." "We have confidence to enter the holy Presence in virtue of the blood of Jesus." He does not make Jesus the object of faith as Paul does, but he argues that only the sacrifice of Jesus opens the way into the presence of God for sinful men.

This is the argument of the central part of the writing (chs. 7–10). Religion is worship, and worship implies sacrifice ; there is no access for man to God without sacrifice, and no

---

[1] "It was by no divine magic, no mere 'breath, turn of eye, wave of hand,' that he 'joined issue with death,' but by the power of that genuinely human faith which had inspired others in the past" (MacNeill, p. 26). Bousset's denial of this (*Theol. Literaturzeitung*, 1915, p. 431 f. : "man wird bei dem Jesus d. Hebräerbriefe so wenig wie bei dem paulinischen noch im strengen Sinne von einem subjectivem Glauben Jesu reden können") is as incomprehensible as his desperate effort to explain He 5⁷⁻¹⁰ from the fixed ideas of the mystery-religions.

religion without a priest (see on 7^{11}). The relations between
God and his People from the first [1] have been on the basis of
sacrifice, as the bible shows, and the new revelation in Jesus
simply changes the old sacrificial order with its priesthood for
another. The writer starts from a profound sense of sin, as an
interruption of fellowship between God and man. He thoroughly
sympathizes with the instinct which underlay the ancient practice
of sacrifice, that fellowship with God is not a matter of course,
that God is accessible and yet difficult of access, and that human
nature cannot find its way unaided into his presence. Thus he
quotes the 40th psalm (see p. xli), not to prove that God's will
is fellowship, and that to do the will of God is enough for man,
apart from any sacrifice, but to illustrate the truth that the will
of God does require a sacrifice, not simply the ethical obedience
of man, but the self-sacrifice with which Jesus offered himself
freely, the perfect victim and the perfect priest. All men now
have to do is to avail themselves of his sacrifice in order to
enjoy access to God in the fullest sense of the term. "Having
a great Highpriest who has passed through the heavens, let us
draw near."

The conception of religion as devotion or worship covers a
wide range in Πρὸς Ἐβραίους. It helps to explain, for example
(see above, p. xxxviii), why the writer represents Jesus after death
not as being raised from the dead, but as passing through the
heavens into the inner Presence or sanctuary of God with the
sacrifice of his blood (4^{14} $9^{11f.}$). It accounts for the elaboration
of a detail like that of 9^{23}, and, what is much more important, it
explains the "sacrificial" delineation of the Christian life. In
this ἀληθινὴ σκηνή (8^2), of God's own making, with its θυσιαστήριον (13^{10}), Christians worship God (λατρεύειν, 9^{14} 12^{28} 13^{10});
their devotion to him is expressed by the faith and loyalty which
detach them from this world ($13^{13.\ 14}$) and enable them to live
and move under the inspiration of the upper world; indeed their
ethical life of thanksgiving (see on 2^{12}) and beneficence is a
sacrifice by which they honour and worship God ($13^{15.\ 16}$), a
sacrifice presented to God by their ἀρχιερεύς Jesus. The writer
never suggests that the worship-regulations of the outworn cultus
are to be reproduced in any rites of the church on earth; he
never dreamed of this, any more than of the ἡγούμενοι being
called "priests." The essence of priesthood, viz. the mediation
of approach to God, had been absolutely fulfilled in Jesus, and
in one sense all believers were enabled to follow him into the
inner σκηνή, where they worshipped their God as the priests of
old had done in their σκηνή, and as the People of old had never

---

[1] *i.e.* from the inauguration of the διαθήκη at Sinai, though he notes that
even earlier there was sacrifice offered (11^3).

been able to do except through the highpriest as their representative and proxy. But, while the worship-idea is drawn out to describe Christians, in Πρὸς Ἑβραίους its primary element is that of the eternal function of Christ as ἀρχιερεύς in the heavenly σκηνή.

(v.)

Symbolism alters as the ages pass. The picture-language in which one age expresses its mental or religious conceptions often ceases to be intelligible or attractive to later generations, because the civic, ritual, or economic conditions of life which had originally suggested it have disappeared or changed their form. This well-known principle applies especially to the language of religion, and it is one reason why some of the arguments in Πρὸς Ἑβραίους are so difficult for the modern mind to follow. There are other reasons, no doubt. The exegetical methods which the author took over from the Alexandrian school are not ours. Besides, historical criticism has rendered it hard for us moderns to appreciate the naive use of the OT which prevails in some sections of Πρὸς Ἑβραίους. But, above all, the sacrificial analogies are a stumbling-block, for we have nothing to correspond to what an ancient understood by a "priest" and sacrifice. Dryden was not poetic when he translated Vergil's "sacerdos" in the third Georgic (489) by "holy butcher," but the phrase had its truth. The business of a priest was often that of a butcher ; blood flowed, blood was splashed about. It was in terms of such beliefs and practices that the author of Πρὸς Ἑβραίους argued, rising above them to the spiritual conception of the self-sacrifice of Jesus, but nevertheless starting from them as axiomatic. The duty of the modern mind is to understand, in the first place, how he came by these notions ; and, in the second place, what he intended to convey by the use of such symbolic terms as "blood," "highpriest," and "sacrifice."

The striking idea of Christ as the eternal ἀρχιερεύς, by whom the access of man to God is finally and fully assured, may have been a flash of inspiration, one of the notes of originality and insight which mark the writer's treatment and restatement of the faith. But originality is not depreciated by the effort to trace anticipations. What led him to this view? After all, the most brilliant flashes depend upon an atmosphere already prepared for them. They are struck out of something. In this case, it is not enough to say that the conception was merely the transference to Jesus of the Philonic predicates of the Logos, or the result of a bible-reading in the pentateuch. In the pentateuch the writer found proofs of what he brought to it, and the arguments in chs. 7–10 really buttress ideas built on other foundations.

(*a*) Once the conception of a heavenly sanctuary became current, the notion of a heavenly ἀρχιερεύς would not be far-fetched for a writer like this. Philo had, indeed, not only spoken of the Logos as a highpriest, in a metaphorical sense, *i.e.* as mediating metaphysically and psychologically the relations between the worlds of thought and sense, but in an allegorical fashion spoken of "two temples belonging to God, one being the world in which the highpriest is his own Son, the Logos, the other being the rational soul" (*de Somniis*, i. 37). Our writer is much less abstract. Like the author of the Apocalypse (see on 4[16]), he thinks of heaven in royal and ritual imagery as well as in civic, but it is the ritual symbolism which is more prominent. During the second century B.C. the ideas of a heavenly sanctuary and a heavenly altar became current in apocalyptic piety, partly owing to the idealistic and yet realistic conception (see on 8[5]) that in heaven the true originals were preserved, the material altar and sanctuary being, like the earthly Jerusalem, inferior representations of transcendent realities. From this it was a natural development to work out the idea of a heavenly highpriest. By "natural" I do not mean to undervalue the poetical and religious originality of the writer of Πρὸς Ἑβραίους. The author of the Apocalypse of John, for example, fails to reach this idea, and even in the enigmatic passage in the vision and confession of Levi (*Testaments of the Twelve Patriarchs*, Test. Levi 5), where the seer tells us, "I saw the holy temple, and upon a throne of glory the Most High. And he said to me, Levi, I have given thee the blessings of priesthood until I come and sojourn in the midst of Israel"—even here, though the levitical priesthood, as in our epistle, is only a temporary substitute for the presence of God, the heavenly sanctuary has no highpriest. Nevertheless it was the idea of the heavenly sanctuary which held one germ of the idea of the heavenly highpriest for the author of Πρὸς Ἑβραίους, as he desired to express the fundamental significance of Jesus for his faith.

(*b*) Another factor was the speculations of Philo about the Logos as highpriest (*de Migrat. Abrah.* 102, *de Fug.* 108 ff.), though the priestly mediation there is mainly between man and the upper world of ideas. The Logos or Reason is not only the means of creating the material cosmos after the pattern of the first and real world, but inherent in it, enabling human creatures to apprehend the invisible. This is Philo's primary use of the metaphor. It is philosophical rather than religious. Yet the increased prestige of the highpriest in the later Judaism prompted him to apply to the Logos functions which resemble intercession as well as interpretation. Vague as they are, they were familiar to the author of our epistle, and it is probable that they helped to fashion his expression of the eternal significance of Jesus as the mediator between man and God. The Logos as highpriest, says Philo (*de Somn.* ii. 28), for example, is not only ἄμωμος, ὁλόκληρος, but μεθόριός τις θεοῦ <καὶ ἀνθρώπου> φύσις, τοῦ μὲν ἐλάττων, ἀνθρώπου δὲ κρείττων. Then he quotes the LXX of Lv 16[17]. The original says that no man is to be with the highpriest when he enters the inner shrine, but the Greek version runs, ὅταν εἰσίῃ εἰς τὰ ἅγια τῶν ἁγίων ὁ ἀρχιερεὺς, ἄνθρωπος οὐκ ἔσται, and Philo dwells on the literal, wrong sense of the last three words, as if they meant "the highpriest is not to be a man." "What will he be, if he is not a man? God? I would not say that (οὐκ ἂν εἴποιμι). . . . Nor yet is he man, but he touches both extremes (ἑκατέρων τῶν ἄκρων, ὡς ἂν βάσεως καὶ κεφαλῆς, ἐφαπτόμενος)." Later (*ibid.* 34) he remarks, "if at that time he is not a man, it is clear he is not God either, but a minister (λειτουργὸς θεοῦ) of God, belonging to creation in his mortal nature and to the uncreated world in his immortal nature." Similarly he pleads, in the *de sacerdot.* 12, that the function of the highpriest was to mediate between God and man, ἵνα διὰ μέσου τινὸς ἄνθρωποι μὲν ἱλάσκωνται θεόν, θεὸς δὲ τὰς χάριτας ἀνθρώποις ὑποδιακόνῳ τινὶ χρώμενος ὀρέγῃ καὶ χορηγῇ. Here we may feel vibrating a need of intercession, even although the idea is still somewhat theosophic.

(c) A third basis for the conception of Christ's priesthood lay in the combination of messianic and sacerdotal functions which is reflected in the 110th psalm (see above, p. xxxiii), which in the *Testaments of the Patriarchs* (Reuben 6[8]) is actually applied to Hyrcanus the Maccabean priest-king, while in the *Test. Levi* (18) functions which are messianic in all but name are ascribed to a new priest, with more spiritual insight than in the psalm itself. The curious thing, however, is that this Priest discharges no sacerdotal functions. The hymn describes his divine attestation and consecration—"and in his priesthood shall sin come to an end, and he shall open the gates of paradise and shall remove the threatening sword against Adam." That is all. Probably the passing phase of expectation, that a messiah would arise from the sacerdotal Maccabees, accounts for such a fusion of messiah and priest. In any case its influence was not wide. Still, the anticipation is not unimportant for the thought of Πρὸς Ἑβραίους, which rests so much upon the mystical significance of that psalm. Paul had seen the fulfilment of Ps 110[1] in the final triumph of Christ as messiah over his foes (1 Co 15[24, 25] δεῖ γὰρ αὐτὸν βασιλεύειν ἄχρις οὗ θῇ πάντας τοὺς ἐχθροὺς ὑπὸ τοὺς πόδας αὐτοῦ). But meantime Christ was in living touch with his church on earth, and Paul can even speak, in a glowing outburst, of his effective intercession (Ro 8[34] ὃς καὶ ἐντυγχάνει ὑπὲρ ἡμῶν). This is at least the idea of the highpriesthood of Christ, in almost everything except name, though Paul says as much of the Spirit (Ro 8²⁷ κατὰ θεὸν ἐντυγχάνει ὑπὲρ ἁγίων). Later, in the Fourth Gospel, a similar thought reappears; Christ is represented in priestly metaphor as interceding for his People (17¹ᶠ·), and the phrases (17¹⁷⁻¹⁹) about Jesus consecrating himself (as priest and victim) that thereby his disciples may be "consecrated" ἐν τῇ ἀληθείᾳ (i.e. in the sphere of Reality), indicate a use of ἁγιάζειν which expresses one of the central ideas of Πρὸς ʽΕβραίους. But in the latter writing the idea is explicit and elaborate, as it is nowhere else in the NT, and explicit on the basis of a later line in the 110th psalm, which Paul ignored. Our author also knew and used the earlier couplet (10¹³), but he draws his cardinal argument from v.⁴ σὺ εἶ ἱερεὺς εἰς αἰῶνα κατὰ τὴν τάξιν Μελχισέδεκ.

(vi.)

There is a partial anticipation of all this in the Enochic conception of the Son of Man. No doubt, as Volz warns us (*Jüdische Eschatologie*, p. 90), we must not read too much into such apocalyptic phrases, since the Son of Man is an x quantity of personal value in the age of expected bliss and salvation. Still, the pre-existent messiah there is Son of Man as transcendent and in some sense as human; he must be human, "Man," in order to help men, and he must be transcendent in order to be a deliverer or redeemer. But the author of Πρὸς ʽΕβραίους, like Paul, significantly avoids the term Son of Man, even in 2⁶ᶠ·; and although he has these two ideas of human sympathy and of transcendency in close connexion, he derives them from his meditation upon the real Jesus ultimately, not from any apocalyptic speculations. What he meant by the term "Son of God" is not quite plain. Philo had regarded the Logos as pre-existent and as active in the history of the people, and so he regards Christ; but while it seems clear (see on 5⁵) that Christ is priest for him because he was already Son, the further questions, when did he become priest? and how is the Sonship compatible with the earthly life?—these are problems which remain unsolved. The interpretation of the function of Jesus through the phrase in the 2nd psalm (see on 1⁵) hardly clears up the matter any more than in the case of Justin Martyr (*Dial.* 88). Later on, Hippolytus, or whoever wrote the homily appended (chs. xi.–xii.) to the *Epist. Diognet.*, faced the problem more boldly and beautifully by arguing that "the Word was from the very beginning, appeared new, was proved to be old, and is ever young as he is born in the hearts of the saints. He is the eternal One, who to-day was accounted Son" (ὁ σήμερον υἱὸς λογισθείς, 11⁵). Here "to-day" refers to the Christian era;

d

evidently the problem left by the author of Πρὸς Ἐβραίους, with his mystical, timeless use of the 2nd psalm, was now being felt as a theological difficulty. But this is no clue to how he himself took the reference. There is a large section in his thought upon Christ as the eternal, transcendental Son which remains obscure to us, and which perhaps was indefinite to himself. He took over the idea of the divine Sonship from the primitive church, seized upon it to interpret the sufferings and sacrificial function of Jesus as well as his eternal value, and linked it to the notion of the highpriesthood; but he does not succeed in harmonizing its implications about the incarnate life with his special γνῶσις of the eternal Son within the higher sphere of divine realities.

At the same time there seems no hiatus [1] between the meta-physical and the historical in the writer's conception of Jesus, no unreconciled dualism between the speculative reconstruction and the historical tradition. In Πρὸς Ἐβραίους we have the ordinary primitive starting-point, how could a divine, reigning Christ ever have become man? The writer never hints that his readers would question this, for they were not tempted by any Jewish ideas. He uses the category of the Son quite frankly, in order to express the absolute value of the revelation in Jesus ; it is his sheer sense of the reality of the incarnate life which prompts him to employ the transcendental ideas. He does not start from a modern humanist view of Jesus, but from a conviction of his eternal divine character and function as Son and as ἀρχιερεύς, and his argument is that this position was only possible upon the human experience, that Jesus became man because he was Son (2[10f.]), and is ἀρχιερεύς because once he was man.

(a) For our author Jesus is the Son, before ever he became man, but there is no definite suggestion (see on 12[2]) that he made a sacrifice in order to become incarnate, no suggestion that he showed his χάρις by entering our human lot (δι᾽ ὑμᾶς ἐπτώχευσεν πλούσιος ὤν, ἑαυτὸν ἐκένωσεν ἐν ὁμοιώματι ἀνθρώπων γενόμενος). Our author feels deeply the suffering of Jesus in the days of his flesh, but it is the final sacrifice at the end of his life which is emphasized. That he suffered as the eternal Son is understood : also, that it was voluntary (10[5f.]), also that it was his human experience which qualified him to offer the perfect sacrifice, by God's χάρις. But, apart from the (2[8f.]) allusion to the temporary inferiority to angels, the writer does not touch the moving idea of the kenotic theories of the incarnation, viz. the "sense of sacrifice on the part of a pre-existent One."[2]

(b) Since he knew nothing of the sombre view of the σάρξ

---

[1] As H. J. Holtzmann (*Neutest. Theologie*[2], ii. 337) and Pfleiderer (p. 287) imagine.

[2] H. R. Mackintosh, *The Person of Christ*, pp. 265 f.

which pervaded the Pauline psychology, he found no difficulty
in understanding how the sinless Jesus could share human flesh
and blood. The sinlessness is assumed, not argued (cp. on
4^{15} 5^7). Yet the writer does not simply transfer it as a dogmatic
predicate of messiahship to Jesus. One of the characteristics
which set Πρὸς Ἑβραίους apart in the early Christian literature is
the idea that Jesus did not possess sinlessness simply as a prerogative of his divine Sonship or as a requisite for the validity
of his priestly function. It was not a mere endowment. The idea
rather is that he had to realize and maintain it by a prolonged
moral conflict ἐν ταῖς ἡμέραις τῆς σαρκὸς αὐτοῦ. This view goes
back to direct historical tradition, with its deeply marked impression of the personality of Jesus, and no sort of justice is done
to Πρὸς Ἑβραίους if its conceptions of the human Son as sinless
are referred to a theoretical interest or dogmatic prepossession.
Such an interpretation is bound up with the view that Πρὸς
Ἑβραίους represents the more or less arbitrary fusion of an historical tradition about Jesus with a pre-Christian christology.
But it is not enough to speak vaguely of materials for such a
christology floating in pre-Christian Judaism and crystallizing
round the person of Jesus, once Jesus was identified with the
messiah. The crystallization was not fortuitous. What Πρὸς
Ἑβραίους contains is a christology which implies features and
characteristics in Jesus too definite to be explained away as
picturesque deductions from messianic postulates or Philonic
speculations. These undoubtedly enter into the statement of
the christology, but the motives and interests of that christology
lie everywhere. The writer's starting-point is not to be sought
in some semi-metaphysical idea like that of the eternal Son as a
supernatural being who dipped into humanity for a brief interval
in order to rise once more and resume his celestial glory; the
mere fact that the eschatology is retained, though it does not
always accord with the writer's characteristic view of Christ, shows
that he was working from a primitive historical tradition about
Jesus (see above, pp. xliv f.). To this may be added the fact
that he avoids the Hellenistic term σωτήρ, a term which had been
associated with the notion of the appearance of a deity hitherto
hidden.[1] The allusions to the historical Jesus are not numerous,
but they are too detailed and direct to be explained away; he
preached σωτηρία, the message of eschatological bliss; he belonged to the tribe of Judah; he was sorely tempted, badly

---

[1] He does not use the technical language of the mystery-religions (cp. on
6^4), and they cannot be shown to have been present continuously to his mind.
If the argument from silence holds here, he probably felt for them the same
aversion as the devout Philo felt (*de Sacrif.* 12), though Philo on occasion
would employ their terminology for his own purposes.

treated, and finally crucified outside Jerusalem. These are the main outward traits. But they are bound up with an interpretation of the meaning of Jesus which is not a mere deduction from messianic mythology or OT prophecies, and it is unreal, in view of a passage like 5[7f.], e.g., to imagine that the writer was doing little more than painting in a human face among the messianic speculations about a divine Son.

(c) Neither is the sinlessness of Jesus connected with the circumstances of his human origin. No explanation at all is offered of how this pre-existent Son entered the world of men. It is assumed that he did not come out of humanity but that he came into it ; yet, like Paul and the author of the Fourth Gospel (1[9f.]), our author is not interested in questions about the human birth. Even when he describes the prototype Melchizedek as " without father and mother " (7[3]), he is not suggesting any parallel to the Christ; the phrase is no more than a fanciful deduction from the wording or rather the silence of the legend, just as the original priest-king Gudea says to the goddess in the Sumerian tale, " I have no mother, thou art my mother ; I have no father, thou art my father." It is impossible to place this allusion beside the happy misquotation in 10[5] "a body thou hast prepared for me," and to argue, as Pfleiderer (p. 287) does, that the incarnation is conceived as purely supernatural. All we need to do is to recall the Alexandrian belief, voiced in a passage like Wisd 8[19] (" I was the child of fine parts : to my lot there fell a good soul, or rather being good I entered a body undefiled "); the good soul is what we call the personality, the thinking self, to which God allots a body, and birth, in the ordinary human way, is not incompatible with the pre-existence of the soul or self which, prior to birth, is in the keeping of God. The author of Πρὸς Ἑβραίους could quite well think of the incarnation of Jesus along such lines, even although for him the pre-existent Christ meant much more than the pre-existent human soul.

The meaning of the incarnation is, in one aspect, to yield a perfect example of faith (12[2f.]) in action ; in another and, for the writer, a deeper, to prepare Jesus, by sympathy and suffering, for his sacrificial function on behalf of the People. The rationalê of his death is that it is inexplicable except upon the fact of his relationship to men as their representative and priest before God (2[11f.]). From some passages like 5[3f.] 7[27], it has been inferred that Jesus had to offer a sacrifice on his own behalf as well as on behalf of men (i.e. his tears and cries in Gethsemane), or that he only overcame his sinful nature when he was raised to heaven. But this is to read into the letter of the argument more than the writer ever intended it to convey. The point of his daring argument is that the sufferings of Jesus were not incompatible with his sinlessness, and at the same time that they rendered his sacrifice of himself absolutely efficacious. The writer is evidently in line with the primitive synoptic tradition, though he never proves the necessity of the sufferings from OT prophecy, as even his contemporary Peter does, preferring, with a fine intuition in the form of a religious reflection, to employ the idea of moral congruity (2^{10}).

(vii.)

The symbolism of the highpriesthood and sacrifice of Jesus in the heavenly sanctuary is therefore designed to convey the truth that the relations of men with God are based finally upon Jesus Christ. In the unseen world which is conceived in this naive idealistic way, Jesus is central; through him God is known and accessible to man, and through him man enjoys forgiveness and fellowship with God. When Paul once wrote, τὰ ἄνω φρονεῖτε, τὰ ἄνω ζητεῖτε, if he had stopped there he would have been saying no more than Epictetus or Marcus Aurelius might have said and did say. But when he added, οὗ ὁ Χριστός ἐστιν (ἐν δεξιᾷ τοῦ θεοῦ καθήμενος), he defined the upper sphere in a new sense. So with the author of Πρὸς Ἑβραίους. In the real world of higher things, "everything is dominated by the figure of the great High Priest at the right hand of the Majesty in the Heavens, clothed in our nature, compassionate to our infirmities, able to save to the uttermost, sending timely succour to those who are in peril, pleading our cause. It is this which faith sees, this to which faith clings as the divine reality behind and beyond all that passes, all that tries, daunts, or discourages the soul: it is this in which it finds the *ens realissimum*, the very truth of things, all that is meant by God."[1]

Yet while this is the central theme (chs. 7–10), which the writer feels it is essential for his friends to grasp if they are to maintain their position, it is one proof of the primitive character of Πρὸς Ἑβραίους that it preserves traces of other and more popular ideas of Christianity. Thus (*a*) there is the primitive idea of the messiah as the heir, who at the resurrection inherits full power as the divine Son or Κληρονόμος. Strictly speaking, this does not harmonize with the conception of the Son as eternal, but it reappears now and then, thrown up from the eschatological tradition which the author retains (see above, pp. xxxiii f.). (*b*) The isolated reference to the overthrow of the devil is another allusion to ideas which were in the background of the writer's mind (see on $2^{14.\,15}$). (*c*) The scanty

[1] Denney, *The Death of Christ*, pp. 239, 240.

use made of the favourite conception of Jesus as the divine
Κύριος (see below, p. lxiii) is also remarkable. This is not one of
the writer's categories; the elements of divine authority and
of a relation between the Κύριος and the divine Community
are expressed otherwise, in the idea of the Highpriest and the
People.

Furthermore the category of the Highpriesthood itself was
not large enough for the writer's full message. (*a*) It could not
be fitted in with his eschatology any more than the idea of the
two worlds could be. The latter is dovetailed into his scheme
by the idea of faith as practically equivalent to hope (in 10³⁵ᶠ·);
the world to come actually enters our experience here and now,
but the full realization is reserved for the end, and meantime
Christians must wait, holding fast to the revelation of God in
the present. The former could not be adjusted to the eschatology, and the result is that when the writer passes to speak in
terms of the primitive expectation of the end (10³⁵–12²⁹), he
allows the idea of the Highpriesthood to fall into the background. In any case the return of Jesus is connected only
with the deliverance of his own People (9²⁸). He does not
come to judge; that is a function reserved for God. The
end is heralded by a cataclysm which is to shake the whole
universe, heaven as well as earth (1¹¹ᶠ· 12²⁶ᶠ·), another conception
which, however impressive, by no means harmonizes with the
idea of the two spheres. But the writer's intense consciousness of
living in the last days proved too strong for his speculative theory
of the eternal and the material orders. (*b*) Again, the Highpriesthood was inadequate to the ethical conceptions of the
writer. It did involve ethical ideas—the cleansing of the conscience and the prompting of devotion and awe, moral consecration, and inward purity (these being the real "worship");
but when he desires to inspire his readers he instinctively turns
to the vivid conception of Jesus as the ἀρχηγός, as the pioneer
and supreme example of faith on earth.

The latter aspect brings out the idea of a contemplation
of Jesus Christ, a vision of his reality (cp. 3¹ 12¹· ²), which,
when correlated with the idea of a participation in the higher
world of reality, as embodied in the Highpriest aspect, raises
the question, how far is it legitimate to speak of the writer as
mystical?

(viii.)

To claim or to deny that he was a mystic is, after all, a
question of words. He is devoid of the faith-mysticism which
characterizes Paul. Even when he speaks once of believers being
μέτοχοι Χριστοῦ (3¹⁴), he means no more than their membership

in the household of God over which Christ presides; there is no hint of the personal trust in Christ which distinguishes "faith" in Paul. As important is the consideration that the writer does not take the sacrifices of the levitical cultus as merely symbolizing union with God. Such is the genuinely mystical interpretation. To him, on the other hand, sacrifice is an action which bears upon man's relation to God, and it is from this point of view that he estimates and criticizes the levitical cultus. But while technically he is not a mystic, even in the sense in which that much-abused term may be applied to any NT writer, he has notes and qualities which might be called "mystical." To call him an "idealist" is the only alternative, and this is misleading, for idealism suggests a philosophical detachment which is not suitable to Πρὸς ʽΕβραίους. On the other hand, his profound sense of the eternal realities, his view of religion as inspired by the unseen powers of God, his conception of fellowship with God as based on the eternal presence of Jesus in heaven—these and other elements in his mind mark him as a definitely unworldly spirit, impatient of any sensuous medium, even of a sacrificial meal, that would interpose between the human soul and God. Not that he uses any pantheistic language; he is more careful to avoid this than a writer like the author of First John. His deep moral nature conceives of God as a transcendent Majestic Being, before whom believers must feel awe and reverence, even as they rejoice and are thankful. He has a wholesome sense of God's authority, and an instinctive aversion to anything like a sentimental, presumptuous piety (see above, pp. xxxv f.). Yet as he speaks of the Rest or the City of God, as he describes the eternal Sanctuary, or the unshaken order of things, or as he delineates the present position of God's People here in their constant dependence on the unseen relation between Christ and God, he almost tempts us to call him "mystical," if "mysticism" could be restricted to the idea that the human soul may be united to Absolute Reality or God. He is certainly not mystical as Philo is;[1] there is no hint in Πρὸς ʽΕβραίους, for example, of an individualistic, occasional rapture, in which the soul soars above sense and thought into the empyrean of the unconditioned. He remains in close touch with moral realities and the historical tradition. But the spirituality of his outlook, with its speculative reach and its steady openness to influences pouring from the unseen realities, hardly deserves to be denied the name of "mystical," simply because it is neither wistful nor emotional.

[1] The soundest account of Philo's "mysticism" is by Professor H. A. A. Kennedy in *Philo's Contribution to Religion*, p. 211 f.

§ 3. STYLE AND DICTION.

(i.)

Πρὸς Ἐβραίους is distinguished, among the prose works of the primitive church, by its rhythmical cadences. The writer was acquainted with the oratorical rhythms which were popularized by Isokrates, and although he uses them freely, when he uses them at all, his periods show traces of this rhetorical method. According to Aristotle's rules upon the use of paeans in prose rhythm (*Rhet.* iii. 8. 6–7), the opening ought to be – ◡◡◡, while ◡◡◡ – should be reserved for the conclusion.

Our author, however, begins with πολυμερῶς, an introductory rhythm (cp. 1⁵ 3¹²) which seems to be rather a favourite with him, *e.g.* 3¹ ὅθεν ἀδελφ, 7¹⁰ ἔτι γαρ εν τη, 12²⁵ βλεπετε μη, 13²⁰ ὁ δε θεος, though he varies it with an anapaest and an iambus ◡◡–◡– (*e.g.* 2¹·⁴·⁵·¹⁴ 11¹⁶ διὸ οὐκ ἐπαισχ, 12¹² etc.), or – – ◡ – – (as in 5¹² 6⁴ 7⁷, see below, 13⁵ αὐτὸς γὰρ εἴρηκ, etc.), or – – – – – (as in 2³ 3⁵ 11⁶ πιστεῦσαι γὰρ δεῖ, 11³⁹ etc.), or even occasionally with three trochees – ◡ – ◡ – ◡ (*e.g.* 12⁸), or – ◡ – – – (12¹¹ 13¹³ etc.), or – ◡◡◡ – – (*e.g.* 1¹³ 4¹²), or even two anapaests (*e.g.* 1⁶ 5¹¹ 13¹⁰), or – – – ◡ – (13³). He also likes to carry on or even to begin a new sentence or paragraph with the same or a similar rhythm as in the end of the preceding, *e.g.* – ◡◡◡ – – ◡◡◡ – in 4¹¹ and 4¹², or ◡◡◡ – – ◡ – – ◡ in 7²¹ and 7²², or as in 8¹³ (– – ◡ – – – ≅ – – – – ≅ ◡◡◡ – – – – – ≅ – – ◡◡◡ – –) and 9¹ (– – ◡ – – – ≅ ◡ – – ◡◡◡ – ≅ ◡◡◡ – – ◡ –), or – – ◡◡◡ – as in 10¹⁰ and 10¹¹, and to repeat a rhythm twice in succession, as, *e.g.*, – ◡ – – ◡ in 2³ (τηλικαύτης ἀ . . . ἥτις ἀρχὴν λα), ◡◡ – – – – – in 4¹⁰ (ὁ γὰρ εἰσελθὼν εἰς τὴν . . . ἀπὸ τῶν ἔργων αὐτοῦ), or – ◡ – ◡ – – in 12¹ (τοιγαροῦν καὶ ἡμεῖς τηλικοῦτ᾽ ἔχοντες). The standard closing rhythm ◡ ◡ – does not clearly occur till 11³ (γεγονέναι), 11⁴ (ἔτι λαλεῖ), 11²³ (βασιλέως), and 12²⁴; it is not so frequent as, *e.g.*, ◡◡ – – (7²⁸·²⁹ 9²⁶ 10³⁴·³⁵ 11¹³·¹⁵·²⁸ 12³ etc.). He also likes to close with a single or an echoing rhythm like ◡ – ◡ – – – in 1³ (σύνης ἐν ὑψηλοῖς), 2¹⁰ (ἅτ ων τελειῶσαι), 2¹⁸ (πέπονθε πειρασθείς . . . μένοις βοηθῆσαι), or – – ◡ – in 7¹⁹ 9²⁸ (ὀφθήσεται . . . σωτηρίαν), 11⁴ (κεν τῷ θεῷ . . . αὐτοῦ τοῦ θεοῦ), 11²¹ etc. A curious variety in almost parallel clauses occurs in 11¹

– – – ◡ – – ◡ ◡ ◡ – ◡ – ◡ –

ἐστιν δε πιστις ελπιζομενων υποστασις

– – ◡ – – ◡ ◡ – ◡ ◡ ◡ – –

πραγματων ελεγχος ου βλεπομενων,

where the cross cadences are plain, as in Isokrates often.   But
at the end of sentences, as a rule, he prefers ‿‿‿–‿ (παραρυῶμεν, 2¹ 8⁶), or –‿–⸜ (ἧς λαλοῦμεν, 2⁵ 7⁶· ⁷ etc.) or –‿–––
(ὠν τελειῶσαι, 2¹⁰ 2¹⁸ 3¹⁴ 4³· ¹¹ 11²¹ etc.), sometimes the weighty
–––– (2¹⁷ 8² 10³⁹ 11⁹ 11¹⁴ etc.), or ‿–‿– (4¹ 5³· ¹² 10²· ¹⁸· ²⁷
11⁸) now and then, or one or even two (5¹¹) anapaests, often
ending on a short syllable.

He is true to the ancient principle of Isokrates, however, that
prose should be mingled with rhythms of all sorts, especially
iambic and trochaic, and there even happen to be two trimeters
in 12¹⁴, besides the similar rhythm in 12¹³· ²⁶.   Also he secures
smoothness often by avoiding the practice of making a word
which begins with a vowel follow a word which ends with a
vowel (δεῖ τὰ φωνήεντα μὴ συμπίπτειν).   Parallelisms in sound,
sense, and form are not infrequent.   These σχήματα of Isokrates
can be traced, e.g., in 1²· ³ where, by ἀντίθεσις, ὃν . . . πάντων
answers to ὃς . . . ὑποστάσεως αὐτοῦ, as δι’ οὖ . . . ἐποίησεν to
φέρων . . . δυνάμεως αὐτοῦ, or as in 11¹, which is, however, a
case of παρίσωσις or parallelism in form.   As in Wisdom, the
accumulation of short syllables, a characteristic of the later

prose, is frequent in Πρὸς Ἑβραίους (e.g. in 2¹· ² ποτε παραρυ . . .

λογος εγενετο βεβαιος, 6⁹· ¹⁰ και εχομενα . . . ου γαρ αδικος ο θεος),
10²⁵ 11¹²· ¹⁹ 12⁸· ⁹ 13⁴ etc.).   At the same time, Πρὸς Ἑβραίους
is not written in parallel rhythm, like Wisdom (cp. Thackeray's
study in *Journal of Theological Studies*, vi. pp. 232 f.); it is
a prose work, and, besides, we do not expect the same
opportunities for using even prose-rhythms in the theological
centre of the writing, though in the opening chapters and
towards the close, the writer has freer play.   One or two samples
may be cited, e.g., in the two parallel clauses of 1² :

ον εθηκεν κληρονομον παντων

δι ου και εποιησεν τους αιωνας,

or in 1³ where ασεως αυτου answers to αμεως αυτου.   In 2¹⁶ the
two clauses begin with ––– and end with επιλαμβανεται, the
verb being obviously repeated to bring out the anapaestic
rhythm.   The "cretic" (–‿–), which is particularly frequent,
is seen clearly in a carefully wrought passage like 4⁸⁻¹⁰ :

ει γαρ αυτους Ιησους κατεπαυσεν

ουκ αν περι αλλης ελαλει μετα ταυτ(α) ημερας

αρ(α) απολειπεται σαββατισμος τω λαω του θεου

ο γαρ εισελθων εις την καταπαυσιν αυτου

και αυτος κατεπαυσεν

απο των εργων αυτου

ωσπερ απο των ιδιων ο θεος.

There is a repeated attempt at balance, *e.g.* of clauses, like
(11^{33}) :

ηργασαντο δικαιοσυνην

επετυχον επαγγελιων,

where both have the same number of syllables and end on the
same rhythm; or, in the next verse, where δυναμιν πυρος is
echoed in εφυγον στομα, while there is a similar harmony of sound
in the closing syllables of

υροι εν πολεμω

ιναν αλλοτριων,

and in vv.[37] and [38] the balancing is obvious in

εν φονω μαχαιρης

περιηλθον εν

υστερουμενοι θλιβ

εν ερημιαις

or in the chiming of [38] and [39] :

και σπηλαιοις και τοις οπαις της γης

και ουτοι παντες μαρτυρηθεντες δ.

As for the bearing of this rhythmical structure on the text, it does not affect the main passages in question (*e.g.* 2^9 6^2); it rather supports and indeed may explain the omission of τῷ before νἱῷ in 1^1, and of ὅλῳ in 2^2, as well as the right of μελλόντων to stand in 9^{11} and in 10^1; it might favour, however, ἀγγέλων γενόμενος instead of γενόμενος τῶν ἀγγέλων in 1^4, and the insertion of ἡ στεῖρα in 11^{11} and of ὄρει in 12^{18}, if it were pressed; while, on the other hand, as employed by Blass, it buttresses the wrong insertion of μέχρι τέλους βεβαίαν in 3^6, and inferior readings like συγκεκερασμένους and ἀκουσθεῖσιν in 4^2, ἐκδεχομένοις (D*) in 9^{28}, εἰ in 12^7, ἐν χολῇ in 12^{15}, and ἀνέχεσθαι in 13^{22}. But the writer is not shackled to στίχοι, though his mind evidently was familiar with the rhythms in question.

(ii.)

There are traces of vernacular Greek, but the language and style are idiomatic on the whole. Thus the perfect is sometimes employed for the sake of literary variety, to relieve a line of aorists (*e.g.* $11^{17.\ 28}$), and indeed is often used aoristically, without any subtle intention (cp. on 7^6 etc.); it is pedantic to press significance into the tenses, without carefully watching the contemporary Hellenistic usage. The definite article is sparingly employed. Μέν . . . δέ, on the other hand, is more common, as we might expect from the antithetical predilections of the author in his dialectic. As for the prepositions, the avoidance of σύν is remarkable (cp. on 12^{14}), all the more remarkable since our author is fond of verbs compounded with σύν. Oratorical imperatives are used with effect (*e.g.* $3^{1.\ 12}$ 7^4 10^{32} etc.), also double (1^5 $1^{13.\ 14}$ 12^{5-7}) and even triple (3^{16-18}) dramatic questions, as well as single ones ($2^{3.\ 4}$ 7^{11} $9^{13.\ 14}$ 10^{29} 11^{32} 12^9). The style is persuasive, neither diffuse nor concise. The writer shows real skill in managing his transitions, suggesting an idea before he develops it (*e.g.* in 2^{17} 5^6). He also employs artistically parentheses and asides, sometimes of considerable length (*e.g.* καθώς . . . κατάπαυσίν μου 3^{7-11} $5^{13.\ 14}$ 8^5 11^{13-16}), now and then slightly irrelevant (*e.g.* 3^4), but occasionally, as in Plato, of real weight (*e.g.* 2^{16} 7^{12}; οὐδὲν . . . νόμος 7^{19} 10^4; πιστὸς γὰρ ὁ ἐπαγγειλάμενος 10^{23}; ὧν οὐκ ἦν ἄξιος ὁ κόσμος 11^{38} 13^{14}); they frequently explain a phrase (τοῦτ' ἔστιν τὸν διάβολον 2^{14}; τοῦτ' ἔστιν τοὺς ἀδελφοὺς αὐτῶν 7^5; ὁ λαὸς γὰρ ἐπ' αὐτῆς νενομοθέτηται 7^{11}; ἥτις . . . ἐνεστηκότα 9^9; τοῦτ' ἔστιν . . . κτίσεως 9^{11}; τοῦτ' ἔστιν τῆς σαρκὸς αὐτοῦ 10^{20} 12^{20}), especially an OT citation (*e.g.* 4^{10} 6^{13} $7^{2.\ 7}$; αἵτινες κατὰ νόμον προσφέρονται 10^8) on which the writer comments in passing. One outstanding feature of the style (for Πρὸς Ἑβραίους is λέξις κατεστραμμένη, not λέξις εἰρόμενη in the sense of rapid dialogue) is the number of long, carefully constructed sentences (*e.g.* 1^{1-4} 2^{2-4} $2^{14.\ 15}$ 3^{12-15} $4^{12.\ 13}$,

5$^{1-8}$ 5$^{7-10}$ 6$^{4-6}$ 6$^{16-20}$ 7$^{1-3}$ 8$^{4-6}$ 9$^{2-5}$ 9$^{6-10}$ 9$^{24-26}$ 10$^{11-13}$ 10$^{19-25}$ 11$^{24-26}$ 12$^{1, 2}$ 12$^{18-24}$). Yet his short sentences are most effective, *e.g.* 2^{18} 4^{8} 10^{18}, and once at least (3$^{16-18}$) there is a touch of the rapid, staccato *diatribe* style, which lent itself to the needs of popular preaching. He loves a play on words or assonance, *e.g.* καρδία πονηρὰ ἀπιστίας ἐν τῷ ἀποστῆναι (3^{12}), παρακαλεῖτε ἑαυτοὺς . . . ἄχρις οὗ τὸ σήμερον καλεῖται (3^{13}), ἔμαθεν ἀφ᾽ ὧν ἔπαθεν (5^{8}), καλοῦ τε καὶ κακοῦ (5^{14}), ἅπαξ προσενεχθεὶς εἰς τὸ πολλῶν ἀνενεγκεῖν ἁμαρτίας (9^{28}), τοσοῦτον ἔχοντες περικείμενον ἡμῖν νέφος μαρτύρων . . . τρέχωμεν τὸν προκείμενον ἡμῖν ἀγῶνα (12^{1}), ἐκλέλησθε τῆς παρακλήσεως . . . μηδὲ ἐκλύου (12^{5}), μένουσαν πόλιν ἀλλὰ τὴν μέλλουσαν (13^{14}). Also he occasionally likes to use a term in two senses, *e.g.* ζῶν γὰρ ὁ λόγος τοῦ θεοῦ . . . πρὸς ὃν ἡμῖν ὁ λόγος (4$^{12. 13}$), and διαθήκη in 9$^{15f.}$ From first to last he is addicted to the gentle practice of alliteration, *e.g.* πολυμερῶς καὶ πολυτρόπως πάλαι ὁ θεὸς λαλήσας τοῖς πατράσιν ἐν τοῖς προφήταις (1^{1}), πᾶσα παράβασις καὶ παρακοή (2^{2}), ἀφῆκεν αὐτῷ ἀνυπότακτον (2^{8}), τὸν ἀπόστολον καὶ ἀρχιερέα (3^{1}), καίτοι . . . ἀπὸ καταβολῆς κόσμου (4^{3}), ἐνθυμήσεων καὶ ἐννοιῶν (4^{12}), ἀπάτωρ, ἀμήτωρ, ἀγενεαλόγητος (7^{3}), διὰ τὸ αὐτῆς ἀσθενὲς καὶ ἀνωφελές (7^{18}), εἰς τὸ παντελὲς . . . τοὺς προσερχομένους . . . πάντοτε ζῶν (7^{25}), οἱ κεκλημένοι τῆς αἰωνίου κληρονομίας (9^{15}), εἰσῆλθεν ἅγια Χριστὸς ἀντίτυπα τῶν ἀληθινῶν, ἀλλ᾽ εἰς αὐτόν (9^{24}), ἐπεὶ ἔδει αὐτὸν πολλάκις παθεῖν ἀπὸ καταβολῆς κόσμου (9^{26}), ἅπαξ ἐπὶ συντελείᾳ τῶν αἰώνων εἰς ἀθέτησιν τῆς ἁμαρτίας (9^{26}), ἀπόκειται τοῖς ἀνθρώποις ἅπαξ ἀποθανεῖν (9^{27}), ἐν αὐταῖς ἀνάμνησις ἁμαρτιῶν (10^{3}), ἀδύνατον γὰρ αἷμα ταύρων καὶ τράγων ἀφαιρεῖν ἁμαρτίας (10^{4}), θλίψεσιν θεατριζόμενοι (10^{33}), εἰ μὲν ἐκείνης ἐμνημόνευον ἀφ᾽ ἧς ἐξέβησαν (11^{15}), πᾶσα μὲν παιδεία πρὸς μὲν τὸ παρόν (12^{11}), περισσοτέρως δὲ παρακαλῶ τοῦτο ποιῆσαι (13^{19}). On the other hand, he seems deliberately to avoid alliteration once by altering διεθέμην into ἐποίησα (8^{9}).

One or two other features of his style are remarkable. There is, for example, the predilection for sonorous compounds like μισθαποδοσία and εὐπερίστατος, and also the love of adjectives in α privative, which Aristotle noted as a mark of the elevated style (*Rhet.* iii. 6. 7); in Πρὸς Ἑβραίους there are no fewer than twenty-four such, while even in the historical romance miscalled 3 Mac. there are no more than twenty. Other items are the fondness for nouns ending in -ις (cp. on 2^{4}), the extensive use of periphrases (cp. on 4^{11}), and of the infinitive and the preposition (see on 3^{12}). The use of a word like τε is also noticeable. Apart from eleven occurrences of τε καί, and one doubtful case of τε . . . τε . . . καί (6^{2}), τε links (*a*) substantives without any preceding καί or δέ; (*b*) principal clauses, as in 12^{2}; and (*c*) participial clauses, as in 1^{3} 6^{4}. Emphasis is generally brought out by throwing a word forward or to the very end of the sentence.

The writer is also in the habit of interposing several words
between the article or pronoun and the substantive ; *e.g.*

1⁴ διαφορώτερον παρ' αὐτοὺς κεκληρονόμηκεν ὄνομα.

4⁸ οὐκ ἂν περὶ ἄλλης ἐλάλει μετὰ ταῦτα ἡμέρας.

10¹¹ τὰς αὐτὰς πολλάκις προσφέρων θυσίας.

10¹² μίαν ὑπὲρ ἁμαρτιῶν προσενέγκας θυσίαν.

10²⁷ πυρὸς ζῆλος ἐσθίειν μέλλοντος τοὺς ὑπεναντίους.

12⁸ τὸν τοιαύτην ὑπομενενηκότα ὑπὸ τῶν ἁμαρτωλῶν εἰς αὐτὸν
ἀντιλογίαν.

Further, his use of the genitive absolute is to be noted, *e.g.*,
in—

2⁴ συνεπιμαρτυροῦντος τοῦ θεοῦ κτλ.

4¹ καταλειπομένης . . . αὐτοῦ (seven words between μή ποτε
and δοκῇ τις).

4³ καίτοι τῶν ἔργων . . . γενηθέντων.

7¹² μετατιθεμένης γὰρ τῆς ἱερωσύνης.

8⁴ ὄντων τῶν προσφερόντων κατὰ νόμον τὰ δῶρα.

9⁶ τούτων δὲ οὕτω κατεσκευασμένων.

9⁸ τοῦτο δηλοῦντος τοῦ Πνεύματος τοῦ Ἁγίου . . . ἔτι τῆς
πρώτης σκηνῆς ἐχούσης στάσιν.

9¹⁵ θανάτου γενομένου . . . παραβάσεων (ten words between
ὅπως and τ. ἐ. λαβῶσιν).

9¹⁹ λαληθείσης γὰρ πάσης ἐντολῆς . . . Μωυσέως.

10²⁶ ἑκουσίως γὰρ ἁμαρτανόντων ἡμῶν.

11⁴ μαρτυροῦντος ἐπὶ τοῖς δώροις αὐτοῦ τοῦ θεοῦ.

Finally, there is an obvious endeavour to avoid harsh hiatus,
sometimes by the choice of a term (*e.g.* διότι for ὅτι, as in
Polybius and Theophrastus, or ἄχρις for ἄχρι, or ὡς for ὅτι), and
a distinct fondness for compound verbs ; Moulton (ii. 11),
reckoning by the pages of WH, finds that while Mark has 5·7
compound verbs per page, Acts 6·25, Hebrews has 8·0, and Paul
only 3·8.

His vocabulary is drawn from a wide range of reading.
Whether he was a Jew by birth or not, he goes far beyond the
LXX. His Greek recalls that of authors like Musonius Rufus
and the philosophical Greek writers, and he affects more or less
technical philosophical terms like αἰσθητήριον, δημιουργός, θέλησις,
μετριοπαθεῖν, τελειόω, τέλος, τιμωρία, and ὑπόδειγμα. He was
acquainted with the books of the Maccabees, Wisdom, Sirach, and
perhaps even Philo. This last affinity is strongly marked. The
more he differs from Philo in his speculative interpretation of
religion, the more I feel, after a prolonged study of Philo, that
our author had probably read some of his works ; it is not easy

to avoid the conclusion that his acquaintance with the Hellenistic
Judaism of Alexandria included an acquaintance with Philo's
writings.   However this may be, the terminology of the Wisdom
literature was as familiar to this early Christian διδάσκαλος as to
the author of James.[1]

As for the LXX, the text he used—and he uses it with some
freedom in quotations—must have resembled that of A (cp.
Buchel in *Studien und Kritiken*, 1906, pp. 508–591), upon the
whole.   It is to his acquaintance with the LXX that occasional
" Semitisms " in his style may be referred, *e.g.* the ἐπ᾽ ἐσχάτου of
1¹, the καρδία ἀπιστίας of 3¹², the ἐν τῷ λέγεσθαι of 3¹⁵, the θρόνος
τῆς χάριτος of 4¹⁶, and the phrases in 5⁷ 9⁵ and 12¹⁵.   But this is a
minor point.   We note rather that (a) he sometimes uses LXX
terms (*e.g.* δυναμεῖς) in a special Hellenistic sense, or in a sense of
his own.   (b) Again, it is the use of the contents of the LXX which
is really significant.   The nearest approach to Πρὸς Ἑβραίους, in
its treatment of the OT, is the speech of Stephen, the Hellenistic
Jewish Christian, in Ac 7¹⁻⁵³, where we have a similar use of the
typological method and a similar freedom in handling the OT
story (cp. *EBi.* 4791, *e.g.* Ac 7²⁹ = He 11²⁷), which proves how
men like these writers, for all their reverence for the LXX, sat
wonderfully free to the letter of the scripture and employed,
without hesitation, later Jewish traditions in order to interpret it
for their own purposes.   But Stephen's reading of the OT is
not that of Πρὸς Ἑβραίους.   The latter never dwells on the
crime of the Jews in putting Jesus to death (12³ is merely a
general, passing allusion), whereas Stephen makes that crime
part and parcel of the age-long obstinacy and externalism which
had characterized Israel.   In Πρὸς Ἑβραίους, again, the κληρονομία of Palestine is spiritualized (3⁷ᶠ·), whereas Stephen merely
argues that its local possession by Israel was not final.   Stephen,
again, argues that believers in Jesus are the true heirs of the OT
spiritual revelation, not the Jews; while in Πρὸς Ἑβραίους the
continuity of the People is assumed, and Christians are regarded
as *ipso facto* the People of God, without any allusion to the Jews
having forfeited their privileges.   Here the author of Πρὸς
Ἑβραίους differs even from the parable of Jesus (cp. on 1¹); he
conveys no censure of the historical Jews who had been
responsible for the crucifixion.   The occasional resemblances
between Stephen's speech and Πρὸς Ἑβραίους are not so significant as the difference of tone and temper between them, *e.g.* in
their conceptions of Moses and of the angels (cp. on He 2²).
For another thing, (c) the conception of God derives largely

[1] On the philosophical background of ideas as well as of words, see A. R.
Eagar in *Hermathena*, xi. pp. 263–287; and H. T. Andrews in *Expositor*⁸,
xiv. pp. 348 f.

from the element of awe and majesty in the OT (see on 1³
4¹³ 10³⁰· ³¹ 12²⁹). This has been already noted (see pp. xxxv f.).
But linguistically there are characteristic elements in the various
allusions to God. Apart altogether from a stately term like
Μεγαλωσύνη (1³ 8¹) or Δόξα (9⁵), we get a singular number of
indirect, descriptive phrases like δι' ὅν τὰ πάντα καὶ δι' οὗ τὰ
πάντα (2¹⁰), τῷ ποιήσαντι αὐτόν (3²), πρὸς ὃν ἡμῖν ὁ λόγος (4¹³),
τὸν δυνάμενον σώζειν αὐτὸν ἐκ θανάτου (5⁷), ὁ ἐπαγγειλάμενος
(10²³ 11¹¹), τὸν ἀόρατον (11²⁷), τὸν ἀπ' οὐρανῶν χρηματίζοντα (12²⁵).
After 1¹, indeed, there is a slight tendency to avoid the use of
ὁ θεός and to prefer such periphrases of a solemn and even
liturgical tone. It is noticeable, e.g., that while ὁ θεός occurs
about seventy-eight times in 2 Co (which is about the same
length as Πρὸς Ἑβραίους), it only occurs fifty-five times in the
latter writing. The title (ὁ) Κύριος is also rare ; it was probably
one of the reasons that suggested the quotation in 1¹⁰ᶠ· (κύριε),
but it is mainly applied to God (12¹⁴), and almost invariably
in connexion with OT quotations (7²¹ 8² 8⁸ᶠ· 10¹⁶ 10³⁰ 12⁶ 13⁶).
Once only it is applied to Jesus (2³), apart from the solitary use of
ὁ κύριος ἡμῶν in 7¹⁴ (+ Ἰησοῦς, 33. 104. 2127) and in the doxology
with Ἰησοῦς (13²⁰). It is not a term to which the author attaches
special significance (cp. on 7²⁴). Ἰησοῦς, as in (i) 2⁹ (τὸν δὲ
βραχύ τι παρ' ἀγγέλους ἠλαττωμένον βλέπομεν Ἰησοῦν), (ii) 3¹
(κατανοήσατε τὸν ἀπόστολον καὶ ἀρχιερέα τῆς ὁμολογίας ἡμῶν
Ἰησοῦν), (iii) 4¹⁴ (ἔχοντες οὖν ἀρχιερέα μέγαν διεληλυθότα τοὺς
οὐρανούς, Ἰησοῦν), (iv) 6²⁰ (ὅπου πρόδρομος ὑπὲρ ἡμῶν εἰσῆλθεν
Ἰησοῦς), (v) 7²² (κατὰ τοσοῦτον καὶ κρείττονος διαθήκης γέγονεν
ἔγγυος Ἰησοῦς), (vi) 10¹⁹ (ἐν τῷ αἵματι Ἰησοῦ), (vii) 12² (τὸν τῆς
πίστεως ἀρχηγὸν καὶ τελειωτὴν Ἰησοῦν), (viii) 12²⁴ (καὶ διαθήκης
νέας μεσίτῃ Ἰησοῦ), (ix) 13¹² (διὸ καὶ Ἰησοῦς), (x) 13²⁰ (τὸν
ποιμένα τῶν προβάτων τὸν μέγαν ἐν αἵματι διαθήκης αἰωνίου, τὸν
κύριον ἡμῶν Ἰησοῦν), is generally the climax of an impressive
phrase or phrases. The unique use of this name in such connexions soon led to liturgical or theological expansions, as, e.g.,
3¹ (+ Χριστόν, Cᶜ K L Ψ 104. 326. 1175 syr arm Orig. Chrys.),
6²⁰ (+ Χριστός, D), 10¹⁹ (+ τοῦ Χριστοῦ, 1827 vg), 13¹² (+ ὁ, 5 [as
Col 3¹⁷]. 330 [as Col 3¹⁷]. 440 [as Ro 8¹¹]. 623. 635. 1867. 2004 :
+ ὁ κύριος, 1836 : Χριστός, 487), 13²⁰ (+ Χριστόν, D Ψ 5. 104. 177.
241. 323. 337. 436. 547. 623ᶜ. 635. 1831. 1837. 1891 latᵈᶠᵗᵒˡ
syrʰᵏˡ Chrys.). Χριστός (3⁶ 9¹¹· ²⁴), or ὁ Χριστός (3¹⁴ 5⁵ 6¹ 9¹⁴· ²⁸·
11²⁶), has also been altered ; e.g. 3¹⁴ (κυρίου, 256. 2127: θεοῦ, 635 :
om. τοῦ, 467), 5⁵ (om. ὁ, 462), 6¹ (θεοῦ, 38. 2005 : om. 429), 9²⁴
(+ ὁ Cᶜ D Ψ 104. 256. 263. 326. 467. 1739. 2127 arm : Ἰησοῦς,
823 vg Orig.), but less seriously. Ἰησοῦς Χριστός only occurs
thrice (10¹⁰ 13⁸· ²¹).

So far as vocabulary and style go, there are certain affinities between Πρὸς Ἐβραίους and (a) the Lucan writings, (b) 1 Peter, and, to a less degree, (c) the Pastoral Epistles; but an examination of the data indicates that the affinities are not sufficient to do more than indicate a common atmosphere of thought and expression at some points. I do not now feel it safe to go beyond this cautious verdict. The author of Πρὸς Ἐβραίους has idiosyncrasies which are much more significant than any such affinities. His literary relations with the other NT writers, if he had any, remain obscure, with two exceptions. Whether he had read Paul's epistles or not, depends in part on the question whether the quotation in 10[30] was derived outright from Ro 12[19] or from some *florilegium* of messianic texts; but, apart from this, there are numerous cases of what seem to be reminiscences of Paul. As for 1 Peter, our author has some connexion, which remains unsolved, with what probably was an earlier document.

To sum up. He has a sense of literary nicety, which enters into his earnest religious argument without rendering it artificial or over-elaborate. He has an art of words, which is more than an unconscious sense of rhythm. He has the style of a trained speaker; it is style, yet style at the command of a devout genius. "Of Hellenistic writers he is the freest from the monotony that is the chief fault of Hellenistic compared with literary Greek; his words do not follow each other in a mechanically necessary order, but are arranged so as to emphasize their relative importance, and to make the sentences effective as well as intelligible. One may say that he deals with the biblical language (understanding by this the Hellenistic dialect founded on the LXX, not merely his actual quotations from it) . . . as a preacher, whose first duty is to be faithful, but his second to be eloquent" (W. H. Simcox, *The Writers of the NT*, p. 43).

§ 4. Text, Commentaries, etc.

(i.)

The textual criticism of Πρὸς Ἐβραίους is bound up with the general criticism of the Pauline text (cp. *Romans* in the present series, pp. lxiii ff.), but it has one or two special features of its own, which are due in part (a) to the fact of its exclusion from the NT Canon in some quarters of the early church, and (b) also to the fact that the Pauline F (Greek text) and G are wholly, while B C H M N W p[13] and 048 are partially, missing. It is accidental that the Philoxenian Syriac version has not survived, but the former phenomenon (a) accounts for the absence of Πρὸς Ἐβραίους not simply from the Gothic version, but also from the old Latin African bible-text for which Tertullian and Cyprian, the pseudo-Augustinian *Speculum* and "Ambrosiaster," furnish such valuable evidence in the case of

the Pauline epistles. The (*b*) defectiveness of B, etc., on the
other hand, is to some extent made up by the discovery of the
two early papyrus-fragments.

The following is a list of the MSS and the main cursives, the
notations of Gregory and von Soden being added in brackets,
for the sake of convenience in reference :

Codicum Index.

ℵ saec. iv. (v.) [01 : δ 2].

A ,, v.   [02 : δ 4].

B ,, iv.   [03 : δ 1] cont. 1^1–9^{13} : for remainder cp. cursive
                 293.

C ,, v.   [04 : δ 3] cont. 2^4–7^{26} 9^{15}–10^{24} 12^{16}–13^{25}.

D ,, (vi.)   [06 : α 1026] cont. 1^1–13^{20}. Codex Claromontanus
                 is a Graeco-Latin MS, whose Greek text is
                 poorly [1] reproduced in the later (saec. ix.-x.)
                 E=codex Sangermanensis. The Greek text of
                 the latter (1^1–12^8) is therefore of no independent
                 value (cp. Hort in WH, §§ 335-337) ; for its
                 Latin text, as well as for that of F=codex
                 Augiensis (saec. ix.), whose Greek text of Πρὸς
                 'Εβραίους has not been preserved, see below,
                 p. lxix.

H ,, vi.   [015 : α 1022] cont. 1^{3-8} 2^{11-16} 3^{13-19} 4^{12-15} $10^{1-7.\ 32-38}$
                 12^{10-15} 13^{24-25} : mutilated fragments, at Moscow
                 and Paris, of codex Coislinianus.

K ,, ix.   [018 : I¹].

L ,, ix.   [020 : α 5] cont. 1^1–13^{10}.

M ,, ix.   [0121 : α 1031] cont. 1^1–4^8 12^{20}–13^{25}.

N ,, ix.   [0122 : α 1030] cont. 5^8–6^{10}.

P ,, ix.   [025 : α 3] cont. 1^1–12^8 12^{11}–13^{25}.

p¹³ ,, iv.   [α 1034] cont. 2^{14}–5^5 10^8–11^{13} 11^{28}–12^{17} : *Oxyrhyn-*
                 chus Papyri, iv. (1904) 36-48. The tendency,
                 in 2^{14}–5^5, to agree with B "in the omission of
                 unessential words and phrases . . . gives the
                 papyrus peculiar value in the later chapters,
                  where B is deficient" ; thus p¹³ partially makes
                 up for the loss of B after 9^{14}. Otherwise the
                 text of the papyrus is closest to that of D.

p¹⁸ ,, iv.   [α 1043] cont. 9^{12-19} : *Oxyrhynchus Papyri*, viii.
                 (1911) 11-13.

Ψ ,, (vi. ?) viii.–ix. [044 : δ 6] cont. 1^1–8^{11} 9^{19}–13^{25}.

W ,, (iv.–vi.) [I] cont. $1^{1-3.\ 9-12}$ $2^{4-7.\ 12-14}$ $3^{4-6.\ 14-16}$ $4^{3-6.\ 12-14}$ 5^{5-7}
                 $6^{1-3.\ 10-13.\ 20}$ $7^{1-2.\ 7-11.\ 18-20.\ 27-28}$ $8^{1.\ 7-9}$ $9^{1-4.\ 9-11.\ 16-19.}$
                 $^{25-27}$ $10^{5-8.\ 16-18.\ 26-29.\ 35-38}$ $11^{6-7.\ 12-15.\ 22-24.\ 31-33.\ 38-40}$
                 $12^{1.\ 7-9.\ 16-18.\ 25-27}$ $13^{7-9.\ 16-18.\ 23-25}$: *NT MSS in*
                 Freer Collection, The Washington MS of the Epp.
                 of Paul (1918), pp. 294-306. Supports Alexan-
                 drian text, and is "quite free from Western
                 readings."

---

[1] An instance may be found in 10^{33}, where a corrector of D obelized the
first and last letters of ὀνειδιζόμενοι and wrote over it θεατριζόμενοι. In E
we get the absurd νιδιζομενοθεατοιζομενοι (cp. Gregory's *Textkritik des NT*,
i. 109).

e

048 saec. v.   [α 1] cont. 11³²–13⁴.   Codex Patiriensis is a
                          palimpsest.
0142 ,, x.   [o⁶].
0151 ,, xii.   [x²¹].

Three specimens of how the MSS group themselves may be
printed. (*a*) shows the relation between M and the papyrus p¹³ :

M agrees with p¹³ in eight places :

$$3^1 \text{ 'Ιησοῦν.}$$
$$3^8 \text{ δόξης οὗτος } (+K \text{ L vg, alone).}$$
$$3^4 \text{ πάντα.}$$
$$3^6 \text{ ἐάν.}$$
$$3^9 \text{ ὑμῶν ἐν δοκιμασίᾳ.}$$
$$3^{10} \text{ ταύτῃ.}$$
$$3^{13} \text{ τις ἐξ ὑμῶν.}$$
$$4^2 \text{ συγκεκ(ε)ρασμένους.}$$

It opposes p¹³ (+B) in

$$3^2 + δλῳ.$$
$$3^6 \text{ ὅς.}$$
$$3^6 + μέχρι τέλους βεβαίαν.$$
$$3^9 + με.$$
$$4^3 \text{ οὖν.}$$
$$4^3 + τήν \text{ before } κατάπαυσιν.$$

M has some remarkable affinities with the text of Origen (*e.g.* 1⁸ 1⁹ 2¹).
(*b*) exhibits the relations of א and D*, showing how A and B agree with them
on the whole, and how p¹³ again falls into this group :

א and D* agree in

1² position of ἐποίησεν	A B M	
1⁸ + καί before ἡ ῥάβδος	A B M	
2¹ παραρυῶμεν	A B*	
2⁷ + καί κατέστησας . . . σου	A	
2¹⁵ δουλίας		
3¹ om. Χριστόν	A B M p¹³	
3⁴ πάντα	A B M p¹³	
3¹⁰ ταύτῃ	A B M p¹³	
3¹⁹ δι' (so 7⁹)	A B M p¹³	
4¹ καταλιπομένης (alone), except for p¹³		
4⁷ προείρηται	A (B)	p¹³
4¹⁵ συνπαθῆσαι	A B*	
4¹⁶ ἔλεος	A B	
5³ δι' αὐτήν	A B	
5³ περὶ ἁμαρτιῶν	A B	
6¹⁰ om. τοῦ κόπου	A B	
6¹⁶ om. μέν	A B	
7⁵ Λευί		
7⁶ om. τόν before 'Αβραάμ	B	
7¹⁰ ,, ὁ ,, Μελχισεδέκ	B	
7¹¹ αὐτῆς	A B	
7¹¹ νενομοθέτηται	A B	
7¹⁶ σαρκίνης	A B	
7¹⁷ μαρτυρεῖται	A B	
8² om. καί before οὐκ ἄνθρωπος	B	

8⁴ οὖν	A B	
8⁴ om. τῶν ἱερέων	A B	
8¹¹ om. αὐτῶν after μικροῦ	A B	
9⁵ χερουβίν (alone of uncials)		
9⁹ καθ' ἥν	A B	
9²¹ ἐράντισεν	A	
9²⁴ om. ὁ before Χριστός	A	
10¹⁰ om. οἱ ,, διά	A	
10¹² οὗτος	A	
10¹⁶ διάνοιαν	A	
10²³ λελουσμένοι		
11³ τὸ βλεπόμενον	A	p¹³
11¹⁹ δυνατός		
11²⁹ + γῆς	A	p¹³
11³⁰ ἔπεσαν	A	p¹³
11³² με γάρ	A	
11³⁴ μαχαίρης (so 11³⁷)	A	
12⁵ παιδίας		
12⁸ position of ἐστε	A	p¹³
12⁹ πολύ (so 12²⁵)	A	
12²¹ ἔκτρομος (alone)		
13³ κακουχουμένων	A M	
13⁴ γάρ	A M	
13⁸ ἐχθές	A M	
13²¹ om. ἔργῳ		

(*c*) exhibits characteristic readings of H, with some of its main allies:

1³ καθαρισμόν	ℵ A B	Dᵇ	H*	P		vg	arm	
2¹⁵ δουλίας	ℵ	D*	H	P				
3¹³ τις ἐξ ὑμῶν	p¹³ ℵ A C		H	M P		vg pesh arm boh		
3¹⁴ τοῦ Χριστοῦ γεγ.	ℵ A B C D W H			M P		vg		
3¹⁷ τίσιν δέ	ℵ B C D		H	P	K L			sah
4¹² ἐνεργής	ℵ A C D		H	P	K L vg			
4¹² ψυχῆς	ℵ A B C		H	P	L (vg	arm boh)		
4¹⁵ συνπαθῆσαι	ℵ A B* C D*		H					
10¹ θυσίας (– αὐτῶν)	A C D		H		K L vg			
10¹ αἷς	D*		H		L			
10¹ δύναται	D		H		K L vg		boh	
10² om. οὐκ			H*		(vg) pesh			
10² κεκαθαρισμένους	ℵ	D	H	P	K			
10⁶ ηὐδόκησας	A	C D* W H		P				
10³⁴ τοῖς δεσμίοις	p¹³ A	D*	H			vg pesh	boh	
10³⁴ ἑαυτούς	p¹³ ℵ A		H			vg	boh	
10³⁴ ὕπαρξιν	p¹³ ℵ* A	D*	H*			vg	boh	
10³⁵ μεγάλην μισθ.	ℵ A	D W H		P				
10³⁷ χρονιεῖ	ℵᶜ A	Dᶜ W H		P	K L			
10³⁸ μου ἐκ πίστεως	ℵ A		H*			vg	arm	
12¹¹ πᾶσα δέ	p¹³ ℵᶜ A	Dᶜ	H		K L	vg pesh	boh	
12¹³ ποιήσατε	ℵ A	D	H		K L			
12¹⁵ αὐτῆς	(p¹³) A		H	P				
12¹⁶ αὐτοῦ	ℵᶜ	D*	H	P	K L			
13²¹ om. τῶν αἰώνων	Cᶜ D		H				arm	
13²³ ἡμῶν	ℵ* A	C D* W H		M		vg pesh arm boh sah		
13²⁵ ἀμήν.	ℵᶜ A	C D	H	P M K		vg pesh (arm) boh		

CURSIVES.

1 saec.	x. [δ 254]	189 saec.	xiii. [Θ δ 30]
2 ,,	xii. [α 253]	203 ,,	xii. [α 203]
5 ,,	xiv. [δ 453]	206 ,,	xiii. [α 365]
6 ,,	xiii. [δ 356] cont. 1¹–9³	209 ,,	xiv. [δ 457]
	10²²–13²⁵	216 ,,	xiv. [α 469]
31 ,,	xi. [α 103]	217 ,,	xi. [α 1065] cont. 1¹–6⁸
33 ,,	ix.–x. [δ 48] Hort's 17	218 ,,	xiii. [δ 300]
35 ,,	xiii. [δ 309]	221 ,,	x. [α 69]
38 ,,	xiii. [δ 355]	226 ,,	xi. [δ 156]
47 ,,	xi. [O π¹⁰³]	227 ,,	xii. [α 258]
69 ,,	xv. [δ 505]	241 ,,	xi. [δ 507]
88 ,,	xii. [α 200]	242 ,,	xii. [δ 206]
90 ,,	xvi. [δ 652]	253 ,,	xi. [δ 152]
93 ,,	x. [α 51]	255 .,	xi. [α 174]
103 ,,	xi. [O ²⁸]	256 ,,	xii. [α 216]
104 ,,	xi. [α 103]	257 ,,	xiv. [α 466]
112 ,,	xi. [E π¹⁰]	263 ,,	xiii.–xiv. [δ 372]
177 ,,	xi. [α 106]	293 ,,	xv. [α 1574] cont. 9¹⁴–13²⁸
181 ,,	xi. [α 101]	296 ,,	xvi. [δ 600]
188 ,,	xii. [α 200]	323 ,,	xi.–xii. [α 157]

326 saec. xii. [α 257]
327 ,, xiii. [O ³⁶]
330 ,, xii. [δ 259]
337 ,, xii. [α 205]
371 ,, xiv. [α 1431] cont. 7³-13²⁵
378 ,, xii. [α 258]
383 ,, xiii. [α 353] cont. 1¹-13⁷
418 ,, xv. (x.) [α 1530] cont. 1¹-13¹⁷
424 ,, xi. [O ¹²] Hort's 67
429 ,, xiii.-xiv. [α 398]
431 ,, xii. [δ 268]
436 ,, xi. [α 172]
440 ,, xii. [δ 260]
442 ,, xiii. [O¹⁸]
456 ,, x. ? [α 52]
460 ,, xiii.-xiv. [α 397]
461 ,, xiii. [α 359]
462 ,, xv. [α 502]
487 ,, xi. [α 171]
489 ,, xiv. [δ 459] Hort's 102
491 ,, xi. [δ 152]
506 ,, xi. [δ 101]
522 ,, xvi. [δ 602]
547 ,, xi. [δ 157]
614 ,, xiii. [α 364]
623 ,, xi. [α 173]
633 ,, xi. [α 161]
639 ,, xi. [α 169]
642 ,, xv. [α 552] cont. 1¹-7¹⁸ 9¹³-13²⁵
794 ,, xiv. [δ 454]
808 ,, xii. [δ 203]
823 ,, xiii. [δ 368]
876 ,, xiii. [α 356]
913 ,, xiv. [α 470]
915 ,, xiii. [α 382]
917 ,, xii. [α 264]
919 ,, xi. [α 113]
920 ,, x. [α 55]
927 ,, xii. [δ 251]

941 saec. xiii. [δ 369]
999 ,, xiii. [δ 353]
1108 ,, xiii. [α 370]
1149 ,, xiii. [δ 370]
1175 ,, x. [α 74] cont. 1¹-3⁵ 6⁸ 13²⁰
1243 ,, xii. [δ 198]
1245 ., xi. [α 158]
1288 (81) xi. [α 162]
1311 ,, xi. [α 170]
1319 ,, xi. [δ 180]
1518 ,, xi. [α 116]
1522 ,, xiv. [α 464]
1525 ,, xiii. [α 361] cont. 1¹-7⁸
1610 ,, xiv. [α 468]
1611 ,, xii. [α 208]
1739 ,, x. [α 78]
1758 ,, xiii. [α 396] cont. 1¹-13¹⁴
1765 ,, xiv. [α 486]
1827 ,, xiii. [α 367]
1831 ,, xiv. [α 472]
1836 ,, x. [α 65]
1837 ,, xi. [α 192]
1838 ,, xi. [α 175]
1845 ,, x. [α 64]
1852 ,, xi. [α 114] cont. 1¹-11¹⁰
1867 ,, xi.-xii. [α 154]
1872 ., xii. [α 209]
1873 ,, xii. [α 252]
1891 ,, x. [α 62]
1898 ,, x. [α 70]
1906 ,, xi. [O π ¹⁰¹]
1908 ,, xi. [O π ¹⁰³]
1912 ,, x.-xi. [α 1066]
2004 ,, x. [α 56]
2055 ,, xiv. [α 1436] cont. 1¹-7²
2127 ,, xii. [δ 202]
2138 ,, xi. [α 116]
2143 ,, xi.-xii. [α 184]
2147 ,, xii. [δ 299]

Of these some like 5 and 33 and 442 and 999 and 1908, are of the first rank; von Soden pronounces 1288 "a very good representative" of his H text. Yet even the best cursives, like the uncials, may stray (see on 4¹⁶). As a specimen of how one good cursive goes, I append this note of some characteristic readings in 424** :

1⁸ om. αὐτοῦ after δυνάμεως		M	Orig	d e f vg
om. ἡμῶν	ℵ* A B D*	M P		
2⁹ χωρίς		M	Orig	
3¹ om. Χριστόν	ℵ A B D* C*	M P		d e f vg sah
3⁶ ὅς	D*	M		d e f vg
3¹⁰ ταύτῃ	ℵ A B D*	M		sah

-4^{14} πίστεως				
-5^{12} ὑμᾶς (om. τινά)				
8^4 om. τῶν ἱερεων	ℵ A B D*	P		d e f vg
9^9 καθ' ἥν	ℵ A B D*			f vg
9^{23} καθαρίζεται (ἀνάγκη)	D*		Orig	
10^1 δύνανται	ℵ A Dᵇ C	P [sc. D*, Orig]		
10^{30} om. λέγει κύριος	ℵ* D*	P		d e f vg
10^{34} δεσμίοις	A H D*	(Orig??)		f vg
11^5 om. αὐτοῦ	ℵ* A D*	P		d e f vg
12^{15} αὐτῆς	A	P		
12^{25} ἀπ' οὐρανοῦ	ℵ	M		b
12^{26} σείσω	ℵ A C M			f vg

LATIN VERSIONS.

A. Old Latin (vt), saec. ii. (?)–iv.

Hebrews is omitted in the pseudo-Augustinian *Speculum* ($=m$) and in codex Boernerianus ($=g$), but included in—

> d (Latin version of D)
> e (,, ,, ,, E)
> f (,, ,, ,, F)
> r (codex Frisingensis: saec. vi., cont. 6^6–7^5 7^8–8^1 9^{27}–11^7)
> x^2 (,, Bodleianus: ,, ix., cont. 1^1–11^{23})

Of these, r (corresponding to the text used by Augustine), with the few quotations by Priscillian, represents the African, d (in the main) [1] and x^2 the European, type of the Old Latin text ; but f is predominantly vulgate, and it is doubtful whether x^2 is really Old Latin. On the other hand, some evidence for the Old Latin text is to be found occasionally in the following MSS of—

B. Vulgate (vg), saec. iv.

> am (Codex Amiatinus : saec. vii.–viii.)
> $fuld$ (,, Fuldensis : ,, vi.)
> cav (,, Cavensis : ,, ix.) ⎫ Spanish
> tol (,, Toletanus : ,, viii.) ⎭
> $harl$ (,, Harleianus : ,, viii.)
> c (,, Colbertinus : ,, xii.)

Though c is an Old Latin text for the gospels, Hebrews and the rest of the NT are vulgate ; but He 10–11 in *harl* (which elsewhere has affinities with *am* and *fuld*) is Old Latin, according to E. S. Buchanan (*The Epistles and Apocalypse from the codex Harleianus* [z = *Wordsworth's* Z_2], *numbered Harl. 1772 in the British Museum Library*, 1913). Both in *harl* and in *e*, 11^{3-33} has a special capitulation ; *harl*, which adds after " the prophets " in

---

[1] The text of d corresponds to that of Lucifer of Cagliari (saec. iv.), who quotes 3^5–4^{10} and 4^{11-13} in his treatise *De non conueniendo cum haereticis*, xi. (*CSEL.*, vol. xiv.). According to Harnack (*Studien zur Vulgata des Hebräerbriefs*, 1920) it is d, not r, which underlies the vulgate (cp. J. Belser on " die Vulgata u. der Griech. Text im Hebräerbrief," in *Theolog. Quartal-schrift*, 1906, pp. 337–369).

11³² —" Ananias azarias misahel daniel helias helisaeus "—apparently points
to 11³⁻³² having been at one time added to the original text which ran
(11². ³³): "in hac enim testimonium habuerunt seniores qui per fidem
uicerunt regna," etc.   Of these MSS, *fuld* represents an Italian text, *cav* and
tol a Spanish (the former with some admixture of Old Latin); *am* (whose text
is akin to *fuld*) is an Italian text, written in Great Britain.   At an early
date the Latin versions were glossed, however (cp. on 7¹ 11²³).

EGYPTIAN VERSIONS.

sah = Sahidic (saec. iii.–iv.) :   *The Coptic Version of the NT in the Southern
                                       Dialect* (Oxford, 1920), vol. v. pp. 1–131.
boh = Bohairic (saec. vi.–vii.) :   *The Coptic Version of the NT in the Northern
                                       Dialect* (Oxford, 1905), vol. iii. pp. 472–
                                       555.

In sah Πρὸς Ἑβραίους comes very early in the Pauline canon, immediately
after Romans and Corinthians, even earlier than in the first (A.D. 400)
Syriac canon, whereas in boh it comes between the Pauline church letters and
the Pastorals.   The latter seems to have been an early (*i.e.* a fourth century)
position in the Eastern or Alexandrian canon, to judge from Athanasius
(*Fest. Ep.* xxxix.); it reappears in the uncials א A B¹ W.   Not long
afterwards, at the Synod of Carthage (can. 39), in A.D. 397, it is put between the Pauline and the Catholic epistles, which seems to have been the
African and even the (or, a) Roman order.   This reflects at least a doubt
about its right to stand under Paul's name, whereas the order in sah and the
primitive Syriac canon reflects a deliberate assertion of its Pauline authorship.
The Alexandrian position is intermediate.

The data of the Egyptian versions are of special interest, as several of the
uncials have Egyptian affinities or an Egyptian origin, and as Πρὸς Ἑβραίους
was early studied at Alexandria.   Thus, to cite only one or two, boh is right,
as against sah, *e.g.* in the rendering of πρός in 1⁷, in omitting ὅλῳ (3⁵), in
rendering ὑποστάσεως as "confidence" in 3¹⁴, in rendering ἐν Δαυείδ (4⁷) "in
David," in reading παθεῖν in 9²⁶, in rendering ὑπόστασις by "assurance"
(so syr arm) in 11¹, in taking καλούμενος by itself (11⁸), in keeping ἐλιθάσθησαν
before ἐπρίσθησαν (11³⁷, though ἐπειράσθησαν, = were tempted, is inferior to
sah's omission of any such term), in reading ἐπαγγελίαν (11³⁹, where sah
agrees with W in reading the plural), etc.   On the other hand, and in a large
number of cases, sah is superior, *e.g.* at 2¹⁷ ("a merciful and faithful highpriest"), at 3⁶ (omitting μέχρι τέλους βεβαίαν), at 4² (συνκεκερασμένος), in
rendering κρατῶμεν (4¹⁴) "let us hold on to," in maintaining θεός in 6³ (for
"Lord" in boh), in omitting τοῦ κόπου in 6¹⁰, in reading ἱερεῖς (with W) in
7²⁸, in reading ὑμῶν in 9¹⁴, in rendering the last words of 9²⁸, in rendering
ἁμ . . . ἀντιλογίαν in 12³ etc.   Note also that sah agrees with arm in
inserting τῆς before ἐπαγγελίας in 4¹, ὕστερον λέγει in 10¹⁶. ¹⁷, and γάρ in 12⁴,
while boh agrees with arm in adding εἶπεν in 1⁸ and αἰώνιος at 5¹⁰, and both
agree with arm in omitting καί in 1⁶.   Both translate εἰσερχόμεθα (4³) as a
future, read ἀπιστίαν in 4⁶ (with vg and arm), omit κατὰ τὴν τ. M. in 7²¹,
take ἅγιον as an adjective in 9¹, read μελλόντων in 9¹¹, take ἧς in 11⁷ to mean
the ark, read ἡ στεῖρα in 11¹¹, render ὄγκον by "pride" in 12¹, take ὑπομένετε
as imperative in 12⁷, and refer αὐτήν to τόπον μετανοίας in 12¹⁷.   Sah has

---

¹ Yet in the archetype of the capitulation system in B Πρὸς Ἑβραίους must
have stood between Galatians and Ephesians, which "is the order given in
the Sahidic version of the 'Festal letter' of Athanasius" (Kirsopp Lake,
The Text of the NT, p. 53).

some curious renderings, *e.g.* "hewed out" for ἐνεκαίνισεν (10²⁰), "the place of the blood" for αἵματος in 12⁴, and actually "hanging for them another time" (ἀνασταυροῦντας ἑαυτοῖς, 6⁶); in general it is rather more vivid and less literal, though boh reads "through the sea of Shari" [? slaughter] in 11²⁹ (sah is defective here), which is singular enough. On the other hand, sah is more idiomatic. Thus it is in sah, not in boh, that νωθροὶ γένησθε (6¹²) is rendered by "become daunted." The differences in a passage like 12²²ᶠ· are specially instructive. Sah takes πανηγύρει with what follows, boh with ἀγγέλων ("myriads of angels keeping festival"); on the other hand, sah is right as against boh's reading of πνεύματι (v.²³), while both render "God the judge of all." In v.²⁶ both render ἐπήγγελται literally by "he promised," but boh translates παραλαμβάνοντες in v.²⁸ as a future and χάριν as "grace," whereas sah renders correctly in both cases. In ch. 13, sah seems to read περιφέρεσθε in v.⁹ ("be not tossed about"), inserts ἔργῳ (as against boh), and reads ἡμῖν in v.²¹; in v.²² it reads ἀνέχεσθε; in v.²³, while boh renders ἀπολελυμένον by "released," sah renders "our brother Timotheos whom I sent" (which confuses the sense of the passage altogether), and, unlike boh, omits the final ἀμήν. It is significant that sah[1] often tallies with *r* as against *d*, *e.g.* in 6¹⁸ (ἰσχυράν), 7²⁷ (ἀρχιερεῖς), though with *d* now and then against *r*, as in 11⁶ (δέ). It agrees with *d* and eth in reading πνεῦμα in 1⁷, ὡς ἱμάτιον in 1¹² (as well as ἑλίξεις), and καὶ τῶν τράγων in 9¹⁹, but differs from *d* almost as often, and from eth in reading ταύτῃ in 3¹⁰, in omitting κατὰ τ. τ. M. in 7²¹, etc. Unexpectedly a collation of sah and of eth yields no material for a clear decision upon the relation of the texts they imply.

SYRIAC VERSIONS.

For the Old Syriac, *i.e.* for the Syriac text of Hebrews prior to the vulgate revision (Peshitta) of the fifth century, we possess even less material than in the case of the Old Latin version. Hebrews belonged to the old Syrian canon, but the primitive text can only be recovered approximately from (i) the Armenian version,[2] which rests in part upon an Old Syriac basis—"readings of the Armenian vulgate which differ from the ordinary Greek text, especially if they are supported by the Peshitta, may be considered with some confidence to have been derived from the lost Old Syriac" (F. C. Burkitt, *EBi.* 5004); from (ii) the homilies of Aphraates (saec. iv), and from (iii) the Armenian translation of Ephraem Syrus (saec. iv.), *Commentarii in Epp. Pauli nunc primum ex armenio in latinum sermonem a patribus Mekitharistis translati* (Venice, 1893, pp. 200-242).

Hebrews is not extant in the Philoxenian version of A.D. 508, but the Harklean revision of that text (A.D. 616-617) is now accessible in complete form, thanks to R. L. Bensly's edition (*The Harklean Version of the Epistle to the Hebrews*, 11²⁸-13²⁵, *now edited for the first time with Introduction and Notes*, Cambridge, 1889). The Peshitta version is now conveniently accessible in the British and Foreign Bible Society's edition of *The New Testament in Syriac* (1920).

---

[1] It rarely goes its own way, but the omission of any adjective at all with πνεύματος in 9¹⁴ is most remarkable; so is the reading of ὑμᾶς for ἡμᾶς in 13⁶ (where M Orig have one of their characteristic agreements in omitting any pronoun).

[2] Mr. F. C. Conybeare kindly supplied me with a fresh collation.

The early evidence for the use of Πρὸς Ἑβραίους may be chronologically tabulated as follows :

	MSS.		VERSIONS.		WRITERS.	
100–200					Clem. Rom.	
200–300			(Old Syriac) (Old Latin)		Clem. Alex.	Tertullian
					Origen (–248)	
300–400	p13 p18				Eusebius (–340)	
					Basil (–379)	Lucifer (–371)
	B		Sahidic (?)		Cyril of Jerus. (–386)	Priscillian (–385)
					Apollinaris (–392)	Ambrose (397)
	ℵ (?)		vulgate (370–383)		Chrysostom (–407)	Jerome (–420)
					Theodore of Mopsuestia	
400–500	W (?)		peshiṭta (411–435)			Augustine (–430)
					Cyril of Alex. (–444)	
	A C			Armenian	Theodoret (–458)	
	048					
500–600	D d					
	fuld		Ethiopic			Fulgentius
	H r					
600–700			harklean (616–617)			
700–800	am		Bohairic (?)			
	Ψ tol					
800–900	K L					
	M N f					Sedulius Scotus
	P cav					
900–1000	e (?)					
	0142					

ℵ A B C H M Ψ W (with p13) would represent von Soden's H text (approximating to WH's Neutral), his I text (corresponding to WH's Western) being represented by K L P among the uncials. But the difference between these in the Pauline corpus are, he admits, less than in the case of the gospels. Bousset (in *Texte und Untersuchungen*, xi. 4, pp. 45 f.) has shown that ℵ^c H (which tend to agree with Origen's text) have affinities with Euthalius ; they carry with them a number of cursives (including 33. 69. 88. 104. 424**. 436 and 1908), and enable us to reconstruct the archetype of codex Pamphili, *i.e.* the third century recension of Origen's text. This group would therefore stand midway between B ℵ A C and the later K L (with majority of cursives). But no exact grouping of the MSS is feasible. The text has suffered early corruption at several places, *e.g.* 2^9 4^2 7^1 10^{34} 11^4 11^{37} 12^3 12^{18} and 13^{21}, though only the first of these passages is of real, religious importance. But, apart from this, the earliest MSS betray serious errors (cp. on 7^1 11^{35}), as though the text had not been well preserved. Thus B, for all its services (*e.g.* in 6^2), goes wrong repeatedly (*e.g.* 1^8 1^8 4^{12}), as does ℵ* (*e.g.* 1^5 om. αὐτῷ, 4^9 6^9 9^{17} τότε, 10^{32} ἁμαρτίας), and even p13 in 4^3 (ἐλεύσονται), 10^{18} (ἁμαρτίαις), 11^1 (ἀπόστασις), etc. The errors of W are mainly linguistic, but it reads ἐνθυμήσεως in 4^{12}, πίστεως in 6^{11} etc. A test passage like 2^{14}, where "blood and flesh" naturally passed into the conventional "flesh and blood," shows the inferior reading supported not only by K and L, as we might expect, but by *f* and *tol*, the peshitta and eth. Similarly the wrong reading μαρτυρεῖ in 7¹⁷ brings out not only K and L again but C D syr and a group of cursives, 256. 326. 436. 1175. 1837. 2127. In 9²⁸ only arm inserts πίστει after ἀπεκδεχομένοις, but the similar homiletic gloss of διὰ πίστεως before or after εἰς σωτηρίαν turns up in A P syr^hkl, and in 38. 69. 218. 256. 263. 330. 436. 440. 462. 823, 1245. 1288. 1611. 1837. 1898. 2005. In 9¹⁴ the gloss καὶ ἀληθινῷ is supported also by A P as well as by boh and one or two cursives like 104. To take another instance, the gloss καὶ δακρύων (in 10²⁸) has only D* among the uncials, but it is an Old Latin reading, though *r* does not support it, and it was read in the original text of the harklean Syriac. Again, in 11¹², what B. Weiss calls the "obvious emendation" ἐγεννήθησαν is supported by ℵ L p¹³ Ψ and 1739, while in the same verse καὶ ὡς ἡ (κάθως, D) carries with it ℵ A D K L P p¹³, and D Ψ omit ἡ παρὰ τὸ χεῖλος. When M resumes at 12²⁰ it is generally in the company of ℵ A D P (as, *e.g.*, 12²³. ²⁴. ²⁵ 13⁵. ⁹. ²⁰), once (12²⁷ om. τήν) with D* arm, once with D* (om. ἐξουσίαν, 13¹⁰), once with K L P (κακοχ. 13³) against ℵ A D*. Such phenomena render the problem of ascertaining any traditional text of Πρὸς Ἑβραίους unusually difficult. Even the data yielded by Clement of Alexandria[1] and the Latin and Egyptian versions do not as yet facilitate a genealogical grouping of the extant MSS or a working hypothesis as to the authorities in which a text free from Western readings may be preserved.

(ii.)

The eighteen homilies by Origen (†253) are lost, though Eusebius (cp. above, pp. xviii–xix) quotes two fragments on the style and authorship. The Ἀπολογία Ὠριγενοῦς of Pamphilus (partially extant in the Latin version of Rufinus) implies that he also wrote a commentary on the epistle, but this is lost, and the Syriac commentary of Ephraem Syrus (†373) is only extant in the Latin version of an Armenian version (cp. above, p. lxxi). We are fortunate, however, in possessing the first important exposition of Πρὸς Ἑβραίους, viz. the homilies of Chrysostom (†407), extant in the form of notes, posthumously published, which the presbyter Constantine had taken down. Chrysostom's comments are drawn upon by most of the subsequent expositors. The foremost of these Greek exegetes is Theodore of Mopsuestia (†428), who is the first to show any appreciation of historical

---

[1] The original text in one place at least (cp. on 11⁴) can be restored by the help of p¹³ and Clement.

criticism (*Theodori Mopsuesteni in NT Commentaria quae reperiri potuerunt, collegit* O. F. *Fritzsche,* 1847, pp. 160–172). The exposition by his contemporary Theodoret of Cyrrhus (†458) is based almost entirely upon Chrysostom and Theodore of Mopsuestia (*Theod. Comm. in omnes Pauli epistolas,* ed. E. B. Pusey, 1870, ii. 132–219). Similarly, the work of Oecumenius of Tricca in Thrace (tenth century) contains large excerpts from previous writers, including Chrysostom, Theodore of Mopsuestia, and Photius (cp. Migne, *PG.* cxviii–cxix). Theophylact, archbishop of Bulgaria (end of eleventh century), also draws upon his predecessors (cp. Migne, *PG.* cxxiv), like Euthymius Zigabenus (beginning of twelfth century), a monk near Constantinople. The latter's commentary on Hebrews is in the second volume (pp. 341 f.) of his *Commentarii* (ed. N. Calogeras, Athens, 1887). In a happy hour, about the middle of the sixth century, Cassiodorus (Migne's *PL.* lxx. p. 1120) employed a scholar called Mutianus to translate Chrysostom's homilies into Latin. This version started the homilies on a fresh career in the Western church, and subsequent Latin expositions, *e.g.* by Sedulius Scotus, W. Strabo, Alcuin, and Thomas of Aquinum, build on this version and on the vulgate. An excellent account of these commentaries is now published by Riggenbach in Zahn's *Forschungen zur Gesch. des NTlichen Kanons,* vol. viii. (1907).

Since F. Bleek's great edition (1828–1840) there has been a continuous stream of commentaries; special mention may be made of those by Delitzsch (Eng. tr. 1867), Lünemann (1867, 1882), Moses Stuart[4] (1860), Alford[2] (1862), Reuss (1860, 1878), Kurtz (1869), Hofmann (1873), A. B. Davidson (1882), F. Rendall (1888), C. J. Vaughan (1890), B. Weiss (in Meyer, 1897), von Soden (1899), Westcott[3] (1903), Hollmann[2] (1907), E. J. Goodspeed (1908), A. S. Peake (*Century Bible,* n.d.), M. Dods (1910), E. C. Wickham (1910), A. Seeberg (1912), Riggenbach (1913, 1922), Windisch (1913), and Nairne (1918).

Other works referred to, in this edition,[1] are as follows :—

Bengel (Bgl.). *J. A. Bengelii Gnomon Novi Testamenti* (1742).

Blass . . F. Blass, *Grammatik des neutestamentlichen Griechisch : vierte, völlig neugearbeitete Auflage, besorgt von Albert Debrunner* (1913); also, *Brief an die Hebräer, Text mit Angabe der Rhythmen* (1903).

---

[1] Some references, in the textual notes, are the usual abbreviations, like Amb. = Ambrose, Ath. or Athan. = Athanasius, Cosm. = Cosmas Indicopleustes (ed. E. O. Winstedt, Cambridge, 1909), Cyr. = Cyril of Alexandria, Euth. = Euthalius, Hil. = Hilary, Lucif. = Lucifer, Sedul. = Sedulius Scotus, Thdt. = Theodoret, Theod. = Theodore of Mopsuestia, etc.

BGU. . . *Aegyptische Urkunden (Griechisch Urkunden)*,
ed. Wilcken (1895).

BM. . . *Greek Papyri in the British Museum* (1893 f.).

Diat. . . E. A. Abbott, *Diatessarica*.

EBi. . . *The Encyclopaedia Biblica* (1899–1903, ed. J. S.
Black and T. K. Cheyne).

Erasmus . *Adnotationes* (1516), *In epist. Pauli apostoli ad
Hebraeos paraphrasis* (1521).

ERE. . . *Encyclopaedia of Religion and Ethics* (ed. J.
Hastings).

Expositor . *The Expositor.* Small superior numbers indicate
the series.

GCP. . . *Grundzüge und Chrestomathie der Papyruskunde*,
von L. Mitteis und U. Wilcken (1912), I.
Band.

Helbing . *Grammatik der Septuaginta, Laut- und Wort-
lehre*, von R. Helbing (1907).

IMA. . . *Inscriptiones Graecae Insul. Maris Aegaei*
(1895 f.).

Josephus . *Flavii Josephi Opera Omnia post Immanuelem
Bekkerum*, recognovit S. A. Naber.

LXX . . *The Old Testament in Greek according to the
Septuagint Version* (ed. H. B. Swete).

Magn. . . *Die Inschriften von Magnesia am Maeander* (ed.
Kern, 1900).

Michel . . *Recueil d'Inscriptions Grecques* (ed. C. Michel,
1900).

Mitteis-Wilcken *Grundzüge u. Chrestomathie der Papyruskunde*
(1912).

Moulton . J. H. Moulton's *Grammar of New Testament
Greek*, vol. i. (2nd edition, 1906).

OGIS. . . Dittenberger's *Orientis Graeci Inscriptiones
Selectae* (1903–1905).

OP. . . *The Oxyrhynchus Papyri* (ed. B. P. Grenfell
and A. Hunt).

Pfleiderer . *Primitive Christianity*, vol. iii. (1910) pp. 272–
299.

Philo . . *Philonis Alexandriai Opera Quae Supersunt*
(recognoverunt L. Cohn et P. Wendland).

Radermacher. *Neutestamentliche Grammatik* (1911), in Lietz-
mann's *Handbuch zum Neuen Testament*
(vol. i.).

Rein. P. . *Papyrus Grecs et Démotiques* (Paris, 1905), ed.
Th. Reinach.

Syll. . . *Sylloge Inscriptionum Graecarum*[2] (ed. W. Dittenberger).

Tebt. P. . . *Tebtunis Papyri* (ed. Grenfell **and** Hunt), 1902.

Thackeray . H. St J. Thackeray, *A Grammar of the Old Testament in Greek* (1909).

Weiss . . B. Weiss, "Textkritik der paulinischen Briefe" (in *Texte und Untersuchungen zur Geschichte der altchristlichen Literatur*, vol. xiv. 3), also *Der Hebräerbrief in Zeitgeschichtlicher Beleuchtung* (1910).

WH . . Westcott and Hort's *New Testament in Greek* (1890, 1896).

Zahn . . Theodor Zahn's *Einleitung in das NT*, §§ 45–47.

COMMENTARY.

———◆———

THE final disclosure of God's mind and purpose has been made in his Son, who is far superior to the angels; beware then of taking it casually and carelessly (1^1–2^4)!

The epistle opens with a long sentence (vv.$^{1-4}$), the subject being first (vv.$^{1. 2}$) God, then (vv.$^{3. 4}$) the Son of God; rhetorically and logically the sentence might have ended with ἐν (+ τῷ arm) υἱῷ, but the author proceeds to elaborate in a series of dependent clauses the pre-eminence of the Son within the order of creation and providence. The main thread on which these clauses about the Son's relation to God and the world are strung is ὃς . . . ἐκάθισεν ἐν δεξιᾷ τῆς μεγαλωσύνης. It is in this (including the purging of men from their sins by His sacrifice) that the final disclosure of God's mind and purpose is made; ὁ θεὸς ἐλάλησεν ἡμῖν ἐν υἱῷ . . . ὃς . . . ἐκάθισεν κτλ. But the cosmic significance of the Son is first mentioned (v.^{2}); he is not created but creative, under God. Here as in 2^{10} the writer explicitly stresses the vital connexion between redemption and creation; the Son who deals with the sins of men is the Son who is over the universe. This is again the point in the insertion of φέρων τε τὰ πάντα κτλ. before καθαρισμὸν ἁμαρτιῶν ποιησάμενος. The object of insisting that the Son is also the exact counterpart of God (ὃς ὢν κτλ. ^{3a}), is to bring out the truth that he is not only God's organ in creation, but essentially divine as a Son. In short, since the object of the divine revelation (λαλεῖν) is fellowship between God and men, it must culminate in One who can deal with sin, as no prophet or succession of prophets could do; the line of revelation ἐν προφήταις has its climax ἐν υἱῷ, in a Son whose redeeming sacrifice was the real and effective manifestation of God's mind for communion.

As it is necessary to break up this elaborate sentence for the purpose of exposition, I print it not only in Greek but in the stately Vulgate version, in order to exhibit at the very outset the style and spirit of Πρὸς Ἑβραίους.

I

Πολυμερῶς καὶ πολυτρόπως πάλαι ὁ θεὸς λαλήσας τοῖς πατράσιν ἐν τοῖς προφήταις ἐπ' ἐσχάτου τῶν ἡμερῶν τούτων ἐλάλησεν ἡμῖν ἐν υἱῷ, ὃν ἔθηκε κληρονόμον πάντων, δι' οὗ καὶ ἐποίησε τοὺς αἰῶνας· ὃς ὢν ἀπαύγασμα τῆς δόξης καὶ χαρακτὴρ τῆς ὑποστάσεως αὐτοῦ, φέρων τε τὰ πάντα τῷ ῥήματι τῆς δυνάμεως αὐτοῦ, καθαρισμὸν τῶν ἁμαρτιῶν ποιησάμενος ἐκάθισεν ἐν δεξιᾷ τῆς μεγαλωσύνης ἐν ὑψηλοῖς, τοσούτῳ κρείττων γενόμενος τῶν ἀγγέλων ὅσῳ διαφορώτερον παρ' αὐτοὺς κεκληρονόμηκεν ὄνομα.

Multifariam et multis modis olim Deus loquens patribus in prophetis novissime diebus istis locutus est nobis in filio, quem constituit heredem universorum, per quem fecit et saecula, qui cum sit splendor gloriae et figura substantiae eius, portans quoque omnia verbo virtutis suae, purgationem peccatorum faciens, sedit ad dexteram majestatis in excelsis, tanto melior angelis effectus quanto differentius prae illis nomen hereditavit.

[1] *Many were the forms and fashions in which God spoke of old to our fathers by the prophets,* [2] *but in these days at the end he has spoken to us by a Son—a Son whom he has appointed heir of the universe, as it was by him that he created the world.*

Greek prefaces and introductions of a rhetorical type were fond of opening with πολύς in some form or other (*e.g.* Sirach prol. πολλῶν καὶ μεγάλων κτλ.; Dion. Halic. *de oratoribus antiquis,* πολλὴν χάριν κτλ., an early instance being the third Philippic of Demosthenes, πολλῶν, ὦ ἄνδρες Ἀθηναῖοι, λόγων γιγνομένων κτλ.). Here πολυμερῶς καὶ πολυτρόπως is a sonorous hendiadys for "variously," as Chrysostom was the first to point out (τὸ γὰρ πολυμερῶς καὶ πολυτρόπως τουτέστι διαφόρως). A similar turn of expression occurs in 2² παράβασις καὶ παρακοή. The writer does not mean to exclude variety from the Christian revelation; he expressly mentions how rich and manysided it was, in 2⁴. Nor does he suggest that the revelation ἐν προφήταις was inferior because it was piecemeal and varied. There is a slight suggestion of the unity and finality of the revelation ἐν υἱῷ, as compared with the prolonged revelations made through the prophets, the Son being far more than a prophet; but there is a deeper suggestion of the unity and continuity of revelation then and now. Πολυμερῶς καὶ πολυτρόπως really "signalises the variety and fulness of the Old Testament word of God" (A. B. Davidson). On the other hand, Christ is God's last word to the world; revelation in him is complete, final and homogeneous.

Compare the comment of Eustathius on *Odyssey,* I¹: πολυτρόπως ἀνεγνωρίσθη πᾶσιν οἷς ἦλθεν εἰς γνῶσιν, μηδενὸς ἀναγνωρισμοῦ συμπεσόντος ἑτέρῳ ἀναγνωρισμῷ τὸ σύνολον· ἄλλως γὰρ τῷ Τελεμάχῳ, ἑτέρως δὲ Εὐρυκλείᾳ, ἑτέρως τοῖς δούλοις, ἄλλον δὲ τρόπον τῷ Λαέρτῃ, καὶ ὅλως ἀνομοίως ἅπασι. Πολυμερῶς, according to Hesychius (= πολυσχέδως), differs from πολυτρόπως (διαφόρως, ποικίλως), and, strictly speaking, is the adverb of πολυμερής = manifold (Wis 7²², where Wisdom is called πνεῦμα μονογενές, πολυμερές). But no such distinction is intended here.

In πάλαι (as opposed to ἐπ' ἐσχάτου τῶν ἡμερῶν τούτων) θεὸς λαλήσας, λαλεῖν, here as throughout the epistle, is practically an equivalent for λέγειν (see Anz's *Subsidia*, pp. 309–310), with a special reference to inspired and oracular utterances of God or of divinely gifted men.   This sense is as old as Menander (ὁ νοῦς γάρ ἐστιν ὁ λαλήσων θεός, Kock's *Comic. Attic. Fragm.* 70).   Οἱ πατέρες in contrast to ἡμεῖς means OT believers in general (cp. Jn 6⁵⁸ 7²²), whereas the more usual NT sense of the term is "the patriarchs" (cp. *Diat.* 1949–1950, 2553*e*), *i.e.* Abraham, etc., though the term (3⁹ 8⁹) covers the ancients down to Samuel or later (Mt 23³⁰).   *Our fathers* or ancestors (Wis 18⁶) means the Hebrew worthies of the far past to whom Christians as God's People, whether they had been born Jews or not (1 Co 10¹ οἱ πατέρες ἡμῶν), look back, as the earlier Sirach did in his πατέρων ὕμνος (Sir 44¹–50²³), or the prophet in Zec 1⁵ (οἱ πατέρες ὑμῶν . . . καὶ οἱ προφῆται).   For οἱ πατέρες = our fathers, cp. Prayer of Manasseh ¹ (θεὸς τῶν πατέρων) and Wessely's *Studien zur Paläographie und Papyruskunde*, i. 64, where boys are reckoned in a list σὺν τοῖς πατράσι.   The insertion of ἡμῶν (p¹² 999. 1836 boh sah Clem. Alex., Chrys. Priscillian) is a correct but superfluous gloss.   As for ἐν τοῖς προφήταις, προφῆται is used here in a broader sense than in 11³²; it denotes the entire succession of those who spoke for God to the People of old, both before and after Moses (Ac 3²² 7³⁷), who is the supreme prophet, according to Philo (*de ebriet.* 21, *de decalogo* 33).   Joshua is a prophet (Sir 46¹), so is David (Philo, *de agric.* 12).   In Ps 105¹⁵ the patriarchs, to whom revelations are made, are both God's προφῆται and χριστοί.   Later on, the term was extended, as in Lk 13²⁸ (Abraham, Isaac, and Jacob, καὶ πάντας τοὺς προφήτας, cp. He 11³²), and still more in Mt 5¹² (τοὺς προφήτας τοὺς πρὸ ὑμῶν).   The reason why there is no contrast between the Son and the prophets is probably because the writer felt there was no danger of rivalry ; prophecy had ceased by the time that the Son came ; the "prophet" belonged to a bygone order of things, so that there was no need to argue against any misconception of their function in relation to that of the Son (Bar 85¹⁻³ "in former times our fathers had helpers, righteous men and holy prophets . . . but now the righteous have been gathered and the prophets have fallen asleep").

As no further use is made of the contrast between Jesus and the prophets (who are only again mentioned incidentally in 11³²), it was natural that ἀγγέλοις should be conjectured (S. Crellius, *Initium Ioannis Evangelii restitutum*, p. 238, independently by Spitta in *Stud. u. Kritiken*, 1913, pp. 106–109) to have been the original reading, instead of προφήταις.   But "the word spoken by angels" (2²) does not refer to divine communications made to the patriarchs ; nor can οἱ πατέρες be identified with the patriarchs, as Spitta contends (cf. U. Holzmeister in *Zeitschrift für kathol. Theologie*, 1913, pp. 805–830), and, even if it could, προφήταις would be quite apposite (cp. Philo, *de Abrah.* 22). Why the writer selects προφήταις is not clear. But ἀνθρώποις would have been an imperfect antithesis, since the Son was human. Philo (*de Monarch.* 9: ἑρμηνεῖς γάρ εἰσιν οἱ προφῆται θεοῦ καταχρωμένου τοῖς ἐκείνων ὀργάνοις πρὸς δήλωσιν ὧν ἂν ἐθελήσῃ) views the prophets as interpreters of God in a sense that might correspond to the strict meaning of ἐν, and even (*Quaest. in Exod.* 23²² τοῦ γὰρ λέγοντος ὁ προφήτης ἄγγελος κυρίου ἐστίν) applies ἄγγελος to the prophet. But ἐν here is a synonym for διά (Chrys. ὁρᾷς ὅτι καὶ τὸ ἐν διὰ ἐστίν), as in 1 S 28⁶ (ἀπεκρίθη αὐτῷ κύριος ἐν τοῖς ἐνυπνίοις καὶ ἐν τοῖς δήλοις καὶ ἐν τοῖς προφήταις).

In Test. Dan 1¹ [acc. to the tenth cent. Paris MS 938]¹ and in LXX of Nu 24¹⁴, Jer 23²⁰ [B: ἐσχάτων, A Q*], 25¹⁹ (49³⁹) [B: ἐσχάτων, A Q], 37 (30) ²⁴ [A Q: ἐσχάτων, B], Ezk 38⁸ (ἐπ' ἐσχάτου ἐτῶν), Dn 10¹⁴ [ἐσχάτῳ ? ἐσχάτων], Hos 3⁵ [Q], ἐπ' ἐσχάτου τῶν ἡμερῶν appears, instead of the more common ἐπ' ἐσχάτων τῶν ἡμερῶν, as a rendering of the phrase בְּאַחֲרִית הַיָּמִים. A similar variety of reading occurs here; Origen, *e.g.*, reads ἐσχάτων without τούτων (on La 4²⁰) and ἐσχάτου (fragm. on John 3³¹), while ἐσχάτων is read by 044, a few minor cursives, d and the Syriac version. The same idea is expressed in 1 P 1²⁰ by ἐπ' ἐσχάτου τῶν χρόνων, but the τούτων here is unique. The messianic mission of Jesus falls at the close of *these days*, or, as the writer says later (9²⁶), ἐπὶ συντελείᾳ τῶν αἰώνων. *These days* correspond to the *present age* (ὁ νῦν αἰών); *the age* (or *world*) *to come* (ὁ μέλλων αἰών, 6⁵) is to dawn at the second coming of Christ (9²⁸ 10³⁷). Meantime, the revelation of God ἐν υἱῷ has been made to the Christian church as God's People (ἐλάλησεν ἡμῖν); the ἡμεῖς does not mean simply the hearers of Jesus on earth, for this would exclude the writer and his readers (2³), and ἐλάλησεν covers more than the earthly mission of Jesus. There is no special reference in ἐλάλησεν to the teaching of Jesus; the writer is thinking of the revelation of God's redeeming purpose in Christ as manifested (vv.³·⁴) by the (resurrection and) intercession in heaven which completed the sacrifice on the cross. This is the final revelation, now experienced by Christians.

The saying of Jesus quoted by Epiphanius (*Haer.* xxiii. 5, xli. 3, lxvi. 42), ὁ λαλῶν ἐν τοῖς προφήταις, ἰδοὺ πάρειμι, was an anti-gnostic logion based partly on this passage and partly on Is 52⁶ ἐγὼ εἰμι αὐτὸς ὁ λαλῶν, πάρειμι. The author of Hebrews is not conscious of any polemic against the OT revelation as inferior to and unworthy of the Christian God. He assumes that it was the same God who spoke in both Testaments: "Sed in hac diversitate unum tamen Deus nobis proponit: nequis putet Legem cum Evangelio pugnare, vel alium esse huius quam illius authorem" (Calvin).

¹ The Armenian reading τούτων after ἡμερῶν, instead of αὐτοῦ, is incorrect, and may even be a reminiscence of He 1¹.

In ὃν ἔθηκεν κληρονόμον πάντων there is a parallel, perhaps even an allusion, to the Synoptic parable: *finally he sent his son* (Mt 21²⁷), or, as Mark (12⁶) and Luke (20¹³) explicitly declare, his *beloved son*, though our author does not work out the sombre thought of the parable. There, the son is the heir (οὗτός ἐστιν ὁ κληρονόμος), though not of the universe. Here, the meaning of ὃν ἔθηκεν κληρονόμον πάντων is the same: he was "appointed" heir, he was heir by God's appointment. It is the fact of this position, not the time, that the writer has in mind, and we cannot be sure that this "appointment" corresponds to the elevation of v.³ (ἐκάθισεν). Probably, in our modern phrase, it describes a pre-temporal act, or rather a relationship which belongs to the eternal order. The force of the aorist ἔθηκεν is best rendered by the English perfect, "has appointed"; no definite time is necessarily intended.

"Nam ideo ille haeres, ut nos suis opibus ditet. Quin hoc elogio nunc eum ornat Apostolus ut sciamus nos sine ipso bonorum omnium esse inopes" (Calvin). The reflection of Sedulius Scotus (alii post patrem haeredes sunt, hic autem vivente Patre haeres est) is pious but irrelevant, for κληρονομεῖν in Hellenistic Greek had come to mean, like its equivalent "inherit" in Elizabethan English, no more than "possess" or "obtain"; a κληρονόμος was a "possessor," with the double *nuance* of certainty and anticipation. "Haeres" in Latin acquired the same sense; "pro haerede gerere est pro domino gerere, veteres enim 'haeredes' pro 'dominis' appellabant" (Justinian, *Instit.* ii. 19. 7).

In δι' οὗ (Griesbach conj. διότι) καὶ ἐποίησε τοὺς αἰῶνας the καί especially [1] suggests a correspondence between this and the preceding statement; what the Son was to possess was what he had been instrumental in making. Τοὺς αἰῶνας here, though never in Paul, is equivalent (*EBi.* 1147) to τὰ πάντα in v.³ (implied in πάντων above), *i.e.* the universe or world (11³). The functions assigned by Jewish speculation to media like the Logos at creation are here claimed as the prerogative of the Son. This passing allusion to the function of Christ in relation to the universe probably originated, as in the case of Paul, in the religious conception of redemption. From the redeeming function of Christ which extended to all men, it was natural to infer His agency in relation to creation as part of his pre-existence. The notion is that "the whole course of nature and grace must find its explanation in God, not merely in an abstract divine *arbitrium*, but in that which befits the divine nature" (W. Robertson Smith), *i.e.* the thought behind 2⁹ᶠ· is connected with the thought behind 1¹⁻³. This may be due to a theological reflection, but the tendency to emphasize the moral rather than the metaphysical aspect, which is noticeable in Πρὸς Ἑβραίους as

[1] An emphasis blurred by the τοὺς αἰῶνας ἐποίησεν of Dᵇ K L P harkl Chrys. Theod. (Blass, von Sod.).

in the Fourth Gospel, and even in Paul, is consonant with Philo's
tendency to show the function of the Logos and the other intermediate powers as religious rather than cosmical (cp. Bréhier's
Les Idées Philos. et Religieuses de Philon d'Alexandrie, pp. 65 f.,
111 f., 152, "il ne s'agit plus chez Philon d'un explication du
monde mais du culte divin"; 174 f., "la thése de Philon, qui
explique et produit la doctrine des intermédiaires, n'est pas
l'impossibilité pour Dieu de produire le monde mais l'impossibilité
pour l'âme d'atteindre Dieu directement"). Yet Philo had
repeatedly claimed for his Logos, that it was the organ of
creation (*e.g. de sacerdot.* 5, λόγος δ' ἐστὶν εἰκὼν θεοῦ, δι' οὗ
σύμπας ὁ κόσμος ἐδημιουργεῖτο), and this is what is here, as by
Paul, claimed for Christ. Only, it is a religious, not a cosmological, instinct that prompts the thought. The early Christian,
who believed in the lordship of Christ over the world, felt, as a
modern would put it, that the end must be implicit in the beginning, that the aim and principle of the world must be essentially Christian. This is not elaborated in "Hebrews" any more
than in the Fourth Gospel (Jn 1³); the author elsewhere prefers
the simple monotheistic expression (2¹⁰ 11³). But the idea is
consonant with his conception of the Son. "If pre-existence is
a legitimate way of expressing the absolute significance of Jesus,
then the mediation of creation through Christ is a legitimate
way of putting the conviction that in the last resort, and in spite
of appearances, the world in which we live is a Christian world,
our ally, not our adversary" (Denney in *ERE.* viii. 516 f.).

[3] *He* (ὃς ὤν) *reflecting God's bright glory and stamped with God's own
character, sustains the universe with his word of power; when he had
secured our purification from sins, he sat down at the right hand of the
Majesty on high;* [4] *and thus he is superior to* (κρείττων) *the angels, as he has
inherited a Name superior* (διαφορώτερον, 8⁶) *to theirs.*

The unique relation of Christ to God is one of the unborrowed
truths of Christianity, but it is stated here in borrowed terms.
The writer is using metaphors which had been already applied in
Alexandrian theology to Wisdom and the Logos. Thus Wisdom
is an unalloyed emanation τῆς τοῦ παντοκράτορος δόξης, ἀπαύγασμα
. . . φωτὸς ἀιδίου (Wis 7²⁵· ²⁶), and ἀπαύγασμα in the same sense
of "reflection" occurs in Philo, who describes the universe as
οἷον ἁγίων ἀπαύγασμα, μίμημα ἀρχετύπου (*de plant.* 12), the human
spirit as τύπον τινὰ καὶ χαρακτῆρα θείας δυνάμεως (*quod deter. pot.
ins. sol.* 83), and similarly the Logos. χαρακτήρ is "the exact
reproduction," as a statue of a person (*OGIS.* 363⁶⁰ χαρακτῆρα
μορφῆς ἐμῆς); literally, the stamp or clear-cut impression made
by a seal, the very facsimile of the original. The two terms
ἀπαύγασμα and χαρακτήρ are therefore intended to bring out the
same idea.

ὑπόστασις = the being or essence of God, which corresponds to his δόξα (= character or nature); it is a philosophical rather than a religious term, in this connexion, but enters the religious world in Wis 16²¹ (ἡ μὲν γὰρ ὑπόστασίς σου κτλ.). Its physical sense emerges in the contemporary *de Mundo*, 4, τῶν ἐν ἀέρι φαντασμάτων τὰ μέν ἐστι κατ᾽ ἔμφασιν τὰ δὲ καθ᾽ ὑπόστασιν. The use of it as a term for the essence or substance of a human being is not uncommon in the LXX (*e.g.* Ps 39⁵ 139¹⁵); cp. Schlatter's *Der Glaube im NT³* (1905), pp. 615 f., where the linguistic data are arranged.

χαρακτήρ had already acquired a meaning corresponding to the modern "character" (*e.g.* in Menander's proverb, ἀνδρὸς χαρακτὴρ ἐκ λόγου γνωρίζεται, *Heauton Timoroumenos*, 11). The idea of χαρακτήρ as replica is further illustrated by the Bereschith rabba, 52. 3 (on Gn 21²): "hence we learn that he (Isaac) was the splendour of his (father's) face, as like as possible to him."

An early explanation of this conception is given by Lactantius (*diuin. instit.* iv. 29), viz. that "the Father is as it were an overflowing fountain, the Son like a stream flowing from it; the Father like the sun, the Son as it were a ray extended from the sun (radius ex sole porrectus). Since he is faithful (cp. He 3²) and dear to the most High Father, he is not separated from him, any more than the stream is from the fountain or the ray from the sun; for the water of the fountain is in the stream, and the sun's light in the ray." But our author is content to throw out his figurative expressions. How the Son could express the character of God, is a problem which he does not discuss; it is felt by the author of the Fourth Gospel, who suggests the moral and spiritual affinities that lie behind such a function of Jesus Christ, by hinting that the Son on earth taught what he had heard from the Father and lived out the life he had himself experienced and witnessed with the unseen Father. This latter thought is present to the mind of Seneca in *Epp.* 6⁵·⁶, where he observes that "Cleanthes could never have exactly reproduced Zeno, if he had simply listened to him; he shared the life of Zeno, he saw into his secret purposes" (vitae eius interfuit, secreta perspexit). The author of Hebrews, like Paul in Col 1¹⁵⁻¹⁷, contents himself with asserting the vital community of nature between the Son and God, in virtue of which (φέρων τε) the Son holds his position in the universe.

In the next clause, φέρων [1] τε τὰ πάντα is not used in the sense in which Sappho (fragm. 95, πάντα φέρων) speaks of the evening star "bringing all things home," the sheep to their fold and children to their mother. The phrase means "upholding the universe as it moves," bearing it and bearing it on. "Thou bearest things on high and things below," Cain tells God in Bereschith rabba, 23. 2, "but thou dost not bear my sins." "Deus ille maximus potentissimusque ipse vehit omnia" (Seneca, *Epist.* 31¹⁰). The idea had been already applied by Philo to the Logos (e.g. *de migrat. Abrah.* 6, ὁ λόγος . . . ὁ τῶν ὅλων κυβερνήτης πηδαλιουχεῖ τὰ σύμπαντα: *de spec. legibus*, i. 81, λόγος δ᾽ ἐστὶν εἰκὼν θεοῦ, δι᾽ οὗ σύμπας ὁ κόσμος ἐδημιουργεῖτο: *de plant.* 8, λόγος δὲ ὁ ἀίδιος θεοῦ τοῦ αἰωνίου τὸ ὀχυρώτατον καὶ βεβαιότατον ἔρεισμα τῶν ὅλων ἐστί). So Chrysostom takes it: φέρων . . . τουτέστι, κυβερνῶν, τὰ διαπίπτοντα συγκρατῶν. It would certainly carry on the thought of δι᾽ οὗ . . . αἰῶνας, however, if φέρειν here could be taken in its regular Philonic sense of "bring into existence" (e g. *quis rer. div. haer.* 7, ὁ τὰ μὴ ὄντα φέρων καὶ τὰ πάντα γεννῶν:

___
[1] φανερῶν is, like ἀπολεῖται in 4⁹, an error of B*.

de mutat. nom. 44, πάντα φέρων σπουδαῖα ὁ θεός); this was the
interpretation of Gregory of Nyssa (*MPG*. xlvi. 265), and it would
give a better sense to "word of power" as the fiat of creative
authority.   But the ordinary interpretation is not untenable.

In τῷ ῥήματι τῆς δυνάμεως αὐτοῦ, the αὐτοῦ (αὑτοῦ ?) refers to the Son,
not as in the preceding clause and in 11³ to God.   Hence perhaps its omission
by M 424** 1739 Origen.

With καθαρισμὸν . . . ὑψηλοῖς the writer at last touches what
is for him the central truth about the Son ; it is not the teaching
of Jesus that interests him, but what Jesus did for sin by his
sacrifice and exaltation.   From this conception the main argument of the epistle flows.   Καθαρισμὸν τῶν ἁμαρτιῶν is a Septuagint expression (*e.g.* Job 7²¹ ποίησω . . . καθαρισμὸν (עָבַר) τῆς
ἁμαρτίας μου), though this application of κ. to sins is much more
rare than that either to persons (Lv 15¹³) or places (1 Ch 23²⁶,
2 Mac 10⁵).   In 2 P 1⁹ (τοῦ καθαρισμοῦ τῶν πάλαι αὐτοῦ ἁμαρτιῶν)
it is filled out with the possessive pronoun, which is supplied here
by some (*e.g.* ἡμῶν Dᶜ K L harkl sah arm Athan. Chrys., ὑμῶν אᶜ).
Grammatically it = (*a*) purgation of sins, as καθαρίζω may be used
of the "removal" of a disease (Mt 8³·⁴), or = (*b*) our cleansing
from sins (9¹⁴ καθαριεῖ τὴν συνείδησιν ἡμῶν ἀπὸ νεκρῶν ἔργων).
Before καθαρισμόν the words δι' ἑαυτοῦ (αὑτοῦ) are inserted by
D H K L M 256 d harkl sah boh eth Orig. Athan. Aug. etc.
Δι' ἑαυτοῦ = ipse, as ἑαυτῷ = sua sponte.   Ἐκάθισεν ἐν δεξιᾷ is a
reminiscence of a favourite psalm (110¹) of the writer, though he
avoids its ἐκ δεξιῶν.   It denotes entrance into a position of divine
authority.   "Sedere ad Patris dexteram nihil aliud est quam
gubernare vice Patris" (Calvin).   Ἐν ὑψηλοῖς, a phrase used by
no other NT writer, is a reminiscence of the Greek psalter and
equivalent to ἐν ὑψίστοις : grammatically it goes with ἐκάθισεν.
(The divine attribute of μεγαλωσύνη is for the first time employed
as a periphrasis for the divine *Majesty*.)   This enthronement
exhibits (v.⁴) the superiority of the Son to the angels.   Ὄνομα is
emphatic by its position at the close of the sentence ; it carries
the general Oriental sense of "rank" or "dignity."   The
precise nature of this dignity is described as that of sonship (v.⁵),
but the conception widens in the following passage (vv.⁶ᶠ·), and
it is needless to identify ὄνομα outright with υἱός, though υἱός
brings out its primary meaning.   In τοσούτῳ κρείττων γενόμενος
(going closely with ἐκάθισεν) τῶν (accidentally omitted by B and
Clem. Rom.) ἀγγέλων (emphatic by position) παρ' αὐτοὺς κεκληρονόμηκεν ὄνομα, the relative use of ὅσος in NT Greek is confined to Mk 7³⁶, but τοσοῦτος . . . ὅσος is a common Philonic
expression.   Κρείττων (for which Clement of Rome in 36² substitutes the synonymous μείζων) is an indefinite term = "superior."

Unlike Paul, the writer here and elsewhere is fond of using παρά after a comparative.

Κρείττων in this sense occurs in the contemporary (?) Aristotelian treatise *de Mundo*, 391a (διὰ τὸ ἀθέατοι τῶν κρειττόνων εἶναι), where τὰ κρειττόνα means the nobler Universe.

The sudden transition to a comparison between the Son and the angels implies that something is before the writer's mind. Were his readers, like the Colossians to whom Paul wrote, in danger of an undue deference to angels in their religion, a deference which threatened to impair their estimate of Christ? Or is he developing his argument in the light of some contemporary belief about angels and revelation? Probably the latter, though this does not emerge till 2². Meanwhile, seven Biblical proofs (cp. W. Robertson Smith, *Expositor*², i. pp. 5 f.) of v.⁴ are adduced; the two in v.⁵ specially explain the διαφορώτερον ὄνομα, while the five in vv.⁶⁻¹⁴ describe the meaning and force of κρείττων τῶν ἀγγέλων.   The first two are:

> ⁵ *For to what angel did God ever say,*
>   "*Thou art my son,*
>   *to-day have I become thy father*"?
> *Or again,*
>   "*I will be a father to him,*
>   *and he shall be a son to me*"?

The first quotation is from the 2nd Psalm (v.⁷), read as a messianic prediction—which may have been its original meaning, and certainly was the meaning attached to it by the early Christians, if not already by some circles of Judaism:¹

> υἱός μου εἶ σύ,
> ἐγὼ σήμερον γεγέννηκά σε.

Did the author take σήμερον here, as perhaps in 3⁷ᶠ·, though not in 13⁸, in (*a*) a mystical sense, or (*b*) with a reference to some special phase in the history of Christ? (*a*) tallies with Philo's usage: σήμερον δ᾽ ἐστὶν ὁ ἀπέρατος καὶ ἀδιεξίτητος αἰών . . . τὸ ἀψευδὲς ὄνομα αἰῶνος (*de fuga*, 11, on Dt 4⁴), ἕως τῆς σήμερον ἡμέρας, τουτέστιν ἀεί· ὁ γὰρ αἰὼν ἅπας τῷ σήμερον παραμετρεῖται (*leg. alleg.* iii. 8 on Gn 35⁴). (*b*) might allude either to the baptism or to the resurrection of Christ in primitive Christian usage; the latter would be more congenial to our author, if it were assumed that he had any special incident in mind. But he simply quotes the text for the purpose of bringing out the title of Son as applied to Christ. When we ask what he meant by σήμερον, we are asking a question which was not present to his mind, unless, indeed, "the idea of a bright radiance streaming forth from God's glory" (v.³) pointed in the direction of (*a*), as

¹ See G. H. Box, *The Ezra-Apocalypse*, pp. lvi, lvii.

Robertson Smith thought. But the second line of the verse is merely quoted to fill out the first, which is the pivot of the proof : υἱός μου εἶ σύ. *Sons of God* is not unknown as a title for angels in the Hebrew Old Testament (see *EBi.* 4691). "Sometimes Moses calls the angels sons of God," Philo observes (*Quaest. in Gen.* 6⁴—as being bodiless spirits). But the LXX is careful to translate : "sons of Elohim" by ἄγγελοι θεοῦ (*e.g.* in Gn 6². ⁴, Job 1⁶ 2¹ 38⁷), except in Ps 29¹ and 89⁷, where *sons of God* are intended by the translator to denote human beings ; and no individual angel is ever called υἱός.[1] As the author of Πρὸς Ἑβραίους and his readers knew only the Greek Bible, the proof holds good.

The second quotation is from 2 S 7¹⁴ :

$$\text{Ἐγὼ ἔσομαι αὐτῷ εἰς πατέρα,}$$
$$\text{καὶ αὐτὸς ἔσται μοι εἰς υἱόν,}$$

a promise cited more exactly than in 2 Co 6¹⁸ and Rev 21⁷, but with equal indifference to its original setting. Paul and the prophet John apply it to the relationship between God and Christians ; our author prefers to treat it as messianic. Indeed he only alludes twice, in OT quotations, to God as the Father of Christians (see Introd. p. xxxv).

The third quotation (v.⁶) clinches this proof of Christ's unique authority and opens up the sense in which he is κρείττων τῶν ἀγγέλων :

> *and further, when introducing the Firstborn into the world, he says,*
> " *Let all God's angels worship him.*"

In ὅταν δὲ πάλιν εἰσαγάγῃ the term πάλιν, rhetorically transferred, answers to the πάλιν of v.⁵ ; it is not to be taken with εἰσαγάγῃ = "reintroduce," as if the first "introduction" of the Son had been referred to in v.²ᶠ·. A good parallel for this usage occurs in Philo (*leg. alleg.* iii. 9 : ὁ δὲ πάλιν ἀποδιδράσκων θεὸν τὸν μὲν οὐδενὸς αἴτιον φησὶν εἶναι, where πάλιν goes with φησίν). Εἰσάγειν might refer to birth,[2] as, *e.g.*, in Epictetus (iv. 1. 104, οὐχὶ ἐκεῖνός σε εἰσήγαγεν) and pseudo-Musonius, ep. 90 (Hercher's *Epist. Graeci*, 401 f. : οὐ τέκνα μόνον εἰς τὸ γένος ἄλλα καὶ τοιάδε τέκνα εἰσήγαγες), or simply for "introduction" (cp. Mitteis-Wilcken, i. 2. 141 (110 B.C.), εἰσάξω τὸν ἐμαυτοῦ υἱὸν εἰς τὴν σύνοδον). Linguistically either the incarnation or the second advent might be intended ; but neither the tense of εἰσαγάγῃ (unless it be taken strictly as futuristic = ubi introduxerit) nor the proximity of

---

[1] It is only Theodotion who ventures in Dan 3²⁵ ⁽⁹²⁾ to retain the literal *son*, since from his christological point of view it could not be misunderstood in this connexion.

[2] Cp. M. Aurelius, v. 1, τοιεῖν ὧν ἕνεκεν γέγονα καὶ ὧν χάριν προῆγμαι εἰς τὸν κόσμον.

πάλιν is decisive in favour of the latter (ὅταν εἰσαγάγῃ might, by a well-known Greek idiom, be equivalent to "when he speaks of introducing, or, describes the introduction of"—Valckenaer, etc.). Πρωτότοκος is Firstborn in the sense of superior. The suggestion of Christ being higher than angels is also present in the context of the term as used by Paul (Col 1¹⁵· ¹⁶), but it is nowhere else used absolutely in the NT, and the writer here ignores any inference that might be drawn from it to an inferior sonship of angels. Its equivalent (cp. the *v.ll.* in Sir 36¹⁷) πρωτόγονος is applied by Philo to the Logos. Here it means that Christ was Son in a pre-eminent sense; the idea of priority passes into that of superiority. A πρωτότοκος υἱός had a relationship of likeness and nearness to God which was unrivalled. As the context indicates, the term brings out the pre-eminent honour and the unique relationship to God enjoyed by the Son among the heavenly host.

The notion of worship being due only to a senior reappears in the *Vita Adae et Evae* (14), where the devil declines to worship Adam : "I have no need to worship Adam . . . I will not worship an inferior being who is my junior. I am his senior in the Creation ; before he was made, I was already made ; it is his duty to worship me." In the *Ascensio Isaiae* (11²³ᶠ·) the angels humbly worship Christ as he ascends through the heavens where they live ; here the adoration is claimed for him as he enters ἡ οἰκουμένη.

The line καὶ προσκυνησάτωσαν αὐτῷ πάντες ἄγγελοι θεοῦ comes from a LXX addition to the Hebrew text of the Song of Moses in Dt 32⁴³, calling upon all angels to pay homage to Yahweh. But the LXX text[1] actually reads υἱοὶ θεοῦ, not ἄγγελοι θεοῦ (into which F corrects it) ! Our author probably changed it into ἄγγελοι θεοῦ, recollecting the similar phrase in Ps 97⁷ (προσκυνήσατε αὐτῷ πάντες οἱ ἄγγελοι αὐτοῦ),[2] unless, indeed, the change had been already made. The fact that Justin Martyr (*Dial.* 130) quotes the LXX gloss with ἄγγελοι, is an indication that this may have been the text current among the primitive Christians.

The last four (vv.⁷⁻¹⁴) quotations carry on the idea of the Son's superiority to the angels :

⁷ *While he says of angels* (πρός = with reference to),
　　" *Who makes his angels into winds,*
　　his servants into flames of fire,"
⁸ *he says of the Son,*
　　" *God is thy throne for ever and ever,*
　　and thy royal sceptre is the sceptre of equity :
⁹ *thou hast loved justice and hated lawlessness,*
　　therefore God, thy God, has consecrated thee
　　with the oil of rejoicing beyond thy comrades"—
¹⁰ *and,*
　　" *Thou didst found the earth at the beginning, O Lord,*

---

[1] As the song appears in A, at the close of the psalter, the reading is ἄγγελοι (υἱοί, R).

[2] Which acquired a messianic application (see *Diat.* 3134).

and the heavens are the work of thy hands:
11 *they will perish, but thou remainest,*
   they will all be worn out like a garment,
12 *thou wilt roll them up like a mantle, and they will be changed,*
   but thou art the same,
   and thy years never fail."

In v.[7] the quotation (ὁ ποιῶν τοὺς ἀγγέλους αὐτοῦ πνεύματα| καὶ τοὺς λειτουργοὺς αὐτοῦ πυρὸς φλόγα) only differs from the LXX by the substitution of πυρὸς φλόγα [1] for πῦρ φλέγον (B : πυρὸς φλέγα Aᵃ). The singular in φλόγα and perhaps the recollection that πνεῦμα elsewhere in NT = " wind " only in the singular, led to the change of πνεύματα into πνεῦμα (D 1. 326. 424**. 1912. 1245. 2005 d sah eth Orig.). The author is taking the LXX translation or mistranslation of Ps 104[4] (ὁ ποιῶν κτλ., a nominative without a verb, as in 1 Co 3[19]) to mean that God can reduce angels to the elemental forces of wind and fire, so unstable is their nature, whereas the person and authority of the Son are above all change and decay. The meaning might also be that God makes angels out of wind and fire ; [2] but this is less apt. Our author takes the same view as the author of 4 Esdras, who (8[21]) writes :

" Before whom the heavenly host stands in terror,
   and at thy word change to wind and fire."

Rabbinic traditions corroborate this interpretation ; *e.g.* " every day ministering angels are created from the fiery stream, and they utter a song and perish " (*Chagiga*, ed. Streane, p. 76), and the confession of the angel to Manoah in *Yalkut Shimeoni*, ii. 11. 3 : " God changes us every hour . . . sometimes he makes us fire, at other times wind."

The interest of rabbinic mysticism in the nature of angels is illustrated by the second century dialogue between Hadrian, that " curiositatum omnium explorator," and R. Joshua ben Chananja (cp. W. Bacher, *Agada der Tannaiten*[2], i. 171–172). The emperor asks the rabbi what becomes of the angels whom God creates daily to sing His praise ; the rabbi answers that they return to the stream of fire which flows eternally from the sweat shed by the Beasts supporting the divine throne or chariot (referring to the vision of Ezekiel and the " fiery stream " of Dn 7[10]). From this stream of fire the angels issue, and to it they return. Λειτουργούς of angels as in Ps 103[21] (λειτουργοὶ αὐτοῦ, ποιοῦντες τὸ θέλημα αὐτοῦ).

The fifth (vv.[8, 9]) quotation is from Ps 45[7, 8]—a Hebrew epithalamium for some royal personage or national hero, which our author characteristically regards as messianic.

---

[1] Aquila has πῦρ λάβρον, Symm. πυρίνην φλόγα.
[2] As in Apoc. Bar. 21[6] (" the holy creatures which thou didst make from the beginning out of flame and fire ") and 48[8] (" Thou givest commandment to the flames and they change into spirits ").

ὁ θρόνος σου ὁ θεὸς εἰς τὸν αἰῶνα τοῦ αἰῶνος,
καὶ¹ ῥάβδος τῆς εὐθύτητος ἡ ῥάβδος τῆς βασιλείας σου.²
ἠγάπησας δικαιοσύνην καὶ ἐμίσησας ἀνομίαν·
διὰ τοῦτο ἔχρισέ σε ὁ θεός, ὁ θεός σου,
ἔλαιον ἀγαλλιάσεως παρὰ³ τοὺς μετόχους σου.

The quotation inserts τῆς before εὐθύτητος, follows A in preferring τὸν αἰῶνα τοῦ αἰῶνος (τοῦ αἰῶνος om. B 33) to αἰῶνα αἰῶνος
(B), but prefers⁴ B's ἀνομίαν (cp. 2 Co 6¹⁴) to A's ἀδικίαν, and
agrees with both in prefixing ἡ to the second (D K L P Cyr. Cosm.
Dam.) instead of to the first (ℵ A B M, etc.) ῥάβδος. The psalm
is not quoted elsewhere in NT (apart from a possible reminiscence of 45⁵· ⁶ in Rev 6²), and rarely cited in primitive Christian
literature, although the messianic reference reappears in Irenaeus
(iv. 34. 11, quoting v.²). ῾Ο θεός (sc. ἐστίν rather than ἔστω) may
be (a) nominative (subject or predicate). This interpretation
("God is thy throne," or, "thy throne is God"), which was
probably responsible for the change of σοῦ after βασιλείας into
αὐτοῦ (ℵ B), has been advocated, e.g., by Grotius, Ewald
("thy throne is divine"), WH ("founded on God, the im-
movable Rock"), and Wickham ("represents God"). Tyndale's
rendering is, "God thy seat shall be." Those who find this
interpretation harsh prefer to (b) take ὁ θεός as a vocative, which
grammatically is possible (= ὦ θεέ, cp. 10⁷ and Ps 3⁸ 138¹⁷ etc.);
"Thy throne, O God (or, O divine One), is for ever and ever."
This (so sah vg, etc.) yields an excellent sense, and may well
explain the attractiveness of the text for a writer who wished to
bring out the divine significance of Christ; ὁ θεός appealed to
him like κύριε in the first line of the next quotation. The sense
would be clear if ὁ θεός were omitted altogether, as its Hebrew
equivalent ought to be in the original; but the LXX text as it
stands was the text before our author, and the problem is
to decide which interpretation he followed. (b) involves the
direct application of ὁ θεός to the Son, which, in a poetical quotation, is not perhaps improbable (see Jn 1¹⁸ 20²⁸); in v.⁹ it may
involve the repetition of ὁ θεός (om. by Irenaeus, Apost. Preaching,
47—accidentally?) as vocative, and does involve the rendering
of ὁ θεός σου as the God of the God already mentioned. The
point of the citation lies in its opening and closing words: (i)
the Son has a royal and lasting authority (as ὁ θεός?), in contrast

¹ The addition of this καί is not to mark a fresh quotation (as in v.¹⁰), but
simply to introduce the parallel line (as in v.¹⁰ καὶ ἔργα κτλ.).
² Cp. Ps 110² ῥάβδον δυνάμεως σου (om. ℵ) ἐξαποστελεῖ κύριος.
³ For παρά with accus. in this sense, cp. above, v.⁴, and Is 53³ ἄτιμον καὶ
ἐκλιπὸν παρὰ τοὺς υἱοὺς τῶν ἀνθρώπων.
⁴ ἀνομίαν, B D (Δ* ἀνομίας) M P lat harkl Ath. Eus., ἀδικίαν ℵ A 33 38
218. 226. 919 Iren. Cosm.

to the angels, and (ii) he is anointed ($\check{\epsilon}\chi\rho\iota\sigma\epsilon$[1] $= \dot{\delta}$ $X\rho\iota\sigma\tau\delta\varsigma$) more highly than his companions—an Oriental metaphor referring here, as in Is 61³ etc., not to coronation but to bliss. If the writer of Hebrews has anything specially in mind, it is angels (12²³) rather than human beings (3¹⁴) as $\mu\acute{\epsilon}\tau o\chi o\iota$ of the royal Prince, whose superior and supreme position is one of intense joy, based on a moral activity (as in 12², where the passive side of the moral effort is emphasized).

The sixth (vv.¹⁰⁻¹²) quotation is from Ps 102²⁶⁻²⁸ which in A runs thus :

$\kappa\alpha\tau$' $\dot{\alpha}\rho\chi\dot{\alpha}\varsigma$[2] $\sigma\acute{v}$, $\kappa\acute{v}\rho\iota\epsilon$,[3] $\tau\dot{\eta}\nu$ $\gamma\dot{\eta}\nu$ $\dot{\epsilon}\theta\epsilon\mu\epsilon\lambda\acute{\iota}\omega\sigma\alpha\varsigma$,
$\kappa\alpha\grave{\iota}$ $\check{\epsilon}\rho\gamma\alpha$ $\tau\hat{\omega}\nu$ $\chi\epsilon\iota\rho\hat{\omega}\nu$ $\sigma o\acute{v}$ $\epsilon\dot{\iota}\sigma\iota\nu$ $o\dot{\iota}$ $o\dot{v}\rho\alpha\nu o\acute{\iota}$·
$\alpha\dot{v}\tau o\grave{\iota}$[4] $\dot{\alpha}\pi o\lambda o\hat{v}\nu\tau\alpha\iota$, $\sigma\grave{v}$ $\delta\grave{\epsilon}$ $\delta\iota\alpha\mu\acute{\epsilon}\nu\epsilon\iota\varsigma$,
$\kappa\alpha\grave{\iota}$ $\pi\acute{\alpha}\nu\tau\epsilon\varsigma$ $\dot{\omega}\varsigma$ $\dot{\iota}\mu\acute{\alpha}\tau\iota o\nu$ $\pi\alpha\lambda\alpha\iota\omega\theta\acute{\eta}\sigma o\nu\tau\alpha\iota$,
$\kappa\alpha\grave{\iota}$ $\dot{\omega}\sigma\epsilon\grave{\iota}$ $\pi\epsilon\rho\iota\beta\acute{o}\lambda\alpha\iota o\nu$ $\dot{\epsilon}\lambda\acute{\iota}\xi\epsilon\iota\varsigma$ $\alpha\dot{v}\tau o\grave{v}\varsigma$ $\kappa\alpha\grave{\iota}$ $\dot{\alpha}\lambda\lambda\alpha\gamma\acute{\eta}\sigma o\nu\tau\alpha\iota$·
$\sigma o\grave{\iota}$ $\delta\grave{\epsilon}$ $\dot{\delta}$ $\alpha\dot{v}\tau\grave{o}\varsigma$ $\epsilon\dot{\iota}$, $\kappa\alpha\grave{\iota}$ $\tau\grave{\alpha}$ $\check{\epsilon}\tau\eta$ $\sigma o v$ $o\dot{v}\kappa$ $\dot{\epsilon}\kappa\lambda\epsilon\acute{\iota}\psi o v\sigma\iota\nu$.

The author, for purposes of emphasis (as in 2¹³), has thrown $\sigma\acute{v}$ to the beginning of the sentence, and in the last line he has reverted to the more natural $\sigma\acute{v}$ (B). In the text of the epistle there are only two uncertain readings, for the proposed change of $\delta\iota\alpha\mu\acute{\epsilon}\nu\epsilon\iota\varsigma$ into the future $\delta\iota\alpha\mu\epsilon\nu\epsilon\hat{\iota}\varsigma$ (vg. permanebis) does not really affect the sense, and D*'s $\dot{\omega}\varsigma$ for $\dot{\omega}\sigma\epsilon\acute{\iota}$ is a merely stylistic alteration. In ¹²ᵃ two small points of textual uncertainty emerge. (a) $\dot{\epsilon}\lambda\acute{\iota}\xi\epsilon\iota\varsigma$ (A B Dᶜ K L P M fu Syr arm sah boh eth Orig. Chrys.) has been altered into $\dot{\alpha}\lambda\lambda\acute{\alpha}\xi\epsilon\iota\varsigma$ (א* D* 327. 919 vt Tert. Ath.). The same variant occurs in LXX, where $\dot{\alpha}\lambda\lambda\acute{\alpha}\xi\epsilon\iota\varsigma$ is read by א for $\dot{\epsilon}\lambda\acute{\iota}\xi\epsilon\iota\varsigma$, which may have crept into the text from Is 34⁴, but is more likely to have been altered into $\dot{\alpha}\lambda\lambda\acute{\alpha}\xi\epsilon\iota\varsigma$ in view of $\dot{\alpha}\lambda\lambda\alpha\gamma\acute{\eta}\sigma o\nu\tau\alpha\iota$ ($\dot{\epsilon}\lambda\iota\gamma\acute{\eta}\sigma o\nu\tau\alpha\iota$, arm). (b) $\dot{\omega}\varsigma$ $\dot{\iota}\mu\acute{\alpha}\tau\iota o\nu$ (א A B D* 1739 vt arm eth) after $\alpha\dot{v}\tau o\acute{v}\varsigma$ is omitted by Dᶜ M vg syr sah boh Chrys. Ath. Cyril Alex. Probably the words are due to homoioteleuton. If retained, a comma needs to be placed after them (so Zimmer.) ; they thus go with the preceding phrase, although one early rendering (D d) runs : " (and) like a garment they will be changed."

The psalm is taken as a messianic oracle (see Bacon in *Zeitschrift für die neutest. Wissenschaft*, 1902, 280–285), which the Greek version implied, or at any rate suggested ; it contained welcome indications of the Son in his creative function and also of his destined triumph. The poetical suggestion of the sky as a mantle of the deity occurs in Philo, who writes (*de fuga*, 20)

---

[1] $\chi\rho\acute{\iota}\omega$, in contrast to $\dot{\alpha}\lambda\epsilon\acute{\iota}\phi\omega$, is exclusively metaphorical in NT (cp. Gray in *EBi.* 173), although neither Latin nor English is able to preserve the distinction.

[2] A classical and Philonic equivalent for $\dot{\epsilon}\nu$ $\dot{\alpha}\rho\chi\hat{\eta}$ (LXX again in Ps 119¹⁵²).

[3] This title, which attracted our author, is an addition of the LXX.

[4] Including $\dot{\eta}$ $\gamma\hat{\eta}$, but with special reference to $o\dot{\iota}$ $o\dot{v}\rho\alpha\nu o\acute{\iota}$.

that the Logos ἐνδύεται ὡς ἐσθῆτα τὸν κόσμον· γῆν γὰρ καὶ ὕδωρ καὶ
ἀέρα καὶ πῦρ καὶ τὰ ἐκ τούτων ἐπαμπίσχεται.   But the quotation is
meant to bring out generally (i) the superiority of the Son as
creative (so v.[2]) to the creation, and (ii) his permanence amid
the decay of nature ;[1] the world wears out,[2] even the sky (12[26])
is cast aside, and with it the heavenly lights, but the Son remains
("thou art thou," boh); nature is at his mercy, not he at
nature's.   The close connexion of angels with the forces of
nature (v.[7]) may have involved the thought that this transiency
affects angels as well, but our author does not suggest this.

The final biblical proof (v.[13]) is taken from Ps 110[1], a psalm
in which later on the writer is to find rich messianic suggestion.
The quotation clinches the argument for the superiority of the Son
by recalling (v.[3]) his unique divine commission and authority :

[13] *To what angel did he ever say,*
  "Sit at my right hand,
    till I make your enemies a footstool for your feet"?
[14] *Are not all angels merely spirits in the divine service, commissioned for*
the benefit of those who are to inherit salvation?

The Greek couplet—

  κάθου ἐκ δεξιῶν μου,
  ἕως ἂν θῶ τοὺς ἐχθρούς σου ὑποπόδιον τῶν ποδῶν σου,

corresponds exactly to the LXX ; D* omits ἄν as in Ac 2[35].   The
martial metaphor is (cp. Introd. pp. xxxiii f.) one of the primitive
Christian expressions which survive in the writer's vocabulary
(cp. 10[12]).

The subordinate position of angels is now (v.[14]) summed up ;
πάντες—all without distinction—are simply λειτουργικὰ πνεύματα
(without any power of ruling) εἰς διακονίαν ἀποστελλόμενα (commissioned, not acting on their own initiative).[3]   According to the
Mechilta on Ex 14[13], the Israelites, when crossing the Red Sea,
were shown "squadrons upon squadrons of ministering angels"
(תּוּרְמִיוֹת תּוּרְמִיוֹת שֶׁל מַלְאֲכֵי הַשָּׁרֵת) ; cp. Heb. of Sir 43[26a], and
Dieterich's *Mithrasliturgie*, p. 6, line 14, ἡ ἀρχὴ τοῦ λειτουργοῦντος
ἀνέμου (see above, v.[7]).   Philo speaks of ἄγγελοι λειτουργοί (*de
virtutibus*, 74), of τοὺς ὑποδιακόνους αὐτοῦ τῶν δυνάμεων ἀγγέλους (*de
templo*, 1), and in *de plantatione*, 4 : Μωσῆς δὲ ὀνόματι εὐθυβόλῳ
χρώμενος ἀγγέλους προσαγορεύει, πρεσβευομένας καὶ διαγγελλούσας

---

[1] A pre-Christian Upanishad (*Sacred Books of East*, xv. 266) cries : "Only
when men shall roll up the sky like a hide, will there be an end of misery,
unless God has first been known."

[2] παλαιοῦσθαι is a common word with ἱμάτιον, and the wearing-out of
clothes is a favourite metaphor for men (Is 50[9], Sir 14[17]) as well as for nature
(Is 51[6]).   Περιβολαῖον is any covering for the body ; not simply a veil (1 Co
11[15]), but a generic term (cp. Ps 104[6] ἄβυσσος ὡς ἱμάτιον τὸ περιβόλαιον αὐτοῦ).

[3] B reads διακονίας, as in 8[9] ἡμέραις for ἡμέρᾳ.

τά τε παρὰ τοῦ ἡγεμόνος τοῖς ὑπηκόοις ἀγαθὰ καὶ τῷ βασιλεῖ ὧν εἰσιν οἱ ὑπήκοοι χρεῖοι. " Angels of the (divine) ministry " was a common rabbinic term, and the writer concludes here that the angels serve God, not, as Philo loved to argue, in the order of nature, but in promoting the interests of God's people ; this is the main object of their existence. He ignores the Jewish doctrine voiced in Test. Levi 3⁵, that in (the sixth?) heaven the angels of the Presence (οἱ λειτουργοῦντες καὶ ἐξιλασκόμενοι πρὸς κύριον ἐπὶ πάσαις ταῖς ἀγνοίαις τῶν δικαίων) sacrifice and intercede for the saints, just as in 11⁴⁰–12¹ he ignores the companion doctrine that the departed saints interceded for the living. Later Christian speculation revived the Jewish doctrine of angels interceding for men and mediating their prayers, but our author stands deliberately apart from this. Heaven has its myriads of angels (12²³), but the entire relation of men to God depends upon Christ. Angels are simply servants (λειτουργοί, v.⁷) of God's saving purpose for mankind ; how these " angels and ministers of grace " further it, the writer never explains. He would not have gone as far as Philo, at any rate (ἄγγελοι . . . ἱεραὶ καὶ θεῖαι φύσεις, ὑποδιάκονοι καὶ ὕπαρχοι τοῦ πρώτου θεοῦ, δι᾽ ὧν οἷα πρεσβευτῶν ὅσα ἂν θελήσῃ τῷ γένει ἡμῶν προσθεσπίσαι διαγγέλλει, de Abrahamo, 23).

In διὰ τοὺς μέλλοντας κληρονομεῖν σωτηρίαν (κλ. σωτ. only here in NT), it is remarkable that σωτηρία is mentioned for the first time without any adjective or explanation. Evidently it had already acquired a specific Christian meaning for the readers as well as for the writer ; no definition was required to differentiate the Christian significance of the term from the current usage. As σωτηρία involves the sacrificial work of Christ (who is never called σωτήρ), it cannot be applied to the pre-Christian period of revelation. Indeed in our epistle σωτηρία is invariably eschatological. The outlook in the messianic oracles already quoted is one of expectation ; some future deliverance at the hands of God or his messianic representative is anticipated. Μέλλοντας implies a divine purpose, as in 8⁵ 11⁸.

The phrase about τοὺς μέλλοντας κληρονομεῖν σωτηρίαν marks a skilful transition to the deeper theme of the next passage, viz. the relation of the Son to this σωτηρία (on 2¹⁻⁹ cp. W. Robertson Smith in Expositor², i. pp. 138 f.). But the transition is worked out in a practical warning (2¹⁻⁴) to the readers, which not only explains the underlying interest of the preceding biblical proofs, but leads up effectively to the next aspect of truth which he has in mind :

¹ We must therefore (διὰ τοῦτο, in view of this pre-eminent authority of the Son) pay closer attention to what we have heard, in case we drift away. ² For if the divine word spoken by angels held good (ἐγένετο βέβαιος, proved valid), if transgression and disobedience met with due (ἔνδικον=adequate, not arbitrary) punishment in every case, ³ how shall we (ἡμεῖς, emphatic) escape

the penalty [1] *for neglecting* (ἀμελήσαντες, if we ignore : Mt 22⁵) *a salvation which* (ἥτις, inasmuch as it) *was originally proclaimed by the Lord himself* (not by mere angels) *and guaranteed to us by those who heard him,* [4] *while God corroborated their testimony with signs and wonders and a variety of miraculous powers, distributing the holy Spirit as it pleased him* (αὐτοῦ emphatic as in Ro 3²⁵).

Apart from the accidental omission of v.¹ by M 1739, Origen, and of τε (M P) in v.⁴, with the variant **παραρρυῶμεν** (Bᶜ Dᶜ) for παραρυῶμεν,[2] the only textual item of any moment, and it is a minor one, is the substitution of ὑπό for διά in v.³ by some cursives (69. 623. 1066. 1845), due either to the following ὑπό, or to the dogmatic desire of emphasizing the initiative of ὁ κύριος. But διά here as in δι᾽ ἀγγέλων, meaning "by," is used to preserve the idea that in λαλεῖν the subject is God (1¹). The order of words (v.¹) δεῖ περισσοτέρως προσέχειν ἡμᾶς has been spoiled in ℵ vg (περισσοτέρως δεῖ) and K L P (ἡμᾶς προσέχειν).

As elsewhere in Hellenistic Greek (*e.g.* Jos. *Apion.* i. 1, ἐπεὶ δὲ συχνοὺς ὁρῶ ταῖς ὑπὸ δυσμενείας ὑπὸ τινων εἰρημέναις προσέχοντας βλασφημίαις καὶ τοῖς περὶ τὴν Ἀρχαιολογίαν ὑπ᾽ ἐμοῦ γεγραμμένοις ἀπιστοῦντας κτλ. ; Strabo, ii. 1. 7, τοῖς μὲν ἀπιστεῖν . . . ἐκείνῃ δὲ προσέχειν), **προσέχειν** (*sc.* τὸν νοῦν) is the opposite of ἀπιστεῖν : to "attend" is to believe and act upon what is heard. This is implied even in Ac 8⁶ and 16¹⁴ (προσέχειν τοῖς λαλουμένοις ὑπὸ Παύλου) where it is the attention of one who hears the gospel for the first time ; here it is attention to a familiar message. **Περισσοτέρως** is almost in its elative sense of "with extreme care" ; "all the more" would bring out its force here as in 13¹⁹ Certainly there is no idea of demanding a closer attention to the gospel than to the Law. **Ἡμᾶς** = we Christians (ἡμῖν, 1¹), you and I, as in v.³. The τὰ ἀκουσθέντα (in τοῖς ἀκουσθεῖσι) is the revelation of the εὐαγγέλιον (a term never used by our author), *i.e.* what ὁ θεὸς ἐλάλησεν ἡμῖν ἐν υἱῷ, 1¹, and this is further defined (in vv.³, ⁴) as consisting in the initial revelation made by Jesus on earth and the transmission of this by divinely accredited envoys to the writer and his readers (εἰς ἡμᾶς ἐβεβαιώθη). In the *Ep. Aristeas,* 127, oral teaching is preferred to reading (τὸ γὰρ καλῶς ζῆν ἐν τῷ τὰ νόμιμα συντηρεῖν εἶναι· τοῦτο δὲ ἐπιτελεῖσθαι διὰ τῆς ἀκροάσεως πολλῷ μᾶλλον ἢ διὰ τῆς ἀναγνώσεως), and the evangelists of v.⁴ include οἵτινες ἐλάλησαν ὑμῖν τὸν λόγον τοῦ θεοῦ (13⁷) ; but while the news was oral, there is no particular emphasis as that here. The author simply appeals for attentive obedience, **μή ποτε παραρυῶμεν** (2 aor. subj.), *i.e.* drift away from (literally, "be carried past" and so lose) the σωτηρία which we have heard. Παραρέω in this sense goes back to Pr 3²¹ υἱέ, μὴ παραρυῇς, τήρησον δὲ ἐμὴν βουλὴν καὶ ἔννοιαν (see Clem. *Paed.* III.

---

[1] ἐκφευξόμεθα, without an object (κρίμα τοῦ θεοῦ, Ro 2³) as 12²⁵, Sir 16¹⁵, 1 Th 5³.

[2] Arm apparently read ὑστερήσωμεν, and P. Junius needlessly conjectured παρασυρῶμεν ("pervert them").

xi. 58, διὸ καὶ συστέλλειν χρὴ τὰς γυναῖκας κοσμίως καὶ περισφίγγειν αἰδοῖ σώφρονι, μὴ παραρρυῶσι τῆς ἀληθείας) ; indeed the writer may have had the line of Proverbs in mind, as Chrys. suggested.

The verb may have lost its figurative meaning, and may have been simply an equivalent for "going wrong," like "labi" in Latin (cp. Cicero, *De Officiis*, i. 6, "labi autem, errare . . . malum et turpe ducimus"). Anyhow προσέχειν must not be taken in a nautical sense (=moor), in order to round off the "drift away" of παραρέω, a term which carries a sombre significance here (=παραπίπτειν, 6⁶) ; μήποτε παραρυῶμεν, τουτέστι μὴ ἀπολώμεθα, μὴ ἐκπέσωμεν (Chrysostom).

In vv.²ᶠ· we have a characteristic (*e.g.* 10²⁸⁻³¹) argument *a minori ad maius* ; if, as we know from our bible (the bible being the Greek OT), every infringement of the Sinaitic legislation was strictly punished—a legislation enacted by means of angels—how much more serious will be the consequences of disregarding such a (great, τηλικαύτη) σωτηρία as that originally proclaimed by the Lord himself! The τηλικαύτη is defined as (*a*) "directly in-augurated by the Κύριος himself," and (*b*) transmitted to us unimpaired by witnesses who had a rich, supernatural endow-ment ; it is as if the writer said, "Do not imagine that the revelation has been weakened, or that your distance from the life of Jesus puts you in any inferior position ; the full power of God's Spirit has been at work in the apostolic preaching to which we owe our faith."

The reference in λόγος is to the Mosaic code, not, as Schoettgen thought, to such specific orders of angels as the admonitions to Lot and his wife.

Λόγος is used, not νόμος, in keeping with the emphasis upon the divine λαλεῖν in the context, and, instead of νόμος Μωσέως (10²⁸), ὁ δι᾽ ἀγγέλων λαληθεὶς λόγος is chosen for argumentative reasons.   Here as in Gal 3¹⁹ and Ac 7³⁸· ⁵³ (ἐλάβετε τὸν νόμον εἰς διαταγὰς ἀγγέλων) the function of angels in the revelation of the Law at Sinai is assumed, but without any disparaging tone such as is overheard in Paul's reference.   The writer and his readers shared the belief, which first appeared in Hellenistic Judaism, that God employed angels at Sinai.   Josephus (*Ant.* xv. 136, ἡμῶν δὲ τὰ κάλλιστα τῶν δογμάτων καὶ τὰ ὁσιώτατα τῶν ἐν τοῖς νόμοις δι᾽ ἀγγέλων παρὰ τοῦ θεοῦ μαθόντων)¹ repeats this tradition, but it went back to the LXX which altered Dt 33² into a definite proof of angelic co-operation (ἐκ δεξιῶν αὐτοῦ ἄγγελοι μετ᾽ αὐτοῦ) and brought this out in Ps 68¹⁸.   Rabbinic tradition elaborated the idea.   The writer, however, would not have claimed, like Philo (*de vita Mosis*, 2³), that the Mosaic legislation was βέβαια, ἀσάλευτα, valid and supreme as long as the world endured.

¹ This is from a speech of Herod inciting the Jews to fight bravely.   "In such a speech," as Robertson Smith observed, "one does not introduce doubtful points of theology."   The tenet was firmly held.

Παράβασις καὶ παρακοή form one idea (see on 1[1]); as παρακοή (which is not a LXX term) denotes a disregard of orders or of appeals (cp. Clem. *Hom.* x. 13, εἰ ἐπὶ παρακοῇ λόγων κρίσις γίνεται, and the use of the verb in Mt 18[17] ἐὰν δὲ παρακούσῃ αὐτῶν κτλ., or in LXX of Is 65[12] ἐλάλησε καὶ παρηκούσατε), it represents the negative aspect, παράβασις the positive. Μισθαποδοσία is a sonorous synonym (rare in this sombre sense of κόλασις) for μισθός or for the classical μισθοδοσία. Some of the facts which the writer has in mind are mentioned in 3[17] and 10[28]. The Law proved no dead letter in the history of God's people; it enforced pains and penalties for disobedience.

In v.[3] ἀρχὴν λαβοῦσα is a familiar Hellenistic phrase; cp. *e.g.* Philo in *Quaest. in Exod.* 12[2] (ὅταν οἱ τῶν σπαρτῶν καρποὶ τελειωθῶσιν, οἱ τῶν δένδρων γενέσεως ἀρχὴν λαμβάνουσιν), and *de vita Mosis*, 1[14] (τὴν ἀρχὴν τοῦ γενέσθαι λάβον ἐν Αἰγύπτῳ). The writer felt, as Plutarch did about Rome, τὰ Ῥωμαίων πράγματα οὐκ ἂν ἐνταῦθα προύβη δυνάμεως, μὴ θείαν τινὰ ἀρχὴν λαβόντα καὶ μηδὲν μέγα μηδὲ παράδοξον ἔχουσαν. The modern mind wonders how the writer could assume that the σωτηρία, as he conceives it, was actually preached by Jesus on earth. But he was unconscious of any such difference. The Christian revelation was made through the Jesus who had lived and suffered and ascended, and the reference is not specifically to his teaching, but to his personality and career, in which God's saving purpose came to full expression. Οἱ ἀκούσαντες means those who heard Jesus himself, the αὐτόπται of Lk 1[1-4] (cp. the shorter conclusion to Mark's gospel: μετὰ δὲ ταῦτα καὶ αὐτὸς ὁ Ἰησοῦς . . . ἐξαπέστειλεν δι᾽ αὐτῶν τὸ ἱερὸν καὶ ἄφθαρτον κήρυγμα τῆς αἰωνίου σωτηρίας). If the Sinaitic Law ἐγένετο βέβαιος, the Christian revelation was also confirmed or guaranteed to us—εἰς ἡμᾶς (1 P 1[25] τὸ ῥῆμα τὸ εὐαγγελισθὲν εἰς ὑμᾶς: Ac 2[22] Ἰησοῦν . . . ἄνδρα ἀπὸ τοῦ θεοῦ ἀποδεδειγμένον εἰς ὑμᾶς) ἐβεβαιώθη. It reached us, accurate and trustworthy. No wonder, when we realize the channel along which it flowed. It was authenticated by the double testimony of men [1] who had actually heard Jesus, and of God who attested and inspired them in their mission. Συνεπιμαρτυρεῖν means "assent" in *Ep. Aristeas*, 191, and "corroborate" in the *de Mundo*, 400a (συνεπιμαρτυρεῖ δὲ καὶ ὁ βίος ἅπας), as usual, but is here a sonorous religious term for συμμαρτυρεῖν (Ro 8[16]). "Coniunctio σύν . . . hunc habet sensum, nos in fide euangelii confirmari symphonia quadam Dei et hominum" (Calvin).

---

[1] In ὑπὸ τῶν ἀκουσάντων, ὑπό is used, as invariably throughout Πρὸς Ἑβραίους, of persons, which is a proof of good Greek. "There is no more certain test of the accuracy of individual Greek writers than their use of the passives (or equivalent forms) with ὑπό and a genitive. In the best writers this genitive almost invariably denotes *personal*, or at least *living* objects" (W. J. Hickie, on *Andocides, De Mysteriis*, § 14).

σημ., τερ., δυν. in the reverse order describe the miracles of Jesus in Ac
2²² ; here they denote the miracles of the primitive evangelists as in 2 Co 12¹².
Philo, speaking of the wonderful feats of Moses before the Pharaoh, declares
that signs and wonders are a plainer proof of what God commands than any
verbal injunction (ἅτε δὴ τοῦ θεοῦ τρανοτέραις χρησμῶν ἀποδείξεσι ταῖς διὰ
σημείων καὶ τεράτων τὸ βούλημα δεδηλωκότος, vit. Mos. i. 16).

As "God" (θεοῦ) is the subject of the clause, αὐτοῦ (for which
D actually reads θεοῦ) refers to him, and πνεύματος ἁγίου is the
genitive of the object after μερισμοῖς (cp. 6⁴). What is distributed is the Spirit, in a variety of endowments. To take
αὐτοῦ with πνεύματος and make the latter the genitive of the
subject, would tally with Paul's description of the Spirit διαιροῦν
ἰδίᾳ ἑκάστῳ καθὼς βούλεται (1 Co 12¹¹), but would fail to explain
what was distributed and would naturally require τῷ μερισμῷ.
A fair parallel lies in Gal 3⁵ ὁ ἐπιχορηγῶν ὑμῖν τὸ πνεῦμα καὶ
ἐνεργῶν δυνάμεις ἐν ὑμῖν, where δυνάμεις also means "miraculous
powers" or "mighty deeds" (a Hellenistic sense, differing from
that of the LXX = "forces"). In κατὰ τὴν αὐτοῦ θέλησιν,
as perhaps even in 7¹⁸ (cp. Blass, 284. 3 ; Abbott's *Johannine
Grammar*, 2558), the possessive αὐτός is emphatic. θέλησιν is
read by אᶜᵃ R for δέησιν in Ps 21³ (cp. Ezk 28²³ μὴ θελήσει
θελήσω). It is not merely a vulgarism for θέλημα. "Θέλημα
n'est pas θέλησις, volonté ; θέλημα désigne le vouloir concentré
sur un moment, sur un acte, l'ordre, le commandment" (Psichari,
Essai sur le grec de la Septante, 1908, p. 171 n.). The writer is
fond of such forms (*e.g.* ἀθέτησις, ἄθλησις, αἴνεσις, μετάθεσις,
πρόσχυσις). Naturally the phrase has a very different meaning
from the similar remark in Lucian, who makes Hesiod (*Dis-
putatio cum Hesiode*, 4) apologize for certain omissions in his
poetry, by pleading that the Muses who inspired him gave their
gifts as they pleased—αἱ θεαὶ δὲ τὰς ἑαυτῶν δωρεὰς οἷς τε ἂν ἐθέλωσι.

The vital significance of the Son as the ἀρχηγός of this
"salvation"[1] by means of his sufferings on earth, is now developed (vv.⁵⁻¹⁸). This unique element in the Son has been already
hinted (1⁸), but the writer now proceeds to explain it as the core of
Christ's pre-eminence. The argument starts from the antithesis
between the Son and angels (v.⁵) ; presently it passes beyond
this, and angels are merely mentioned casually in a parenthesis
(v.¹⁶). The writer is now coming to the heart of his theme, how
and why the Son or Lord, of whom he has been speaking,
suffered, died, and rose. Vv.⁵⁻⁹ are the prelude to vv.¹⁰⁻¹⁸. The
idea underlying the whole passage is this : λαλεῖσθαι διὰ τοῦ κυρίου
meant much more than λαλεῖσθαι δι᾽ ἀγγέλων, for the Christian
revelation of σωτηρία had involved a tragic and painful experience for the Son on earth as he purged sins away. His present
superiority to angels had been preceded by a period of mortal

[1] In A אᶜᵃ of Is 9⁶ the messiah is called πατὴρ τοῦ μέλλοντος αἰῶνος.

experience on earth ἐν ταῖς ἡμέραις τῆς σαρκὸς αὐτοῦ. But this sojourn was only for a time; it was the vital presupposition of his triumph; it enabled him to die a death which invested him with supreme power on behalf of his fellow-men; and it taught him sympathy (cp. Zimmer, in *Studien und Kritiken*, 1882, pp. 413 f., on 2¹⁻⁵, and in *NTlichen Studien*, i. pp. 20–129, on 2⁶⁻¹⁸).

⁵ *For the world to come, of which I* (ἡμεῖς of authorship) *am speaking, was not put under the control of angels* (whatever may be the case with the present world). ⁶ *One writer, as we know, has affirmed,*
   "*What is man, that thou art mindful of him?*
   or the son of man, that thou carest for him?
⁷ *For a little while thou hast put him lower than the angels,*
   crowning him with glory and honour,
⁸ *putting all things under his feet.*"
Now by ¹ "*putting all things under him*" ² *the writer meant to leave nothing out of his control. But, as it is, we do not yet see "all things controlled" by man;* ⁹ *what we do see is Jesus "who was put lower than the angels for a little while" to suffer death, and who has been "crowned with glory and honour," that by God's grace he might taste death for everyone.*

Οὐ γὰρ ἀγγέλοις (γάρ, as in Greek idiom, opening a new question; almost equivalent to "now": οὐ γάρ = non certe, Valckenaer) ὑπέταξε (*i.e.* ὁ θεός, as C vg add)—the writer is already thinking of ὑπέταξας in the quotation which he is about to make. In the light of subsequent allusions to μέλλοντα ἀγαθά (9¹¹ 10¹) and ἡ μέλλουσα πόλις (13¹⁴), we see that τὴν οἰκουμένην τὴν μέλλουσαν means the new order of things in which the σωτηρία of 1¹⁴ 2². ³ is to be realized (see 9²⁸), and from which already influences are pouring down into the life of Christians. The latter allusion is the pivot of the transition. The powers and spiritual experiences just mentioned (in v.⁴) imply this higher, future order of things (cp. 6⁴. ⁵ especially δυνάμεις τε μέλλοντος αἰῶνος), from which rays stream down into the present. How the ministry of angels is connected with them, we do not learn. But the author had already urged that this service of angels was rendered to the divine authority, and that it served to benefit Christians (1¹⁴). This idea starts him afresh. Who reigns in the new order? Not angels but the Son, and the Son who has come down for a time into human nature and suffered death. He begins by quoting a stanza from a psalm which seems irrelevant, because it compares men and angels. In reality this is not what occupies his mind; otherwise he might have put his argument differently and used, for example, the belief that Christians would hold sway over angels in the next world (1 Co 6². ³).

¹ ἐν τῷ (*sc.* λέγειν, as 8¹³).
² The omission of this αὐτῷ by B d e arm does not alter the sense.

Philo (*de opificio*, 29, οὐ παρ' ὅσον ὕστατον γέγονεν ἄνθρωπος, διὰ τὴν τάξιν ἠλάττωται) argues that man is not inferior in position because he was created last in order ; but this refers to man in relation to other creatures, not in relation to angels, as here.

The quotation (vv.⁶⁻⁸ᵃ) from the 8th psalm runs :

τί ἐστιν ἄνθρωπος ὅτι μιμνήσκῃ¹ αὐτοῦ,
ἢ υἱὸς ἀνθρώπου ὅτι ἐπισκέπτῃ αὐτόν ;
ἠλάττωσας αὐτὸν βραχύ τι παρ' ἀγγέλους,
δόξῃ καὶ τιμῇ ἐστεφάνωσας αὐτόν.
πάντα ὑπέταξας ὑποκάτω τῶν ποδῶν αὐτοῦ.

The LXX tr. אלהים not incorrectly by ἀγγέλους, since *the elohim* of the original probably included angels. This was the point of the quotation, for the author of Hebrews. The text of the quotation offers only a couple of items. (*a*) τί is changed into τίς (LXX A) by C* P 104. 917. 1288. 1319. 1891. 2127 vt boh, either in conformity to the preceding τις or owing to the feeling that the more common τίς (in questions, *e.g.* 12⁷, Jn 12³⁴) suited the reference to Christ better (Bleek, Zimmer). (*b*) The quotation omits καὶ κατέστησας αὐτὸν ἐπὶ τὰ ἔργα τῶν χειρῶν σου before πάντα : it is inserted by א A C D* M P syr lat boh arm eth Euth. Theodt. Sedul. to complete the quotation. It is the one line in the sentence on which the writer does not comment ; probably he left it out as incompatible with 1¹⁰ (ἔργα τῶν χειρῶν σού εἰσιν οἱ οὐρανοί), although he frequently quotes more of an OT passage than is absolutely required for his particular purpose.

In διεμαρτύρατο δέ πού τις (v.⁶), even if the δέ is adversative, it need not be expressed in English idiom. διαμαρτύρεσθαι in Greek inscriptions "means primarily to address an assembly or a king " (Hicks, in *Classical Review*, i. 45). Here, the only place where it introduces an OT quotation, it = attest or affirm. Πού τις in such a formula is a literary mannerism familiar in Philo (*De Ebriet.* 14 : εἶπε γάρ πού τις), and που later on (4⁴) recurs in a similar formula, as often in Philo. The τις implies no modification of the Alexandrian theory of inspiration ; his words are God's words (v.⁸). The psalm intends no contrast between ἠλάττωσας κτλ. and δόξῃ . . . ἐστεφάνωσας αὐτόν. The proof that this wonderful being has been created in a position only slightly inferior to that of the divine host lies in the fact that he is crowned king of nature, invested with a divine authority over creation. The psalm is a panegyric on man, like Hamlet's ("What a piece of work is man ! how noble in reason ! how infinite in faculties ! in form and moving how express and admirable ! in action how like an angel !" etc.), but with a religious note of wonder and gratitude to God. In applying the psalm, however, our writer takes βραχύ τι

¹ μιμνήσκῃ means mindfulness shown in act, and ἐπισκέπτῃ, as always in the NT, denotes personal care.

in the sense of "temporarily" rather than "slightly," and so has
to make the "inferiority" and "exaltation" two successive phases,
in applying the description to the career of Jesus. He does not take
this verse as part of a messianic ode; neither here nor elsewhere
does he use the term "Son of Man." He points out, first of
all (v.[8]) that, as things are (νῦν δὲ οὔπω: οὐ πω = οὐ πως might be
read, *i.e.* "in no wise," and νῦν taken logically instead of temporally;
but this is less natural and pointed), the last words are still unfulfilled; οὔπω ὁρῶμεν αὐτῷ (*i.e.* man) τὰ "πάντα" (*i.e.* ἡ οἰκουμένη
ἡ μέλλουσα) ὑποτεταγμένα. Human nature is not "crowned with
glory and honour" at present. How can it be, when the terror
of death and the devil (v.[15]) enslaves it? What is to be said,
then? This, that although we do not see man triumphant, there
is something that we do see: βλέπομεν Ἰησοῦν dealing triumphantly with death on man's behalf (v.[9]). The Ἰησοῦν comes in
with emphasis, as in 3[1] and 12[2], at the end of a preliminary
definition τὸν . . . ἠλαττωμένον.

It is less natural to take the messianic interpretation which
involves the reference of αὐτῷ already to him. On this view, the
writer frankly allows that the closing part of the prophecy is still
unfulfilled. "We do not yet see τὰ πάντα under the sway of Jesus
Christ, for *the world to come* has not yet *come*; it has only been
inaugurated by the sacrifice of Christ (1[3] καθαρισμὸν τῶν ἁμαρτιῶν
ποιησάμενος ἐκάθισεν ἐν δεξιᾷ τῆς μεγαλωσύνης ἐν ὑψηλοῖς). Though
the Son is crowned (1[8, 9]) and enthroned (1[13] κάθου ἐκ δεξιῶν μου),
his foes are still to be subdued (ἕως ἂν θῶ τοὺς ἐχθρούς σου ὑποπόδιον
τῶν ποδῶν σου), and we must be content to wait for our full σωτηρία
(9[28]) at his second coming; under the οὔπω ὁρῶμεν κτλ. of experience there is a deeper experience of faith." The writer rather
turns back in v.[9] to the language of v.[7]; this at least has been
fulfilled. *Jesus* has been put lower than the angels and he has been
crowned. How and why? The writer answers the second question first. Or rather, in answering the second he suggests the
answer to the first. At this point, and not till then, the messianic
interpretation becomes quite natural and indeed inevitable. It
is the earlier introduction of it which is unlikely. The application
to the messiah of words like those quoted in v.[6] is forced, and
"Hebrews" has no room for the notion of Christ as the ideal or
representative Man, as is implied in the messianic interpretation
of αὐτῷ in v.[8]. That interpretation yields a true idea—the
thought expressed, *e.g.*, in T. E. Brown's poem, "Sad! Sad!"—

> "One thing appears to me—
> The work is not complete;
> One world I know, and see
> It is not at His feet—
> Not, not! Is this the sum?"

No, our author hastens to add, it is not the sum; our outlook is not one of mere pathos; we do see Jesus enthroned, with the full prospect of ultimate triumph. But the idea of the issues of Christ's triumph being still incomplete is not true here. What is relevant, and what is alone relevant, is the decisive character of his sacrifice. The argument of v.[8. 9], therefore, is that, however inapplicable to man the rhapsody of the psalm is, at present, the words of the psalm are true, notwithstanding. For we see the Jesus who was "put lower than the angels for a little while" to suffer death (διὰ τὸ πάθημα τοῦ θανάτου must refer to the death of Jesus himself,[1] not to the general experience of death as the occasion for his incarnation), now "crowned with glory and honour." When διὰ τὸ πάθημα τοῦ θανάτου is connected with what follows (δόξῃ καὶ τιμῇ ἐστεφανωμένον), it gives the reason for the exaltation, not the object of the incarnation (= εἰς τὸ πάσχειν). But διά . . . θανάτου is elucidated in a moment by ὅπως . . . θανάτου. V.[9] answers the question why Jesus was lowered and exalted—it was for the sake of mankind. In v.[10] the writer proceeds to explain how he was "lowered"—it was by suffering that culminated in death. Then he recurs naturally to the "why." The mixture of quotation and comment in v.[9] leaves the meaning open to some dubiety, although the drift is plain. "But one Being referred to in the psalm (τὸν . . . ἠλαττωμένον) we do see—it is Jesus, and Jesus as ἠλαττωμένον for the purpose of suffering death, and δόξῃ καὶ τιμῇ ἐστεφανωμένον. Why did he die? Why was he thus humiliated and honoured? For the sake of every man; his death was ὑπὲρ παντός, part of the divine purpose of redemption." Thus ὅπως . . . θανάτου explains and expounds the idea of διὰ τὸ πάθημα (which consists in) τοῦ θανάτου, gathering up the full object and purpose of the experience which has just been predicated of Jesus. This implies a pause after ἐστεφανωμένον, or, as Bleek suggests, the supplying of an idea like ὃ ἔπαθεν before ὅπως κτλ., if γεύσηται is to be taken, as it must be, as = "he might taste." How a ὅπως clause follows and elucidates διά κτλ. may be seen in *Ep. Arist.* 106 (διὰ τοὺς ἐν ταῖς ἁγνείαις ὄντας, ὅπως μηδενὸς θιγγάνωσιν).

As for v.[8a], Paul makes a similar comment (1 Co 15[27]), but excludes God from the τὰ πάντα. The curiously explicit language here is intended to reiterate what is possibly hinted at in v.[5], viz., that the next world has no room for the angelic control which characterizes the present. (The τὰ πάντα includes even angels!) This belief was familiar to readers of the Greek bible, where Dt 32[8] voices a conception of guardian-angels over the non-Jewish nations which became current in some circles of the later Judaism. Non-Jewish Christians, like the readers of our epistle, would be likely to appreciate the point of an argument which dealt with this. Note that ἀνυπότακτον occurs in a similar antithesis in Epictetus, ii. 10. 1, ταύτῃ τὰ

---

[1] But not, as the Greek fathers, etc., supposed, as if it was the fact of his death (and stay in the underworld) that lowered him (διά = on account of).

ἄλλα ὑποτεταγμένα, αὐτὴν δ᾽ ἀδούλευτον καὶ ἀνυπότακτον. Our author's language reads almost like a tacit repudiation of Philo's remark on Gn 1²⁶ in *de opificio Mundi* (28), that God put man over all things with the exception of the heavenly beings—ὅσα γὰρ θνητὰ ἐν τοῖς τρισὶ στοιχείοις γῇ ὕδατι ἀέρι πάντα ὑπέταττεν αὐτῷ, τὰ κατ᾽ οὐρανὸν ὑπεξελόμενος ἅτε δειοτέρας μοίρας ἐπιλαχόντα.

The closing clause of v.⁹ (ὅπως χάριτι θεοῦ ὑπὲρ παντὸς γεύσηται θανάτου), therefore, resumes and completes the idea of διὰ τὸ πάθημα τοῦ θανάτου. Each follows a phrase from the psalm ; but ὅπως . . . θανάτου does not follow ἐστεφανωμένον logically. The only possible method of thus taking ὅπως κτλ. would be by applying δόξῃ καὶ τιμῇ ἐστεφανωμένον to Christ's life prior to death, either (*a*) to his pre-incarnate existence, when "in the counsels of heaven" he was, as it were, "crowned for death" (so Rendall, who makes γεύσασθαι θανάτου cover the "inward dying" of daily self-denial and suffering which led up to Calvary), or (*b*) to his incarnate life (so, *e.g.*, Hofmann, Milligan, Bruce), as if his readiness to sacrifice himself already threw a halo round him, or (*c*) specifically to God's recognition and approval of him at the baptism and transfiguration (Dods). But the use of δόξα in v.¹⁰ tells against such theories ; it is from another angle altogether that Jesus is said in 2 P 1¹⁷ to have received τιμὴν καὶ δόξαν from God at the transfiguration. The most natural interpretation, therefore, is to regard δόξῃ . . . ἐστεφανωμένον as almost parenthetical, rounding off the quotation from the psalm. It is unnecessary to fall back on such suggestions as (i) to assume a break in the text after ἐστεφανωμένον, some words lost which led up to ὅπως . . . θανάτου (Windisch), or (ii) to translate ὅπως by "how," as in Lk 24²⁰, *i.e.* "we see how Jesus tasted death" (so Blass, boldly reading ἐγεύσατο), or by "after that" or "when" (Moses Stuart), as in Soph. *Oed. Col.* 1638 (where, however, it takes the indicative as usual), etc.

In ὑπὲρ παντός, παντός was at an early stage taken as neuter, practically = the universe. This was a popular idea in Egyptian Christianity. "You know," says the risen Christ to his disciples, in a Bohairic narrative of the death of Joseph (*Texts and Studies*, iv. 2. 130), "that many times now I have told you that I must needs be crucified and taste death for the universe." The interpretation occurs first in Origen, who (*in Joan.* i. 35) writes : "He is a 'great highpriest' [referring to Heb 4¹⁵], having offered himself up in sacrifice once (ἅπαξ) not for human beings alone, but for the rest of rational creatures as well (ἀλλὰ καὶ ὑπὲρ τῶν λοιπῶν λογικῶν). 'For without God he tasted death for everyone' (χωρὶς γὰρ θεοῦ ὑπὲρ παντὸς ἐγεύσατο θανάτου). In some copies of the epistle to the Hebrews this passage runs : 'for by the grace of God' (χάριτι γὰρ θεοῦ). Well, if 'without God he tasted death for everyone,' he did not die simply for human beings, but for the rest of rational creatures as well ; and if 'by the grace of God he tasted the death for everyone,'[1] he died for all except for God (χωρὶς θεοῦ)— for 'by the grace of God he tasted death for everyone.' It would indeed be

---

[1] Reading τοῦ before ὑπέρ.

preposterous (ἄτοπον) to say that he tasted death for human sins and not also for any other being besides man who has fallen into sin—*e.g.* for the stars. Even the stars are by no means pure before God, as we read in the book of Job: 'The stars are not pure before him,' unless this is said hyperbolically. For this reason he is a 'great highpriest,' because he restores (ἀποκαθίστησι) all things to his Father's kingdom, ordering it so that what is lacking in any part of creation is completed for the fulness of the Father's glory (πρὸς τὸ χωρῆσαι δόξαν πατρικήν)." The Greek fathers adhered steadily to this interpretation of παντός as equivalent to the entire universe, including especially angels. But the neuter is always expressed in "Hebrews" by the plural, with or without the article, and, as v.[16] shows, the entire interest is in human beings.

Γεύσηται after ὑπὲρ παντός has also been misinterpreted. Γεύειν in LXX, as a rendering of טעם, takes either genitive (1 S 14[24], cp. 2 Mac 6[20]) or accusative (1 S 14[29], Job 34[3]), but γεύεσθαι θανάτου never occurs; it is the counterpart of the rabbinic phrase מיתה טעם, and elsewhere in the NT (Mk 9[1]=Mt 16[28]=Lk 9[27], Jn 8[52]) is used not of Jesus but of men. It means to experience (=ἰδεῖν θάνατον, 11[5]). Here it is a bitter experience, not a rapid sip, as if Jesus simply "tasted" death (Chrysostom, Theophyl., Oecumenius: οὐ γὰρ ἐνέμεινεν τῷ θανάτω ἀλλὰ μόνον αὐτὸν τρόπον τινὰ ἀπεγεύσατο) quickly, or merely sipped it like a doctor sipping a drug to encourage a patient. The truer comment would be: "When I think of our Lord as tasting death it seems to me as if He alone ever truly tasted death" (M'Leod Campbell, *The Nature of the Atonement*, p. 259); γεύσηται does not echo βραχύ τι, as though all that Jesus experienced of death was slight or short.

The hardest knot of the hard passage lies in χάριτι θεοῦ. In the second century two forms of the text were current, χωρις θεου and χαριτι θεου. This is plain from Origen's comment (see above); he himself is unwilling to rule out the latter reading, but prefers the former, which he apparently found to be the ordinary text. Theodoret assumed it to be original, as Ambrose did in the West. Jerome knew both (on Gal 3[10]), and the eighth century Anastasius Abbas read χωρίς ("absque deo: sola enim divina natura non egebat"), *i.e.*, in the sense already suggested by Fulgentius and Vigilius, that Christ's divine nature did not die. On the other hand, writers like Eusebius, Athanasius, and Chrysostom never mention any other reading than χάριτι. Of all the supporters of χωρίς, the most emphatic is Theodore of Mopsuestia, who protests that it is most absurd (γελοιότατον) to substitute χάριτι θεοῦ for χωρὶς θεοῦ, arguing from passages like 1 Co 15[10] and Eph 2[8. 9] that Paul's custom is not to use the former phrase ἁπλῶς, ἀλλὰ πάντως ἀπό τινος ἀκολουθίας λόγου. The reading suited the Nestorian view of the person of Christ, and probably the fact of its popularity among the Nestorians tended to compromise χωρίς in the eyes of the later church; it survives only in M 424**, though there is a trace of it (a Nestorian gloss?) in three codices of the Peshitto. But Oecumenius and Theophylact are wrong in holding that it originated among the Nestorians. This is dogmatic prejudice;

χωρίς was read in good manuscripts, if not in the best, by
Origen's time, and the problem is to determine whether it or
χάριτι was original. The one may be a transcriptional error for
the other. In this case, the textual canon "potior lectio
difficillima" would favour χωρίς. But the canon does not apply
rigidly to every such case, and the final decision depends upon
the internal probabilities. Long associations render it difficult
for a modern to do justice to χωρὶς θεοῦ. Yet χωρίς is elsewhere
used by our author in a remarkable way, e.g. in 9²⁸ χωρὶς
ἁμαρτίας ὀφθήσεται, and the question is whether χωρὶς θεοῦ here
cannot be understood in an apt, although daring, sense. It
may be (i) "forsaken by God," an allusion to the "dereliction"
of Mk 15³⁴ (B. Weiss, Zimmer), though this would rather be put
as ἄτερ θεοῦ. (ii) "Apart from his divinity" (see above), i.e.
when Christ died, his divine nature survived. But this would
require a term like τῆς θεότητος. (iii) Taken with παντός, "die
for everyone (everything?) except God" (Origen's view, adopted
recently by moderns like Ewald and Ebrard). Of these (i) and
(iii) are alone tenable. Even if (iii) be rejected, it furnishes
a clue to the problem of the origin of the reading. Thus
Bengel and others modify it by taking ὑπὲρ παντός = to master
everything, χωρὶς θεοῦ being added to explain that "everything"
does not include God. It is possible, of course, that in the
Latin rendering (ut gratia Dei pro omnibus gustaret mortem)
gratia is an original nominative, not an ablative, and represents χάρις (Christ = the Grace of God),[1] which came to be
altered into χωρίς and χάριτι. But, if χωρὶς θεοῦ is regarded as
secondary, its origin probably lies in the dogmatic scruple of
some primitive scribe who wrote the words on the margin as
a gloss upon παντός, or even on the margin of v.⁸ opposite οὐδὲν
ἀφῆκεν αὐτῷ ἀνυπότακτον, whence it slipped lower down into the
text. Upon the whole, it seems fairest to assume that at some
very early stage there must have been a corruption of the text,
which cannot be explained upon the available data. But at
any rate χάριτι fits in well with ἔπρεπει, which immediately
follows, and this is one point in its favour. It was χάριτι θεοῦ
that Jesus died for everyone, and this was consonant with God's
character (ἔπρεπει γὰρ αὐτῷ, i.e. θεῷ). The nearest Latin
equivalent for πρέπον, as Cicero (de Officiis, i. 26) said, was
"decorum" (dulce et decorum est pro patria mori), and in this
high sense the divine χάρις (4¹⁶), shown in the wide range and
object of the death of Jesus, comes out in the process and
method.

[1] It was so taken by some Latin fathers like Primasius and by later
theologians of the Western church like Thomas of Aquinum and Sedulius
Scotus, who depended on the Vulgate version.

The writer now explains (vv.¹⁰⁻¹⁸) why Jesus had to suffer
and to die. Only thus could he save his brother men who lay
(whether by nature or as a punishment, we are not told) under
the tyranny of death. To die for everyone meant that Jesus had
to enter human life and identify himself with men ; suffering is
the badge and lot of the race, and a Saviour must be a sufferer,
if he is to carry out God's saving purpose. The sufferings of
Jesus were neither an arbitrary nor a degrading experience, but
natural, in view of what he was to God and men alike. For the
first time, the conception of suffering occurs, and the situation
which gave rise to the author's handling of the subject arose out
of what he felt to be his readers' attitude. " We are suffering
hardships on account of our religion." But so did Jesus, the
writer replies. " Well, but was it necessary for him any more
than for us ? And if so, how does that consideration help us in
our plight ? " To this there is a twofold answer. (a) Suffering
made Jesus a real Saviour ; it enabled him to offer his perfect
sacrifice, on which fellowship with God depends. (b) He suffered
not only for you but like you, undergoing the same temptations
to faith and loyalty as you have to meet. The threefold
inference is : (i) do not give way, but realize all you have
in his sacrifice, and what a perfect help and sympathy you
can enjoy. (ii) Remember, this is a warning as well as an
encouragement ; it will be a fearful thing to disparage a
religious tie of such privilege. (iii) Also, let his example
nerve you.

¹⁰ *In bringing many sons to glory, it was befitting that He for whom and
by whom the universe exists, should perfect the Pioneer of their salvation by
suffering* (διὰ παθημάτων, echoing διὰ τὸ πάθημα τοῦ θανάτου). ¹¹ *For
sanctifier and sanctified have all one origin* (ἐξ ἑνός, sc. γενοῦς : neuter as Ac
17²⁶). *That is why he* (ὁ ἁγιάζων) *is not ashamed to call them brothers,*
¹² *saying,*

" *I will proclaim thy name to my brothers,*
        in the midst of the church I will sing of thee " ;
¹³ *and again,*
            " *I will put my trust in him* " ;
    and again,
        " *Here am I and the children God has given me.* "

¹⁴ *Since the children then* (οὖν, resuming the thought of v.¹¹ᵃ) *share blood
and flesh,¹ he himself participated in their nature,² so that by dying he might
crush him who wields the power of death* (*that is to say, the devil*), ¹⁵ *and
release from thraldom those who lay under a life-long fear of death.* ¹⁶ (*For
of course it is not angels that* " *he succours,*" *it is* " *the offspring of Abraham* "). ¹⁷ *He had to resemble his brothers in every respect, in order to prove
a merciful and faithful high priest in things divine, to expiate the sins of the*

───────────

¹ αἵματος καὶ σαρκός (Eph 6¹²) is altered into the more conventional σαρκὸς
καὶ αἵματος by, *e.g.*, K L f vg syr pesh eth boh Theodoret, Aug. Jerome.
² αὐτῶν, *i.e.* αἵματος καὶ σαρκός, not παθημάτων, which is wrongly added
by D* d syrᵖᵃˡ Eus. Jerome, Theodoret.

People. [18] *It is as he suffered by his temptations that he is able to help the tempted.*

It is remarkable (cp. Introd. p. xvi) that the writer does not connect the sufferings of Jesus with OT prophecy, either generally (as, *e.g.*, Lk 24²⁶ οὐχὶ ταῦτα ἔδει[1] παθεῖν τὸν Χριστόν κτλ.), or with a specific reference to Is 53. He explains them on the ground of moral congruity. Here they are viewed from God's standpoint, as in 12² from that of Jesus himself. God's purpose of grace made it befitting and indeed inevitable that Jesus should suffer and die in fulfilling his function as a Saviour (v.¹⁰); then (vv.¹¹ᶠ·) it is shown how he made common cause with those whom he was to rescue.

Ἔπρεπεν γάρ κτλ. (v.¹⁰). Πρέπειν or πρέπον, in the sense of "seemly," is not applied to God in the LXX, but is not uncommon in later Greek, *e.g.* Lucian's *Prometheus*, 8 (οὔτε θεοῖς πρέπον οὔτε ἄλλως βασιλικόν), and the *de Mundo*, 397*b*, 398*a* (ὃ καὶ πρέπον ἐστὶ καὶ θεῷ μάλιστα ἁρμόζον—of a theory about the universe, however). The writer was familiar with it in Philo, who has several things to say about what it behoved God to do,[2] though never this thing; Philo has the phrase, not the idea. According to Aristotle (*Nic. Ethics*, iv. 2. 2, τὸ πρέπον δὴ πρὸς αὐτόν, καὶ ἐν ᾧ καὶ περὶ ὅ), what is "befitting" relates to the person himself, to the particular occasion, and to the object. Here, we might say, the idea is that it would not have done for God to save men by a method which stopped short of suffering and actual death. "Quand il est question des actes de Dieu, ce qui est *convenable* est toujours *nécessaire* au point de vue métaphysique" (Reuss). In the description of God (for αὐτῷ cannot be applied to Jesus in any natural sense) δι' ὃν τὰ πάντα καὶ δι' οὗ τὰ πάντα, the writer differs sharply from Philo. The Alexandrian Jew objects to Eve (Gn 4¹) and Joseph (Gn 40¹⁸) using the phrase διὰ τοῦ θεοῦ (*Cherubim*, 35), on the ground that it makes God merely instrumental; whereas, ὁ θεὸς αἴτιον, οὐκ ὄργανον. On the contrary, we call God the creative cause (αἴτιον) of the universe, ὄργανον δὲ λόγον θεοῦ δι' οὗ κατεσκευάσθη. He then quotes Ex 14¹³ to prove, by the use of παρά, that οὐ διὰ[3] τοῦ θεοῦ ἀλλὰ παρ' αὐτοῦ ὡς αἰτίου τὸ σῴζεσθαι. But our author has no such scruples about διά, any more than Aeschylus had (*Agamemnon*, 1486, διαὶ Διὸς παναιτίου πανεργέτα). Like Paul (Ro 11³⁶) he can say δι' οὗ τὰ πάντα of God, adding, for the sake of paronomasia, δι' ὃν to cover what Paul meant by ἐξ αὐτοῦ καὶ εἰς αὐτόν. Or rather, starting with δι' ὃν τὰ πάντα he

---

[1] The ὤφειλεν of v.¹⁷ is not the same as this ἔδει.

[2] Thus: πρέπει τῷ θεῷ φυτεύειν καὶ οἰκοδομεῖν ἐν ψυχῇ τὰς ἀρετάς (*Leg. alleg.* i. 15)

[3] When he does use διά (*de opificio*, 24) it is δι' αὐτοῦ μόνου, of creation.

prefers another διά with a genitive, for the sake of assonance, to the more usual equivalent ἐξ οὗ or ὑφ' οὗ. To preserve the assonance, Zimmer proposes to render: "um dessentwillen das All, und durch dessen Willen das All."

The ultimate origin of the phrase probably lies in the mystery-cults; Aristides (Εἰς τὸν Σάραπιν, 51 : ed. Dindorf, i. p. 87), in an invocation of Serapis, writes to this effect, πάντα γὰρ πανταχοῦ διὰ σοῦ τε καὶ διὰ σε ἡμῖν γίγνεται. But Greek thought in Stoicism had long ago played upon the use of διά in this connexion. Possibly διά with the accusative was the primitive and regular expression, as Norden contends.[1] We call Zeus "Ζῆνα καὶ Δία" ὡς ἂν εἰ λέγοιμεν δι' ὃν ζῶμεν, says the author of de Mundo (401a), like the older Stoics (see Arnim's Stoicorum veterum Fragmenta, ii. pp. 305, 312), and διά with the accusative might have the same causal sense here,[2] i.e. "through," in which case the two phrases δι' ὅν and δι' οὗ would practically be a poetical reduplication of the same idea, or at least = "by whom and through whom." But the dominant, though not exclusive, idea of δι' ὅν here is final, "for whom"; the end of the universe, of all history and creation, lies with Him by whom it came into being and exists; He who redeems is He who has all creation at His command and under His control.

The point in adding δι' ὅν . . . τὰ πάντα to αὐτῷ is that the sufferings and death of Jesus are not accidental; they form part of the eternal world-purpose of God. Philo had explained that Moses was called up to Mount Sinai on the seventh day, because God wished to make the choice of Israel parallel to the creation of the world (Quaest. in Exod. 24[16] βουλόμενος ἐπιδεῖξαι ὅτι αὐτὸς καὶ τὸν κόσμον ἐδημιούργησε καὶ τὸ γένος εἵλετο. Ἡ δὲ ἀνάκλησις τοῦ προφήτου δευτέρα γένεσίς ἐστι τῆς προτέρας ἀμείνων). But our author goes deeper; redemption, he reiterates (for this had been hinted at in 1[1-4]), is not outside the order of creation. The distinction between the redeeming grace of God and the created universe was drawn afterwards by gnosticism. There is no conscious repudiation of such a view here, only a definite assertion that behind the redeeming purpose lay the full force of God the creator, that God's providence included the mysterious sufferings of Jesus His Son, and that these were in line with His will.

In πολλοὺς υἱούς the πολλοί is in antithesis to the one and only ἀρχηγός, as in Ro 8[29], Mk 14[24]. For the first time the writer calls Christians God's sons. His confidence towards the Father is in sharp contrast to Philo's touch of hesitation in De Confus. Ling. 28 (κἂν μηδέπω μέντοι τυγχάνῃ τις ἀξιόχρεως ὢν υἱὸς θεοῦ προσαγορεύεσθαι . . . καὶ γὰρ εἰ μήπω ἱκανοὶ θεοῦ παῖδες νομίζεσθαι γεγόναμεν). Ἀγαγόντα is devoid of any reference to

---

[1] Agnostos Theos, 347 f. ("Das ist die applikation der logisch-grammatischen Theorie über den Kasus, der in ältester Terminologie, ἡ κατ' αἰτίαν πτῶσις, heisst, auf die Physik : die Welt ist das Objekt der durch die höchste αἰτία ausgeübten Tätigkeit").

[2] As in Apoc. 4[11] and Epist. Aristeas, 16 : δι' ὃν ζωοποιοῦνται τὰ πάντα καὶ γίνεται (quoting Ζῆνα καὶ Δία).

past time. The aorist participle is used adverbially, as often, to denote "an action evidently in a general way coincident in time with the action of the verb, yet not identical with it. The choice of the aorist participle rather than the present in such cases is due to the fact that the action is thought of, not as in progress, but as a simple event or fact" (Burton, *Moods and Tenses*, 149). It is accusative instead of dative, agreeing with an implied αὐτόν instead of αὐτῷ, by a common Greek assimilation (cp. *e.g.* Ac 11¹² 15²² 22¹⁷ 25²⁷). The accusative and infinitive construction prompted ἀγαγόντα instead of ἀγαγόντι. Had ἀγαγόντα been intended to qualify ἀρχηγόν, πολλούς would have been preceded by τόν. The thought is: thus do men attain the δόξα which had been their destiny (v.⁷), but only through a Jesus who had won it for them by suffering.

The mistaken idea that ἀγαγόντα must refer to some action previous to τελειῶσαι, which gave rise to the Latin rendering "qui adduxerat" (vg) or "multis filiis adductis" (vt), is responsible for the ingenious suggestion of Zimmer that δόξα denotes an intermediate state of bliss, where the δίκαιοι of the older age await the full inheritance of the messianic bliss. It is possible (see below on 11⁴⁰ 12²³) to reconstruct such an idea in the mind of the writer, but not to introduce it here.

The general idea in ἀρχηγόν is that of originator or personal source; τουτέστι, τὸν αἴτιον τῆς σωτηρίας (Chrysostom). It is doubtful how far the writer was determined, in choosing the term, by its varied associations, but the context, like that of 12², suggests that the "pioneer" meaning was present to his mind; Jesus was ἀρχηγὸς τῆς σωτηρίας αὐτῶν in the sense that he led the way, broke open the road for those who followed him. This meaning, common in the LXX, recurs in Ac 5³¹ (ἀρχηγὸν καὶ σωτῆρα), and suits ἀγαγόντα better than the alternative sense of the head or progenitor—as of a Greek clan or colony. In this sense ἀρχηγός is applied to heroes, and is even a divine title of Apollo as the head of the Seleucidae (*OGIS.* 212¹³, 219²⁶), as well as a term for the founder (= conditor) or head of a philosophical school (Athenaeus, xiii. 563 E, τὸν ἄρχηγον ὑμῶν τῆς σοφίας Ζήνωνα). But the other rendering is more relevant. Compare the confession (in the Acts of Maximilianus) of the soldier who was put to death in 295 A.D. (Ruinart, *Acta Martyrum*, pp. 340 f.): "huic omnes Christiani servimus, hunc sequimur vitae principem, salutis auctorem." The sufferings of Jesus as ἀρχηγὸς σωτηρίας had, of course, a specific value in the eyes of the writer. He did not die simply in order to show mortals how to die; he experienced death ὑπὲρ παντός, and by this unique suffering made it possible for "many sons" of God to enter the bliss which he had first won for them. Hence, to "perfect" (τελειῶσαι) the ἀρχηγὸς σωτηρίας is to make him adequate,

completely effective. What this involved for him we are not yet
told; later on (5^9 7^{28}) the writer touches the relation between
the perfect ability of Christ and his ethical development through
suffering (see below, v.[14]), but meantime he uses this general
term. God had to "perfect" Jesus by means of suffering, that
he might be equal to his task as ἀρχηγός or ἀρχιερεύς (v.[17]); the
addition of αὐτῶν to σωτηρίας implies (see 7^{26}) that he himself
had not to be saved from sin as they had. The underlying idea
of the whole sentence is that by thus "perfecting" Jesus through
suffering, God carries out his purpose of bringing "many sons"
to bliss.

The verb had already acquired a tragic significance in connexion with
martyrdom; in 4 Mac 7^{15} (ὃν πιστὴ θανάτου σφραγὶς ἐτελείωσεν) it is used of
Eleazar's heroic death, and this reappeared in the Christian vocabulary, as,
e.g., in the title of the Passio S. Perpetuae (μαρτύριον τῆς ἁγίας Περπετούας καὶ
τῶν σὺν αὐτῇ τελειωθέντων ἐν 'Αφρικῇ). But, although Philo had popularized the idea of τελευτᾶν=τελεῖσθαι, this is not present to our writer's
mind; he is thinking of God's purpose to realize a complete experience of
forgiveness and fellowship (σωτηρία) through the Son, and this includes and
involves (as we shall see) a process of moral development for the Son.

The writer now (v.[11]) works out the idea suggested by πολλοὺς
υἱούς. Since Jesus and Christians have the same spiritual origin,
since they too in their own way are "sons" of God, he is proud
to call them brothers and to share their lot (vv.[11-13]). The
leader and his company are a unit, members of the one family of
God. It is implied, though the writer does not explain the
matter further, that Christ's common tie with mankind goes back
to the pre-incarnate period; there was a close bond between
them, even before he was born into the world; indeed the incarnation was the consequence of this solidarity or vital tie (ἐξ
ἑνός, cp. Pindar, Nem. vi. 1, ἓν ἀνδρῶν, ἓν θεῶν γένος). Ὁ ἁγιάζων
and οἱ ἁγιαζόμενοι are participles used as substantives, devoid of
reference to time. Here, as at 13^{12}, Jesus is assigned the divine
prerogative of ἁγιάζειν (cp. Ezk 20^{12} ἐγὼ κύριος ὁ ἁγιάζων αὐτούς,
2 Mac 1^{25}, etc.), i.e. of making God's People His very own, by
bringing them into vital relationship with Himself. It is another
sacerdotal metaphor; the thought of 1^3 (καθαρισμὸν τῶν ἁμαρτιῶν
ποιησάμενος) is touched again, but the full meaning of ἁγιάζειν is
not developed till $9^{13f.}$, where we see that to be "sanctified" is
to be brought into the presence of God through the self-sacrifice
of Christ; in other words, ἁγιάζεσθαι=προσέρχεσθαι or ἐγγίζειν
τῷ θεῷ, as in Nu 16^5 where the ἅγιοι are those whom God
προσηγάγετο πρὸς ἑαυτόν.

According to (Akiba?) Mechilta, 71b (on Ex 20^{18}), God said to the angels
at Sinai, "Go down and help your brothers" (רְדוּ וְסִיעוּ אֶת־אֲחֵיכֶם); yet it
was not merely the angels, but God himself, who helped them (the proof-text
being Ca 2^6 !).

Δι' ἣν αἰτίαν—a phrase only used elsewhere in the NT by the author of the Pastoral epistles—οὐκ ἐπαισχύνεται κτλ.   Ἐπαισχύνεσθαι implies that he was of higher rank, being somehow υἱὸς θεοῦ as they were not.   The verb only occurs three times in LXX, twice of human shame (Ps 119⁶, Is 1²⁹), and once perhaps of God (= אֵשׁב) in Job 34¹⁹.   In *Test. Jos.* 2⁵ it is used passively (οὐ γὰρ ὡς ἄνθρωπος ἐπαισχύνεται ὁ θεός).   In the gospels, besides Mk 3³⁴ᶠ. and Mt 25⁴⁰, there are slight traditions of the risen Jesus calling the disciples his ἀδελφοί (Mt 28¹⁰, Jn 20¹⁷); but the writer either did not know of them or preferred, as usual, to lead biblical proofs.   He quotes three passages (vv.¹². ¹³), the first from the 22nd psalm (v.²³) taken as a messianic cry, the only change made in the LXX text being the alteration of διηγήσομαι into ἀπαγγελῶ (a synonym, see Ps 55¹⁸).   The Son associates himself with his ἀδελφοί in the praise of God offered by their community (a thought which is echoed in 12²⁸ 13¹⁵).

According to Justin Martyr (*Dial.* 106), Ps 22²². ²³ foretells how the risen Jesus stood ἐν μέσῳ τῶν ἀδελφῶν αὐτοῦ, τῶν ἀποστόλων . . . καὶ μετ' αὐτῶν διάγων ὕμνησε τὸν θεόν, ὡς καὶ ἐν τοῖς ἀπομνημονεύμασιν τῶν ἀποστόλων δηλοῦται γεγενημένον, and in the *Acta Joannis* (11) Jesus, before going out to Gethsemane, says, *Let us sing a hymn to the Father* (ἐν μέσῳ δὲ αὐτὸς γενόμενος).   The couplet is quoted here for the sake of the first line ; the second fills it out.   Our author only uses ἐκκλησία (12²³) of the heavenly host, never in its ordinary sense of the "church."

The second quotation (v.¹³ᵃ) is from Is 8¹⁷ ἔσομαι πεποιθὼς (a periphrastic future) ἐπ' αὐτῷ, but the writer prefixes ἐγώ to ἔσομαι for emphasis.   The insertion of ἐρεῖ by the LXX at the beginning of Is 8¹⁷ helped to suggest that the words were not spoken by the prophet himself.   The fact that Jesus required to put faith in God proves that he was a human being like ourselves (see 12²).

In Philo trustful hope towards God is the essential mark of humanity ; e.g. *quod det. pot.* 38 (on Gn 4²⁶), τοῦ δὲ κατὰ Μωυσῆν ἀνθρώπου διάθεσις ψυχῆς ἐπὶ τὸν ὄντως ὄντα θεὸν ἐλπιζούσης.

The third quotation (v.¹³ᵇ) is from the words which immediately follow in Is 8¹⁸, where the LXX breaks the Hebrew sentence into two, the first of which is quoted for his own purposes by the writer.   The παιδία are God's children, the fellow υἱοί of Christ.   It is too subtle to treat, with Zimmer, the three quotations as (a) a resolve to proclaim God, as a man to men ; (b) a resolve to trust God amid the sufferings incurred in his mission, and (c) an anticipation of the reward of that mission. On the other hand, to omit the second καὶ πάλιν as a scribal gloss (Bentley) would certainly improve the sense and avoid the necessity of splitting up an Isaianic quotation into two, the first of which is not strictly apposite.   But καὶ πάλιν is similarly [1]

<hr>

[1] It is a literary device of Philo in making quotations (cp. *quis rer. div.* 1).

used in 10³⁰ ; it is more easy to understand why such words should be omitted than inserted ; and the deliberate addition of ἐγώ in the first points to an intentional use of the sentence as indirectly a confession of fellow-feeling with men on the part of the Son.

The same words of the 22nd psalm are played upon by the Od. Sol 31⁴ : "and he (*i.e.* messiah or Truth) lifted up his voice to the most High, and offered to Him the sons that were with him (or, in his hands)."

In v.¹⁴ κεκοινώνηκεν (here alone in the NT) takes the classical genitive, as in the LXX. An apt classical parallel occurs in the military writer Polyaenus (*Strateg.* iii. 11. 1), where Chabrias tells his troops to think of their foes merely as ἀνθρώποις αἷμα καὶ σάρκα ἔχουσι, καὶ τῆς αὐτῆς φύσεως ἡμῖν κεκοινωνηκόσιν. The following phrase παραπλησίως (= "similarly," *i.e.* almost "equally" or "also," as, *e.g.*, in Maxim. Tyr. vii. 2, καὶ ἐστὶν καὶ ὁ ἄρχων πόλεως μέρος, καὶ οἱ ἀρχόμενοι παραπλησίως) μετέσχεν . . . ἵνα κτλ. answers to the thought of ἠλαττωμένον . . . διὰ τὸ πάθημα κτλ. above. The verb is simply a synonym for κοινωνεῖν ; in the papyri and the inscriptions μετέχειν is rather more common, but there is no distinction of meaning between the two.

This idea (ἵνα κτλ.) of crushing the devil as the wielder of death is not worked out by the writer. He alludes to it in passing as a belief current in his circle, and it must have had some context in his mind ; but what this scheme of thought was, we can only guess. Evidently the devil was regarded as having a hold upon men somehow, a claim and control which meant death for them. One clue to the meaning is to be found in the religious ideas popularized by the Wisdom of Solomon, in which it is pretty clear that man was regarded as originally immortal (1¹³, ¹⁴), that death did not form part of God's scheme at the beginning, and that the devil was responsible for the introduction of death into the world (2²³, ²⁴) ; those who side with the devil encounter death (πειράζουσιν δὲ αὐτὸν οἱ τῆς ἐκείνου μερίδος ὄντες), which they bring upon themselves as a result of their sins. Robertson Smith (*Expositor²*, iii. pp. 76 f.) suggests another ex- planation, viz., that Jesus removes the fear of death by acting as our Highpriest, since (cp. Nu 18⁵) the OT priests were respon- sible for averting death from the people, "the fear of death" being "specially connected with the approach of an impure worshipper before God." This certainly paves the way for v.¹⁷, but it does not explain the allusion to the devil, for the illustra- tion of Zech 3⁵ᶠ· is too remote.

Corroborations of this idea are to be found in more quarters than one. (*a*) There is the rabbinic notion that the angel of death has the power of inflicting death, according to Pes. Kahana, 32. 189*b* ; Mechilta, 72*a* on Ex 20²⁰ (where Ps 82⁶ is applied to Israel at Sinai, since obedience to the Torah would have exempted them from the power of the angel of death), the angel of death being identified with the devil. (*b*) There is also the apocalyptic hope that

messiah at the end would crush the power of the devil, a hope expressed
in the second-century conclusion (Freer-Codex) to Mark, where the risen
Christ declares that "the limit (or term, ὁ ὅρος) of years for Satan's power has
now expired." (c) Possibly the author assumed and expanded Paul's view of
death as the divine punishment for sin executed by the devil, and of Christ's
death as a satisfaction which, by removing this curse of the law, did away
with the devil's hold on sinful mortals. Theodoret's explanation (*Dial.* iii.) is
that the sinlessness of Christ's human nature freed human nature from sin,
which the devil had employed to enslave men: ἐπειδὴ γὰρ τιμωρία τῶν ἁμαρ-
τηκότων ὁ θάνατος ἦν, τὸ δὲ σῶμα τὸ Κυριακὸν οὐκ ἔχον ἁμαρτίας κηλῖδα ὃ παρὰ
τὸν θεῖον νόμον ὁ θάνατος ἀδίκως ἐξήρπασεν, ἀνέστησε μὲν πρῶτον τὸ παρανόμως
κατασχεθέν· ἔπειτα δὲ καὶ τοῖς ἐνδίκως καθειργμένοις ὑπέσχετο τὴν ἀπαλλαγήν.

The force of the paradox in διὰ τοῦ θανάτου (to which the
Armenian version needlessly adds αὐτοῦ) is explained by
Chrysostom : δι' οὗ ἐκράτησεν ὁ διάβολος, διὰ τούτου ἡττήθη. As
the essence of σωτηρία is life, its negative aspect naturally
involves emancipation from death. Ἔχειν τὸ κράτος τοῦ θανάτου
means to wield the power of death, *i.e.* to have control of death.
ἔχειν τὸ κράτος with the genitive in Greek denoting lordship in
a certain sphere, *e.g.* Eurip. *Helena*, 68 (τίς τῶνδ' ἐρυμνῶν δωμάτων
ἔχει κράτος;). Ἀπαλλάξῃ goes with δουλείας (as in Joseph. *Ant.*
13. 13 (363), τῆς ὑπὸ τοῖς ἐχθροῖς αὐτοὺς δουλείας . . . ἀπαλ-
λάττειν, etc.), which is thrown to the end of the sentence for
emphasis, after ὅσοι . . . ἦσαν which qualifies τούτους. Ἔνοχοι
is a passive adjective, equivalent to ἐνεχόμενοι, "bound by" (as
in Demosthenes, 1229), and goes with φόβῳ θανάτου, which is
not a causal dative. Ὅσοι in Hellenistic Greek is no more than
the ordinary relative οἵ. Διὰ παντὸς τοῦ ζῆν, not simply in old
age, as Musonius (ed. Hense, xvii.) thinks : καὶ τό γε ἀθλιώτατον
ποιοῦν τὸν βίον τοῖς γέρουσιν αὐτὸ ἐστιν, ὁ τοῦ θανάτου φόβος.
Aristeas (130, 141, 168) uses δι' ὅλου τοῦ ζῆν, but διὰ παντὸς τοῦ
ζῆν is an unparalleled (in NT Greek) instance of an attribute in
the same case being added to the infinitive with a preposition.
There is a classical parallel in the Platonic διὰ παντὸς τοῦ εἶναι
(*Parmenides*, 152 E); but τὸ ζῆν had already come to be
equivalent to ὁ βίος.

The enslaving power of fear in general is described by
Xenophon in the *Cyropaedia*, iii. 1. 23 f.: οἴει οὖν τι μᾶλλον
καταδουλοῦσθαι ἀνθρώπους τοῦ ἰσχυροῦ φόβου; . . . οὕτω πάντων
τῶν δεινῶν ὁ φόβος μάλιστα καταπλήττει τὰς ψυχάς. Here it is the
fear of death, or rather of what comes after death, which is
described. The Greek protest against the fear of death (cp.
Epict. iii. 36. 28), as unworthy of the wise and good, is echoed
by Philo (*quod omnis probus liber*, 3, ἐπαινεῖται παρά τισιν ὁ
τρίμετρον ἐκεῖνο ποιήσας· "τίς ἐστι δοῦλος, τοῦ θανεῖν ἄφροντις ὤν;"
ὡς μάλα συνιδὼν τὸ ἀκόλουθον. Ὑπέλαβε γάρ, ὅτι οὐδὲν οὕτω
δουλοῦσθαι πέφυκε διάνοιαν, ὡς τὸ ἐπὶ θανάτῳ δέος, ἕνεκα τοῦ πρὸς
τὸ ζῆν ἱμέρου). But the fear persisted, as we see from writers

like Seneca ("optanda mors est sine metu mortis mori," *Troades*, 869) and Cicero; the latter deals with the fear of death in *De Finibus*, v. 11, as an almost universal emotion ("fere sic afficiuntur omnes"). Lucretius as a rationalist had denounced it magnificently in the *De Rerum Natura*, which "is from end to end a passionate argument against the fear of death and the superstition of which it was the basis. The fear which he combated was not the fear of annihilation, but one with which the writer of this Epistle could sympathize, the fear of what might come after death; 'aeternas quoniam poenas in morte timendum est' (i. 111)" (Wickham). The fear of death as death (cp. Harnack's *History of Dogma*, iii. 180) has been felt even by strong Christians like Dr. Johnson. But our author has more in view. Seneca's epistles, for example, are thickly strewn with counsels against the fear of death; he remonstrates with Lucilius on the absurdity of it, discusses the legitimacy of suicide, if things come to the worst, points out that children and lunatics have no such fear (*Ep.* xxxvi. 12), and anticipates most of the modern arguments against this terror. Nevertheless, he admits that it controls human life to a remarkable extent, even though it is the thought of death, not death itself, that we dread (*Ep.* xxx. 17); he confesses that if you take anyone, young, middle-aged, or elderly, "you will find them equally afraid of death" (xxii. 14). And his deepest consolation is that death cannot be a very serious evil, because it is the last evil of all ("quod extremum est," *Ep.* iv. 3). Now the author of Πρὸς Ἑβραίους sees more beyond death than Seneca. "After death, the judgment." The terror which he notes in men is inspired by the fact that death is not the final crisis (9²⁷). "Ultra (*i.e.* post mortem) neque curae neque gaudio locum esse," said Sallust. It was because a primitive Christian did see something "ultra mortem," that he was in fear, till his hope reassured him (9²⁸).

It is noteworthy that here (vv.¹⁴·¹⁵) and elsewhere our author, not unlike the other διδάσκαλος who wrote the epistle of James, ignores entirely the idea of the devil as the source of temptation; he does not even imply the conception of the devil, as 1 Peter does, as the instigator of persecution.

In one of his terse parentheses the writer now (v.¹⁶) adds, οὐ γὰρ δήπου ἀγγέλων ἐπιλαμβάνεται. Δήπου is the classical term for "it need hardly be said" or "of course," and ἐπιλαμβάνεσθαι means "to succour" (Sir 4¹¹ ἡ σοφία υἱοὺς ἑαυτῇ ἀνύψωσεν, καὶ ἐπιλαμβάνεται τῶν ζητούντων αὐτήν). If it meant "seize" or "grip," θάνατος (*i.e.* either death, or the angel of death, cp. v.¹⁴) might be taken as the nominative, the verse being still a parenthesis. This idea, favoured by some moderns, seems to lie behind the Syriac version (cp. A. Bonus, *Expository Times*, xxxiii. pp. 234–236); but ἐπιλαμβάνεσθαι here corresponds to

βοηθῆσαι in v.[18], and is used in the same good sense as in the
other quotation in 8[9]. The words ἀλλὰ σπέρματος Ἀβραὰμ
ἐπιλαμβάνεται may be a reminiscence of Is 41[8. 9] where God
reassures Israel: σπέρμα Ἀβραὰμ . . . οὗ ἀντελαβόμην. The
archaic phrase was perhaps chosen, instead of a term like
ἀνθρώπων,[1] on account of Abraham's position as the father of the
faithful (see 11[8f.]). Paul had already claimed it as a title for
all Christians, irrespective of their birth: οὐκ ἔνι Ἰουδαῖος οὐδὲ
Ἕλλην . . . εἰ δὲ ὑμεῖς Χριστοῦ, ἄρα τοῦ Ἀβραὰμ σπέρμα ἐστέ
(Gal 3[28. 29]), and our author likes these archaic, biblical periphrases. He repeats ἐπιλαμβάνεται after Ἀβραάμ to make a
rhetorical antistrophe (see Introd. p. lvii).

It is a warning against the habit of taking the Greek fathers as absolute
authorities for the Greek of Πρὸς Ἑβραίους, that they never suspected the real
sense of ἐπιλαμβάνεται here. To them it meant "appropriates" (the nature
of). When Castellio (Chatillon), the sixteenth century scholar, first pointed
out the true meaning, Beza pleasantly called his opinion a piece of cursed
impudence ("execranda Castellionis audacia qui ἐπιλαμβάνεται convertit
'opitulatur,' non modo falsa sed etiam inepta interpretatione"). The mere
fact that the Greek fathers and the versions missed the point of the word is
a consideration which bears, e.g., upon the interpretation of a word like
ὑπόστασις in 3[14] and 11[1].

The thought of vv.[14. 15] is now resumed in v.[17]; ὅθεν (a
particle never used by Paul) ὤφειλεν (answering to ἔπρεπεν)
κατὰ πάντα (emphatic by position) τοῖς ἀδελφοῖς ὁμοιωθῆναι—
resembling them in reality, as one brother resembles another
(so *Test. Naphtali* 1[8] ὅμοιός μου ἦν κατὰ πάντα Ἰωσήφ). In
what follows, ἐλεήμων [2] is put first for emphasis (as the writer is
about to speak of this first), and goes like πιστός with ἀρχιερεύς.
"Quae verba sic interpretor: ut misericors esset, ideoque
fidelis," Calvin argues. But this sequence of thought is not
natural; loyalty to God's purpose no doubt involved compassion
for men, but Christ was πιστός as he endured stedfastly the
temptations incurred in his τελείωσις as ἀρχηγός. He suffered,
but he never swerved in his vocation. Nor can πιστός here
mean "reliable" (Seeberg, *Der Tod Christi*, 17), i.e. reliable because merciful; the idea of his sympathy as an encouragement
to faith is otherwise put (cp. 4[14f.] 12[1f.]). The idea of τελειῶσαι
in v.[10] is being explicitly stated; the sufferings of Christ on earth
had a reflex influence upon himself as Saviour, fitting him for
the proper discharge of his vocation. But the vocation is
described from a new angle of vision; instead of ἀρχηγός or
ὁ ἁγιάζων, Jesus is suddenly (see Introd. p. xxv) called ἀρχιερεύς,

---

[1] Cosmas Indicopleustes correctly interpreted the phrase: τουτέστι
σώματος καὶ ψυχῆς λογικῆς (372 B).

[2] The seer in Enoch 40[1-10] has a vision of the four angels who intercede
for Israel before God ; the first is "Michael, the merciful and longsuffering."

evidently a term familiar to the readers (ἀρχιερέα τῆς ὁμολογίας ἡμῶν, 3²). The prestige of the highpriest in the later Judaism is plain in rabbinic (e.g. *Berachoth, Joma*) tradition and also in apocalyptic. The Maccabean highpriests assumed the title of ἱερεὺς τοῦ θεοῦ τοῦ ὑψίστου (Ass. Mosis, 6¹; Jubilees, 32¹), and the ritual of the day of atonement, when he officiated on behalf of the people, was invested with a special halo. This is the point of the allusion here, to the ἀρχιερεύς expiating the sins of the people. Philo had already used the metaphor to exalt the functions of his Logos as a mediator : ὁ δ᾽ αὐτὸς ἱκέτης μέν ἐστι τοῦ θνητοῦ κηραίνοντος ἀεὶ πρὸς τὸ ἄφθαρτον, πρεσβευτὴς δὲ τοῦ ἡγεμόνος πρὸς τὸ ὑπήκοον (*quis rerum div. heres*, 42). But, while the term ἱκέτης does imply some idea of intercession, this is not prominent in Philo's cosmological and metaphysical scheme, as it is in our epistle, which carefully avoids the Philonic idea that men can propitiate God (βούλεται γὰρ αὐτὸν ὁ νόμος μείζονος μεμοιρᾶσθαι φύσεως ἢ κατ᾽ ἄνθρωπον, ἐγγυτέρω προσιόντα τῆς θείας, μεθόριον, εἰ δεῖ τἀληθὲς λέγειν, ἀμφοῖν, ἵνα διὰ μέσου τινὸς ἄνθρωποι μὲν ἱλάσκωνται θεόν, θεὸς δὲ τὰς χάριτας ἀνθρώποις ὑποδιακόνῳ τινὶ χρώμενος ὀρέγῃ καὶ χορηγῇ, *De Spec. Leg.* i. 12). Again, Philo explains (*de sacerdot.* 12) that the highpriest was forbidden to mourn, when a relative died, ἵνα . . . κρείττων οἴκτου γενόμενος, ἄλυπος εἰς ἀεὶ διατελῇ. This freedom from the ordinary affections of humanity was part of his nearer approximation to the life of God (ἐγγυτέρω προσιόντα τῆς θείας [φύσεως]). But our author looks at the function of Christ as ἀρχιερεύς differently ; the first word to be used about him in this connexion is ἐλεήμων, and, before passing on to develop the idea of πιστός, the writer adds (v.¹⁸) another word upon the practical sympathy of Christ. In resembling his ἀδελφοὶ κατὰ παντά Christ πέπονθεν πειρασθείς. His death had achieved for them an emancipation from the dread of death (v.¹⁴) ; by entering into glory he had expiated the sins of God's People, thereby securing for them a free and intimate access to God. But the process by means of which he had thus triumphed was also of value to men ; it gave him the experience which enabled him by sympathy to enter into the position of those who are tempted as he was, and to furnish them with effective help. The connexion between v.¹⁸ (with its γάρ) and v.¹⁷ does not rest upon the idea of Christ as ἐλεήμων καὶ πιστὸς ἀρχιερεύς, as though the effective help received from Christ were a constant proof that he expiates sins, *i.e.* maintains us in the favour and fellowship of God (Seeberg). It rests on the special idea suggested by ἐλεήμων. "His compassion is not mere pity for men racked . . . by pain in itself, however arising ; it is compassion for men tempted by sufferings towards sin or unbelief" (A. B.

Davidson). What the writer has specially in mind is the agony in Gethsemane (cp. 5⁷ᶠ·) as the culminating experience of sorrow caused by the temptation to avoid the fear of death or the cross.

The adverbial accusative τὰ πρὸς τὸν θεόν here, as in 5¹, is a fairly common LXX phrase (*e.g.* Ex 4¹⁶ (of Moses), σὺ δὲ αὐτῷ ἔσῃ τὰ πρὸς τὸν θεόν). Ἱλάσκεσθαι τὰς ἁμαρτίας is also a LXX phrase, an expression for pardon or expiation, as in Ps 65⁴ (τὰς ἀσεβείας ἡμῶν σὺ ἱλάσῃ), which never occurs again in the NT. When the verb (middle voice) is used of God's dealings with men, it generally takes the person of the sinner as its object in the dative (as Lk 18¹³, the only other NT instance of ἱλάσκεσθαι) or else sins in the dative (ταῖς ἁμαρτίαις is actually read here by A 5. 33. 623. 913, Athan. Chrys. Bentley, etc.). This removal of sins as an obstacle to fellowship with God comes under the function of ὁ ἁγιάζων. The thought reappears in 7²⁵ and in 1 Jn 2² (καὶ αὐτὸς ἱλασμός ἐστιν).

ὁ λαός (τοῦ θεοῦ) is the writer's favourite biblical expression for the church, from the beginning to the end ; he never distinguishes Jews and Gentiles.

The introduction of the πειρασμοί of Jesus (v.¹⁸) is as abrupt as the introduction of the ἀρχιερεύς idea, but is thrown out by way of anticipation. Ἐν ᾧ γάρ = ἐν τούτῳ ἐν ᾧ (causal) or ὅτι, explaining not the sphere, but the reason of his "help," πέπονθεν αὐτὸς πειρασθείς—the participle defining the πάσχειν (a term never applied to Jesus by Paul) : he suffered by his temptations, the temptations specially in view being temptations to avoid the suffering that led to the cross. This is the situation of the readers. They are in danger of slipping into apostasy, of giving up their faith on account of the hardships which it involved. Οἱ πειραζόμενοι are people tempted to flinch and falter under the pressure of suffering. Life is hard for them, and faith as hard if not harder. Courage, the writer cries, Jesus understands ; he has been through it all, he knows how hard it is to bear suffering without being deflected from the will of God. Grammatically, the words might also read : "For he himself, having been tempted by what he suffered, is able to help those who are tempted." The sense is really not very different, for the particular temptations in view are those which arise out of the painful experience of having God's will cross the natural inclination to avoid pain. But the πειρασμοί of Jesus were not simply due to what he suffered. He was strongly tempted by experiences which were not painful at all—*e.g.* by the remonstrance of Simon Peter at Caesarea Philippi. As Ritschl puts it, "Christ was exposed to temptation simply because a temptation is always bound up with an inclination which is at the outset morally legitimate or permissible. It was the impulse, in itself lawful, of self-preservation which led to Christ's desire to be spared the suffering of death. And this gave rise to a temptation to sin, because the wish collided with his duty in his vocation. Christ, however, did not consent to this temptation. He renounced his self-preservation, because he assented to the Divine disposal of the end of his life as a consequence of his vocation" (*Rechtfertigung u. Versöhnung*, iii. 507; Eng. tr. p. 573). On the suffering that such temptation involved, see below on 5⁸.

Βοηθεῖν and ἱλάσκεσθαι ταῖς ἁμαρτίαις occur side by side in the prayer of Ps 79⁹ (LXX). Are they synonymous here? Is the meaning of τὸ ἱλάσκεσθαι τὰς ἁμαρτίας τοῦ λαοῦ that Christ constantly enables us to overcome the temptations that would keep us at a distance from God or hinder us from being at peace with God? (so, *e.g.*, Kurtz and M'Leod Campbell, *The Nature of the Atonement*, pp. 172–174). The meaning is deeper. The help conveyed by the sympathy of Jesus reaches back to a sacrificial relationship, upon which everything turns. Hence the ideas of ἐλεήμων and πιστός are now developed, the latter in 3¹⁻⁶ᵃ, the former in 4¹⁴ᶠ, 3⁶ᵇ–4¹³ being a practical application of what is urged in 3¹⁻⁶ᵃ. But the writer does not work out the thought of Christ as πιστός in connexion with his function as ἀρχιερεύς, even though he mentions the latter term at the outset of his appeal, in which the stress falls on the expiatory work of Christ.

¹ *Holy brothers* (ἅγιοι = οἱ ἁγιαζόμενοι, 2¹¹), *you who participate in a heavenly calling, look at Jesus then* (ὅθεν in the light of what has just been said), *at the apostle and highpriest of our confession;* ² *he is "faithful" to Him who appointed him. For while "Moses" also was "faithful in every department of God's house,"* ³ *Jesus* (οὗτος, as in 10¹²) *has been adjudged greater glory* (δόξης) *than* (παρά, as 1⁴) *Moses, inasmuch as the founder of a house enjoys greater honour* (τιμήν, a literary synonym for δόξην) *than the house itself.* ⁴ (*Every house is founded by some one, but God is the founder of all.*) ⁵ *Besides, while "Moses" was "faithful in every department of God's house" as an attendant—by way of witness to the coming revelation—* ⁶ *Christ is faithful as a son over God's house.*

In v.² ὅλῳ (om. p¹³ B sah boh Cyr. Amb.) may be a gloss from v.⁵. In v.³ the emphasis on πλείονος is better maintained by οὗτος δόξης (א A B C D P vt Chrys.) than by δόξης οὗτος (p¹³ K L M 6. 33. 104. 326. 1175. 1288 vg) or by the omission of οὗτος altogether (467 arm Basil). In v.⁴ πάντα has been harmonized artificially with 1³ 2¹⁰ by the addition of τά (Cᶜ L P Ψ 104. 326. 1175. 1128 Athan.).

For the first time the writer addresses his readers, and as ἀδελφοὶ ἅγιοι (only here in NT, for ἁγίοις in 1 Th 5²⁷ is a later insertion), κλήσεως ἐπουρανίου μέτοχοι (6⁴ etc., cp. Ps 119⁶³ μέτοχος ἐγώ εἰμι πάντων τῶν φοβουμένων σε, *Ep. Arist.* 207; *de Mundo*, 401*b*). In Ph 3¹⁴ the ἄνω κλῆσις is the prize conferred at the end upon Christian faith and faithfulness. Here there may be a side allusion to 2¹¹ (ἀδελφοὺς αὐτοὺς καλεῖν). In κατανοήσατε (a verb used in this general sense by *Ep. Aristeas*, 3, πρὸς τὸ

περιέργως τὰ θεῖα κατανοεῖν) κτλ., the writer summons his readers
to consider Jesus as πιστός; but, instead of explaining why or
how Jesus was loyal to God, he uses this quality to bring out
two respects (the first in vv.²ª⁻⁴, the second in vv.⁵⁻⁶ª) in which
Jesus outshone Moses, the divinely-commissioned leader and
lawgiver of the People in far-off days, although there is no tone
of disparagement in the comparison with Moses, as in the comparison with the angels.

In the description of Jesus as τὸν ἀπόστολον καὶ ἀρχιερέα τῆς
ὁμολογίας ἡμῶν, ὁμολογία is almost an equivalent for "our religion," as in 4¹⁴ (cp. 10²³).¹　Through the sense of a vow (LXX)
or of a legal agreement (papyri and inscriptions), it had naturally
passed into the Christian vocabulary as a term for the common
and solemn confession or creed of faith.　Ἡμῶν is emphatic.
In "*our* religion" it is Jesus who is ἀπόστολος καὶ ἀρχιερεύς, not
Moses.　This suits the context better than to make the antithesis
one between the law and the gospel (Theophyl. οὐ γὰρ τῆς κατὰ
νόμον λατρείας ἀρχιερεύς ἐστιν, ἀλλὰ τῆς ἡμετέρας πίστεως).　Possibly
the writer had in mind the Jewish veneration for Moses which
found expression during the second century in a remark of rabbi
Jose ben Chalafta upon this very phrase from Numbers (Sifre,
§ 110): "God calls Moses 'faithful in all His house,' and thereby
he ranked higher than the ministering angels themselves."　The
use of ἀπόστολος as an epithet for Jesus shows "the fresh creative genius of the writer and the unconventional nature of his
style" (Bruce).　Over half a century later, Justin (in *Apol.* 1¹²)
called Jesus Christ τοῦ πατρὸς πάντων καὶ δεσπότου θεοῦ υἱὸς καὶ
ἀπόστολος ὤν, and in *Apol.* 1⁶³ described him as ἄγγελος καὶ
ἀπόστολος· αὐτὸς γὰρ ἀπαγγέλλει ὅσα δεῖ γνωσθῆναι, καὶ ἀποσ-
τέλλεται, μηνύσων ὅσα ἀγγέλλεται (the connexion of thought here
possibly explains the alteration of διηγήσομαι into ἀπαγγελῶ in
He 2¹²).　Naturally Jesus was rarely called ἄγγελος; but it was
all the easier for our author to call Jesus ἀπόστολος, as he avoids
the term in its ecclesiastical sense (cp. 2³).　For him it carries
the usual associations of authority; ἀπόστολος is Ionic for πρεσ-
βευτής, not a mere envoy, but an ambassador or representative
sent with powers, authorized to speak in the name of the person
who has dispatched him.　Here the allusion is to 2³, where the
parallel is with the Sinaitic legislation, just as the allusion to
Jesus as ἀρχιερεύς recalls the ὁ ἁγιάζων of 2¹¹· ¹⁷.　On the other
hand, it is not so clear that any explicit antithesis to Moses is
implied in ἀρχιερέα, for, although Philo had invested Moses with

¹ Had it not been for these other references it might have been possible to
take τ. ὁ. ἡ. here as = "whom we confess."　The contents of the ὁμολογία
are suggested in the beliefs of 6¹ᵗ·, which form the fixed principles and standards of the community, the Truth (10²⁶) to which assent was given at baptism.

highpriestly honour (*praem. et poen.* 9, τυγχάνει . . . ἀρχιερωσύνης, *de vita Mosis*, ii. 1, ἐγένετο γὰρ προνοίᾳ θεοῦ . . . ἀρχιερεύς), this is never prominent, and it is never worked out in "Hebrews."

The reason why they are to look at Jesus is (v.[2]) his faithfulness τῷ ποιήσαντι αὐτόν, where ποιεῖν means "to appoint" to an office (as 1 S 12[6] κύριος ὁ ποιήσας τὸν Μωυσῆν καὶ τὸν Ἀαρών, Mk 3[14] καὶ ἐποίησεν δώδεκα). This faithfulness puts him above Moses for two reasons. First (vv.[2b-4]), because he is the founder of the House or Household of God, whereas Moses is part of the House. The text the writer has in mind is Nu 12[7] (οὐχ οὕτως ὁ θεράπων μου Μωυσῆς· ἐν ὅλῳ τῷ οἴκῳ μου πιστός ἐστιν), and the argument of v.[3], where οἶκος, like our "house," includes the sense of household or family,[1] turns on the assumption that Moses belonged to the οἶκος in which he served so faithfully. How Jesus "founded" God's household, we are not told. But there was an οἶκος θεοῦ before Moses, as is noted later in 11[2. 25], a line of πρεσβύτεροι who lived by faith ; and their existence is naturally referred to the eternal Son. The founding of the Household is part and parcel of the creation of the τὰ πάντα (1[2. 3]). Κατασκευάζειν includes, of course (see 9[2. 6]), the arrangement of the οἶκος (cp. Epict. i. 6. 7–10, where κατασκευάζω is similarly used in the argument from design). The author then adds an edifying aside, in v.[4], to explain how the οἶκος was God's (v.[2] αὐτοῦ), though Jesus had specially founded it. It would ease the connexion of thought if θεός meant (as in 1[8] ?) "divine" as applied to Christ (so, *e.g.*, Cramer, M. Stuart), or if οὗτος could be read for θεός, as Blass actually proposes. But this is to rewrite the passage. Nor can we take αὐτοῦ in v.[6a] as "Christ's" ; there are not two Households, and πᾶς (v.[4]) does not mean "each" (so, *e.g.*, Reuss). Αὐτοῦ in vv.[2. 5] and [6a] must mean "God's." He as creator is ultimately responsible for the House which, under him, Jesus founded and supervises.

This was a commonplace of ancient thought. Justin, *e.g.*, observes : Μενάνδρῳ τῷ κωμικῷ καὶ τοῖς ταῦτα φήσασι ταὐτὰ φράζομεν· μείζονα γὰρ τὸν δημιουργὸν τοῦ σκευαζομένου ἀπεφήνατο (*Apol.* 1[20]). It had been remarked by Philo (*De Plant.* 16) : ὅσῳ γὰρ ὁ κτησάμενος τὸ κτῆμα τοῦ κτήματος ἀμείνων καὶ τὸ πεποιηκὸς τοῦ γεγονότος, τοσούτῳ βασιλικώτεροι ἀκεῖνοι, and in *Legum Allegor.* iii. 32 he argues that just as no one would ever suppose that a furnished mansion had been completed ἄνευ τέχνης καὶ δημιουργοῦ, so anyone entering and studying the universe ὥσπερ εἰς μεγίστην οἰκίαν ἢ πόλιν would naturally conclude that ἦν καὶ ἔστιν ὁ τοῦδε τοῦ παντὸς δημιουργὸς ὁ θεός.

The usual way of combining the thought of v.[4] with the context is indicated by Lactantius in proving the unity of the Father and the Son (*diuin. instit.* iv. 29) : " When anyone has a son of whom he is specially fond (quem unice diligat), a son who is still in the house and under his father's authority (in manu patris)—he may grant him the name and power of lord (nomen

---

[1] Our author avoids (see on 2[12]) ἐκκλησία, unlike the author of 1 Ti 3[15] who writes ἐν οἴκῳ θεοῦ, ἥτις ἐστὶν ἐκκλησία τοῦ θεοῦ.

domini potestatemque), yet by civil law (civili iure) the house is one, and one is called lord. So this world is one house of God, and the Son and the Father, who in harmony (unanimos) dwell in the world, are one God."

The second ($^{5-6a}$) proof of the superiority of Jesus to Moses is now introduced by καί. It rests on the term θεράπων used of Moses in the context (as well as in Nu 11^{11} 12$^{7.\ 8}$ etc.; of Moses and Aaron in Wis 10^{16} 18^{21}); θεράπων is not the same as δοῦλος, but for our author it is less than υἱός, and he contrasts Moses as the θεράπων ἐν τῷ οἴκῳ with Jesus as the Son ἐπὶ τὸν οἶκον, ἐπί used as in 10^{21} (ἱερέα μέγαν ἐπὶ τὸν οἶκον τοῦ θεοῦ) and Mt 25$^{21.\ 23}$ (ἐπὶ ὀλίγα ἧς πιστός). Moses is "egregius domesticus fidei tuae" (Aug. *Conf.* xii. 23). The difficult phrase εἰς τὸ μαρτύριον τῶν λαληθησομένων means, like 9^9, that the position of Moses was one which pointed beyond itself to a future and higher revelation; the tabernacle was a σκήνη τοῦ μαρτυρίου (Nu 12^5) in a deep sense. This is much more likely than the idea that the faithfulness of Moses guaranteed the trustworthiness of anything he said, or even that Moses merely served to bear testimony of what God revealed from time to time (as if the writer was thinking of the words στόμα κατὰ στόμα λαλήσω αὐτῷ which follow the above-quoted text in Numbers).

The writer now passes into a long appeal for loyalty, which has three movements (3^{6b-19} 4$^{1-10}$ 4$^{11-13}$). The first two are connected with a homily on Ps 95$^{7-11}$ as a divine warning against the peril of apostasy, the story of Israel after the exodus from Egypt being chosen as a solemn instance of how easy and fatal it is to forfeit privilege by practical unbelief. It is a variant upon the theme of 2$^{2.\ 3}$, suggested by the comparison between Moses and Jesus, but there is no comparison between Jesus and Joshua; for although the former opens up the Rest for the People of to-day, the stress of the exhortation falls upon the unbelief and disobedience of the People in the past.

[6] *Now we are this house of God* (οὖ, from the preceding αὐτοῦ), *if we will only keep confident and proud of our hope.* [7] *Therefore, as the holy Spirit says* :
"*Today, when* (ἐάν, as in 1 Jn 2^{28}) *you hear his voice,*
[8] *harden not* (μὴ σκληρύνητε, aor. subj. of negative entreaty) *your hearts as at the Provocation,*
on the day of the Temptation in the desert,
[9] *where* (οὖ = ὅπου as Dt 8^{15}) *your fathers put me to the proof,*
[10] *and for forty years felt what I could do.*"
Therefore "*I grew exasperated with that generation,*
I said, 'They are always astray in their heart' ;
they would not learn my ways ;
[11] *so* (ὡς consecutive) *I swore in my anger*
'*they shall never* (εἰ = the emphatic negative אם in oaths) *enter my Rest.*'"
[12] *Brothers, take care in case there is a wicked, unbelieving heart in any of you, moving you to apostatize from the living God.* [13] *Rather admonish one another* (ἑαυτούς = ἀλλήλους) *daily, so long as this word* "*Today*" *is uttered, that none of you may be deceived by sin and* "*hardened.*" [14] *For we only*

*participate in Christ provided that we keep firm to the very end the confidence
with which we started,* [15] *this word ever sounding in our ears :*
  "*Today, when you hear his voice,
  harden not your hearts as at the Provocation.*"
[16] *Who heard and yet "provoked" him? Was it not all who left Egypt
under the leadership of Moses?* [17] *And with whom was he exasperated for
forty years? Was it not with those who sinned, whose "corpses*[1] *fell in the
desert"?* [18] *And to whom "did he swear that they (sc. αὐτούς) would never
enter his Rest"? To whom but those who disobeyed (ἀπειθήσασιν, cp. Ac 19⁹)?*
[19] *Thus (καὶ consecutive) we see it was owing to unbelief that they could not
enter.*

In v.⁶ (*a*) οὖ is altered into ὅς by D* M 6. 424 Lat Lucifer, Ambr. Priscillian, probably owing to the erroneous idea that the definite article (supplied
by 440. 2005) would have been necessary between οὖ and οἶκος. (*b*) ἐάν is
assimilated to the text of v.¹⁴ by a change to ἐάνπερ in אᶜ A C Dᶜ K L W
syrʰᵏˡ Lucifer, Chrys. etc. (von Soden). (*c*) After ἐλπίδος the words μέχρι
τέλους βεβαίαν are inserted from v.¹⁴ by a number of MSS ; the shorter,
correct text is preserved in p¹³ B 1739 sah eth Lucifer, Ambrose.

V.⁶ᵇ introduces the appeal, by a transition from ⁶ᵃ. When
Philo claims that παρρησία is the mark of intelligent religion
(*quis rer. div. haeres*, 4, τοῖς μὲν οὖν ἀμαθέσι συμφέρον ἡσυχία,
τοῖς δὲ ἐπιστήμης ἐφιεμένοις καὶ ἅμα φιλοδεσπότοις ἀναγκαιότατον ἡ
παρρησία κτῆμα), he means by παρρησία the confidence which is
not afraid to pray aloud: cp. *ib.* 5 (παρρησία δὲ φιλίας συγγενές,
ἐπεὶ πρὸς τίνα ἄν τις ἢ πρὸς τὸν ἑαυτοῦ φίλον παρρησιάσαιτο;), where
the prayers and remonstrances of Moses are explained as a proof
that he was God's friend. But here as elsewhere in the NT
παρρησία has the broader meaning of "confidence" which already
appears in the LXX (*e.g.* in Job 27¹⁰ μὴ ἔχει τινὰ παρρησίαν
ἐναντίον αὐτοῦ). This confidence is the outcome of the Christian
ἐλπίς (for τῆς ἐλπίδος goes with τὴν παρρησίαν as well as with τὸ
καύχημα); here as in 4¹⁶ and 10¹⁹. ³⁵ it denotes the believing
man's attitude to a God whom he knows to be trustworthy.
The idea of τὸ καύχημα τῆς ἐλπίδος is exactly that of Ro 5²
(καυχώμεθα ἐπ' ἐλπίδι τῆς δόξης τοῦ θεοῦ), and of a saying like
Ps 5¹² (καὶ εὐφρανθήτωσαν ἐπὶ σοὶ πάντες οἱ ἐλπίζοντες ἐπὶ σέ).

Διό in v.⁷ goes most naturally with μὴ σκληρύνητε (v.⁸), the
thought of which recurs in v.¹³ as the central thread. The
alternative, to take it with βλέπετε in v.¹², which turns the whole
quotation into a parenthesis, seems to blunt the direct force of
the admonition; it makes the parenthesis far too long, and
empties the second διό of its meaning. βλέπετε is no more
abrupt in v.¹² than in 12²⁵; it introduces a sharp, sudden
warning, without any particle like οὖν or δέ, and requires no previous term like διό. The quotation is introduced as in 10¹⁵ by
"the holy Spirit" as the Speaker, a rabbinic idea of inspiration.
The quotation itself is from Ps 95⁷⁻¹¹ which in A runs as follows:

_____

[1] κῶλα in this sense is from Nu 14²⁹⋅ ³², a passage which the writer has
in mind.

σήμερον ἐὰν τῆς φωνῆς αὐτοῦ ἀκούσητε,
  μὴ σκληρύνητε τὰς καρδίας ὑμῶν ὡς ἐν τῷ παραπικρασμῷ
  κατὰ τὴν ἡμέραν τοῦ πειρασμοῦ ἐν τῇ ἐρήμῳ·
οὗ ἐπείρασαν[1] οἱ πατέρες ὑμῶν,
  ἐδοκίμασαν με καὶ ἴδον τὰ ἔργα μου.
τεσσεράκοντα ἔτη προσώχθισα τῇ γενεᾷ ἐκείνῃ,[2]
  καὶ εἶπον·[3] ἀεὶ[4] πλανῶνται τῇ καρδίᾳ,
  αὐτοὶ δὲ οὐκ ἔγνωσαν τὰς ὁδούς μου.
ὡς ὤμοσα ἐν τῇ ὀργῇ μου,
  εἰ εἰσελεύσονται εἰς τὴν κατάπαυσίν μου.

In vv.[9, 10], though he knew (v.[17]) the correct connexion of the LXX (cp. v.[17a]), he alters it here for his own purpose, taking τεσσαράκοντα ἔτη with what precedes instead of with what follows, inserting διό (which crept into the text of R in the psalm) before προσώχθισα for emphasis, and altering ἐδοκίμασαν με into ἐν δοκιμασίᾳ.[5] The LXX always renders the place-names "Meriba" and "Massa" by generalizing moral terms, here by παραπικρασμός and πειρασμός, the former only here in the LXX (Aquila, 1 Sam 15[33]; Theodotion, Prov 17[11]). The displacement of τεσσεράκοντα ἔτη was all the more feasible as εἶδον τὰ ἔργα μου meant for him the experience of God's punishing indignation. (Τεσσαράκοντα is better attested than τεσσεράκοντα (Moulton, ii. 66) for the first century.) There is no hint that the writer was conscious of the rabbinic tradition, deduced from this psalm, that the period of messiah would last for forty years, still less that he had any idea of comparing this term with the period between the crucifixion and 70 A.D. What he really does is to manipulate the LXX text in order to bring out his idea that the entire forty years in the desert were a "day of temptation,"[6] during which the People exasperated God. Hence (in v.[9]) he transfers the "forty years" to εἶδον τὰ ἔργα μου, in order to emphasize the truth that the stay of the People in the desert was one long provocation of God; for εἶδον τὰ ἔργα μου is not an aggravation of their offence

---

[1] א^{ca} adds με (so T), which has crept (needlessly, for πειράζειν may be used absolutely as in 1 Co 10[9]) into the text of Hebrews through א^c D^c M vg pesh harkl boh arm Apollin.

[2] In some texts of Hebrews (p[13] א A B D* M 33. 424** vg Clem. Apollin.) this becomes (under the influence of the literal view of forty years?) ταύτῃ (ἐκείνῃ in C D^c K L P syr sah boh arm eth Eus. Cyril, Chrys.).

[3] The Ionic form εἶπα (B) has slipped into some texts of Hebrews (A D 33. 206. 489. 1288. 1518. 1836).

[4] The LXX is stronger than the Hebrew; it appears to translate not the עם of the MT, but עלם (cp. Flashar in Zeits. für alt. Wiss., 1912, 84–85).

[5] ἐδοκίμασαν (με) is read in the text of Hebrews, by assimilation, in א^c D^c K L vg syr arm eth Apollin. Lucifer, Ambr. Chrys. etc. i.e. ΕΔΟΚΙΜΑCΙΑ was altered into ΕΔΟΚΙΜΑCΑ.

[6] The κατά in κατὰ τὴν ἡμέραν (v.[8]) is temporal as in 1[10] 7[27], not "after the manner of" ("secundum," vg).

("though they felt what I could do for them"), but a reminder that all along God let them feel how he could punish them for their disobedience. Finally, their long-continued obstinacy led him to exclude them from the land of Rest. This "finally" does not mean that the divine oath of exclusion was pronounced at the end of the forty years in the desert, but that as the result of God's experience he gradually killed off (v.[17]) all those who had left Egypt. This retribution was forced upon him by the conviction αὐτοὶ δὲ οὐκ ἔγνωσαν τὰς ὁδούς μου (*i.e.* would not learn my laws for life, cared not to take my road).

The rabbinic interpretation of Ps 95 as messianic appears in the legend (T.B. *Sanhedrim*, 98a) of R. Joshua ben Levi and Elijah. When the rabbi was sent by Elijah to messiah at the gates of Rome, he asked, " *Lord, when comest thou?*" *He answered,* "*To-day.*" *Joshua returned to Elijah, who inquired of him:* "*What said He to thee?*" *Joshua:* "*Peace be with thee, son of Levi.*" *Elijah:* "*Thereby He has assured to thee and thy father a prospect of attaining the world to come.*" *Joshua:* "*But He has deceived me, by telling me He would come to-day.*" *Elijah:* "*Not so, what He meant was, To-day, if you will hear His voice.*" The severe view of the fate of the wilderness-generation also appears in *Sanh.* 110b, where it is proved that the generation of the wilderness have no part in the world to come, from Nu 14[35] and also from Ps 95 (*as I swore in my anger that they should not enter into my Rest*). This was rabbi Akiba's stern reading of the text. But rabbinic opinion, as reflected in the Mishna (cp. W. Bacher, *Agada der Tannaiten*[2], i. 135 f.), varied on the question of the fate assigned to the generation of Israelites during the forty years of wandering in the desert. While some authorities took Ps 95[11] strictly, as if the "rest" meant the rest after death, and these Israelites were by the divine oath excluded from the world to come, others endeavoured to minimize the text ; God's oath only referred to the incredulous spies, they argued, or it was uttered in the haste of anger and recalled. In defence of the latter milder view Ps 50[5] was quoted, and Isa 35[10]. Our author takes the sterner view, reproduced later by Dante (*Purgatorio*, xviii. 133-135), for example, who makes the Israelites an example of sloth ; "the folk for whom the sea opened were dead ere Jordan saw the heirs of promise." He never speaks of men "tempting God," apart from this quotation, and indeed, except in 11[17], God's πειρασμός or probation of men is confined to the human life of Jesus.

For διό in v.[10] Clem. Alex. (*Protrept.* 9) reads δι' ὅ. Προσωχθίζειν is a LXX term for the indignant loathing excited by some defiance of God's will, here by a discontented, critical attitude towards him. In v.[11] κατάπαυσις is used of Canaan as the promised land of settled peace, as only in Dt 12[9] (οὐ γὰρ ἥκατε . . . εἰς τὴν κατάπαυσιν) and 1 K 8[56] (εὐλογητὸς Κύριος σήμερον, ὃς ἔδωκεν κατάπαυσιν τῷ λαῷ αὐτοῦ). The mystical sense is developed in 4[3f.].

The application (vv.[12f.]) opens with βλέπετε (for the classical ὁρᾶτε) μὴ . . . ἔσται (as in Col 2[8] (βλέπετε μὴ . . . ἔσται), the reason for the future being probably "because the verb εἰμί has no aorist, which is the tense required," Field, *Notes on Translation of N.T.*, p. 38) ἐν τινι ὑμῶν—the same concern for individuals

as in 4^{11} 10^{25} 12^{15}—καρδία ἀπιστίας (genitive of quality—a
Semitism here). Ἀπιστία must mean more than "incredulity";
the assonance with ἀποστῆναι was all the more apt as ἀπιστία
denoted the unbelief which issues in action, ἐν τῷ ἀποστῆναι—the
idea as in Ezk 20^8 καὶ ἀπέστησαν ἀπ' ἐμοῦ, καὶ οὐκ ἠθέλησαν
εἰσακοῦσαί μου, though the preposition ἀπό was not needed, as may
be seen, e.g., in Wis 3^{10} (οἱ . . . τοῦ κυρίου ἀποστάντες). Our
author is fond of this construction, the infinitive with a preposition.
"The living God" suggests what they lose by their apostasy,
and what they bring upon themselves by way of retribution
(10^{31}), especially the latter (cp. 4^{12}). There is no real distinction
between θεοῦ ζῶντος and τοῦ θεοῦ ζῶντος, for the article could be
dropped, as in the case of θεὸς πατήρ and κύριος Ἰησοῦς, once the
expression became stamped and current.

In v.[13] παρακαλεῖτε . . . καθ' ἑκάστην ἡμέραν (cp. Test. Levi 9^8
ἣν καθ' ἑκάστην ἡμέραν συνετίζων με) emphasizes the keen, constant
care of the community for its members, which is one feature of
the epistle. In ἄχρις οὗ (elsewhere in NT with aorist or future),
which is not a common phrase among Attic historians and
orators, ἄχρις is a Hellenistic form of ἄχρι (p[13] M) used sometimes
when a vowel followed. Σήμερον is "God's instant men call
years" (Browning), and the paronomasia in καλεῖται[1] . . . παρακαλεῖτε led the writer to prefer καλεῖται to a term like κηρύσσεται.
The period (see 4^7) is that during which God's call and opportunity still hold out, and the same idea is expressed in ἐν τῷ
λέγεσθαι Σήμερον κτλ. (v.[15]). ἐξ ὑμῶν is sufficiently emphatic as it
stands, without being shifted forward before τις (B D K L d e etc.
harkl Theodt. Dam.) in order to contrast ὑμεῖς with οἱ πατέρες
ὑμῶν (v.[9]). As for ἡ ἁμαρτία, it is the sin of apostasy (12^4), which
like all sin deceives men (Ro 7^{11}), in this case by persuading them
that they will be better off if they allow themselves to abandon the
exacting demands of God. The responsibility of their position is
expressed in ἵνα μὴ σκληρυνθῇ, a passive with a middle meaning;
men can harden themselves or let lower considerations harden
them against the call of God. As Clement of Alexandria
(Protrept. ix.) explains: ὁρᾶτε τὴν ἀπειλήν· ὁρᾶτε τὴν προτροπήν·
ὁρᾶτε τὴν τιμήν. τί δὴ οὖν ἔτι τὴν χάριν εἰς ὀργὴν μεταλλάσσομεν . . . ;
μεγάλη γὰρ τῆς ἐπαγγελίας αὐτοῦ ἡ χάρις, "ἐὰν σήμερον τῆς φωνῆς
αὐτοῦ ἀκούσωμεν"· τὸ δὲ σήμερον τῆς φωνῆς αὐτοῦ αὔξεται τὴν ἡμέραν,
ἔστ' ἂν ἡ σήμερον ὀνομάζηται.

In v.[14] μέτοχοι τοῦ Χριστοῦ (which is not an equivalent for the
Pauline ἐν Χριστῷ, but rather means to have a personal interest
in him) answers to μέτοχοι κλήσεως ἐπουρανίου in v.[1] and to
μετόχους πνεύματος ἁγίου in 6^4; γεγόναμεν betrays the predilection
of the writer for γέγονα rather than its equivalent εἶναι. Ἐάνπερ

---

[1] The common confusion between αι and ει led to the variant καλεῖτε (A C).

an intensive particle (for ἐάν, v.⁹) τὴν ἀρχὴν τῆς ὑποστάσεως
(genitive of apposition)—*i.e.* " our initial confidence " (the idea
of 10³²)—κατάσχωμεν (echoing v.⁶ᵇ).   The misinterpretation of
ὑποστάσεως as (Christ's) "substance"¹ led to the addition of
αὐτοῦ (A 588. 623. 1827. 1912 vg).   But ὑπόστασις here as in
11¹ denotes a firm, confident conviction or resolute hope (in
LXX, *e.g.*, Ru 1¹² ἔστιν μοι ὑπόστασις τοῦ γενηθῆναι με ἀνδρί,
rendering תקוה, which is translated by ἐλπίς in Pr 11⁷), with the
associations of steadfast patience under trying discouragements.
This psychological meaning was already current (cp. 2 Co 9⁴
μὴ . . . καταισχυνθῶμεν ἡμεῖς ἐν τῇ ὑποστάσει ταύτῃ), alongside
of the physical or metaphysical.   What a man bases himself on,
as he confronts the future, is his ὑπόστασις, which here in sound
and even (by contrast) in thought answers to ἀποστῆναι.

It is possible to regard v.¹⁴ as a parenthesis, and connect
ἐν τῷ λέγεσθαι (v.¹⁵) closely with παρακαλεῖτε or ἵνα μὴ . . .
ἁμαρτίας (v.¹³), but this is less natural ; ἐν τῷ λέγεσθαι (" while it
is said," as in Ps 42⁴ ἐν τῷ λέγεσθαι) connects easily and aptly
with κατάσχωμεν, and vv.¹⁴˙ ¹⁵ thus carry on positively the thought
of v.¹³, viz. that the writer and his readers are still within the
sound of God's call to his οἶκος to be πιστός.

The pointed questions which now follow (vv.¹⁶⁻¹⁸) are a
favourite device of the diatribe style.   Παραπικραίνειν (Hesych.
παροργίζειν)² in v.¹⁶ seems to have been coined by the LXX
to express "rebellious" with a further sense of provoking or
angering God ; *e.g.* Dt 31²⁷ παραπικραίνοντες ἦτε τὰ πρὸς τὸν θεόν
(translating מרה), and Dt 32¹⁶ ἐν βδελύγμασιν αὐτῶν παρεπίκρανάν
με (translating כעם).   The sense of " disobey" recurs occasionally
in the LXX psalter (*e.g.* 104²⁸, 106¹¹) ; indeed the term involves
a disobedience which stirs up the divine anger against rebels,
the flagrant disobedience (cp. παραβαίνειν for מרה in Dt 1⁴³,
Nu 27¹⁴) which rouses exasperation in God.   Ἀλλ', one rhetorical
question being answered by another (as Lk 17⁸), logically
presupposes τινές, but τίνες must be read in the previous question.
By writing πάντες the writer does not stop to allow for the faithful minority, as Paul does (1 Co 10⁷ᶠ· τινες αὐτῶν).   In the grave
conclusion (v.¹⁹) δι' ἀπιστίαν (from v.¹²) is thrown to the end for
the sake of emphasis.

But, the author continues (4¹ᶠ·), the promised rest is still
available; it is open to faith, though only to faith (¹⁻³).   No
matter how certainly all has been done upon God's part (³⁻⁵),
and no matter how sure some human beings are to share his

---

¹ Another early error was to regard it as " our substance," so that ἡ ἀρχὴ
τῆς ὑποστάσεως meant faith as "the beginning of our true nature" (a view
already current in Chrysostom).

² In Dt 32¹⁶ it is paraîiel to παροξύνειν ; cp. Flashar's discussion in *Zeitschrift für alt. Wiss.*, 1912, 185 f.   It does not always require an object (God).

Rest (v.⁶), it does not follow that *we* shall, unless we take warning
by this failure of our fathers in the past and have faith in God.
Such is the urgent general idea of this paragraph.   But the
argument is compressed; the writer complicates it by defining
the divine Rest as the sabbath-rest of eternity, and also by
introducing an allusion to Joshua.   That is, he (*a*) explains
God's κατάπαυσις in Ps 95 by the σαββατισμός of Gn 2², and
then (*b*) draws an inference from the fact that the psalm-promise
is long subsequent to the announcement of the σαββατισμός.
He assumes that there is only one Rest mentioned, the κατάπαυσις
into which God entered when he finished the work of creation,
to which οἱ πατέρες ὑμῶν were called under Moses, and to which
Christians are now called.   They must never lose faith in it,
whatever be appearances to the contrary.

   [1] *Well then, as the promise of entrance into his Rest is still left to us, let*
us be afraid of anyone being judged to have missed it.   [2] *For* (καὶ γάρ = etenim)
we have had the good news as well as they (ἐκεῖνοι = 3⁸⁻¹⁹); *only, the message*
they heard was of no use to them, because it did not meet with faith in the
hearers.   [3] *For we do "enter the Rest" by our faith : according to his word,*
            "As I swore in my anger,
               they shall never enter my Rest"—
although "his works" were all over by the foundation of the world.   [4] *For he*
says somewhere about the seventh (sc. ἡμέρας) *day : "And God rested from all*
his works on the seventh day."   [5] *And again in this* (ἐν τούτῳ, sc. τόπῳ)
passage, "they shall never enter my Rest."   [6] *Since then it is reserved*
(ἀπολείπεται, a variant for καταλειπ. v.¹) *for some "to enter it," and since*
those who formerly got the good news failed to "enter" owing to their disobedi-
ence,[1] [7]*he again fixes a day; "today"—as he says in "David" after so long*
an interval, and as has been already quoted:
            "Today, when you hear his voice,
               harden not your hearts."
   [8] *Thus if Joshua had given them Rest, God would not speak later about another*
day.   There is a sabbath-Rest, then, reserved (ἀπολείπεται, as in ⁶) *still for*
the People of God (for once "a man enters his (αὐτοῦ, *i.e.* God's) *rest," he*
"rests from work" just as God did).

Ἐπαγγελία (v.¹) is not common in the LXX, though it mis-
translates סִפְרָה in Ps 56⁸, and is occasionally the term for a
human promise.   In the Prayer of Manasseh (⁶) it is the divine
promise (τὸ ἔλεος τῆς ἐπαγγελίας σου), and recurs in the plural,
of the divine promises, in *Test. Jos.* 20¹ (ὁ θεὸς ποιήσει τὴν
ἐκδίκησιν ὑμῶν καὶ ἐπάξει ὑμᾶς εἰς τὰς ἐπαγγελίας τῶν πατέρων
ὑμῶν) and Ps. Sol 12⁸ (ὅσιοι κυρίου κληρονομήσαιεν ἐπαγγελίας
κυρίου—the first occurrence of this phrase κλ. ἐπ., cp. below on
6¹²).   Καταλειπομένης ἐπαγγελίας (+τῆς D* 255, from 6¹⁵· ¹⁷ 11⁹)
is a genitive absolute.   Ἐπαγγελίας εἰσελθεῖν (like ὁρμὴ . . . ὑβρίσαι
in Ac 14⁵) κτλ. : the basis of the appeal is (*a*) that the divine
promise of Rest has been neither fulfilled nor withdrawn (still τὸ
"σήμερον" καλεῖται); and (*b*) that the punishment which befalls

   [1] Ἀπείθειαν, altered into ἀπιστίαν by א* vg sah boh arm Cyr.

others is a warning to ourselves (cp. Philo, *ad Gaium*, I : αἱ γὰρ ἑτέρων τιμωρίαι βελτιοῦσι τοὺς πολλούς, φόβῳ τοῦ μὴ παραπλήσια παθεῖν). By a well-known literary device μή ποτε, like μή in 12¹⁵, takes a present (δοκῇ), instead of the more usual aorist, subjunctive. Δοκῇ means "judged" or "adjudged," as in Josephus, *Ant.* viii. 32, κἂν ἀλλότριον δοκῇ. This is common in the LXX, *e.g.* in Pr 17²⁸ ἐνεὸν δέ τις ἑαυτὸν ποιήσας δόξει φρόνιμος εἶναι (where δόξει is paralleled by λογισθήσεται), 27¹⁴ (καταρωμένου οὐδὲν διαφέρειν δόξει); indeed it is an ordinary Attic use which goes back to Plato (*e.g. Phaedo*, 113 D, of the souls in the under-world, οἳ μὲν ἂν δόξωσι μέσως βεβιωκέναι) and Demosthenes (629. 17, οἱ δεδογμένοι ἀνδροφόνοι = the convicted murderers). The searching scrutiny which passes this verdict upon lack of faith is the work of the divine Logos (in v.¹²).

In v.² εὐηγγελισμένοι is remarkable. Our author, who never uses εὐαγγέλιον (preferring ἐπαγγελία here as an equivalent), employs the passive of εὐαγγελίζειν ¹ (as in v.⁶) in the broad sense of "having good news brought to one." The passive occurs in LXX of 2 S 18³¹ (εὐαγγελισθήτω ὁ κύριός μου ὁ βασιλεύς) and in Mt 11⁵ (πτωχοὶ εὐαγγελίζονται). The καί after καθάπερ emphasizes as usual the idea of correspondence. The reason for the failure of the past generation was that they merely heard what God said, and did not believe him; ὁ λόγος τῆς ἀκοῆς (ἀκοῆς, passive = "sermo auditus," vg), which is another (see 3¹²) instance of the Semitic genitive of quality, is defined as μή (causal particle as in 11²⁷ μὴ φοβηθείς) συγκεκ(ε)ρα(σ)μένος τῇ πίστει τοῖς ἀκούσασιν, since it did not get blended with faith in (the case of) those who heard it. Or τῇ πίστει may be an instrumental dative : "since it did not enter vitally into the hearers by means of the faith which it normally awakens in men." The fault lies, as in the parable of the Sower, not with the message but with the hearers. The phrase λόγος . . . συγκεκρασμένος may be illustrated from Menander (Stob. *Serm.* 42, p. 302), τὴν τοῦ λόγου μὲν δύναμιν οὐκ ἐπίφθονον ἤθει δὲ χρηστῷ συγκεκραμένην ἔχειν, and Plutarch, *non posse suauiter vivi secundum Epicurum*, 1101, βέλτιον γὰρ ἐνυπάρχειν τι καὶ συγκεκρᾶσθαι τῇ περὶ θεῶν δόξῃ κοινὸν αἰδοῦς καὶ φόβου πάθος κτλ. The use of λόγος with such verbs is illustrated by Plutarch, *Vit. Cleom.* 2 (ὁ δὲ Στωϊκὸς λόγος . . . βάθει δὲ καὶ πράῳ κεραννύμενος ἤθει μάλιστα εἰς τὸ οἰκεῖον ἀγαθὸν ἐπιδίδωσιν). Κρᾶσις occurs in Philo's definition of φιλία (*Quaest. in Gen.* 2¹⁸) as consisting [οὐκ] ἐν τῷ χρειώδει μᾶλλον ἢ κράσει καὶ συμφωνίᾳ βεβαίῳ τῶν ἠθῶν, and συγκεκρᾶσθαι in his description of the union of spirit and blood in the human body (*Quaest. in Gen.* 9⁴ πνεῦμα . . . ἐμφέρεσθαι καὶ συγκεκρᾶσθαι αἵματι).

---

¹ An almost contemporary instance (εὐαγγελίζοντι τὰ τῆς νείκης αὐτοῦ καὶ προκοπῆς) of the active verb is cited by Mitteis-Wilcken, i. 2. 29.

The original reading συγκεκ(ε)ρα(σ)μένος (א 114 vt pesh Lucif.) was soon
assimilated (after ἐκείνους) into the accusative -ους (p¹³ A B C D K L M P vg
boh syrʰᵏˡ etc. Chrys. Theod.-Mops. Aug.), and this led to the alteration of
τοῖς ἀκούσασιν into τῶν ἀκουσάντων (D* 104. 1611. 2005 d syrʰᵏˡ ᵐᵍ Lucif.),
or τοῖς ἀκουσθεῖσιν (1912 vg Theod.-Mops.), or τοῖς ἀκούουσιν (1891). The
absence of any allusion elsewhere to the faithful minority (Caleb, Joshua)
tells decisively against συγκεκρασμένους ("since they did not mix with the
believing hearers"); for the writer (see above) never takes them into account,
and, to make any sense, this reading implies them. How could the majority
be blamed for not associating with believing hearers when *ex hypothesi* there
were none such ?

The writer now (vv.[3-10]) lays emphasis upon the reality of
the Rest. "We have had this good news too as well as they,"
for (γάρ) we believers do enter into God's Rest; it is prepared
and open, it has been ready ever since the world began—ἄρα
ἀπολείπεται σαββατισμὸς τῷ λαῷ τοῦ θεοῦ. Εἰσερχόμεθα is the
emphatic word in v.³: "we do (we are sure to) enter," the futuristic
present ("ingrediemur," vg). When God excluded that unbelieving generation from his Rest, he was already himself in his
Rest. The κατάπαυσις was already in existence; the reason
why these men did not gain entrance was their own unbelief, not
any failure on God's part to have the Rest ready. Long ago it
had been brought into being (this is the force of καίτοι in v.³),
for what prevents it from being realized is not that any ἔργα of
God require still to be done. Κατάπαυσις is the sequel to ἔργα.
The creative ἔργα leading up to this κατάπαυσις have been completed centuries ago; God enjoys his κατάπαυσις, and if his
People do not, the fault lies with themselves, with man's disbelief.

Here, as in Ro 3[28], there is a choice of reading between οὖν (א A C M
1908 boh) and γάρ (p¹³ B D K L P Ψ 6. 33 lat syrʰᵏˡ eth Chrys. Lucif.
etc.); the colourless δέ (syrᵖᵉˢʰ arm) may be neglected. The context is decisive in favour of γάρ. Probably the misinterpretation which produced οὖν
led to the change of εἰσερχόμεθα into εἰσερχώμεθα [1] (A C 33. 69* : future in
vg sah boh Lucif.). The insertion of τήν (the first) may be due to the same
interpretation, but not necessarily; p¹³ B D* om., but B omits the article
sometimes without cause (*e.g.* 7[15]). The omission of εἰ (p¹³ D* 2. 330. 440.
623. 642. 1288. 1319. 1912) was due to the following εἰ in εἰσελεύσονται.

Καίτοι (with gen. absol., as *OP.* 898[26]) is equivalent here to
καίτοιγε for which it is a *v.l.* in Ac 17[27] (A E, with ptc.). "Καίτοι,
ut antiquiores καίπερ, passim cum participio iungunt scriptores
aetatis hellenisticae" (Herwerden, *Appendix Lexici Graeci*, 249).
Καταβολή is not a LXX term, but appears in *Ep. Aristeas*, 129
and 2 Mac 2[29] (τῆς ὅλης καταβολῆς = the entire edifice); in the
NT always, except He 11[11], in the phrase ἀπό or πρὸ καταβολῆς
κόσμου.

The writer then (v.⁴) quotes Gn 2², inserting ὁ θεὸς ἐν (exactly
as Philo had done, *de poster. Caini*, 18), as a proof that the κατά-

[1] A similar error of A C in 6².

παυσις had originated immediately after the six days of creation. In εἴρηκε που the που is another literary mannerism (as in Philo); instead of quoting definitely he makes a vague allusion (cp. 2⁶). The psalm-threat is then (v.⁵) combined with it, and (v.⁶) the deduction drawn, that the threat (v.⁷) implies a promise (though not as if v.¹ meant, "lest anyone imagine he has come too late for it"—an interpretation as old as Schöttgen, and still advocated, e.g., by Dods).

The title of the 92nd psalm, "for the sabbath-day," was discussed about the middle of the 2nd century by R. Jehuda and R. Nehemia; the former interpreted it to mean the great Day of the world to come, which was to be one perfect sabbath, but R. Nehemia's rabbinical tradition preferred to make it the seventh day of creation on which God rested (see W. Bacher's *Agada der Tannaiten*², i. pp. 328–329). The author of the Epistle of Barnabas (15) sees the fulfilment of Gn 2² in the millennium: "he rested on the seventh day" means that "when his Son arrives he will destroy the time of the lawless one, and condemn the impious, and alter sun and moon and stars; then he will really rest on the seventh day," and Christians cannot enjoy their rest till then. Our author's line is different—different even from the Jewish interpretation in the *Vita Adae et Evae* (li. 1), which makes the seventh day symbolize "the resurrection and the rest of the age to come; on the seventh day the Lord rested from all his works."

In v.⁷ μετὰ τοσοῦτον χρόνον, like μετὰ ταῦτα (v.⁸), denotes the interval of centuries between the desert and the psalm of David, for ἐν Δαυείδ means "in the psalter" (like ἐν Ἠλίᾳ, Ro 11²); the 95th psalm is headed αἶνος ᾠδῆς τῷ Δαυείδ in the Greek bible, but the writer throughout (3⁷ᶠ·) treats it as a direct, divine word. Προείρηται (the author alluding to his previous quotation) is the original text (p¹³ A C D* P 6. 33. 1611. 1908. 2004. 2005 lat syr Chrys. Cyr. Lucif.); προείρηκεν (B 256. 263. 436. 442. 999. 1739. 1837 arm sah boh Orig.) suggests that God or David spoke these words before the oath (v.⁷ comes before v.¹¹!), while εἴρηται (Dᶜ K L eth etc. Theophyl.) is simply a formula of quotation. From the combination of Ps 95⁷· ⁸ with Ps 95¹¹ and Gn 2² (vv.³⁻⁷) the practical inference is now drawn (v.⁸ᶠ·). Like Sirach (46¹· ² κραταιὸς ἐν πολέμοις Ἰησοῦς Ναυή . . . ὃς ἐγένετο κατὰ τὸ ὄνομα αὐτοῦ μέγας ἐπὶ σωτηρίᾳ ἐκλεκτῶν αὐτοῦ), Philo (de mutatione nominum, 21, Ἰησοῦς δὲ [ἑρμηνεύεται] σωτηρία κυρίου, ἕξεως ὄνομα τῆς ἀρίστης) had commented on the religious significance of the name Joshua; but our author ignores this, and even uses the name Ἰησοῦς freely, since Ἰησοῦς is never applied by him to Christ before the incarnation (Aquila naturally avoids Ἰησοῦς and prefers Ἰωσονα). The author of Ep. Barnabas plays on the fact that "Joshua" and "Jesus" are the same names: ἐλπίσατε ἐπὶ τὸν ἐν σαρκὶ μέλλοντα φανεροῦσθαι ὑμῖν Ἰησοῦν (6⁹), i.e. not on the "Jesus" who led Israel into the land of rest, but on the true, divine "Joshua." Such, he declares, is the inner

meaning of Is 28¹⁶ (ὃς ἐλπίσει ἐπ' αὐτὸν ζήσεται εἰς τὸν αἰῶνα).
But the author of Πρὸς Ἑβραίους takes his own line, starting from
the transitive use of καταπαύειν (Jos 1¹³ κύριος ὁ θεὸς ὑμῶν κατέ-
παυσεν ὑμᾶς καὶ ἔδωκεν ὑμῖν τὴν γῆν ταύτην, etc.); not that he
reads subtle meanings into the transitive and intransitive usages
of καταπαύειν, like Philo. Nor does he philosophize upon the
relevance of κατάπαυσις to God. Philo, in *De Cherubim* (26),
explains why Moses calls the sabbath (ἑρμηνεύεται δ' ἀνάπαυσις)
the "sabbath of God" in Ex 20¹⁰ etc.; the only thing which
really rests is God—"rest (ἀνάπαυλαν) meaning not inactivity
in good (ἀπραξίαν καλῶν)—for the cause of all things which is
active by nature never ceases doing what is best, but—an energy
devoid of laboriousness, devoid of suffering, and moving with
absolute ease." The movement and changes of creation point
to labour, but "what is free from weakness, even though it
moves all things, will never cease to rest: ὥστε οἰκειοτότατον
μόνῳ θεῷ τὸ ἀναπαύεσθαι." So in *De Sacrif. Abelis et Caini*, 8,
τὸν τοσοῦτον κόσμον ἄνευ πόνων πάλαι μὲν εἰργάζετο, νυνὶ δὲ καὶ
εἰσαεὶ συνέχων οὐδέποτε λήγει [cp. He 1³ φέρων τε τὰ πάντα], θεῷ
γὰρ τὸ ἀκάματον ἁρμοδιώτατον. All such speculations are remote
from our author. He simply assumes (*a*) that God's promise of
κατάπαυσις is spiritual; it was not fulfilled, it was never meant
to be fulfilled, in the peaceful settlement of the Hebrew clans
in Canaan; (*b*) as a corollary of this, he assumes that it is
eschatological.

In v.⁹ ἄρα, as in 12⁸, Lk 11⁴⁸, Ac 11¹⁸, Ro 10¹⁷, is thrown to
the beginning by an unclassical turn ("müsste dem gebildeten
Hellenen hochgradig anstössig erscheinen," Radermacher, 20).
Σαββατισμός, apparently [1] a word coined by the writer, is a Sem-
itic-Greek compound. The use of σαββατισμός for κατάπαυσις is
then (v.¹⁰) justified in language to which the closest parallel is
Apoc 14¹³. "Rest" throughout all this passage—and the writer
never refers to it again—is the blissful existence of God's faithful
in the next world. As a contemporary apocalyptist put it, in
4 Es 8⁵²: "for you paradise is opened, the tree of life planted,
the future age prepared, abundance made ready, a City built, a
Rest appointed" (κατέσταθη?). In ἀπὸ τῶν ἰδίων, as in διὰ τοῦ
ἰδίου αἵματος (13¹²), ἴδιος is slightly emphatic owing to the context;
it is not quite equivalent to the possessive pronoun.

When Maximus of Tyre speaks of life as a long, arduous path to the goal
of bliss and perfection, he describes in semi-mystical language how tired
souls, longing for the land to which this straight and narrow and little-
frequented way leads, at length reach it and "rest from their labour"
(*Dissert.* xxiii.).

---

[1] The only classical instance is uncertain; Bernadakis suspects it in the
text of Plutarch, *de superstit.* 166 A.

The lesson thus drawn from the reading of the OT passages is pressed home (vv.¹¹⁻¹³) with a skilful blend of encouragement and warning.

¹¹ *Let us be eager then to "enter that Rest," in case anyone falls into the same sort of disobedience.* ¹² *For the Logos of God is a living thing, active and more cutting than any sword with double edge, penetrating to the very division of soul and spirit, joints and marrow—scrutinizing the very thoughts and conceptions of the heart.* ¹³ *And no created thing is hidden from him; all things lie open and exposed before the eyes of him with whom we have to reckon (ὁ λόγος).*

In v.¹¹ the position of τις, as, *e.g.*, in Lk 18¹⁸, is due to "the tendency which is to be noted early in Greek as well as in cognate languages, to bring unemphasized (enclitic) pronouns as near to the beginning of the sentence as possible" (Blass, § 473. 1). For πίπτειν ἐν, cp. Epict. iii. 22. 48, πότε ὑμῶν εἶδέν μέ τις . . . ἐν ἐκκλίσει περιπίπτοντα. This Hellenistic equivalent for πίπτειν εἰς goes back to earlier usage, *e.g.* Eurip. *Herc.* 1091, 1092, ἐν κλύδωνι καὶ φρενῶν ταράγματι πέπτωκα δεινῷ. In Hellenistic Greek ὑπόδειγμα came to have the sense of παράδειγμα, and is used here loosely for "kind" or "sort"; take care of falling into disobedience like that of which these πατέρες ὑμῶν yield such a tragic example. The writer, with his fondness for periphrases of this kind, writes ἐν τῷ αὐτῷ ὑποδείγματι τῆς ἀπειθείας, where ἐν τῇ αὐτῇ ἀπειθείᾳ would have served. In passing away from the text about Rest, he drops this last warning reference to the classical example of ἀπείθεια in the far past of the People.

The connexion of thought in vv.¹¹ᶠ· is suggested by what has been already hinted in v.¹, where the writer pled for anxiety, μή ποτε δοκῇ τις ἐξ ὑμῶν ὑστερηκέναι. He repeats ἵνα μὴ . . . τις . . . πέσῃ, and enlarges upon what lies behind the term δοκῇ. Then, after the passage on the relentless scrutiny of the divine Logos, he effects a transition to the direct thought of God (v.¹³), with which the paragraph closes. Σπουδάσωμεν—we have to put heart and soul into our religion, for we are in touch with a God whom nothing escapes; ζῶν γάρ κτλ. (v.¹²). The term ζῶν echoes θεὸς ζῶν in 3¹² (men do not disobey God with impunity), just as καρδίας echoes καρδία πονηρὰ ἀπιστίας. God is swift to mark any departure from his will in human thought—the thought that issues in action.

The personifying of the divine λόγος, in a passage which described God in action, had already been attempted. In Wis 18¹⁵, for example, the plagues of Egypt are described as the effect of God's λόγος coming into play: ὁ παντοδύναμός σου λόγος ἀπ' οὐρανῶν . . . ξίφος ὀξὺ τὴν ἀνυπόκριτον ἐπιταγήν σου φέρων. In Wis 1⁶, again, the φιλάνθρωπον πνεῦμα σοφία, which cannot tolerate blasphemy, reacts against it: ὅτι τῶν νεφρῶν αὐτοῦ (the blasphemer) μάρτυς ὁ θεός, καὶ τῆς καρδίας αὐτοῦ ἐπίσκοπος ἀληθής, so that no muttering of rebellion is unmarked. Here the writer poetically personifies the revelation of God for a moment. Ὁ λόγος τοῦ θεοῦ is God speaking, and speaking in words which are charged with doom and promise (3⁷ᶠ·). The revelation, however, is broader than the scripture ; it includes the revelation of God's purpose in Jesus (1¹ᶠ·). The free application of ὁ λόγος (τοῦ θεοῦ) in primitive Christianity is seen in 1 P 1²³ᶠ·, Ja 1¹⁸ᶠ·, quite apart from the specific application of the term to the person of Christ (Jn 1¹⁻¹⁸). Here it denotes the Christian gospel declared authoritatively by men like the writer, an inspired message which carries on the OT revelation of God's promises and threats, and which is vitally effective. No dead letter, this λόγος ! The rhetorical outburst in vv.¹²ᶠ· is a preacher's equivalent for the common idea that the sense of God's all-seeing scrutiny should deter men from evil-doing, as, *e.g.*, in Plautus (*Captivi*, ii. 2. 63, "est profecto deu', qui quae nos gerimus auditque et uidet"). This had been deepened by ethical writers like Seneca (*Ep.* lxxxiii. 1, "nihil deo clusum est, interest animis nostris et cogitationibus mediis intervenit"), Epictetus (ii. 14. 11, οὐκ ἔστι λαθεῖν αὐτὸν οὐ μόνον ποιοῦντα ἀλλ' οὐδὲ διανοούμενον ἢ ἐνθυμούμενον), and the author of the *Epistle of Aristeas* (132–133 : Moses teaches ὅτι μόνος ὁ θεός ἐστι . . . καὶ οὐθὲν αὐτὸν λανθάνει τῶν ἐπὶ γῆς γινομένων ὑπ' ἀνθρώπων κρυφίως . . . κἂν ἐννοηθῇ τις κακίαν ἐπιτελεῖν, οὐκ ἂν λάθοι, μὴ ὅτι καὶ πράξας, and 210 : the characteristic note of piety is τὸ διαλαμβάνειν ὅτι πάντα διαπαντὸς ὁ θεὸς ἐνεργεῖ καὶ γινώσκει, καὶ οὐθὲν ἂν λάθοι ἄδικον ποιήσας ἢ κακὸν ἐργασάμενος ἄνθρωπος), as well as by apocalyptists like the author of Baruch (83³ : He will assuredly examine the secret thoughts and that which is laid up in the secret chambers of all the members of man). But our author has one particular affinity. Take Philo's interpretation of διεῖλεν αὐτὰ μέσα in Gn 15¹⁰. Scripture means, he explains (*quis rer. div. haeres*, 26) that it was God who divided them, τῷ τομεῖ τῷ συμπάντων ἑαυτοῦ λόγῳ, ὃς εἰς τὴν ὀξυτάτην ἀκονηθεὶς ἀκμὴν διαιρῶν οὐδέποτε λήγει. τὰ γὰρ αἰσθητὰ πάντα ἐπειδὰν μέχρι τῶν ἀτόμων καὶ λεγομένων ἀμερῶν διεξέλθῃ, πάλιν ἀπὸ τούτων τὰ λόγῳ θεωρητὰ εἰς ἀμυθήτους καὶ ἀπεριγράφους μοίρας ἄρχεται διαιρεῖν οὗτος ὁ τομεύς. He returns (in 48) to this analytic function of the Logos in God and man, and in *De mutatione nominum* (18) speaks of ἠκονημένον καὶ ὀξὺν λόγον, μαστεύειν καὶ ἀναζητεῖν ἕκαστα ἱκανόν. Still, the Logos is τομεύς as the principle of differentiation in the universe, rather than as an ethical force ; and when Philo connects the latter with ὁ λόγος, as he does in *quod deter. pot.* 29, *Cherub.* 9, etc., ὁ λόγος is the human faculty of reason. Obviously, our author is using Philonic language rather than Philonic ideas.

Ἐνεργής (for which B, by another blunder, has ἐναργής =

evidens) is not a LXX term, but denotes in Greek vital activity (cp. Schol. on Soph. *Oed. Tyr.* 45, ζώσας ἀντὶ ἐνεργεστέρας). Neither is τομώτερος a LXX term; the comparison of ὁ λόγος to a sword arose through the resemblance between the tongue and a "dagger," though μάχαιρα had by this time come to mean a sword of any size, whether long (ῥομφαία) or short.[1] The comparative is followed (cp. Lk 16⁸) by ὑπέρ, as elsewhere by παρά, and the "cutting" power of ὁ λόγος extends or penetrates to the innermost recesses of human nature—ἄχρι μερισμοῦ ψυχῆς καὶ πνεύματος,[2] ἁρμῶν τε καὶ μυελῶν (the conj. μελῶν = limbs is neat but superfluous, for μυελῶν was in the text known to Clem. Alex. *quis dives*, 41).   D K here (as in 11³²) insert τε before the first καί, but there is no idea of distinguishing the psychical and the physical spheres; ἁρμῶν . . . μυελῶν is merely a metaphorical equivalent for ψυχῆς καὶ πνεύματος. Μερισμός (only in LXX in Jb 11²³, 2 Es 6¹⁸) means here "division," not "distribution" (2⁴); the subtlest relations of human personality, the very border-line between the ψυχή and the πνεῦμα, all this is open to ὁ λόγος. The metaphorical use of μυελῶν in this sense is as old as Euripides, who speaks of μὴ πρὸς ἄκρον μυελὸν ψυχῆς (*Hippolytus*, 255).

According to Philo (*De Cherubim*, 8. 9), the flaming sword of Gn 3²⁴ is a symbol either of the sun, as the swiftest of existences (circling the whole world in a single day), or of reason, ὀξυκινητότατον γὰρ καὶ θέρμον λόγος καὶ μάλιστα ὁ τοῦ αἰτίου. Learn from the fiery sword, o my soul, he adds, to note the presence and power of this divine Reason, ὃς οὐδέποτε λήγει κινούμενος σπουδῇ πάσῃ πρὸς αἵρεσιν μὲν τῶν καλῶν, φυγὴν δὲ τῶν ἐναντίων. But there is a still better parallel to the thought in Lucian's account of the impression made by the address (ὁ λόγος) of a philosopher : οὐ γὰρ ἐξ ἐπιπολῆς οὐδ᾽ ὡς ἔτυχεν ἡμῶν ὁ λόγος καθίκετο, βαθεῖα δὲ καὶ καίριος ἡ πληγὴ ἐγένετο, καὶ μάλα εὐστόχως ἐνεχθεὶς ὁ λόγος αὐτήν, εἰ οἷόν τε εἰπεῖν, διέκοψε τὴν ψυχήν (*Nigr.* 35).   Only, Lucian proceeds to compare the soul of a cultured person to a target at which the words of the wise are aimed. Similarly, in pseudo-Phocylides, 124 : ὅπλον τοι λόγος ἀνδρὶ τομώτερον ἐστι σιδήρου, and Od. Sol. 12⁵ : for the swiftness of the Word is inexpressible, and like its expression is its swiftness and force, and its course knows no limit.

The μερισμοῦ . . . μυελῶν passage is "a mere rhetorical accumulation of terms to describe the whole mental nature of man" (A. B. Davidson); the climax is καρδία, for what underlies human failure is καρδία πονηρὰ ἀπίστιας (3¹²), and the writer's warning all along has been against hardening the heart, *i.e.* obdurate disobedience. Hence the point of καὶ κριτικός κτλ. Κριτικός is another of his terms which are classical, not religious ; it is used by Aristotle (*Eth. Nik.* vi. 10) of ἡ σύνεσις, the intelligence of man being κριτική in the sense that it discerns. If

[1] The description was familiar to readers of the LXX, *e.g.* Pr 5⁴ ἠκονημένον μᾶλλον μαχαίρας διστόμου.

[2] The subtlety of thought led afterwards to the change of πνεύματος into σώματος (2. 38. 257. 547. 1245).

there is any distinction between ἐνθυμήσεων (ἐνθυμήσεως C* D* W vt Lucifer) and ἐννοιῶν, it is between impulses and reflections, but contemporary usage hardly distinguished them; indeed ἔννοια could mean "purpose" as well as "conception." The two words are another alliterative phrase for "thought and conception," ἔννοια, unlike ἐνθύμησις, being a LXX term.

In v.¹³ καὶ οὐκ ἔστιν κτίσις ἀφανής κτλ., κτίσις means anything created (as in Ro 8³⁹), and αὐτοῦ is "God's." The negative side is followed by the positive, πάντα δὲ γυμνὰ καὶ τετραχηλισμένα. The nearest verbal parallel is in En 9⁵ πάντα ἐνώπιόν σου φανερὰ καὶ ἀκάλυπτα, where the context points as here to secret sins. The general idea was familiar; *e.g.* (above, p. 55) "nihil deo clusum est, interest animis nostris et cogitationibus mediis intervenit." Μόνῳ γὰρ ἔξεστι θεῷ, ψυχὴν ἰδεῖν (Philo, *de Abrahamo*, 21). But what the writer had in mind was a passage like that in *de Cherub*. 5, where Philo explains Dt 29²⁹ (τὰ κρυπτὰ κυρίῳ τῷ θεῷ, τὰ δὲ φανερὰ γενέσει γνώριμα) by arguing, γενητὸς δὲ οὐδεὶς ἱκανὸς γνώμης ἀφανοῦς κατιδεῖν ἐνθύμημα, μόνος δὲ ὁ θεός. Hence, he adds, the injunction (Nu 5¹⁸) τὴν ψυχὴν "ἐναντίον τοῦ θεοῦ στῆσαι" with head uncovered; which means, the soul τὸ κεφάλαιον δόγμα γυμνωθεῖσαν καὶ τὴν γνώμην ᾗ κέχρηται ἀπαμφιασθεῖσαν, ἵν' ὄψεσι ταῖς ἀκριβεστάταις ἐπικριθεῖσα τοῦ ἀδεκάστου θεοῦ κτλ., the closing description of God being τῷ μόνῳ γυμνὴν ψυχὴν ἰδεῖν δυναμένῳ. For γυμνά see also M. Aurel. 12² ὁ θεὸς πάντα τὰ ἡγεμονικὰ γυμνὰ τῶν ὑλικῶν ἀγγείων . . . ὁρᾷ. Τετραχηλισμένα must mean something similar, "exposed" or "bared" ("aperta," vg; πεφανερωμένα, Hesych.).

Though τραχηλίζω does not occur in the LXX, the writer was familiar with it in Philo, where it suggests a wrestler "downing" his opponent by seizing his throat. How this metaphorical use of throttling or tormenting could yield the metaphorical passive sense of "exposed," is not easy to see. The Philonic sense of "depressed" or "bent down" would yield here the meaning "abashed," *i.e.* hanging down the head in shame ("conscientia male factorum in ruborem aguntur caputque mittunt," Wettstein). But this is hardly on a level with γυμνά. The most probable clue is to be found in the practice of exposing an offender's face by pushing his head back, as if the word were an equivalent for the Latin "resupinata" in the sense of "manifesta." The bending back of the neck produced this exposure. Thus when Vitellius was dragged along the Via Sacra to be murdered, it was "reducto coma capite, ceu noxii solent, atque etiam mento mucrone gladii subrecto, ut visendam praeberet faciem" (Suet. *Vit. Vitell.* 17).

In the last five words, πρὸς ὃν ἡμῖν ὁ λόγος, which are impressive by their bare simplicity, there is a slight play on the term λόγος here and in v.¹², although in view of the flexible use of the term, *e.g.* in 5¹¹ and 13¹⁷, it might be even doubtful if the writer intended more than a verbal assonance. The general sense of the phrase is best conveyed by "with whom we have to reckon." (*a*) This rendering, "to whom we have to account (or, to render our account)," was adopted without question by the Greek fathers from

Chrysostom (αὐτῷ μέλλομεν δοῦναι εὐθύνας τῶν πεπραγμένων) onwards, and the papyri support the origin of the phrase as a com-
mercial metaphor; e.g. OP. 1188⁵ (A.D. 13) ὡς πρὸς σὲ τοῦ περὶ
τῶν ἀγνοη[θέντων] ζη[τήματος] ἐσο[μένου] (sc. λόγου), and Hibeh
Papyri, 53⁴ (246 B.C.) πειρῶ οὖν ἀσφολῶς ὡς πρὸς σὲ τοῦ λόγου
ἐσομένου. (b) The alternative rendering, "with whom we have to
do," has equal support in Gk. usage; e.g. in the LXX phrase λόγος
μοι πρός σε (1 K 2¹⁴, 2 K 9⁵) and in Jg 17⁷ (μακράν εἰσιν Σιδωνίων,
καὶ λόγον οὐκ ἔχουσιν πρὸς ἄνθρωπον). The former idea is predominant, however, as the context suggests (cp. Ignat. ad Magn. 3,
τὸ δὲ τοιοῦτον οὐ πρὸς σάρκα ὁ λόγος, ἀλλὰ πρὸς θεὸν τὸν τὰ κρύφια
εἰδότα), and includes the latter. It is plainly the view of the
early anti-Marcionite treatise, which has been preserved among
the works of Ephraem Syrus (cp. Preuschen, Zeitschrift für die
neutest. Wissenschaft, 1911, pp. 243–269), where the passage is
quoted from a text like this: ὡς καὶ ὁ Παῦλος λέγει, ζῶν ὁ λόγος
τοῦ θεοῦ καὶ τομώτερος ὑπὲρ πασὰν μάχαιραν δίστομον, διϊκνούμενον
μέχρι μερισμοῦ πνεύματος καὶ σαρκός, μέχρι ἁρμῶν τε καὶ μυελῶν,
καὶ κριτικός ἐστιν ἐνθυμήσεων καὶ ἐννοιῶν καρδίας· καὶ οὐκ ἔστιν
κτίσις ἀφανὴς ἐνώπιον αὐτοῦ, ἀλλὰ πάντα ἐμφανῆ ἐνώπιον αὐτοῦ, ὅτι
γυμνοὶ καὶ τετραχηλισμένοι ἐσμὲν ἐν τοῖς ὀφθαλμοῖς αὐτοῦ ἕκαστος
ἡμῶν λόγον αὐτῷ ἀποδιδόναι. The rendering, "who is our subject,
of whom we are speaking" (πρός = with reference to, and ἡμῖν ὁ
λόγος as in 5¹¹), is impossibly flat.

At this point the writer effects a transition to the main theme,
which is to occupy him till 10¹⁸, i.e. Christ as ἀρχιερεύς. He begins,
however, by a practical appeal (vv.¹⁴⁻¹⁶) which catches up the
ideas of 2¹⁷·¹⁸ 3¹.

¹⁴As we have a great highpriest, then, who has passed through the heavens,
Jesus the Son of God, let us hold fast to our confession; ¹⁵ for ours is no high
priest who is incapable (μὴ δυν. as in 9⁹) of sympathizing with our weaknesses,
but one who has been tempted in every respect like ourselves (sc. πρὸς ἡμᾶς), yet
without sinning. ¹⁶ So let us approach the throne of grace with confidence
(μετὰ παρρησίας, 3⁶), that we may receive mercy and find grace to help us in
the hour of need.

Μέγας is a favourite adjective for ἀρχιερεύς in Philo,[1] but when
the writer adds, ἔχοντες οὖν ἀρχιερέα μέγαν διεληλυθότα τοὺς
οὐρανούς, he is developing a thought of his own. The greatness
of Jesus as ἀρχιερεύς consists in his access to God not through
any material veil, but through the upper heavens; he has pene-
trated to the very throne of God, in virtue of his perfect self-
sacrifice. This idea is not elaborated till later (cp. 6¹⁹ᶠ· 9²⁴ᶠ·), in
the sacerdotal sense. But it has been already mentioned in 2⁹·¹⁰,
where Jesus the Son of God saves men by his entrance into the
full divine glory. Κρατῶμεν here as in 6¹⁸ with the genitive

[1] ὁ μὲν δὴ μέγας ἀρχιερεύς (de Somn. i. 38), even of the Logos.

(ὁμολογιάς, see 3[1]); in Paul it takes the accusative. The writer now (v.[15]) reiterates the truth of 2[11f.]; the exalted Jesus is well able to sympathize with weak men on earth, since he has shared their experience of temptation. It is put negatively, then positively. Συμπαθῆσαι is used of Jesus [1] as in *Acta Pauli et Theclae*, 17 (ὃς μόνος συνεπάθησεν πλανωμένῳ κόσμῳ); see below, on 10[34]. Origen (*in Matt.* xiii. 2) quotes a saying of Jesus: διὰ τοὺς ἀσθενοῦντας ἠσθένουν καὶ διὰ τοὺς πεινῶντας ἐπείνων καὶ διὰ τοὺς διψῶντας ἐδίψων, the first part of which may go back to Mt 8[17] (αὐτὸς τὰς ἀσθενείας ἔλαβεν); cp. also Mt 25[35f.]. Philo uses the term even of the Mosaic law (*de spec. leg.* ii. 13, τῷ δὲ ἀπόρως ἔχοντι συνεπάθησε), but here it is more than "to be considerate." The aid afforded by Jesus as ἀρχιερεύς is far more than official; it is inspired by fellow-feeling ταῖς ἀσθενείαις ἡμῶν. "Verius sentiunt qui simul cum externis aerumnis comprehendunt animi affectus, quales sunt metus, tristitia, horror mortis, et similes" (Calvin). These ἀσθένειαι are the sources of temptation. Ἡ σὰρξ ἀσθενής, as Jesus had said to his disciples, warning them against temptation. Jesus was tempted κατὰ πάντα (2[17. 18]) καθ' ὁμοιότητα (a psychological Stoic term; the phrase occurs in *OP.* ix. 1202[24] and *BGU.* 1028[15], in second-century inscriptions) χωρὶς ἁμαρτίας, without yielding to sin. Which is a real ground for encouragement, for the best help is that afforded by those who have stood where we slip and faced the onset of temptation without yielding to it. The special reference is to temptations leading to apostasy or disobedience to the will of God. It is true that χωρὶς ἁμαρτίας does exclude some temptations. Strictly speaking, κατὰ πάντα is modified by this restriction, since a number of our worst temptations arise out of sin previously committed. But this is not in the writer's mind at all. He is too eager, to enter into any psychological analysis.

Philo deduces from Lv 4[3] (μόνον οὐκ ἄντικρυς ἀναδιδάσκων, ὅτι ὁ πρὸς ἀλήθειαν ἀρχιερεὺς καὶ μὴ ψευδώνυμος ἀμέτοχος ἁμαρτημάτων ἐστίν) that the ideal highpriest is practically sinless (*de Victimis*, 10); but this is a thought with which he wistfully toys, and the idea of the Logos as unstained by contact with the material universe is very different from this conception of Jesus as actually tempted and scatheless. Nor would the transference of the idea of messiah as sinless account for our writer's view. To him and his readers Jesus is sinless, not in virtue of a divine prerogative, but as the result of a real human experience which proved successful in the field of temptation.

Hence (v.[16]) προσερχώμεθα οὖν μετὰ παρρησίας. Philo (*quis rer. div. haeres*, 2) makes παρρησία the reward of a good conscience, which enables a loyal servant of God to approach him frankly.

---

[1] Of God in 4 Mac 5[25] κατὰ φύσιν ἡμῖν συμπαθεῖ νομοθετῶν ὁ τοῦ κτίστης, but in the weaker sense of consideration. It is curious that 4 Mac., like Hebrews, uses the word twice, once of God and once of men (cp. 4 Mac 13[23] οὕτως δὴ τοίνυν καθεστηκυίας τῆς φιλαδελφίας συμπαθούσης).

But here (cp. *ERE*. ii. 786) παρρησία is not freedom of utterance so much as resolute confidence (cp. on 3⁶). Our writer certainly includes prayer in this conception of approaching God, but it is prayer as the outcome of faith and hope. Seneca bids Lucilius pray boldly to God, if his prayers are for soundness of soul and body, not for any selfish and material end: "audacter deum roga; nihil illum de alieno rogaturus es" (*Ep*. x. 4). But even this is not the meaning of παρρησία here. The Roman argues that a man can only pray aloud and confidently if his desires are such as he is not ashamed to have others hear, whereas the majority of people "whisper basest of prayers to God." Our author does not mean "palam" by παρρησία.

Our approach (προσερχώμεθα: the verb in the sense of applying to a court or authority, *e.g.* in *OP*. 1119⁸ προσήλθομεν τῇ κρατίστῃ βουλῇ, *BGU*. 1022) is τῷ θρόνῳ τῆς χάριτος, for grace is now enthroned (see 2⁹ᶠ·). For the phrase see Is 16⁵ διορθωθή-σεται μετ' ἐλέους θρόνος. Our author (cp. Introd. p. xlvii), like those who shared the faith of apocalyptic as well as of rabbinic piety, regarded heaven as God's royal presence and also as the σκηνή where he was worshipped, an idea which dated from Is 6¹ᶠ· and Ps 29 (cp. Mechilta on Ex 15¹⁷), though he only alludes incidentally (12²²) to the worship of God by the host of angels in the upper sanctuary. He is far from the pathetic cry of Azariah (Dn 3³⁸): ὡκ ἔστιν ἐν τῷ καιρῷ τούτῳ . . . οὐδὲ τόπος τοῦ καρπῶσαι ἐνώπιόν σου καὶ εὑρεῖν ἔλεος. He rather shares Philo's feeling (*de Exsecrat*. 9) that οἱ ἀνασωζόμενοι can rely upon the compassionate character of God (ἑνὶ μὲν ἐπιεικείᾳ καὶ χρηστότητι τοῦ παρακαλουμένου συγγνώμην πρὸ τιμωρίας ἀεὶ τιθέντος), though he regards this mercy as conditioned by the sacrifice of Jesus. The twofold object of the approach is (*a*) λαμβάνειν ἔλεος, which is used for the passive of ἐλεῶ (which is rare), and (*b*) χάριν εὑρίσκειν κτλ., an echo of the LXX phrase (*e.g.* Gn 6⁸) εὑρίσκειν χάριν ἐναντίον κυρίου (τοῦ θεοῦ). In the writer's text (A) of the LXX, Prov 8¹⁷ ran οἱ δὲ ἐμὲ ζητοῦντες εὑρήσουσι χάριν.¹ Εἰς εὔκαιρον βοήθειαν recalls τοῖς πειραζομένοις βοηθῆσαι in 2¹⁸; it signifies "for assistance in the hour of need." Εὔκαιρος means literally "seasonable," as in Ps 104²⁷ (δοῦναι τὴν τροφὴν αὐτοῖς εὔκαιρον), "fitting" or "opportune" (*Ep. Aristeas*, 203, 236). The "sympathy" of Jesus is shown by practical aid to the tempted, which is suitable to their situation, suitable above all because it is timely (εὔκαιρον being almost equivalent to ἐν καιρῷ

¹ Aristotle argues that χάρις or benevolence must be spontaneous and disinterested; also, that its value is enhanced by necessitous circumstances (ἔστω δὴ χάρις, καθ' ἣν ὁ ἔχων λέγεται χάριν ὑπουργεῖν δεομένῳ μὴ ἀντί τινος, μηδ' ἵνα τι αὐτῷ τῷ ὑπουργοῦντι ἀλλ' ἵν' ἐκείνῳ τι· μεγάλη δ' ἂν ᾖ σφόδρα δεομένῳ, ἢ μεγάλων καὶ χαλεπῶν, ἢ ἐν καιροῖς τοιουτοῖς, ἢ μόνος ἢ πρῶτος ἢ μάλιστα, *Rhet*. ii. 7. 2).

χρείας, Sir 8⁹). Philo (*de sacrificantibus*, 10) shows how God, for all his greatness, cherishes compassion (ἔλεον καὶ οἶκτον λαμβάνει τῶν ἐν ἐνδείαις ἀπορωτάτων) for needy folk, especially for poor proselytes, who, in their devotion to him, are rewarded by his help (καρπὸν εὑράμενοι τῆς ἐπὶ τὸν θεὸν καταφυγῆς τὴν ἀπ᾽ αὐτοῦ βοήθειαν). But the best illustration of the phrase is in Aristides, Εἰς τὸν Σάραπιν 50 : σὲ γὰρ δὴ πᾶς τις ἐν παντὶ καιρῷ βοηθὸν καλεῖ, Σάραπι.

How widely even good cursives may be found supporting a wrong reading is shown by the evidence for προσερχόμεθα : 6. 38. 88. 104. 177. 206*. 241. 255. 263. 337. 378. 383. 440. 462. 467. 487. 489. 623. 635. 639. 642. 915. 919. 920. 927. 1149. 1245. 1288. 1518. 1836. 1852. 1872. 1891. 2004. For ἔλεος (the Hellenistic neuter, cp. Cronert's *Memoria Graeca Herculanensis*, 176¹), the Attic ἔλεον (ἔλεος, masc.) is substituted by L and a few minuscules (Chrys. Theodoret). B om. εὕρωμεν.

He now (5¹⁻¹⁰) for the first time begins to explain the qualifications of the true ἀρχιερεύς.

(*a*) First, he must be humane as well as human :
¹ *Every highpriest who is selected from men and appointed to act on behalf of men in things divine, offering gifts and sacrifices for sin,* ² *can deal gently with those who err through ignorance, since he himself is beset with weakness—* ³ *which obliges him to present offerings for his own sins as well as for those of the People.*

(*b*) Second, he must not be self-appointed.
⁴ *Also, it is an office which no one elects to take for himself ; he is called to it by God, just as Aaron was.*

The writer now proceeds to apply these two conditions to Jesus, but he takes them in reverse order, beginning with (*b*).

⁵ *Similarly Christ was not raised to the glory of the priesthood by himself, but by Him who declared to him,*

        " *Thou art my son,*
        to-day have I become thy father."
⁶ *Just as elsewhere* (ἐν ἑτέρῳ, sc. τόπῳ) *he says,*
    " *Thou art a priest for ever, with the rank of Melchizedek.*"

He then goes back to (*a*) :
⁷ *In the days of his flesh, with bitter cries and tears, he offered prayers and supplications to Him who was able to save him from death ; and he was heard, because of his godly fear.* ⁸ *Thus, Son though he was, he learned by* (ἀφ᾽ ὧν = ἀπὸ τούτων ἅ) *all he suffered how to obey,* ⁹ *and by being thus perfected he became the source of eternal salvation for all who obey him,* ¹⁰ *being designated by God highpriest " with the rank of Melchizedek.*"

Πᾶς γὰρ ἀρχιερεύς (dealing only with Hebrew highpriests, and only with what is said of them in the LXX) ἐξ ἀνθρώπων λαμβανόμενος (Nu 8⁶ λάβε τοὺς Λευείτας ἐκ μέσου υἱῶν Ἰσραήλ) καθίσταται—passive, in the light of 7²⁸ (ὁ νόμος γὰρ ἀνθρώπους καθίστησιν ἀρχιερεῖς ἔχοντας ἀσθένειαν) and of the Philonic usage (e.g. *de vit. Mosis*, ii. 11, τῷ μέλλοντι ἀρχιερεῖ καθίστασθαι). The middle may indeed be used transitively, as, *e.g.*, in Eurip. *Supplic.* 522 (πόλεμον δὲ τοῦτον οὐκ ἐγὼ καθίσταμαι), and is so taken here by some (*e.g.* Calvin, Kypke). But τὰ πρὸς τὸν θεόν is an adverbial accusative as in 2¹⁷, not the object of καθίσταται in an active sense. In δωρά τε καὶ θυσίας, here as in 8³ and 9⁹, the

writer goes back to the LXX (A) rendering of 1 K 8⁶⁴ (καὶ τὸ
δῶρον καὶ τὰς θυσίας). The phrase recurs in *Ep. Aristeas*, 234 (οὐ
δώροις οὐδὲ θυσίαις), and is a generic term for sacrifices or offerings, without any distinction. The early omission of τε (B Dᵇ
K Lat boh pesh) was due to the idea that θυσίας should be
closely connected with ἁμαρτιῶν ("ut offerat dona, et sacrificia pro
peccatis," vg). Instead of writing εἰς τὸ προσφέρειν, our author
departs from his favourite construction of εἰς with the infinitive
and writes ἵνα προσφέρῃ, in order to introduce μετριοπαθεῖν
δυνάμενος. This, although a participial clause, contains the leading idea of the sentence. The ἀρχιερεύς is able to deal gently
with the erring People whom he represents, since he shares
their ἀσθένεια, their common infirmity or liability to temptation.

Μετριοπαθεῖν in v.² is a term coined by ethical philosophy.
It is used by Philo to describe the mean between extravagant
grief and stoic apathy, in the case of Abraham's sorrow for the
death of his wife (τὸ δὲ μέσον πρὸ τῶν ἄκρων ἑλόμενον μετριοπαθεῖν,
De Abrah. 44) ; so Plutarch (*Consol. ad Apoll.* 22) speaks of τῆς
κατὰ φύσιν ἐν τοιούτοις μετριοπαθείας. But here it denotes
gentleness and forbearance, the moderation of anger in a person
who is provoked and indignant—as in Plut. *de Cohib. ira*, 10,
ἀναστῆσαι δὲ καὶ σῶσαι, καὶ φείσασθαι καὶ καρτερῆσαι, πραότητός
ἐστι καὶ συγγνώμης καὶ μετριοπαθείας. Josephus (*Ant.* xii. 3. 2)
praises this quality in Vespasian and Titus (μετριοπαθησάντων),
who acted magnanimously and generously towards the unruly
Jews ; Dionysius Halicarnassus accuses Marcius (*Ant.* 8. 529)
of lacking τὸ εὐδιάλλακτον καὶ μετριοπαθές, ὁπότε δι᾽ ὀργῆς τῷ
γένοιτο. And so on. The term is allied to πραότης. The sins
of others are apt to irritate us, either because they are repeated
or because they are flagrant ; they excite emotions of disgust,
impatience, and exasperation, and tempt us to be hard and harsh
(Gal 6¹). The thought of excess here is excessive severity rather
than excessive leniency. The objects of this μετριοπαθεῖν are
τοῖς ἀγνοοῦσιν καὶ πλανωμένοις, *i.e.*, people who sin through yielding to the weaknesses of human nature. For such offenders
alone the *piacula* of atonement-day (which the writer has in mind)
availed. Those who sinned ἑκουσίως (10²⁶), not ἀκουσίως, were
without the pale ; for such presumptuous sins, which our writer
regards specially under the category of deliberate apostasy (3¹²
10²⁶), there is no pardon possible. The phrase here is practically a hendiadys, for τοῖς ἐξ ἀγνοίας πλανωμένοις : the People err
through their ἄγνοια. Thus ἀγνοεῖν becomes an equivalent for
ἁμαρτάνειν (Sir 23² etc.), just as the noun ἀγνόημα comes to
imply sin (cp. 9⁷ and Jth 5²⁰ εἰ μέν ἐστιν ἀγνόημα ἐν τῷ λαῷ τούτῳ
καὶ ἁμαρτάνουσι εἰς τὸν θεὸν αὐτῶν, with Tebt. Pap. 124⁴ (118 B.C.)
and 5³—a proclamation by king Euergetes and queen Cleopatra

declaring "an amnesty to all their subjects for all errors, crimes," etc., except wilful murder and sacrilege). In the *Martyr. Pauli*, 4, the apostle addresses his pagan audience as ἄνδρες οἱ ὄντες ἐν τῇ ἀγνωσίᾳ καὶ τῇ πλάνῃ ταύτῃ.

(*a*) Strictly speaking, only such sins could be pardoned (Lv 4² 5²¹· ²², Nu 15²²⁻³¹, Dt 17¹²) as were unintentional. Wilful sins were not covered by the ordinary ritual of sacrifice (10²⁶, cp. Nu 12¹¹).

(*b*) The term περίκειμαι only occurs in the LXX in Ep. Jer. 23. 57 and in 4 Mac 12³ (τὰ δεσμὰ περικείμενον), and in both places in its literal sense (Symm. Is 61¹⁰), as in Ac 28²⁰. But Seneca says of the body, " hoc quoque natura ut quemdam vestem animo circumdedit " (*Epist.* 92), and the metaphorical sense is as old as Theocritus (23¹³· ¹⁴ φεῦγε δ᾽ ἀπὸ χρὼς ὕβριν τὰς ὀργᾶς περικείμενος).

The ἀρχιερεύς, therefore (v.³), requires to offer sacrifice for his own sins as well as for those of the People, καθὼς περὶ τοῦ λαοῦ οὕτω καὶ περὶ ἑαυτοῦ. This twofold sacrifice is recognized by Philo (*de vit. Mosis*, ii. 1), who notes that the holder of the ἱερωσύνη must ἐπὶ τελείοις ἱεροῖς beseech God for blessing αὐτῷ τε καὶ τῆς ἀρχομένοις. The regulations for atonement-day (Lv 16⁶⁻¹⁷) provided that the ἀρχιερεύς sacrificed for himself and his household as well as for the People (καὶ προσάξει ᾽Ααρὼν τὸν μόσχον τὸν περὶ τῆς ἁμαρτίας αὐτοῦ καὶ ἐξιλάσεται περὶ αὐτοῦ καὶ τοῦ οἴκου αὐτοῦ . . . καὶ περὶ πάσης συναγωγῆς υἱῶν ᾽Ισραήλ). But our author now turns from the idea of the solidarity between priest and People to the idea of the priest's commission from God. Τὴν τιμήν (in v.⁴) means position or office, as often, *e.g.* ἐπίτροπος λαμβάνει ταύτην τὴν τιμήν (*i.e.* of supervising the household slaves), Arist. *Pol.* i. 7, τιμὰς γὰρ λέγομεν εἶναι τὰς ἀρχάς, *ib.* iii. 10, περὶ τῶν ἀρχιερέων πῶς τ᾽ ἤρξαντο καὶ τίσιν ἔξεστι τῆς τιμῆς ταύτης μεταλαμβάνειν, Joseph. *Ant.* xx. 10. 1. ᾽Αλλὰ (*sc.* λαμβάνει) καλούμενος, but takes it when (or, as) he is called. The terseness of the phrase led to the alteration (Cᶜ L) of ἀλλά into ἀλλ᾽ ὁ (as in v.⁵). Καθώσπερ καὶ ᾽Ααρών. In Josephus (*Ant.* iii. 8. 1), Moses tells the Israelites, νῦν δ᾽ αὐτὸς ὁ θεὸς ᾽Ααρῶνα τῆς τιμῆς ταύτης ἄξιον ἔκρινε καὶ τοῦτον ᾔρηται ἱερέα.

περὶ (before ἁμαρτιῶν in v.³) has been changed to ὕπερ in Cᵉ Dᶜ K L etc. (conforming to 5¹). There is no difference in meaning (cp. περί, Mt 26²⁸ = ὕπερ, Mk. and Lk.), for περί (see 10⁶· ⁸· ¹⁸· ²⁶ 13¹¹) has taken over the sense of ὕπερ. For καθώσπερ (א* A B D* 33) in v.⁴, אᶜ Dᶜ K L P Ψ 6. 1288. 1739 read the more obvious καθάπερ (C ? syrʰᵏˡ Chrys. Cyr. Alex. Procopius : καθώς).

In v.⁵ οὐχ ἑαυτὸν ἐδόξασεν, while the term δόξα was specially applicable to the highpriestly office (cf. 2 Mac 14⁷ ὅθεν ἀφελόμενος τὴν προγονικὴν δόξαν, λέγω δὴ τὴν ἀρχιερωσύνην), the phrase is quite general, as in the parallel Jn 8⁵⁴. The following γενηθῆναι is an epexegetic infinitive, which recurs in the Lucan writings (Lk 1⁵⁴· ⁷², Ac 15¹⁰) and in the earlier Psalter of Solo-

mon (2²⁸·⁴⁰ etc.). After ἀλλ' we must supply some words like
αὐτὸν ἐδόξασεν.

The argument runs thus : We have a great ἀρχιερεύς, Jesus
the Son of God (4¹⁴), and it is as he is Son that he carries out
the vocation of ἀρχιερεύς. There is something vital, for the
writer's mind, in the connexion of ἀρχιερεύς and Υἱός. Hence he
quotes (v.⁵) his favourite text from Ps 2⁷ before the more apposite
one (in v.⁶) from Ps 110⁴, implying that the position of divine
Son carried with it, in some sense, the rôle of ἀρχιερεύς. This
had been already suggested in 1²·³ where the activities of the
Son include the purification of men from their sins. Here the
second quotation only mentions ἱερεύς, it is true ; but the writer
drew no sharp distinction between ἱερεύς and ἀρχιερεύς. In
κατὰ τὴν τάξιν Μελχισεδέκ, τάξις for the writer, as 7¹⁵ proves
(κατὰ τὴν ὁμοιότητα Μελχισεδέκ), has a general meaning ;[1] Jesus
has the rank of a Melchizedek, he is a priest of the Melchizedek
sort or order, though in the strict sense of the term there was no
τάξις or succession of Melchizedek priests.

Τάξις in the papyri is often a list or register ; in *OP.* 1266²⁴ (A.D. 98)
ἐν τάξει means "in the class" (of people). It had acquired a sacerdotal
nuance, *e.g.* Michel 735¹²⁵ᶠ· (the regulations of Antiochus I.), ὅστις τε ἂν
ὑστέρωι χρόνωι τάξιν λάβῃ ταύτην, and occasionally denoted a post or office
(*e.g.* Tebt. P 297⁸, A.D. 123).

Ὅς κτλ. Some editors (*e.g.* A. B. Davidson, Lünemann,
Peake, Hollmann) take vv.⁷⁻¹⁰ as a further proof of (*b*). But
the writer is here casting back to (*a*), not hinting that the
trying experiences of Jesus on earth proved that his vocation was
not self-sought, but using these to illustrate the thoroughness
with which he had identified himself with men. He does this,
although the parallel naturally broke down at one point. Indeed
his conception of Christ was too large for the categories he had
been employing, and this accounts for the tone and language of
the passage. (*a*) Jesus being χωρὶς ἁμαρτίας did not require to
offer any sacrifices on his own behalf ; and (*b*) the case of
Melchizedek offered no suggestion of suffering as a vital element
in the vocation of an ἀρχιερεύς. As for the former point, while
the writer uses προσενέγκας in speaking of the prayers of Jesus,
this is at most a subconscious echo of προσφέρειν in vv.¹⁻³ ; there
is no equivalent in Jesus to the sacrifice offered by the OT
ἀρχιερεύς, περὶ ἑαυτοῦ . . . περὶ ἁμαρτιῶν. The writer starts with
his parallel, for ἐν ταῖς ἡμέραις τῆς σαρκὸς αὐτοῦ corresponds to
περίκειται ἀσθένειαν (v.²) ; but instead of developing the idea of
sympathy in an official (μετριοπαθεῖν δυνάμενος κτλ.), he passes to
the deeper idea that Jesus qualified himself by a moral discipline

[1] As in 2 Mac 9¹⁸ ἐπιστολὴν ἔχουσαν ἱκετηρίας τάξιν, *Ep. Arist.* 69,
κρηπῖδος ἔχουσα τάξιν.

to be ἀρχιερεύς in a pre-eminent sense.　He mentions the prayers and tears of Jesus here, as the faith of Jesus in 2[12f.], for the express purpose of showing how truly he shared the lot of man on earth, using δεήσεις τε καὶ ἱκετηρίας, a phrase which the writer may have found in his text (A) of Jb 40[22] [(27)] δεήσεις καὶ ἱκετηρίας, but which was classical (*e.g.* Isokrates, *de Pace*, 46, πολλὰς ἱκετηρίας καὶ δεήσεις ποιούμενοι).　Ἱκετηρία had become an equivalent for ἱκεσία, which is actually the reading here in 1 (δεήσεις τε καὶ ἱκεισίας).　The phrase recurs in a Ptolemaic papyrus (Brunet de Presle et E. Egger's *Papyrus Grecs du Musée du Louvre*, 27[22]), χαίρειν σε ἀξιῶ μετὰ δεήσεως καὶ ἱκετείας, though in a weakened sense.　The addition of μετὰ κραυγῆς (here a cry of anguish) ἰσχυρᾶς καὶ δακρύων may be a touch of pathos, due to his own imagination,[1] or suggested by the phraseology of the 22nd psalm, which was a messianic prediction for him (cp. above, 2[12]) as for the early church; the words of v.[3] in that psalm would hardly suit (κεκράξομαι ἡμέρας πρὸς σὲ καὶ οὐκ εἰσακούσῃ), but phrases like that of v.[6] (πρὸς σὲ ἐκέκραξαν καὶ ἐσώθησαν) and v.[25] (ἐν τῷ κεκραγέναι με πρὸς αὐτὸν ἐπήκουσέν μου) might have been in his mind.　Tears were added before long to the Lucan account of the passion, at 22[44] (Epiph. *Ancor.* 31, ἀλλὰ "καὶ ἔκλαυσεν" κεῖται ἐν τῷ κατὰ Λουκᾶν εὐαγγελίῳ ἐν τοῖς ἀδιορθώτοις ἀντιγράφοις).　It is one of the passages which prove how deeply the writer was impressed by the historical Jesus; the intense faith and courage and pitifulness of Jesus must have deeply moved his mind.　He seeks to bring out the full significance of this for the saving work of Jesus as Son.　His methods of proof may be remote and artificial, to our taste, but the religious interest which prompted them is fundamental.　No theoretical reflection on the qualification of priests or upon the dogma of messiah's sinlessness could have produced such passages as this.

Later Rabbinic piety laid stress on tears, *e.g.* in Sohar Exod. fol. 5. 19, " Rabbi Jehuda said, all things of this world depend on penitence and prayers, which men offer to God (Blessed be He !), especially if one sheds tears along with his prayers "; and in Synopsis Sohar, p. 33, n. 2, " There are three kinds of prayers, entreaty, crying, and tears.　Entreaty is offered in a quiet voice, crying with a raised voice, but tears are higher than all."

In ἀπὸ τῆς εὐλαβείας, the sense of εὐλαβεία in 12[28] and of εὐλαβεῖσθαι in 11[7] shows that ἀπό here means " on account of " (as is common in Hellenistic Greek), and that ἀπὸ τῆς εὐλαβείας must be taken, as the Greek fathers took it, " on account of his reverent fear of God," *pro sua reverentia* (vg), " because he had

---

[1] Like that of Hos 12[4], where tears are added to the primitive story (Gn 32[26]) of Jacob's prayer (ἐνίσχυσεν μετὰ ἀγγέλου καὶ ἠδυνάσθη· ἔκλαυσαν καὶ ἐδεήθησάν μου).　In 2 Mac 11[6] the Maccabean army μετὰ ὀδυρμῶν καὶ δακρύων ἱκέτευον τὸν κύριον.

5

God in reverence" (Tyndale; "in honour," Coverdale). The
writer is thinking of the moving tradition about Jesus in Gethsemane, which is now preserved in the synoptic gospels, where
Jesus entreats God to be spared death: Ἀββᾶ ὁ πατήρ, πάντα
δυνατά σοι· παρένεγκε τὸ ποτήριον ἀπ' ἐμοῦ τοῦτο (Mk 14³⁶). This
repeated supplication corresponds to the "bitter tears and cries."
Then Jesus adds, ἀλλ' οὐ τί ἐγὼ θέλω, ἀλλὰ τί σύ. This is his
εὐλάβεια, the godly fear which leaves everything to the will of
God. Such is the discipline which issues in ὑπακοή. Compare
Ps. Sol 6⁸ καὶ κύριος εἰσήκουσε προσευχὴν παντὸς ἐν φόβῳ θεοῦ.

(a) The alternative sense of "fear" appears as early as the Old Latin
version (d=exauditus a metu). This meaning of εὐλαβεία (Beza: "liberatus
ex metu") occurs in Joseph. *Ant.* xi. 6. 9, εὐλαβείας αὐτὴν (Esther) ἀπολύων.
Indeed εὐλαβεία (cp. Anz, 359) and its verb εὐλαβεῖσθαι are common in this
sense; cp. *e.g.* 2 Mac 8¹⁶ μὴ καταπλαγῆναι τοῖς δεσμίοις μηδὲ εὐλαβεῖσθαι
τὴν . . . πολυπληθείαν: Sir 41³ μὴ εὐλαβοῦ κρῖμα θανάτου: Wis 17⁸ οὗτοι
καταγέλαστον εὐλάβειαν ἐνόσουν. But here the deeper, religious sense is more
relevant to the context. "In any case the answer consisted . . . in courage
given to face death. . . . The point to be emphasized is, not so much that
the prayer of Jesus was heard, as that it *needed* to be heard" (A. B. Bruce,
p. 186).

(b) Some (*e.g.* Linden in *Studien und Kritiken*, 1860, 753 f., and Blass,
§ 211) take ἀπὸ τῆς εὐλαβείας with what follows; this was the interpretation of
the Peshitto ("and, although he was a son, he learned obedience from fear
and the sufferings which he bore"). But the separation of ἀπὸ τῆς εὐλαβείας
from ἀφ' ὧν and the necessity of introducing a καί before the latter phrase
point to the artificiality of this construction.

In v.⁸ καίπερ ὢν υἱός (καίπερ being used with a participle as
in 7⁵ 12¹⁷) means, "Son though he was," not "son though he
was." The writer knows that painful discipline is to be expected
by all who are sons of God the Father; he points out, in 12⁵ᶠ·,
that every son, because he is a son, has to suffer. Here the
remarkable thing is that Jesus had to suffer, not because but
although he was υἱός, which shows that Jesus is Son in a unique
sense; as applied to Jesus υἱός means something special. As
divine υἱός in the sense of 1¹ᶠ·, it might have been expected that
he would be exempt from such a discipline. Ὅς . . . ἔμαθεν
. . . ὑπακοήν is the main thread of the sentence, but καίπερ ὢν
υἱός attaches itself to ἔμαθεν κτλ. rather than to the preceding
participles προσενέγκας and εἰσακουσθείς (Chrys. Theophyl.).
With a daring stroke the author adds, ἔμαθεν ἀφ' ὧν ἔπαθε τὴν
ὑπακοήν. The paronomasia goes back to a common Greek
phrase which is as old as Aeschylus (*Agam.* 177 f.), who describes Zeus as τὸν πάθει μάθος θέντα κυρίως ἔχειν, and tells how
(W. Headlam)—

"The heart in time of sleep renews
    Aching remembrance of her bruise,
And chastening wisdom enters wills that most refuse"—

which, the poet adds, is a sort of χάρις βίαιος from the gods.
This moral doctrine, that πάθος brings μάθος, is echoed by
Pindar (*Isthm.* i. 40, ὁ πονήσαις δὲ νόῳ καὶ προμάθειαν φέρει) and
other writers, notably by Philo (*de vit. Mos.* iii. 38, τούτους οὐ
λόγος ἀλλ᾽ ἔργα παιδεύει· παθόντες εἴσονται τὸ ἐμὸν ἀψευδές, ἐπεὶ
μαθόντες οὐκ ἔγνωσαν: *de spec. leg.* iii. 6, ἵν᾽ ἐκ τοῦ παθεῖν μάθῃ
κτλ.: *de somn.* ii. 15, ὁ παθὼν ἀκριβῶς ἔμαθεν, ὅτι τοῦ θεοῦ (Gn
50¹⁹) ἐστιν). But in the Greek authors and in Philo it is almost
invariably applied to "the thoughtless or stupid, and to open and
deliberate offenders" (Abbott, *Diat.* 3208a), to people who can
only be taught by suffering. Our writer ventures, therefore, to
apply to the sinless Jesus an idea which mainly referred to young
or wilful or undisciplined natures. The term ὑπακοή only occurs
once in the LXX, at 2 S 22³⁶ (καὶ ὑπακοή σου ἐπλήθυνέν με, A),
where it translates עֲנָוָה. The general idea corresponds to that
of 10⁵⁻⁹ below, where Jesus enters the world submissively to do
the will of God, a vocation which involved suffering and self-
sacrifice. But the closest parallel is the argument of Paul in Ph
2⁶⁻⁸, that Jesus, born in human form, ἐταπείνωσεν ἑαυτὸν γενόμενος
ὑπήκοος (*sc.* τῷ θεῷ) μέχρι θανάτου, and the conception of the
ὑπακοή of Jesus (Ro 5¹⁸·¹⁹) in contrast to the παρακοή of Adam.
What our writer means to bring out here, as in 2¹⁰ᶠ·, is the
practical initiation of Jesus into his vocation for God and men.
"Wherever there is a vocation, growth and process are inevitable. . . . Personal relations are of necessity relations into which
one grows; the relation can be fully and practically constituted
only in the practical exercise of the calling in which it is involved.
So it was with Christ. He had, so to speak, to work Himself
into His place in the plan of salvation, to go down among the
brethren whom He was to lead to glory and fully to identify
Himself with them, not of course by sharing their individual
vocation, but in the practice of obedience in the far harder
vocation given to Him. That obedience had to be learned, not
because His will was not at every moment perfect . . . but
simply because it was a concrete, many-sided obedience" (W.
Robertson Smith, *Expositor²*, ii. pp. 425, 426). Τελειωθείς in v.⁹
recalls and expands the remark of 2¹⁰, that God "perfected"
Jesus by suffering as τὸν ἀρχηγὸν τῆς σωτηρίας αὐτῶν, and the
argument of 2¹⁷·¹⁸. The writer avoids the technical Stoic terms
προκόπτειν and προκοπή. He prefers τελειοῦν and τελείωσις, not
on account of their associations with the sacerdotal consecration
of the OT ritual, but in order to suggest the moral ripening
which enabled Jesus to offer a perfect self-sacrifice, and also
perhaps with a side-allusion here to the death-association of
these terms.

Philo (*de Abrah.* 11) observes that nature, instruction, and practice are the three things essential πρὸς τελειότητα τοῦ βιοῦ, οὔτε γὰρ διδασκαλίαν ἄνευ φύσεως ἢ ἀσκήσεως τελειωθῆναι δυνατὸν οὔτε φύσις ἐπὶ πέρας ἐστὶν ἐλθεῖν ἱκανὴ δίχα τοῦ μαθεῖν.

Αἴτιος σωτηρίας was a common Greek phrase. Thus Philo speaks of the brazen serpent as αἴτιος σωτηρίας γενόμενος παντελοῦς τοῖς θεασαμένοις (*de Agric.* 22), Aeschines (*in Ctesiph.* 57) has τὴς μὲν σωτηρίαν τῇ πόλει τοὺς θεοὺς αἰτίους γεγενήμενους, and in the *de Mundo,* 398b, the writer declares that it is fitting for God αἴτιον τε γίνεσθαι τοῖς ἐπὶ τῆς γῆς σωτηρίας. Σωτηρία αἰώνιος is a LXX phrase (Is 45¹⁷), but not in the sense intended here (cp. 2³). The collocation of Jesus learning how to obey God and of thus proving a saviour τοῖς ὑπακούουσιν αὐτῷ is remarkable. At first sight there is a clue to the sense in Philo, who declares that "the man who is morally earnest," receiving God's kingdom, "does not prove a source of evil to anyone (αἴτιος γίνεται), but proves a source of the acquisition and use of good things for all who obey him" (πᾶσι τοῖς ὑπηκόοις, *de Abrah.* 45). This refers to Abraham, but to the incident of Gn 23⁶, not to that of Melchizedek; Philo is spiritualizing the idea of the good man as king, and the ὑπηκόοι are the members of his household under his authority. The parallel is merely verbal. Here by πᾶσιν τοῖς ὑπακούουσιν αὐτῷ the writer means οἱ πιστεύσαντες (4³), but with a special reference to their loyalty to Christ. Disobedience to Christ or to God (3¹⁸ 4⁶·¹¹) is the practical expression of disbelief. It is a refusal to take Christ for what he is, as God's appointed ἀρχιερεύς. The writer then adds (v.¹⁰) προσαγορευθεὶς ὑπὸ τοῦ θεοῦ ἀρχιερεὺς κατὰ τὴν τάξιν Μελχισεδέκ, in order to explain how, thus commissioned, he brought the σωτηρία αἰώνιος. The paragraph is thus rounded off, like that of vv.⁵·⁶, with a reference to the Melchizedek priesthood, which the writer regards as of profound importance, and to which he now proposes to advance. Though προσαγορεύω is not used in this sense ("hail," "designate") in the LXX, the usage is common in Hellenistic writings like 2 Maccabees (1³⁶ 4⁷ 10⁹) and Josephus (e.g. *c. Apion.* i. 311). But the Melchizedek type of priesthood is not discussed till 6²⁰ 7¹ᶠ·. The interlude between 5¹⁰ and 6²⁰ is devoted to a stirring exhortation; for this interpretation of the Son as priest is a piece of γνῶσις which can only be imparted to those who have mastered the elementary truths of the Christian religion, and the writer feels and fears that his readers are still so immature that they may be unable or unwilling to grasp the higher and fuller teaching about Christ. The admonition has three movements of thought, 5¹¹⁻¹⁴, 6¹⁻⁸, and 6⁹⁻¹⁹.

¹¹ *On this point I* (ἡμῖν, plural of authorship, as 2⁵) *have a great deal to say, which it is hard to make intelligible to you. For* (καὶ γάρ=etenim) *you have*

grown dull of hearing. ¹² *Though by this time you should be teaching other people, you still need someone to teach you once more the rudimentary prin-ciples of the divine revelation.* **You are in need of milk, not of solid food.** ¹³ *(For anyone who is fed on milk is unskilled in moral truth; he is* ¹ *a mere babe.* ¹⁴ *Whereas solid food is for the mature, for those who have their faculties trained by exercise to distinguish good and evil.)* 6¹ *Let us pass on then to what is mature, leaving elementary Christian doctrine behind, instead of laying the foundation over again with repentance from dead works, with faith in God,* ² *with instruction about ablutions and the laying on of hands, about the resurrection of the dead and eternal punishment.* ³ *With God's permission we will take this step.*

Περὶ οὖ (*i.e.* on ἀρχιερεὺς κατὰ τὴν τάξιν M.) πολύς κτλ. (v.¹¹). The entire paragraph (vv.¹¹⁻¹⁴) is full of ideas and terms current in the ethical and especially the Stoic philosophy of the day. Thus, to begin with, πολύς (*sc.* ἔστι) ὁ λόγος is a common literary phrase for "there is much to say"; *e.g.* Dion. Hal. *ad Amm.* i. 3, πολὺς γὰρ ὁ περὶ αὐτῶν λόγος, and Lysias *in Pancleonem*, 11, ὅσα μὲν οὖν αὐτόθι ἐρρήθη, πολὺς ἂν εἴη μοι λόγος δεηγεῖσθαι. Πολύς and δυσερμήνευτος are separated, as elsewhere adjectives are (*e.g.* 2¹⁷). For the general sense of δυσερμήνευτος λέγειν, see Philo, *de migrat. Abrah.* 18, ἧς τὰ μὲν ἄλλα μακροτέρων ἢ κατὰ τὸν παρόντα καιρὸν δεῖται λόγων καὶ ὑπερθετέον, and Dion. Halic. *de Comp.* viii. περὶ ὧν καὶ πολὺς ὁ λόγος καὶ βαθεῖα ἡ θεωρία. Δυσερμήνευτος occurs in an obscure and interpolated passage of Philo's *de Somniis* (i. 32, ἀλέκτῳ τινι καὶ δυσερμηνεύτῳ θέᾳ), and Artemidorus (*Oneirocr.* iii. 67, οἱ ὄνειροι . . . ποικίλοι καὶ πολλοῖς δυσερμήνευτοι) uses it of dreams. Ἐπεί κτλ. (explaining δυσερμή-νευτοι) for the fault lies with you, not with the subject. Νωθρός only occurs once in the LXX, and not in this sense (Pr 22²⁹ ἀνδράσι νωθροῖς, tr. עָצֵל); even in Sir 4²⁹ 11¹² it means no more than slack or backward (as below in 6¹²). It is a common Greek ethical term for sluggishness, used with the accusative or the (locative) dative. With ἀκοή it denotes dulness. The literal sense occurs in Heliodorus (v. 10: ἐγὼ μὲν οὖν ᾐσθόμην . . . τάχα μέν που καὶ δι᾽ ἡλικίαν νωθρότερος ὢν τὴν ἀκοήν· νόσος γὰρ ἄλλων τε καὶ ὤτων τὸ γῆρας), and the metaphorical sense of ἀκοαί is illustrated by Philo's remark in *quis rer. div. haer.* 3: ἐν ἀψύχοις ἀνδριᾶσιν, οἷς ὦτα μὲν ἔστιν, ἀκοαὶ δ᾽ οὐκ ἔνεισιν.

Why (καὶ γάρ, v.¹²), the writer continues, instead of being teachers you still need a teacher. For χρεία with the article and infinitive (τοῦ διδάσκειν ² κτλ.), cp. the similar use of χρέων in *OP.* 1488²⁵. In what follows, τινά, the masculine singular, gives a better sense than τίνα, the neuter plural. "Ye again have need of (one) to teach you what are the elements" (sah boh); but it

---

¹ D* inserts ἀκμήν (Mt 15¹⁶) between γάρ and ἐστιν: "he is *still* a mere babe." Blass adopts this, for reasons of rhythm.
² 1912 and Origen read (with 462) διδάσκεσθαι, and omit ὑμᾶς.

is the elementary truths themselves, not what they are, that need
to be taught. Τὰ στοιχεῖα here means the ABC or elementary
principles (see Burton's *Galatians*, pp. 510 f.), such as he mentions in 6¹·². He defines them further as τῆς ἀρχῆς τῶν λογίων
θεοῦ, where τὰ λογία θεοῦ means not the OT but the divine
revelation in general, so that τὰ σ. τ. ἀρχῆς corresponds to the
Latin phrase "prima elementa." The words ὀφείλοντες εἶναι
διδάσκαλοι simply charge the readers with backwardness. "The
expression, 'to be teachers,' affirms no more than that the
readers ought to be ripe in Christian knowledge. Once a man
is ripe or mature, the qualification for teaching is present"
(Wrede, p. 32). The use of the phrase in Greek proves that it
is a general expression for stirring people up to acquaint themselves with what should be familiar. See Epict. *Enchir.* 51,
ποῖον οὖν ἔτι διδάσκαλον προσδοκᾷς; . . . οὐκ ἔτι εἶ μειράκιον, ἀλλὰ
ἀνὴρ ἤδη τέλειος. It was quite a favourite ethical maxim in
antiquity. Thus Cyrus tells the Persian chiefs that he would be
ashamed to give them advice on the eve of battle : οἶδα γὰρ ὑμᾶς
ταῦτα ἐπισταμένους καὶ μεμελετηκότας καὶ ἀσκοῦντας διὰ τέλους
οἷάπερ ἐγώ, ὥστε κἂν ἄλλους εἰκότως ἂν διδάσκοιτε (*Cyrop.* iii. 3.
35). Similarly we have the remark of Aristophanes in Plato,
Sympos. 189*d*, ἐγὼ οὖν πειράσομαι ὑμῖν εἰσηγήσασθαι τὴν δύναμιν
αὐτοῦ, ὑμεῖς δὲ τῶν ἄλλων διδάσκαλοι ἔσεσθε, and the reply given
by Apollonius of Tyana to a person who asked why he never put
questions to anybody : ὅτι μειράκιον ὢν ἐζήτησα, νῦν δὲ οὐ χρὴ
ζητεῖν ἀλλὰ διδάσκειν ἃ εὕρηκα (Philostratus, *Vita Apoll.* i. 17).
Seneca tells Lucilius the same truth : "quousque disces ? iam et
praecipe (*Ep.* 33⁹). Thus the phrase here offers no support
whatever to any theories about the readers of Πρὸς Ἑβραίους
being a group of teachers, or a small, specially cultured community. The author, himself a διδάσκαλος, as he is in possession
of this mature γνῶσις, is trying to shame his friends out of their
imperfect grasp of their religion. That is all. Γεγόνατε χρείαν
ἔχοντες is a rhetorical variant for χρείαν ἔχετε, due to the writer's
fondness for γεγόνα. If there is any special meaning in the
larger phrase, it is that detected by Chrysostom, who argues that
the writer chose it deliberately : τουτέστιν, ὑμεῖς ἠθελήσατε, ὑμεῖς
ἑαυτοὺς εἰς τοῦτο κατεστήσατε, εἰς ταύτην τὴν χρείαν. They are
responsible for this second childhood of theirs. The comparison [1]
of milk and solid food is one of the most common in Greek

---

[1] Origen (*Philocalia*, xviii. 23) uses this passage neatly to answer Celsus,
who had declared that Christians were afraid to appeal to an educated and
intelligent audience. He quotes 5¹²ᶠ· as well as 1 Co 3²ᶠ·, arguing that in
the light of them it must be admitted ἡμεῖς, ὅση δύναμις, πάντα πράττομεν
ὑπὲρ τοῦ φρονίμων ἀνδρῶν γενέσθαι τὸν σύλλογον ἡμῶν· καὶ τὰ ἐν ἡμῖν μάλιστα
καλὰ καὶ θεῖα τότε τολμῶμεν ἐν τοῖς πρὸς τὸ κοινὸν διαλόγοις φέρειν εἰς μέσον,
ὅτ᾽ εὐποροῦμεν συνετῶν ἀκροατῶν.

ethical philosophy, as in Epictetus, *e.g.* ii. 16. 39, οὐ θέλεις ἤδη ὡς τὰ παιδία ἀπογαλακτισθῆναι καὶ ἅπτεσθαι τροφῆς στερεωτέρας, and iii. 24. 9, οὐκ ἀπογαλακτίσομεν ἤδη ποθ᾽ ἑαυτούς, and particularly in Philo. A characteristic passage from the latter writer is the sentence in *de agric.* 2 : ἐπεὶ δὲ νηπίοις μὲν ἐστι γάλα τροφή, τελείοις δὲ τὰ ἐκ πυρῶν πέμματα, καὶ ψυχῆς γαλακτώδεις μὲν ἂν εἶεν τροφαὶ κατὰ τὴν παιδικὴν ἡλικίαν τὰ τῆς ἐγκυκλίου μουσικῆς προπαιδεύματα, τέλειαι δὲ καὶ ἀνδράσιν ἐμπρεπεῖς αἱ διὰ φρονήσεως καὶ σωφροσύνης καὶ ἁπάσης ἀρετῆς ὑφηγήσεις. Our writer adopts the metaphor, as Paul had done (1 Co 3[1, 2]), and adds a general aside (vv.[13, 14]) in order to enforce his remonstrance. He does not use the term γνῶσις, and the plight of his friends is not due to the same causes as operated in the Corinthian church, but he evidently regards his interpretation of the priesthood of Christ as mature instruction, στερεὰ τροφή. Ὁ μετέχων γάλακτος is one whose only food (μετέχειν as in 1 Co 10[17] etc.) is milk ; ἄπειρος is "inexperienced," and therefore "unskilled," in λόγου δικαιοσύνης—an ethical phrase for what moderns would call "moral truth," almost as in Xen. *Cyrop.* i. 6. 31, ἀνὴρ διδάσκαλος τῶν παίδων, ὃς ἐδίδασκεν ἄρα τοὺς παῖδας τὴν δικαιοσύνην κτλ., or in M. Aurelius xi. 10, xii. 1. Thus, while δικαιοσύνη here is not a religious term, the phrase means more than (*a*) "incapable of talking correctly" (Delitzsch, B. Weiss, von Soden), which is, no doubt, the mark of a νήπιος, but irrelevant in this connexion ; or (*b*) "incapable of understanding normal speech," such as grown-up people use (Riggenbach). Τελείων δέ κτλ. (v.[14]). The clearest statement of what contemporary ethical teachers meant by τέλειος as mature, is (cp. p. 70) in Epict. *Enchirid.* 51, "how long (εἰς ποῖον ἔτι χρόνον) will you defer thinking of yourself as worthy of the very best . . .? You have received the precepts you ought to accept, and have accepted them. Why then do you still wait for a teacher (διδάσκαλον προσδοκᾷς), that you may put off amending yourself till he comes? You are a lad no longer, you are a full-grown man now (οὐκ ἔτι εἶ μειράκιον, ἀλλὰ ἀνὴρ ἤδη τέλειος). . . . Make up your mind, ere it is too late, to live ὡς τέλειον καὶ προκόπτοντα." Then he adds, in words that recall He 12[1f.] : "and when you meet anything stiff or sweet, glorious or inglorious, remember that νῦν ὁ ἀγὼν καὶ ἤδη πάρεστι τὰ Ὀλύμπια." As Pythagoras divided his pupils into νήπιοι and τέλειοι, so our author distinguishes between the immature and the mature (cp. 1 Co 2[6] ἐν τοῖς τελείοις, 3[1] νηπίοις). In διὰ τὴν ἕξιν (vg. "pro consuetudine") he uses ἕξις much as does the writer of the prologue to Sirach (ἱκανὴν ἕξιν περιποιησάμενος), for facility or practice.[1] It is not an equivalent for mental faculties here,

---

[1] "Firma quaedam facilitas quae apud Graecos ἕξις nominatur" (Quint. *Instit. Orat.* 10. 1).

but for the exercise of our powers. These powers or faculties
are called τὰ αἰσθητήρια. Αἰσθητήριον was a Stoic term for an
organ of the senses, and, like its English equivalent "sense,"
easily acquired an ethical significance, as in Jer 4¹⁹ τὰ αἰσθητήρια
τῆς καρδίας μου. The phrase γεγυμνασμένα αἰσθητήρια may be
illustrated from Galen (*de dign. puls.* iii. 2, ὃς μὲν γὰρ ἂν εὐαισθητό-
τατον φύσιν τε καὶ τὸ αἰσθητήριον ἔχῃ γεγυμνασμένον ἱκανῶς . . .
οὗτος ἂν ἄριστος εἴη γνώμων τῶν ἐντὸς ὑποκειμένων, and *de complexu*,
ii. : λελογισμένον μὲν ἐστιν ἀνδρὸς τοὺς λογισμοὺς οὓς εἴρηκα καὶ
γεγυμνασμένα τὴν αἴσθησιν ἐν πολλῇ τῇ κατὰ μέρος ἐμπειρίᾳ κτλ.),
γεγυμνασμένα being a perfect participle used predicatively, like
πεφυτευμένην in Lk 13⁶, and γεγυμνασμένον above. Compare
what Marcus Aurelius (iii. 1) says about old age; it may come
upon us, bringing not physical failure, but a premature decay of
the mental and moral faculties, *e.g.*, of self-control, of the sense
of duty, καὶ ὅσα τοιαῦτα λογισμοῦ συγγεγυμνασμένου πάνυ χρῄζει.
Elsewhere (ii. 13) he declares that ignorance of moral distinctions
(ἄγνοια ἀγαθῶν καὶ κακῶν) is a blindness as serious as any inability
to distinguish black and white. The power of moral discrimination (πρὸς διάκρισιν καλοῦ τε καὶ κακοῦ) is the mark of maturity,
in contrast to childhood (cp. *e.g.* Dt 1³⁹ πᾶν παιδίον νέον ὅστις
οὐκ οἶδεν σήμερον ἀγαθὸν ἢ κακόν). Compare the definition of
τὸ ἠθικόν in Sextus Empiricus (*Hyp. Pyrrh.* iii. 168): ὅπερ δοκεῖ
περὶ τὴν διάκρισιν τῶν τε καλῶν καὶ κακῶν καὶ ἀδιαφόρων κατα-
γίγνεσθαι.

In spite of Resch's arguments (*Texte u. Untersuchungen*, xxx. 3. 112 f.),
there is no reason to hear any echo of the well-known saying attributed to
Jesus : γίνεσθε δὲ δόκιμοι τραπεζῖται, τὰ μὲν ἀποδοκιμάζοντες, τὸ δὲ καλὸν
κατέχοντες.

Διὸ—well then (as in 12¹². ²⁸)—ἐπὶ τὸν τελειότητα φερώμεθα
(6¹). It is a moral duty to grow up, and the duty involves an
effort. The τελειότης in question is the mature mental grasp of
the truth about Christ as ἀρχιερεύς, a truth which the writer is
disappointed that his friends still find it difficult to understand.
However, διὰ τὸν χρόνον they ought to understand it. He has every
reason to expect an effort from them, and therefore he follows
up his remonstrance with a word of encouragement. Instead of
the sharp, severe tone of vv.¹¹ᶠ·, he now speaks more hopefully.
The connexion is not easy. We expect "however" instead of
"well then." But the connexion is not made more easy by
regarding 6¹ᶠ· as a resolve of the writer: "since you are so immature, I am going on myself to develop the higher teaching."
It would be senseless for a teacher to take this line, and it is not
facilitated by reading φερόμεθα. The plural is not the literary
plural as in 5¹¹. The writer wishes to carry his readers along
with him. "If you want anyone to instruct you over again in

rudimentary Christianity, I am not the man; I propose to carry
you forward into a higher course of lessons. Come, let us
advance, you and I together." The underlying thought, which
explains the transition, is revealed in the next paragraph (vv.⁴ᶠ·),
where the writer practically tells his readers that they must either
advance or lose their present position of faith,[1] in which latter
case there is no second chance for them. In spite of his un-
qualified censure in 5¹², he shows, in 6⁹ᶠ·, that they are really
capable of doing what he summons them to try in 6¹ᶠ·, *i.e.* to
think out the full significance of Jesus in relation to faith and
forgiveness. Only thus, he argues, can quicken the faint pulse of
your religious life. "Religion is something different from mere
strenuous thinking on the great religious questions. Yet it still
remains true that faith and knowledge are inseparable, and that
both grow stronger as they react on one another. More often
than we know, the failure of religion, as a moral power, is due to
no other cause than intellectual sloth" (E. F. Scott, p. 44).
After the parenthesis of 5¹³·¹⁴, the writer resumes the thought
with which he started in 5¹¹ᵃ "you must make an effort to enter
into this larger appreciation of what Christ means." Ἀφέντες . . .
φερώμεθα is a phrase illustrated by Eurip. *Androm.* 392-393,
τὴν ἀρχὴν ἀφεὶς | πρὸς τὴν τελευτὴν ὑστέραν οὖσαν φέρῃ : by
ἀφέντες the writer means "leaving behind," and by φερώμεθα
"let us advance." Ἀφίημι might even mean "to omit" ("not
mentioning"); it is so used with λόγον (= to pass over without
mentioning), *e.g.* in Plutarch's *an seni respublica gerenda sit*, 18,
ἀλλ' ἀφέντες, εἰ βούλει, τὸν ἀποσπῶντα τῆς πολιτείας λόγον ἐκεῖνο
σκοπῶμεν ἤδη κτλ., and even independently (cp. Epict. iv. 1. 15, τὸν
μὲν Καίσαρα πρὸς τὸ παρὸν ἀφῶμεν, and Theophrastus, *prooem.* ἀφεὶς
τὸ προοιμιάζεσθαι καὶ πολλὰ περὶ τοῦ πράγματος λέγειν). In what
follows, τὸν τῆς ἀρχῆς τοῦ Χριστοῦ λόγον is a variant for τὰ στοιχεῖα
τῆς ἀρχῆς τῶν λογίων τοῦ θεοῦ (5¹²). Τοῦ Χριστοῦ is an objective
genitive; the writer is not thinking of injunctions issued by
Christ (so Harnack, *Constitution and Law of the Church*, p. 344).
Blass follows L in reading λοιπόν after λόγον—needlessly.

The use of the θεμέλιον metaphor after τῆς ἀρχῆς was natural ;
it occurs in Epictetus (ii. 15. 8, οὐ θέλεις τὴν ἀρχὴν στῆσαι καὶ τὸν
θεμέλιον) and in Philo (*de spec. leg.* ii. 13, ἀρχὴν ταύτην βαλλό-
μενος ὥσπερ θεμέλιόν τινα). Indeed the θεμέλιον metaphor is
particularly common in Philo, as, *e.g.*, in the *de vita contempl.*
476 (ἐγκράτειαν δὲ ὥσπερ τινὰ θεμέλιον προκαταβαλλόμενοι ψυχῆς).
This basis (θεμέλιον) of Christian instruction is now described ;
the contents are arranged in three pairs, but, as the middle pair
are not distinctively Christian ideas (v.²), the writer puts in

---

[1] Compare the motto which Cromwell is said to have written on his
pocket-bible, "qui cessat esse melior cessat esse bonus."

διδαχήν or διδαχῆς. The θεμέλιον of instruction consists of
μετανοίας . . . καὶ πίστεως (genitives of quality), while διδαχήν,
which is in apposition to it ("I mean, instruction about"),
controls the other four genitives. Μετάνοια and πίστις, βαπτισμοί
and ἐπιθέσις χειρῶν, ἀνάστασις and κρίμα αἰώνιον, are the fundamental truths. Μετάνοια[1] ἀπό is like μετανοεῖν ἀπό (Ac 8²²), and
πίστις ἐπὶ θεόν like πιστεύειν ἐπί (e.g. Wis 12² ἵνα ἀπαλλαγέντες τῆς
κακίας πιστεύσωμεν ἐπὶ σέ, κύριε). These two requirements were
foremost in the programme of the Christian mission. The other
side of repentance is described in 9¹⁴ πόσῳ μᾶλλον τὸ αἷμα τοῦ
Χριστοῦ . . . καθαριεῖ τὴν συνείδησιν ἡμῶν ἀπὸ νεκρῶν ἔργων εἰς τὸ
λατρεύειν θεῷ ζῶντι, where the last word indicates that νεκρὰ ἔργα
mean the conduct of those who are outside the real life and
service of God. Practically, therefore, νεκρὰ ἔργα are sins, as the
Greek fathers assumed; the man who wrote 11²⁵ (θεοῦ . . .
ἁμαρτίας) would hardly have hesitated to call them such. He
has coined this phrase to suggest that such ἔργα have no principle
of life in them,[2] or that they lead to death. The origin of the
phrase has not been explained, though Chrysostom and Oecumenius were right in suggesting that the metaphor of 9¹⁴ was
derived from the contamination incurred by touching a corpse
(see Nu 19¹ᶠ· 31¹⁹). Its exact meaning is less clear. The one
thing that is clear about it is that these ἔργα νεκρά were not
habitual sins of Christians; they were moral offences from which
a man had to break away, in order to become a Christian at all.
They denote not the lifeless, formal ceremonies of Judaism, but
occupations, interests, and pleasures, which lay within the sphere
of moral death, where, as a contemporary Christian writer put it
(Eph 2¹), pagans lay νεκροὶ τοῖς παραπτώμασιν καὶ ταῖς ἁμαρτίαις.
The phrase might cover Jewish Christians, if there were any
such in the community to which this homily is addressed, but it is
a general phrase. Whatever is evil is νεκρόν, for our author, and
ἔργα νεκρά render any Christian πίστις or λατρεύειν impossible
(cp. *Expositor*, Jan. 1918, pp. 1–18), because they belong to the
profane, contaminating sphere of the world.

In v.² διδαχήν is read, instead of διδαχῆς, by B syr^harkl and
the Old Latin, a very small group—yet the reading is probably

---

[1] According to Philo (*de Abrah.* 2, 3), next to hope, which is the ἀρχὴ
μετουσίας ἀγαθῶν, comes ἡ ἐπὶ ἁμαρτανομένοις μετάνοια καὶ βελτίωσις. Only,
he adds (*ibid.* 4), repentance is second to τελειότης, ὥσπερ καὶ ἀνόσου σώματος
ἡ πρὸς ὑγιείαν ἐξ ἀσθενείας μεταβολή . . . ἡ δ' ἀπό τινος χρόνου βελτίωσις ἴδιον
ἀγαθὸν εὐφυοῦς ψυχῆς ἐστι μὴ τοῖς παιδικοῖς ἐπιμενούσης ἀλλ' ἀδροτέροις καὶ
ἀνδρὸς ὄντως φρονήμασιν ἐπιζητούσης εὔδιον κατάστασιν [ψυχῆς] καὶ τῇ φαντασίᾳ
τῶν καλῶν ἐπιτρεχούσης.

[2] Cp. the use of νεκρός in Epict. iii. 23. 28, καὶ μὴν ἂν μὴ ταῦτα ἐμποιῇ ὁ
τοῦ φιλοσόφου λόγος, νεκρός ἐστι καὶ αὐτὸς καὶ ὁ λέγων. This passage indicates
how νεκρός could pass from the vivid application to persons (Mt 8²², Lk 15³²,
cp. Col 2¹³), into a secondary application to their sphere and conduct.

original; the surrounding genitives led to its alteration into
διδαχῆς. However, it makes no difference to the sense, which
reading is chosen. Even διδαχῆς depends on θεμέλιον as a
qualifying genitive. But the change of διδαχήν into διδαχῆς is
much more likely than the reverse process. Διδαχήν follows
βαπτισμῶν like κόσμος in 1 P 3³ (ἐνδύσεως ἱματίων κόσμος).
Βαπτισμοί by itself does not mean specifically Christian baptism
either in this epistle (9¹⁰) or elsewhere (Mk 7⁴), but ablutions or
immersions such as the mystery religions and the Jewish cultus
required for initiates, proselytes, and worshippers in general.
The singular might mean Christian baptism (as in Col 2¹²), but
why does the writer employ the plural here? Not because
in some primitive Christian circles the catechumen was thrice
sprinkled or immersed in the name of the Trinity (Didache 7¹⁻³),
but because ancient religions, such as those familiar to the
readers, had all manner of purification rites connected with
water (see on 10²²). The distinctively Christian uses of water
had to be grasped by new adherents. That is, at baptism, *e.g.*,
the catechumen would be specially instructed about the difference between this Christian rite, with its symbolic purification
from sins of which one repented, and (*a*) the similar rites in
connexion with Jewish proselytes on their reception into the
synagogue or with adherents who were initiated into various
cults, and (*b*) the ablutions which were required from Christians
in subsequent worship. The latter practice may be alluded to
in 10²² (λελουσμένοι τὸ σῶμα ὕδατι καθαρῷ). Justin (*Apol.* i. 62)
regards these lustrations of the cults as devilish caricatures of
real baptism : καὶ τὸ λουτρὸν δὴ τοῦτο ἀκούσαντες οἱ δαίμονες . . .
ἐνήργησαν καὶ ῥαντίζειν ἑαυτοὺς τοὺς εἰς τὰ ἱερὰ αὐτῶν ἐπιβαίνοντας
καὶ προσιέναι αὐτοῖς μέλλοντας, λοιβὰς καὶ κνίσας ἀποτελοῦντας
τέλεον δὲ καὶ λούεσθαι ἐπιόντας πρὶν ἐλθεῖν ἐπὶ τὰ ἱερά, ἔνθα
ἵδρυνται, ἐνεργοῦσι. The ἐπιθέσις χειρῶν which often followed
baptism in primitive days (*e.g.* Ac 8¹⁷ᶠ· 19⁶), though it is ignored
by the Didache and Justin, was supposed to confer the holy
Spirit (see v.⁴). Tertullian witnesses to the custom (*de baptismo*,
18, *de carnis resurrectione*, 8), and Cyprian corroborates it (*Ep.*
lxxiv. 5, "manus baptizato imponitur ad accipiendum spiritum
sanctum "). The rite was employed in blessing, in exorcising,
and at "ordination," afterwards at the reception of penitents
and heretics ; here it is mentioned in connexion with baptism
particularly (*ERE.* vi. 494*b*).

The subject is discussed in monographs like A. J. Mason's *The Relation
of Confirmation to Baptism* (1891), and J. Behm's *Die Handauflegung im
Urchristenthum* (1911).

The final pair of doctrines is ἀναστάσεως νεκρῶν καὶ κρίματος
(2¹⁴· ¹⁵ 9²⁷) αἰωνίου (as in Ac 24¹⁵· ²⁵). Τε is added after ἀνασ-

τάσεως mechanically (to conform with the preceding τε) by ℵ A C K L Lat arm syr[hkl pesh], just as it is added after βαπτισμῶν by harkl.   In the rather elliptical style and loose construction of the whole sentence, "notwithstanding its graceful rhythmical structure," it is possible to see, with Bruce (p. 203), "an oratorical device to express a feeling of impatience" with people who need to have such *principia* mentioned.   At any rate the writer hastens forward.   V.[3] is not a parenthesis ("I will do this," *i.e.* go over such elementary truths with you, "if God permits," when I reach you, 13[23]); the τοῦτο refers to the advance proposed in v.[1], and after ποιήσομεν the author adds reverently, "if God permits," ἐάνπερ ἐπιτρέπῃ ὁ θεός, almost as a contemporary rhetorician might say in a pious aside : ἐὰν δὲ σώζῃ τὸ δαιμόνιον ἡμᾶς (Dion. Halicarn. *De Admir. Vi dicendi in Dem.* 58), or θεῶν ἡμᾶς φυλαττόντων ἀσινεῖς τε καὶ ἀνόσους (*De Composit. Verborum*, 1). The papyri show that similar phrases were current in the correspondence of the day (cp. Deissmann's *Bible Studies*, p. 80), and Josephus (*Ant.* xx. 11. 2) uses κἂν τὸ θεῖον ἐπιτρεπῇ.

ποιήσομεν (ℵ B K L N 1. 2. 5. 6. 33. 69. 88. 216. 218. 221. 226. 242. 255. 337. 429. 489. 919. 920. 1149. 1518. 1739. 1758. 1827. 1867. 2127. 2143. Lat sah boh Chrys.) has been changed into ποιήσωμεν by A C D P arm, etc., though the latter may have been originally, like φερόμεθα in v.[1], an orthographical variant, ο and ω being frequently confused.

[4] *For in the case of people who have been once enlightened, who tasted the heavenly Gift, who participated in the holy Spirit,* [5] *who tasted the goodness of God's word and the powers of the world to come,* [6] *and then fell away—it is impossible to make them repent afresh, since they crucify the Son of God in their own persons and hold him up to obloquy.* [7] *For "land" which absorbs the rain that often falls on it, and bears "plants" that are useful to those for whom it is tilled, receives a blessing from God;* [8] *whereas, if it (sc. ἡ γῆ) "produces thorns and thistles," it is reprobate and on the verge of being cursed—its fate is to be burned.*

Vv.[4-6] put the reason for τοῦτο ποιήσομεν (v.[3]), and vv.[7. 8] give the reason for ἀδύνατον . . . ἀνακαινίζειν εἰς μετάνοιαν (vv.[4-6]). Ἀδύνατον γάρ κτλ. (v.[4]); there are four impossible things in the epistle : this and the three noted in vv.[18] 10[4] and 11[6].   Τοὺς . . . αἰῶνος ([4. 5a]) is a long description of people who have been initiated into Christianity; then comes the tragic καὶ παραπεσόντας.   What makes the latter so fatal is explained in (v.[6]) ἀνασταυροῦντας . . . παραδειγματίζοντας.   Logically πάλιν ἀνακαινίζειν εἰς μετάνοιαν ought to come immediately after ἀδύνατον γάρ, but the writer delayed the phrase in order to break up the sequence of participles.   The passage is charged with an austerity which shows how seriously the writer took life.   Seneca quotes (*Ep.* xxiii. 9-11) to Lucilius the saying of Epicurus, that "it is irksome always to be starting life over again," and that "they live badly who are always beginning to live."   The reason is : "quia

semper illis imperfecta vita est." But our writer takes a much
more sombre view of the position of his friends. He urges
them to develop their ideas of Christianity. "You need some
one to teach you the rudimentary lessons of the faith all over
again," he had said. "Yes," he now adds, "and in some cases
that is impossible. Relaying a foundation of repentance, etc.!
That cannot be done for deliberate apostates." The implication
is that his readers are in danger of this sin, as indeed he has
hinted already (in 3^7–4^{14}), and that one of the things that is
weakening them is their religious inability to realize the supreme
significance of Jesus. To remain as they are is fatal; it means
the possibility of a relapse altogether. "Come on," the writer
bids them, "for if you do not you will fall back, and to fall back
is to be ruined." The connexion between this passage and the
foregoing, therefore, is that to rest content with their present
elementary hold upon Christian truth is to have an inadequate
grasp of it; the force of temptation is so strong that this rudimentary acquaintance with it will not prevent them from falling
away altogether, and the one thing to ensure their religious
position is to see the full meaning of what Jesus is and does.
This meaning he is anxious to impart, not as an extra but as an
essential. The situation is so serious, he implies, that only
those who fully realize what Jesus means for forgiveness and
fellowship will be able to hold out. And once you relapse, he
argues, once you let go your faith, it is fatal; people who deliberately abandon their Christian confession of faith are beyond
recovery. Such a view of apostasy as a heinous offence, which
destroyed all hope of recovery, is characteristic of Πρὸς Ἑβραίους.
It was not confined to this writer. That certain persons could
not repent of their sins was, *e.g.*, an idea admitted in rabbinic
Judaism. "Over and over again we have the saying: 'For him
who sins and causes others to sin no repentance is allowed or
possible' (Aboth v. 26; Sanhedrin, 107*b*). 'He who is wholly
given up to sin is unable to repent, and there is no forgiveness
to him for ever' (Midrash Tehillim on Ps 1 *ad fin.*)."[1] There
is a partial parallel to this passage in the idea thrown out by
Philo in *de agricultura*, 28, as he comments upon Gn 9^{20}:
"Noah began to till the earth." Evidently, says Philo, this
means that he was merely working at the ἄρχαι of the subject.
Ἀρχὴ δ', ὁ τῶν παλαιῶν λόγος, ἥμισυ τοῦ πάντος, ὡς ἂν ἡμίσει πρὸς
τὸ τέλος ἀφεστηκυῖα, οὗ μὴ προσγενομένου καὶ τὸ ἄρξασθαι
πολλάκις μεγάλα πολλοὺς ἔβλαψεν. His point is that it
is dangerous to stop short in any moral endeavour. But our
author is more rigorous in his outlook. His warning is modified,
however. (*a*) It is put in the form of a general statement.

[1] C. G. Montefiore, in *Jewish Quarterly Review* (1904), p. 225.

(*b*) It contains a note of encouragement in v.[7]; and (*c*) it is at
once followed up by an eager hope that the readers will disappoint their friend and teacher's fear (v.[9]). In the later church
this feature of Πρὸς Ἑβραίους entered into the ecclesiastical
question of penance (cp. *ERE.* ix. 716, and *Journal of Theological Studies*, iv. 321 f.), and seriously affected the vogue of the
epistle (cp. Introd. p. xx).

The fourfold description of believers ([4, 5a]) begins with ἅπαξ
φωτισθέντας, where φωτισθέντας corresponds to λαβεῖν τὴν ἐπίγνωσιν τῆς ἀληθείας (10[26]), in the general sense of LXX (*e.g.*
Ps 118[130] ἡ δήλωσις τῶν λόγων σου φωτιεῖ, καὶ συνετεῖ νηπίους),
i.e. "enlightened" in the sense of having their eyes opened
(Eph 1[18]) to the Christian God. Subsequently, earlier even than
Justin Martyr, the verb, with its noun φωτισμός, came to be used
of baptism specifically (cp. *ERE.* viii. 54, 55). Ἅπαξ is prefixed, in contrast to πάλιν (v.[6]); once for all men enter Christianity, it is an experience which, like their own death (9[27]) and
the death of Jesus (9[28]), can never be repeated. In καλὸν γευσαμένους θεοῦ ῥῆμα ("experienced how good the gospel is") the construction resembles that of Herod. vii. 46, where the active voice
is used with the accusative (ὁ δὲ θεὸς γλυκὺν γεύσας τὸν αἰῶνα,
φθονερὸς ἐν αὐτῷ εὑρίσκεται ἐών), and the adj. is put first : "the
deity, who let us taste the sweetness of life (or, that life is
sweet), is found to be spiteful in so doing." The similar use of
the middle here as in Pr 29[36] and Jn 2[9] probably points to the
same meaning (cp., however, *Diat.* 2016–2018), *i.e.*, practically
as if it were ὅτι κτλ. (cp. Ps 34[8] γεύσασθε καὶ ἴδετε ὅτι χρηστὸς
ὁ κύριος, 1 P 2[3]), in contrast to the more common construction
with the genitive (v.[4] 2[9]). The writer uses genitive and accusative indifferently, for the sake of literary variety ; and καλόν here
is the same as καλοῦ in 5[14]. Γευσαμένους κτλ. recalls the parti-
ality of Philo for this metaphor (e.g. *de Abrah.* 19 ; *de Somniis*,
i. 26), but indeed it is common (cp. *e.g.* Jos. *Ant.* iv. 6. 9, ἅπαξ
τὸ νέον γευσαμένον ξενικῶν ἐθισμῶν ἀπλήστως αὐτῶν ἐνεφορεῖτο)
throughout contemporary Hellenistic Greek as a metaphor for
experiencing. Probably γευσαμένους . . . ἐπουρανίου, μετόχους
. . . ἁγίου, and καλὸν γευσαμένους αἰῶνος are three rhetorical
expressions for the initial experience described in ἅπαξ φωτισθέντας. "The heavenly Gift" (τῆς δωρεᾶς τῆς ἐπουρανίου) may be
the Christian salvation in general, which is then viewed as the
impartation of the holy Spirit, and finally as the revelation of the
higher world which even already is partly realized in the experience of faith. Note that φωτισθέντας is followed by γευσαμένους
κτλ., as the light-metaphor is followed by the food-metaphor
in Philo's (*de fuga et invent.* 25) remarks upon the manna
(Ex 16[15, 16]): ἡ θεία σύνταξις αὕτη τὴν ὁρατικὴν ψυχὴν φωτίζει τε

καὶ ὁμοῦ καὶ γλυκαίνει . . . τοὺς διψῶντας καὶ πεινῶντας καλοκἀγαθίας ἐφηδύνουσα. Also, that δυνάμεις τε μέλλοντος αἰῶνος[1] includes the thrilling experiences mentioned in 2⁴. The dramatic
turn comes in (v.⁶) καὶ παραπεσόντας. Παραπίπτειν is here used
in its most sinister sense; it corresponds to ἀποστῆναι (3¹²), and
indeed both verbs are used in the LXX to translate the same
term מעל. The usage in Wis 6⁹ (μὴ παραπέσητε) 12² (τοὺς
παραπίπτοντας) paves the way for this sense of a deliberate
renunciation of the Christian God, which is equivalent to ἑκουσίως
ἁμαρτάνειν in 10²⁶. The sin against the holy Spirit, which Jesus
regarded as unpardonable, the mysterious ἁμαρτία πρὸς θάνατον
of 1 Jn 5¹⁶, and this sin of apostasy, are on the same level. The
writer never hints at what his friends might relapse into.
Anything that ignored Christ was to him hopeless.

Ἀδύνατον (sc. ἐστι) is now (v.⁶) taken up in ἀνακαινίζειν (for
which Paul prefers the form ἀνακαινοῦν), a LXX term (e.g. Ps
51¹²) which is actually used for the Christian start in life by
Barnabas (6¹¹ ἀνακαινίσας ἡμᾶς ἐν τῇ ἀφέσει τῶν ἁμαρτιῶν), and
naturally of the divine action. Πάλιν is prefixed for emphasis,
as in Isokr. Areopag. 3, τῆς ἔχθρας τῆς πρὸς τὸν βασιλέα πάλιν
ἀνακεκαινισμένης.

There have been various, vain efforts to explain the apparent harshness of
the statement. Erasmus took ἀδύνατον (like d = difficile) as "difficult";
Grotius said it was impossible "per legem Mosis"; others take ἀνακαινίζειν
to mean "keep on renewing," while some, like Schoettgen, Bengel, and
Wickham, fall back on the old view that while men could not, God might
effect it. But even the last-named idea is out of the question. If the writer
thought of any subject to ἀνακαινίζειν, it was probably a Christian διδάσκαλος
like himself; but the efforts of such a Christian are assumed to be the channel
of the divine power, and no renewal could take place without God. There
is not the faintest suggestion that a second repentance might be produced by
God when human effort failed. The tenor of passages like 10²⁸ᵗ· and 12¹⁷
tells finally against this modification of the language. A similarly ominous
tone is heard in Philo's comment on Nu 30¹⁰ in quod deter. pot. insid. 40:
φήσομεν διάνοιαν . . . ἐκβεβλῆσθαι καὶ χήραν θεοῦ, ἥτις ἢ γονὰς θείας οὐ
παρεδέξατο ἢ παραδεξαμένη ἑκουσίως αὖθις ἐξήμβλωσε . . . ἡ δ' ἅπαξ διαζευχ-
θεῖσα καὶ διοικισθεῖσα ὡς ἄσπονδος μέχρι τοῦ παντὸς αἰῶνος ἐκτετόξευται, εἰς τὸν
ἀρχαῖον οἶκον ἐπανελθεῖν ἀδυνατοῦσα.

The reason why a second repentance is impossible is given
in ἀνασταυροῦντας . . . παραδειγματίζοντας, where ἀνασταυροῦντας
is used instead of σταυροῦντας, for the sake of assonance (after
ἀνακαινίζειν), but with the same meaning. Ἀνασταυροῦν simply
means "to crucify," as, e.g., in Plato's Gorgias, 28 (τοὺς αὑτοῦ ἐπιδὼν

[1] Tertullian's translation, "occidente iam aevo" (de Pudicitia, 20) shows
that his Greek text had omitted a line by accident:

ΝΟΥΣΘΥΡΗΜΑΔΥΝ
ΑΜΕΙΣΤΕΜΕΛΛ
ΟΝΤΟΣΑΙΩΝΟΣΚΑΙ,

i.e. δυν[άμεις τε μέλλ]οντος αἰῶνος.

παῖδας τε καὶ γυναῖκα τὸ ἔσχατον ἀνασταυρωθῇ ἢ καταπιττωθῇ);
Thucyd. i. 110 ('Ινάρως . . . προδοσίᾳ ληφθεὶς ἀνεσταυρώθη);
Josephus (*Ant.* xi. 6. 10, ἀνασταυρῶσαι τὸν Μαρδοχαῖον), etc. The
ἀνα = sursum, not rursum, though the Greek fathers (*e.g.* Chrys.
τὶ δέ ἐστιν ἀνασταυροῦντας; ἄνωθεν πάλιν σταυροῦντας), and several
of the versions (*e.g.* vg "rursum crucifigentes"), took it in the sense
of re-crucify. Ἑαυτοῖς: it is *their* crucifixion of Jesus. "The
thought is that of wilfulness rather than of detriment" (Vaughan).

In the story of Jesus and Peter at Rome, which Origen mentions as part
of the Acts of Paul (*in Joh.* xx. 12), the phrase, "to be crucified over again"
occurs in a different sense (*Texte u. Unters.* xxx. 3, pp. 271-272). Καὶ ὁ
κύριος αὐτῷ εἶπεν· εἰσέρχομαι εἰς τὴν Ῥώμην σταυρωθῆναι. Καὶ ὁ Πέτρος εἶπεν
αὐτῷ· Κύριε, πάλιν σταυροῦσαι; εἶπεν αὐτῷ· ναί, Πέτρε, πάλιν σταυροῦμαι.
Origen, quoting this as Ἄνωθεν μέλλω σταυροῦσθαι, holds that such is the
meaning of ἀνασταυροῦν in He 6⁵.

The meaning of the vivid phrase is that they put Jesus out
of their life, they break off all connexion with him; he is dead to
them. This is the decisive force of σταυροῦσθαι in Gal 6¹⁴. The
writer adds an equally vivid touch in καὶ παραδειγματίζοντας
(= τὸν υἱὸν θεοῦ καταπατήσας κτλ., 10²⁹)—as if he is not worth
their loyalty! Their repudiation of him proclaims to the world
that they consider him useless, and that the best thing they can
do for themselves is to put him out of their life. Παραδειγ-
ματίζειν is used in its Hellenistic sense, which is represented by
τιθέναι εἰς παράδειγμα in the LXX (Nah 3⁶). Possibly the term
was already associated with impaling (cp. Nu 25⁴ παραδειγμάτισον
αὐτοὺς Κυρίῳ),[1] but our author does not use it in the LXX sense
of "make an example of" (by punishing); the idea is of exposing
to contemptuous ignominy, in public (as in Mt 1¹⁹).

The Bithynians who had renounced Christianity proved to Pliny their
desertion by maligning Christ—one of the things which, as he observed, no
real Christian would do ("quorum nihil posse cogi dicuntur qui sunt re vera
Christiani"). "Omnes . . . Christi male dixerunt." When the proconsul
urges Polykarp to abandon Christianity, he tells the bishop, λοιδόρησον τὸν
Χριστόν (*Mart. Polyk.* ix. 3). The language of Πρὸς Ἑβραίους is echoed in
the saying of Jesus quoted in *Apost. Const.* vi. 18 : οὗτοί εἰσι περὶ ὧν καὶ ὁ
κύριος πικρῶς καὶ ἀποτόμως ἀπεφήνατο λέγων ὅτι εἰσὶ ψευδόχριστοι καὶ ψευδοδι-
δάσκαλοι, οἱ βλασφημήσαντες τὸ πνεῦμα τῆς χάριτος καὶ ἀποπτύσαντες τὴν παρ'
αὐτοῦ δωρεὰν μετὰ τὴν χάριν, οἷς οὐκ ἀφεθήσεται οὔτε ἐν τῷ αἰῶνι τούτῳ οὔτε ἐν
τῷ μέλλοντι. In Sir 31³⁰ (βαπτιζόμενος ἀπὸ νεκροῦ καὶ πάλιν ἁπτόμενος αὐτοῦ,
τί ὠφέλησεν τῷ λουτρῷ αὐτοῦ;) the allusion is to the taboo-law of Nu 19¹¹, ¹² ;
the parallel is verbal rather than real. But there is a true parallel in
Mongolian Buddhism, which ranks five sins as certain "to be followed by a
hell of intense sufferings, and that without cessation . . . patricide, matricide,
killing a Doctor of Divinity (*i.e.* a lama), bleeding Buddha, sowing hatred
among priests. . . . Drawing blood from the body of Buddha is a figurative
expression, after the manner of He 6⁶" (J. Gilmour, *Among the Mongols*,
pp. 233, 234).

---

[1] In alluding to the gibbeting law of Dt 21²²ᶠ·, Josephus (*Bell. Jud.* iv.
5. 2) speaks of ἀνασταυροῦν.

In the little illustration (vv.⁷·⁸), which corresponds to what Jesus might have put in the form of a parable, there are reminiscences of the language about God's curse upon the ground (Gn 3¹⁷·¹⁸) : ἐπικατάρατος ἡ γῆ . . . ἀκάνθας καὶ τριβόλους ἀνατελεῖ, and also of the words in Gn 1¹² καὶ ἐξήνεγκεν ἡ γῆ βοτάνην χόρτου, though the writer uses ἐκφέρειν for ἀνατέλλειν, and prefers τίκτειν to ἐκφέρειν (in v.⁷). The image of a plot or field is mentioned by Quintilian (*Instit. Orat.* v. 11. 24) as a common instance of the παραβολή : "ut, si animum dicas excolendum, similitudine utaris terrae quae neglecta spinas ac dumos, culta fructus creat." The best Greek instance is in Euripides (*Hecuba*, 592 f. : οὔκουν δεινόν, εἰ γῆ μὲν κακὴ | τυχοῦσα καιροῦ θεόθεν εὖ στάχυν φέρει, | χρηστὴ δ' ἁμαρτοῦσ' ὧν χρεὼν αὐτὴν τυχεῖν | κακὸν δίδωσι καρπόν κτλ.). Πιοῦσα of land, as, *e.g.*, in Dt 11¹¹ γῆ . . . ἐκ τοῦ ὑετοῦ τοῦ οὐρανοῦ πίεται ὕδωρ : Is 55¹⁰ᶠ· etc. As εὔθετος generally takes εἰς with the accusative, it is possible that τίκτουσα was meant to go with ἐκείνοις. Γεωργεῖται, of land being worked or cultivated, is a common term in the papyri (*e.g. Syll.* 429⁹ τά τε χωρία εἰ γεωργεῖται) as well as in the LXX.

(*a*) Origen's homiletical comment (*Philocalia*, xxi. 9) is, τὰ γινόμενα ὑπὸ τοῦ θεοῦ τεράστια οἱονεὶ ὑετός ἐστιν· αἱ δὲ προαιρέσεις αἱ διάφοροι οἱονεὶ ἡ γεγεωργημένη γῆ ἐστὶ καὶ ἡ ἠμελημένη, μιᾷ τῇ φύσει ὡς γῆ τυγχάνουσα—an idea similar to that of Jerome (*tractatus de psalmo xcvi.*, Anecdota Maredsolana, iii. 3. 90 : "apostolorum epistolae nostrae pluviae sunt spiritales. Quid enim dicit Paulus in epistola ad Hebraeos ? Terra enim saepe venientem super se bibens imbrem, et reliqua "). (*b*) The Mishna directs that at the repetition of the second of the Eighteen Blessings the worshipper should think of the heavy rain and pray for it at the ninth Blessing (Berachoth, 5¹), evidently because the second declares, "Blessed art thou, O Lord, who restorest the dead " (rain quickening the earth), and the ninth runs, "Bless to us, O Lord our God, this year and grant us a rich harvest and bring a blessing on our land." Also, " on the occasion of the rains and good news, one says, Blessed be He who is good and does good " (Berachoth, 9²). Cp. Marcus Aurelius, v. 7, εὐχὴ Ἀθηναίων· ὗσον, ὗσον, ὦ φίλε Ζεῦ, κατὰ τῆς ἀρούρας τῆς Ἀθηναίων καὶ τῶν πεδίων.

Μεταλαμβάνει (= participate in) is not a LXX term, but occurs in this sense in Wis 18⁹ etc. ; εὐλογίας occurs again in 12¹⁷ (of Esau the apostate missing his εὐλογία), and there is a subtle suggestion here, that those alone who make use of their divine privileges are rewarded. What the writer has in mind is brought out in v.¹⁰ ; that he was thinking of the Esau-story here is shown by the reminiscence of ἀγροῦ ὃν ηὐλόγησεν Κύριος (Gn 27²⁷).

The reverse side of the picture is now shown (v.⁸).

Commenting on Gn 3¹⁸ Philo fancifully plays on the derivation of the word τρίβολος (like " trefoil ") : ἕκαστον δὲ τῶν παθῶν τριβόλια εἴρηκεν, ἐπειδὴ τριττά ἐστιν, αὐτό τε καὶ τὸ ποιητικὸν καὶ τὸ ἐκ τούτων ἀποτέλεσμα (*leg. alleg.* 3⁸⁹). He also compares the eradication of evil desires in the soul to a gardener or farmer burning down weeds (*de Agric.* 4, πάντ' ἐκκόψω, ἐκτεμῶ . . . καὶ ἐπικαύσω καὶ τὰς ῥίζας αὐτῶν ἐφιεὶς ἄχρι τῶν ὑστάτων τῆς γῆς φλογὸς ῥιπήν) ; but in our epistle, as in Jn 15⁶, the burning is a final doom, not a process of severe discipline.

6

Ἀδόκιμος is used as in 1 Co 9²⁷; the moral sense breaks through, as in the next clause, where the meaning of εἰς καῦσιν may be illustrated by Dt 29²² and by Philo's more elaborate description of the thunderstorm which destroyed Sodom (*de Abrah.* 27); God, he says, showered a blast οὐχ ὕδατος ἀλλά πυρός upon the city and its fields, by way of punishment, and everything was consumed, ἐπεὶ δὲ τὰ ἐν φανερῷ καὶ ὑπὲρ γῆς ἅπαντα κατανάλωσεν ἡ φλόξ, ἤδη καὶ τὴν γῆν αὐτὴν ἔκαιε . . . ὑπὲρ τοῦ μηδ᾽ αὖθίς ποτε καρπὸν ἐνεγκεῖν ἢ χλοηφορῆσαι τὸ παράπαν δονηθῆναι. The metaphor otherwise is inexact, for the reference cannot be to the burning of a field in order to eradicate weeds; our author is thinking of final punishment (= κρίματος αἰωνίου, 6²), which he associates as usual with fire (10²⁶· ²⁷ 12²⁹). The moral application thus impinges on the figurative sketch. The words κατάρας ἐγγύς actually occur in Aristides (*Orat. in Rom.* 370: τὸ μὲν προχωρεῖν αὐτοῖς ἃ ἐβούλοντο, ἀμήχανον καὶ κατάρας ἐγγύς).[1] There is no thought of mildness in the term ἐγγύς, it being used, as in 8¹³, of imminent doom, which is only a matter of time. Meanwhile there is the ἐκδοχή (10²⁷).

Later on, this conception of unpardonable sins led to the whole system of penance, which really starts from the discussion by Hermas in the second century. But for our author the unpardonable sin is apostasy, and his view is that of a missionary. Modern analogies are not awanting. Thus, in Dr. G. Warneck's book, *The Living Forces of the Gospel* (p. 248), we read that "the Battak Christians would have even serious transgressions forgiven; but if a Christian should again sacrifice to ancestors or have anything to do with magic, no earnest Christian will speak in his favour; he is regarded as one who has fallen back into heathenism, and therefore as lost."

⁹ *Though I say this, beloved, I feel sure you will take the better* ² *course that means salvation.* ¹⁰ *God is not unfair; he will not forget what you have done, or the love you have shown for his sake in ministering, as you still do, to the saints.* ¹¹ *It is my heart's desire that each of you would prove equally keen upon realizing your full* (πληροφορίαν, 10²²) *hope to the very end,* ¹² *so that instead of being slack you may imitate those who inherit the promises by their steadfast faith.*

The ground for his confident hope about his "dear friends" (Tyndale, v.⁹) lies in the fact that they are really fruitful (v.⁷) in what is the saving quality of a Christian community, viz. brotherly love (v.¹⁰). The God who blesses a faithful life (v.⁷) will be sure to reward them for that; stern though he may be, in punishing the disloyal, he never overlooks good service. Only (vv.¹¹· ¹²),

[1] Cp. Eurip. *Hippolytus*, 1070: αἰαῖ, πρὸς ἧπαρ· δακρύων ἐγγὺς τόδε.

[2] For some reason the softer linguistic form κρείσσονα is used here, as at 10³⁴, in preference to κρείττονα.

the writer adds, put as much heart and soul into your realization
of what Christianity means as you are putting into your brotherly
love; by thus taking the better course, you are sure of God's
blessing. As ἀγαπητοί indicates (the only time he uses it), the
writer's affection leads him to hope for the best; he is deeply
concerned about the condition of his friends, but he does not
believe their case is desperate (v.⁴). He has good hopes of them,
and he wishes to encourage them by assuring them that he still
believes in them. We may compare the remarks of Seneca to
Lucilius, *Ep.* xxix. 3, about a mutual friend, Marcellinus, about
whom both of them were anxious. Seneca says he has not yet
lost hope of Marcellinus. For wisdom or philosophy " is an art ;
let it aim at some definite object, choosing those who will make
progress (profecturos) and withdrawing from those of whom it
despairs—yet not abandoning them quickly, rather trying drastic
remedies when everything seems hopeless." Elsewhere, he
encourages Lucilius himself by assuring him of his friend's
confidence and hope (*Ep.* xxxii. 2 : " habeo quidem fiduciam non
posse te detorqueri mansurumque in proposito "), and, in connexion with another case, observes that he will not be deterred
from attempting to reform certain people (*Ep.* xxv. 2) : " I would
rather lack success than lack faith."

In καὶ (epexegetic) ἐχόμενα (*sc.* πράγματα) σωτηρίας, ἐχόμενα,
thus employed, is a common Greek phrase (cp. *e.g.* Marc.
Aurel. i. 6, ὅσα τοιαῦτα τῆς Ἑλληνικῆς ἀγωγῆς ἐχόμενα : Musonius
(ed. Hense), xi., ζητεῖν παιδείας ἐχόμενα (*v.l.* ἐχόμενον) : Philo, *de
Agric.* 22, τὰ δὲ καρτερίας καὶ σωφροσύνης . . . ἐχόμενα) for what
has a bearing upon, or is connected with ; here, for what pertains
to and therefore promotes σωτηρία (the opposite of κατάρα
and καῦσις). The reason for this confidence, with which he
seeks to hearten his readers, lies in their good record of practical
service (τοῦ ἔργου ὑμῶν κτλ.) which God is far too just to ignore.
After all, they had some fruits as well as roots of Christianity
(v.¹⁰). Ἐπιλαθέσθαι is an infinitive of conceived result (Burton's
Moods and Tenses, 371c; Blass, § 391. 4), instead of ἵνα c. subj.,
as, *e.g.*, in 1 Jn 1⁹, or ὥστε c. infinitive; cp. Xen. *Cyrop.* iv. 1. 20,
δίκαιος εἶ ἀντιχαρίζεσθαι.¹ The text of τοῦ ἔργου ὑμῶν καὶ τῆς
ἀγάπης was soon harmonized with that of 1 Th 1³ by the insertion of τοῦ κόπου after καὶ (so D^c K L 69*. 256. 263. 1611*.
2005. 2127 boh Theodoret, etc.). The relative ἥν after ἀγάπης
has been attracted into the genitive ἧς (as in 9²⁰). One practical form of this διακονεῖν is mentioned in 10³³·³⁴. Here εἰς
τὸ ὄνομα αὐτοῦ goes closely with διακονήσαντες κτλ., as well as
with ἐνεδείξασθε, in the sense of " for his sake." In *Pirke Aboth*,

---

¹ See Dolon's remark in the *Rhesus* of Euripides (161, 162) : οὐκοῦν πονεῖ
μὲν χρή, πονοῦντα δ᾽ ἄξιον μισθὸν φέρεσθαι.

2¹⁶, R. Jose's saying is quoted, "Let all thy works be done for the sake of heaven" (literally לְשֵׁם, *i.e.* εἰς ὄνομα, as here and in Ign. *Rom.* 9³ ἡ ἀγάπη τῶν ἐκκλησιῶν τῶν δεξαμένων με εἰς ὄνομα Ἰησοῦ Χριστοῦ). Τοῖς ἁγίοις, the only place (except 13²⁴) where the writer uses this common term for "fellow-Christians"; God will never be so unjust as to overlook kindness shown to "his own."

The personal affection of the writer comes out not only in the ἀγαπητοί of v.⁹, but again (v.¹¹) in the deep ἐπιθυμοῦμεν, a term charged with intense yearning (as Chrysostom says, πατρικῆς φιλοστοργίας), and in the individualizing ἕκαστον (cp. 3¹². ¹³). He is urgent that they should display τὴν αὐτὴν σπουδήν with regard to their Christian ἐλπίς as they display in the sphere of their Christian ἀγάπη. This does not mean that he wishes them to be more concerned about saving their own souls or about heaven than about their duties of brotherly love; his point is that the higher knowledge which he presses upon their minds is the one security for a Christian life at all. Just as Paul cannot assume that the warm mutual affection of the Thessalonian Christians implied a strict social morality (see below on 13⁴), or that the same quality in the Philippian Christians implied moral discrimination (Ph 1⁹), so our author pleads with his friends to complete their brotherly love by a mature grasp of what their faith implied. He reiterates later on the need of φιλαδελφία (13¹), and he is careful to show how it is inspired by the very devotion to Christ for which he pleads (10¹⁹⁻²⁴). Πληροφορία (not a LXX term) here is less subjective than in 10²², where it denotes the complete assurance which comes from a realization of all that is involved in some object. Here it is the latter sense of fulness, scope and depth in their—ἐλπίς.¹ This is part and parcel of the τελειότης to which he is summoning them to advance (6¹). The result of this grasp of what is involved in their faith will be (v.¹²) a vigorous constancy, without which even a kindly, unselfish spirit is inadequate. For ἐνδείκνυσθαι σπουδήν compare Herodian's remark that the soldiers of Severus in A.D. 193 πᾶσαν ἐνεδείκνυντο προθυμίαν καὶ σπουδήν (ii. 10. 19), Magn. 53⁶¹ (iii. B.C.), ἀπόδειξιν ποιούμενος τῆς περὶ τὰ μέγιστα σπουδῆς, and *Syll.* 342⁴¹ (i. B.C.) τὴν μεγίστην ἐνδείκνυται σπουδὴν εἰς τὴν ὑπὲρ τῆς πατρίδος σωτηρίαν. The Greeks used the verb as we use "display," in speaking of some inward quality. This ardour has to be kept up ἄχρι τέλους (cp. pseudo-Musonius, *Epp.* 1, in Hercher's *Epistolog. Graeci*, 401 f. : τηροῦντας δὲ ἣν ἔχουσι νῦν πρόθεσιν ἄχρι τέλους φιλοσοφῆσαι) ; it is the sustained interest in essential Christian truth which issues practically in μακροθυμία (v.¹²), or in the confident attitude of hope (3⁶, ¹⁴).

¹ For ἐλπίδος, πίστεως is read in W 1867.

Aristotle, in *Rhet.* ii. 19. 5, argues that οὗ ἡ ἀρχὴ δύναται γενέσθαι, καὶ τὸ τέλος· οὐδὲν γὰρ γίγνεται οὐδ' ἄρχεται γίγνεσθαι τῶν ἀδυνάτων, a paradox which really means that "if you want to know whether the end of any course of action, plan, scheme, or indeed of anything—is possible, you must look to the beginning : beginning implies end : if it can be begun, it can also be brought to an end " (Cope).

In v.¹² the appeal is rounded off with ἵνα μὴ νωθροὶ γένησθε, that you may not prove remiss (repeating νωθροί from 5¹¹, but in a slightly different sense : they are to be alert not simply to understand, but to act upon the solid truths of their faith), μιμηταὶ δέ κτλ. Hitherto he has only mentioned people who were a warning ; now he encourages them by pointing out that they had predecessors in the line of loyalty. This incentive is left over for the time being ; the writer returns to it in his panegyric upon faith in chapter 11. Meanwhile he is content to emphasize the steadfast faith (πίστεως καὶ μακροθυμίας, a hendiadys) that characterizes this loyalty. Μακροθυμία means here (as in Ja 5⁷ᶠ·) the tenacity with which faith holds out. Compare Menander's couplet (Kock's *Com. Attic. Fragm.* 549), ἄνθρωπος ὢν μηδέποτε τὴν ἀλυπίαν | αἰτοῦ παρὰ θεῶν, ἀλλὰ τὴν μακροθυμίαν, and *Test. Jos.* 2⁷ μέγα φάρμακόν ἐστιν ἡ μακροθυμία | καὶ πολλὰ ἀγαθὰ δίδωσιν ἡ ὑπομονή. But this aspect of πίστις is not brought forward till 10³⁵ᶠ·, after the discussion of the priest-hood and sacrifice of Christ. In κληρονομούντων τὰς ἐπαγγελίας the writer implies that hope is invariably sustained by a promise or promises. He has already mentioned ἡ ἐπαγγελία (4¹). Κληρονομεῖν τὰς ἐπαγγελίας can hardly mean "get a promise of something"; as the appended διὰ πίστεως καὶ μακροθυμίας suggests, it denotes "coming into possession of what is promised." This is proved by the equivalent ἐπέτυχε τῆς ἐπαγγελίας in v.¹⁵.

Taking Abraham as the first or as a typical instance of steadfast faith in God's promises, the writer now (vv.¹³⁻¹⁹) lays stress not upon the human quality, but upon the divine basis for this undaunted reliance. Constancy means an effort. But it is evoked by a divine revelation ; what stirs and sustains it is a word of God. From the first the supreme Promise of God has been guaranteed by him to men so securely that there need be no uncertainty or hesitation in committing oneself to this Hope. The paragraph carries on the thought of vv.¹¹· ¹² ; at the end, by a dexterous turn, the writer regains the line of argument which he had dropped when he turned aside to incite and reprove his readers (5¹¹ᶠ·).

¹³ *For in making a promise to Abraham God " swore by himself" (since he could swear by none greater),* ¹⁴ *" I will indeed bless you and multiply you."* ¹⁵ *Thus it was (i.e.* thanks to the divine Oath) *that Abraham by his steadfast-ness obtained* (so 11³³) *what he had been promised.* ¹⁶ *For as* ¹ *men swear by*

¹ To make the connexion clear, some inferior texts (C Dᶜ K L 6. 33. 104 1610, etc.) add μέν.

a greater than themselves, and as an oath means to them a guarantee that ends any dispute, [17] *God, in his desire to afford the heirs of the Promise a special proof of the solid character of his purpose, interposed with an oath ;* [18] *so that by these two solid facts* (the Promise and the Oath), *where it is impossible for God to be false, we refugees might have strong encouragement* (παράκλησιν, see on 12⁵) *to seize the hope set before us,* [19] *anchoring the soul to it safe and sure, as it " enters the inner " Presence " behind the veil."*

As usual, he likes to give a biblical proof or illustration (vv.¹³·¹⁴), God's famous promise to Abraham, but the main point in it is that God ratified the promise with an oath.

Our author takes the OT references to God's oath quite naively. Others had felt a difficulty, as is shown by Philo's treatise *de Abrahamo* (46): "God, enamoured of this man [*i.e.* Abraham], for his faith (πίστιν) in him, gives him in return a pledge (πίστιν), guaranteeing by an oath (τὴν δι' ὅρκου βεβαίωσιν) the gifts he had promised . . . for he says, 'I swear by myself' (Gn 22¹⁶)— and with him a word is an oath—for the sake of confirming his mind more steadfastly and immovably than ever before." But the references to God's oaths were a perplexity to Philo ; his mystical mind was embarrassed by their realism. In *de sacrif. Abelis et Caini* (28, 29) he returns to the subject. Hosts of people, he admits, regard the literal sense of these OT words as inconsistent with God's character, since an oath implies (μαρτυρία θεοῦ περὶ πράγματος ἀμφισβητουμένου) God giving evidence in a disputed matter ; whereas θεῷ οὐδὲν ἄδηλον οὐδὲ ἀμφισβητούμενον, God's mere word ought to be enough : ὁ δὲ θεὸς καὶ λέγων πιστός ἐστιν, ὥστε καὶ τοὺς λόγους αὐτοῦ βεβαιότητος ἕνεκα μηδὲν ὅρκων διαφέρειν. He inclines to regard the OT references to God's oaths as a condescension of the sacred writer to dull minds rather than as a condescension upon God's part. In *Leg. Allegor.* iii. 72 he quotes this very passage (Gn 22¹⁶·¹⁷), adding : εὖ καὶ τὸ ὅρκῳ βεβαιῶσαι τὴν ὑπόσχεσιν καὶ ὅρκῳ θεοπρεπεῖ· ὁρᾷς γὰρ ὅτι οὐ καθ' ἑτέρου ὀμνύει θεός, οὐδὲν γὰρ αὐτοῦ κρεῖττον, ἀλλὰ καθ' ἑαυτοῦ, ὅς ἐστι πάντων ἄριστος. But he feels bound to explain it. Some of his contemporaries had begun to take exception to such representations of God, on the ground that God's word required no formal confirmation—it confirmed itself by being fulfilled—and that it was absurd (ἄτοπον) to speak of God swearing by himself, in order to bear testimony to himself.[1] Philo (*ibid.* 73) attempts to meet this objection by urging that only God can bear testimony to himself, since no one else knows the divine nature truly ; consequently it is appropriate for him to add confirmation to his word, although the latter by itself is amply deserving of belief. In Berachoth, 32. 1 (on Ex 32¹³), it is asked, "What means בך? R. Eleazar answered : 'Thus saith Moses to God (Blessed be He !), 'Lord of all the world, hadst thou sworn by heaven and earth, I would say, even as heaven and earth shall perish, so too thine oath shall perish. But now thou hast sworn by thy Great Name, which lives and lasts for ever and ever ; so shall thine oath also last for ever and ever.'"

Εἶχε (v.¹³) with infin. = ἐδύνατο as usual. Ὤμοσεν. . . . εἰ μήν . . . εὐλογήσω. Both the LXX (Thackeray, pp. 83, 84) and the papyri (Deissmann, *Bible Studies*, 205 f.) show that εἰ μήν after ὀμνύειν in oaths is common as an asseveration ; in some cases, as here, the classical form ἦ μήν, from which εἰ μήν arose by itacism, is textually possible. The quotation (v.¹⁴) is from the promise made to Abraham after the sacrifice of Isaac (Gn 22¹⁶·¹⁷): κατ' ἐμαυτοῦ ὤμοσα . . . εἰ μὴν εὐλογῶν εὐλογήσω σε, καὶ πλη-

---

[1] This is the point raised in Jn 8¹³ᶠ.

θύνων πληθυνῶ τὸ σπέρμα σου. The practical religious value of God's promise being thus (v.[15]) confirmed is now brought out for the present generation (vv.[16f.]—another long sentence). Κατὰ τοῦ μείζονος, *i.e.* by God. Which, Philo argues, is irreverent: ἀσεβεῖς ἂν νομισθεῖεν οἱ φάσκοντες ὀμνύναι κατὰ θεοῦ (*Leg. Allegor.* iii. 73), since only swearing by the Name of God is permissible (cp. Dt 6[13]). But our author has no such scruples (see above). And he is quite unconscious of any objection to oaths, such as some early Christian teachers felt (*e.g.* Ja 5[12]); he speaks of the practice of taking oaths without any scruples. "Hic locus . . . docet aliquem inter Christianos jurisjurandi usum esse legitimum . . . porro non dicit olim fuisse in usu, sed adhuc vigere pronuntiat" (Calvin). Ἀντιλογίας, dispute or quarrel (the derived sense in 7[7] χωρὶς πάσης ἀντιλογίας, there is no disputing). Εἰς βεβαίωσιν only occurs once in the LXX (Lv 25[23]), but is a current phrase in the papyri (cp. Deissmann's *Bible Studies*, 163 f.) for "by way of guarantee"; it is opposed to εἰς ἀθέτησιν, and used here as in Wis 6[19] προσοχὴ δὲ νόμων βεβαίωσις ἀφθαρσίας. In Philo (see on v.[13]) it is the oath which is guaranteed; here the oath guarantees. The general idea of v.[17] is that of *OGIS.* (ii. B.C.), ὅπως ἂν εἰς τὸν ἄπαντα χρόνον ἀκίνητα καὶ ἀμετάθετα μένηι τά τε πρὸς τὸν θεὸν τίμια καὶ τὰ πρὸς τὸν Ἀθήναιον φιλάνθρωπα. Ἐν ᾧ (= διό, Theophylact), such being the case. Περισσότερον, which goes with ἐπιδεῖξαι, is illustrated by what Philo says in *de Abrahamo,* 46 (see above): "abundantius quam sine juramento factum videretur" (Bengel). It is an equivalent for περισσοτέρως, which, indeed, B reads here. Ἐπιδεῖξαι (cp. Elephantine-Papyri [1907] 1[7] (iv. B.C.) ἐπιδειξάτω δὲ Ἡρακλείδης ὅτι ἂν ἐγκαλῆι Δημητρίαι ἐναντίον ἀνδρῶν τριῶν): the verb, which is only once used of God in the LXX (Is 37[26] νῦν δὲ ἐπέδειξα ἐξερημῶσαι ἔθνη κτλ.), means here "to afford proof of." The writer uses the general plural, τοῖς κληρονόμοις τῆς ἐπαγγελίας,[1] instead of the singular "Abraham," since the Promise in its mystical sense applied to the entire People, who had faith like that of Abraham. The reference is not specifically to Isaac and Jacob, although these are called his συγκληρονόμοι in 11[9]. In τὸ ἀμετάθετον τῆς βουλῆς our author evidently chooses βουλῆς for the sake of the assonance with βουλόμενος. Ἀμετάθετος is a synonym for ἀκίνητος (cp. above on v.[17] and Schol. on Soph. *Antig.* 1027), and, as the papyri show, had a frequent connexion with wills in the sense of "irrevocable." Here, in connexion with βουλῆς, it implies final determination (cp. 3 Mac 5[11. 12]); the purpose had a fixed

---

[1] Eusebius once (*Dem.* iv. 15. 40) omits τῆς ἐπαγγελίας, and once (*ibid.* v. 3. 21) reads τῆς βασιλείας, either accidentally or with a recollection of Ja 2[5].

character or solidity about it. The verb ἐμεσίτευσεν ("intervened") does not occur in the LXX, and is here used intransitively, instead of, as usual (cp. *e.g.* Dion. Halic. *Ant.* ix. 59. 5; *OGIS.* 437[76] etc.), with some accusative like συνθήκας. In Jos. *Ant.* vii. 8. 5 it is used intransitively, but in the sense of "interceding" (πεισθεὶς δ' ὁ Ἰωαβος καὶ τὴν ἀνάγκην αὐτοῦ κατοικτείρας ἐμεσίτευσε πρὸς τὸν βασιλέα). The oath is almost certainly that just mentioned. Less probable is the interpretation (Delitzsch, Hofmann, M. Stuart, von Soden, Peake, Seeberg, Wickham) which regards the oath referred to in vv.[16f.] as the oath in the writer's favourite psalm, 110[4]:

> ὤμοσεν Κύριος καὶ οὐ μεταμεληθήσεται
> Σὺ εἶ ἱερεὺς εἰς τὸν αἰῶνα κατὰ τὴν τάξιν Μελχισέδεκ.

This oath does refer to the priesthood of Jesus, which the writer is about to re-introduce (in v.[20]); but it is not a thought which is brought forward till 7[20. 21. 28]; and the second line of the couplet has been already quoted (5[6]) without any allusion to the first.

In v.[18] καταφεύγειν and ἐλπίς are connected, but not as in Wis 14[6] (Noah = ἡ ἐλπὶς τοῦ κόσμου ἐπὶ σχεδίας, καταφυγοῦσα). Here, as ἐλπίς means what is hoped for, *i.e.* the object of expectation, "the only thought is that we are moored to an immoveable object" (A. B. Davidson). The details of the anchor-metaphor are not to be pressed (v.[19]); the writer simply argues that we are meant to fix ourselves to what has been fixed for us by God and in God. To change the metaphor, our hope roots itself in the eternal order. What we hope for is unseen, being out of sight, but it is secure and real, and we can grasp it by faith.

(*a*) Philo (*Quaest. in Exod.* 22[20]) ascribes the survival and success of the Israelites in Egypt διὰ τὴν ἐπὶ τὸν σωτῆρα θεὸν καταφυγήν, ὃς ἐξ ἀπόρων καὶ ἀμηχάνων ἐπιπέμψας τὴν εὐεργέτιν δύναμιν ἐρρύσατο τοὺς ἱκέτας. (*b*) τόν is inserted in v.[18] before θεόν (by א* A C P 33. 1245. 1739. 1827. 2005 Ath. Chrys.), probably to harmonize with ὁ θεός in v.[17] (where 1912 omits ὁ). But θεόν ("one who is God") is quite apposite.

Παράκλησιν goes with κρατῆσαι (aor. = "seize," rather than "hold fast to," like κρατεῖν in 4[14]), and οἱ καταφυγόντες stands by itself, though there is no need to conjecture οἱ κατὰ φυγὴν ὄντες = in our flight (so J. J. Reiske, etc.). Is not eternal life, Philo asks, ἡ πρὸς τὸ ὂν καταφυγή (*de fuga*, 15)? In τῆς προκειμένης ἐλπίδος, προκειμένης must have the same sense as in 12[2]; the colloquial sense of "aforesaid," which is common in the papyri (*e.g.* *OP.* 1275[25] εἰς τὴν προκιμένην κώμην), would be flat. Ἀσφαλῆ τε καὶ βεβαίαν reflects one of the ordinary phrases in Greek ethics which the writer is so fond of employing. Cp.

Plutarch, *de comm. not.* 1061*c*, καίτοι πᾶσα κατάληψις ἐν τῷ σοφῷ καὶ μνήμη τὸ ἀσφαλὲς ἔχουσα καὶ βέβαιον κτλ. : Sextus Empir. *adv. log.* ii. 374, ἐς τὸ ὑποτιθέμενον ἢ ὑποτίθεται βέβαιον ἐστι καὶ ἀσφαλές : and Philo, *quis rer. div.* 62, κατάληψις ἀσφαλὴς καὶ βεβαία. The ἄγκυρα of hope is safe and sure, as it is fixed in eternity. All hope for the Christian rests in what Jesus has done in the eternal order by his sacrifice.

Chrysostom's comment on the "anchor" metaphor is all that is needed : ὥσπερ γὰρ ἡ ἄγκυρα ἐξαρτηθεῖσα τοῦ πλοίου, οὐκ ἀφίησεν αὐτὸ περιφέρεσθαι, κἂν μυρίοι παρασαλεύωσιν ἄνεμοι, ἀλλ' ἐξαρτηθεῖσα ἑδραῖον ποιεῖ· οὕτω καὶ ἡ ἐλπίς. The anchor of hope was a fairly common metaphor in the later Greek ethic (*e.g.* Heliod. vii. 25, πᾶσα ἐλπίδος ἄγκυρα παντοίως ἀνέσπασται, and Epict. *Fragm.* (30) 89, οὔτε ναῦν ἐξ ἑνὸς ἀγκυρίου οὔτε βίον ἐκ μιᾶς ἐλπίδος ὁρμιστέον), but our author may have taken the religious application from Philo, who writes (*de Somniis*, i. 39),[1] οὐ χρὴ κατεπτηχέναι τὸν ἐλπίδι θείας συμμαχίας ἐφορμοῦντα (lies moored to). He does not use it as a metaphor for stability, however, like most of the Greeks from Euripides (*e.g. Helena*, 277, ἄγκυρα δ' ἤ μου τὰς τύχας ὤχει μόνη) and Aristophanes (*e.g. Knights*, 1244, λεπτή τις ἐλπίς ἐστ' ἐφ' ἧς ὀχούμεθα) onwards, as, *e.g.*, in the most famous use of the anchor-metaphor,[2] that by Pythagoras (Stob. *Eclog.* 3 : πλοῦτος ἀσθενὴς ἄγκυρα, δόξα ἔτι ἀσθενεστέρα . . . τίνες οὖν ἄγκυραι δύναται; φρόνησις, μεγαλοψυχία, ἀνδρία· ταύτας οὐθεὶς χειμὼν σαλεύει).

Suddenly he breaks the metaphor,[3] in order to regain the idea of the priesthood of Jesus in the invisible world. Hope enters the unseen world ; the Christian hope, as he conceives it, is bound up with the sacrifice and intercession of Jesus in the Presence of God, and so he uses language from the ritual of Lv 16²ᶠ· about Aaron "passing inside the veil," or curtain that screened the innermost shrine. To this conception he returns in 9³ᶠ· after he has described the vital functions of Jesus as ἱερεύς (6²⁰ᶠ·). For at last he has reached what he regards as the cardinal theme of his homily. The first paragraph (7¹⁻³), which is one long sentence in Greek, applies and expands εἰς τὸν αἰῶνα, the first note of Melchizedek's priesthood being that it is perpetual, thus typifying the priesthood of Jesus. The next is (7⁴⁻¹⁰), that it is prior and superior to the levitical priesthood ; this is

[1] The comparison between hope and a voyage in *de Abrahamo*, 9, is different : ὁ δὲ ἐλπίζων, ὡς αὐτὸ δηλοῖ τοὔνομα, ἐλλιπής, ἐφιέμενος μὲν ἀεὶ τοῦ καλοῦ, μήπω δ' ἐφικέσθαι τούτου δεδυνημένος, ἀλλ' ἐοικὼς τοῖς πλέουσιν, οἳ σπεύδοντες εἰς λιμένας καταίρειν θαλαττεύουσιν ἐνορμίσασθαι μὴ δυνάμενοι. This is nearer to the thought of Ro 8²⁴·²⁵.

[2] For the anchor as a symbol on tombs, pagan and Christian, see Le Blant's *Inscr. Chrét. de Gaule*, ii. 158, 312. Contrast with He 6¹⁸·¹⁹ the bitter melancholy of the epitaph in the Greek Anthology (ix. 49): ἐλπὶς καὶ σύ, Τύχη, μέγα χαίρετε· τὸν λιμέν' εὗρον | οὐδὲν ἐμοὶ χ' ὑμῖν· παίζετε τοὺς μετ' ἐμέ.

[3] A similar mixture of metaphor in *Ep. Aristeas*, 230 (σὲ μὲν οὐ δυνατόν ἐστι πταῖσαι, πᾶσι γὰρ χάριτας ἔσπαρκας αἳ βλαστάνουσιν εὔνοιαν, ἢ τὰ μέγιστο. τῶν ὅπλων κατισχύουσα περιλαμβάνει τὴν μεγίστην ἀσφάλειαν), and Philo, *de praemiis*, 2 (ταύτης δ' ὁ πρῶτος σπόρος ἐστὶν ἐλπίς, ἡ πηγὴ τῶν βίων).

implied in the former claim, but the writer works it out fancifully
from the allusion to tithes.

> [20] *There* (ὅπου for the classical ὅποι) *Jesus entered for us in advance, when
> he became highpriest "for ever with the rank of Melchizedek."* [1] *For
> "Melchizedek, the king of Salem, a priest of the Most High God," who "met
> Abraham on his return from the slaughter of the kings and blessed him".* -
> [2] *who had "a tenth part* (δεκάτην, sc. μοῖραν) *of everything" assigned him by
> Abraham—this Melchizedek is* (sc. ὤν) *primarily a "king of righteousnes."*
> (*that is the meaning of his name*); *then, besides that, "king of Salem"*
> (*which means, king of peace*). [3] *He has neither father nor mother nor gene-
> alogy, neither a beginning to his days nor an end to his life, but, resembling
> the Son of God, continues to be "priest" permanently.*

This paragraph and that which follows (vv.[4-10]) are another
little sermon, this time on the story of Gn 14[18-20]. In 6[20]-7[3]
the writer starts from the idea that Jesus is ἀρχιερεὺς εἰς τὸν
αἰῶνα κατὰ τὴν τάξιν Μελχισεδέκ, and shows how the Melchizedek
priesthood was εἰς τὸν αἰῶνα, *i.e.* explaining Ps 110[4] from Gn
14[18-20]. Εἰσῆλθεν in 6[20] is explained later, in 9[12f]. Πρόδρομος
recalls ἀρχηγός (2[10]), with its suggestion of pioneering. The
term is only used in the LXX of the days ἔαρος, πρόδρομοι
σταφυλῆς (Nu 13[22]), or of early fruit (ὡς πρόδρομος σύκου, Is 28[4]);
the present sense occurs, however, in Wis 12[8], where wasps or
hornets are called the πρόδρομοι of God's avenging host. The
thought here is of Christ entering heaven as we are destined to
do, after him, once like him (5[9]) we are "perfected." Vv.[1-3]
in ch. 7 are another of the writer's long sentences : οὗτος ὁ Μελχισεδέκ . . . μένει ἱερεὺς εἰς τὸ διηνεκές is the central thought,
but the subject is overloaded with quotations and comments,
including a long μέν . . . δέ clause. The length of the sentence
and the difficulty of applying μένει ἱερεὺς εἰς τὸ διηνεκές to
Melchizedek have led some editors to make Jesus the subject of
the sentence : οὗτος (Jesus) γὰρ (ὁ Μελχισεδέκ . . . τῷ υἱῷ θεοῦ)
μένει ἱερεὺς εἰς τὸν αἰῶνα. But the οὗτος, as v.[4] shows, is
Melchizedek, and the theory is wrecked upon v.[8], for it is quite
impossible to take ἐκεῖ κτλ. as " in the upper sanctuary (sc. ἐστιν)
there is One of whom the record is that He lives." There is a
slight but characteristic freedom at the very outset in the use of
the story, *e.g.* in ὁ συναντήσας κτλ. The story implies this, but
does not say it. It was the king of Sodom who ἐξῆλθεν εἰς
συνάντησιν αὐτῷ μετὰ τὸ ὑποστρέψαι αὐτὸν ἀπὸ τῆς κοπῆς, but as
Melchizedek is immediately said to have brought the conquering
hero bread and wine, our writer assumed that he also met
Abraham.

An interesting example of the original reading being preserved in an
inferior group of MSS is afforded by ὁ συναντήσας (C* L P). The variant
ὃς συναντήσας (א A B C² D K W 33. 436. 794. 1831. 1837. 1912), which
makes a pointless anacolouthon, was due to the accidental reduplication of C

(OCCYN for OCYN), though attempts have been made to justify this reading by assuming an anacolouthon in the sentence, or a parenthesis in ὅς . . . Ἀβραάμ, or carelessness on the part of the writer who began with a relative and forgot to carry on the proper construction. Some curious homiletic expansions have crept into the text of vv.[1, 2]. After βασιλέων two late minuscules (456, 460) read ὅτι ἐδίωξεν τοὺς ἀλλοφύλους καὶ ἐξείλατο Λὼτ μετὰ πάσης αἰχμαλωσίας, and after αὐτόν, D* vt 330. 440. 823 put καὶ (Ἀβραὰμ) εὐλογηθεὶς ὑπ' αὐτοῦ. The latter is another (cp. 11²³) of the glosses which were thrown up by the Latin versions.

In v.[2] ἐμέρισεν is substituted for the ἔδωκεν of the LXX (which reappears in v.[4]), in order to make it clear that Abraham's gift was a sort of tithe. Tithes were not paid by the Hebrews from spoils of war; this was a pagan custom. But such is the interpretation of the story in Philo, *e.g.* in his fragment on Gn 14[18] (*Fragments of Philo*, ed. J. Rendel Harris, p. 72): τὰ γὰρ τοῦ πολέμου ἀριστεῖα δίδωσι τῷ ἱερεῖ καὶ τὰς τῆς νίκης ἀπαρχάς. ἱεροπρεπεστάτη δὲ καὶ ἁγιωτάτη πασῶν ἀπαρχῶν ἡ δεκάτη διὰ τὸ παντέλειον εἶναι τὸν ἀριθμόν, ἀφ' οὗ καὶ τοῖς ἱερεῦσι καὶ νεωκόροις αἱ δεκάται προστάξει νόμου καρπῶν καὶ θρεμμάτων ἀποδίδονται, ἄρξαντος τῆς ἀπαρχῆς Ἀβραάμ, ὃς καὶ τοῦ γένους ἀρχηγέτης ἐστίν. Or again in *de congressu*, 17, where he describes the same incident as Abraham offering God τὰς δεκάτας χαριστήρια τῆς νίκης.

The fantastic interpretation of the Melchizedek episode is all the writer's own. What use, if any, was made of Melchizedek in pre-Christian Judaism, is no longer to be ascertained. Apparently the book of Jubilees contained a reference to this episode in Abraham's career, but it has been excised for some reason (see R. H. Charles' note on Jub 13²⁵). Josephus makes little of the story (*Ant.* i. 10. 2). He simply recounts how, when Abraham returned from the rout of the Assyrians, ἀπήντησε δ' αὐτῷ ὁ τῶν Σοδομιτῶν βασιλεὺς εἰς τόπον τινὰ ὃν καλοῦσι Πεδίον βασιλικόν· ἔνθα ὁ τῆς Σολυμᾶ πόλεως ὑποδέχεται βασιλεὺς αὐτὸν Μελχισεδέκης. σημαίνει δὲ τοῦτο βασιλεὺς δίκαιος· καὶ ἦν δὲ τοιοῦτος ὁμολογουμένως, ὡς διὰ ταύτην αὐτὸν τὴν αἰτίαν καὶ ἱερέα γινέσθαι τοῦ θεοῦ. τὴν μέντοι Σολυμᾶ ὕστερον ἐκάλεσαν Ἱεροσόλυμα. ἐχορήγησε δὲ οὗτος ὁ Μελχισεδέκης τῷ Ἀβράμου στρατῷ ξένια καὶ πολλὴν ἀφθονίαν τῶν ἐπιτηδείων παρέσχε, καὶ παρὰ τὴν εὐωχίαν αὐτὸν τ' ἐπαινεῖν ἤρξατο καὶ τὸν θεὸν εὐλογεῖν ὑποχειρίους αὐτῷ ποιήσαντα τοὺς ἐχθρούς. Ἀβράμου δὲ διδόντος καὶ τὴν δεκάτην· τῆς λείας αὐτῷ, προσδέχεται τὴν δόσιν κτλ. In the later Judaism, however, more interest was taken in Melchizedek (cp. M. Friedländer in *Revue des Études Juives*, v. pp. 1 f.). Thus some applied the 110th psalm to Abraham (Mechilta on Ex 15⁷, r. Gen. 55. 6), who was ranked as the priest after the order of Melchizedek, while Melchizedek was supposed to have been degraded because he (Gn 14¹⁹) mentioned the name of Abraham before that of God! This, as Bacher conjectures, represented a protest against the Christian view of Melchizedek (*Agada der Tannaiten*², i. p. 259). It denotes the influence of Πρὸς Ἑβραίους. Philo, as we might expect, had already made more of the episode than Josephus, and it is Philo's method of interpretation which gives the clue to our writer's use of the story. Thus in *Leg. Alleg.* iii. 25, 26. he points out (*a*) that Μελχισεδὲκ βασιλέα τε τῆς εἰρήνης—Σαλὴμ τοῦτο γὰρ ἑρμηνεύεται—καὶ ἱερέα ἑαυτοῦ πεποίηκεν[1] ὁ θεός (in Gn 14¹⁸), and allegorizes the reference into a panegyric upon the peaceful, persuasive influence of the really royal mind. He then (*b*) does the same with the sacerdotal reference. Ἀλλ'

---

[1] The same sort of perfect as recurs in Πρὸς Ἑβραίους (*e.g.* 7⁶ and 11²⁸).

ὁ μὲν Μελχισεδὲκ ἀντὶ ὕδατος οἶνον προσφερέτω καὶ ποτιζέτω καὶ ἀκρατιζέτω ψυχάς, ἵνα κατάσχετοι γένωνται θείᾳ μέθῃ νηφαλεωτέρᾳ νήψεως αὐτῆς. ἱερεὺς γάρ ἐστι λόγος κλῆρον ἔχων τὸν ὄντα καὶ ὑψηλῶς περὶ αὐτοῦ καὶ ὑπερόγκως καὶ μεγαλοπρεπῶς λογιζόμενος· τοῦ γὰρ ὑψίστου ἐστὶν ἱερεύς, quoting Gn 14[18] and hastening to add, οὐχ ὅτι ἐστί τις ἄλλος οὐχ ὕψιστος. Philo points out thus the symbolism of wine (not water) as the divine intoxication which raises the soul to lofty thought of God; but our author does not even mention the food and drink, though later on there was a tendency to regard them as symbolizing the elements in the eucharist. His interest in Melchizedek lies in the parallel to Christ. This leads him along a line of his own, though, like Philo, he sees immense significance not only in what scripture says, but in what it does not say, about this mysterious figure in the early dawn of history.

In vv.[1, 2] the only points in the original tale which are specially noted are (a) that his name means βασιλεὺς δικαιοσύνης; (b) that Σαλήμ, his capital, means εἰρήνη; and (c) inferentially that this primitive ideal priest was also a king. Yet none of these is developed. Thus, the writer has no interest in identifying Σαλήμ. All that matters is its meaning. He quotes ἱερεὺς τοῦ θεοῦ τοῦ ὑψίστου, but it is ἱερεύς alone that interests him. The fact about the tithes (ᾧ καὶ δεκάτην ἀπὸ πάντων ἐμέρισεν Ἀβραάμ) is certainly significant, but it is held over until v.[4]. What strikes him as far more vital is the silence of the record about the birth and death of Melchizedek (v.[3]). Δικαιοσύνη as a royal characteristic (see Introd. pp. xxxii f.) had been already noted in connexion with Christ (1[8f.]); but he does not connect it with εἰρήνη, as Philo does, though the traditional association of δικαιοσύνη καὶ εἰρήνη with the messianic reign may have been in his mind. In the alliteration (v.[3]) of ἀπάτωρ, ἀμήτωρ, ἀγενεαλόγητος, the third term is apparently coined by himself; it does not mean "of no pedigree," nor "without successors," but simply (cp. v.[6]) "devoid of any genealogy." Having no beginning (since none is mentioned), M. has no end. Ἀπάτωρ and ἀμήτωρ are boldly lifted from their pagan associations. In the brief episode of Gn 14[18-20], this mysterious Melchizedek appears only as a priest of God; his birth is never mentioned, neither is his death; unlike the Aaronic priests, with whom a pure family descent was vital, this priest has no progenitors. Reading the record in the light of Ps 110[4], and on the Alexandrian principle that the very silence of scripture is charged with meaning, the writer divines in Melchizedek a priest who is permanent. This method of interpretation had been popularized by Philo. In *quod det. pot.* 48, *e.g.*, he calls attention to the fact that Moses does not explain in Gn 4[15] what was the mark put by God upon Cain. Why? Because the mark was to prevent him from being killed. Now Moses never mentions the death of Cain διὰ πάσης τῆς νομοθεσίας, suggesting that ὥσπερ ἡ μεμυθευμένη Σκύλλα, κακὸν ἀθάνατον ἐστιν ἀφροσύνη. Again (*de Ebriet.* 14) εἶπε γάρ πού τις "καὶ γὰρ ἀληθῶς ἀδελφή μού ἐστιν ἐκ πατρός, 'ἀλλ' οὐκ ἐκ μητρός" (Gn 20[12])—

Abraham's evasive description of Sarah—is most significant; she had no mother, *i.e.* she had no connexion with the material world of the senses.

'Απάτωρ and ἀμήτωρ were applied to (*a*) waifs, whose parents were unknown ; or (*b*) to illegitimate children ; or (*c*) to people of low origin ; or (*d*) to deities who were supposed to have been born, like Athenê and Hephaestus, from only one sex. Lactantius (*diuin. instit.* i. 7) quotes the Delphic oracle, which described Apollo as ἀμήτωρ, and insists that such terms refer only to God (*ibid.* iv. 13). "As God the Father, the origin and source of things, is without parentage, he is most accurately called ἀπάτωρ and ἀμήτωρ by Trismegistus, since he was not begotten by anyone. Hence it was fitting that the Son also should be twice born, that he too should become ἀπάτωρ and ἀμήτωρ." His argument apparently[1] is that the pre-existent Son was ἀμήτωρ and that He became ἀπάτωρ by the Virgin-birth (so Theodore of Mopsuestia). Lactantius proves the priesthood of Christ from Ps 110[4] among other passages, but he ignores the deduction from the Melchizedek of Gn 14 ; indeed he gives a rival derivation of Jerusalem as if from ἱερὸν Σολομών. Theodoret, who (*Dial.* ii.) explains that the incarnate Son was ἀμήτωρ, with respect to his divine nature, and ἀγενεαλόγητος in fulfilment of Is 53[8], faces the difficulty of Melchizedek with characteristic frankness. Melchizedek, he explains, is described as ἀπάτωρ, ἀμήτωρ, simply because scripture does not record his parentage or lineage. Εἰ ἀληθῶς ἀπάτωρ ἦν καὶ ἀμήτωρ, οὐκ ἂν ἦν εἰκών, ἀλλ' ἀλήθεια. Ἐπειδὴ δὲ οὐ φύσει ταῦτ' ἔχει, ἀλλὰ κατὰ τὴν τῆς θείας Γραφῆς οἰκονομίαν, δείκνυσι τῆς ἀληθείας τὸν τύπον. In his commentary he explains that μένει ἱερεὺς εἰς τὸ διηνεκὲς means τὴν ἱερωσύνην οὐ παρέπεμψεν εἰς παῖδας, καθάπερ Ἀαρὼν καὶ Ἐλεάζαρ καὶ Φινεές.

'Αφωμοιωμένος in v.[3] means "resembling," as, *e.g.*, in *Ep. Jerem.*[70] νεκρῷ ἐρριμμένῳ ἐν σκότει ἀφωμοίωνται οἱ θεοὶ αὐτῶν, though it might even be taken as a strict passive, "made to resemble" (*i.e.* in scripture), the Son of God being understood to be eternal. Εἰς τὸ διηνεκές is a classical equivalent for εἰς τὸν αἰῶνα, a phrase which is always to be understood in the light of its context. Here it could not be simply "ad vitam"; the foregoing phrases and the fact that even the levitical priests were appointed for life, rule out such an interpretation.

The writer now (vv.[4-10]) moralizes upon the statement that Abraham paid tithes to Melchizedek and received his blessing, which proves the supreme dignity of the Melchizedek priesthood, and, inferentially, its superiority to the levitical.

[4] *Now mark the dignity of this man. The patriarch "Abraham paid" him "a tenth" of the spoils.* [5] *Those sons of Levi, who receive the priestly office, are indeed ordered by law to tithe the people (that is, their brothers), although the latter are descended from Abraham ;* [6] *but he who had no levitical (ἐξ αὐτῶν = ἐκ τῶν υἱῶν Λευεί) genealogy actually tithed Abraham and "blessed" the possessor of the promises !* [7] (*And there is no question that it is the inferior who is blessed by the superior.*) [8] *Again, it is mortal men in the one case who receive tithes, while in the other it is one of whom the witness is that "he lives."* [9] *In fact, we might almost say that even Levi the receiver of tithes paid tithes through Abraham ;* [10] *for he was still in the loins of his father when Melchizedek met him.*

---

[1] In iv. 25 he says that "as God was the Father of his spirit without a mother, so a virgin was the mother of his body without a father."

Θεωρεῖτε (v.⁴) is an oratorical imperative as in 4 Mac 14¹³ (θεωρεῖτε δὲ πῶς πολύπλοκός ἐστιν ἡ τῆς φιλοτεκνίας στοργή); πηλίκος is a rare word, often used for ἡλίκος after vowels, though not in Zec 2⁶ (τοῦ ἰδεῖν πηλίκον τὸ πλάτος αὐτῆς ἐστιν), where alone it occurs in the LXX. The οὗτος (om. D* 67**. 1739 Blass) repeats the οὗτος of v.¹. We have now a triple proof of the inferiority of the levitical priesthood to Melchizedek. (a) Melchizedek, though not in levitical orders, took tithes from and gave a blessing to Abraham himself (vv.⁴⁻⁷); (b) he is never recorded to have lost his priesthood by death (v.⁸); and (c) indeed, in his ancestor Abraham, Levi yet unborn did homage to Melchizedek (⁹·¹⁰). Τὰ ἀκροθίνια (v.⁴), which this alone of NT writers has occasion to use, explains the πάντα of v.²; it is one of the classical terms for which he went outside the LXX. Ὁ πατριάρχης is thrown to the end of the sentence for emphasis. In v.⁵ ἱερατείαν is chosen instead of ἱερωσύνην for the sake of assonance with Λευεί. The LXX does not distinguish them sharply. The general statement about tithing, κατὰ τὸν νόμον (the ἐντολή of Nu 18²⁰·²¹), is intended to throw the spontaneous action of Abraham into relief; ἀποδεκατοῦν of "tithing" persons occurs in 1 S 8¹⁵ᶠ·, but usually means "to pay tithes," like the more common δεκατοῦν (v.⁶), the classical form being δεκατεύειν. In v.⁶ the perfect εὐλόγηκε is like the Philonic perfect (see above). In describing the incident (de Abrahamo, 40), Philo lays stress upon the fact that ὁ μέγας ἱερεὺς τοῦ μεγίστου θεοῦ offered ἐπινίκια and feasted the conquerors; he omits both the blessing and the offering of tithes, though he soon allegorizes the latter (41).

Moulton calls attention to "the beautiful parallel in Plato's *Apol.* 28c, for the characteristic perfect in Hebrews, describing what *stands written* in Scripture," holding that "ὅσοι ἐν Τροίᾳ τετελευτήκασι (as is written in the Athenians' Bible) is exactly like He 7⁶ 11¹⁷·²⁸." But these perfects are simply aoristic (see above, p. 91, note).

V.⁷ is a parenthetical comment on what blessing and being blessed imply; the neuter (ἔλαττον) is used, as usual in Greek (cp. Blass, § 138. 1), in a general statement, especially in a collective sense, about persons. Then the writer rapidly summarizes, from vv.¹⁻⁴, the contrast between the levitical priests who die off and Melchizedek whose record (μαρτυρούμενος in scripture, cp. 11⁵) is "he lives" (μήτε ζωῆς τέλος . . . μένει εἰς τὸ διηνεκές). Finally (vv.⁹·¹⁰), he ventures (ὡς ἔπος εἰπεῖν, a literary phrase, much affected by Philo) on what he seems to feel may be regarded as a forced and fanciful remark, that Levi was committed δι' Ἀβραάμ (genitive) to a position of respectful deference towards the prince-priest of Salem. In v.⁵ καίπερ ἐληλυθότας ἐκ τῆς ὀσφύος Ἀβραάμ (the Semitic expression for descendants, chosen here in view of what he was going to say in

v.[10] ἐν τῇ ὀσφύϊ τοῦ πατρός) is another imaginative touch added
in order to signalize the pre-eminent honour of the levitical
priests over their fellow-countrymen. Such is their high authority.
And yet Melchizedek's is higher still!

(a) In v.[6] "forte legendum, ὁ δὲ μὴ γενεαλογούμενος αὐτὸν δεδεκάτωκε τὸν
Ἀβραάμ, ipsum Abrahamam" (Bentley). But ἐξ αὐτῶν explains itself, and
the stress which αὐτόν would convey is already brought out by the emphatic
position of Ἀβραάμ, and by the comment καὶ τὸν ἔχοντα κτλ. (b) In v.[4] καὶ
is inserted after ᾧ, in conformity with v.[2], by א A C D[c] K L P syr[hkl] arm,
etc. For ἀποδεκατοῦν in v.[5] the termination (cp. Thackeray, 244) ἀποδεκα-
τοῖν is read by B D (as κατασκηνοῦν in Mt 13[32]). In v.[6] the more common
(11[20]) aorist, εὐλόγησε, is read by A C P 6. 104. 242. 263. 326. 383. 1288.
1739. 2004. 2143, Chrys. for εὐλόγηκε.

He now (vv.[11f.]) turns to prove his point further, by glancing
at the text from the 110th psalm. "It is no use to plead that
Melchizedek was succeeded by the imposing Aaronic priesthood; this priesthood belonged to an order of religion which
had to be superseded by the Melchizedek-order of priesthood."
He argues here, as already, from the fact that the psalter is later
than the pentateuch; the point of 7[11] is exactly that of 4[7f.].

[11] *Further, if the levitical priesthood had been the means of reaching perfection (for it was on the basis of that priesthood that the Law was enacted for
the People), why was it still necessary for another sort of priest to emerge
"with the rank of Melchizedek," instead of simply with the rank of Aaron
([12] for when the priesthood is changed, a change of law necessarily follows)?*
[13] *He who is thus (i.e. "with the rank of M.") described belongs to another
tribe, no member of which ever devoted himself to the altar;* [14] *for it is evident
that our Lord sprang from Judah, and Moses never mentioned priesthood in
connexion with that tribe.* [15] *This becomes all the more plain when* (εἰ = ἐπεί)
another priest emerges "resembling Melchizedek," [16] *one who has become a
priest by the power of an indissoluble* (ἀκαταλύτου, i.e. by death) *Life and
not by the Law of an external command;* [17] *for the witness to him is,*
"*Thou art priest for ever, with the rank of Melchizedek."*
[18] *A previous command is set aside on account of its weakness and uselessness*
[19] *(for the Law made nothing perfect), and there is introduced a better Hope,
by means of which we can draw near to God.*

Εἰ μέν οὖν (without any δέ to follow, as in 8[4]) τελείωσις
("perfection" in the sense of a perfectly adequate relation to
God; see v.[19]) διὰ τῆς Λευειτικῆς ἱερωσύνης κτλ. Λευειτικῆς is a
rare word, found in Philo (*de fuga*, ἡ Λευιτικὴ μόνη), but never in
the LXX except in the title of Leviticus; ἱερωσύνη does occur in
the LXX, and is not distinguishable from ἱερατεία (v.[5]). In the
parenthetical remark ὁ λαὸς γὰρ ἐπ᾽ αὐτῆς νενομοθέτηται, αὐτῆς
was changed into αὐτήν (6. 242. 330. 378. 383. 440. 462. 467.
489. 491. 999. 1610. 1836 Theophyl.), or αὐτῇ (K L 326. 1288,
etc. Chrys.) after 8[6] (where again we have this curious passive),
and νενομοθέτηται altered into the pluperfect ἐνενομοθέτητο
(K L, etc.). The less obvious genitive (cp. Ex. 34[27] ἐπὶ γὰρ
τῶν λόγων τούτων τέθειμαι σοὶ διαθήκην καὶ τῷ Ἰσραήλ) ἐπ᾽ αὐτῆς

is not "in the time of," for the levitical priesthood was not in
existence prior to the Law; it might mean "in connexion with,"
since ἐπί and περί have a similar force with this genitive, but the
incorrect dative correctly explains the genitive.   The Mosaic
νόμος could not be worked for the λαός without a priesthood, to
deal with the offences incurred.   The idea of the writer always
is that a νόμος or διαθήκη depends for its validity and effectiveness upon the ἱερεύς or ἱερεῖς by whom it is administered.   Their
personal character and position are the essential thing.   Every consideration is subordinated to that of the priesthood.   As a change
in that involves a change in the νόμος (v.¹²), the meaning of the
parenthesis in v.¹¹ must be that the priesthood was the basis for the
νόμος, though, no doubt, the writer has put his points in vv.¹¹·¹²
somewhat intricately; this parenthetical remark would have been
better placed after the other in v.¹², as indeed van d. Sande
Bakhuyzen proposes.   Three times over (cp. v.¹⁹) he puts in
depreciatory remarks about the Law, the reason being that the
Law and the priesthood went together.   It is as if he meant
here: "the levitical priesthood (which, of course, implies the
Law, for the Law rested on the priesthood)."   The inference
that the νόμος is antiquated for Christians reaches the same end
as Paul does by his dialectic, but by a very different route.
Ἀνίστασθαι (= appear on the scene, as v.¹⁵) and λέγεσθαι refer to
Ps 110⁴, which is regarded as marking a new departure, with
far-reaching effects, involving (v.¹²) an alteration of the νόμος as
well as of the ἱερωσύνη.   In καὶ οὐ . . . λέγεσθαι the οὐ negatives
the infinitive as μή usually does; Ἀαρών, like Κανᾶ (Jn 21²), has
become indeclinable, though Josephus still employs the ordinary
genitive Ἀαρῶνος.   In v.¹² μετάθεσις, which is not a LXX term,
though it occurs in 2 Mac 11²⁴, is practically equivalent here
(cp. 12²⁷) to ἀθέτησις in v.¹⁸.   A close parallel occurs in de
Mundo, 6, νόμος μὲν γὰρ ἡμῖν ἰσοκλινὴς ὁ θεός, οὐδεμίαν ἐπιδεχό-
μενος διόρθωσιν ἢ μετάθεσιν, and a similar phrase is employed by
Josephus to describe the arbitrary transference of the highpriesthood (Ant. xii. 9. 7, ὑπὸ Λυσίου πεισθείς, μεταθεῖναι τὴν τιμὴν ἀπὸ
ταύτης τῆς οἰκίας εἰς ἕτερον).

    We now (vv.¹³ᶠ·) get an account of what was meant by οὐ
κατὰ τὴν τάξιν Ἀαρών or ἕτερος ("another," in the sense of "a
different") ἱερεύς in v.¹¹; Jesus, this ἱερεὺς κατὰ τὴν τάξιν Μελχισεδέκ, came from the non-sacerdotal tribe of Judah, not from that
of Levi.   Ἐφ' ὅν is another instance of the extension of this
metaphorical use of ἐπί from the Attic dative to the accusative.
The perfect μετέσχηκεν may be used in an aoristic sense, like
ἔσχηκα, or simply for the sake of assonance with προσέσχηκεν,
and it means no more than μετέσχεν in 2¹⁴; indeed μετέσχεν is
read here by P 489. 623*. 1912 arm, as προσέσχεν is (by A C

33. 1288) for προσέσχηκεν. The conjecture of Erasmus, προσέσ-
τηκεν, is ingenious, but προσέχειν in the sense of "attend" is
quite classical. The rule referred to in εἰς ἢν φυλήν (ἐξ ἧς φυλῆς,
arm?), *i.e.* ἐκ φυλῆς εἰς ἢν (as Lk 10¹⁰) κτλ. is noted in Josephus,
Ant. xx. 10. 1, πάτριόν ἐστι μηδένα τοῦ θεοῦ τὴν ἀρχιερωσύνην
λαμβάνειν ἢ τὸν ἐξ αἵματος τοῦ Ἀαρῶνος. No tribe except Levi
supplied priests. (Πρόδηλον in v.¹⁴ is not a LXX term, but
occurs in this sense in 2 Mac 3¹⁷ (δι' ὧν πρόδηλον ἐγίνετο) and
14³⁹, as well as in Judith 8²⁹.) In *Test. Levi* 8¹⁴ it is predicted
(cp. Introd. p. xlviii) that βασιλεὺς ἐκ τοῦ Ἰούδα ἀναστήσεται καὶ
ποιήσει ἱερατείαν νέαν: but this is a purely verbal parallel, the
βασιλεύς is Hyrcanus and the reference is to the Maccabean
priest-kings who succeed the Aaronic priesthood. Ἀνατέλλειν is
a synonym for ἀνίστασθαι (v.¹⁵), as in Nu 24¹⁷, though it is just
possible that ἀνατέταλκεν is a subtle allusion to the messianic
title of Ἀνατολή in Zec 6¹²; in commenting on that verse Philo
observes (*de confus. ling.* 14): τοῦτον μὲν γὰρ πρεσβύτατον υἱὸν ὁ
τῶν ὅλων ἀνέτειλε πατήρ. (For ἱερέων the abstract equivalent
ἱερωσύνης, from v.¹², is substituted by Dᶜ K L.) The title
ὁ κύριος ἡμῶν is one of the links between the vocabulary of this
epistle and that of the pastorals (1 Ti 1¹⁴, 2 Ti 1⁸). As the
result of all this, what is it that becomes (v.¹⁵) περισσότερον
(for περισσότερως) κατάδηλον?[1] The provisional character of the
levitical priesthood, or the μετάθεσις νόμου? Probably the
latter, though the writer would not have distinguished the one
from the other. In v.¹⁵ κατὰ τὴν ὁμοιότητα linguistically has the
same sense as ἀφωμοιωμένος (v.³). In v.¹⁶ σαρκίνης (for which
σαρκικῆς is substituted by Cᶜ D K Ψ 104. 326. 1175, etc.) hints at
the contrast which is to be worked out later (in 9¹⁻¹⁴) between
the external and the inward or spiritual, the sacerdotal ἐντολή
being dismissed as merely σαρκίνη, since it laid down physical
descent as a requisite for office. Hereditary succession is
opposed to the inherent personality of the Son (= 9¹⁴). The distinction between σαρκικός (= fleshly, with the nature and qualities
of σάρξ) and σάρκινος (fleshy, composed of σάρξ) is blurred in
Hellenistic Greek of the period, where adjectives in -ινος tend to
take over the sense of those in -ικος, and *vice versa*. In v.¹⁷
μαρτυρεῖται (cp. μαρτυρούμενος, v.⁸) is altered to the active (10¹⁵)
μαρτυρεῖ by C D K L 256. 326. 436. 1175. 1837. 2127 syrʰᵏˡ vg
arm Chrys.

The μετάθεσις of v.¹² is now explained negatively (ἀθέτησις)
and positively (ἐπεισαγωγή) in vv.¹⁸· ¹⁹. Ἀθέτησις (one of his juristic
metaphors, cp. 9²⁶) γίνεται (*i.e.* by the promulgation of Ps 110⁴)
προαγούσης (cp. *IMA*. iii. 247, τὰ προάγοντα ψηφίσματα: προάγειν is

---

[1] Κατάδηλον is the classical intensive form of δῆλον, used here for the sake
of assonance with the following κατά.

not used by the LXX in this sense of "fore-going") ἐντολῆς (v.¹⁶)
διὰ τὸ αὐτῆς (unemphatic) ἀσθενὲς καὶ ἀνωφελές (alliteration).
Ἀνωφελές is a word common in such connexions, e.g. *Ep. Arist.*
253, ὅπερ ἀνωφελὲς καὶ ἀλγεινόν ἐστιν : Polyb. xii. 25⁹ ἄζηλον καὶ
ἀνωφελές. The uselessness of the Law lay in its failure to secure
an adequate forgiveness of sins, without which a real access or
fellowship (ἐγγίζειν τῷ θεῷ) was impossible ; οὐδὲν ἐτελείωσεν, it led
to no absolute order of communion between men and God, no
τελείωσις. The positive contrast (v.¹⁹) is introduced by the striking compound ἐπεισαγωγή (with γίνεται), a term used by Josephus
for the replacing of Vashti by Esther (*Ant.* xi. 6. 2, σβέννυσθαι γὰρ
τὸ πρὸς τὴν προτήραν φιλόστοργον ἑτέρας ἐπεισαγωγῇ, καὶ τὸ πρὸς ἐκείνην εὔνουν ἀποσπώμενον κατὰ μικρὸν γίγνεσθαι τῆς συνούσης) ; there
is no force here in the ἐπει, as if it meant "fresh" or "further."
The new ἐλπίς is κρείττων by its effectiveness (6¹⁸) ; it accomplishes
what the νόμος and its ἱερωσύνη had failed to realize for men, viz.
a direct and lasting access to God. In what follows the writer
ceases to use the term ἐλπίς, and concentrates upon the ἐγγίζειν
τῷ θεῷ, since the essence of the ἐλπίς lies in the priesthood and
sacrifice of Jesus the Son. With this allusion to the κρείττων ἐλπίς,
he really resumes the thought of 6¹⁸· ¹⁹ ; but he has another
word to say upon the superiority of the Melchizedek priest, and
in this connexion he recalls another oath of God, viz. at the
inauguration or consecration mentioned in Ps 110⁴, a solemn
divine oath, which was absent from the ritual of the levitical
priesthood, and which ratifies the new priesthood of Jesus as
permanent (vv.²⁰⁻²²), enabling him to do for men what the levitical
priests one after another failed to accomplish (vv.²³⁻²⁵).

²⁰ *A better Hope, because it was not promised apart from an oath. Previous
priests* (οἱ μέν=levitical priests) *became priests apart from any oath,* ²¹ *but
he has an oath from Him who said to him,*

"*The Lord has sworn, and he will not change his mind,
thou art a priest for ever.*"

²² *And this makes Jesus surety for a superior covenant.* ²³ *Also, while they* (οἱ
μέν) *became priests in large numbers, since death prevents them from continuing
to serve,* ²⁴ *he holds his priesthood without any successor, since he continues for
ever.* ²⁵ *Hence for all time he is able to save those who approach God through
him, as he is always living to intercede on their behalf.*

The long sentence (vv.²⁰⁻²²) closes with Ἰησοῦς in an emphatic
position. After καὶ καθ' ὅσον οὐ χωρὶς ὁρκωμοσίας, which connect
(*sc.* τοῦτο γίνεται) with ἐπεισαγωγὴ κρείττονος ἐλπίδος, there is a long
explanatory parenthesis οἱ μὲν γὰρ . . . εἰς τὸν αἰῶνα, exactly in
the literary style of Philo (e.g. *quis rer. div.* 17, ἐφ' ὅσον γὰρ οἶμαι
κτλ.—νοῦς μὲν γὰρ . . . αἴσθησις—ἐπὶ τοσοῦτον κτλ.). In v.²⁰
ὁρκωμοσία (oath-taking) is a neuter plural (cp. *Syll.* 593²⁹, *OGIS.*
229⁸²) which, like ἀντωμοσία, has become a feminine singular of
the first declension, and εἰσὶν γεγονότες is simply an analytic form

of the perfect tense, adopted as more sonorous than γεγόνασι. As
we have already seen (on 6¹³), Philo (*de sacrific.* 28–29) discusses
such references to God swearing. Thousands of people, he observes, regard an oath as inconsistent with the character of God, who
requires no witness to his character. " Men who are disbelieved
have recourse to an oath in order to win credence, but God's mere
word must be believed (ὁ δὲ θεὸς καὶ λέγων πιστός ἐστιν); hence,
his words are in no sense different from oaths, as far as assurance
goes." He concludes that the idea of God swearing an oath is
simply an anthropomorphism which is necessary on account of
human weakness. Our author takes the OT language in Ps 110⁴
more naively, detecting a profound significance in the line ὤμοσεν
κύριος καὶ οὐ μεταμεληθήσεται (in the Hellenistic sense of " regret "
= change his mind). The allusion is, of course, to the levitical
priests. But Roman readers could understand from their former
religion how oaths were needful in such a matter. Claudius,
says Suetonius (*Vit. Claud.* 22), " in co-optandis per collegia
sacerdotibus neminem nisi juratus (*i.e.* that they were suitable)
nominavit."

The superfluous addition of κατὰ τὴν τάξιν Μελχιζεδέκ was soon made,
after εἰς τὸν αἰῶνα, by אᶜ A D K L P vt Syrᵖᵉˢʰ ʰᵏˡ boh eth Eus (Dem. iv.
15. 40), etc.

Παραμένειν means to remain in office or serve (a common
euphemism in the papyri). The priestly office could last in a
family (cp. Jos. *Ant.* xi. 8. 2, τῆς ἱερατικῆς τιμῆς μεγίστης οὔσης καὶ
ἐν τῷ γένει παραμενούσης), but mortal men (ἀποθνήσκοντες, v.⁸) could
not παραμένειν as priests, whereas (v.²⁴) Jesus remains a perpetual
ἱερεύς, διὰ τὸ μένειν (= πάντοτε ζῶν, v.²⁵) αὐτόν (superfluous as in Lk 2⁴
διὰ τὸ αὐτὸν εἶναι). Ἀπαράβατον, a legal adjective for " inviolable,"
is here used in the uncommon sense of non-transferable (boh
Chrys. οὐκ ἔχει διάδοχον, Oecumenius, etc. ἀδιάδοχον), as an equivalent for μὴ παραβαίνουσαν εἰς ἄλλον, and contrasts Jesus with the
long succession of the levitical priests (πλείονές). The passive
sense of " not to be infringed " (cp. Justin Martyr, *Apol.* i. 43,
εἱμαρμένην φαμὲν ἀπαράβατον ταύτην εἶναι, where the adjective
= ineluctabile) or " unbroken " does not suit the context, for
Jesus had no rivals and the word can hardly refer to the invasion
of death. Like γεγυμνασμένα in 5¹⁴, also after ἔχειν, it has a pre-
dicative force, marked by the absence of the article. Philo (*quis
rer. div. heres*, 6) finds a similar significance in the etymology of
κύριος as a divine title: κύριος μὲν γὰρ παρὰ τὸ κῦρος, ὃ δὴ βέβαιόν
ἐστιν, εἴρηται, κατ᾽ ἐναντιότητα ἀβεβαίου καὶ ἀκύρου. But our author
does not discover any basis for the perpetuity of ὁ κύριος ἡμῶν in
the etymology of κύριος, and is content (in vv.²²⁻²⁴) to stress the
line of the psalm, in order to prove that Jesus guaranteed a superior
διαθήκη (*i.e.* order of religious fellowship). Ἔγγυος is one of the

juristic terms (vg, sponsor) which he uses in a general sense ; here it is "surety" or "pledge." Διαθήκη is discussed by him later on ; it is a term put in here as often to excite interest and anticipation. How readily ἔγγυος could be associated with a term like σώζειν (v.[25]) may be understood from Sir 29[15f.] :

χάριτας ἐγγύου μὴ ἐπιλάθῃ,
ἔδωκεν γὰρ τὴν ψυχὴν αὐτοῦ ὑπὲρ σου.
ἀγαθὰ ἐγγύου ἀνατρέψει ἁμαρτωλός,
καὶ ἀχάριστος ἐν διανοίᾳ ἐγκαταλείψει ῥυσάμενον.

Our author might have written μεσίτης here as well as in 8[6] ; he prefers ἔγγυος probably for the sake of assonance with γέγονεν or even ἐγγίζομεν. As μεσιτεύειν means to vouch for the truth of a promise or statement (cp. 6[17]), so ἔγγυος means one who vouches for the fulfilment of a promise, and therefore is a synonym for μεσίτης here. The conclusion (v.[25]) is put in simple and effective language. Εἰς τὸ παντελές is to be taken in the temporal sense of the phrase, as in *BM*. iii. 161[11] (A.D. 212) ἀπὸ τοῦ νῦν εἰς τὸ παντελές, being simply a literary variant for πάντοτε. The alternative rendering "utterly" suits Lk 13[11] better than this passage. This full and final ἱερωσύνη of Jesus is the κρείττων ἐλπίς (v.[19]), the τελείωσις which the levitical priesthood failed to supply, a perfect access to God's Presence. His intercession (ἐντυγχάνειν, *sc.* θεῷ as in Ro 8[34] ὃς καὶ ἐντύγχανει ὑπὲρ ἡμῶν) has red blood in it, unlike Philo's conception, *e.g.* in *Vit. Mos.* iii. 14, ἀναγκαῖον γὰρ ἦν τὸν ἱερωμένον (the highpriest) τῷ τοῦ κόσμου πατρὶ παρακλήτῳ χρῆσθαι τελειοτάτῳ τὴν ἀρετὴν υἱῷ (*i.e.* the Logos) πρός τε ἀμνηστίαν ἁμαρημάτων καὶ χορηγίαν ἀφθονωτάτων ἀγαθῶν, and in *quis rer. div.* 42, where the Logos is ἱκέτης τοῦ θνητοῦ κηραίνοντος ἀεὶ πρὸς τὸ ἄφθαρτον παρὰ δὲ τῷ φύντι πρὸς εὐελπιστίαν τοῦ μήποτε τὸν ἵλεω θεὸν περιιδεῖν τὸ ἴδιον ἔργον. The function of intercession in heaven for the People, which originally (see p. 37) was the prerogative of Michael the angelic guardian of Israel, or generally of angels (see on 1[14]), is thus transferred to Jesus, to One who is no mere angel but who has sacrificed himself for the People. The author deliberately excludes any other mediator or semi-mediator in the heavenly sphere (see p. xxxix).

A triumphant little summary (vv.[26-28]) now rounds off the argument of 6[19f.]–7[25] :

[26] *Such was the highpriest for us, saintly, innocent, unstained, far from all contact with the sinful, lifted high above the heavens,* [27] *one who has no need, like yonder highpriests, day by day to offer sacrifices first for their own sins and then for* (the preposition is omitted as in Ac 26[18]) *those of the People— he did that once for all in offering up himself.* [28] *For the Law appoints human beings in their weakness to the priesthood ; but the word of the Oath* {which came after the Law) *appoints a Son who is made perfect for ever.*

4 6 8 0 4

The text of this paragraph has only a few variants, none of any importance. After ἡμῖν in v.[26] καί is added by A B D 1739 syr[pesh hkl] Eusebius
("was exactly the one for us "). In v.[27] it makes no difference to the sense
whether προσενέγκας (א A W 33. 256. 436. 442. 1837. 2004. 2127 arm Cyr.)
or ἀνενέγκας (B C D K L P etc. Chrys.) is read ; the latter may have been
suggested by ἀναφέρειν, or προσενέγκας may have appealed to later scribes as
the more usual and technical term in the epistle. The technical distinction
between ἀναφέρειν (action of people) and προσφέρειν (action of the priest)
had long been blurred ; both verbs mean what we mean by "offer up" or
"sacrifice." In v.[28] the original ἱερεῖς (D* 1 r vg) was soon changed (to conform with ἀρχιερεῖς in v.[27]) into ἀρχιερεῖς. The reason why ἱερεύς and
ἱερεῖς have been used in 7[1f.] is that Melchizedek was called ἱερεύς, not
ἀρχιερεύς. Once the category is levitical, the interchange of ἀρχιερεύς and
ἱερεύς becomes natural.

The words τοιοῦτος γὰρ ἡμῖν ἔπρεπεν (another daring use of
ἔπρεπεν, cp. 2[10]) ἀρχιερεύς (v.[26]) might be bracketed as one of
the author's parentheses, in which case ὅσιος κτλ. would carry on
πάντοτε ζῶν . . . αὐτῶν. But ὅς in Greek often follows τοιοῦτος,
and the usual construction is quite satisfactory. Γάρ is intensive,
as often. It is generally misleading to parse a rhapsody, but there
is a certain sequence of thought in ὅσιος κτλ., where the positive
adjective ὅσιος is followed by two negative terms in alliteration
(ἄκακος, ἀμίαντος), and κεχωρισμένος ἀπὸ τῶν ἁμαρτωλῶν is further
defined by ὑψηλότερος τῶν οὐρανῶν γενόμενος (the same idea as in
4[14] διεληλυθότα τοὺς οὐρανούς). He is ὅσιος, pious or saintly
(cp. *ERE*. vi. 743), in virtue of qualities like his reverence,
obedience, faith, loyalty, and humility, already noted. Ἄκακος
is innocent (as in Job 8[20], Jer 11[19]), one of the LXX equivalents
for םָתּ or םיִמָתּ, not simply = devoid of evil feeling towards men ;
like ἀμίαντος, it denotes a character χωρὶς ἁμαρτίας. Ἀμίαντος is
used of the untainted Isis in *OP*. 1380 (ἐν Πόντῳ ἀμίαντος).
The language may be intended to suggest a contrast between
the deep ethical purity of Jesus and the ritual purity of the
levitical highpriest, who had to take extreme precautions against
outward defilement (cp. Lv 21[10-15] for the regulations, and the
details in Josephus, *Ant*. iii. 12. 2, μὴ μόνον δὲ περὶ τὰς ἱερουργίας
καθαροὺς εἶναι, σπουδάζειν δὲ καὶ περὶ τὴν αὐτῶν δίαιταν, ὡς αὐτὴν
ἄμεμπτον εἶναι· καὶ διὰ ταύτην τὴν αἰτίαν, οἱ τὴν ἱερατικὴν στολὴν
φοροῦντες ἄμωμοί τε εἰσι καὶ περὶ πάντα καθαροὶ καὶ νηφάλιοι), and
had to avoid human contact for seven days before the ceremony
of atonement-day. The next two phrases go together. Κεχωρισμένος ἀπὸ τῶν ἁμαρτωλῶν is intelligible in the light of 9[28] ; Jesus
has ἅπαξ sacrificed himself for the sins of men, and in that sense
his connexion with ἁμαρτωλοί is done. He is no levitical highpriest who is in daily contact with them, and therefore obliged
to sacrifice repeatedly. Hence the writer at once adds (v.[27]) a
word to explain and expand this pregnant thought ; the sphere
in which Jesus now lives (ὑψηλότερος κτλ.) is not one in which,

as on earth, he had to suffer the contagion or the hostility of
ἁμαρτωλοί (12²) and to die for human sins.

> " He has outsoared the shadow of our night ;
> Envy and calumny and hate and pain . . .
> Can touch him not and torture not again ;
> From the contagion of the world's slow stain
> He is secure."

This is vital[1] to the sympathy and intercession of Jesus ; it is
in virtue of this position before God that he aids his people,
as τετελειωμένος, and therefore able to do all for them.   His
priesthood is, in modern phrase, absolute.   As eternal ἀρχιερεύς
in the supreme sense, and as no longer in daily contact with
sinners, Jesus is far above the routine ministry of the levitical
ἀρχιερεῖς.   The writer blends loosely in his description (v.²⁷) the
annual sacrifice of the highpriest on atonement-day (to which
he has already referred in 5³) and the daily sacrifices offered by
priests.   Strictly speaking the ἀρχιερεῖς did not require to offer
sacrifices καθ' ἡμέραν, and the accurate phrase would have been κατ'
ἐνιαυτόν.   According to Lv 6¹⁹⁻²³ the highpriest had indeed to offer
a cereal offering morning and evening ; but the text is uncertain,
for it is to be offered both on the day of his consecration and
also διὰ πάντος.   Besides, this section was not in the LXX text
of A, so that the writer of Hebrews did not know of it.   Neither
had he any knowledge of the later Jewish ritual, according to
which the highpriest did offer this offering twice a day.
Possibly, however, his expression here was suggested by Philo's
statement about this offering, viz. that the highpriest did offer a
daily sacrifice (*quis rer. div.* 36 : τὰς ἐνδελεχεῖς θυσίας . . . ἥν τε
ὑπὲρ ἑαυτῶν οἱ ἱερεῖς προσφέρουσι τῆς σεμιδάλεως καὶ τὴν ὑπὲρ τοῦ
ἔθνους τῶν δυεῖν ἀμνῶν, *de spec. leg.* iii. 23, ὁ ἀρχιερεύς . . . εὐχὰς
δὲ καὶ θυσίας τελῶν καθ' ἑκάστην ἡμέραν).   It is true that this
offering ὑπέρ ἑαυτῶν was not a sin-offering, only an offering of
cereals ; still it was reckoned a θυσία, and in Sir 45¹⁴ it is counted
as such.   Τοῦτο γὰρ ἐποίησεν refers then to his sacrifice for sins
(9²⁸), not, of course, including any sins of his own (see on 5³) ;
it means ὑπὲρ τῶν ἁμαρτιῶν τοῦ λαοῦ, and the writer could afford
to be technically inexact in his parallelism without fear of being
misunderstood.   " Jesus offered his sacrifice," " Jesus did all
that a highpriest has to do,"—this was what he intended.   The
Greek fathers rightly referred τοῦτο to ἔπειτα τῶν τοῦ λαοῦ, as if
the writer meant "*this*, not that πρότερον."   It is doubtful if he
had such a sharp distinction in his mind, but when he wrote τοῦτο

---

[1] Thus Philo quotes (*de Fug.* 12) with enthusiasm what Plato says in the
Theatetus : οὔτ' ἀπολέσθαι τὰ κακὰ δυνατόν—ὑπεναντίον γάρ τι τῷ ἀγαθῷ ἀεὶ
εἶναι ἀνάγκη—οὔτε ἐν θείοις αὐτὰ ἱδρῦσθαι.

he was thinking of τῶν τοῦ λαοῦ, and of that alone. An effort is sometimes made to evade this interpretation by confining καθ' ἡμέραν to ὅς οὐκ ἔχει and understanding "yearly" after οἱ ἀρχιερεῖς, as if the idea were that Christ's daily intercession required no daily sacrifice like the annual sacrifice on atonement-day. But, as the text stands, ἀνάγκην is knit to καθ' ἡμέραν, and these words must all be taken along with ὥσπερ οἱ ἀρχιερεῖς (ἔχουσι).

Compare the common assurance of the votaries of Serapis, *e.g.* BGU. ii. 385 (ii/iii A.D.), τὸ προσκύνημά σου ποιῶ κατ' ἑκάστην ἡμέραν παρὰ τῷ κυρίῳ Σαράπιδι καὶ τοῖς συννέοις θεοῖς.

A deep impression is made by the words ἑαυτὸν ἀνενέγκας, "pro nobis tibi uictor et uictima, et ideo uictor, quia uictima, pro nobis tibi sacerdos et sacrificium, et ideo sacerdos, quia sacrificium" (Aug. *Conf.* x. 43). What is meant by this the writer holds over till he reaches the question of the sacrifice of Jesus as ἀρχιερεύς (9¹ᶠ·). As usual, he prepares the way for a further idea by dropping an enigmatic allusion to it. Meantime (v.²⁸) a general statement sums up the argument. Καθίστησιν is used as in 1 Mac 10²⁰ (καθεστάκαμέν σε σήμερον ἀρχιερέα τοῦ ἔθνους σου), and ἀσθένειαν recalls 5² (περίκειται ἀσθένειαν), in the special sense that such weakness involved a sacrifice for one's personal sins (ὑπὲρ τῶν ἰδίων ἁμαρτιῶν). Whereas Jesus the Son of God (as opposed to ἀνθρώπους ἀσθενεῖς) was appointed by a divine order which superseded the Law (μετὰ τὸν νόμον = vv.¹¹⁻¹⁹), and appointed as one who was τετελειωμένος (in the sense of 2¹⁰) εἰς τὸν αἰῶνα. It is implied that he was appointed ἀρχιερεύς, between which and ἱερεύς there is no difference.

The writer now picks up the thought (7²²) of the superior διαθήκη which Jesus as ἀρχιερεύς in the eternal σκηνή or sanctuary mediates for the People. This forms the transition between the discussion of the priesthood (5–8) and the sacrifice of Jesus (9¹–10¹⁷). The absolute sacrifice offered by Jesus as the absolute priest (vv.¹⁻⁶) ratifies the new διαθήκη which has superseded the old (vv.⁷⁻¹³) with its imperfect sacrifices.

¹ *The point of all this is, we do have such a highpriest, one who is "seated at the right hand" of the throne of Majesty (see* 1³) *in the heavens,* ² *and who officiates in the sanctuary or "true tabernacle set up by the Lord" and not by man.* ³ *Now, as every highpriest is appointed to offer gifts and sacrifices, he too must have something to offer.* ⁴ *Were he on earth, he would not be a priest at all, for there are priests already to offer the gifts prescribed by Law* (⁵ *men who serve a mere outline and shadow of the heavenly—as Moses was instructed when he was about to execute the building of the tabernacle: "see," God said, "that* (sc. ὅπως) *you make everything on the pattern shown you upon the mountain"*). ⁶ *As it is, however, the divine service he has obtained is superior, owing to the fact that he mediates a superior covenant, enacted with superior promises.*

The terseness of the clause ἣν ἔπηξεν ὁ κύριος, οὐκ ἄνθρωπος (v.¹) is spoiled by the insertion of καί before οὐκ (A K L P vg boh syr arm eth Cosm.). In v.[4] οὖν becomes γάρ in D[c] K L syr[hkl] arm Chrys. Theod., and a similar group of authorities add ἱερέων after ὄντων. Τόν is prefixed needlessly to νόμον by ℵ[c] D K L P Chrys. Dam. to conform to the usage in 7[5] 9[22]; but the sense is really unaffected, for the only legal regulation conceivable is that of the Law. In v.[6] νῦν and νυνί (9[26]) are both attested; the former is more common in the papyri. The Hellenistic (from Aristotle onwards) form τέτευχεν (ℵ[c] B D[c] 5. 226. 467. 623. 920. 927. 1311. 1827. 1836. 1873. 2004. 2143, etc. : or τέτυχεν, ℵ[c] A D* K L) has been corrected in P Ψ 6. 33. 1908 Orig. to the Attic τετύχηκεν. Before κρείττονός, καί is omitted by D* 69. 436. 462 arm Thdt.

Κεφάλαιον ("the pith," Coverdale), which is nominative absolute, is used as in Cic. *ad Attic.* v. 18 : "et multa, immo omnia, quorum κεφάλαιον," etc., Dem. xiii. 36 : ἔστι δ᾽, ὦ ἄνδρες Ἀθηναῖοι, κεφάλαιον ἁπάντων τῶν εἰρημένων (at the close of a speech); Musonius (ed. Hense, 67 f.) βίου καὶ γενέσεως παίδων κοινωνίαν κεφάλαιον εἶναι γάμου, etc. The word in this sense is common throughout literature and the more colloquial papyri, here with ἐπὶ τοῖς λεγομένοις (concerning what has been said). In passing from the intricate argument about the Melchizedek priesthood, which is now dropped, the writer disentangles the salient and central truth of the discussion, in order to continue his exposition of Jesus as highpriest. "Such, I have said, was the ἀρχιερεύς for us, and such is the ἀρχιερεύς we have—One who is enthroned, ἐν τοῖς οὐρανοῖς, next to God himself." While Philo spiritualizes the highpriesthood, not unlike Paul (Ro 12[1f.]), by arguing that devotion to God is the real highpriesthood (τὸ γὰρ θεραπευτικὸν γένος ἀνάθημά ἐστι θεοῦ, ἱερώμενον τὴν μεγάλην ἀρχιερωσύνην αὐτῷ μόνῳ, *de Fug.* 7), our author sees its essential functions transcended by Jesus in the spiritual order.

The phrase in v.[2] τῶν ἁγίων λειτουργός, offers two points of interest. First, the linguistic form λειτουργός. The ει form stands between the older η or ηι, which waned apparently from the third cent. B.C., and the later ι form ; " λειτουργός sim. socios habet omnium temporum papyros praeter perpaucas recentiores quae sacris fere cum libris conspirantes λιτουργὸς λιτουργία scribunt" (Crönert, *Memoria Graeca Hercul.* 39). Then, the meaning of τῶν ἁγίων. Philo has the phrase, in *Leg. Alleg.* iii. 46, τοιοῦτος δὲ ὁ θεραπευτὴς καὶ λειτουργὸς τῶν ἁγίων, where τῶν ἁγίων means "sacred things," as in *de Fug.* 17, where the Levites are described as priests οἷς ἡ τῶν ἁγίων ἀνάκειται λειτουργία. This might be the meaning here. But the writer uses τὰ ἄγια elsewhere (9[8f.] 10[19] 13[11]) of "the sanctuary," a rendering favoured by the context. By τὰ ἄγια he means, as often in the LXX, the sanctuary in general, without any reference to the distinction (cp. 9[2f.]) between the outer and the inner shrine. The LXX avoids the pagan term ἱερόν in this connexion, though τὸ ἅγιον itself was already in use among ethnic writers (*e.g.* the edict of

Ptolemy III., καὶ καθιδρῦσαι ἐν τῶν ἀγίωι = "in sacrario templi,"
Dittenberger, *OGIS.* 56⁵⁹). It is here defined (καί epexegetic) as
the true or real σκηνή, ἣν ¹ ἔπηξεν ὁ κύριος (a reminiscence of Nu
24⁶ σκηναὶ ἃς ἔπηξεν Κύριος, and of Ex 33⁷ καὶ λαβὼν Μωυσῆς τὴν
σκηνὴν αὐτοῦ ἔπηξεν). The reality and authenticity of the writer's
faith come out in a term like ἀληθινός. What he means by it
he will explain in a moment (v.⁵). Meanwhile he turns to the
λειτουργία of Jesus in this ideal sanctuary. This ἀρχιερεύς of
ours, in his vocation (v.⁸, cp. 5¹), must have (ἀναγκαῖον, *sc.* ἐστίν)
some sacrifice to present before God, though what this offering is,
the writer does not definitely say, even later in 9²⁴. The analogy
of a highpriest carrying the blood of an animal inside the sacred
shrine had its obvious limitations, for Jesus was both ἀρχιερεύς
and offering, by his self-sacrifice. Προσενέγκῃ is the Hellenistic
aorist subjunctive, where classical Greek would have employed
a future indicative (Radermacher, 138). The writer proceeds
to argue that this λειτουργία is far superior to the levitical cultus
(vv.⁴ᶠ·). Even in the heavenly sanctuary there must be sacrifice
of some kind—for sacrifice is essential to communion, in his
view. It is not a sacrifice according to the levitical ritual;
indeed Jesus on this level would not be in levitical orders at all.
But so far from that being any drawback or disqualification to
our ἀρχιερεύς, it is a proof of his superiority, for the bible itself
indicates that the levitical cultus is only an inferior copy of the
heavenly order to which Jesus belongs.

Instead of contrasting at this point (v.⁴) τὰ δῶρα (sacrifices,
as in 11⁴) of the levitical priests with the spiritual sacrifice of
Jesus, he hints that the mere fact of these sacrifices being made
ἐπὶ γῆς is a proof of their inferiority. This is put into a parenthesis (v.⁵); but, though a grammatical aside, it contains one of
the writer's fundamental ideas about religion (Eusebius, in *Praep.
Evang.* xii. 19, after quoting He 8⁵, refers to the similar Platonic
view in the sixth book of the *Republic*). Such priests (οἵτινες,
the simple relative as in 9² 10⁸·¹¹ 12⁵) λατρεύουσι (with dative as
in 13¹⁰) ὑποδείγματι καὶ σκιᾷ τῶν ἐπουρανίων (cp. 9²³). Ὑπόδειγμα
here as in 9²³ is a mere outline or copy (the only analogous
instance in the LXX being Ezk 42¹⁵ τὸ ὑπόδειγμα τοῦ οἴκου); the
phrase is practically a hendiadys for "a shadowy outline," a
second-hand, inferior reproduction. The proof of this is given
in a reference to Ex 25⁴⁰: Καθὼς κεχρημάτισται Μωυσῆς—
χρηματίζω,² as often in the LXX and the papyri, of divine

---

¹ ἦν is not assimilated, though ἧς might have been written; the practice
varied (cp. *e.g.* Dt 5³¹ ἐν τῇ γῇ ἣν ἐγὼ δίδωμι, and 12¹ ἐν τῇ γῇ ᾗ Κύριος
δίδωσιν).

² Passively in the NT in Ac 10²², but the exact parallel is in Josephus,
Ant. iii. 8. 8, Μωϋσῆς . . . εἰς τὴν σκηνὴν εἰσιὼν ἐχρηματίζετο περὶ ὧν ἐδεῖτο
παρὰ τοῦ θεοῦ.

revelations as well as of royal instructions—μέλλων ἐπιτελεῖν τὴν σκηνήν. The subject of the φησι is God, understood from κεχρημάτισται, and the γάρ[1] introduces the quotation, in which the writer, following Philo (*Leg. Alleg.* iii. 33), as probably codex Ambrosianus (F) of the LXX followed him, adds πάντα. He also substitutes δειχθέντα for δεδειγμένον, which Philo keeps (κατὰ τὸ παράδειγμα τὸ δεδειγμένον σοι ἐν τῷ ὄρει πάντα ποιήσεις), and retains the LXX τύπον (like Stephen in Ac 7⁴⁴). The idea was current in Alexandrian Judaism, under the influence of Platonism, that this σκηνή on earth had been but a reproduction of the pre-existent heavenly sanctuary. Thus the author of Wisdom makes Solomon remind God that he had been told to build the temple (νάον . . . καὶ θυσιαστήριον) as μίμημα σκηνῆς ἁγίας ἣν προητοίμασας ἀπ᾽ ἀρχῆς (9⁸), where σκηνὴ ἁγία is plainly the heavenly sanctuary as the eternal archetype. This idealism determines the thought of our writer (see Introd. pp. xxxi f.). Above the shows and shadows of material things he sees the real order of being, and it is most real to him on account of Jesus being there, for the entire relationship between God and man depends upon this function and vocation of Jesus in the eternal sanctuary.

Such ideas were not unknown in other circles. Seneca (*Ep.* lviii. 18-19) had just explained to Lucilius that the Platonic ideas were "what all visible things were created from, and what formed the pattern for all things," quoting the Parmenides, 132 D, to prove that the Platonic idea was the everlasting pattern of all things in nature. The metaphor is more than once used by Cicero, e.g. *Tusc.* iii. 2. 3, and in *de Officiis*, iii. 17, where he writes : "We have no real and life-like (solidam et expressam effigiem) likeness of real law and genuine justice ; all we enjoy is shadow and sketch (umbra et imaginibus). Would that we were true even to these ! For they are taken from the excellent patterns provided by nature and truth." But our author's thought is deeper. In the contemporary Syriac Apocalypse of Baruch the idea of Ex 25⁴⁰ is developed into the thought that the heavenly Jerusalem was also revealed to Moses along with the patterns of the σκηνή and its utensils (4⁴ᶠ·) ; God also showed Moses "the pattern of Zion and its measures, in the pattern of which the sanctuary of the present time was to be made" (Charles' tr.). The origin of this notion is very ancient ; it goes back to Sumerian sources, for Gudea the prince-priest of Lagash (*c.* 3000 B.C.) receives in a vision the plan of the temple which he is commanded to build (cp. A. Jeremias, *Babylonisches im NT*, pp. 62 f.). It is to this fundamental conception that the author of Πρὸς Ἑβραίους recurs, only to elaborate it in an altogether new form, which went far beyond Philo. Philo's argument (*Leg. Alleg.* iii. 33), on this very verse of Exodus, is that Bezaleel only constructed an imitation (μιμήματα) of τὰ ἀρχέτυπα given to Moses ; the latter was called up to the mountain to receive the direct idea of God, whereas the former worked simply ἀπὸ σκιᾶς τῶν γενομένων. In *de Plant.* 6 he observes that the very name of Bezaleel (בְּצַלְאֵל) means "one who works in shadows" (ἐν σκιαῖς ποιῶν) ; in *De Somniis*, i. 35, he defines it as "in the shadow of God," and again contrasts Bezaleel with Moses : ὁ μὲν οἷα σκιὰς ὑπεγράφετο, ὁ δ᾽ οὐ σκιάς,

---

[1] Put before φησι, because the point is not that the oracle was given, but what the oracle contained.

αὐτὰς δὲ τὰς ἀρχετύπους ἐδημιούργει φύσεις. In *Vit. Mos.* iii. 3 he argues that in building the σκηνή Moses designed to produce καθάπερ ἀπ' ἀρχετύπου γραφῆς καὶ νοητῶν παραδειγμάτων αἰσθητὰ μιμήματα . . . ὁ μὲν οὖν τύπος τοῦ παραδείγματος ἐνεσφραγίζετο τῇ διανοίᾳ τοῦ προφήτου . . . τὸ δ' ἀποτέλεσμα πρὸς τὸν τύπον ἐδημιουργεῖτο.

He then continues (v.^{6} νῦν δέ, logical as in 2^8 9^{26}, answering to εἰ μέν in v.^{4}) the thought of Christ's superior λειτουργία by describing him again (cp. 7^{22}) in connexion with the superior διαθήκη, and using now not ἔγγυος but μεσίτης. Μεσίτης (see on Gal 3^{19}) commonly means an arbitrator (*e.g.* Job 9^{33}, *Rein. P.* 44^3 [A.D. 104] ὁ καταστάθεὶς κριτὴς μεσίτης) or intermediary in some civil transaction (*OP.* 1298^{19}); but this writer's use of it, always in connexion with διαθήκη (9^{15} 12^{24})^1 and always as a description of Jesus (as in 1 Ti 2^5), implies that it is practically (see on 7^{22}) a synonym for ἔγγυος. Indeed, linguistically, it is a Hellenistic equivalent for the Attic μετέγγυος, and in Diod. Siculus, iv. 54 (τοῦτον γὰρ μεσίτην γεγονότα τῶν ὁμολογιῶν ἐν Κόλχοις ἐπηγγέλθαι βοηθήσειν αὐτῇ παρασπονδουμένῃ), its meaning corresponds to that of ἔγγυος. The sense is plain, even before the writer develops his ideas about the new διαθήκη, for, whenever the idea of reconciliation emerges, terms like μεσίτης and μεσιτεύειν are natural. Μεσίτης καὶ διαλλάκτης is Philo's phrase^2 for Moses (*Vit. Mos.* iii. 19). And as a διαθήκη was a gracious order of religious fellowship, inaugurated upon some historical occasion by sacrifice, it was natural to speak of Jesus as the One who mediated this new διαθήκη of Christianity. He gave it (Theophyl. μεσίτης καὶ δότης); he it was who realized it for men and who maintains it for men. All that the writer has to say meantime about the διαθήκη is that it has been enacted (v.^{6}) ἐπὶ κρείττοσιν ἐπαγγελίαις. This passive use of νομοθετεῖν is not unexampled; cf. *e.g.* *OGIS.* 493^{55} (ii A.D.) καὶ ταῦτα μὲν ὑμεῖν ὀρθῶς καὶ καλῶς . . . νενομοθετήσθω. It 's implied, of course, that God is ὁ νομοθετῶν (as in LXX Ps 83^7). What the "better promises" are, he now proceeds to explain, by a contrast between their διαθήκη and its predecessor. The superiority of the new διαθήκη is shown by the fact that God thereby superseded the διαθήκη with which the levitical cultus was bound up; the writer quotes an oracle from Jeremiah, again laying stress on the fact that it came after the older διαθήκη (vv.$^{7-13}$), and enumerating its promises as contained in a new διαθήκη.

---

^{1} In these two latter passages, at least, there may be an allusion to the contemporary description of Moses as "mediator of the covenant" ("arbiter testamenti," *Ass. Mosis*, i. 14). The writer does not contrast Jesus with Michael, who was the great angelic mediator in some circles of Jewish piety (cp. Jub 1^{29}, Test. Dan 6).

^{2} Josephus (*Ant.* xvi. 2. 2) says that Herod τῶν παρ' Ἀγρίππα τισὶν ἐπιζητουμένων μεσίτης ἦν, and that his influence moved πρὸς τὰς εὐεργεσίας οὐ βραδύνοντα τὸν Ἀγρίππαν. Ἰλιεῦσι μὲν γὰρ αὐτὸν διήλλαξεν ὀργιζόμενον.

⁷ *For if that first covenant had been faultless, there would have been no occasion for a second.* ⁸ *Whereas God does find fault with the people of that covenant, when he says :*

" The day is coming, saith the Lord,
*   when I will conclude a new covenant with the house of Israel and with the house of Judah.*
⁹ *It will not be on the lines of the covenant I made with their fathers,*
*   on the day when I took them by the hand to lead them out of Egypt's Land ;*
for they would not hold to my covenant,
*   so I left them alone, saith the Lord.*
¹⁰ *This is the covenant I will make with the house of Israel when that*
*   ("the day" of v.⁸) day comes, saith the Lord ;*
I will set my laws within their mind,
*   inscribing them upon their hearts ;*
I will be a God (εἰς θεόν, *i.e.* all that men can expect a God to be) *to them,*
*   and they shall be a People to me ;*
¹¹ *one citizen will no longer teach his fellow,*
*   one man will no longer teach his brother* (τὸν ἀδελφὸν αὐτοῦ, *i.e.* one another, Ex 10²³),
saying, " Know the Lord."
*   for all shall know me, low and high together.*
¹² *I will be merciful to their iniquities,*
*   and remember their sins no more.*
¹³ *By saying " a new covenant," he antiquates the first.   And whatever is antiquated and aged is on the verge of vanishing.*

The contents of the prediction of a καινὴ διαθήκη by God, and the very fact that such was necessary, prove the defectiveness of the first διαθήκη.   The writer is struck by the mention of a new διαθήκη even in the OT itself, and he now explains the significance of this.   As for ἡ πρώτη (*sc.* διαθήκη) ἐκείνη, εἰ . . . ἄμεμπτος (if no fault could have been found with it), οὐκ ἂν δευτέρας ἐζητεῖτο τόπος.   Δευτέρας is replaced by ἑτέρας in B* (so B. Weiss, Blass) ; but, while ἕτερος could follow πρῶτος (Mt 21⁸⁰), δεύτερος is the term chosen in 10⁹, and B* is far too slender evidence by itself.   Ζητεῖν τόπον is one of those idiomatic phrases, like εὑρεῖν τόπον and λαβεῖν τόπον, of which the writer was fond. The force of the γάρ after μεμφόμενος is : "and there was occasion for a second διαθήκη, the first was not ἄμεμπτος, since," etc.   It need make little or no difference to the sense whether we read αὐτοῖς (אᶜ B Dᶜ L 6. 38. 88. 104. 256. 436. 467. 999. 1311. 1319. 1739. 1837. 1845. 1912. 2004. 2127 Origen) or αὐτούς (א* A D* K P W 33 vg arm), for μεμφόμενος can take a dative as well as an accusative (cf. Arist. *Rhet.* i. 6. 24, Κορινθίοις δ' οὐ μέμφεται τὸ Ἴλιον : Aesch. *Prom.* 63, οὐδεὶς ἐνδίκως μέμψαιτο μοι) in the sense of "censuring" or "finding fault with," and μεμφόμενος naturally goes with αὐτοῖς or αὐτούς.   The objection to taking αὐτοῖς with λέγει [1]

---

[1] μεμφόμενος is then "by way of censure," and some think the writer purposely avoided adding αὐτήν.   Which, in view of what he says in v.¹³, is doubtful ; besides, he has just said that the former διαθήκη was not ἄμεμπτος.

is that the quotation is not addressed directly to the people, but spoken at large. Thus the parallel from 2 Mac 2⁷ ($\mu\epsilon\mu\psi\acute{a}\mu\epsilon\nu os \ a\mathring{v}\tau o\hat{i}s \ \epsilon\hat{i}\pi\epsilon\nu$) is not decisive, and the vg is probably correct in rendering " vituperans enim eos dicit."   The context explains here as in 4⁸ and 11²⁸ who are meant by $a\mathring{v}\tau o\acute{v}s$.   The real interest of the writer in this Jeremianic oracle is shown when he returns to it in 10¹⁶⁻¹⁸; what arrests him is the promise of a free, full pardon at the close.   But he quotes it at length, partly because it did imply the supersession of the older $\delta\iota a\theta\acute{\eta}\kappa\eta$ and partly because it contained high promises (vv.¹⁰⁻¹²), higher than had yet been given to the People.   No doubt it also contains a warning (v.⁹), like the text from the 95th psalm (3⁷ᶠ·), but this is not why he recites it (see p. xl).

The text of Jer 38³¹⁻³⁴ (31³¹⁻³⁴) as he read it in his bible (*i.e.* in A) ran thus :

ἰδοὺ ἡμέραι ἔρχονται, λέγει Κύριος,
καὶ διαθήσομαι τῷ οἴκῳ Ἰσραὴλ καὶ τῷ οἴκῳ Ἰούδα διαθήκην
 καινήν,
οὐ κατὰ τὴν διαθήκην ἣν διεθέμην τοῖς πατράσιν αὐτῶν
ἐν ἡμέρᾳ ἐπιλαβομένου μου τῆς χειρὸς αὐτῶν ἐξαγαγεῖν αὐτοὺς ἐκ
 γῆς Αἰγύπτου,
ὅτι αὐτοὶ οὐκ ἐνέμειναν ἐν τῇ διαθήκῃ μου,
κἀγὼ ἠμέλησα αὐτῶν, φησὶν Κύριος.
ὅτι αὕτη ἡ διαθήκη ἣν διαθήσομαι τῷ οἴκῳ Ἰσραὴλ
μετὰ τὰς ἡμέρας ἐκείνας, φησὶν Κύριος,
διδοὺς νόμους μου εἰς τὴν διάνοιαν αὐτῶν
καὶ ἐπιγράψω αὐτοὺς ἐπὶ τὰς καρδίας αὐτῶν,
καὶ ὄψομαι αὐτοὺς
καὶ ἔσομαι αὐτοῖς εἰς θεὸν.
καὶ αὐτοὶ ἔσονταί μοι εἰς λαόν.
καὶ οὐ μὴ¹ διδάξωσιν ἕκαστος τὸν ἀδελφὸν αὐτοῦ
καὶ ἕκαστος τὸν πλησίον αὐτοῦ λέγων· γνῶθι τὸν Κύριον,
ὅτι πάντες ἰδήσουσιν με
ἀπὸ μικροῦ ἕως μεγάλου αὐτῶν,
ὅτι ἵλεως ἔσομαι ταῖς ἀδικίαις αὐτῶν
καὶ τῶν ἁμαρτιῶν αὐτῶν οὐ μὴ μνησθῶ ἔτι.

Our author follows as usual the text of A upon the whole (*e.g.* λέγει for φησίν in v.³¹, κἀγώ in v.³², the omission of μου after διαθήκη and of δώσω after διδούς in v.³³, οὐ μὴ διδάξωσιν for οὐ διδάξουσιν in v.³⁴ and the omission of αὐτῶν after μικροῦ), but substitutes συντελέσω ἐπὶ τὸν οἶκον (bis) for διαθήσομαι τῷ οἴκῳ in v.³¹, reads λέγει for φησίν in v.³² and v.³³, alters διεθέμην into ἐποίησα (Q*), and follows B in reading καὶ ἐπὶ κ. αὐτῶν before the verb (v.³³), and πολίτην . . . ἀδελφόν in v.³⁴, as well as in omitting καὶ ὄψ. αὐτούς (A א) in the former verse ; in v.³⁴ he reads εἰδήσουσιν (א Q) instead of

¹ οὐ μή only occurs in Hebrews in quotations (here, 10¹⁷ 13⁵) ; out of about ninety-six occurrences in the NT, only eight are with the future.

ἰδήσουσιν, the forms of οἶδα and εἶδον being repeatedly confused (cp. Thackeray, 278). These minor changes may be partly due to the fact that he is quoting from memory. In some cases his own text has been conformed to other versions of the LXX ; *e.g.* A D Ψ boh restore μου in v.¹⁰, א* K vg Clem. Chrys. read καρδίαν (with א in LXX), though the singular¹ is plainly a con- formation to διανοιαν (" Für den Plural sprechen ausser A D L noch B, wo nur das C in ε verschrieben und daraus επι καρδια εαυτων geworden ist, und P, wo der Dat. in den Acc. verwandelt," B. Weiss in *Texte u. Unter- suchungen*, xiv. 3. 16, 55) ; B Ψ arm revive the LXX (B) variant γράψω ; the LXX (Q) variant πλησίον is substituted for πολίτην by P vg syrʰᵏˡ eth 38. 206. 218. 226. 257. 547. 642. 1288. 1311. 1912, etc. Cyril, and the LXX (B Q א) αὐτῶν restored after μικροῦ by Dᶜ L syr boh eth, etc. On the other hand, a trait like the reading ἐποίησα in the LXX text of Q* may be due to the influence of Hebrews itself. The addition of καὶ τῶν ἀνομιῶν αὐτῶν after or before καὶ τῶν ἁμαρτιῶν αὐτῶν in v.¹² is a homiletic gloss from 10¹⁷, though strongly entrenched in אᶜ A C D K L P Ψ 6. 104. 326, etc. vg pesh arm Clem

Συντελέσω διαθήκην, a literary LXX variant for ποιήσω διαθήκην, recalls the phrase συντελέσαι διαθήκην (Jer 41⁸ (34⁸)), and, as 12²⁴ (νέας διαθήκης) shows, the writer draws no distinction between καινός and νέος (v.⁸). In v.⁹ the genitive absolute (ἐπιλαβομένου μου) after ἡμέρᾳ, instead of ἐν ᾗ ἐπελαβόμην (as Justin correctly puts it, *Dial.* xi.), is a Hellenistic innovation, due here to trans- lation, but paralleled in Bar 2²⁸ ἐν ἡμέρᾳ ἐντειλαμένου σου αὐτῷ) ; in ὅτι (causal only here and in v.¹⁰) . . . ἐνέμειναν, the latter is our " abide by," in the sense of obey or practise, exactly as in Isokrates, κατὰ τῶν Σοφιστῶν, 20: οἷς εἰ τις ἐπὶ τῶν πράξεων ἐμμείνειεν. Bengel has a crisp comment on αὐτοὶ . . . κἀγώ here and on ἔσομαι . . . καὶ αὐτοί (" correlata . . . sed ratione inversa ; populus fecerat initium tollendi foederis prius, in novo omnia et incipit et perficit Deus ") ; and, as it happens, there is a dramatic contrast between ἠμέλησα here and the only other use of the verb in this epistle (2³). In v.¹⁰ διδούς, by the omission of δώσω, is left hanging in the air ; but (cp. Moulton, 222) such participles could be taken as finite verbs in popular Greek of the period (cp. *e.g.* χειροτονηθείς in 2 Co 8¹⁹). The καινὴ διαθήκη is to be on entirely fresh lines, not a mere revival of the past ; it is to realize a knowledge of God which is inward and intuitive (vv.¹⁰·¹¹). There is significance in the promise, καὶ ἔσομαι αὐτοῖς . . . εἰς λαόν. A διαθήκη was always between God and his people, and this had been the object even of the former διαθήκη (Ex. 6⁷) ; now it is to be realized at last. Philo's sentence (" even if we are sluggish, however, He is not sluggish about taking to Himself those who are fit for His service ; for He says, ' I will take you to be a people for myself, and I will be your God,'" *De Sacrif. Abelis et Caini*, 26) is an apt comment ; but our author, who sees the new διαθήκη fulfilled in Christianity, has

¹ That ἐπί takes the accusative here is shown by 10¹⁶ ; καρδίας cannot be the genitive singular alongside of an accusative.

his own views about how such a promise and purpose was attainable, for while the oracle ignores the sacrificial ritual altogether, he cannot conceive any pardon apart from sacrifice, nor any διαθήκη apart from a basal sacrifice. These ideas he is to develop in his next paragraphs, for it is the closing promise of pardon [1] which is to him the supreme boon. Meanwhile, before passing on to explain how this had been mediated by Jesus, he (v. [13]) drives home the truth of the contrast between old and new (see Introd., p. xxxix). Ἐν τῷ λέγειν (same construction as in 2⁸)—when the word καινήν (sc. διαθήκην) was pronounced, it sealed the doom of the old διαθήκη. Παλαιόω (πεπαλαίωκε) in this transitive sense ("he hath abrogat," Tyndale) is known to the LXX (Job 9⁵, La 3⁴, both times of God in action); γηράσκειν is practically equivalent to μαραίνεσθαι, and implies decay (see Wilamowitz on Eur. *Herakles*, 1223). The two words ἐγγύς (as in 6⁸) ἀφανισμοῦ, at the end of the paragraph, sound like the notes of a knell, though they have no contemporary reference ; the writer simply means that the end of the old διαθήκη was at hand (p. xxii). The new would soon follow, as it had done ἐν υἱῷ (1¹). The verb ἀφανίζειν (-εσθαι) is applied to legislation (*e.g.*, Lysias, 868, τὴν ὑμετέραν νομοθεσίαν ἀφανίζοντας) in the sense of abolition, lapsing or falling into desuetude, Dion. Hal. *Ant.* iii. 178, ἃς (*i.e.* Numa's laws) ἀφανισθῆναι συνέβη τῷ χρόνῳ, the opposite of ἀφανίζειν being γράφειν (*ibid.* ix. 608, κατὰ τοὺς νόμους, οὓς οὐ νεωστὶ δεήσει γράφειν πάλαι γὰρ ἐγράφησαν, καὶ οὐδεὶς αὐτοὺς ἠφάνιζε χρόνος), and the sense of disappearance in ἀφανισμός appears already in the LXX (*e.g.* Jer 28³⁷ καὶ ἔσται Βαβυλὼν εἰς ἀφανισμόν).

But the new διαθήκη is also superior to the old by its sacrifice (9¹ᶠ·), sacrifice being essential to any forgiveness such as has been promised. The older διαθήκη had its sanctuary and ritual (vv.¹⁻⁵), but even these (vv.⁶ᶠ·) indicated a defect.

---

[1] *The first covenant had indeed its regulations for worship and a material sanctuary.* [2] *A tent was set up (κατασκευάζω as in 3³), the outer tent, containing the lampstand, the table, and the loaves of the Presence ; this is called the Holy place.* [3] *But behind (μετά only here in NT of place) the second veil was the tent called the Holy of Holies,* [4] *containing the golden altar of incense, and also the ark of the covenant covered all over with gold, which held the golden pot of manna, the rod of Aaron that once blossomed, and the tablets of the covenant ;* [5] *above this were the cherubim of the Glory overshadowing the mercy-seat—matters which (i.e. all in ²⁻⁵) it is impossible for me to discuss at present in detail.*

---

[1] With τῶν ἁμαρτιῶν αὐτῶν οὐ μὴ μνησθῶ ἔτι compare the parable of R. Jochanan and R. Eliezer on God's readiness to forget the sinful nature of his servants : "There is a parable concerning a king of flesh and blood, who said to his servants, Build me a great palace on the dunghill. They went and built it for him. It was not thenceforward the king's pleasure to remember the dunghill which had been there" (Chagiga, 16 a. i. 27).

The καινὴ διαθήκη of 8⁷⁻¹³ had been realized by the arrival of Christ (9¹¹); hence the older διαθήκη was superseded, and the writer speaks of it in the past tense, εἶχε. As for ἡ πρώτη (*sc.* διαθήκη) of which he has been just speaking (8¹³), the antithesis of the entire passage is between ἡ πρώτη διαθήκη (vv.¹⁻¹⁰) and ἡ καινὴ διαθήκη (vv.¹¹⁻²²), as is explicitly stated in v.¹⁵. The καί (om. B 38. 206*. 216*. 489. 547. 1739. 1827 boh pesh Origen) before ἡ πρώτη emphasizes the fact that the old had this in common with the new, viz. worship and a sanctuary. This is, of course, out of keeping with the Jeremianic oracle of the new διαθήκη, which does not contemplate any such provision, but the writer takes a special view of διαθήκη which involves a celestial counterpart to the ritual provisions of the old order.

The former διαθήκη, then, embraced δικαιώματα, *i.e.* regulations, as in Lk 1⁶ and 1 Mac 2²¹·²² (ἵλεως ἡμῖν καταλείπειν νόμον καὶ δικαιώματα τὸν νόμον τοῦ βασιλέως οὐκ ἀκουσόμεθα, παρελθεῖν τὴν λατρίαν ἡμῶν), rather than rights or privileges (as, *e.g.*, *OP.* 1119¹⁵ τῶν ἐξαιρέτων τῆς ἡμετέρας πατρίδος δικαιωμάτων), arrangements for the cultus. Λατρείας grammatically might be accusative plural (as in v.⁶), but is probably the genitive, after δικαιώματα, which it defines. Λατρεία or (as spelt in W) λατρία (cp. Thackeray, 87) is the cultus (Ro 9⁴), or any specific part of it (Ex 12²⁵·²⁷). The close connexion between worship and a sanctuary (already in 8²·³) leads to the addition of τό τε (as in 1³ 6⁵) ἅγιον κοσμικόν. By τὸ ἅγιον the author means the entire sanctuary (so, *e.g.*, Ex 36³, Nu 3³⁸), not the innermost sacred shrine or ἅγια ἁγίων. This is clear. What is not so clear is the meaning of κοσμικόν, and the meaning of its position after the noun without an article. Primarily κοσμικός here as in Ti 2¹² (τὰς κοσμικὰς ἐπιθυμίας) is an equivalent for ἐπὶ γῆς (8³), *i.e.* mundane or material, as opposed to ἐπουράνιον or οὐ ταύτης τῆς κτίσεως (v.¹¹). A fair parallel to this occurs in *Test. Jos.* 17⁸, διὰ τὴν κοσμικήν μου δόξαν. But did our author use it with a further suggestion? It would have been quite irrelevant to his purpose to suggest the "public" aspect of the sanctuary, although Jews like Philo and Josephus might speak of the temple as κοσμικός in this sense, *i.e.* in contrast to synagogues and προσευχαί, which were of local importance (Philo, *ad Caium*, 1019), or simply as a place of public worship (*e.g.* Jos. *Bell.* iv. 5. 2, τῆς κοσμικῆς θρησκείας κατάρχοντας, προσκυνουμένους τε τοῖς ἐκ τῆς οἰκουμένης παραβάλλουσιν εἰς τὴν πόλιν). Neither would our author have called the sanctuary κοσμικός as symbolic of the κόσμος, though Philo (*Vit. Mosis*, iii. 3–10) and Josephus (*Ant.* iii. 6. 4, iii. 7. 7, ἕκαστα γὰρ τούτων εἰς ἀπομίμησιν καὶ διατύπωσιν τῶν ὅλων) also play with this fancy. He views the sanctuary as a dim representation of the divine sanctuary, not of the universe. Yet he might have employed κοσμικόν in a similar sense, if we interpret the obscure phrase μυστήριον κοσμικὸν ἐκκλησίας in Did. 11¹¹ (see the notes of Dr. C. Taylor and Dr. Rendel Harris in their editions) as a spiritual or heavenly idea, "depicted in the world of sense by emblematic actions or material objects," "a symbol or action wrought upon the stage of this world to illustrate what was doing or to be done on a higher plane." Thus, in the context of the Didache, marriage would be a μυστήριον κοσμικόν (cp. Eph 5³²) of the spiritual relation between Christ and his church. This early Christian usage may have determined the choice of κοσμικόν here, the sanctuary being κοσμικόν because it is the material representation or parabolic outward expression of the true, heavenly sanctuary. But at best it is a secondary suggestion; unless κοσμικόν could be taken as "ornamented," the controlling idea is that the sanctuary and its ritual were external and material (δικαιώματα σαρκὸς, χειροποιήτου, χειροποίητα). The very position of κοσμικόν denotes, as often in Greek, a stress such as might be conveyed in English by "a sanctuary, material indeed."

The ἅγιον is now described (v.²ᶠ·), after Ex 25-26. It consisted of two parts, each called a σκηνή. The large outer tent, the first (ἡ πρώτη) to be entered, was called Ἅγια (neut. plur., not fem. sing.). The phrase, ἥτις λέγεται Ἅγια¹ would have been in a better position immediately after ἡ πρώτη, where, indeed, Chrysostom (followed by Blass) reads it, instead of after the list of the furniture. The lampstand stood in front (to the south) of the sacred table on which twelve loaves or cakes of wheaten flour were piled (ἡ πρόθεσις τῶν ἄρτων = οἱ ἄρτοι τῆς προθέσεως), the Hebrew counterpart of the well-known lectisternia: ἡ τράπεζα . . . ἄρτων is a hendiadys for "the table with its loaves of the Presence." Such was the furniture of the outer σκηνή. Then (vv.³⁻⁵) follows a larger catalogue (cp. *Joma* 2⁴) of what lay inside the inner shrine (ἅγια ἁγίων) behind the curtain (Ex 27¹⁶) which screened this from the outer tent, and which is called δεύτερον καταπέτασμα, δεύτερον, because the first was a curtain hung at the entrance to the larger tent, and καταπέτασμα, either because that is the term used in Ex 26³¹ᶠ· (the particular passage the writer has in mind here), the term elsewhere being usually κάλυμμα or ἐπίσπαστρον (Ex 26³⁶ etc.), or because Philo had expressly distinguished the outer curtain as κάλυμμα, the inner as καταπέτασμα (*de vita Mosis*, iii. 9). This inner shrine contained (v.⁴) χρυσοῦν θυμιατήριον, *i.e.* a wooden box, overlaid with gold, on which incense (θυμίαμα) was offered twice daily by the priests. The LXX calls this θυσιαστήριον τοῦ θυμιάματος (Ex 30¹⁻¹⁰), but our writer follows the usage of Philo, which is also,

¹ Τὰ Ἅγια (B arm) is an attempt to reproduce exactly the LXX phrase.

on the whole, that of Josephus, in calling it θυμιατήριον (so
Symm. Theodotion, Ex 30¹ 31⁸); θυμιατήριον, in the non-biblical
papyri, denotes articles like censers in a sanctuary, but is never
used in the LXX of levitical censers, though Josephus occasionally describes them thus, like the author of 4 Mac 7¹¹.   The
ordinary view was that this θυμιατήριον stood beside the λυχνία
and the sacred τράπεζα in the outer sanctuary.   Both Philo (e.g.
quis rer. div. 46, τριῶν ὄντων ἐν τοῖς ἁγίοις σκευεῶν, λυχνίας,
τραπέζης, θυμιατηρίου: de vita Mos. iii. 9 f., in the outer tent, τὰ
λοιπὰ τρία σκευή . . . μέσον μὲν τὸ θυμιατήριον . . . τὴν δὲ λυχνίαν
. . . ἡ δὲ τράπεζα) and Josephus (Ant. iii. 6. 4 f.; cp. viii. 4. 1 for
the reproduction in Solomon's temple) are quite explicit on this.
Indeed no other position was possible for an altar which required
daily service from the priests; inside the ἅγια τῶν ἁγίων it would
have been useless.   But another tradition, which appears in the
contemporary (Syriac) apocalypse of Baruch (6⁷), placed the
altar of incense¹ inside the ἅγια ἁγίων, a view reflected as early
as the Samaritan text of the pentateuch, which put Ex 30¹⁻¹⁰
(the description of the altar of incense) after 26³⁵, where logically
it ought to stand, inserting a לפני יהוה in Ex 40²⁷ (where the
altar of incense is placed " before the veil ").   The earliest hint
of this tradition seems to be given in the Hebrew text of 1 K 6²²,
where Solomon is said to have overlaid with gold " the altar that
is by the oracle" (i.e. the ἅγια ἁγίων).   But our author could not
have been influenced by this, for it is absent from the LXX text.
His inaccuracy was rendered possible by the vague language of
the pentateuch about the position of the altar of incense, ἀπέναντι
τοῦ καταπετάσματος τοῦ ὄντος ἐπὶ τῆς κιβωτοῦ τῶν μαρτυριῶν
(Ex 30⁶), where ἀπέναντι may mean "opposite" or "close in
front of" the curtain—but on which side of it?   In Ex 37 the
τράπεζα, the λυχνία, and the altar of incense are described
successively after the items in the ἅγια ἁγίων; but then the LXX
did not contain the section on the altar of incense, so that this
passage offered no clue to our writer.   In Ex 40⁵ it is merely put
ἐναντίον τῆς κιβωτοῦ.   This vagueness is due to the fact that in
the original source the sketch of the σκηνή had no altar of
incense at all; the latter is a later accretion, hence the curious
position of Ex 30¹⁻¹⁰ in a sort of appendix, and the ambiguity
about its site.

After all it is only an antiquarian detail for our author.   It has been
suggested that he regarded the ἅγια τῶν ἁγίων, irrespective of the veil, as
symbolizing the heavenly sanctuary, and that he therefore thought it must
include the altar of incense as symbolizing the prayers of the saints.   But
there is no trace of such a symbolism elsewhere in the epistle; it is confined to
the author of the Apocalypse (8³ᶠ·).   The suggestion that he meant ἔχουσα

¹ Whether the language means this or a censer is disputed.

to express only a close or ideal connexion between the inner shrine and the altar of incense, is popular (*e.g.* Delitzsch, Zahn, Peake, Seeberg) but quite unacceptable ; ἔχουσα as applied to the other items could not mean this,[1] and what applies to them applies to the θυμιατήριον. Besides, the point of the whole passage is to distinguish between the contents of the two compartments. Still less tenable is the idea that θυμιατήριον really means "censer" or "incense pan." This way out of the difficulty was started very early (in the peshiṭta, the vulgate), but a censer is far too minor a utensil to be included in this inventory ; even the censer afterwards used on atonement-day did not belong to the ἅγια τῶν ἁγίων, neither was it golden. What the σκηνή had was merely a brazier (πυρεῖον, Lv 16¹²). Since it is not possible that so important an object as the altar of incense could have been left out, we may assume without much hesitation that the writer did mean to describe it by θυμιατήριον,[2] and that the irregularity of placing it on the wrong side of the curtain is simply another of his inaccuracies in describing what he only knew from the text of the LXX. In B the slip is boldly corrected by the transference of (καὶ) χρυσοῦν θυμιατήριον to v.², immediately after ἄρτων (so Blass).

The second item is τὴν κιβωτὸν τῆς διαθήκης covered with gold all over (πάντοθεν: Philo's phrase is ἔνδοθεν καὶ ἔξωθεν, *de Ebriet.* 21), a chest or box about 4 feet long and 2½ feet broad and high (Ex 25¹⁰ᶠ.), which held three sacred treasures, (*a*) the golden pot (στάμνος, Attic feminine) of manna (Ex 16³²⁻³⁴) ; (*b*) Aaron's rod ἡ βλαστήσασα (in the story of Nu 17¹⁻¹¹, which attested the sacerdotal monopoly of the clan of Levi); and (*c*) αἱ πλάκες τῆς διαθήκης (Ex 25¹⁶ᶠ· 31¹⁸), *i.e.* the two stone tablets on which the decalogue was written (πλάκας διαθήκης, Dt 9⁹; ἐνέβαλον τὰς πλάκας εἰς τὴν κιβωτόν, 10⁵), the decalogue summarizing the terms of the διαθήκη for the People. In adding χρυσῆ to στάμνος the writer follows the later tradition of the LXX and of Philo (*de congressu*, 18) ; the pot is not golden in the Hebrew original. He also infers, as later Jewish tradition did, that the ark contained this pot, although, like Aaron's rod, it simply lay in front of the ark (Ex 16³³· ³⁴, Nu 17¹⁰). He would gather from 1 K 8⁹ that the ark contained the tablets of the covenant. He then (v.⁵) mentions the χερουβείν (Aramaic form) or χερουβεὶμ (Hebrew form) δόξης, two small winged figures (Ex 25¹⁸⁻²⁰), whose pinions extended over a rectangular gold slab, called τὸ ἱλαστήριον, laid on the top of the ark, which it fitted exactly. They are called cherubim Δόξης, which is like Μεγαλωσύνης (1³ 8¹) a divine title, applied to Jesus in Ja 2¹, but here used as in Ro 9⁴. The cherubim on the ἱλαστήριον represented the divine Presence as accessible in mercy ; the mystery of this is suggested by the couplet in Sir 49⁸ ⁽¹⁰⁾:

Ἰεζεκιήλ, ὃς εἶδεν ὅρασιν Δόξης
ἣν ὑπέδειξεν αὐτῷ ἐπὶ ἅρματος χερουβείμ.

---

[1] The change from ἐν ᾗ to ἔχουσα is purely stylistic, and ἔχουσα in both instances means "containing."

[2] χρυσοῦν θυμιατήριον lacks the article, like στάμνος χρυσῆ.

Philo's account of τὸ ἱλαστήριον is given in *de vita Mosis*, iii. 8, ἡ δὲ κιβωτὸς . . . κεχρυσωμένη πολυτελῶς ἔνδοθέν τε καὶ ἔξωθεν, ἧς ἐπίθεμα ὡσανεὶ πῶμα τὸ λεγόμενον ἐν ἱεραῖς βίβλοις ἱλαστήριον . . . ὅπερ ἔοικεν εἶναι σύμβολον φυσικώτερον μὲν τῆς ἵλεω τοῦ θεοῦ δυνάμεως. Lower down, in the same paragraph, he speaks of τὸ ἐπίθεμα τὸ προσαγορευόμενον ἱλαστήριον, and τὸ ἱλαστήριον is similarly used in *De Cherub.* 8 (on the basis of Ex 25[19]). The ἐπίθεμα or covering of the ark was splashed with blood on atonement-day; perhaps, even apart from that, its Hebrew original meant "means of propitiation," and was not incorrectly named ἱλαστήριον (cp. Deissmann in *EBi.* 3027–3035), but our author simply uses it in its LXX sense of "mercy-seat." He does not enter into any details about its significance; in his scheme of sacrificial thought such a conception had no place. Philo also allegorizes the overshadowing wings of the cherubim as a symbol of God's creative and royal powers protecting the cosmos, and explains Ex 25[22] as follows (*Quaest. in Exod.* 25[22]): τὰ μὲν οὖν περὶ τὴν κιβωτὸν κατὰ μέρος εἴρηται· δεῖ δὲ συλλήβδην ἄνωθεν ἀναλαβόντα τοῦ γνωρίσαι χάριν τίνων ταῦτά ἐστι σύμβολα διεξελθεῖν· ἦν δὲ ταῦτα συμβολικά· κιβωτὸς καὶ τὰ ἐν αὐτῇ θησαυριζόμενα νόμιμα καὶ ἐπὶ ταύτης τὸ ἱλαστήριον καὶ τὰ ἐπὶ τοῦ ἱλαστηρίου Χαλδαίων γλώττῃ λεγόμενα χερουβίμ, ὑπὲρ δὲ τούτων κατὰ τὸ μέσον φωνὴ καὶ λόγος καὶ ὑπεράνω ὁ λέγων κτλ. But our author does not enter into any such details. He has no time for further discussion of the furniture, he observes; whether he would have allegorized these items of antiquarian ritual, if or when he had leisure, we cannot tell. The only one he does employ mystically is the κατα-πέτασμα (10[20]), and his use of it is not particularly happy. He now breaks off, almost as Philo does (*quis rer. div.* 45, πολὺν δ' ὄντα τὸν περὶ ἑκάστου λόγον ὑπερθέτεον εἰσαῦθις) on the same subject. Κατὰ μέρος is the ordinary literary phrase in this connexion (*e.g.* 2 Mac 2[30]; Polybius, i. 67. 11, περὶ ὧν οὐχ οἷόν τε διὰ τῆς γραφῆς τὸν κατὰ μέρος ἀποδοῦναι λόγον, and Poimandres [ed. Reitzenstein, p. 84] περὶ ὧν ὁ κατὰ μέρος λόγος ἐστὶ πολύς). Οὐκ ἔστιν as in 1 Co 11[20].

Worship in a sanctuary like this shows that access to God was defective (vv.[6-8]), as was inevitable when the sacrifices were external (vv.[8-10]). Having first shown this, the writer gets back to the main line of his argument (8[2]), viz. the sacrifice of Jesus as pre-eminent and final (v.[11f.]).

---

[6] *Such were the arrangements for worship. The priests constantly enter the first tent* (v.[2]) *in the discharge of their ritual duties,* [7] *but the second tent is entered only once a year by the highpriest alone—and it must not be without blood, which he presents on behalf of* (cp. 5[3]) *himself and the errors of the People.* [8] *By this the holy Spirit means that the way into the Holiest Presence was not yet disclosed so long as the first tent* [9] (*which foreshadowed the present age*) *was still standing, with its offerings of gifts and sacrifices which cannot* (μή *as in* 4[2]) *possibly make the conscience of the worshipper*

perfect, [10] *since they relate (sc. οὖσαι) merely to food and drink and a variety of ablutions—outward regulations for the body, that only hold till the period of the New Order.*

In v.[6] διὰ παντός = continually, as in *BM.* i. 42[6] (ii B.C.) οἱ ἐν οἴκῳ πάντες σου διαπαντὸς μνείαν ποιούμενοι. Εἰσίασιν (which might even be the present with a futuristic sense, the writer placing himself and his readers back at the inauguration of the sanctuary : " Now, this being all ready, the priests will enter," etc.) ἐπιτελοῦντες (a regular sacerdotal or ritual term in Philo) λατρείας (morning and evening, to trim the lamps and offer incense on the golden altar, Ex 27[21] 30[7f.] etc. ; weekly, to change the bread of the Presence, Lv 24[8f.], Jos. *Ant.* iii. 6. 6). The ritual of the inner shrine (v.[8]) is now described (v.[7], cp. *Joma* 5[3]) ; the place is entered by the highpriest ἅπαξ τοῦ ἐνιαυτοῦ, on the annual day of atonement (Lv 16[29. 34], Ex 30[10]) : only once, and he must be alone (μόνος, Lv 16[17]), this one individual out of all the priests. Even he dare not enter χωρὶς αἵματος (Lv 16[14f.]), *i.e.* without carrying in blood from the sacrifice offered for his own and the nation's ἀγνοημάτων. In Gn 43[12] ἀγνόημα is "an oversight," but in Jg 5[20] Tob 3[3], 1 Mac 13[39], Sir 23[2] ἀγνοήματα and "sins" are bracketed together (see above on 5[2]), and the word occurs alone in Polyb. xxxviii. 1. 5 as an equivalent for "offences" or "errors" in the moral sense. There is no hint that people were not responsible for them, or that they were not serious ; on the contrary, they had to be atoned for. Ὑπέρ κτλ. ; for a similarly loose construction cp. 1 Jn 2[2] (οὐ περὶ ἡμετέρων [ἁμαρτιῶν] δὲ μόνον, ἀλλὰ καὶ περὶ ὅλου τοῦ κόσμου).

Rabbi Ismael b. Elischa, the distinguished exegete of i–ii A.D., classified sins as follows (*Tos. Joma* 5[6]) : Transgressions of positive enactments were atoned for by repentance, involving a purpose of new obedience, according to Jer 22[23] (" Return, ye backsliding children, and I will heal your backslidings "). The day of atonement, however, was necessary for the full pardon of offences against divine prohibitions : according to Lv 16[30] (" On that day shall the priest make atonement for you, to cleanse you, that ye may be clean from all your sins "). An offender whose wrongdoing deserved severe or capital punishment could only be restored by means of sufferings : according to Ps 89[32] (" Then will I visit their transgression with the rod, and their iniquity with stripes "). But desecration of the divine Name could not be atoned for by any of these three methods ; death alone wiped out this sin (Jer 24[4]).

The author now (v.[8]) proceeds to find a spiritual significance in this ceremonial. Δηλοῦντος is used of a divine meaning as in 12[27], here conveyed by outward facts. In 1 P 1[11] the verb is again used of the Spirit, and this is the idea here ; Josephus (*Ant.* iii. 7. 7, δηλοῖ δὲ καὶ τὸν ἥλιον καὶ τὴν σελήνην τῶν σαρδονύχων ἑκάτερος) uses the same verb for the mystic significance of the jewels worn by the highpriest, but our author's interpretation of the significance of the σκηνή is naturally very different from that

of Josephus, who regards the unapproachable character of the
ἄδυτον or inner shrine as symbolizing heaven itself (*Ant.* iii. 6. 4
and 7. 7, ὃ τοῖς ἱερεῦσιν ἦν ἄβατον, ὡς οὐρανὸς ἄνειτο τῷ θεῷ . . .
διὰ τὸ καὶ τὸν οὐρανὸν ἀνεπίβατον εἶναι ἀνθρώποις). For ὁδόν with
gen. in sense of "way to," cp. Gn 3²⁴ (τὴν ὁδὸν τοῦ ξύλου τῆς
ζωῆς), Jg 5¹⁴ (εἰς ὁδὸν τοῦ Σινά). Τῶν ἁγίων here (like τὰ ἅγια in
vv.¹². ²⁵, cp. 13¹¹) as in 10¹⁹ means the very Presence of God, an
archaic liturgical phrase suggested by the context. The word
φανεροῦσθαι was not found by the writer in his text of the LXX;
it only occurs in the LXX in Jer 40 (33)⁶, and the Latin phrase
"iter patefieri" (*e.g.* Caesar, *de Bello Gall.* iii. 1) is merely a
verbal parallel. In τῆς πρώτης σκηνῆς ἐχούσης στάσιν (v.⁹), the
writer has chosen στάσιν for the sake of assonance with ἐνεστηκότα,
but ἔχειν στάσιν is a good Greek phrase for "to be in existence."
The parenthesis ἥτις ¹ παραβολὴ (here = τύπος, as Chrysostom saw)
εἰς τὸν καιρὸν τὸν ἐνεστηκότα means that the first σκηνή was merely
provisional, as it did no more than adumbrate the heavenly
reality, and provisional εἰς (as in Ac 4³ εἰς τὴν αὔριον) τὸν
καιρὸν τὸν ἐνεστηκότα, *i.e.* the period in which the writer and his
readers lived, the period inaugurated by the advent of Jesus with
his new διαθήκη. This had meant the supersession of the older
διαθήκη with its sanctuary and δικαιώματα, which only lasted
μέχρι καιροῦ διορθώσεως. But, so long as they lasted, they were
intended by God to foreshadow the permanent order of religion;
they were, as the writer says later (v.²³), ὑποδείγματα τῶν ἐν τοῖς
οὐρανοῖς, mere copies but still copies. This is why he calls the
fore-tent a παραβολή. For now, as he adds triumphantly, in a
daring, imaginative expression, our ἀρχιερεύς has passed through
his heavenly fore-tent (v.¹¹), and his heavenly sanctuary corresponds to a heavenly (*i.e.* a full and final) sacrifice. In the
levitical ritual the highpriest on atonement-day took the blood
of the victim through the fore-tent into the inner shrine. Little
that accomplished! It was but a dim emblem of what our highpriest was to do and has done, in the New Order of things.

When readers failed to see that ἥτις . . . ἐνεστηκότα was a parenthesis, it
was natural that καθ' ἥν should be changed into καθ' ὅν (Dᶜ K L P, so Blass).

The failure of animal sacrifices (⁹ᵇ⁻¹⁰) lies κατὰ συνείδησιν. As
the inner consciousness here is a consciousness of sin, "conscience" fairly represents the Greek term συνείδησις. Now, the
levitical sacrifices were ineffective as regards the conscience of
worshippers; they were merely ἐπὶ βρώμασιν καὶ πόμασιν καὶ διαφό-
ροις βαπτισμοῖς, a striking phrase (cp. 13⁹) of scorn for the mass of

---

¹ *Sc.* ἦν. The construction was explained by the addition of καθέστηκεν
after ἐνεστηκότα (so 69. 104. 330. 436. 440. 462. 491. 823. 1319. 1836. 1837.
1898. 2005. 2127, etc.).

minute regulations about what might or might not be eaten or drunk, and about baths, etc.   Food and ablutions are intelligible ; a book like Leviticus is full of regulations about them.   But πόμασιν ?   Well, the writer adds this as naturally as the author of *Ep. Aristeas* does, in describing the levitical code.   "I suppose most people feel some curiosity about the enactments of our law περί τε τῶν βρωτῶν καὶ ποτῶν " (128) ; it was to safeguard us from pagan defilement that παντόθεν ἡμᾶς περιέφραξεν ἀγνείαις καὶ διὰ βρωτῶν καὶ ποτῶν (142), ἐπὶ τῶν βρωτῶν καὶ ποτῶν ἀπαρξαμένους εὐθέως τότε συγχρῆσθαι κελεύει (158).   It is curious that this defence of the levitical code contains an allusion which is a verbal parallel to our writer's disparaging remark here ; the author asserts that intelligent Egyptian priests call the Jews "men of God," a title only applicable to one who σέβεται τὸν κατὰ ἀλήθειαν θεόν, since all others are ἄνθρωποι βρωτῶν καὶ ποτῶν καὶ σκέπης, ἡ γὰρ πᾶσα διάθεσις αὐτῶν ἐπὶ ταῦτα καταφεύγει.   τοῖς δὲ παρ᾿ ἡμῶν ἐν οὐδενὶ ταῦτα λελόγισται (140. 141).   Libations of wine accompanied certain levitical sacrifices (*e.g.* Nu 5[15] 6[15. 17] 28[7f.]), but no ritual regulations were laid down for them, and they were never offered independently (cp. *EBi.* 4193, 4209).   It is because the whole question of sacrifice is now to be restated that he throws in these disparaging comments upon the δῶρά τε καὶ θυσίαι and their accompaniments in the older σκηνή.   Such sacrifices were part and parcel of a system connected with (v.[10]) external ritual, and in concluding the discussion he catches up the term with which he had opened it : all such rites are δικαιώματα σαρκός, connected with the sensuous side of life and therefore provisional, μέχρι καιροῦ διορθώ-σεως ἐπικείμενα.   Here ἐπικείμενα is "prescribed," as in the description of workmen on strike, in *Tebt. P.* 26[17] (114 B.C.) ἐγκαταλείποντας τὴν ἐπικειμένην ἀσχολίαν.   Διόρθωσις means a "reconstruction" of religion, such as the new διαθήκη (8[13]) involved ; the use of the term in Polybius, iii. 118. 12 (πρὸς τὰς τῶν πολιτευμάτων διορθώσεις), indicates how our author could seize on it for his own purposes.

The comma might be omitted after βαπτισμοῖς, and δικαιώματα taken closely with μόνον : "gifts and sacrifices, which (μόνον κτλ. in apposition) are merely (the subject of) outward regulations for the body," ἐπί being taken as cumulative (Lk 3[20])—"besides," etc.   This gets over the difficulty that the levitical offerings had a wider scope than food, drink, and ablutions ; but ἐπί is not natural in this sense here, and ἐπὶ . . . βαπτισμοῖς is not a parenthetical clause.   The insertion of καί before δικαιώματα (by אᶜ B Dᶜ etc. vg hkl Chrys.), = "even" or "in particular" (which is the only natural sense), is pointless. Δικαιώμασιν (Dᶜ K L vg hkl) was an easy conformation to the previous datives, which would logically involve ἐπικειμένοις (as the vg implies : "et justitiis carnis usque ad tempus correctionis impositis"), otherwise ἐπικείμενα would be extremely awkward, after δυνάμεναι, in apposition to δῶρα τε καὶ θυσίαι.

Now for the better sanctuary and especially the better sacri-fice of Christ as our ἀρχιερεύς (vv.[11-28]) !

[11] *But when Christ arrived as the highpriest of the bliss that was to be, he passed through the greater and more perfect tent which no hands had made (no part, that is to say, of the present order),* [12] *not* (οὐδέ = nor yet) *taking any blood of goats and calves but his own blood, and entered once for all into the Holy place.   He secured an eternal redemption.* [13] *For if the blood of goats and bulls and the ashes of a heifer, sprinkled on defiled persons, give them a holiness that bears on bodily purity,* [14] *how much more shall* (καθαριεῖ, logical future) *the blood of Christ, who in the spirit of the eternal offered himself as an unblemished sacrifice to God, cleanse your conscience from dead works to serve a living God."*

This paragraph consists of two long sentences (vv.[11. 12], [13. 14]). The second is an explanation of αἰωνίαν λύτρωσιν εὑράμενος at the close of the first.   In the first, the sphere, the action, and the object of the sacrifice are noted, as a parallel to vv.[6. 7]; but in vv.[13. 14] the sphere is no longer mentioned, the stress falling upon the other two elements.   The writer does not return to the question of the sphere till vv.[21f.]

Χριστὸς δὲ παραγενόμενος (v.[11]).   But Christ came on the scene,[1] and all was changed.   He arrived as ἀρχιερεύς, and the author carries on the thought by an imaginative description of him passing through the upper heavens (no hand-made, mundane fore-court this!) into the innermost Presence.   It is a more detailed account of what he had meant by ἔχοντες ἀρχιερέα μέγαν διεληλυθότα τοὺς οὐρανούς (4[14]). Χειροποιήτου, like χειροποίητα (v.[24]), means "manufactured," not "fictitious" (as applied to idols or idol-temples by the LXX and Philo).   Τουτ' ἔστιν οὐ ταύτης τῆς κτίσεως reads like the gloss of a scribe, but the writer is fond of this phrase τουτ' ἔστιν, and, though it adds nothing to οὐ χειρο-ποιήτου, it may stand. Κτίσις, in this sense of creation or created order, was familiar to him (e.g. Wis 5[17] 19[6]). Μελλόντων, before ἀγαθῶν, was soon altered into γενομένων (by B D* 1611. 1739. 2005 vt syr Orig. Chrys.), either owing to a scribe being misled by παραγενόμενος or owing to a pious feeling that μελλόντων here (though not in 10[1]) was too eschatological.   The ἄγαθα were μέλλοντα in a sense even for Christians, but already they had begun to be realized; e.g. in the λύτρωσις.   This full range was still to be disclosed (2[5] 13[14]), but they were realities of which Christians had here and now some vital experience (see on 6[5]).

Some editors (e.g. Rendall, Nairne) take τῶν γενομένων ἀγαθῶν with what follows, as if the writer meant to say that "Christ appeared as highpriest of the good things which came by the greater and more perfect tabernacle (not made with hands—that is, not of this creation)."   This involves, (a) the interpretation of οὐδέ as = "not by the blood of goats and calves either," the term carrying on παραγενόμενος; and (b) διά in a double sense.   There is no objection to (b), but (a) is weak; the bliss and benefit are mediated not through the sphere but through what Jesus does in the sphere of the eternal σκηνή.   Others (e.g. Westcott, von Soden, Dods, Seeberg) take διὰ τῆς

---

[1] Παραγενόμενος (as Lk 12[51], Mt 3[1] suggest) is more active than the πεφα-νέρωται of v.[26].

σκηνῆς with Χριστός, "Christ by means of the . . . sanctuary." This sense
of διά is better than that of (a) above, and it keeps διά the same for vv.[11]
and [12]. But the context (παραγενόμενος . . . εἰσῆλθεν) points to the local use
of διά in διὰ τῆς . . . σκηνῆς, rather than to the instrumental ; and it is no
objection that the writer immediately uses διά in another sense (δι' αἵματος),
for this is one of his literary methods (cp. διά with gen. and accus. in 2[1, 2]
2[9, 10] 7[18, 19, 23, 24, 25]).

Continuing the description of Christ's sacrifice, he adds (v.[12])
οὐδὲ δι' αἵματος τράγων (for the People) καὶ μόσχων (for himself),
which according to the programme in Lv 16 the priest smeared
on the east side of the ἱλαστήριον. The later Jewish procedure
is described in the Mishna tractate *Joma*, but our author simply
draws upon the LXX text, though (like Aquila and Symmachus)
he uses μόσχων instead of χίμαρων. Διά is graphically used in
διὰ τοῦ ἰδίου αἵματος, as in δι' αἵματος τράγων καὶ μόσχων, but the
idea is the self-sacrifice, the surrender of his own life, in virtue
of which[1] he redeemed his People, the αἷμα or sacrifice being
redemptive as it was his. The single sacrifice had eternal value,
owing to his personality. The term ἐφάπαξ, a stronger form of
ἅπαξ, which is unknown to the LXX, is reserved by our author
for the sacrifice of Jesus, which he now describes as issuing in
a λύτρωσις—an archaic religious term which he never uses elsewhere ; it is practically the same as ἀπολύτρωσις (v.[15]), but he
puts into it a much deeper meaning than the LXX or than Luke
(1[68] 2[38]), the only other NT writer who employs the term.
Though he avoids the verb, his meaning is really that of 1 P 1[18]
(ἐλυτρώθητε τιμίῳ αἵματι ὡς ἀμνοῦ ἀμώμου καὶ ἀσπίλου Χριστοῦ)
or of Ti 2[14] (ὃς ἔδωκεν ἑαυτὸν ὑπὲρ ἡμῶν, ἵνα λυτρώσηται ἡμᾶς ἀπὸ
πάσης ἀνομίας καὶ καθαρίσῃ ἑαυτῷ λαὸν περιούσιον).

In this compressed phrase, **αἰωνίαν λύτρωσιν εὑράμενος,** (a) αἰωνίαν
offers the only instance of αἰώνιος being modified in this epistle. (b) Εὑράμενος, in the sense of Dion. Hal. *Ant.* v. 293 (οὔτε διαλλαγὰς εὕρατο τοῖς
ἀνδράσιν καὶ κάθοδον), and Jos. *Ant.* i. 19. 1 (πάππου δόξαν ἀρετῆς μεγάλης
εὑράμενου), is a participle (for its form,[2] cp. Moulton, i. p. 51), which, though
middle, is not meant to suggest any personal effort like "by himself," much
less "for himself" ; the middle in Hellenistic Greek had come to mean what
the active meant. What he secured, he secured for us (cp. Aelian, *Var. Hist.*
iii. 17, καὶ αὐτοῖς σωτηρίαν εὕραντο). The aorist has not a past sense ; it
either means "to secure" (like εὑράμενοι in 4 Mac 3[13] and ἐπισκεψάμενοι in
2 Mac 11[36]), after a verb of motion (cp. Ac 25[13]), or "securing" (by what
grammarians call "coincident action").

The last three words of v.[12] are now (vv.[13, 14]) explained by
an *a fortiori* argument. Why was Christ's redemption eternal?
What gave it this absolute character and final force? In v.[13]

---

[1] The διά here as in διὰ πνεύματος αἰωνίου suggest the state in which a
certain thing is done, and inferentially the use becomes instrumental, as we
say, "he came *in* power."

[2] The Attic form εὑρόμενος is preferred by D* 226. 436. 920.

τράγων καὶ ταύρων reverses the order in 10⁴, and ταύρων is now
substituted for μόσχων. The former led to ταύρων καὶ τράγων
being read (by the K L P group, Athanasius, Cyril, etc.), but
"the blood of goats and bulls" was a biblical generalization
(Ps 50¹³, Is 1¹¹), chosen here as a literary variation, perhaps for
the sake of the alliteration, though some editors see in ταύρων a
subtle, deliberate antithesis to the feminine δάμαλις. According
to the directions of Nu 19⁹ᶠ· a red cow was slaughtered and then
burned; the ashes (ἡ σπόδος τῆς δαμάλεως) were mixed with fresh
water and sprinkled upon any worshipper who had touched a
dead body and thus incurred ceremonial impurity, contact with
the dead being regarded as a disqualification for intercourse with
men or God (see above on 6¹). This mixture was called ὕδωρ
ῥαντισμοῦ. The rite supplies the metaphors of the argument in
vv.¹⁴· ¹⁵; it was one of the ablutions (v.¹⁰) which restored the
contaminated person (τοὺς κεκοινωμένους) to the worshipping
community of the Lord. The cow is described as ἄμωμον, the
purified person as καθαρός; but our author goes ouside the LXX
for κεκοινωμένους, and even ῥαντίζειν is rare in the LXX. "The
red colour of the cow and the scarlet cloth burnt on the pyre
with the aromatic woods, suggest the colour of blood; the aromatic woods are also probably connected with primitive ideas of
the cathartic value of odours such as they produce" (R. A. S.
Macalister in *ERE.* xi. 36a). The lustration had no connexion
whatever with atonement-day, and it was only in later rabbinic
tradition that it was associated with the functions of the highpriest. According to *Pesikta* 40a, a pagan inquirer once pointed
out to Rabbi Jochanan ben Zakkai the superstitious character of
such rites. His disciples considered his reply unsatisfactory,
and afterwards pressed him to explain to them the meaning of
the ashes and the sprinkling, but all he could say was that it had
been appointed by the Holy One, and that men must not
inquire into His reasons (cp. Bacher's *Agada d. Pal. Amoräer*,
i. 556; *Agada der Tannaiten²*, i. 37, 38). Our author does not go
into details, like the author of *Ep. Barnabas* (8), who allegorizes
the ritual freely in the light of the Jewish tradition; he merely
points out that, according to the bible, the rite, like the similar
rite of blood on atonement-day, restored the worshipper to outward communion with God. Ἁγιάζει means this and no more.

The removal of the religious tabu upon persons contaminated by contact
with the dead was familiar to non-Jews. The writer goes back to the OT
for his illustration, but it would be quite intelligible to his Gentile Christian
readers (cp. Marett's *The Evolution of Religion*, pp. 115 f.; *ERE.* iv. 434,
x. 456, 483, 485, 501), in a world where physical contact with the dead was
a μίασμα. Philo's exposition (*de spec. legibus*, i. περὶ θυόντων, 1 f.) of the rite
is that the primary concern is for the purity of the soul; the attention
needed for securing that the victim is ἄμωμον, or, as he says, παντελῶς

μούμων ἀμέτοχον, is a figurative expression for moral sensitiveness on the part of the worshipper; it is a regulation really intended for rational beings. Οὐ τῶν θυομένων φροντίς ἐστιν . . . ἀλλὰ τῶν θυόντων, ἵνα περὶ μηδὲν πάθος κηραίνωσι. The bodily cleansing is only secondary, and even this he ingeniously allegorizes into a demand for self-knowledge, since the water and ashes should remind us how worthless our natures are, and knowledge of this kind is a wholesome purge for conceit! Thus, according to Philo, the rite did purge soul as well as body: ἀναγκαῖον τοὺς μέλλοντας φοιτᾶν εἰς τὸ ἱερὸν ἐπὶ μετουσίᾳ θυσίας τό τε σῶμα φαιδρύνεσθαι καὶ τὴν ψυχὴν πρὸ τοῦ σώματος. Our author does not share this favourable view (cp. Seeberg's *Der Tod Christi*, pp. 53 f.; O. Schmitz's *Die Opferanschauung des späteren Judentums*, pp. 281 f.). He would not have denied that the levitical cultus aimed at spiritual good; what he did deny was that it attained its end. Till a perfect sacrifice was offered, such an end was unattainable. The levitical cultus "provided a ritual cleansing for the community, a cleansing which, for devout minds that could penetrate beneath the letter to the spirit, must have often meant a sense of restoration to God's community. But at best the machinery was cumbrous : at best the pathway into God's presence was dimly lighted" (H. A. A. Kennedy, *The Theology of the Epistles*, p. 213).

Our author does not explain how the blood of goats and bulls could free the worshiper from ceremonial impurity; the cathartic efficacy of blood is assumed. From the comparative study of religion we know now that this belief was due to the notion that "the animal that has been consecrated by contact with the altar becomes charged with a divine potency, and its sacred blood, poured over the impure man, absorbs and disperses his impurity" (Marett, *The Evolution of Religion*, p. 121). But in Πρὸς Ἑβραίους, (*a*) though the blood of goats and bulls is applied to the people as well as to the altar, and is regarded as atoning (see below), the writer offers no rationale of sacrifice. Χωρὶς αἱματεκχυσίας οὐ γίνεται ἄφεσις. He does not argue, he takes for granted, that access to God involves sacrifice, *i.e.* blood shed. (*b*) He uses the rite of Nu 19 to suggest the cathartic process, the point of this lustration being the use of "water made holy by being mingled with the ashes of the heifer that had been burnt." "The final point is reached," no doubt (Marett, *op. cit.* 123), "when it is realized that the blood of bulls and goats cannot wash away sin, that nothing external can defile the heart or soul, but only evil thoughts and evil will." Yet our writer insists that even this inward defilement requires a sacrifice, the sacrifice of Christ's blood. This is now (v.[14]) urged in the phrase ἑαυτὸν προσήνεγκεν, where we at last see what was intended by προσφέρειν τι in 8³. We are not to think of the risen or ascended Christ presenting himself to God, but of his giving himself up to die as a sacrifice. The blood of Christ means his life given up for the sake of men. He did die, but it was a voluntary death—not the slaughter of an unconscious, reluctant victim; and he who died lives. More than that, he lives with the power of that death or sacrifice. This profound thought is further developed by (a) the term ἄμωμον, which is in apposition to ἑαυτόν; and (b) by διὰ πνεύματος αἰωνίου, which goes with προσή-νεγκεν. (a) Paul calls Christians, or calls them to be, ἄμωμοι; but our writer, like the author of 1 P (1¹⁹), calls Christ ἄμωμος as a victim. It is a poetic synonym for ἀμώμητος, taken over as the technical term (LXX) for the unblemished (מוּם) animals which alone could be employed in sacrifice; here it denotes the stainless personality, the sinless nature which rendered the self-sacrifice of Jesus eternally valid. Then (b) the pregnant phrase διὰ πνεύματος αἰωνίου, which qualifies ἑαυτὸν προσήνεγκεν, means that this sacrifice was offered in the realm or order of the inward spirit, not of the outward and material; it was no δικαίωμα σαρκός, but carried out διὰ πνεύματος, i.e. in, or in virtue of, his spiritual nature. What the author had called ζωὴ ἀκατάλυτος (7¹⁶) he now calls πνεῦμα αἰώνιον. The sacrificial blood had a mystical efficacy; it resulted in an eternal λύτρωσις because it operated in an eternal order of spirit, the sacrifice of Jesus purifying the inner personality (τὴν συνείδησιν) because it was the action of a personality, and of a sinless personality which belonged by nature to the order of spirit or eternity. Christ was both priest and victim; as Son of God he was eternal and spiritual, unlike mortal highpriests (7¹⁶), and, on the other side, unlike a mortal victim. The implication (which underlies all the epistle) is that even in his earthly life Jesus possessed eternal life. Hence what took place in time upon the cross, the writer means, took place really in the eternal, absolute order. Christ sacrificed himself ἐφάπαξ, and the single sacrifice needed no repetition, since it possessed absolute, eternal value as the action of One who belonged to the eternal order. He died—he had to die—but only once (9¹⁵–10¹⁸), for his sacrifice, by its eternal significance, accomplished at a stroke what no amount of animal sacrifices could have secured, viz. the forgiveness of sins. It is as trivial to exhaust the meaning of πνεῦμα αἰώνιον in a contrast with the animal sacrifices of the levitical cultus as it is irrele-vant to drag in the dogma of the trinity. Αἰωνίου closely describes πνεύματος (hence it has no article). What is in the writer's mind is the truth that what Jesus did by dying can never be exhausted or transcended. His sacrifice, like his διαθήκη, like the λύτρωσις or σωτηρία which he secures, is αἰώνιος or lasting, because it is at the heart of things. It was because Jesus was what he was by nature that his sacrifice had such final value; its atoning significance lay in his vital connexion with the realm of absolute realities; it embodied all that his divine personality meant for men in relation to God. In short, his self-sacrifice "was something beyond which nothing could be, or could be conceived to be, as a response to God's mind and requirement

in relation to sin ... an intelligent and loving response to the
holy and gracious will of God, and to the terrible situation of
man" (Denney, *The Death of Christ*, p. 228).

A later parallel from rabbinic religion occurs in the Midrash Tehillim on
Ps 31: "formerly you were redeemed with flesh and blood, which to-day is
and to-morrow is buried; wherefore your redemption was temporal (גאולת שעה).
But now I will redeem you by myself, who live and remain for ever; wherefore your redemption will be eternal redemption (גאולת עולם, cp. Is 45¹⁷)."

One or two minor textual items may be noted in v.¹⁴.

πνεύματος] J. J. Reiske's conjecture ἀγνεύματος (purity) is singularly
prosaic. Αἰωνίου (א* A B Dᶜ K L syrᵛᵍ ʰᵏˡ arm Ath) is altered into the conventional ἁγίου by אᶜ D* P 35. 88. 206. 326. 547, etc. lat boh Chrys. Cyril.
Liturgical usage altered ὑμῶν into ἡμῶν (A D* P 5. 38. 218. 241. 256. 263.
378. 506. 1319. 1831. 1836*. 1912. 2004. 2127 vt syrᵛᵍ boh Cyr.), and, to
ζῶντι, καὶ ἀληθινῷ (a gloss from 1 Th 1⁹) is added in A P 104 boh Chrys. etc.

In the closing words of v.¹⁴ καθαριεῖ is a form which is rare
(Mt 3¹², Ja 4⁸?) in the NT, so rare that καθαρίσει is read here
by 206. 221. 1831 Did. Ath. It is a Hellenistic verb, used in
the inscriptions (with ἀπό) exactly in the ceremonial sense underlying the metaphor of this passage (Deissmann, *Bible Studies*,
216 f.). The cleansing of the conscience (cp. v.⁹) is ἀπὸ νεκρῶν
ἔργων, from far more serious flaws and stains than ceremonial
pollution by contact with a corpse (see above, and in 6¹). As
Dods puts it, "a pause might be made before ἔργων, from dead—
(not bodies but) works." The object is εἰς τὸ λατρεύειν θεῷ ζῶντι.
The writer uses the sacerdotal term (8⁵) here as in 10² and 12²⁸,
probably like Paul in a general sense; if he thought of Christians as priests, *i.e.* as possessing the right of access to God, he
never says so. Religion for him is access to God, and ritual
metaphors are freely used to express the thought. When others
would say "fellowship," he says "worship." It is fundamental
for him that forgiveness is essential to such fellowship, and forgiveness is what is meant by "purifying the conscience." As
absolute forgiveness was the boon of the new διαθήκη (8¹²),
our author now proceeds (vv.¹⁵ᶠ·) to show how Christ's sacrifice
was necessary and efficacious under that διαθήκη. A sacrifice,
involving death, is essential to any διαθήκη: this principle,
which applies to the new διαθήκη (v.¹⁵), is illustrated first
generally (vv.¹⁶· ¹⁷) and then specifically, with reference to the
former διαθήκη (vv.¹⁸⁻²²).

¹⁵ *He mediates a new covenant for this reason, that those who have been
called may obtain the eternal inheritances they have been promised, now that a
death has occurred which redeems them from the transgressions involved in
the first covenant.* ¹⁶ *Thus in the case of a will, the death of the testator must
be announced.* ¹⁷ *A will only holds in cases of death, it is never valid so long
as the testator is alive.* ¹⁸ *Hence even the first (ἡ πρώτη, sc. διαθήκη as in 9¹)
covenant of God's will was not inaugurated apart from blood;* ¹⁹ *for after
Moses had announced every command in the Law to all the people, he took the*

blood of calves and goats, together with water, scarlet wool and hyssop, sprinkl-
ing the book and all the people, and saying, 20 *" This is the blood of that*
covenant which is God's command for you." 21 *He even* (καὶ . . . δέ, only
here in Heb.) *sprinkled with blood the tent and all the utensils of worship in*
the same way. 22 *In fact, one might almost say that by Law everything is*
cleansed with blood. No blood shed no remission of sins !

The writer thus weaves together the idea of the new διαθήκη
(9^15 echoes 8^6) and the idea of sacrifice which he has just been
developing. In v.^15 διὰ τοῦτο carries a forward reference (" now
this is why Christ mediates a new διαθήκη, ὅπως κτλ."), as, *e.g.*,
in Xen. *Cyrop.* ii. 1. 21, οἱ σύμμαχοι οὐδὲ δι' ἓν ἄλλο τρέφονται ἢ
ὅπως μαχοῦνται ὑπὲρ τῶν τρεφόντων. As the climax of the promises in the new διαθήκη is pardon (8^12), so here its purpose is
described as ἀπολύτρωσις, which obviously is equivalent to full
forgiveness (Eph 1^7 τὴν ἀπολύτρωσιν διὰ τοῦ αἵματος αὐτοῦ, τὴν
ἄφεσιν τῶν παραπτωμάτων). Ἀπολύτρωσιν τῶν . . . παραβάσεων is
like καθαρισμὸν τῶν ἁμαρτιῶν in 1^3. But pardon is only the
means to fellowship, and the full scope of what has been promised is still to be realized. Yet it is now certain ; the " bliss to
be " is an eternal κληρονομία, assured by Christ. Note that the
ἐπί in ἐπὶ τῇ πρώτῃ διαθήκῃ is not exactly temporal = " under,"
i.e. during the period of (cp. ἐπὶ συντελείᾳ τῶν αἰώνων in v.^26), but
causal. The transgressions, which had arisen " in connexion
with " the first διαθήκη, like unbelief and disobedience, are
conceived as having taken their place among men ; they are the
standing temptations of life towards God. The writer does not
say, with Paul, that sin became guilt in view of the law, but
this is near to his meaning ; with the first διαθήκη sins started,
the sins that haunt the People. They are removed, for the
penitent, by the atoning death of Jesus, so that the People are
now unencumbered. There is a similar thought in Ac 13^38. 39,
where Paul tells some Jews that through Jesus Christ ὑμῖν ἄφεσις
ἁμαρτιῶν καταγγέλλεται, καὶ ἀπὸ πάντων ὧν οὐκ ἠδυνήθητε ἐν νόμῳ
Μωϋσέως δικαιωθῆναι, ἐν τούτῳ πᾶς ὁ πιστεύων δικαιοῦται. For the
sake of emphasis, τὴν ἐπαγγελίαν is thrown forward, away from
κληρονομίας, like θάνατον in the next verse.

Ἀπολύτρωσις, which in 11^35 is used in its non-technical sense of "release"
from death (at the cost of some unworthy compliance), is used here in its LXX
religious sense of a redemption which costs much, which can only be had at
the cost of sacrifice. The primitive idea of "ransom" had already begun to
fade out of it (cp. Dn 4^32 ; Philo, *quod omnis probus*, 17), leaving "liberation"
at some cost as the predominant idea (so in Clem. Alex. *Strom.* vii. 56).
Here it is a synonym for λύτρωσις (v.^12), or as Theophylact put it, for
deliverance. But its reference is not eschatological ; the retrospective reference is uppermost.

For the first and only time he employs οἱ κεκλημένοι to
describe those whom he had already hailed as κλήσεως ἐπουρανίου

μέτοχοι (3¹). To be "called" was indispensable to receiving
God's boon (11⁸), so that κεκλημένοι here is an appropriate term
for those who are no longer hampered by any obstacles of an
inadequate pardon. The κεκλημένοι are the faithful People;
"the objects of redemption are united in one category, for the
One and Only Sacrifice is not of the sphere of time" (Wickham).
It is not an aoristic perfect (= κλήθεντες), as if the κεκλημένοι
were simply those under the old διαθήκη, though these are included, for the sacrificial death of Jesus has a retrospective value;
it clears off the accumulated offences of the past. The writer
does not work out this, any more than Paul does in Ro 3²⁵ᶠ·; but
it may be implied in 11⁴⁰ 12²³ (see below), where the "perfecting"
of the older believers is connected with the atonement. However, the special point here of θανάτου . . . παραβάσεων is that the
death which inaugurates the new διαθήκη deals effectively with the
hindrances left by the former διαθήκη. Not that this is its exclusive function. That the death inaugurates an order of grace
in which forgiveness is still required and bestowed, is taken for
granted (e.g. 4¹⁶); but the κληρονομία, which from the beginning
has been held out to the People of God, has only become attainable since the sacrifice of Jesus, and therefore (a) his death
avails even for those who in the past hoped for it, yet could not
obtain it, and also (b) deals with the παράβασεις set up by the
older διαθήκη among men.

But how was a death necessary to a διαθήκη? The answer
is given in v.¹⁶ᶠ· through a characteristic play on the term. In
ὅπου γὰρ (sc. ἐστι) διαθήκη κτλ. he uses διαθήκη as equivalent to
"will" or testamentary disposition, playing effectively upon the
double sense of the term, as Paul had already done in Gal 3¹⁵ᶠ·.
The point of his illustration (vv.¹⁶· ¹⁷) depends upon this; βεβαία
and ἰσχύει are purposely used in a juristic sense, applicable to
wills as well as to laws, and ὁ διαθέμενος is the technical term for
"testator." The illustration has its defects, but only when it is
pressed beyond what the writer means to imply. A will does
not come into force during the lifetime of the testator, and yet
Jesus was living! True, but he had died, and died inaugurating
a διαθήκη in words which the writer has in mind (v.²⁰); indeed,
according to one tradition he had spoken of himself figuratively
as assigning rights to his disciples (κἀγὼ διατίθεμαι ὑμῖν, Lk 22²⁹).
The slight incongruity in this illustration is not more than that
involved in making Jesus both priest and victim. It is a curious
equivoque, this double use of διαθήκη, the common idea of
both meanings being that benefits are "disponed," and that the
διαθήκη only takes effect after a death. The continuity of argument is less obvious in English, where no single word conveys
the different nuances which διαθήκη bore for Greek readers.

Hence in v.[18] some periphrasis like "the first covenant of God's will" is desirable.

That διαθήκη in vv.[16, 17] is equivalent to "testamentary disposition," is essential to the argument. No natural interpretation of vv.[15-20] is possible, when διαθήκη is understood rigidly either as "covenant" or as "will." The classical juristic sense is richly illustrated in the papyri and contemporary Hellenistic Greek, while the "covenant" meaning prevails throughout the LXX; but Philo had already used it in both senses, and here the juristic sense of κληρονομία (v.[15]) paved the way for the juristic sense which v.[17] demands. The linguistic materials are collected, with a variety of interpretations, by Norton in *A Lexicographical and Historical Study of* Διαθήκη (Chicago, 1908), Behm (*Der Begriff* Διαθήκη *im Neuen Testament*, Naumburg, 1912), Lohmeyer (Διαθήκη: *ein Beitrag zür Erklärung des Neutestamentlichen Begriffs*, Leipzig, 1913), and G. Vos in *Princeton Theological Review* (1915, pp. 587 f.; 1916, pp. 1–61).

In v.[16] φέρεσθαι is "announced," almost in the sense of "proved" (as often in Greek); in v.[17] μή ποτε (cp. on οὔπω in 2[8]) is not equivalent to μήπω (nondum, vg) but simply means "never" (non unquam), as, *e.g.*, in Eurip. *Hipp.* 823, ὥστε μήποτε ἐκπνεῦσαι πάλιν, μή here following the causal particle ἐπεί, like ὅτι in Jn 3[18]; it had begun to displace οὐ in later Greek. Moulton quotes *BGU.* 530 (i A.D.), μέμφεταί σε ἐπ(ε)ὶ μὴ ἀντέγραψας αὐτῇ, and Radermacher (171) suggests that the change was sometimes due to a desire of avoiding the hiatus. Ἰσχύει has the same force as in Gal 5[6], cp. *Tebt. P.* 286[7] (ii A.D.) νομὴ ἄδικος [οὐ]δὲν εἰσχύει. Some needless difficulties have been felt with regard to the construction of the whole sentence. Thus (*a*) ἐπεὶ . . . διαθέμενος might be a question, it is urged: "For is it ever valid so long as the testator is alive?" In Jn 7[26] μήποτε is so used interrogatively, but there it opens the sentence. This construction goes back to the Greek fathers Oecumenius and Theophylact; possibly it was due to the feeling that μήποτε could not be used in a statement like this. (*b*) Isidore of Pelusium (*Ep.* iv. 113) declares that πότε is a corruption of τότε (Π from T, a stroke being added by accident), and that he found τότε "ἐν παλαιοῖς ἀντιγράφοις." Two old MSS (א* D*) do happen to preserve this reading, which is in reality a corruption of πότε.

Why, it may be asked, finally, does not the writer refer outright to the new διαθήκη as inaugurated at the last supper? The reason is plain. Here as throughout the epistle he ignores the passover or eucharist. As a non-sacerdotal feast, the passover would not have suited his argument. Every Israelite was his own priest then, as Philo remarks (*De Decalogo*, 30, πάσχα . . . ἐν ᾗ θύουσι πανδημεὶ αὐτῶν ἕκαστος τοὺς ἱερεῖς αὐτῶν οὐκ ἀναμένοντες, ἱερωσύνην τοῦ νόμου χαρισαμένου τῷ ἔθνει παντὶ κατὰ μίαν ἡμέραν κτλ.). Hence the absence of a passover ritual from the entire argument of the epistle, and also perhaps his failure to employ it here, where it would have been extremely apt.

Reverting now to the other and biblical sense of διαθήκη, the writer (vv.¹⁸ᶠ·) recalls how the διαθήκη at Sinai was inaugurated with blood. Ὅθεν—since διαθήκη and θάνατος are correlative—οὐδὲ ἡ πρώτη (sc. διαθήκη) χωρὶς αἵματος ἐνκεκαίνισται (the verb here and in 10²⁰ being used in its ordinary LXX sense, e.g., 1 K 11¹⁴ ἐγκαινίσωμεν ἐκεῖ τὴν βασιλείαν, 1 Mac 4³⁶ ἀναβῶμεν καθαρίσαι τὰ ἅγια καὶ ἐνκαινίσαι). This fresh illustration of death or blood being required in order to inaugurate a διαθήκη, is taken from the story in Ex 24³ᶠ·, but he treats it with characteristic freedom. Five points may be noted. (i) He inserts¹ τὸ αἷμα . . . τῶν τράγων, a slip which was conscientiously corrected by a number of MSS which omitted καὶ τῶν τράγων (א° K L Ψ 5. 181. 203. 242. 487. 489. 506. 623. 794. 917. 1311. 1319. 1739. 1827. 1836. 1845. 1898. 2143) as well as by syr Origen and Chrysostom. Moses merely had μοσχάρια slaughtered ; our author adds goats, perhaps because the full phrase had become common for OT sacrifices (see on v.¹³). (ii) He inserts μετὰ ὕδατος καὶ ἐρίου κοκκίνου καὶ ὑσσώπου, as these were associated in his mind with the general ritual of sprinkling ; water, hyssop, and scarlet thread (κόκκινον), for example, he remembered from the description of another part of the ritual in Nu 19. The water was used to dilute the blood ; and stems of a small wall plant called "hyssop" were tied with scarlet wool (κεκλωσμένον κόκκινον) to form a sprinkler in the rite of cleansing a leper (Lv 14⁶ᶠ·), or for sprinkling blood (Ex 12²²). But of this wisp or bunch there is not a word in Ex 24³ᶠ·. (iii) Nor is it said in the OT that Moses sprinkled² αὐτὸ τὸ βιβλίον. He simply splashed half of the blood πρὸς τὸ θυσιαστήριον, καὶ λαβὼν τὸ βιβλίον (i.e. the scroll containing the primitive code) τῆς διαθήκης, read it aloud to the people, who promised obedience ; whereupon λαβὼν δὲ Μωυσῆς τὸ αἷμα κατεσκέδασεν τοῦ λαοῦ καὶ εἶπεν κτλ. An ingenious but impracticable attempt to correct this error is to take αὐτό τε τὸ βιβλίον with λαβών, but the τε goes with the next καὶ πάντα τὸν λαόν. The βιβλίον may have been included, since as a human product, for all its divine contents, it was considered to require cleansing ; in which case the mention of it would lead up to v.²¹, and αὐτό τε τὸ βιβλίον might be rendered "the book itself." This intensive use of αὐτός occurs just below in αὐτὰ τὰ ἐπουράνια. But αὐτός may be, according to the usage of Hellenistic Greek,

¹ In πάσης ἐντολῆς κατὰ τὸν (om. א* K P) νόμον ("lecto omni mandato legis," vg) the κατά means "throughout" rather than "by."

² For κατεσκέδασεν he substitutes ἐρράντισεν, from ῥαντίζω, which is comparatively rare in the LXX (Lv 6²⁷, 2 K 9³³, Ps 51⁷, Aquila and Symm. in Is 63³, Aquila and Theodotion in Is 52¹⁵).

unemphatic, as, *e.g.*, in 11¹¹ καὶ αὐτὴ Σάρρα, Jn 2²⁴ αὐτὸς δὲ ὁ
Ἰησοῦς. (iv) In quoting the LXX ἰδοὺ τὸ αἷμα τῆς διαθήκης ἧς
διέθετο Κύριος πρὸς ὑμᾶς (= ὑμῖν), he changes ἰδού into τοῦτο
(possibly a reminiscence of the synoptic tradition in Mk 14²²),
διέθετο into ἐνετείλατο (after ἐντολῆς in v.¹⁹; but the phrase
occurs elsewhere, though with the dative, *e.g.* Jos 23¹⁶), and
κύριος πρὸς ὑμᾶς into πρὸς ἡμᾶς ὁ θεός. This is a minor alteration. It is more significant that, (v) following a later Jewish
tradition, which reappears in Josephus (*Ant*. iii. 8. 6 [Moses
cleansed Aaron and his sons] τήν τε σκηνὴν καὶ τὰ περὶ αὐτὴν
σκεύη ἐλαίῳ τε προθυμιωμένῳ καθὼς εἶπον, καὶ τῷ αἵματι τῶν ταύρων
καὶ κριῶν σφαγέντων κτλ.), he makes Moses use blood to sprinkle
the σκηνή and all τὰ σκεύη τῆς λειτουργίας (a phrase from 1 Ch 9²⁸).
The account of Ex 40⁹·¹⁰ mentions oil only; Josephus adds
blood, because the tradition he followed fused the oil-dedication
of the σκηνή in Ex 40⁹·¹⁰ with the (oil) sprinkling at the consecration of the priests (Lv 8¹⁰ᶠ·), which was followed by a blood-
sprinkling of the altar alone. Philo had previously combined
the oil-dedication of the σκηνή with the consecration of the
priests (*vit. Mos.* iii. 17); but he, too, is careful to confine any
blood-sprinkling to the altar. Our author, with his predilection
for blood as a cathartic, omits the oil altogether, and extends
the blood to everything.

This second illustration (vv.¹⁸ᶠ·) is not quite parallel to the
first; the death in the one case is of a human being in the course
of nature, in the other case of animals slaughtered. But **αἷμα**
and **θάνατος** were correlative terms for the writer. The vital
necessity of αἷμα in this connexion is reiterated in the summary
of v.²². **Σχεδόν**, he begins—for there were exceptions to the rule
that atonement for sins needed an animal sacrifice (*e.g.* Lv 5¹¹⁻¹³,
where a poverty-stricken offender could get remission by presenting a handful of flour, and Nu 31²²ᶠ·, where certain articles, spoils
of war, are purified by fire or water). But the general rule was
that **πάντα**, *i.e.* everything connected with the ritual and every
worshipper, priest, or layman, had to be ceremonially purified by
means of blood (**καθαρίζεται** as the result of **ἐρράντισεν**). The
Greek readers of the epistle would be familiar with the similar
rite of αἱμάσσειν τοὺς βωμούς (Theokr. *Epigr.* i. 5, etc.). Finally,
he sums up the position under the first διαθήκη by coining a term
αἱματεκχυσία (from ἔκχυσις αἵματος, 1 K 18²⁸ etc.) for the shedding
of an animal victim's blood in sacrifice; **χωρὶς αἱματεκχυσίας οὐ
γίνεται ἄφεσις,** *i.e.* even the limited pardon, in the shape of
"cleansing," which was possible under the old order. Ἄφεσις
here as in Mk 3²⁹ has no genitive following, but the sense is
indubitable, in view of 10¹⁸ ὅπου δὲ ἄφεσις τούτων (*i.e.* of sins).
The latter passage voices a feeling which seems to contradict the

possibility of any forgiveness prior to the sacrifice of Christ (cp. 9¹⁵ 10⁴ᶠ·), but the writer knew from his bible that there had been an ἄφεσις under the old régime as the result of animal sacrifice ; καὶ ἐξιλάσεται περὶ (or περὶ τῆς ἁμαρτίας) αὐτοῦ ὁ ἱερεύς . . . καὶ ἀφεθήσεται αὐτῷ was the formula (cp. Lv 5¹⁰. ¹⁶. ¹⁸ etc.). The underlying principle of the argument is practically (cp. Introd., p. xlii) that laid down in the Jewish tract *Joma* v. 1 ("there is no expiation except by blood"), which quotes Lv 17¹¹, a text known to the writer of Hebrews in this form : ἡ γὰρ ψυχὴ πάσης σαρκὸς αἷμα αὐτοῦ ἐστίν, καὶ ἐγὼ δέδωκα αὐτὸ ὑμῖν ἐπὶ τοῦ θυσιαστηρίου ἐξιλάσκεσθαι περὶ τῶν ψυχῶν ὑμῶν· τὸ γὰρ αἷμα αὐτοῦ ἀντὶ τῆς ψυχῆς ἐξιλάσεται. Blood as food is prohibited, since blood contains the vital principle ; as there is a mysterious potency in it, which is to be reserved for rites of purification and expiation, by virtue of the life in it, this fluid is efficacious as an atonement. The Greek version would readily suggest to a reader like our author that the piacular efficacy of αἷμα was valid universally, and that the αἷμα or sacrificial death of Christ was required in order that human sin might be removed. Why such a sacrifice, why sacrifice at all, was essential, he did not ask. It was commanded by God in the bible ; that was sufficient for him. The vital point for him was that, under this category of sacrifice, the αἷμα of Christ superseded all previous arrangements for securing pardon.

After the swift aside of v.²², the writer now pictures the appearance of Christ in the perfect sanctuary of heaven with the perfect sacrifice (vv.²⁵ᶠ·) which, being perfect or absolute, needs no repetition.

²³ *Now, while the copies of the heavenly things had* (ἀνάγκη, sc. ἦν or ἐστίν) *to be cleansed with sacrifices like these, the heavenly things themselves required nobler sacrifices.* ²⁴ *For Christ has not entered a holy place which human hands have made* (*a mere type of the reality !*) ; *he has entered heaven itself, now to appear in the presence of God on our behalf.* ²⁵ *Nor was it* (sc. εἰσῆλθεν) *to offer himself repeatedly, like the highpriest entering the holy place every year with blood that was not his own :* ²⁶ *for in that case he would have had to suffer repeatedly ever since the world was founded. Nay, once for all, at the end of the world, he has appeared with his self-sacrifice to abolish sin.* ²⁷ *And just as it is appointed for men to die once and after that to be judged,* ²⁸ *so Christ, after being once sacrificed to bear the sins of many, will appear again, not to deal with sin, but for the saving of those who look out for him.*

The higher σκηνή requires a nobler kind of sacrifice than its material copy on earth (v.²³).[1] This would be intelligible enough ;

---

[1] For ἀνάγκη . . . καθαρίζεσθαι an early variant was ἀνάγκῃ . . . καθαρίζεται (D* 424** Origen), which Blass adopts. But our author prefers the nominative (v.¹⁶) to the dative, and καθαρίζεται is no more than a conformation to the καθαρίζεται of v.²². The τε, which some cursives (33. 1245. 2005) substitute for δέ between αὐτά and τὰ ἐπουράνια, is due to alliteration.

but when the writer pushes the analogy so far as to suggest that the sacrifice of Christ had, among other effects, to purify heaven itself, the idea becomes almost fantastic.   The nearest parallel to this notion occurs in Col 1²⁰ ; but the idea here is really unique, as though the constant work of forgiving sinners in the upper σκηνή rendered even that in some sense defiled.   The slight touch of disparagement in τούτοις (= τοῖς ἀλόγοις, Theodoret) may be conveyed by "like these" or "such," and θυσίαις is the plural of category (like νεκροῖς in v.¹⁷).   After this passing lapse into the prosaic, the writer quickly recovers himself in a passage of high insight (vv.²⁴ᶠ·) upon the nobler sacrifice of Jesus.   Indeed, even as he compares it with the levitical sacrifices, its incomparable power becomes more and more evident.   In v.²⁴ (= vv.¹¹· ¹²) by ἀντίτυπα τῶν ἀληθινῶν he means a counterpart (ἀντίτυπον in reverse sense in 1 P 3²¹) of reality (cp. 8²), ἀντίτυπα being a synonym here for ὑποδείγματα, literally = "answering to the τύπος" which was shown to Moses (cp. 2 Clem. 14³ οὐδεὶς οὖν τὸ ἀντίτυπον φθείρας τὸ αὐθεντικὸν μεταλήψεται).   Christ has entered the heavenly sphere νῦν (emphatic, "now at last " = 1²) ἐμφανισθῆναι κτλ.   In ἐμφανισθῆναι τῷ προσώπῳ τοῦ θεοῦ (cp. Ps 42³ ὀφθήσομαι τῷ προσώπῳ τοῦ θεοῦ) we have ἐμφανίζειν used in its Johannine sense (14²¹· ²²), though passively as in Wis 1² (ἐμφανίζεται τοῖς μὴ πιστεύουσιν αὐτῷ).   But the appearance is before God on behalf of men, and the meaning is brought out in 7²⁶ 10¹²ᶠ·.   Christ's sacrifice, it is held, provides men with a close and continuous access to God such as no cultus could effect ; it is of absolute value, and therefore need not be repeated (vv.²⁵· ²⁶), as the levitical sacrifices had to be.   Οὐδ' ἵνα πολλάκις προσφέρῃ ἑαυτόν] What is meant precisely by προσφέρειν ἑαυτόν here (as in v.¹⁴) is shown by παθεῖν in v.²⁶.   "There is no difference between entering in and offering.   The act of entering in and offering is one highpriestly act" (A. B. Davidson), and προσφέρειν ἑαυτόν is inseparably connected with the suffering of death upon the cross.   The contrast between his self-sacrifice and the highpriest entering with αἵματι ἀλλοτρίῳ (as opposed to ἰδίῳ, v.¹²) is thrown in, as a reminiscence of vv.⁷ᶠ·, but the writer does not dwell on this ; it is the ἅπαξ (cp. v.¹² and 1 P 3¹⁸ Χριστὸς ἅπαξ περὶ ἁμαρτιῶν ἀπέθανεν) which engrosses his mind in v.²⁶, ἐπεὶ (" alioquin," vg) ἔδει (the ἄν being omitted as, e.g., in 1 Co 5¹⁰ ἐπεὶ ὠφείλετε . . . ἐξελθεῖν) κτλ.   According to his outlook, there would be no time to repeat Christ's incarnation and sacrifice before the end of the world, for that was imminent ; hence he uses the past, not the future, for his *reductio ad absurdum* argument.   If Christ's sacrifice had not been of absolute, final value, *i.e.* if it had merely availed for a brief time, as a temporary provision, it would have had to be done over and over again in previous ages, since from the first sinful man has needed sacrifice ; whereas the only time he was seen on earth was once, late in the evening of the world. It is implied that Christ as the Son of God was eternal and pre-existent; also that when his sacrifice did take place, it covered sins of the past (see v.[15]), the single sacrifice of Christ in our day availing for all sin, past as well as present and future. Had it not been so, God could not have left it till so late in the world's history ; it would have had to be done over and over again to meet the needs of men from the outset of history. Νυνὶ δέ (logical, as in 8[6], not temporal) ἐπὶ συντελείᾳ (for which Blass arbitrarily reads τέλει) τῶν αἰώνων (= ἐπ' ἐσχάτου τῶν ἡμερῶν τούτων, 1[2]) κτλ. Συντέλεια is employed in its ordinary Hellenistic sense of "conclusion" (e.g. *Test. Benj.* xi. 3, ἕως συντελείας τοῦ αἰῶνος : *Test. Levi* x. 2, ἐπὶ τῇ συντελείᾳ τῶν αἰώνων) ; in Matthew's gospel, where alone in the NT it occurs, the genitive is τοῦ αἰῶνος. Πεφανέρωται, as in the primitive hymn or confession of faith (1 Ti 3[16] ἐφανερώθη ἐν σαρκί) ; but the closest parallel is in 1 P 1[20] Χριστοῦ προεγνωσμένου μὲν πρὸ καταβολῆς κόσμου, φανερωθέντος δὲ ἐπ' ἐσχάτου τῶν χρόνων. The object of the incarnation is, as in 2[9], the atonement.

The thought of the first "appearance" of Christ naturally suggests that of the second, and the thought of Jesus dying ἅπαξ also suggests that men have to die ἅπαξ as well. Hence the parenthesis of vv.[27. 28], for 10[1] carries on the argument from 9[26]. It is a parenthesis, yet a parenthesis of central importance for the primitive religious eschatology which formed part of the writer's inheritance, however inconsistent with his deeper views of faith and fellowship. "As surely as men have once to die and then to face the judgment, so Christ, once sacrificed for the sins of men, will reappear to complete the salvation of his own." Ἀπόκειται (cp. Longinus, *de sublim.* 9[7] ἀλλ' ἡμῖν μὲν δυσδαιμονοῦσιν ἀπόκειται λιμὴν κακῶν ὁ θάνατος, and 4 Mac 8[11] οὐδὲν ὑμῖν ἀπειθήσασιν πλὴν τοῦ μετὰ στρεβλῶν ἀποθανεῖν ἀπόκειται) τοῖς ἀνθρώποις ἅπαξ ἀποθανεῖν. The ἅπαξ here is not by way of relief, although the Greeks consoled themselves by reflecting that they had not to die twice ; as they could only live once, they drew from this the conclusion that life must be "all the sweeter, as an experience that never can be repeated" (A. C. Pearson on Sophocles' *Fragments*, n. 67). But our author (see on 2[14]) sees that death is not the last thing to be faced by men ; μετὰ δὲ τοῦτο κρίσις. This was what added seriousness to the prospect of death for early Christians. The Greek mind was exempt from such a dread ; for them death ended the anxieties of life, and if there was one thing of which the Greek was sure, it was that "dead men rise up never."

Aeschylus, for example, makes Apollo declare (*Eumenides*, 647, 648):

> ἀνδρὸς δ᾽ ἐπειδὰν αἷμ᾽ ἀνασπάσῃ κόνις
> ἅπαξ θανόντος, οὔτις ἔστ᾽ ἀνάστασις.

Even in the sense of a return to life, there is no ἀνάστασις (Eurip. *Heracles*, 297; *Alcestis*, 1076; *Supplices*, 775). Κρίσις in En 1[7f.] (καὶ κρίσις ἔσται κατὰ πάντων), as the context shows, is the eschatological catastrophe which spares the elect on earth, just as in En 5[6], which parallels He 9[28], sinners are threatened thus: πᾶσιν ὑμῖν τοῖς ἁμαρτωλοῖς οὐχ ὑπάρξει σωτηρία ἀλλὰ ἐπὶ πάντας ὑμᾶς κατάλυσις, κατάρα. In 10[27] below κρίσις means the doom of the rebellious, but that is due to the context; here it is judgment in general, to which all ἄνθρωποι alike are liable (12[23] κριτῇ θεῷ πάντων). Only, some have the happy experience of Christ's return (v.[28]), in the saving power of his sacrifice. There is (as in 1 P 2[24]) an echo of Is 53[12] (καὶ αὐτὸς ἁμαρτίας πολλῶν ἀνήνεγκεν) in εἰς τὸ πολλῶν (cp. above on 2[10]) ἀνενεγκεῖν ἁμαρτίας. Προσενεχθείς may be chosen to parallel men's passive experience of death. At any rate his suffering of death was vicarious suffering; he took upon himself the consequences and responsibilities of our sins. Such is the Christ who ἐκ δευτέρου ὀφθήσεται. In 1 P 5[4] φανεροῦσθαι is used of the second appearance as well as of the first, but our author prefers a variety (see on v.[26]) of expression. The striking phrase χωρὶς ἁμαρτίας rests on the idea that the one atonement had been final (εἰς ἀθέτησιν τῆς ἁμαρτίας), and that Christ was now κεχωρισμένος ἀπὸ τῶν ἁμαρτωλῶν (7[26]). He is not coming back to die, and without death sin could not be dealt with. The homiletic (from 2 Ti 3[15]) addition of διὰ (τῆς, 1611. 2005) πίστεως, either after ἀπεκδεχομένοις (by 38. 68. 218. 256. 263. 330. 436. 440. 462. 823. 1837 arm. etc.) or after σωτηρίαν (by A P 1245. 1898 syr[hkl]), is connected with the mistaken idea that εἰς σωτηρίαν goes with ἀπεκδεχομένοις (cp. Phil 3[20]) instead of with ὀφθήσεται. There is a very different kind of ἐκδοχή (10[27]) for some ἄνθρωποι, even for some who once belonged to the People!

He now resumes the idea of 9[25. 26], expanding it by showing how the personal sacrifice of Jesus was final. This is done by quoting a passage from the 40th psalm which predicted the supersession of animal sacrifices (vv.[5-10]). The latter are inadequate, as is seen from the fact of their annual repetition; and they are annual because they are animal sacrifices.

---

[1] *For as the Law has a mere shadow of the bliss that is to be, instead of representing the reality of that bliss, it never can perfect those who draw near with the same annual sacrifices that are perpetually offered.* [2] *Otherwise, they would have surely ceased to be offered; for the worshippers, once cleansed, would no longer be conscious of sins!* [3] *As it is, they are an annual reminder*

of sins ⁴ *(for the blood of bulls and goats cannot possibly remove sins!).*
⁵ *Hence, on entering the world he says,*

> " *Thou hast no desire for sacrifice or offering ;*
> *it is a body thou hast prepared for me—*
> ⁶ *in holocausts and sin-offerings* (περὶ ἁμαρτίας as 13¹¹) *thou*
> *takest no delight.*
> ⁷ *So* (τότε) *I said, 'Here I come—in the roll of the book this*
> *is written of me—*
> *I come to do thy will, O God.'*"

⁸ *He begins by saying,* " *Thou hast no desire for, thou takest no delight in,*
sacrifices and offerings and holocausts and sin-offerings" *(and those are what*
are offered in terms of the Law) ; ⁹ *he then* (τότε) *adds,* " *Here I come to do*
thy will." *He does away with the first in order to establish the second.*
¹⁰ *And it is by this* "*will*" *that we are consecrated, because Jesus Christ once*
for all has "*offered*" *up his* "*body.*"

This is the author's final verdict on the levitical cultus,
"rapid in utterance, lofty in tone, rising from the didactic style
of the theological doctor to the oracular speech of the Hebrew
prophet, as in that peremptory sentence : 'It is not possible that
the blood of bulls and of goats should take away sins.' The
notable thing in it is, not any new line of argument, though that
element is not wanting, but the series of spiritual intuitions it
contains, stated or hinted, in brief, pithy phrases " (A. B. Bruce,
pp. 373, 374). In σκιὰν . . . οὐκ εἰκόνα τῶν πραγμάτων (v.¹) the
writer uses a Platonic phrase (Cratylus, 306 E, εἰκόνας τῶν πραγμάτων) ; εἰκών (= ἀλήθεια, Chrysostom) is contrasted with σκιά
as the real expression or representation of substance is opposed
to the faint shadow. The addition of τῶν πραγμάτων (= τῶν
μέλλοντων ἀγαθῶν) emphasizes this sense ; what represents solid
realities is itself real, as compared to a mere σκιά. The μέλλοντα
ἀγαθά (9¹¹) are the boons and blessings still to be realized in
their fulness for Christians, being thought of from the standpoint of the new διαθήκη, not of the Law. The Law is for
the writer no more than the regulations which provided for the
cultus ; the centre of gravity in the Law lies in the priesthood
(7¹¹) and its sacrifices, not in what were the real provisions of
the Law historically. The writer rarely speaks of the Law by
itself. When he does so, as here, it is in this special ritual
aspect, and what really bulks in his view is the contrast between
the old and the new διαθήκη, *i.e.* the inadequate and the adequate
forms of relationship to God. Once the former was superseded,
the Law collapsed, and under the new διαθήκη there is no new
Law. Even while the Law lasted, it was shadowy and ineffective,
i.e. as a means of securing due access to God. And this is the
point here made against the Law, not as Paul conceived it, but
as the system of atoning animal sacrifices.

The text of v.¹ has been tampered with at an early stage, though the
variants affect the grammar rather than the general sense. Unless δύναται

(D H K L Ψ 2. 5. 35. 88. 181. 206. 226. 241. 242. 255. 326. 383. 429. 431.
547. 623. 794. 915. 917. 927. 1311. 1518. 1739. 1827. 1836. 1845. 1867.
1873. 1898. 2143 lat boh Orig. Chrys. Thdt. Oec.) is read for δύνανται, ὁ
νόμος is a hanging nominative, and an awkward anacolouthon results. Hort
suggests that the original form of the text was : καθ᾽ ἣν κατ᾽ ἐνιαυτὸν τὰς αὐτὰς
θυσίας προσφέρουσιν, αἱ εἰς τὸ διηνεκὲς οὐδέποτε δύνανται τοὺς προσερχομένους
τελειῶσαι. As in 9⁹, καθ᾽ ἤν (dropped out by a scribe accidentally, owing to
the resemblance between ΚΑΘΗΝ and ΚΑΘΕΝ) would connect with a previous
noun (here σκιάν), ΑΙ similarly fell out before ΕΙ (ΕΙΣ), and ΑΣ was changed
into ΑΙΣ in the three consecutive words after ἐνιαυτόν. This still leaves ὁ
νόμος without a verb, however, and is no improvement upon the sense gained
either (a) by treating ὁ νόμος as a nominative absolute, and δύνανται as an
irregular plural depending on αἱ understood¹ from θυσίαις ; or (b) by simply
reading δύναται (so Delitzsch, Weiss, Westcott, Peake, Riggenbach, Blass),
which clears up everything. A desire to smooth out the grammar or to
bring out some private interpretation may be underneath changes like the
addition of αὐτῶν after θυσίαις (ℵ P), or the substitution of αὐτῶν for αὐταῖς
(69. 1319), or the omission of αὐταῖς altogether (2. 177. 206. 642. 920. 1518.
1872), as well as the omission of ἅς (A 33. 1611. 2005) or αἷς altogether, like
the Syriac and Armenian versions, and the change of τελειῶσαι (τελεῶσαι,
Blass) into καθαρίσαι (D vt).

Προσφέρουσιν is an idiomatic use of the plural (Mt 2²⁰ τεθνή-
κασιν, Lk 12²⁰ αἰτοῦσιν), "where there is such a suppression of the
subject in bringing emphasis upon the action, that we get the
effect of a passive, or of French *on*, German *man*" (Moulton, i.
58). The allusion is to the yearly sacrifice on atonement-day,
for προσφέρουσιν goes with κατ᾽ ἐνιαυτόν, the latter phrase being
thrown forward for the sake of emphasis, and also in order to
avoid bringing εἰς τὸ διηνεκές too near it. Εἰς τὸ διηνεκές also
goes with προσφέρουσιν, not (as in v.¹⁴) with τελειοῦν. Οὐδέποτε
here as in v.¹¹ before δύνα(ν)ται (never elsewhere in the epistle) is
doubly emphatic from its position. The constant repetition of
these sacrifices proves that their effect is only temporary ; they
cannot possibly bring about a lasting, adequate relationship to
God. So our author denies the belief of Judaism that atonement-day availed for the pardon of the People, a belief explicitly
put forward, *e.g.*, in Jub 5¹⁷·¹⁸ ("If they turn to Him in righteousness, He will forgive all their transgressions, and pardon all their
sins. It is written and ordained that He will show mercy to all
who turn from their guilt once a year"). He reiterates this in
v.², where ἐπεί (as in 9²⁶ = alioquin) is followed by οὐκ, which
implies a question. "Would they not, otherwise, have ceased
to be offered?" When this was not seen, either οὐκ was omitted
(H* vg? syr 206. 1245. 1518 Primasius, etc.), leaving ἄν out of
its proper place, or it was suggested—as would never have
occurred to the author—that the OT sacrifices ceased to be valid

¹ It is inserted by A** 31. 366. 472. 1319 syrʰᵏˡ arm. If the relative
pronoun were assimilated, *i.e.* if αἷς (D* H L 5. 88. 257. 547, etc.) were read
for ἅς, the accidental omission of αἱ would be more intelligible.

when the Christian sacrifice took place. In οὐκ ἂν ἐπαύσαντο προσφερόμεναι (for construction see Gn 11⁸ ἐπαύσαντο οἰκοδο-μοῦντες) the ἄν is retained (see on 9²⁶). Κεκαθαρισμένους has been altered into κεκαθάρμενους (L), but καθαρίζω, not the Attic καθαίρω, is the general NT form. If our author spelt like his LXX codex, however, κεκαθερισμένους would be original (cp. Thackeray, 74). Συνείδησις is again used (9⁹) in connexion with "the worshipper(s)," but the writer adds ἁμαρτιῶν (*i.e.* sins still needing to be pardoned). For the genitive, compare Philo's fine remark in *quod det. pot.* 40, ἱκετεύωμεν οὖν τὸν θεὸν οἱ συνειδήσει τῶν οἰκείων ἀδικημάτων ἐλεγχόμενοι, κολάσαι μᾶλλον ἡμᾶς ἢ παρεῖναι. In v.³ ἀνάμνησις means that public notice had to be taken of such sins ("commemoratio," vg).

There is possibly an echo here of a passage like Nu 5¹⁵ (θυσία μνημοσύνου ἀναμιμνήσκουσα ἁμαρτίαν), quoted by Philo in *de Plant.* 25 to illustrate his statement that the sacrifices of the wicked simply serve to recall their misdeeds (ὑπομιμνήσκουσαι τὰς ἑκάστων ἀγνοίας τε καὶ διαμαρτίας). In *vita Mosis*, iii. 10, he repeats this ; if the sacrificer was ignorant and wicked, the sacrifices were no sacrifices (. . . οὐ λύσιν ἁμαρτημάτων, ἀλλ' ὑπόμνησιν ἐργάζονται). What Philo declares is the result of sacrifices offered by the wicked, the author of Hebrews declares was the result of all sacrifices ; they only served to bring sin to mind. So in *de Victimis*, 7, εὔηθες γὰρ τὰς θυσίας ὑπόμνησιν ἁμαρτημάτων ἀλλὰ μὴ λήθην αὐτῶν κατασκευάζειν—what Philo declares absurd, our author pronounces inevitable.

The ringing assertion of v.⁴ voices a sentiment which would appeal strongly to readers who had been familiar with the classical and contemporary protests (cp. *ERE.* iii. 770ᵃ), against ritual and external sacrifice as a means of moral purification (see above on 9¹³). Ἀφαιρεῖν, a LXX verb in this connexion (*e.g.* Num 14¹⁸ ἀφαιρῶν ἀνομίας καὶ ἀδικίας καὶ ἁμαρτίας), becomes ἀφελεῖν in L (so Blass), the aoristic and commoner form ; the verb is never used elsewhere in the NT, though Paul once quotes Is 27⁹ ὅταν ἀφέλωμαι ἁμαρτίας (Ro 11²⁷). All this inherent defectiveness of animal sacrifices necessitated a new sacrifice altogether (v.⁵ διό), the self-sacrifice of Jesus. So the writer quotes Ps 40⁷⁻⁹, which in A runs as follows :

> θυσίαν καὶ προσφορὰν οὐκ ἠθέλησας,
>> σῶμα δὲ κατηρτίσω μοι·
> ὁλοκαυτώματα καὶ περὶ ἁμαρτίας οὐκ ἐζήτησας.
> τότε εἶπον· ἰδοὺ ἥκω,
>> (ἐν κεφαλίδι βιβλίου γέγραπται περὶ ἐμοῦ)
> τοῦ ποιῆσαι τὸ θέλημά σου, ὁ θεός μου, ἠβουλήθην.

Our author reads εὐδόκησας for ἐζήτησας,[1] shifts ὁ θεός (omitting μου) to

---

[1] Which is replaced in the text of Hebrews by Ψ (ἐκζητήσεις) 623*. 1836. The augment spelling ηὐδόκησας reappears here as occasionally at v.⁸ in a small group (A C D* W, etc.), and the singular θυσίαν κ. προσφοράν is kept at v.⁸ by אᶜ Dᶜ K L W, etc.

a position after ποιῆσαι, in order to emphasize τὸ θέλημά σου, and by omitting ἐβουλήθην (replaced by W in v.⁷), connects τοῦ ποιῆσαι closely with ἥκω. A recollection of Ps 51¹⁸ εἰ ἠθέλησας θυσίαν . . . ὁλοκαυτώματα οὐκ εὐδοκήσεις may have suggested εὐδόκησας, which takes the accusative as often in LXX. Κεφαλίς is the roll or scroll, literally the knob or tip of the stick round which the papyrus sheet was rolled (cp. Ezek 2⁹ κεφαλὶς βιβλίου).

This is taken as an avowal of Christ on entering the world, and the LXX mistranslation in σῶμα is the pivot of the argument. The more correct translation would be ὠτία δέ, for the psalmist declared that God had given him ears for the purpose of attending to the divine monition to do the will of God, instead of relying upon sacrifices. Whether ὠτία was corrupted into σῶμα, or whether the latter was an independent translation, is of no moment; the evidence of the LXX text is indecisive. Our author found σῶμα in his LXX text and seized upon it; Jesus came with his body to do God's will, *i.e.* to die for the sins of men. The parenthetical phrase ἐν κεφαλίδι βιβλίου γέγραπται περὶ ἐμοῦ, which originally referred to the Deuteronomic code prescribing obedience to God's will, now becomes a general reference to the OT as a prediction of Christ's higher sacrifice; that is, if the writer really meant anything by it (he does not transcribe it, when he comes to the interpretation, vv.⁸ᶠ·). Though the LXX mistranslated the psalm, however, it did not alter its general sense. The Greek text meant practically what the original had meant, and it made this interpretation or application possible, namely, that there was a sacrifice which answered to the will of God as no animal sacrifice could. Only, our author takes the will of God as requiring some sacrifice. The point of his argument is not a contrast between animal sacrifices and moral obedience to the will of God; it is a contrast between the death of an animal which cannot enter into the meaning of what is being done, and the death of Jesus which means the free acceptance by him of all that God requires for the expiation of human sin. To do the will of God is, for our author, a sacrificial action, which involved for Jesus an atoning death, and this is the thought underlying his exposition and application of the psalm (vv.⁸⁻¹⁰). In v.⁸ ἀνώτερον is "above" or "higher up" in the quotation (v.⁶). The interpretation of the oracle which follows is plain; there are no textual variants worth notice,[1] and the language is clear. Thus εἴρηκεν in v.⁹ is the perfect of a completed action, = the saying stands on record, and ἀναιρεῖ has its common juristic sense of "abrogate," the opposite of ἵστημι. The general idea is: Jesus entered the world fully conscious that the various sacrifices of the Law were unavailing as means of atonement, and ready to sacrifice himself in order

---

[1] The vocative ὁ θεός is sometimes repeated after ποιῆσαι by אᶜ L 104. 1288. 1739 vg syrʰᵏˡ ᵃⁿᵈ ᵖᵉˢʰ etc., or after σου (*e.g.* 1. 1311 harl, arm).

to carry out the redeeming will of God. God's will was to
bring his People into close fellowship with himself (2¹⁰); this
necessitated a sacrifice such as that which the σῶμα of Christ
could alone provide. The triumphant conclusion is that this
divine will, which had no interest in ordinary sacrifices, has been
fulfilled in the προσφορά of Christ; what the Law could not do
(v.¹) has been achieved by the single self-sacrifice of Christ; it
is by what he suffered in his body, not by any animal sacrifices,
that we are ἡγιασμένοι (v.¹⁰). Jesus chose to obey God's will;
but, while the Psalmist simply ranked moral obedience higher
than any animal sacrifice, our writer ranks the moral obedience
of Jesus as redeemer above all such sacrifices. "Christ did not
come into the world to be a good man : it was not for this that
a body was prepared for him. He came to be a great High
Priest, and the body was prepared for him, that by the offering
of it he might put sinful men for ever into the perfect religious
relation to God" (Denney, *The Death of Christ*, p. 234).

In conclusion (¹¹⁻¹⁸) the writer interprets (¹¹⁻¹⁴) a phrase which
he has not yet noticed expressly, namely, that Christ *sat down
at the right hand of God* (1⁸⋅¹³); this proves afresh that his
sacrifice was final. Then, having quoted from the pentateuch
and the psalter, he reverts to the prophets (¹⁵⁻¹⁸), citing again
the oracle about the new διαθήκη with its prediction, now fulfilled,
of a final pardon.

¹¹ *Again, while every priest stands daily at his service, offering the same
sacrifices repeatedly, sacrifices which never can take sins away—* ¹² *He offered
a single sacrifice for sins and then "seated himself" for all time "at the
right hand of God,"* ¹³ *to wait "until his enemies are made a footstool for his
feet."* ¹⁴ *For by a single offering he has made the sanctified perfect for all
time.* ¹⁵ *Besides, we have the testimony of the holy Spirit ; for after saying,*
¹⁶ *"This is the covenant I will make with them when that day comes,*
    saith the Lord,
    I will set my laws upon their hearts,
    inscribing them upon their minds,"

he adds,

¹⁷ *"And their sins and breaches of the law I will remember no more."*
¹⁸ *Now where these are remitted* (ἄφεσις, as 9²²)*, an offering for sin exists* (sc.
ἐστι) *no longer.*

One or two textual difficulties emerge in this passage. In v.¹¹ ἱερεύς was
altered (after 5¹ 8³) into ἀρχιερεύς (A C P 5. 69. 88. 206. 241. 256. 263. 436.
462. 467. 489. 623. 642. 794. 917 920. 927. 999. 1836. 1837. 1898 syrʰᵏˡ˙
sah arm eth Cyr. Cosm.). In v.¹² αὐτός (K L 104. 326 boh Theod. Oec.
Theophyl.) is no improvement upon οὗτος. A curious variant (boh Ephr.)
in the following words is ἑαυτὸν μίαν ὑπὲρ ἁμαρτιῶν προσενέγκας θυσίαν.
In v.¹⁴ boh (" for one offering will complete them, who will be sanctified,
for ever ") appears to have read μιὰ γὰρ προσφορά (so Bgl.) τελειώσει κτλ.
In v.¹⁶ τῶν διανοιῶν is read by K L Ψ d r syr sah boh arm.

The decisive consideration in favour of ἱερεύς (v.¹¹) is not that the ἀρχιερεύς did not sacrifice daily (for the writer believed this, see on 7²⁷), but the adjective πᾶς. Περιελεῖν is a literary synonym for ἀφαιρεῖν (v.⁴); there is no special emphasis in the verb here any more than, e.g., in 2 Co 3¹⁶, for the (Zeph 3¹⁵ περιεῖλε κύριος τὰ ἀδικήματά σου) metaphorical idea of stripping no longer attached to the term, and the περί had ceased to mean "entirely" or "altogether." The contrast between this repeated and ineffective ritual of the priests and the solitary, valid sacrifice of Jesus is now drawn in v.¹², where εἰς τὸ διηνεκές goes more effectively with ἐκάθισεν than with προσενέγκας θυσίαν, since the idea in the latter collocation is at once expressed in v.¹⁴ At the opening of the writer's favourite psalm (110¹) lay a promise of God to his Son, which further proved that this sacrifice of Christ was final:

εἶπεν ὁ κύριος τῷ κυρίῳ μου Κάθου ἐκ δεξιῶν μου
ἕως ἂν θῶ τοὺς ἐχθρούς σου ὑποπόδιον τῶν ποδῶν σου.

Κάθου—a unique privilege; so Christ's priestly sacrifice must be done and over, all that remains for him being to await the submission and homage of his foes. As for the obedient (5⁹), they are perfected "finally," i.e. brought into the closest relation to God, by what he has done for them; no need for him to stand at any priestly service on their behalf, like the levitical drudges! The contrast is between ἐκάθισεν and ἕστηκεν (the attitude of a priest who has to be always ready for some sacrifice). Who the foes of Christ are, the writer never says.[1] This militant metaphor was not quite congruous with the sacerdotal metaphor, although he found the two side by side in the 110th psalm. If he interpreted the prediction as Paul did in 1 Co 15²⁵ᶠ, we might think of the devil (2¹⁴) and such supernatural powers of evil; but this is not an idea which is worked out in Πρὸς Ἑβραίους. The conception belonged to the primitive messianic faith of the church, and the writer takes it up for a special purpose of his own, but he cannot interpret it, as Paul does, of an active reign of Christ during the brief interval before the end. Christ must reign actively, Paul argues. Christ must sit, says our writer.

The usual variation between the LXX ἐκ δεξιῶν and ἐν δεξιᾷ is reproduced in Πρὸς Ἑβραίους: the author prefers the latter, when he is not definitely quoting from the LXX as in 1¹³. As this is a reminiscence rather than a citation, ἐν δεξιᾷ is the true reading, though ἐκ δεξιῶν is introduced by A 104 Athanasius. The theological significance of the idea is discussed in Dr. A. J. Tait's monograph on The Heavenly Session of our Lord (1912), in which he points out the misleading influence of the Vulgate's mistranslation of 10¹² ("hic autem unam pro peccatis offerens hostiam in sempiternum sedit") upon the notion that Christ pleads his passion in heaven.

[1] In Clem. Rom. 36⁵· ⁶ they are οἱ φαῦλοι καὶ ἀντιτασσόμενοι τῷ θελήματι αὐτοῦ.

After reiterating the single sacrifice in v.¹⁴ (where τοὺς ἁγιαζο-
μένους is "the sanctified," precisely as in 2¹¹), he adds (v.¹⁵) an
additional proof from scripture. Μαρτυρεῖ δὲ ἡμῖν καὶ τὸ πνεῦμα
τὸ ἅγιον, a biblical proof as usual clinching the argument. Ἡμῖν
is "you and me," "us Christians," not the literary plural, as if
he meant "what I say is attested or confirmed by the inspired
book." Μαρτυρεῖν is a common Philonic term in this connexion,
e.g. *Leg. Alleg.* iii. 2, μαρτυρεῖ δὲ καὶ ἐν ἑτέροις λέγων κτλ. (introducing Dt 4³⁹ and Ex 17⁶); similarly in Xen. *Mem.* i. 2. 20,
μαρτυρεῖ δὲ καὶ τῶν ποιητῶν ὁ λέγων. The quotation, which is
obviously from memory, is part of the oracle already quoted
upon the new διαθήκη (8⁸⁻¹²); the salient sentence is the closing
promise of pardon in v.¹⁷, but he leads up to it by citing some
of the introductory lines. The opening, μετὰ γὰρ τὸ εἰρηκέναι,
implies that some verb follows or was meant to follow, but the
only one in the extant text is λέγει κύριος (v.¹⁶). Hence, before
v.¹⁷ we must understand something like μαρτυρεῖ or λέγει or
προσέθηκεν καί φησιν (Oecumenius) or τότε εἴρηκεν, although the
evidence for any such phrase, *e.g.* for ὕστερον λέγει (31. 37. 55.
67. 71. 73. 80. 161) is highly precarious. In v.¹⁷ μνησθήσομαι
has been corrected into μνησθῶ by אᶜ Dᶜ K L P, etc., since μνησθῶ
was the LXX reading and also better grammar, the future after
οὐ μή being rare (cp. *Diat.* 2255, and above on 8¹¹). The oracle,
even in the LXX version, contemplates no sacrifice whatever
as a condition of pardon; but our author (see above, p. 131)
assumes that such an absolute forgiveness was conditioned by
some sacrifice.

The writer now (10¹⁹–12²⁹) proceeds to apply his arguments
practically to the situation of his readers, urging their privileges
and their responsibilities under the new order of religion which
he has just outlined. In 10¹⁹⁻³¹, which is the first paragraph,
encouragement (vv.¹⁹⁻²⁵) passes into warning (²⁶⁻³¹).

¹⁹ *Brothers* (ἀδελφοί, not since 3¹· ¹²), *since we have confidence to enter the
holy Presence in virtue of the blood of Jesus,* ²⁰ *by the fresh, living way which
he has inaugurated for us through the veil* (*that is, through his flesh*), ²¹ *and
since we have "a great Priest over the house of God,"* ²² *let us draw near with
a true heart, in absolute assurance of faith, our hearts sprinkled clean from
a bad conscience, and our bodies washed in pure water;* ²³ *let us hold the hope
we avow without wavering* (*for we can rely on him who gave us the Promise*);
²⁴ *and let us consider how to stir one another up to love and good deeds—* ²⁵ *not
ceasing to meet together, as is the habit of some, but admonishing one another*
(sc. ἑαυτούς, as 3¹³), *all the more so, as you see the Day coming near.*

The writer (ἔχοντες οὖν) presses the weighty arguments of
6²⁰–10¹⁸, but he returns with them to reinforce the appeal of
3¹–4¹⁶; after 10¹⁹⁻²¹ the conception of Jesus as the ἱερεύς falls
more into the background. The passage is one long sentence,

ἔχοντες . . . προσερχώμεθα . . . κατέχωμεν . . . καὶ κατανοῶμεν
. . . Ἔχοντες οὖν (as in 4¹⁴) since the way is now open (9⁸)
through the sacrifice of Jesus, whose atoning blood is for us the
means of entering God's presence; παρρησίαν, "a fre sure
intraunce" (Coverdale), echoing 4¹⁶. But the writer fills out
the appeal of 4¹⁴⁻¹⁶ with the idea of the sanctuary and the
sacrifice which he had broken off, in 5¹ᶠ, to develop. Though
the appeal still is προσερχώμεθα (²³ = 4¹⁶), the special motives are
twofold : (a) παρρησία for access in virtue of the sacrifice of Jesus
(vv.¹⁹· ²⁰), and (b) the possession of Jesus as the supreme ἱερεύς
(v.²¹). (a) The religious sense of παρρησία emerges in the early
gloss inserted after Sir 18²⁹ :

κρείσσων παρρησία ἐν δεσπότῃ μόνῳ
ἢ νεκρὰ καρδία νεκρῶν ἀντέχεσθαι.

Here παρρησία means confident trust, the unhesitating adherence
of a human soul to God as its only Master, but our author
specially defines it as παρρησία εἰς (cp. 2 P 1¹¹ ἡ εἴσοδος εἰς τὴν
αἰώνιον βασιλείαν) εἴσοδον (with gen. as ὁδόν in 9⁸, but not a
synonym for ὁδόν), i.e. for access to (τῶν ἁγίων) the holy Presence,
ἐν τῷ αἵματι Ἰησοῦ (qualifying εἴσοδον).[1] This resumes the
thought of 9²⁴⁻²⁶ 10¹⁰⁻¹² (ἐν αἵματι as in 9²⁵). Compare for the
phrase and general idea the words on the self-sacrifice of Decius
Mus in Florus, i. 15. 3 : "quasi monitu deorum, capite uelato,
primam ante aciem dis manibus se devoverit, ut in confertissima
se hostium tela iaculatus nouum ad uictoriam iter sanguinis sui
semita aperiret." This εἴσοδος τῶν ἁγίων ἐν τῷ αἵματι Ἰησοῦ is
further described in v.²⁰; we enter by (ἥν, with ὁδόν . . . ζῶσαν
in apposition) a way which Jesus has inaugurated by his sacrifice
(9¹⁸· ²⁴· ²⁵). This way is called recent or fresh and also living.
In πρόσφατος, as in the case of other compounds (e.g. κελαινεφής),
the literal sense of the second element had been long forgotten
(cp. Holden's note on Plutarch's Themistocles, 24); πρόσφατος
simply means "fresh," without any sacrificial allusion ("freshly-
killed"). Galen (de Hipp. et Plat. plac. iv. 7) quotes the well-
known saying that λύπη ἐστὶ δόξα πρόσφατος κακοῦ παρουσίας,
and the word (i.e. τὸ ἀρτίως γενόμενον, νέον, νεαρόν, Hesychius), as
is plain from other passages like Arist. Magna Moralia, 1203b
(ὁ ἐκ τῆς προσφάτου φαντασίας ἀκρατής κτλ.), and Eccles 1⁹ (οὐκ
ἔστιν πᾶν πρόσφατον ὑπὸ τὸν ἥλιον), had no longer any of the
specific sacrificial sense suggested etymologically by its second
part. It is the thought of ἐχθές in 13⁸, though the writer means

---

[1] Hence the idea is not put in quite the same way as in Eph 3¹² (ἐν ᾧ
ἔχομεν τὴν παρρησίαν καὶ τὴν προσαγωγήν). In Sir 25²⁵ μηδὲ (δῷς) γυναικὶ
πονηρᾷ ἐξουσίαν, א A read παρρησίαν for B's ἐξουσίαν, which proves how deeply
the idea of liberty was rooted in παρρησία.

particularly (as in 1¹⁻² 9⁸⁻¹¹) to suggest that a long period had
elapsed before the perfect fellowship was inaugurated finally ; it
is πρόσφατος, not ἀρχαῖος. Ζῶσαν means, in the light of 7²⁵ (cp.
Jn 14⁶), that access to God is mediated by the living Christ in
virtue of his sacrificial intercession ; the contrast is not so much
with what is transient, as though ζῶσαν were equivalent to μένουσαν
(Chrysostom, Cosm. 415a), as with the dead victims of the
OT cultus or "the lifeless pavement trodden by the highpriest"
(Delitzsch).   He entered God's presence thus διὰ τοῦ καταπετάσματος (6¹⁹ 9⁸), τοῦτ' ἔστιν τοῦ σαρκὸς αὐτοῦ—a ritual expression
for the idea of 6¹⁹.   Διά is local, and, whether a verb like
εἰσελθών is supplied or not, διὰ τ. κ. goes with ἐνεκαίνισεν, the idea
being that Jesus had to die, in order to bring us into a living
fellowship with God ; the shedding of his blood meant that he
had a body (10⁵⁻¹⁰) to offer in sacrifice (cp. 9¹⁴).   The writer,
however, elaborates his argument with a fresh detail of
symbolism, suggested by the ritual of the tabernacle which he
has already described in 9²ᶠ.   There, the very existence of a veil
hanging between the outer and the inner sanctuary was interpreted
as a proof that access to God's presence was as yet imperfectly
realized.   The highpriest carried once a year inside the veil the
blood of victims slain outside it ; that was all.   Jesus, on the
other hand, sheds his own blood as a perfect sacrifice, and thus
wins entrance for us into the presence of God.   Only, instead of
saying that his sacrificial death meant the rending of the veil
(like the author of Mk 15³⁸), *i.e.* the supersession of the OT
barriers between God and man, he allegorizes the veil here as
the flesh of Christ ; this had to be rent before the blood could
be shed, which enabled him to enter and open God's presence
for the people.   It is a daring, poetical touch, and the parallelism
is not to be prosaically pressed into any suggestion that the
human nature in Jesus hid God from men ἐν ταῖς ἡμέραις τῆς
σαρκὸς αὐτοῦ, or that he ceased to be truly human when he
sacrificed himself.

   The idea already suggested in ζῶσαν is now (*b*) developed
(in v.²¹) by (ἔχοντες) καὶ ἱερέα μέγαν ἐπὶ τὸν οἶκον τοῦ θεοῦ, another
echo of the earlier passage (cp. 3¹⁻⁶ 4¹⁴), ἱερεὺς μέγας being a
sonorous LXX equivalent for ἀρχιερεύς.   Then comes the triple
appeal, προσερχώμεθα . . . κατέχωμεν . . . καὶ κατανοῶμεν . . .
The metaphor of προσερχώμεθα κτλ. (v.²²), breaks down upon the
fact that the Israelites never entered the innermost shrine, except
as represented by their highpriest who entered once a year ἐν
αἵματι ἀλλοτρίῳ (9⁷· ²⁵), which he took with him in order to atone
for the sins that interrupted the communion of God and the
people.   In Πρὸς Ἑβραίους the point is that, in virtue of the
blood of Christ, Christians enjoy continuous fellowship with

God; the sacrifice of Christ enables them to approach God's presence, since their sins have been once and for all removed The entrance of the OT highpriest therefore corresponds both to the sacrifice of Christ and to that access of Christians which the blood of Christ secures. On the one hand, Christ is our high-priest (v.²¹); through his self-sacrifice in death the presence of God has been thrown open to us (vv.¹⁹· ²⁰). This is the primary thought. But in order to express our use of this privilege, the writer has also to fall back upon language which suggests the entrance of the OT highpriest (cp. v.¹⁹ ἐν τῷ αἵματι Ἰησοῦ with 9²⁵). He does not mean that Christians are priests, with the right of entry in virtue of a sacrifice which they present, but, as to approach God was a priestly prerogative under the older order, he describes the Christian access to God in sacerdotal metaphors. Προσερχώμεθα is one of these. It is amplified first by a μετά clause, and then by two participial clauses. The approach to God must be whole-hearted, μετὰ ἀληθινῆς καρδίας,[1] without any hesitation or doubt, ἐν πληροφορίᾳ (6¹¹) πίστεως.[2] This thought of πίστις as man's genuine answer to the realities of divine revelation, is presently to be developed at length (10³⁸ᶠ·). Meantime the writer throws in the double participial clause, ῥεραντισμένοι . . . καθαρῷ. The metaphors are sacer-dotal; as priests were sprinkled with blood and bathed in water, to qualify them for their sacred service, so Christians may approach God with all confidence, on the basis of Christ's sacrifice, since they have been ῥεραντισμένοι (i.e. sprinkled and so purified from—a frequent use of the verb) ἀπὸ συνειδήσεως πονηρᾶς (= συνειδήσεως ἁμαρτιῶν, 10²) in their hearts (τὰς καρδίας —no external cleansing). Then the writer adds, καὶ λελουσμένοι τὸ σῶμα ὕδατι καθαρῷ, suggesting that baptism corresponded to the bathing of priests (e.g. in Lev 16⁴). Once and for all, at baptism (cp. 1 P 3²¹), Christians have been thus purified from guilty stains by the efficacy of Christ's sacrifice.[3] What room then can there be in their minds for anything but faith, a confident faith that draws near to Him, sure that there is no longer anything between Him and them?

The distinctive feature which marked off the Christian βαπτισμός from all similar ablutions (6² 9¹⁰) was that it meant something more than a cleansing of the body; it was part and parcel of an inward cleansing of the καρδία, effected by τὸ αἷμα

---

[1] The phrase ἐν ἀληθινῇ καρδίᾳ occurs in Test. Dan 5³ (v.l. καθαρᾷ) and in Is 38³ (ἐν. κ. ἀ.).

[2] There is a verbal parallel in the account of Isis-worship given by Apuleius (Metamorph. xi. 28: "ergo igitur cunctis adfatim praeparatis . . . principalis dei nocturnis orgiis inlustratus, plena iam fiducia germanae religionis obsequium diuinum frequentabam").

[3] More specifically, by the αἷμα ῥαντισμοῦ of 12²⁴.

τῆς διαθήκης (v.²⁹).[1] Hence this as the vital element is put first, though the body had also its place and part in the cleansing experience. The καρδία and the σῶμα are a full, plastic expression for the entire personality, as an ancient conceived it. Ancient religious literature [2] is full of orders for the penitent to approach the gods only after moral contrition and bodily cleansing, with a clean heart and a clean body, in clean clothes even. But, apart from other things, such ablutions had to be repeated, while the Christian βαπτισμός was a single ceremony, lying at the source and start of the religious experience. And what our author is thinking of particularly is not this or that pagan rite, but the OT ritual for priests as described in Ex 29²⁰ᶠ·, Lv 8²³ᶠ· 14⁵ᶠ· etc. (cp. *Joma* 3).

Three specimens of the anxious care for bodily purity in ancient religious ritual may be given. First (i) the ritual directions for worship in *Syll.* 567 (ii A.D.) : πρῶτον μὲν καὶ τὸ μέγιστον, χεῖρας καὶ γνώμην καθαροὺς καὶ ὑγιεῖς ὑπάρχοντας καὶ μηδὲν αὐτοῖς δεινὸν συνειδότας. Second (ii) the stress laid on it by a writer like Philo, who (*quod deus sit immutabilis*, 2), after pleading that we should honour God by purifying ourselves from evil deeds and washing off the stains of life, adds : καὶ γὰρ εὔηθες εἰς μὲν τὰ ἱερὰ μὴ ἐξεῖναι βαδίζειν, ὃς ἂν μὴ πρότερον λουσάμενος φαιδρύνηται τὸ σῶμα, εὔχεσθαι δὲ καὶ θύειν ἐπιχειρεῖν ἔτι κηλιδωμένῃ καὶ πεφυρμένῃ διανοίᾳ. His argument is that if the body requires ablutions (περιρραντηρίοις καὶ καθαρσίοις ἁγνευτικοῖς) before touching an external shrine, how can anyone who is morally impure draw near (προσελθεῖν τῷ θεῷ) the most pure God, unless he means to repent? Ὁ μὲν γὰρ πρὸς τῷ μηδὲν ἐπεξεργάσασθαι κακὸν καὶ τὰ παλαιὰ ἐκνίψασθαι δικαιώσας γεγηθὼς προσίτω [cp. He 10¹⁹·²²], ὁ δ' ἄνευ τούτων δυσκάθαρτος ὢν ἀφιστάσθω· λήσεται γὰρ οὐδέποτε τὸν τὰ ἐν μυχοῖς τῆς διανοίας ὁρῶντα [cp. He 4¹³] καὶ τοῖς ἀδύτοις αὐτῆς ἐμπεριπατοῦντα. Or again in *de Plant.* 39 : σώματα καὶ ψυχὰς καθηράμενοι, τὰ μὲν λουτροῖς, τὰ δὲ νόμων καὶ παιδείας ὀρθῆς ρεύμασι. In *de Cherub.* 28 he denounces the ostentatious religion of the worldly, who in addition to their other faults, τὰ μὲν σώματα λουτροῖς καὶ καθαρσίοις ἀπορρύπτονται, τὰ δὲ ψυχῆς ἐκνίψασθαι πάθη, οἷς καταρρυπαίνεται ὁ βίος, οὔτε βούλονται οὔτε ἐπιτηδεύουσι, are very particular about their outward religious practices [3] but careless about a clean soul. Finally, (iii) there is the saying of Epictetus (iv. 10. 3): ἐπεὶ γὰρ ἐκεῖνοι (*i.e.* the gods) φύσει καθαροὶ καὶ ἀκήρατοι, ἐφ' ὅσον ἠγγίκασιν αὐτοῖς οἱ ἄνθρωποι κατὰ τὸν λόγον, ἐπὶ τοσοῦτον καὶ τοῦ καθαροῦ καὶ τοῦ καθαρίου εἰσὶν ἀνθεκτικοί.

For the exceptional ῥεραντισμένοι (א* A C D*), אᶜ Dᶜ etc. have substituted ἐρραντισμένοι (so Theodoret). The λελουσμένοι of א B D P is the more common κοινή form of the Attic λελουμένοι (A C Dᶜ etc.).

The next appeal (v.²³), κατέχωμεν τὴν ὁμολογίαν τῆς ἐλπίδος (to which א* vg pesh eth add the gloss of ἡμῶν), echoes 4¹⁴

---

[1] Τὸ αἷμα τῆς διαθήκης ἐν ᾧ ἡγιάσθη, as 1 Co 6¹¹ ἀλλὰ ἀπελούσασθε, ἀλλὰ ἡγιάσθητε.

[2] Cp. Eugen Fehrle's *Die Kultische Keuschheit im Altertum* (1910), pp. 26 f., 131 f. ; Sir J. G. Frazer's *Adonis, Attis, Osiris* (1907), pp. 407 f.

[3] According to a recently discovered (first century) inscription on a Palestinian synagogue (cp. *Revue Biblique*, 1921, pp. 247 f.), the synagogue was furnished with τὸν ξενῶνα (for hospitality, cp. below, 13²) καὶ τὰ χρηστήρια τῶν ὑδάτων (baths for ritual ablutions).

(κρατῶμεν τῆς ὁμολογίας) and 3⁶ (ἐὰν τὴν παρρησίαν καὶ τὸ
καύχημα τῆς ἐλπίδος . . . κατάσχωμεν). This hope for the future
was first confessed at baptism, and rests upon God's promise [1]
(as already explained in 6¹⁷·¹⁸). It is to be held ἀκλινής, a term
applied by Philo to the word of a good man (ὁ γὰρ τοῦ σπουδαίου,
φησί, λόγος ὅρκος ἔστω, βέβαιος, ἀκλινής, ἀψευδέστατος, ἐρηρεισμένος
ἀληθείᾳ, de Spec. Leg. ii. 1); in Irenaeus it recurs in a similar
connexion (i. 88, ed. Harvey: ὁ τὸν κανόνα τῆς ἀληθείας ἀκλινῆ
ἐν ἑαυτῷ κατέχων, ὃν διὰ τοῦ βαπτίσματος εἴληφε). The old
Wycliffite version translates finely: "hold we the confessioun of
oure hope bowynge to no side." The close connexion between
ῥεραντισμένοι κτλ. and λελουσμένοι κτλ. makes it inadvisable to
begin the second appeal with καὶ λελουσμένοι τὸ σῶμα ὕδατι καθαρῷ
(Erasmus, Beza, Bengel, Lachmann, Lünemann, von Soden, B.
Weiss, etc.). A more plausible suggestion, first offered by
Theodoret and adopted recently by Hofmann and Seeberg, is to
begin the second appeal after πίστεως, making κατεχῶμεν carry
ῥεραντισμένοι . . . καθαρῷ. This yields a good sense, for it
brings together the allusions to the baptismal confession. But
the ordinary view is more probable; the asyndeton in κατεχῶμεν
is impressive, and if it is objected that the κατεχῶμεν clause is
left with less content than the other two, the answer is that its
eschatological outlook is reiterated in the third clause, and that
by itself its brevity has a telling force. Besides, ἔχοντες κτλ.
(¹⁹⁻²¹) introduce κατεχῶμεν as well as προσερχώμεθα.

The third appeal (²⁴·²⁵) turns on love (cp. 6¹⁰), as the first on
faith, and the second on hope. The members of the circle or
community are to stir up one another to the practice of Christian love. Since this is only possible when common worship
and fellowship are maintained, the writer warns them against
following the bad example of abandoning such gatherings; καὶ
κατανοῶμεν ἀλλήλους, for, if we are to κατανοεῖν Christ (3¹), we
are also bound to keep an eye on one another εἰς παροξυσμὸν
ἀγάπης καὶ καλῶν ἔργων (i.e. an active, attractive moral life,
inspired by Christian love). This good sense of παροξυσμός as
stimulus seems to be an original touch; in Greek elsewhere it
bears the bad sense of provocation or exasperation (cp. Ac 15³⁹),
although the verb παροξύνειν had already acquired a good sense
(e.g. in Josephus, Ant. xvi. 125, παροξῦναι τὴν εὔνοιαν: in Pr 6³
ἴσθι μὴ ἐκλυόμενος, παρόξυνε δὲ καὶ τὸν φίλον σου ὃν ἐνεγγυήσω: and
in Xen. Cyrop. vi. 2. 5, καὶ τούτους ἐπαινῶν τε παρώξυνε). Pliny's
words at the close of his letter to Caninius Rufus (iii. 7) illustrate what is meant by παροξυσμός in this sense: "Scio te
stimulis non egere; me tamen tui caritas evocat ut currentem

---

[1] An instance of this is quoted in 11¹¹.

quoque instigem, sicut tu soles me. Ἀγαθὴ δ' ἔρις, cum invicem
se mutuis exhortationibus amici ad amorem immortalitatis
exacuunt." How the παροξυσμός is to be carried out, the writer
does not say. By setting a good example? By definite exhorta-
tions (παρακαλοῦντες, v.[25], like 13[1])? Μὴ ἐγκαταλείποντες—do not
do to one another what God never does to you (13[5]), do not
leave your fellow-members in the lurch (the force of ἐγκαταλείπειν,
especially in the κοινή)—τὴν ἐπισυναγωγὴν ἑαυτῶν (reflexive pronoun in the genitive = ἡμῶν). Ἐπισυναγωγή in the κοινή (cp. Deissmann's *Light from the East*, 102 f.) means a collection (of money),
but had already in Jewish Greek (*e.g.* 2 Mac 2[7] ἕως ἂν συνάγῃ ὁ
θεὸς ἐπισυναγωγὴν τοῦ λαοῦ) begun to acquire the present sense
of a popular "gathering." Καθὼς ἔθος (*sc.* ἔστιν) τισίν. But who
are these? What does this abandonment of common fellowship
mean? (*a*) Perhaps that some were growing ashamed of their
faith; it was so insignificant and unpopular, even dangerous to
anyone who identified himself with it openly. They may have
begun to grow tired of the sacrifices and hardships involved in
membership of the local church. This is certainly the thought
of 10[32f.], and it is better than to suppose (*b*) the leaders were a small
group of teachers or more intelligent Christians, who felt able, in
a false superiority, to do without common worship; they did not
require to mix with the ordinary members! The author in any
case is warning people against the dangers of individualism, a
warning on the lines of the best Greek and Jewish ethics, *e.g.*
Isokrates, *ad Demon.* 13, τιμὰ τὸ δαιμόνιον ἀεὶ μὲν, μάλιστα δὲ μετὰ
τῆς πόλεως, and the rabbinic counsel in Taanith, 11. 1 (" whenever
the Israelites suffer distress, and one of them withdraws from the
rest, two angels come to him and, laying their hands upon his
head, say, this man who separates himself from the assembly
shall not see the consolation which is to visit the congregation"),
or in Hillel's saying (*Pirke Aboth* 2[5]): " Separate not thyself
from the congregation, and trust not in thyself until the day of
thy death." The loyal Jews are described in Ps.-Sol 17[18] as
οἱ ἀγαπῶντες συναγωγὰς ὁσίων, and a similar thought occurs also
(if " his " and not " my " is the correct reading) in Od. Sol 3[2]:
" His members are with Him, and on them do I hang." Any
early Christian who attempted to live like a pious particle without
the support of the community ran serious risks in an age when
there was no public opinion to support him. His isolation, whatever its motive—fear, fastidiousness, self-conceit, or anything else
—exposed him to the danger of losing his faith altogether. These
are possible explanations of the writer's grave tone in the passage before us. Some critics, like Zahn (§ 46), even think that
(*c*) such unsatisfactory Christians left their own little congregation for another, in a spirit of lawless pique, or to gratify their

own tastes selfishly ; but ἑαυτῶν is not emphatic, and in any
congregation of Christians the duties of love would be pressed.
Separatist tendencies were not absent from the early church ;
thus some members considered themselves too good to require
common worship, as several warnings prove, *e.g.* in Barn 4¹⁰
μὴ καθ᾽ ἑαυτοὺς ἐνδύνοντες μονάζετε ὡς ἤδη δεδικαιωμένοι, ἀλλ᾽ ἐπὶ
τὸ αὐτὸ συνερχόμενοι συνζητεῖτε περὶ τοῦ κοινῇ συμφέροντος) and
Ign. *Eph.* 5³ (ὁ οὖν μὴ ἐρχόμενος ἐπὶ τὸ αὐτὸ οὗτος ἤδη ὑπερηφανεῖ
καὶ ἑαυτὸν διέκρινεν). But in our epistle (*d*) the warning is directed
specially against people who combined Christianity with a
number of mystery-cults, patronizing them in turn, or who withdrew from Christian fellowship, feeling that they had exhausted
the Christian faith and that it required to be supplemented by
some other cult. " At first and indeed always there were
naturally some people who imagined that one could secure the
sacred contents and blessings of Christianity as one did those of
Isis or the Magna Mater, and then withdraw " (Harnack,
Expansion of Christianity, bk. iii. c. 4 ; cp. Reitzenstein's *Hellen.
Mysterienreligionen*, 94). This was serious, for, as the writer
realized, it implied that they did not regard Christianity as the
final and full revelation ; their action proved that the Christian
faith ranked no higher with them than one of the numerous
Oriental cults which one by one might interest the mind, but
which were not necessarily in any case the last word on life.
The argument of the epistle has been directed against this misconception of Christianity, and the writer here notes a practical
illustration of it in the conduct of adherents who were holding aloof, or who were in danger of holding aloof, from the
common worship. Hence the austere warning which follows.
Such a practice, or indeed any failure to " draw near " by
the way of Jesus, is an insult to God, which spells hopeless
ruin for the offender. And evidently this retribution is near.
Christians are to be specially on their guard against conduct
that means apostasy, for βλέπετε (how, he does not say)
ἐγγίζουσαν (as in Ro 13¹²) τὴν ἡμέραν (here, as in 1 Co 3¹³,
without ἐκείνη or τοῦ κυρίου). This eschatological setting
distinguishes the next warning (vv.²⁶⁻³¹) from the earlier
in 6⁴⁻⁶.

²⁶ *For if we sin deliberately after receiving the knowledge of the Truth,
there is no longer any sacrifice for sins left,* ²⁷ *nothing but an awful outlook of
doom, that " burning Wrath " which will " consume the foes "* (see v.¹³) *of
God.* ²⁸ *Anyone who has rejected the law of Moses " dies " without mercy,
" on the evidence of two or of three witnesses."* ²⁹ *How much heavier, do you
suppose, will be the punishment assigned* (*i.e.* by God) *to him who has spurned
the Son of God, who has profaned " the covenant-blood "* (9²⁰) *with which he
was sanctified* (10¹⁰), *who has insulted the Spirit of grace?* ³⁰ *We know who
said, " Vengeance is mine, I will exact a requital " : and again* (πάλιν, as in

2¹³), "*The Lord will pass sentence on his people.*" ³¹ *It is an awful thing to fall into the hands of the living God.*

Apostasy like withdrawal from the church on the ground already mentioned, is treated as one of the deliberate (ἑκουσίως) sins which (cp. on 5²), under the OT order of religion, were beyond any atonement. Wilful offences, like rebellion and blasphemy against God, were reckoned unpardonable. "In the case of one who, by his sin, intentionally disowns the covenant itself, there can be no question of sacrifice. He has himself cut away the ground on which it would have been possible for him to obtain reconciliation" (Schultz, *OT Theology*, ii. 88). There is an equivalent to this, under the new διαθήκη, our author declares. To abandon Christianity is to avow that it is in-adequate, and this denial of God's perfect revelation in Jesus Christ is fatal to the apostate. In ἑκουσίως ἁμαρτόντων ἡμῶν (²⁶), ἑκουσίως is put first for the sake of emphasis, and ἁμαρτόντων means the sin of ἀποστῆναι ἀπὸ θεοῦ ζῶντος (3¹²) or of παρα-πίπτειν (6⁶), the present tense implying that such people persist in this attitude. Ἑκουσίως is the keynote to the warning. Its force may be felt in a passage like Thuc. iv. 98, where the Athenians remind the Boeotians that God pardons what is done under the stress of war and peril, καὶ γὰρ τῶν ἀκουσίων ἁμαρτη-μάτων καταφυγὴν εἶναι τοὺς βωμούς, and that it is wanton and presumptuous crimes alone which are heinous. Philo (*vit. Mos.* i. 49) describes Balaam praying for forgiveness from God on the ground that he had sinned ὑπ' ἀγνοίας ἀλλ' οὐ καθ' ἑκούσιον γνώμην. The adverb occurs in 2 Mac 14³ ("Αλκιμος . . . ἑκουσίως δὲ μεμολυσμένος). The general idea of the entire warning is that the moral order punishes all who wantonly and wilfully flout it; as Menander once put it (Kock's *Com. Attic. Fragm.* 700):

> νόμος φυλαχθεὶς οὐδέν ἐστιν ἢ νόμος·
> ὁ μὴ φυλαχθεὶς καὶ νόμος καὶ δήμιος.

Our author expresses this law of retribution in personal terms drawn from the OT, which prove how deeply moral and reverent his religious faith was, and how he dreaded anything like pre-suming upon God's kindness and mercy. The easy-going man thinks God easy going; he is not very serious about his religious duties, and he cannot imagine how God can take them very seriously either. "We know" better, says the author of Πρὸς Ἑβραίους!

Christianity is described (in v.²⁶) as τὸ λαβεῖν τὴν ἐπίγνωσιν τῆς ἀληθείας, a semi-technical phrase of the day, which recurs in the Pastoral Epistles (though with ἐλθεῖν εἰς instead of λαβεῖν). It is not one of our author's favourite expressions,[1] but the phrase

---

[1] Here it is an equivalent for the phrases used in 6⁴ ⁵; there is no dis-tinction between ἐπίγνωσις and γνῶσις (θεοῦ) any more than in the LXX, and

is partly used by Epictetus in its most general sense (λαβών τις παρὰ τῆς φύσεως μέτρα καὶ κανόνας εἰς ἐπίγνωσιν τῆς ἀληθείας κτλ., ii. 20. 21), when upbraiding the wretched academic philosophers (οἱ ἀταλαίπωροι ᾿Ακαδημαϊκοί) for discrediting the senses as organs of knowledge, instead of using and improving them. All that renegades can expect (v.²⁷) is φοβερά τις (= quidam, deepening the idea with its touch of vagueness) ἐκδοχή (a sense coined by the writer for this term, after his use of ἐκδέχεσθαι in 10¹³) κρίσεως, for they have thrown over the only sacrifice that saves men from κρίσις (9²⁷). This is expanded in a loose[1] reminiscence of Is 26¹¹ (ζῆλος λήμψεται λαὸν ἀπαίδευτον, καὶ νῦν πῦρ τοὺς ὑπεναντίους ἔδεται), though the phrase πυρὸς ζῆλος recalls Zeph 1¹⁹ (3⁸) ἐν πυρὶ ζήλου αὐτοῦ καταναλωθήσεται πᾶσα ἡ γῆ. The contemporary Jewish Apocalypse of Baruch (48³⁹· ⁴⁰) contains a similar threat to wilful sinners :

"Therefore shall a fire consume their thoughts,
   and in flame shall the meditations of their reins be tried;
   for the Judge shall come and will not tarry—
   because each of earth's inhabitant knew when he was trans-
      gressing."

The penalty for the wilful rejection (ἀθετήσας) of the Mosaic law[2] was severe (Dt 17²⁻¹⁷), but not more severe than the penalty to be inflicted on renegades from Christianity (vv.²⁸⁻³¹). The former penalty was merciless, χωρὶς οἰκτιρμῶν (to which, at an early period, καὶ δακρύων was added by D, most old Latin texts, and syrʰᵏˡ). It is described in a reminiscence of Dt 17⁶ ἐπὶ δυσὶν μάρτυσιν ἢ ἐπὶ τρισὶν μάρτυσιν ἀποθανεῖται ὁ ἀποθνήσκων (i.e. the apostate who has yielded to idolatry). The witnesses executed the punishment for the sin of which they had given evidence (Dt 17⁷, Ac 7⁵⁷ᶠ·, Jn 8⁷, Sanhedrim 6⁴), but this is not before the writer's mind; ἐπί with the dative simply means "on the ground of (the evidence given by)." In πόσῳ δοκεῖτε κτλ. (v.²⁹), δοκεῖτε is intercalated as in Aristoph. Acharn. 12 (πῶς τοῦτ᾽ ἔσεισέ μου δοκεῖς τὴν καρδίαν;), and Herm. Sim. ix. 28. 8 (εἰ τὰ ἔθνη τοὺς δούλους αὐτῶν κολάζουσιν, ἐάν τις ἀρνήσηται τὸν κύριον ἑαυτοῦ, τί δοκεῖτε ποιήσει ὁ κύριος ὑμῖν;). Πόσῳ (cp. 9¹⁴) introduces an

ἀλήθεια had been already stamped by Philo (e.g. de Justitia, 6, where the proselyte is said μετανάστὰς εἰς ἀλήθειαν) as a term for the true religion, which moulds the life of those who become members of the People. Compare the study of the phrase by M. Dibelius in NT Studien für G. Heinrici (1914), pp. 176-189.

[1] Probably it was the awkwardness of ζῆλος, coming after πυρός, which led to its omission in W. Sah reads simply "the flame of the fire."

[2] According to the later rabbinic theory of inspiration, even to assert that Moses uttered one word of the Torah on his own authority was to despise the Torah (Sifre 112, on Nu 15³¹).

argument from the less to the greater, which was the first of
Hillel's seven rules for exegesis, and which is similarly used by
Philo in *de Fuga*, 16, where, after quoting Ex 21¹⁵, he adds that
Moses here practically denies that there is any pardon for those
who blaspheme God (εἰ γὰρ οἱ τοὺς θνητοὺς κακηγορήσαντες γονεῖς
ἀπάγονται τὴν ἐπὶ θανάτῳ, τίνος ἀξίους χρὴ νομίζειν τιμωρίας τοὺς
τῶν ὅλων πατέρα καὶ ποιητὴν βλασφημεῖν ὑπομένοντας ;). There
is also a passage in *de Spec. Legibus* (ii. 254, 255) where Philo
asks, "If a man μὴ προσηκόντως ὀμνύς is guilty, πόσης ἄξιος
τιμωρίας ὁ τὸν ὄντως ὄντα θεὸν ἀρνούμενος ; "

τιμωρία originally meant vengeance. Διαφέρει δὲ τιμωρία καὶ κόλασις· ἡ
μὲν γὰρ κόλασις τοῦ πάσχοντος ἕνεκα ἐστιν, ἡ δὲ τιμωρία τοῦ ποιοῦντος, ἵνα
ἀποπληρωθῇ (Arist. *Rhetoric*, i. 10. 11 ; see Cope's *Introduction*, p. 232).
But it became broadened into the general sense of punishment, and this
obtained in Hellenistic Greek.

The threefold description of what is involved in the sin of
apostasy begins : ὁ τὸν υἱὸν τοῦ θεοῦ καταπατήσας, another expression for the thought of 6⁶, which recalls Zec 12³ (λίθον
καταπατούμενον πᾶσιν τοῖς ἔθνεσιν· πᾶς ὁ καταπατῶν αὐτὴν ἐμπαίζων
ἐμπαίξεται). Καταπατεῖν ὅρκια was the phrase for breaking oaths
(*Iliad*, 4¹⁵⁷) ; with a personal object, the verb denotes contempt of the most flagrant kind. Another aspect of the sin is
that a man has thereby κοινὸν ¹ ἡγησάμενος the sacrifice of Jesus ;
his action means that it is no more to him than an ordinary death
("communem," *d*), instead of a divine sacrifice which makes him
a partaker of the divine fellowship (see p. 145). Where Christ is
rejected, he is first despised ; outward abandonment of him
springs from some inward depreciation or disparagement. The
third aspect, καὶ τὸ πνεῦμα τῆς χάριτος (not τὸν νόμον Μωυσέως)
ἐνύβρισας, suggests that the writer had in mind the language of
Zec 12¹⁰ (ἐκχεῶ . . . πνεῦμα χάριτος καὶ οἰκτιρμοῦ), but πνεῦμα
χάριτος (contrasted here, as in Jn 1¹⁷, with the νόμος Μωυσέως)
is a periphrasis for πνεῦμα ἅγιον (6⁴), χάρις being chosen (4¹⁶ 12¹⁵)
to bring out the personal, gracious nature of the power so wantonly insulted.² Ἐνυβρίζειν is not a LXX term, and it generally
takes the dative. (Ἐν ᾧ ἡγιάσθη after ἡγησάμενος is omitted by
A and some MSS of Chrysostom.)

The sombre close (vv.³⁰· ³¹) of the warning is a reminder
that the living God punishes renegades. Φοβερόν (v.³¹) re-echoes
the φοβερά of v.²⁷, and the awful nature of the doom is brought
out by two quotations adapted from the OT. Ἐμοὶ ἐκδίκησις,

---

¹ Once in the LXX (Pr 15²³) in this sense.
² In *Test. Jud.* 18² the πνεῦμα χάριτος poured out upon men is the Spirit
as a gracious gift of God. But in He 10²⁹, as in Eph 4³⁰, it is the divine Spirit
wounded or outraged, the active retribution, however, being ascribed not to
the Spirit itself but to God.

ἐγὼ ἀνταποδώσω, is the same form of Dt 32³⁵ as is quoted in Ro
12¹⁹; it reproduces the Hebrew original more closely than the
LXX (ἐν ἡμέρᾳ ἐκδικήσεως ἀνταποδώσω), perhaps from some
current Greek version, unless the author of Hebrews borrowed
it from Paul.[1] Some of the same authorities as in 8¹² indeed
add, from Ro 12¹⁹, λέγει κύριος (‭א‬ᶜ A Dᶜ K L arm Theodoret,
Damasus, etc.). Κρινεῖ Κύριος τὸν λαὸν αὐτοῦ is from Dt 32³⁶. The
thought of the original, in both passages, is God avenging his
people on their foes and championing them, not punishing them;
but here this fate is assigned to all who put themselves outside
the range of God's mercy in the sacrifice of Jesus Christ; they fall
under God's retribution. Τὸ ἐμπεσεῖν εἰς χεῖρας θεοῦ is a phrase
used in a very different sense in 2 S 24¹⁴, Sir 2¹⁸; here it means,
to fall into the grasp of the God who punishes the disloyal[2]
or rebels against his authority. Thus the tyrant Antiochus is
threatened, in 2 Mac 7³¹, οὐ μὴ διαφύγῃς τὰς χεῖρας τοῦ θεοῦ. As
in 3¹², ζῶντος is added to θεοῦ to suggest that he is quick and
alive to inflict retribution. The writer is impressively reticent
on the nature of God's τιμωρία, even more reticent than Plato, in
one of the gravest warnings in Greek literature, the famous
passage in the Leges (904, 905) about the divine δίκη: Ταύτης
τῆς δίκης οὔτε σὺ μὴ πότε οὔτε εἰ ἄλλος ἀτυχὴς γενόμενος ἐπεύξηται
περιγενέσθαι θεῶν· ἣν πασῶν δικῶν διαφερόντως ἔταξάν τε οἱ τάξαντες
χρεών τε ἐξευλαβεῖσθαι τὸ παράπαν. οὐ γὰρ ἀμεληθήσῃ ποτὲ ὑπ'
αὐτῆς· οὐχ οὕτω σμικρὸς ὢν δύσῃ κατὰ τὸ τῆς γῆς βάθος, οὐδ' ὑψηλὸς
γενόμενος εἰς τὸν οὐρανὸν ἀναπτήσῃ, τείσεις δὲ αὐτῶν τὴν προσήκουσαν
τιμωρίαν εἴτ' ἐνθάδε μένων εἴτε καὶ ἐν Ἅιδου διαπορευθείς. Plato
altered the Homeric term δίκη θεῶν to suit his purpose; what
meant "way" or "habit," he turned into a weighty word for
"justice." The alteration is justified from his "preaching"
point of view, and the solemn note of the Greek sage's warning
is that of He 10²⁶ᶠ·; you cannot play fast and loose with God.

Yet, as at 6⁹, so here, the writer swiftly turns from warning to
encouragement, appealing to his readers to do better than he
feared, and appealing to all that was best in them. "Why
throw away the gains of your fine record in the past? You have
not long to wait for your reward. Hold on for a little longer."
This is the theme of vv.³²⁻³⁹:

[1] Paul cites the saying to prove that private Christians need not and must
not take revenge into their own hands, since God is sure to avenge his people
on their adversaries. Which is close to the idea of the original. Our author
uses the text to clinch a warning that God will punish (κρινεῖ= "punibit," not
"judicabit") his people for defying and deserting him.
[2] So the martyr Eleazar protests in 2 Mac 6²⁶, as he refuses to save his
life by unworthy compromise: εἰ γὰρ καὶ ἐπὶ τοῦ παρόντος ἐξελοῦμαι τὴν ἐξ
ἀνθρώπων τιμωρίαν, ἀλλὰ τὰς τοῦ παντοκράτορος χεῖρας οὔτε ζῶν οὔτε ἀποθανὼν
ἐκφεύξομαι.

[32] *Recall the former days when, after you were enlightened* (φωτισθέντες, as 6⁴), *you endured a hard struggle of suffering,* [33] *partly by being held up yourselves to obloquy and anguish, partly by making common cause with those who fared in this way ;* [34] *for you did sympathize with the prisoners, and you took the confiscation of your own belongings cheerfully, conscious that elsewhere you had higher, you had lasting possessions.* [35] *Now do not drop that confidence of yours ; it* (ἥτις, as in 2³) *carries with it a rich hope of reward.* [36] *Steady patience is what you need, so that after doing the will of God you may* (like Abraham, 6¹⁵) *get what you have been promised.* [37] *For "in a little, a very little" now,*

"*The Coming One* (9²⁹) *will arrive without delay.*
[38] *Meantime my just man shall live on by his faith ;
if he shrinks back, my soul takes no delight in him."*

[39] *We are not the men to shrink back and be lost, but to have faith and so to win our souls.*

The excellent record of these Christians in the past consisted in their common brotherliness (6¹⁰), which is now viewed in the light of the hardships they had had to endure, soon after they became Christians. The storm burst on them early; they weathered it nobly ; why give up the voyage, when it is nearly done ? It is implied that any trouble at present is nothing to what they once passed through. Ἀναμιμνήσκεσθε δὲ τὰς πρότερον ἡμέρας (v.³²): memory plays a large part in the religious experience, and is often as here a stimulus. In these earlier days they had (vv.³². ³³) two equally creditable experiences (τοῦτο μέν . . . τοῦτο δέ, a good classical idiom) ; they bore obloquy and hardship manfully themselves, and they also made common cause with their fellow-sufferers. By saying ἄθλησιν παθημάτων, the writer means, that the παθήματα made the ἄθλησις which tested their powers (2¹⁰). Ἄθλησις—the metaphor is athletic, as in 12¹ —came to denote a martyr's death in the early church ; but no such red significance attaches to it here. Apparently the persecution was not pushed to the last extreme (12⁴); all survived it. Hence there can be no allusion to the "ludibria" of Nero's outburst against the Roman Christians, in (v.³³) θεατριζόμενοι, which is used in a purely figurative sense (so θέατρον in 1 Co 4⁹), like ἐκθεατρίζειν in Polybius (e.g. iii. 91. 10, διόπερ ἔμελλον . . . ἐκθεατριεῖν δὲ τοὺς πολεμίους φυγομαχοῦντας). The meaning is that they had been held up to public derision, scoffed and sneered at, accused of crime and vice, unjustly suspected and denounced. All this had been, the writer knew, a real ordeal, particularly because the stinging contempt and insults had had to be borne in the open. Ὅταν μὲν γάρ τις ὀνειδίζηται καθ᾽ ἑαυτόν, λυπηρὸν μέν, πολλῷ δὲ πλέον, ὅταν ἐπὶ πάντων (Chrysostom). They had been exposed to ὀνειδισμοῖς τε καὶ θλίψεσι, taunts and scorn that tempted one to feel shame (an experience which our author evidently felt keenly), as well as to wider hardships, both insults and injuries. All this they had stood manfully. Better still, their personal troubles had not rendered them indisposed to care for their fellow-sufferers, τῶν οὕτως (*i.e.* in the παθήματα) ἀναστρεφομένων (13¹⁸). They exhibited the virtue of practical sympathy, urged in 13³, at any risk or cost to themselves (κοινωνοὶ . . . γενηθέντες with the genitive, as in LXX of Pr 28¹⁴, Is 1²³).

The ideas of v.³³ are now (v.³⁴) taken up in the reverse order (as in 5¹·⁷). Καὶ γὰρ τοῖς δεσμίοις συνεπαθήσατε, imprisonment being for some a form of their παθήματα. Christians in prison had to be visited and fed by their fellow-members. For συμπαθεῖν (cp. 4¹⁵) as between man and man, see *Test. Sym.* 3⁶ καὶ λοιπὸν συμπαθεῖ τῷ φθονουμένῳ: *Test. Benj.* 4⁴ τῷ ἀσθενοῦντι συμπάσχει: Ign. *Rom.* 6⁴ συμπαθείτω μοι: and the saying which is quoted in Meineke's *Frag. Comic. Graec.* iv. 52, ἐκ τοῦ παθεῖν γίγνωσκε καὶ τὸ συμπαθεῖν· καὶ σοὶ γὰρ ἄλλος συμπαθήσεται παθών. They had also borne their own losses with more than equanimity,[1] with actual gladness (μετὰ χαρᾶς, the same thought as in Ro 5³, though differently worked out), γινώσκοντες (with accus. and infinitive) ἔχειν ἑαυτούς (=ὑμᾶς, which is actually read here by Cosmas Indicopleustes, 348*a*; ἑαυτούς is not emphatic any more than ἑαυτῶν in v.²⁵) κρείσσονα (a favourite term of the author) ὕπαρξιν (Ac 2³⁵) καὶ μένουσαν (13¹⁴, the thought of Mt 6²⁰). Τὴν ἁρπαγὴν τῶν ὑπαρχόντων ὑμῶν (cp. Polybius, iv. 17. 4, ἁρπαγὰς ὑπαρχόντων) implies that their own property had been either confiscated by the authorities or plundered in some mob-riot. Note the paronomasia of ὑπαρχόντων and ὕπαρξιν, and the place of this loss in the list of human evils as described in the *Laches*, 195 E (εἴτε τῷ θάνατος εἴτε νόσος εἴτε ἀποβολὴ χρημάτων ἔσται).

There is no question of retaliation; the primitive Christians whom the author has in view had no means of returning injuries for injuries, or even of claiming redress. Thus the problem raised and solved by contemporary moralists does not present itself to the writer; he does not argue, as, *e.g.*, Maximus of Tyre did in the next century (*Dissert.* ii.), that the good man should treat the loss of property as a trifle, and despise the futile attempts of his enemies to injure him thus, the soul or real self being beyond the reach of such evil-doers. The tone is rather that of Tob 4²¹ (μὴ φοβοῦ, παιδίον, ὅτι ἐπτωχεύσαμεν· ὑπάρχει σοὶ πολλά, ἐὰν φοβηθῇς τὸν θεόν κτλ.), except that our author notes the glow (μετὰ χαρᾶς) of an enthusiastic unworldliness, which was more than any Stoic resignation or even any quiet acquiescence in providence; he suggests in ἑαυτούς that, while others might seize and hold their property, they themselves had a possession of which no one could rob them. Seneca (*Ep.* ix. 18-19) quotes the famous reply of the philosophic Stilpo to Demetrius Poliorketes, who asked him, after the siege and sack of Megara, if he had lost anything in the widespread ruin, Stilpo answered that he had suffered no loss; "omnia bona mecum sunt." That is, Seneca explains, he did not consider anything as "good" which could be taken from him. This helps to illustrate what the author of Πρὸς Ἑβραίους means. As Epictetus put it, there are more losses than the loss of property (ii. 10. 14,

---

[1] This is not conveyed in προσεδέξασθε, which here, as in 11³⁵, simply means "accepted," not "welcomed."

ἀλλὰ δεῖ σε κέρμα ἀπολέσαι, ἵνα ζημιωθῇς, ἄλλου <δ'> οὐδενὸς ἀπώλεια ζημιοῖ τὸν ἄνθρωπον ;). A similar view pervades the fine homiletic misinterpretation of Dt 6⁵ in *Berachoth* 9⁵ "Man is bound to bless [God] for evil as for good, for it is said, *Thou shalt love Jahweh thy God with all thy heart and with all thy soul and with all thy strength. With all thy heart* means, with both yetzers, the good and the bad alike : *with all thy soul* means, even if he deprive thee of thy soul : *with all thy strength* means, with all thy possessions." A similar view is cited in Sifre 32. Apollonius, in the last quarter of the second century, declares : "We do not resent having our goods taken from us, because we know that, whether we live or die, we are the Lord's " (Conybeare, *Monuments of Early Christianity*, p. 44).

No persecution known to us in the primitive church answers to the data of this passage. But some sidelights are thrown upon it by Philo's vivid account of the earlier anti-Semite riots in Alexandria. He notes that even those who sympathized with the persecuted were punished : τῶν δ' ὡς ἀλθῶς πεπονθότων φίλοι καὶ συγγενεῖς, ὅτι μόνον ταῖς τῶν προσηκόντων συμφόραις συνήλγησαν, ἀπήγοντο, ἐμαστιγοῦντο, ἐτροχίζοντο, καὶ μετὰ πάσας τὰς αἰκίας, ὅσας ἐδύνατο χωρῆσαι τὰ σώματα αὐτοῖς, ἡ τελευταία καὶ ἔφεδρος τιμωρία σταυρὸς ἦν (*in Flaccum*, 7 : *n. b.* neither here nor in 11³⁵ᶠ· does the author of Πρὸς Ἑβραίους mention the cross as a punishment for sufferers). Philo (*ibid.* 9) continues : πενία χαλεπὸν μὲν, καὶ μάλισθ' ὅταν κατασκευάζηται πρὸς ἐχθρῶν, ἔλαττον δὲ τῆς εἰς τὰ σώματα ὕβρεως, κἂν ᾖ βραχυτάτη. He repeats this (10), telling how Flaccus maltreated Jews who had been already stripped of their property, ἵνα οἱ μὲν ὑπομενῶσι διττὰς συμφοράς, πενίαν ὁμοῦ καὶ τὴν ἐν τοῖς σώμασιν ὕβριν, καὶ οἱ μὲν δρῶντες, ὥσπερ ἐν τοῖς θεατρίκοις μίμοις καθυπερκρίνοντο τοὺς πάσχοντας.

Three items of textual corruption occur in v.³⁴. (*a*) δεσμίοις (p¹³ A D* H 33. 104. 241. 424**. 635. 1245. 1288. 1739. 1908. 1912. 2005 r vg syrʰᵏˡ boh arm Chrys.) was eventually corrupted into δεσμοῖς (μου) in ℵ Dᶜ Ψ 256. 1288* etc. vt eth Clem. Orig.), a misspelling (*i.e.* δεσμοῖς) which, with *μου* added to make sense, contributed to the impression that Paul had written the epistle (Ph 1⁷· ¹⁵ᶠ·, Col 4¹⁸). Compare the text implied in the (Pelagian ?) prologue to Paul's epp. in vg : "nam et vinctis compassi estis, et rapinam bonorum vestrorum cum gaudio suscepistis."

(*b*) ἑαυτούς (p¹³ ℵ A H lat boh Clem. Orig. etc.) suffered in the course of transmission ; it was either omitted (by C) or altered into ἑαυτοῖς (D K L Ψ, etc., Chrys.) or ἐν ἑαυτοῖς (1. 467. 489. 642. 920. 937. 1867. 1873), the dative being an attempt to bring out the idea that they had in their own religious personalities a possession beyond the reach of harm and loss, an idea pushed by some editors even into ἑαυτούς, but too subtle for the context.

(*c*) ὕπαρξιν was eventually defined by the addition of ἐν (τοῖς) οὐρανοῖς (from Ph 3²⁰ ?) in ℵᶜ Dᶜ H** Ψ 6. 203. 326. 506. 1288. 1739 syr arm Chrys. etc.

The reminder of vv.³²⁻³⁴ is now (³⁵⁻³⁹) pressed home. Μὴ ἀποβάλητε οὖν τὴν παρρησίαν ὑμῶν, as evinced in μετὰ χαρᾶς . . . γινώσκοντες κτλ. The phrase occurs in Dio Chrys. *Orat.* 34³⁹ (δέδοικα μὴ τελέως ἀποβάλητε τὴν παρρησίαν) and elsewhere in the

sense of losing courage, but παρρησία retains its special force
(3⁶) here, and ἀποβάλλειν is the opposite of κατέχειν ("nolite
itaque amittere," vg). The παρρησία is to be maintained, ἥτις
ἔχει μεγάλην μισθαποδοσίαν (as 11²⁶), it is so sure of bringing
its reward in the bliss promised by God to cheerful loyalty.
Compare the saying of the contemporary rabbi Tarphon : "faithful is the Master of thy work, who will pay thee the reward of
thy work, and know thou that the recompense of the reward of
the righteous is for the time to come" (*Pirke Aboth* 2¹⁹).

Epictetus makes a similar appeal, in iv. 3. 3 f., not to throw away all that
one has gained in character by failing to maintain one's philosophical
principles when one has suffered some loss of property.   When you lose any
outward possession, recollect what you gain instead of it (τί ἀντ' αὐτοῦ
περιποιῇ) ; otherwise, you imperil the results of all your past conscientiousness
(ὅσα νῦν προσέχεις σεαυτῷ, μέλλεις ἐκχεῖν ἅπαντα ταῦτα καὶ ἀνατρέπειν).   And
it takes so little to do this ; a mere swerve from reasonable principle (μικρᾶς
ἀποστροφῆς τοῦ λόγου), a slight drowsiness, and all is lost (ἀπῆλθεν πάντα τὰ
μέχρι νῦν συνειλεγμένα).   No outward possession is worth having, Epictetus
continues, if it means that one ceases to be free, to be God's friend, to serve
God willingly.   I must not set my heart on anything else ; God does not
allow that, for if He had chosen, He would have made such outward goods
good for me (ἀγαθὰ πεποιήκει αὐτὰ ἂν ἐμοί).   Maximus of Tyre again argued
that while, for example, men might be willing to endure pain and discomfort
for the sake and hope of regaining health, "if you take away the hope of good
to come, you also take away the power of enduring present ills" (εἰ ἀφέλοις
τινὰ ἐλπίδα τῶν μελλόντων ἀγαθῶν, ἀφαιρήσεις καὶ τινὰ αἵρεσιν τῶν παρόντων
κακῶν, *Diss.* xxxiii).

To retain the Christian παρρησία means still ὑπομένειν, no
longer perhaps in the earlier sense (ὑπεμείνατε, v.³²), and yet sometimes what has to be borne is harder, for sensitive people, than
any actual loss.   Such obedience to the will of God assumes
many phases, from endurance of suffering to sheer waiting, and
the latter is now urged (v.³⁶). Ὑπομονῆς γὰρ ἔχετε χρείαν (5¹²) ἵνα
τὸ θέλημα τοῦ θεοῦ ποιήσαντες (suggested by 10⁷⁻⁹) κομίσησθε τὴν
ἐπαγγελίαν (6¹² 10²³).   "Though the purpose of ὑπομονή is
contained in the clause ἵνα . . . ἐπαγγελίαν, yet the function of
this clause in the sentence is not telic.   Its office is not to
express the purpose of the principal clause, but to set forth a
result (conceived, not actual) of which the possesion of ὑπομονή
is the necessary condition" (Burton, *NT Moods and Tenses*,
p. 93). Ὑπομονή and ὑπομένειν echo through this passage and
12¹⁻⁷, the idea of tenacity being expressed in 10³⁸–11⁴⁰ by πίστις.
Ὑπομονή here as in the LXX (cp. *Diat.* 3548a–c) implies the
conviction of "hope that the evil endured will be either remedied
or proved to be no evil." Κομίσησθε does not mean to get back
or recover, nor to gather in, but simply as in the κοινή to receive,
to get what has been promised (τὴν ἐπαγγελίαν) rather than to
get it as our due (which is the idea of μισθαποδοσίαν), though

what is promised is in one sense our due, since the promise can
only be fulfilled for those who carry out its conditions (6¹⁰). And
it will soon be fulfilled. "Have patience; it is not long now."
Again he clinches his appeal with an OT word, this time from the
prophets (vv.³⁷·³⁸). Ἔτι γὰρ (om. p¹³) μικρὸν (sc. ἔστιν) ὅσον ὅσον.
In *de mutat. nomin.* 44, Philo comments upon the aptness and
significance of the word ναί in the promise of Gn 17¹⁹ (τί γὰρ
εὐπρεπέστερον ἢ τἀγαθὰ ἐπινεύειν θεῷ καὶ ταχέως ὁμολογεῖν;). Our
author has a similar idea in mind, though he is eschatological, as
Philo is not. Ὅσον ὅσον is a variant in D (on Lk 5³) for ὀλίγον.
The phrase occurs in Aristoph. *Wasps*, 213 (τί οὐκ ἀπεκοιμηθήσαν
ὅσον ὅσον στίλην), and elsewhere, but here it is a reminiscence of
the LXX of Is 26²⁰ (μικρὸν ὅσον ὅσον). Hence, although μικρὸν
ὅσον is also used, as by Philo, the omission of the second ὅσον in
the text of Hebrews by some cursives (*e.g.* 6. 181. 326. 1836)
and Eusebius is unjustified. The words serve to introduce the
real citation, apparently suggested by the term ὑπομονῆς (v.³⁶),
from Hab 2³·⁴ ἐὰν ὑστερήσῃ, ὑπόμεινον αὐτόν, ὅτι ἐρχόμενος ἥξει
καὶ οὐ μὴ χρονίσῃ· ἐὰν ὑποστείληται, οὐκ εὐδοκεῖ ἡ ψυχή μου ἐν αὐτῷ·
ὁ δὲ δίκαιος ἐκ πίστεώς μου ζήσεται, especially as the LXX makes
the object of patient hope not the fulfilment of the vision, *i.e.*
the speedy downfall of the foreign power, but either messiah
or God. (*a*) The author of Hebrews further adds ὁ to ἐρχόμενος,
applying the words to Christ; (*b*) changes οὐ μὴ χρονίσῃ into οὐ
χρονεῖ:[1] (*c*) reverses the order of the last two clauses, and (*d*)
shifts μου in front of ἐκ πίστεως, as in the A text of the LXX.
In the MSS of Hebrews, μου is entirely omitted by p¹³ D H K
L P W cop eth Chrys. etc., to conform the text to the Pauline
quotation (Ro 1¹⁷, Gal 3¹¹), while the original LXX text, with
μου after πίστεως, is preserved in D* d syrᵖᵉˢʰ ʰᵏˡ etc. This text,
or at any rate its Hebrew original, meant that the just man (*i.e.*
the Israelite) lived by God being faithful to his covenant with
the nation. In Πρὸς Ἑβραίους the idea is that the just man of
God is to live by his own πίστις or loyalty, as he holds on and
holds out till the end, timidity meaning ἀπώλεια (v.³⁹), while the
ζωή promised by God as the reward of human loyalty is the
outcome of πίστις (ἐκ πίστεως). But our author is interested in
πίστις rather than in ζωή. The latter is not one of his categories,
in the sense of eternal life; this idea he prefers to express
otherwise. What he quotes the verse for is its combination of
God's speedy recompense and of the stress on human πίστις,
which he proceeds to develop at length. The note struck in ὁ
δὲ δίκαιός μου also echoes on and on through the following
passage (11⁴ Ἄβελ . . . ἐμαρτυρήθη εἶναι δίκαιος, 11⁷ Νῶε . . .

---

[1] This second future, or χρονίσει, p¹³ א* D*, is read by some editors (*e.g.*
Tregelles, W-H, B. Weiss).

τῆς κατὰ πίστιν δικαιοσύνης, 11³³ ἠργάσαντο δικαιοσύνην, 12¹¹ καρπὸν
ἀποδίδωσιν δικαιοσύνης, 12²³ πνεύμασι δικαίων τετελειωμένων).   The
aim of (c) was to make it clear, as it is not clear in the LXX,
that the subject of ὑποστείληται was ὁ δίκαιος, and also to make
the warning against apostasy the climax.   Καὶ ἐὰν ὑποστείληται—
not simply in fear (as, e.g., Dem. adv. Pant. 630, μηδὲν ὑποστελ-
λόμενον μηδ᾿ αἰσχυνόμενον), but in the fear which makes men (cp.
Gal 2¹²) withdraw from their duty or abandon their convictions—
οὐκ εὐδοκεῖ ἡ ψυχή μου ἐν αὐτῷ.   It is a fresh proof of the freedom
which the writer uses, that he refers these last seven words to
God as the speaker; in Habakkuk the words are uttered by the
prophet himself.   Then, with a ringing, rallying note, he expresses
himself confident about the issue.   Ἡμεῖς δὲ οὐκ ἐσμὲν ὑποστολῆς
(predicate genitive, as in 12¹¹, unless ἄνδρες or ἐκ is supplied) εἰς
ἀπώλειαν, ἀλλὰ πίστεως εἰς περιποίησιν ψυχῆς (=ζήσεται, v.³⁸).
Περιποίησις occurs three times in the LXX (2 Ch 14¹³, Hag 2⁹,
Mal 3¹⁷) and several times in the NT, but never with ψυχῆς,
though the exact phrase was known to classical Greek as an
equivalent for saving one's own life.   Ὑποστόλη, its antithesis,
which in Jos. B.J. ii. 277 means dissimulation, has this new
sense stamped on it, after ὑποστείληται.

The exhortation is renewed in 12¹ᶠ·, but only after a long
paean on πίστις, with historical illustrations, to prove that πίστις
has always meant hope and patience for loyal members of the
People (11¹⁻⁴⁰).   The historical résumé (11³⁻⁴⁰), by which the
writer seeks to kindle the imagination and conscience of his
readers, is prefaced by a brief introduction (11¹⁻³):

¹ Now faith means we are confident of what we hope for, convinced of what
we do not see.   ² It was for this that the men of old won their record.   ³ It
is by faith we understand that the world was fashioned by the word of God,
and thus the visible was made out of the invisible.

Calvin rightly protested against any division here, as an interruption to the thought: "quisquis hic fecit initium capitis
undecimi, perperam contextum abrupit."   The following argument of 11¹⁻⁴⁰ flows directly out of 10³⁵⁻³⁹: ὑπομονή is justified
and sustained by πίστις, and we have now a λόγος παρακλήσεως
on μιμηταὶ τῶν διὰ πίστεως καὶ μακροθυμίας κληρονομούντων τὰς
ἐπαγγελίας (6¹²).   Hitherto the only historical characters who
have been mentioned have been Abraham, Melchizedek, Moses,
Aaron, and Joshua; and Abraham alone has been mentioned
for his πίστις; now a long list of heroes and heroines of πίστει
is put forward, from Abel to the Maccabean martyrs.   But first
(vv.¹⁻³) a general word on faith.   Ἔστιν δὲ πίστις κτλ. (v.¹).   It
is needless to put a comma after πίστις, i.e., "there is such a
thing as faith, faith really exists."   Εἰμί at the beginning of a

sentence does not necessarily carry this meaning ; cp. *e.g.* Wis
7¹ εἰμὶ μὲν κἀγὼ θνητός, Lk 8¹¹ ἔστιν δὲ αὕτη ἡ παραβολή (Jn 21²⁵
and 1 Jn 5¹⁷ etc.). Ἔστιν here is simply the copula, πίστις being
the subject, and ἐλπιζομένων ὑπόστασις the predicate. This turn
of phrase is common in Philo, who puts ἔστι first in descriptions
or definitions (e.g. *Leg. Allegor.* iii. 75, ἔστι δὲ στεναγμὸς σφοδρὰ
καὶ ἐπιτεταμένη λύπη : *quod deus immut.* 19, ἔστι δὲ εὐχὴ μὲν
αἴτησις ἀγαθῶν παρὰ θεοῦ κτλ.). Needless difficulties have been
raised about what follows. Ὑπόστασις is to be understood in the
sense of 3¹⁴ "une assurance certaine" (Ménégoz) ; "faith is a
sure confidence of thynges which are hoped for, and a certaynetie
of thynges which are not seyne" (Tyndale), the opposite of
ὑποστόλη. In the parallel clause, πράγματων ἔλεγχος οὐ βλεπομένων (which in Attic Greek would have been ὧν ἄν τις μὴ ὁρᾷ),
grammatically πράγματων might go with ἐλπιζομένων instead of
with βλεπομένων, for the sake of emphasis (so Chrysostom,
Oecumenius, von Soden, etc.) ; the sense would be unaffected,
but the balance of the rhythm would be upset. Ἔλεγχος is used
in a fresh sense, as the subjective "conviction" (the English
word has acquired the same double sense as the Greek) ; as
Euthymius said, it is an equivalent for πραγμάτων ἀοράτων πληροφορία (so syr arm eth). The writer could find no Greek term
for the idea, and therefore struck out a fresh application for
ἔλεγχος. As for ἐλπιζομένων . . . οὐ βλεπομένων (ὃ γὰρ βλέπει τις,
τί ἐλπίζει ; εἰ δὲ ὃ οὐ βλέπομεν ἐλπίζομεν δι᾽ ὑπομονῆς ἀπεκδεχόμεθα,
Ro 8²⁴· ²⁵), the unseen realities of which faith is confident are
almost entirely in the future as promised by God, though, as the
sequel shows, τὰ οὐ βλεπόμενα (*e.g.* vv.³· ⁷· ⁸· ²⁷) are not precisely
the same as τὰ ἐλπιζόμενα. It cannot be too emphatically
pointed out that the writer did not mean to say : (*a*) that faith
gave substance or reality to unseen hopes, though this is the
interpretation of the Greek fathers (Chrysostom, for example,
argues : ἐπειδὴ τὰ ἐν ἐλπίδι ἀνυπόστατα εἶναι δοκεῖ, ἡ πίστις ὑπόστασιν αὐτοῖς χαρίζεται· μᾶλλον δὲ οὐ χαρίζεται ἀλλ᾽ αὐτό ἐστιν
οὐσία αὐτῶν). When the writer declares that it is by faith we
understand that the world was created, he does not mean that
faith imparts reality to the creation ; nor, when he says, *e.g.*, the
patriarchs lived in the expectation of a celestial Fatherland,
that they thereby made this more real to themselves. No doubt
this was true in a sense ; but the author's point is that just
because these objects of hope were real, because, *e.g.*, God had
prepared for them a City, therefore they were justified in having
faith. It is faith as the reflex of eternal realities or rewards
promised by God which is fundamental in this chapter, the faith
by which a good man lives. (*b*) Similarly, faith is not the ἔλεγχος
of things unseen in the sense of "proof," which could only mean

that it tests, or rather attests, their reality. The existence of
human faith no doubt proves that there is some unseen object
which calls it out, but the writer wishes to show, not the reality
of these unseen ends of God—he assumes these—but the fact
and force of believing in them with absolute confidence. Such
erroneous interpretations arise out of the notion that the writer
is giving an abstract definition of πίστις, whereas he is describing
it, in view of what follows, as an active conviction which moves
and moulds human conduct. The happiest description of it is,
"seeing Him who is invisible" (v.²⁷); and this idea is applied
widely; sometimes it is belief in God as against the world and its
forces, particularly the forces of human injustice or of death,
sometimes belief in the spirit as against the senses, sometimes
again (and this is prominent in 11⁵ᶠ·) belief in the future as
against the present.

In the papyri (e.g. in OP. ii. pp. 153, 176, where in the plural it = "the
whole body of documents bearing on the ownership of a person's property . . .
deposited in the archives, and forming the evidence of ownership") ὑπόστασις means occasionally the entire collection of title-deeds by which a man
establishes his right to some property (cp. Moulton in Manchester Theological
Essays, i. 174; Expositor, Dec. 1903, pp. 438 f.); but while this might
suggest the metaphor, the metaphor means "confident assurance." The
original sense of substance or reality, as in the de Mundo, 4 (συλλήβδην δὲ τῶν
ἐν ἀέρι φαντασμάτων τὰ μέν ἐστι κατ᾿ ἔμφασιν τὰ δὲ καθ᾿ ὑπόστασιν), survives
in Dante's interpretation (Paradiso, xxiv. 61 f.). He quotes the words as a
definition of faith :

"Fede è sustanzia di cose sperate,
   ed argumento delle non parventi,"

adding that he understands this to be its "quidity" or essence. But the
notion that faith imparts a real existence to its object is read into the text.
Faith as ὑπόστασις is "realization" of the unseen, but "realization" only in
our popular, psychological sense of the term. The legal or logical sense of
ἔλεγχος, as proof (in classical Greek and elsewhere, e.g. Jos. BJ. iv. 5. 4,
ἦν δ᾿ οὔτ᾿ ἔλεγχός τις τῶν κατηγορουμένων, οὔτε τεκμήριον) is out of place
here. The existence of human faith is in one sense a proof that an invisible
order exists, which can alone explain men acting as they do ἐν πίστει. But
the writer assumes that, and declares that πίστις lives and moves in the
steady light of the unseen realities. The sense of "test," as in Epictetus,
iii. 10. 11 (ἐνθάδ᾿ ὁ ἔλεγχος τοῦ πράγματος, ἡ δοκιμασία τοῦ φιλοσοφοῦντος),
is as impossible here as that of "rebuke"; the force of πίστις in 11³⁻⁴⁰
rests on its subjective sense as an inner conviction, which forms a motive for
human life, and this determines the meaning of ὑπόστασις and ἔλεγχος as
applied to it in the introductory description.

This connexion of faith with the future is emphasized by
Philo in de Migratione Abrahami, 9, commenting on Gn 12¹ ἥν
σοι δείξω. It is δείξω, not δείκνυμι, he points out—εἰς μαρτυρίαν
πίστεως ἣν ἐπίστευσεν ἡ ψυχὴ θεῷ, οὐκ ἐκ τῶν ἀποτελεσμάτων
ἐπιδεικνυμένη τὸ εὐχάριστον, ἀλλ᾿ ἐκ προσδοκίας τῶν μελλόντων
. . . νομίσασα ἤδη παρεῖναι τὰ μὴ παρόντα διὰ τὴν τοῦ ὑποσχο-

μένου βεβαιότητα πίστιν [cp. He 10²³], ἀγαθὸν τέλειον, ἆθλον
εὕρηται. Faith thus relies upon God's promise and eagerly expects what is to come; indeed it lives for and in the future.
So our writer uses πίστις, almost as Paul used ἐλπίς (psychologically the two being often indistinguishable). Nor is this πίστις
a novelty in our religion (v.²), he adds, ἐν ταύτῃ γὰρ ἐμαρτυρήθησαν
(7⁸) οἱ πρεσβύτεροι. Ἐν = διὰ (ταύτης) as in 4⁶ 6¹⁶ 9²² 10¹⁰; δι'
ἧς ἐμαρτυρήθη (v.⁴), μαρτυρηθέντες διὰ τῆς πίστεως (v.³⁹). Οἱ
πρεσβύτεροι (= οἱ πατέρες, 1¹) never bears this exact sense elsewhere in the NT, the nearest¹ parallel being Mt 15² = Mk 7³·⁵
(τὴν παράδοσιν τῶν πρεσβυτέρων). Philo (de Abrahamo 46),
indeed, noting that Abraham the man of faith is the first man
called πρεσβύτερος in scripture (Gn 24¹), reflects that this is
significant; ὁ γὰρ ἀληθείᾳ πρεσβύτερος οὐκ ἐν μήκει χρόνων ἀλλ' ἐν
ἐπαινετῷ καὶ τελείῳ βίῳ θεωρεῖται. Aged worldly people can only
be called longlived children, τὸν δὲ φρονήσεως καὶ σοφίας καὶ τῆς
πρὸς θεὸν πίστεως ἐρασθέντα λέγοι τις ἂν ἐνδίκως εἶναι πρεσβύτερον.
But our author weaves no such fancies round the word, though
he probably understood the term in an honorific sense (cp.
Philo, de Sobrietate, 4, πρεσβύτερον . . . τὸν γέρως καὶ τιμῆς ἄξιον
ὀνομάζει). For ἐμαρτυρήθησαν in this sense of getting a good
report, cp. B. Latyschev's Inscript. Antiquae Orae Septent. i.
21²⁶ᶠ· ἐμαρτυρήθη τοὺς ὑπὲρ φιλίας κινδύνους . . . παραβολευσά-
μενος: Syll. 366²⁸ (i A.D.) ἀρχιτέκτονας μαρτυρηθέντας ὑπὸ τῆς
ὀ͙εμνοτάτης [βουλῆς], and the instances quoted in Deissmann's
Bible Studies (265).

Before describing the scriptural record of the πρεσβύτεροι,
however, the writer pauses to point out the supreme proof of
πίστις as πραγμάτων ἔλεγχος οὐ βλεπομένων. The very world
within which they showed their faith and within which we are to
show our faith, was the outcome of what is invisible (v.³), and
this conviction itself is an act of faith. Πίστει νοοῦμεν (cp.
Ro 1²⁰: "νοεῖν is in Hellenistic Greek the current word for the
apprehension of the divine in nature," A. T. Goodrick on Wis
13⁴) κατηρτίσθαι (of creation, Ps 73¹⁶ σὺ κατηρτίσω ἥλιον καὶ
σελήνην) τοὺς αἰῶνας (1²) ῥήματι θεοῦ (the divine fiat here), εἰς
(with consecutive infinitive) τὸ μὴ ἐκ φαινομένων τὸ βλεπόμενον
γεγονέναι (perfect of permanence). The μή goes with φαινομένων,
but is thrown before the preposition as, e.g., in Ac 1⁵ οὐ μετὰ
πολλὰς ταύτας ἡμέρας (according to a familiar classical construction, Blass, § 433. 3).² Faith always answers to revelation,

---

¹ W. Brandt (Jüdische Reinheitslehre und ihre Beschreibung in den
Evangelien, 1910, pp. 2, 3) thinks that this expression might apply to the
more recent teachers as well as to the ancient authorities.

² In 2 Mac 7²⁸ οὐκ ἐξ ὄντων ἐποίησεν αὐτὰ ὁ θεός (A), the οὐκ goes with
the verb.

and creation is the first revelation of God to man.   Creation by
the fiat of God was the orthodox doctrine of Judaism, and
anyone who read the OT would accept it as the one theory
about the origin of the world (cp. *e.g.* the description of God in
the Mechilta, 33*b*, on Ex 14³¹ etc. as "He who spoke and the
world was," שָׁאָמַן וְהָיָה הָעוֹלָם, and Apoc. Bar. 14¹⁷: "when of old
there was no world with its inhabitants, Thou didst devise and
speak with a word, and forthwith the works of creation stood
before Thee").   But the explicitness of this sentence about
creation out of what is invisible, suggests that the writer had
other views in mind, which he desired to repudiate.   Possibly
Greek theories like those hinted at in Wis 10¹⁷ about the world ¹
being created ἐξ ἀμόρφου ὕλης, or the statement in the *de
aeternitate mundi*, 2, where Philo declares ἐκ τοῦ μὴ ὄντος οὐδὲν
γίνεται, quoting Empedocles to this effect, though elsewhere Philo
does agree that the world was made out of nothing, as, *e.g.*, in the
de Somniis, i. 13 (ὁ θεὸς τὰ πάντα γεννήσας οὐ μόνον εἰς τοὐμφανὲς
ἤγαγεν ἀλλὰ καὶ ἃ πρότερον οὐκ ἦν ἐποίησεν, οὐ δημιουργὸς μόνον
ἀλλὰ καὶ κτίστης αὐτὸς ὤν, cp. also Apoc. Bar. 21⁴: "O Thou
. . . that hast called from the beginning of the world that which
did not yet exist," and Slav. En. 24²: "I will tell thee now what
things I created from the non-existent, and what visible things
from the invisible").   What the μὴ φαινόμενα were, our author
does not suggest.   R. Akiba is said to have applied the words
of Ps 101⁷ to anyone who rashly speculated on the original
material of the world.   Our author does not speculate; it is
very doubtful if he intends (Windisch, M'Neill) to agree with
Philo's idea (in the *de opificio Mundi*, 16, *de confus. ling.* 34) of the
φαινόμενος οὗτος κόσμος being modelled on the ἀσώματος καὶ
νοητός or archetypal ideas, for the language of 8⁵ is insufficient
to bear the weight of this inference.

To take εἰς τὸ . . . γεγονέναι as final, is a forced construction.   The
phrase does not describe the motive of κατηρτίσθαι, and if the writer had
meant, "so that we might know the seen came from the unseen," ² he would
have written this, instead of allowing the vital words *might know* to be
supplied.

The roll-call of the πρεσβύτεροι (vv.⁴ᶠ·) opens with Abel and
Enoch, two men who showed their πίστις before the deluge
(vv.⁴⁻⁶).   One was murdered, the other, as the story went, never
died ; and the writer uses both tales to illustrate his point about
πίστις.

¹ LXX of Gn 1² ἡ δὲ γῆ ἦν ἀόρατος καὶ ἀκατασκεύαστος.
² At an early period τὸ βλεπόμενον was altered into τὰ βλεπόμενα
(D K L Ψ 6. 104. 218. 326. 1288. r vg syr arm), to conform with the previous
plurals βλεπομένων and φαινομένων.

⁴ *It was by faith* (πίστει, the rhetorical anaphora repeated throughout the section) *that Abel offered God a richer sacrifice than Cain did, and thus* (δι' ἧς, sc. πίστεως) *won from God the record of being "just," on the score of what he gave ; he died, but by his faith he is speaking to us still.* ⁵ *It was by faith that Enoch was taken to heaven, so that he never died* ("*he was not overtaken by death, for God had taken him away*"). *For before he was taken to heaven, his record was that* "*he had satisfied God*"; ⁶ *and apart from faith it is impossible* (ἀδύνατον, sc. ἐστι) "*to satisfy him," for the man who draws near to God must believe that he exists, and that he does reward those who seek him.*

The faith of Abel and of Enoch is not πίστις ἐλπιζομένων, which is not introduced till v.⁷. In 4 Mac 16²⁰ᶠ· the illustrations of steadfast faith are (*a*) Abraham sacrificing Isaac, (*b*) Daniel in the den of lions, and (*c*) the three men in the fiery furnace ; but in 18¹¹ᶠ· the list of noble sufferers includes (*a*) Abel, (*b*) Isaac, (*c*) Joseph in prison, (*d*) Phinehas, (*e*) the three men in the fiery furnace, and (*f*) Daniel. Sirach's eulogy of famous men in Israel (44–50) has a wider sweep : Enoch, Noah, Abraham, Isaac, Jacob, Moses, Aaron, Phinehas, Joshua, Caleb, the judges, Samuel, David, Solomon, Elijah, Elisha, Hezekiah, Isaiah, Josiah, Jeremiah, Ezekiel, Job, the twelve prophets, Zerubbabel, Joshua the son of Josedek, Nehemiah, and the highpriest Simon (*i.e.* down to the second century B.C.).

The first illustration (v.⁴) is much less natural than most of those that follow. In the story of Gn 4⁴⁻⁸, ἔπιδεν ὁ θεὸς ἐπὶ Ἄβελ καὶ ἐπὶ τοῖς δώροις αὐτοῦ. But why God disregarded Cain's sacrifice and preferred Abel's, our author does not explain. Josephus (*Ant.* i. 54) thought that an offering of milk and animals was more acceptable to God as being natural (τοῖς αὐτομάτοις καὶ κατὰ φύσιν γεγονόσι) than Cain's cereal offering, which was wrung out of the ground by a covetous man ; our author simply argues that the πλείων θυσία of Abel at the very dawn of history was prompted by faith. He does not enter into the nature of this πλείονα (in sense of Mt 6²⁵ or Mk 12⁴³ ἡ χήρα αὕτη ἡ πτωχὴ πλεῖον πάντων βέβληκεν) θυσίαν παρὰ (as in 1⁴) Κάϊν, offered at the first act of worship recorded in scripture. What seems to be implied is that faith must inspire any worship that is to be acceptable to God from anyone who is to be God's δίκαιος (10³⁸). Josephus held that Abel δικαιοσύνης ἐπιμελεῖτο, the blood of Ἄβελ τοῦ δικαίου is noted in Mt 23³⁵, and the Genesis-words ἔπιδεν ὁ θεός are here expanded by our author into ἐμαρτυρήθη εἶναι δίκαιος. Note the practical equivalence of δῶρα and θυσία, as already in 5¹ etc. There is nothing in Πρὸς Ἑβραίους like Philo's effort (*Quaest. in Gen.* 4⁴) to distinguish between δῶρα and θυσίας as follows : ὁ μὲν θύων ἐπιδιαιρεῖ, τὸ μὲν αἷμα τῷ βωμῷ προχέων, τὰ δὲ κρέα οἴκαδε κομίζων· ὁ δὲ δωρούμενος ὅλον ἔοικε παραχωρεῖν τῷ λαμβάνοντι· ὁ μὲν οὖν φίλαυτος διανομεὺς οἷος ὁ Κάϊν, ὁ δὲ φιλόθεος δώρηται οἷον ὁ Ἄβελ.

Πλείονα : of the conjectural emendations, ΠΙΟΝΑ and ΗΔΙΟΝΑ (Cobet, Vollgraff), the latter is favoured by Justin's reference in *Dial.* 29 (εὐδόκησε γὰρ καὶ εἰς τὰ ἔθνη, καὶ τὰς θυσίας ἥδιον παρ' ἡμῖν ἢ παρ' ὑμῶν λαμβάνει· τίς οὖν ἔτι μοὶ περιτομῆς λόγος, ὑπὸ τοῦ θεοῦ μαρτυρηθέντι;), and is admitted into the text by Baljon and Blass (so Maynard in *Exp.*[7] vii. 164 f., who infers from μαρτυρηθέντι that Justin knew Πρὸς 'Εβραίους, the original text of the latter being αὐτῷ τοῦ θεοῦ). In Demosth. *Prooem.* 23, ἥδιον has been corrupted into πλεῖον.

In what follows, (*a*) the original text (μαρτυροῦντος . . . αὐτῷ τοῦ θεοῦ) is preserved in p[13] Clem. (om. τῷ θεῷ). (*b*) αὐτῷ then became αὐτοῦ under the influence of the LXX, and τῷ θεῷ was inserted after προσήνεγκε to complete the sense (א[c] D[c] K L P r vg syr boh arm Orig. Chrys. etc.). Finally, (*c*) τοῦ θεοῦ became assimilated to the preceding τῷ θεῷ, and μαρτυροῦντος . . . αὐτοῦ τῷ θεῷ (א* A D* 33. 104. 326. 1311. 1836. eth) became current, as though Abel witnessed to God, instead of God witnessing to Abel. Thus after προσήνεγκε the Greek originally ran : δι' ἧς ἐμαρτυρήθη εἶναι δίκαιος, μαρτυροῦντος ἐπὶ τοῖς δώροις αὐτῷ τοῦ θεοῦ. Then another application of the LXX was added. The phrase in Gn 4[10] (φωνὴ αἵματος τοῦ ἀδελφοῦ σου βοᾷ πρός με) had already suggested to Philo that Abel was in a sense still living (*quod det. potiori insid. soleat*, 14 : ὁ Ἄβελ, τὸ παραδοξότατον, ἀνῄρηταί τε καὶ ζῇ· ἀνῄρηται μὲν ἐκ τῆς τοῦ ἄφρονος διανοίας, ζῇ δὲ τὴν ἐν θεῷ ζωὴν εὐδαίμονα· μαρτυρήσει δὲ τὸ χρησθὲν λόγιον, ἐν ᾧ "φωνῇ" χρώμενος καὶ "βοῶν" (Gen 4[10]) ἃ πέπονθεν ὑπὸ κακοῦ συνδέτου τηλαυγῶς εὑρίσκεται· πῶς γὰρ ὁ μηκέτ' ὢν διαλέγεσθαι δυνατός;). Our author takes a similar line here : καὶ δι' αὐτῆς (*i.e.* πίστεως) ἀποθανὼν ἔτι λαλεῖ. Even after death, Abel's cry is represented as reaching God, so Philo puts it (*ibid.* 20), ζῇ μὲν γάρ, ὡς καὶ πρότερον ἔφην, ὁ τεθνάναι δοκῶν, εἴ γε καὶ ἱκέτης ὢν θεοῦ καὶ φωνῇ χρώμενος εὑρίσκεται. Only, it is not the fact that the cry was one for retribution (12[24]) which is stressed here, not the fact that his blood cried to God after he died ; but, as λαλεῖν is never used of speaking to God, what the writer means to suggest (as in 3[15]) is that Abel's faith still speaks to us (λαλεῖ, not the historic present, but = in the record). Not even in 12[24] does he adopt the idea of a divine nemesis for the sufferings of the pious in past generations. He does not represent the blood of martyrs like Abel as crying from the ground for personal vengeance ; he has nothing of the spirit which prompted the weird vision of the wronged souls under the altar crying out for retribution (Rev 6[10]). Ἔτι λαλεῖ means, in a general sense, that he is an eloquent, living witness to all ages (so recently Seeberg). Primasius ("qui enim alios suo exemplo admonet ut justi sint, quomodo non loquitur?") and Chrysostom (τοῦτο καὶ τοῦ ζῆν σημεῖόν ἐστι, καὶ τοῦ παρὰ πάντων ᾄδεσθαι, θαυμάζεσθαι καὶ μακαρίζεσθαι· ὁ γὰρ παραινῶν τοῖς ἄλλοις δικαίοις εἶναι λαλεῖ) put this well. The witness is that πίστις may

have to face the last extreme of death (12⁴), and that it is not
abandoned by God; ἀποθανών is never the last word upon a
δίκαιος. Compare Tertullian's argument from Abel, in *De Scor-
piace*, 8 : "a primordio enim justitia vim patitur. Statim ut coli
Deus coepit, invidiam religio sortita est: qui Deo placuerat,
occiditur, et quidem a fratre; quo proclivius impietas alienum
sanguinem sectaretur, a suo auspicata est. Denique non modo
justorum, verum etiam et prophetarum."

The difficulty of λαλεῖ led to the tame correction λαλεῖται in D K L d eth,
etc. Λαλεῖται as passive (=λέγεται) is nearly as impossible as middle ; to say
that Abel, even after death, is still spoken of, is a tepid idea. The writer of
Hebrews meant more than an immortal memory, more even than Epictetus
when he declared that by dying ὅτε ἔδει καὶ ὡς ἔδει one may do even more
good to men than he did in life, like Socrates (iv. 1. 169, καὶ νῦν Σωκράτους
ἀποθανόντος οὐθὲν ἧττον ἢ καὶ πλεῖον ὠφέλιμός ἐστιν ἀνθρώποις ἡ μνήμη ὧν ἔτι
ζῶν ἔπραξεν ἢ εἶπεν).

The πίστις ᾽Ενώχ (vv.⁵·⁶) is conveyed in an interpretation
of the LXX of Gn 5²⁴ καὶ εὐηρέστησεν ᾽Ενὼχ τῷ θεῷ· καὶ οὐχ
ηὑρίσκετο, διότι μετέθηκεν αὐτὸν ὁ θεός. The writer takes the two
clauses in reverse order. Enoch μετετέθη τοῦ (with infinitive of
result) μὴ ἰδεῖν θάνατον (Lk 2²⁶) καὶ ("indeed," introducing the
quotation) οὐχ ηὑρίσκετο (on this Attic augmented form, which
became rare in the κοινή, see Thackeray, 200) διότι μετέθηκεν
αὐτὸν ὁ θεός, πρὸ γὰρ (resuming πίστει μετετέθη) τῆς μεταθέσεως
μεμαρτύρηται (in the scripture record; hence the perfect, which
here is practically aoristic) εὐηρεστηκέναι τῷ θεοῦ (εὐαρεστεῖν in its
ordinary Hellenistic sense of a servant giving satisfaction to his
master). For εὑρίσκεσθαι = die (be overtaken or surprised by
death),[1] cp. Epict. iii. 5. 5 f., οὐκ οἶδας ὅτι καὶ νόσος καὶ θάνατος
καταλαβεῖν ἡμᾶς ὀφείλουσίν τί ποτε ποιοῦντας; . . . ἐμοὶ μὲν γὰρ
καταληφθῆναι γένοιτο μηδενὸς ἄλλου ἐπιμελουμένῳ ἢ τῆς προαιρέσεως
τῆς ἐμῆς . . . ταῦτα ἐπιτηδεύων θέλω εὑρεθῆναι: iv. 10. 12, ἀγαθὸς
ὢν ἀποθανῇ, γενναίαν πρᾶξιν ἐπιτελῶν. ἐπεὶ γὰρ δεῖ πάντως ἀποθανεῖν,
ἀνάγκη τί ποτε ποιοῦντα εὑρεθῆναι . . . τί οὖν θέλεις ποιῶν εὑρεθῆναι
ὑπὸ τοῦ θανάτου; Here εὑρεθῆναι (with or without τοῦ θανάτου)
is a synonym for καταληφθῆναι or ἀποθανεῖν, as in Ph 3⁹ (εὑρεθῶ
ἐν αὐτῷ).

Both Clem. Rom. (9²) and Origen, like Tertullian, appear to have read
οὐχ εὑρέθη αὐτοῦ θάνατος in Gn 5²⁴; and Blass therefore reads here οὐχ
ηὑρίσκετ(ο) αὐτοῦ θάνατος, especially as it suits his scheme of rhythm. This
is linguistically possible, as εὑρίσκεσθαι = be (cp. Fr. *se trouver*), *e.g.* in Lk
17¹⁸, Ph 2⁸. Μετέθηκεν was turned into the pluperfect μετετέθηκεν by ℵ*
Dᶜ L 5. 203. 256. 257. 326. 337. 378. 383. 491. 506. 623. 1611, etc.

Traditions varied upon Enoch (*EBi.* 1295*a*), and even Alexandrian Judaism did not always canonize him in this way. (*a*)

---

[1] In Sifre Deut. 304, the angel of death sought Moses, but found him not
(ואינם מצאו).

The author of Wis 4[10f.], without mentioning his name, quotes
Gn 5[24] as if it meant that God removed Enoch from life early
(καὶ ζῶν μεταξὺ ἁμαρτωλῶν μετετέθη) in order to prevent him from
sharing the sin of his age (ἡρπάγη, μὴ κακία ἀλλάξῃ σύνεσιν αὐτοῦ,
ἢ δόλος ἀπατήσῃ ψυχὴν αὐτοῦ); he departed young, but his
removal was a boon mercifully granted by God to his youthful
piety. (b) Philo views him in de Abrahamo, 3 (cp. de praem.
3–4), as a type of μετάνοια. Quoting Gn 5[24] he points out that
μετάθεσις means a change for the better, and that οὐχ ηὑρίσκετο
is therefore appropriate, τῷ τὸν ἀρχαῖον καὶ ἐπίληπτον ἀπαληλίφθαι
βίον καὶ ἠφανίσθαι καὶ μηκέθ᾽ εὑρίσκεσθαι, καθάπερ εἰ μηδὲ τὴν
ἀρχὴν ἐγένετο.   The Greek version of Sir 44[16] echoes the same
tradition ("Ἐνωχ εὐηρέστησεν Κυρίῳ καὶ μετετέθη, ὑπόδειγμα
μετανοίας ταῖς γενεαῖς), viz. that μετέθηκεν implies the effacement
of Enoch's blameable past, or at any rate that he was enrolled in
better company.   Our author does not share this view.   His
general deduction in v.[6] expands the description of πίστις in v.[1].
To say that a man has satisfied God is to pronounce the highest
possible eulogy upon him, says Philo [1] (de Abrahamo, 6, "τῷ θεῷ
εὐηρέστησεν᾽ " οὗ τί γένοιτ᾽ ἂν ἐν τῇ ψύσει κρεῖττον; τίς καλοκἀγαθίας
ἐναργέστερος ἔλεγχος;), though he is referring to Noah, not to
Enoch.   Our author explains that to satisfy God necessarily
implies πίστις (v.[6]) in the sense of 10[35]. Πιστεῦσαι γὰρ δεῖ τὸν
προσερχόμενον τῷ θεῷ (4[16] etc.) ὅτι ἔστιν (so Epict. iii. 26. 15,
ὅτι καὶ ἔστι καὶ καλῶς διοικεῖ τὰ ὅλα) καὶ τοῖς ἐκζητοῦσιν αὐτὸν
μισθαποδότης (cf. v.[26] 10[35]) γίνεται.   As for the first element of
belief, in the existence of God (ὅτι ἔστιν), the early commentators,
from Chrysostom (ὅτι ἔστιν· οὐ τὸ τί ἐστιν: cp. Tert. adv. Marc.
i. 17, "primo enim quaeritur an sit, et ita qualis sit ") and Jerome
(on Is 6[1-7], in Anecdota Maredsolana, iii. 3. 110: "cumque idem
apostolus Paulus scribit in alio loco, Credere oportet accedentem
ad Deum quia est, non posuit quis et qualis sit debere cognosci,
sed tantum quod sit.   Scimus enim esse Deum, scimusque quid
non sit; quid autem et qualis sit, scire non possumus ") onwards,
emphasize the fact that it is God's existence, not his nature,
which is the primary element of faith.   Philo does declare that
the two main problems of enquiry are into God's existence and
into his essence (de Monarch. i. 4–6), but our author takes the
more practical, religious line, and he does not suggest how faith in

---

[1] Philo fancifully allegorizes the phrase in the de mutat. nomin. 4:
φθείρεται οὖν εἰκότως τὸ γεῶδες καὶ καταλύεται, ὅταν ὅλος δι᾽ ὅλων ὁ νοῦς
εὐαρεστεῖν προέληται θεῷ· σπάνιον δὲ καὶ τὸ γένος καὶ μόλις εὑρισκόμενον,
πλὴν οὐκ ἀδύνατον γενέσθαι· δηλοῖ δὲ τὸ χρησθὲν ἐπὶ τοῦ Ἐνὼχ λόγιον τόδε·
εὐηρέστησε δὲ Ἐνὼχ τῷ θεῷ καὶ οὐχ εὑρίσκετο· ποῦ γὰρ <ἂν> σκεψάμενός τις
εὗροι τἀγαθὸν τοῦτο; . . . οὐχ εὑρίσκετο ὁ εὐαρηστήσα στρόπος τῷ θεῷ, ὡς
ἂν δήπου ὑπαρκτὸς μὲν ὤν, ἀποκρυπτόμενος δὲ καὶ τὴν εἰς ταὐτὸ σύνοδον ἡμῶι
ἀποδιδράσκων, ἐπειδὴ καὶ μετατεθῆναι λέγεται.

God's existence is to be won or kept. When objectors asked him why he believed in the existence of the gods, Marcus Aurelius used to reply: πρῶτον μὲν καὶ ὄψει ὁρατοί εἰσιν· ἔπειτα μέντοι οὐδὲ τὴν ψυχὴν τὴν ἐμαυτοῦ ἑώρακα καὶ ὅμως τιμῶ· οὕτως οὖν καὶ τοὺς θεούς, ἐξ ὧν τῆς δυνάμεως αὐτῶν ἑκάστοτε πειρῶμαι, ἐκ τούτων ὅτι τε εἰσὶ καταλαμβάνω καὶ αἰδοῦμαι (xii. 28). We have no such argument against atheism here; only the reminder that faith does imply a belief in the existence of God—a reminder which would appeal specially to those of the readers who had been born outside Judaism. Belief in the existence of God is for our author, however, one of the elementary principles of the Christian religion (6[1]); the stress here falls on the second element, καὶ . . . μισθαποδότης γίνεται. When the Stoics spoke about belief in the divine existence, they generally associated it with belief in providence; both Seneca (*Ep.* xcv. 50, "primus est deorum cultus deos credere . . . scire illos esse qui praesident mundo, quia universa vi sua temperant, qui humani generis tutelam gerunt interdum curiosi singulorum") and Epictetus (*e.g.* ii. 14. 11, λέγουσιν οἱ φιλόσοφοι ὅτι μαθεῖν δεῖ πρῶτον τοῦτο, ὅτι ἔστι θεὸς καὶ προνοεῖ τῶν ὅλων : *Enchir.* xxxi. 1, τῆς περὶ τοὺς θεοὺς εὐσεβείας ἴσθω ὅτι τὸ κυριώτατον ἐκεῖνό ἐστιν ὀρθὰς ὑπολήψεις περὶ αὐτῶν ἔχειν ὡς ὄντων καὶ διοικούντων τὰ ὅλα καλῶς καὶ δικαίως) are contemporary witnesses to this connexion of ideas, which, indeed, is as old as Plato (*Leges,* 905d, ὅτι μὲν γὰρ θεοί τ᾽ εἰσὶν καὶ ἀνθρώπων ἐπιμελοῦνται).

Τοῖς ἐκζητοῦσιν αὐτόν (for which p[13] P read the simple ζητοῦσιν) denotes, not philosophic enquiry, but the practical religious quest, as in the OT (*e.g.* Ac 15[17], Ro 3[11]). This is not Philo's view, *e.g.*, in the *Leg. Alleg.* 3[15] εἰ δὲ ζητοῦσα εὑρήσεις θεὸν ἄδηλον, πολλοῖς γὰρ οὐκ ἐφανέρωσεν ἑαυτόν, ἀλλ᾽ ἀτελῆ τὴν σπουδὴν ἄχρι παντὸς ἔσχον· ἐξαρκεῖ μέντοι πρὸς μετουσίαν ἀγαθῶν καὶ ψιλὸν τὸ ζητεῖν μόνον, ἀεὶ γὰρ αἱ ἐπὶ τὰ καλὰ ὁρμαὶ κἂν τοῦ τέλους ἀτυχῶσι τοὺς χρωμένους προευφραίνουσιν. But our author has a simpler belief; he is sure that the quest of faith is always successful. By God's reward he means that the faith of man reaching out to God is never left to itself, but met by a real satisfaction; God proves its rewarder. Such faith is a conviction which illustrates 11[1], for the being of God is an unseen reality and his full reward is at present to be hoped for.

A still more apt illustration of πίστις as the ἔλεγχος πράγματων οὐ βλεπομένων which becomes a motive in human life, now occurs in (v.[7]) the faith which Noah showed at the deluge when he believed, against all appearances to the contrary, that he must obey God's order and build an ark, although it is true that in this case the unseen was revealed and realized within the lifetime of the δίκαιος. Like Philo, our author passes from Enoch to

Noah, although for a different reason. Philo ranks Noah as the
lover of God and virtue, next to Enoch the typical penitent (*de
Abrah.* 3, 5, εἰκότως τῷ μετανενοηκότι τάττει κατὰ τὸ ἑξῆς τὸν θεοφιλῆ
καὶ φιλάρετον); here both are grouped as examples of πίστις.
Sirach (44¹⁷ᶠ·) also passes at once from Enoch to Noah the δίκαιος.

> ⁷ *It was by faith* (πίστει) *that Noah, after being told by God* (χρηματισθείς,
> 8⁵, sc. παρὰ τοῦ θεοῦ) *of what was still unseen* (τῶν μηδέπω βλεπομένων, *i.e.*
> the deluge), *reverently* (εὐλαβηθείς, cp. 5⁷) *constructed* (κατεσκεύασεν, as 1 P
> 3²⁰) *an ark to save his household; thus he condemned the world and became
> heir of the righteousness that follows faith.*

The writer recalls, though he does not quote from, the story
of Gn 6¹³ᶠ·. Πίστει goes closely with εὐλαβηθεὶς κατεσκεύασεν,
and περὶ τ. μ. βλεπομένων goes with χρηματισθείς (as Jos. *Ant.* iv.
102, ἐχρηματίζετο περὶ ὧν ἐδεῖτο), not with εὐλαβηθείς, which is not
a synonym for φοβηθείς—the writer is at pains always to exclude
fear or dread from faith (cp. vv.²³·²⁷). Εἰς σωτηρίαν is to be
taken as = "to save alive" (Ac 27²⁰ πᾶσα ἐλπὶς τοῦ σώζεσθαι ἡμᾶς,
27³⁴ τοῦτο γὰρ πρὸς τῆς ὑμετέρας σωτηρίας ὑπάρχει). Δι᾽ ἧς (*i.e.* by
the faith he thus exhibited; as both of the following clauses
depend on this, it cannot refer to the ark, which would suit only
the first) κατέκρινε τὸν κόσμον, where κατέκρινεν corresponds to
what is probably the meaning of Wis 4¹⁶ κατακρινεῖ δὲ δίκαιος
καμὼν τοὺς ζῶντας ἀσεβεῖς, though καμών (= θανών) is not the
point of Hebrews, which regards Noah's action as shaming the
world, throwing its dark scepticism into relief against his own
shining faith in God (Josephus, in *Ant.* i. 75, puts it less
pointedly: ὁ δὲ θεὸς τοῦτον μὲν τῆς δικαιοσύνης ἠγάπησε, κατεδίκαζε
δ᾽ ἐκείνους); κόσμος here (as in v.³⁸) means sinful humanity,
almost in the sense so common in the Johannine vocabulary,
the κόσμος ἀσεβῶν of 2 P 2⁵. Philo (*de congressu erudit.* 17)
notes that Noah was the first man in the OT to be specially
called (Gn 6⁹) δίκαιος; but our author, who has already called
Abel and Noah δίκαιος, does not use this fact; he contents
himself with saying that τῆς κατὰ πίστιν δικαιοσύνης ἐγένετο κληρό-
νομος, *i.e.* he became entitled to, came into possession of, the
δικαιοσύνη which is the outcome or property (κατά κτλ., as in
Hellenistic Greek, cp. Eph 1¹⁵, a periphrasis for the possessive
genitive) of such faith as he showed. Δικαιοσύνη here is the
state of one who is God's δίκαιος (ὁ δίκαιος μου, 10³⁸). A vivid
description of Noah's faith is given in Mark Rutherford's novel,
The Deliverance, pp. 162, 163.

The faith of Abraham, as might be expected, receives more
attention than that of any other (cp. Ac 7²ᶠ·). It is described in
three phases (⁸·⁹⁻¹⁰·¹⁷⁻¹⁹); the faith of his wife Sara is attached to
his (¹¹⁻¹²), and a general statement about his immediate descend-

ants is interpolated (¹³⁻¹⁶) before the writer passes from the second
to the third phase. As in Sirach and Philo, Abraham follows
Noah. "Ten generations were there from Noah to Abraham,
to show how great was His longsuffering; for all the generations
were provoking Him, till Abraham our father came and received
the reward of them all" (*Pirke Aboth* 5³).

⁸ *It was by faith that Abraham obeyed his call to go forth to a place
which he would receive as an inheritance; he went forth, although he did not
know where he was to go.* ⁹ *It was by faith that he "sojourned" in the
promised land, as in a foreign country, residing in tents, as did Isaac and
Jacob, who were co-heirs with him of the same promise;* ¹⁰ *he was waiting for
the City with its fixed foundations, whose builder and maker is God.*

The first phase (v.⁸) is the call to leave Mesopotamia and
travel West, which is described in Gn 12¹ᶠ. The writer does not
dwell, like Philo (*de Abrahamo*, 14), on the wrench of tearing
oneself from one's home. But, as Philo says that Abraham
started ἅμα τῷ κελευσθῆναι, our author begins with καλούμενος.
When the call came, he obeyed it—ὑπήκουσεν ἐξελθεῖν (epexegetic
infinitive), a reminiscence of Gn 12¹·⁴ καὶ εἶπεν κύριος τῷ
Ἀβράμ, Ἔξελθε . . . καὶ ἐπορεύθη Ἀβράμ καθάπερ ἐλάλησεν αὐτῷ
κύριος. He went out from Mesopotamia, μὴ ἐπιστάμενος ποῦ
ἔρχεται, his faith being tested by this uncertainty. So Philo (*de
Migr. Abrah.* 9) notes the point of the future δείξω in Gn 12¹;
it is εἰς μαρτυρίαν πίστεως ἣν ἐπίστευσεν ἡ ψυχὴ θεῷ.

The insertion of ὁ before καλούμενος (A D 33. 256. 467. 1739. 2127 sah
boh arm Thdt.) turns the phrase into an allusion to Abraham's change of
name in Gn 17⁵, which is irrelevant to his earlier call to leave the far East.

The second phase (vv.⁹·¹⁰) is the trial of patience. He did
not lose heart or hope, even when he did reach the country
appointed to him, although he had to wander up and down it as
a mere foreigner, εἰς (= ἐν, Mk 13¹⁶, Ac 8⁴⁰) . . . ἀλλοτρίαν.
He found the land he had been promised still in the hands of
aliens, and yet he lived there, lived as an alien in his own
country! Παρῴκησεν is the opposite of κατῴκησεν (as in Gn 37¹),
and with a fine touch of paradox the writer therefore goes on to
describe Abraham as ἐν σκηναῖς κατοικήσας, contented patiently
to lead a wandering, unsettled life. Such was all the "residence"
he ever had! What sustained him was his πίστις (v.¹⁰), his eager
outlook for the City, ἧς τεχνίτης καὶ δημιουργὸς ὁ θεός. Compare
the scholion on Lucian's *Jov. Trag.* 38: ὃν δὴ θεὸν καὶ δημιουργὸν
ὁ εὐσεβὴς ἀνευρηκὼς λογισμὸς ἔφορον καὶ τεχνίτην τοῦ παντὸς
προευτρέπισεν. Τεχνίτης is not a LXX term, and only began to
be used of God in Alexandrian Judaism (*e.g.* in Wis 13¹). This
is the one place in the NT where it is applied to God; afterwards (*e.g.* Did. 12³; Diognetus, 7²) it became more common.
Δημιουργός is equally unique as a NT term for God, but it occurs

in 2 Mac 4¹, and was used in classical literature frequently for a
subordinate deity (cp. Schermann, *Texte u. Untersuchungen*,
xxxiv. 2*b*. 23). In Apoc. Esdrae (ed. Tisch. 32) the phrase
occurs, ὁ πάσης τῆς κτίσεως δημιουργός. Our author simply writes
τεχνίτης καὶ δημιουργός as a rhetorical expression for maker or
creator (8²), without differentiating the one term from the other,
as "designer" and "constructor" (cp. Philo, *quis rer. div.* 27,
ὁ τεχνίτης . . . ἡνίκα τὸν κόσμον ἐδημιούργει: *de mut. nom.* 4,
ἔθηκε τὰ πάντα ὁ γεννήσας καὶ τεχνιτεύσας πατήρ, ὥστε τὸ "ἐγώ εἰμι
θεὸς σὸς" ἴσον ἐστὶ τῷ "ἐγώ εἰμι ποιητὴς καὶ δημιουργός").

In ⁹ᵇ the writer adds a new touch (as if to suggest that
Abraham propagated his πίστις) in μετὰ Ἰσαὰκ καὶ Ἰακώβ ¹—who
shared the same outlook—τῶν συγκληρονόμων (a κοινή, though
not a LXX, term for co-heir) τῆς ἐπαγγελίας τῆς αὐτῆς. Their
individual faith is noted later (vv.²⁰·²¹). In sketching his fine
mystical interpretation of Abraham's hope, the author ignores
the fact that Jacob, according to Gn 33¹⁷ (ἐποίησεν αὐτῷ ἐκεῖ
οἰκίας), did erect a permanent settlement for himself at Sukkoth.
His immediate interest is not in Isaac and Jacob but in
Abraham, and in the contrast of the tent-life with the stable,
settled existence in a city—the idea which recurs in 12²² 13¹⁴.
It is a Philonic thought in germ, for Philo (*Leg. Alleg.* 3²⁷)
declares that the land promised by God to Abraham is a πόλις
ἀγαθὴ καὶ πολλὴ καὶ σφόδρα εὐδαίμων, typifying the higher contemplation of divine truth in which alone the soul is at home, or
that the soul lives for a while in the body as in a foreign land
(*de Somniis*, 1³¹), till God in pity conducts it safe to μητρόπολις or
immortality. The historical Abraham never dreamed of a πόλις,
but our author imaginatively allegorizes the promised land once
more (cp. 4³ᶠ·), this time as (12²²) a celestial πόλις or Jerusalem,
like Paul and the apocalyptists. According to later tradition
in Judaism, the celestial Jerusalem was shown in a vision to
Abraham at the scene of Gn 15⁹⁻²¹ (Apoc. Bar. 4⁴), or to Jacob at
Bethel (Beresh. rabba on Gn 28¹⁷). Ἐξεδέχετο γάρ—and this
showed the steady patience(10³⁶) and inward expectation (11¹) of
his faith—τὴν τοὺς θεμελίους (τούς, because it was such foundations
that the tents lacked) ἔχουσαν πόλιν. No doubt there was something promised by God which Abraham expected and did get, in
this life; the writer admits that (6¹³⁻¹⁵). But, in a deeper sense,
Abraham had yearnings for a higher, spiritual bliss, for heaven
as his true home. The fulfilment of the promise about his
family was not everything; indeed, his real faith was in an
unseen future order of being (11¹). However, the realization of
the one promise about Isaac (6¹³⁻¹⁵) suggests a passing word
upon the faith of Sara (vv.¹¹·¹²).

---

¹ According to Jubilees 19¹⁶ᶠ· Abraham lived to see Jacob's manhood.

[11] *It was by faith that even* (καὶ) *Sara got strength to conceive, bearing a son when she was past the age for it—because she considered she could rely on Him who gave the promise.* [12] *Thus a single man, though* (καὶ ταῦτα) *he was physically impotent, had issue in number "like the stars in heaven, countless as the sand on the seashore."*

This is the first instance of a woman's faith recorded, and she is a married woman. Paul (Ro 4[19f.]) ignores any faith on her part. Philo again praises Sarah, but not for her faith; it is her loyalty and affection for her husband which he singles out for commendation, particularly her magnanimity in the incident of Gn 16[2] (*de Abrahamo*, 42–44). Our author declares that even in spite of her physical condition (καὶ αὐτὴ Σάρρα), she believed God when he promised her a child. The allusion is to the tale of Gn 17[15]–21[7], which the readers are assumed to know, with its stress on the renewal of sexual functions in a woman of her age. This is the point of καὶ αὐτή, not "mere woman that she was" (Chrysostom, Oec., Bengel), nor "in spite of her incredulity" (Bleek), nor "Sara likewise," *i.e.* as well as Abraham (Delitzsch, Hofmann, von Soden, Vaughan), owing to her close connexion with Abraham (Westcott, Seeberg), though the notion of "likewise" is not excluded from the author's meaning, since the husband also was an old man. A gloss (στεῖρα, ἡ στεῖρα, ἡ στεῖρα οὖσα) was soon inserted by D* P, nearly all the versions, and Origen. This is superfluous, however, and probably arose from dittography (ΣΑΡΡΑΣΤΕΙΡΑ). The general idea is plain, though there is a difficulty in δύναμιν ἔλαβεν (*i.e.* from God) εἰς καταβολὴν σπέρματος = εἰς τὸ καταβάλλεσθαι σπέρμα, *i.e.* for Abraham the male to do the work of generation upon her. This is how the text was understood in the versions, *e.g.* the Latin ("in conceptionem seminis"). Probably it was what the writer meant, though the expression is rather awkward, for καταβολὴ σπέρματος means the act of the male; εἰς ὑποδοχὴν σπέρματος would have been the correct words. This has been overcome (*a*) by omitting καὶ αὐτὴ Σάρρα as a gloss, or (*b*) by reading αὐτῇ Σάρρᾳ. (*a*) certainly clears up the verse, leaving Abraham as the subject of both verses (so Field in *Notes on Transl. of NT*, p. 232, and Windisch); (*b*) is read by Michaelis, Storr, Rendall, Hort, and Riggenbach, the latter interpreting it not as "dativus commodi," but = "along with." If the ordinary text is retained, the idea suggested in καὶ αὐτὴ Σάρρα is made explicit in παρὰ καιρὸν ἡλικίας. What rendered such faith hard for her was her physical condition. Philo (*de Abrah.* 22) applies this to both parents (ἤδη γὰρ ὑπερήλικες γεγονότες διὰ μακρὸν γῆρας ἀπέγνωσαν παιδὸς σποράν), and a woman in the period of life described in Gn 18[11, 12] is called by Josephus γύναιον τὴν ἡλικίαν ἤδη προβεβληκός (*Ant.* vii. 8. 4).

Εἰς τὸ τεκνῶσαι (D* P 69. 436. 462. 1245. 1288. 2005 syr^hkl) after ἔλαβεν is a harmless gloss. The addition of ἔτεκεν (א° K L P lat arm) after ἡλικίας was made when the force of καί (=even) before παρὰ καιρόν was missed.

Πιστὸν ἡγήσατο τὸν ἐπαγγειλάμενον (10^23) is an assertion which shows that the author ignores her sceptical laughter in Gn 18^12; he does not hesitate (cp. v.^27) to deal freely with the ancient story in order to make his point, and indeed ignores the equally sceptical attitude of Abraham himself (Gn 17^17). To be πιστός in this connexion is to be true to one's word, as Cicero observes in the *de Officiis* (i. 7 : "fundamentum autem justitiae fides, id est dictorum conventorumque constantia et veritas "). The promise was fulfilled in this life, so that Sara's faith resembles that of Noah (v.^7). The fulfilment is described in v.^12, where, after διὸ καὶ ἀφ' ἑνὸς (*i.e.* Abraham),[1] ἐγεννήθησαν (p^13 א L Ψ 1739, etc.) is read by some authorities for ἐγενήθησαν (A D K P etc.), though the latter suits the ἀπό in ἀφ' ἑνός rather better. In either case something like τέκνα must be understood. 'Αφ' ἑνός is resumed in καὶ ταῦτα (a *v.l.* in 1 Co 6^8 for the less common καὶ τοῦτο) νενεκρωμένου (in the sense of Ro 4^19). Gen. r. on Gn 25^1 applies Job 14^7-9 to Abraham, but the plain sense is given in Augustine's comment (*Civit. Dei*, xvi. 28) : "sicut aiunt, qui scripserunt interpretationes nominum Hebraeorum, quae his sacris literis continentur, Sara interpretatur princeps mea, Sarra autem uirtus. Unde scriptum est in epistula ad Hebraeos : Fide et ipsa Sarra uirtutem accepit ad emissionem seminis. Ambo enim seniores erant, sicut scriptura testatur; sed illa etiam sterilis et cruore menstruo iam destituta, propter quod iam parere non posset, etiam si sterilis non fuisset. Porro si femina sit prouectioris aetatis, ut ei solita mulierum adhuc fluant, de iuuene parere potest, de seniore non potest; quamuis adhuc possit ille senior, sed de adulescentula gignere, sicut Abraham post mortem Sarrae de Cettura potuit [Gn 25^1], quia uiuidam eius inuenit aetatem. Hoc ergo est, quod mirum commendat apostolus, et ad hoc dicit Abrahae iam fuisse corpus emortuum, quoniam non ex omni femina, cui adhuc esset aliquod pariendi tempus extremum, generare ipse in illa aetate adhuc posset." This elucidates He 11^11. 12a. In what follows, the author is quoting from the divine promise in Gn 22^17, a passage much used in later Jewish literature,[2] though this is the only full allusion to it in the NT (cf. Ro 9^27).

Before passing to the third phase of Abraham's faith, the writer adds (vv.^13-16) a general reflection on the faith of the patriarchs, an application of vv.^9. 10. There were promises which

[1] Is 51^2 ἐμβλέψατε εἰς 'Αβραὰμ τὸν πατέρα ὑμῶν . . . ὅτι εἷς ἦν.
[2] The comparison of a vast number to stars and sands is common in Greek and Latin literature ; cp. *e.g.* Pindar's *Olymp.* 2^98, and Catullus, 61^202f.

could not be fulfilled in the present life, and this aspect of faith is now presented.

> [13] (*These all died in faith without obtaining the promises; they only saw them far away and hailed them, owning they were "strangers and exiles" upon earth.* [14] *Now people who speak in this way plainly show they are in search of a fatherland.* [15] *If they thought of the land they have left behind, they would have time to go back,* [16] *but they really aspire to the better land in heaven. That is why God is not ashamed to be called their God; he has prepared a City for them.*)

Οὖτοι πάντες (those first mentioned in [9-12], particularly the three patriarchs) died as well as lived κατὰ πίστιν, which is substituted here for πίστει either as a literary variety of expression, or in order to suggest πίστις as the sphere and standard of their characters. The writer argues that the patriarchs already possessed a πίστις in eternal life beyond the grave; their very language proves that. Μὴ κομισάμενοι explains the πίστις in which they died; this is the force of μή. All they had was a far-off vision of what had been promised them, but a vision which produced in them a glad belief—ἰδόντες καὶ ἀσπασά-μενοι, the latter ptc. meaning that they hailed the prospect with delight, sure that it was no mirage. The verb here is less metaphorical than, *e.g.*, in Musonius (ed. Hense), vi. : τὴν δὲ ζωὴν ὡς τῶν ἀγαθῶν μέγιστον ἀσπαζόμεθα, or Philo (ἀγάπησον οὖν ἀρετὰς καὶ ἄσπασαι ψυχῇ τῇ σεαυτοῦ, *quis rer. div. heres*, 8). Two interesting classical parallels may be cited, from Euripides (*Ion*, 585-587 :

> οὐ ταὐτὸν εἶδος φαίνεται τῶν πραγμάτων
> πρόσωθεν ὄντων ἐγγύθεν θ' ὁρωμένων.
> ἐγὼ δὲ τὴν μὲν συμφορὰν ἀσπάζομαι)

and Vergil (*Aen.* 3[524] "Italiam laeto socii clamore salutant "). Chrysostom prettily but needlessly urges that the whole metaphor is nautical (τῶν πλεόντων καὶ πόρρωθεν ὁρώντων τὰς πόλεις τὰς ποθουμένας, ἃς πρὶν ἢ εἰσελθεῖν εἰς αὐτὰς τῇ προσρήσει λαβόντες αὐτὰς οἰκειοῦνται).

Κομισάμενοι (p[13] א* P W 33, etc.) is more likely to be original than a conformation to 10[36] 11[39]; the sense is unaffected if we read the more common λαβόντες (א[c] D K L Ψ 6. 104. 1739, Orig.). The reading of A arm (προσδεξά-μενοι) makes no sense.

Καὶ ὁμολογήσαντες, for to reside abroad carried with it a certain stigma, according to ancient opinion (cp. e.g. *Ep. Aristeae*, 249, καλὸν ἐν ἰδίᾳ καὶ ζῆν καὶ τελευτᾶν. ἡ δὲ ξενία τοῖς μὲν πένησι καταφρόνησιν ἐργάζεται, τοῖς δὲ πλουσίοις ὄνειδος, ὡς διὰ κακίαν ἐκπεπτωκόσιν : Sir 29[22-28] etc.). The admission, ὅτι ξένοι καὶ παρεπίδημοί εἰσιν ἐπὶ γῆς, is a generalization from the Oriental deprecation of Jacob in Gn 47[9] (εἶπεν Ἰακὼβ τῷ Φαραώ, αἱ ἡμέραι τῶν ἐτῶν τῆς ζωῆς μου ἃς παροικῶ κτλ.), and the similar confession of Abraham in Gn 23[4] to the sons of Heth, πάροικος

καὶ παρεπίδημος ἐγώ εἰμι μεθ' ὑμῶν. The ἐπὶ γῆς is a homiletic
touch, as in Ps 119¹⁹ (πάροικός εἰμι ἐν τῇ γῇ). In both cases this
ὁμολογία τῆς ἐλπίδος (10²³) is made before outsiders, and the
words ἐπὶ τῆς γῆς start the inference (vv.¹⁴⁻¹⁶ᵃ) that the true home
of these confessors was in heaven. Such a mystical significance
of ξένοι καὶ παρεπίδημοι, which had already been voiced in the
psalter, is richly and romantically developed by Philo, but it never
became prominent in primitive Christianity. Paul's nearest
approach to it is worded differently (Phil 3²⁰, where τὸ πολίτευμα
corresponds to πατρίς here). In Eph 2¹²⁻¹⁹, indeed, Christians are
no longer ξένοι καὶ πάροικοι, for these terms are applied literally
to pagans out of connexion with the chosen People of God. The
only parallel to the thought of Hebrews is in 1 P, where Christians
are παρεπιδήμοι (1¹) and πάροικοι καὶ παρεπιδήμοι (2¹¹). The term
ξένοι is used here as a synonym for πάροικοι, which (cp. Eph 2¹². ¹⁹)
would be specially intelligible to Gentile Christians. Παρεπίδημος only occurs in the LXX in Gn 23⁴, Ps 39¹³; in the
Egyptian papyri παρεπιδημοῦντες (consistentes) denotes foreigners
who settled and acquired a domicile in townships or cities like
Alexandria (*GCP*. i. 40, 55; cp. A. Peyron's *Papyri graeci R.
Taur. Musei Aegyptii*, 8¹³ τῶν παρεπιδημοῦντων καὶ [κα]τοικούντων
ἐ[ν] [τ]αύται[ς] ξένων), and for ξένοι=peregrini, *Ep. Arist.* 109 f.
The use of such metaphorical terms became fairly common in
the moral vocabulary of the age, quite apart from the OT, *e.g.*
Marcus Aurelius, ii. 17 (ὁ δὲ βίος πόλεμος καὶ ξένου ἐπιδημία). A
similar symbolism recurs in the argument of Epictetus (ii. 23, 36 f.)
against the prevalent idea that logic, style, and eloquence are the
end of philosophy: οἷον εἴ τις ἀπιὼν εἰς τὴν πατρίδα τὴν ἑαυτοῦ
καὶ διοδεύων πανδοκεῖον καλὸν ἀρέσαντος αὐτῷ τοῦ πανδοκείου κατα-
μένοι ἐν τῷ πανδοκείῳ. ἄνθρωπε, ἐπελάθου σου τῆς προθέσεως· οὐκ εἰς
τοῦτο ὥδευες, ἀλλὰ διὰ τούτου . . . τὸ δὲ προκείμενον ἐκεῖνο· εἰς τὴν
πατρίδα ἐπανελθεῖν. In a more specifically religious sense, it is
expressed in the saying of Anaxagoras quoted by Diogenes
Laertius (ii. 3. 7, πρὸς τὸν εἰπόντα, "οὐδέν σοι μέλει τῆς πατρίδος,"
"εὐφήμει" ἔφη, "ἔμοι γὰρ καὶ σφόδρα μέλει τῆς πατρίδος," δείξας
τὸν οὐρανόν). According to Philo, the confession that they were
strangers and pilgrims meant that the soul in this world longed
to return to its pre-existent state in the eternal order, and could
never feel at home among things material. So, e.g., *de confus.
ling.* 17, διὰ τοῦτο οἱ κατὰ Μωυσῆν σοφοὶ πάντες εἰσάγονται "παροι-
κοῦντες·" αἱ γὰρ τούτων ψυχαὶ στέλλονται μὲν ἀποικίαν οὐδέποτε τὴν
ἐξ οὐρανοῦ, εἰώθασι δὲ ἕνεκα τοῦ φιλοθεάμονος καὶ φιλομαθοῦς
εἰς τὴν περίγειον φύσιν ἀποδημεῖν . . . ἐπανέρχονται ἐκεῖσε πάλιν,
ὅθεν ὡρμήθησαν τὸ πρῶτον, πατρίδα μὲν τὸν οὐράνιον χῶρον ἐν ᾧ
πολιτεύονται, ξένην δὲ τὸν περίγειον ἐν ᾧ παρῴκησαν νομίζουσαι κτλ.
In *Cherub.* 33, 34, commenting on πάροικοι in Lv 25²³, he argues

that this is the real position of all wise souls towards God, since each of us is a stranger and sojourner in the foreign city of the world where God has for a time placed us till we return to Him.

The metaphor had been applied, in a derogatory sense, by Sallust to the lazy and sensual men who never know what real life means, but who pass through it heedlessly: "many human beings, given over to sensuality and sloth ('ventri atque somno'), uneducated, and uncultured, have gone through life like travellers" ("vitam sicuti peregrinantes transiere," *Catil.* 2).

Such a confession proves (v.[14]) that the men in question are not satisfied with the present outward order of things; ἐμφανί-ζουσιν (Esth 2[22] καὶ αὐτὴ ἐνεφάνισεν τῷ βασιλεῖ τὰ τῆς ἐπιβουλῆς: Ac 23[15], *OGIS.* (iii A.D.) 42[9], *Syll.* 226[85] τήν τε παρουσίαν ἐμφανί-σάντων τοῦ βασίλεως), they thus avow or affirm, ὅτι πατρίδα ἐπιζητοῦσιν (Valckenaer's conjecture, ἔτι ζητοῦσι, is ingenious but needless, cp. 13[14]). For πάτρις in a mystical sense, compare Philo, *de Agric.* 14, commenting on Gn 47[4]): τῷ γὰρ ὄντι πᾶσα ψυχὴ σοφοῦ πατρίδα μὲν οὐρανόν, ξένην δὲ γῆν ἔλαχε, καὶ νομίζει τὸν μὲν σοφίας οἶκον ἴδιον, τὸν δὲ σώματος ὀθνεῖον, ᾧ καὶ παρεπιδημεῖν οἴεται. Here it is "heaven, the heart's true home." The creditable feature in this kind of life was that these men had deliberately chosen it.[1] Had they liked, they might have taken another and a less exacting line (v.[15]). Εἰ μὲν (as in 8[4]) ἐμνη-μόνευον (referring to the continuous past) κτλ. The μνημονεύουσιν of א* D* was due to the influence of the preceding presents, just as ἐμνημόνευσαν (33. 104. 216 Cosm.) to the influence of ἐξέβησαν, which in turn was smoothed out into the usual NT term ἐξῆλθον (א^c D K L Ψ 436. 919. 1288. 1739). Μνημόνευειν here has the sense of "giving a thought to," as in Jos. *Ant.* vi. 37, οὔτε τροφῆς ἐμνημόνευσεν οὔθ᾽ ὕπνου, and below in v.[22]. Time (as Ac 24[25]), as elsewhere in Hebrews, rather than opportunity (1 Mac 15[34] ἡμεῖς δὲ καιρὸν ἔχοντες ἀντεχόμεθα τῆς κληρονομίας ἡμῶν καὶ τῶν πατέρων ἡμῶν), is the idea of εἶχον ἂν καιρόν, καιρός taking an infinitive ἀνακάμψαι (so Codex A in Jg 11[39] καὶ ἀνεκά-μψεν πρὸς τὸν πατέρα αὐτῆς, for the ἀπέστρεψεν of B), as in Eurip. *Rhesus,* 10 (καιρὸς γὰρ ἀκοῦσαι).

Philo remarks of Abraham: τίς δ᾽ οὐκ ἂν μετατραπόμενος παλινδρόμησεν οἴκαδε, βραχέα μὲν φροντίσας τῶν μελλουσῶν ἐλπίδων, τὴν δὲ παροῦσαν ἀπορίαν σπεύδων ἐκφυγεῖν (*de Abrahamo,* 18).

> "Sometimes he wished his aims had been
> To gather gain like other men;
> Then thanked his God he'd traced his track
> Too far for wish to drag him back."
> (THOMAS HARDY, *The Two Men.*)

On the contrary (v.[16]), so far from that, they held on, the writer

---

[1] Cp. *Test. Job* xxxiii. (οὕτω κἀγὼ ἡγησάμην τὰ ἐμά, ἀπ᾽ οὐδένος πρὸς ἐκείνην τὴν πόλιν περὶ ἧς λελάληκέν μοι ὁ ἄγγελος).

adds ; νῦν δέ (logical, as in 8⁶, not temporal) κρείττονος ὀρέγονται, τοῦτ' ἔστιν ἐπουρανίου (so God is described in 2 Mac 3³⁹ as ὁ τὴν κατοικίαν ἐπουράνιον ἔχων). Διὸ οὐκ ἐπαισχύνεται (compare 2¹¹) αὐτοὺς ὁ θεὸς " θεὸς " ἐπικαλεῖσθαι (epexegetic infinitive) " αὐτῶν," referring to Ex 3⁶, Ἐγώ εἰμι . . . θεὸς Ἀβραὰμ καὶ θεὸς Ἰσαὰκ καὶ θεὸς Ἰακώβ, which the writer ¹ interprets (cp. Mk 12²⁶·²⁷) as an assurance of immortality. Their hope of a πατρίς or heavenly home was no illusion ; it was because God had such a πόλις (v.¹⁰) all ready for them that he could call himself their God. He might have been ashamed to call himself such, had he not made this provision for their needs and prepared this reward for their faith (ἡτοίμασεν, cp. Mt 23³⁴).

The third phase of the faith of Abraham (vv.¹⁷⁻¹⁹) is now chronicled, followed by three instances of faith at the end of life, in Isaac, Jacob, and Joseph (vv.²⁰⁻²²).

¹⁷ *It was by faith* (πίστει), *" when Abraham was put to the test, that he sacrificed Isaac " ; he was ready to sacrifice " his only son," although he had received the promises,* ¹⁸ *and had been told* (πρὸς ὅν, as 5⁵) *that* (ὅτι recitative) *" it is through Isaac* (not Ishmael) *that your offspring shall be reckoned"—* ¹⁹ *for he considered God was able even to raise men from the dead. Hence* (ὅθεν, causal) *he did get him back, by what was a parable of the resurrection.* ²⁰ *It was by faith that Isaac blessed Jacob and Esau in connection with the future.* ²¹ *It was by faith that, when Jacob was dying* (ἀποθνῄσκων), *he blessed each of the sons of Joseph, " bending in prayer over the head of his staff."* ²² *It was by faith that Joseph at his end* (τελευτῶν only here) *thought about the exodus of the sons of Israel, and gave orders about his own bones.*

The supreme test of Abraham's πίστις is found in the story of Gn 22¹⁻¹⁸, which Jewish tradition always reckoned as the last and sorest of his ten trials (*Pirke Aboth* 5⁴). It is cited in 4 Mac 16¹⁸⁻²⁰ as a classical example of ὑπομονή (ὀφείλετε πάντα πόνον ὑπομένειν διὰ τὸν θεόν, δι' ὅν καὶ ὁ πατὴρ ἡμῶν Ἀβραὰμ ἔσπευδεν τὸν ἐθνοπάτορα υἱὸν σφαγιάσαι Ἰσαάκ κτλ.). In v.¹⁷ the perfect tense προσενήνοχεν may mean "the ideally accomplished sacrifice, as permanently recorded in scripture" (Moulton, so *Diat.* 2751) ; but it is more likely to be aoristic (cp. Simcox, *Lang. of NT.*, pp. 104, 126). Πειραζόμενος echoes Gn 22¹ (ὁ θεὸς ἐπείραζεν τὸν Ἀβραάμ). Καὶ (epexegetic) τὸν μονογενῆ (a Lucan use of the term in the NT)² προσέφερεν (conative imperfect of interrupted action, like ἐκάλουν in Lk 1⁵⁹) ὁ τὰς ἐπαγγελίας ἀναδεξάμενος, *i.e.* the promises of a son, of a numerous line of descendants (v.¹²), and of a blessing thus coming to all nations.

¹ Origen (*Joh.* ii. 17) : μεγάλη γὰρ δωρεὰ τοῖς πατριάρχαις τὸ τὸν θεὸν ἀντὶ ὀνόματος προσάψαι τὴν ἐκείνων ὀνομασίαν τῇ >θεὸς< ἰδίᾳ αὐτοῦ προσηγορίᾳ.

² The LXX of Gn 22² reads τὸν ἀγαπητόν, but perhaps the writer of Πρὸς Ἑβραίους read a text like that underlying Aquila (τὸν μονογενῆ), Josephus (τὸν μονογενῆ, *Ant.* i. 3. 1), and Symmachus (τὸν μόνον). Μονογενής and ἀγαπητός, as applied to a son, tended to shade into one another. Philo reads ἀγαπητὸς καὶ μόνος (*quod deus immut.* 4, etc.).

This is made explicit in v.[18], with its quotation from Gn 21[12]. For ἀναδέχομαι in the sense of "secure," see the line from Sophocles' "Ichneutae," in *Oxyrh. Papyri*, vii. 25 (ὃν Φοῖβος ὑμῖν εἶπε κ[ὰ]νεδέξατο).

In v.[19] λογισάμενος (as Ro 8[18] etc.) explains why he had the courage to sacrifice Isaac, although the action seemed certain to wreck the fulfilment of what God had promised him. He held ὅτι καὶ ἐκ νεκρῶν ἐγείρειν (weakened into ἐγεῖραι by A P, etc.) δυνατός (Dan 3[17] ὅς ἐστι δυνατὸς ἐξελέσθαι ἡμᾶς κτλ., and Ro 4[21]) *sc.* ἔστιν ὁ θεός. Abraham, says Philo (*de Abrahamo*, 22), πάντα ᾔδει θεῷ δυνατὰ σχεδὸν ἐξ ἔτι σπαργάνων τουτὶ τὸ δόγμα προμαθοῦσα. Later (32) he speaks of this sacrifice as the most outstanding action in Abraham's life—ὀλίγου γὰρ δέω φάναι πάσας ὅσαι θεοφιλεῖς ὑπερβάλλει. It was "a complicated and brilliant act of faith" (A. B. Davidson), for God seemed to contradict God, and the command ran counter to the highest human affection (Wis 10[6] σοφία . . . ἐπὶ τέκνου σπλάγχνοις ἰσχυρὸν ἐφύλαξεν). As Chrysostom put it, this was the special trial, τὰ γὰρ τοῦ θεοῦ ἐδόκει τοῖς τοῦ θεοῦ μάχεσθαι, καὶ πίστις ἐμάχετο πίστει, καὶ πρόσταγμα ἐπαγγελίᾳ. Hence (ὅθεν, in return for this superb faith) ἐκομίσατο, he did recover him (κομίζεσθαι, as in Gn 38[20] etc., of getting back what belongs to you),[1] in a way that prefigured the resurrection (κρείττονος ἀναστάσεως, v.[35]). Such is the meaning of ἐν παραβολῇ (cp. 9[9]). Isaac's restoration was to Abraham a sort[2] of resurrection (v.[35a] "quaedam resurrectionis fuit species, quod subito liberatus fuit ex media morte," Calvin). Ἐν παραβολῇ has been taken sometimes in two other ways. (*a*) = παραβολῶς, *i.e.* beyond all expectation, almost παραδόξως, παρ' ἐλπίδα(ς), or in a desperate peril, as Polybius says of Hannibal (i. 23. 7, ἀνελπίστως καὶ παραβόλως αὐτὸς ἐν τῇ σκάφῃ διέφυγε). This is at any rate less far-fetched than—(*b*) "whence he had originally got him, figuratively-speaking," as if the allusion was to νενεκρωμένου (in v.[12])! Against (*a*) is the fact that παραβολή never occurs in this sense.

Augustine's comment is (*Civit. Dei*, xvi. 32): "non haesitauit, quod sibi reddi poterat immolatus, qui dari potuit non speratus. Sic intellectum est et in epistula ad Hebraeos, et sic expositum [He 11[17-19]] . . . cuius similitudinem, nisi illius unde dicit apostolus: Qui proprio filio non pepercit, sed pro nobis omnibus tradidit eum?" He makes Isaac carrying the wood a type of Christ carrying his cross, and the ram caught in the thicket typical of Christ crowned with thorns. According to the later Jewish tradition (*Pirqe R. Eliezer*, 31), Isaac's soul, which had left his body as his father's sword

---

[1] Josephus (*Ant.* i. 13. 4) describes the father and son as παρ' ἐλπίδας ἑαυτοὺς κεκομισμένοι. Philo (*de Josepho*, 35, τὸ κομίσασθαι τὸν ἀδελφόν) has the same usage.

[2] Aelian (*Var. Hist.* iii. 33) speaks of Satyrus the flautist, τρόπον τινὰ τὴν τέχνην ἐκφαυλίζων παραβολῇ τῇ πρὸς φιλοσοφίαν.

was falling, returned at the words, "Lay not thy hand on the lad"; thus Abraham and Isaac "learned that God would raise the dead."

The next three instances are of πίστις as ὑπόστασις ἐλπιζομένων, the hope being one to be realized in the destiny of the race (vv.²⁰⁻²²).

The solitary instance of πίστις in Isaac (v.²⁰) is that mentioned in Gn 27²⁸· ²⁹· ³⁹· ⁴⁰, a faith which (11¹) anticipated a future for his two sons. Εὐλόγησεν, of one man blessing another, as in 7¹ᶠ· In καὶ περὶ μελλόντων (sc. πραγμάτων), where μέλλειν refers to a future in this world, the καί simply ¹ emphasizes περὶ μελλόντων εὐλόγησεν, and the whole phrase goes with εὐλόγησεν, not with πίστει. The very fact that he blessed his two sons proved that he believed the divine promises to them would be realized in the future. The next two instances of faith are taken from death-beds; it is faith, not in personal immortality, but in the continuance of the chosen race. In v.²¹ the writer quotes from Gn 47³¹ καὶ προσεκύνησεν Ἰσραὴλ ἐπὶ τὸ ἄκρον τῆς ῥάβδου αὐτοῦ, where the LXX by mistake has read הַמַּטֶּה (staff) instead of הַמִּטָּה (bed), and the incident is loosely transferred to the later situation (Gn 48⁹ᶠ·), when Jacob blessed the two sons of Joseph. Supporting himself on ² his staff, he bowed reverently before God, as he blessed the lads. (In the Ep. Barnabas 13⁴⁻⁶, the writer interprets Jacob's preference for the younger son as a proof that Christians, not Jews, were the real heirs of God's blessing!) In v.²² the argument draws upon Gn 50²⁴· ²⁵ (Ex 13¹⁹, Jos 24³²), where Joseph makes the Israelites swear to remove his remains from Egypt to the promised land, so confident was he that God's promise to the people would one day be fulfilled. Τελευτῶν (Gn 50²⁶ καὶ ἐτελεύτησεν Ἰωσήφ) περὶ τῆς ἐξόδου (only here in this sense in NT) τῶν υἱῶν Ἰσραὴλ ἐμνημόνευσε (called to mind, as v.¹⁵) καὶ περὶ τῶν ὀστέων (uncontracted form as in LXX and Mt 23²⁷, Lk 24³⁹; cp. Crönert, Mem. Graeca Hercul. 166⁴) αὐτοῦ ἐνετείλατο. Joseph's faith also was shown in his conviction of the future promised by God to Israel, but it found a practical expression in the instructions about conveying his mummy out of Egypt (Sir 49¹⁸ καὶ τὰ ὀστᾶ αὐτοῦ ἐπεσκέπησαν).

The ninth example of πίστις is Moses, of whom almost as much is made as of Abraham. Five instances of faith are mentioned in connexion with his career (vv.²³⁻²⁹).

²³ *It was by faith that Moses was "hidden for three months"* (τρίμηνον, sc. χρόνον) *after birth by his parents, because "they saw" the child was*

---

¹ To suggest that it means "even" is flat for a blessing, *ex hypothesi,* referred to the future. Its omission (by א K L P, the eastern versions, etc.) is more easily explained than its insertion.

² 1 K 1⁴⁷ προσεκύνησεν ὁ βασιλεὺς ἐπὶ τὴν κοίτην, ἐπί has the same local sense.

"beautiful" (Ac 7²⁰), *and had no fear of the royal decree.* ²⁴ *It was by faith that Moses refused, "when he had grown up," to be called the son of Pharaoh's daughter;* ²⁵ *ill-treatment with God's people he preferred to the passing pleasures of sin,* ²⁶ *considering obloquy with the messiah to be richer wealth than all Egypt's treasures—for he had an eye to the Reward.* ²⁷ *It was by faith that he left Egypt, not from any fear of the king's wrath; like one who saw the King Invisible, he never flinched.* ²⁸ *It was by faith that he celebrated "the passover" and performed the sprinkling by blood, so that "the destroying angel"* (cf. 1 Co 10¹⁰) *might not touch Israel's firstborn.* ²⁹ *It was by faith that they crossed the Red Sea* (Ac 7³⁶) *like dry land—and when the Egyptians attempted it, they were drowned.*

Moses (v.²³) owed the preservation of his life as an infant to the courageous πίστις of his parents (πατέρων = γονεῖς, *parentes*, like *patres* in Ovid's *Metam.* 4⁶¹, and Plato's *Leges*, vi. 772 E, ἀγαθῶν πατέρων φύντι). The writer quotes from Ex 2². ³, adding that, as the result of their faith, they had no fear of the royal edict (διάταγμα as in Jos. *Ant.* xvi. 16. 5; Wis 11⁷ etc.). This is the main point of their πίστις. On ἀστεῖον see Philo's *vit. Mos.* i. 3: γεννηθεὶς οὖν ὁ παῖς εὐθὺς ὄψιν ἐνέφαινεν ἀστειοτέραν ἢ κατ᾽ ἰδιώτην, ὡς καὶ τῶν τοῦ τυράννου κηρυγμάτων, ἐφ᾽ ὅσον οἷόν τε ἦν, τοὺς γονεῖς ἀλογῆσαι). The Hebrew text makes the mother act alone, but the LXX gives the credit to both parents; and this tradition is followed by Philo and Josephus (*Ant.* ii. 9. 4), as by our author.

The parents of Moses are the first anonymous people in the roll-call of faith's representatives. Calvin rather severely ranks their faith on a lower level, because the parents of Moses were moved by the external appearance of their child, and because they ought to have brought him up themselves ("notandum est fidem quae hîc laudatur ualde fuisse imbecillam. Nam quum posthabito mortis suae metu Mosen deberent educare, eum exponunt. Patet igitur illorum fidem breui non tantum uacillasse sed fuisse collapsam"). Still, he reflects that this is after all an encouragement, since it proves that even weak faith is not despised by God. Chrysostom's comment is kinder; the writer, he thinks, means to afford additional encouragement to his readers by adducing not only heroes, but commonplace people as examples of faith (ἀσήμων, ἀνωνύμων).

Another (7²) gloss has been inserted here, after v.²³, by D* 1827 and nearly all the MSS of the Latin versions, viz. πίστει μέγας γενόμενος Μωυσῆς ἀνεῖλεν τὸν Αἰγύπτιον κατανοῶν τὴν ταπείνωσιν τῶν ἀδελφῶν αὐτοῦ, a homiletical application of Ex 2¹¹. ¹² (used in Ac 7²³ᶠ.).

The second item of faith (v.²⁴) is the first individual proof by Moses himself. Josephus (*Ant.* ii. 9. 7) makes Moses refuse the Pharaoh's crown when a baby. The Pharaoh's daughter placed the child in her father's arms; he took it, pressed it to his bosom, and to please his daughter graciously put the crown upon its head. But the child threw it to the ground and stamped on it. Which seemed ominous to the king! The writer of Hebrews avoids such fancies, and simply summarizes Ex 2¹¹ᶠ, where Moses μέγας γενόμενος (from Ex 2¹¹; *i.e.*, as Calvin points out, when his refusal could not be set down to childish ignorance

of the world, nor to youthful impetuousness) ἠρνήσατο (with
infinitive as in Wis 12²⁷ 16¹⁶ 17¹⁰) λέγεσθαι υἱὸς θυγατρὸς Φαραώ.
His religious motive in declining the title and position of son to
an Egyptian princess (Jub 47⁹) is now given (v.²⁵); μᾶλλον
ἑλόμενος (for the construction and idea, cp. *OGIS.* 669¹⁵ μᾶλλον
τὴν τῶν προτέρων ἐπάρχων αἰώνιον συνήθειαν φυλάσσων ἢ <ι> τὴν
πρόσκαιρόν τινος ἀδικίαν μειμησάμενος) συγκακουχεῖσθαι (a new
compound, unknown to the LXX) τῷ λαῷ τοῦ θεοῦ ἢ πρόσκαιρον (a
non-LXX term [1] which first occurs in 4 Mac 15². ⁸. ²³, and passed
into the early Christian vocabulary as an antithesis to αἰώνιος)
ἔχειν ἁμαρτίας ἀπόλαυσιν. The ἁμαρτία is the sin which he
would have committed in proving disloyal to the People of God;
that might have been pleasant for the time being, but πίστις
looks to higher and lasting issues (10⁸⁴ 11¹). It would have
been "sin" for him to choose a high political career at court,
the "sin" of apostasy; he did what others in their own way had
done afterwards (10³⁵, cp. 13⁸).

For ἀπόλαυσις see Antipater of Tarsus (Stob. *Florileg.* lxvii. 25) : τὸν δ'
ἤθεον <βίον>, ἐξουσίαν διδόντα πρὸς ἀκολασίαν καὶ ποικίλων ἡδονῶν ἀπόλαυσιν
ἀγεννῶν καὶ μικροχαρῶν, ἰσόθεον νομίζουσι, and 4 Mac 5⁸, where the tyrant
taunts the conscientious Jews, καὶ γὰρ ἀνόητον τοῦτο τὸ μὴ ἀπολαύειν τῶν χωρὶς
ὀνείδους ἡδέων. Philo (*vit. Mos.* i. 6 : γενόμενός τε διαφερόντως ἀσκητὴς
ὀλιγοδεείας καὶ τὸν ἁβροδίαιτον βίον ὡς οὐδεὶς ἕτερος χλευάσας—ψυχῇ γὰρ
ἐπόθει μόνῃ ζῆν, οὐ σώματι) praises the asceticism of Moses in the palace
of the Pharaoh, but gives an interpretation of his reward which is lower
than that of our author; he declares (i. 27) that as Moses renounced the
high position of authority which he might have enjoyed in Egypt (ἐπειδὴ γὰρ
τὴν Αἰγύπτου κατέλιπεν ἡγεμονίαν, θυγατριδοῦς τοῦ τότε βασιλεύοντος ὤν),
because he disapproved of the local injustice, God rewarded him with
authority over a greater nation.

In v.²⁶ the reason for this renunciation of the world is
explained. Μείζονα πλοῦτον ἡγησάμενος (cp. v.¹¹ and λογισάμενος
in v.¹⁹) τῶν Αἰγύπτου θησαυρῶν τὸν ὀνειδισμὸν τοῦ Χριστοῦ (as
involved in συγκακουχεῖσθαι τῷ λαῷ τοῦ θεοῦ). This is one of
the writer's dinting phrases. There is a special obloquy in being
connected with Christ. It is one of the things which Christians
have to face to-day (13¹³), and, the writer argues, it has always
been so; Moses himself, the leader of God's people at the first,
showed his πίστις by deliberately meeting it. The obloquy was
part of the human experience of Jesus himself (12² 13¹²), but the
point here in τὸν ὀνειδισμὸν τοῦ Χριστοῦ is that, by identifying
himself with God's people in Egypt, Moses encountered the
same ὀνειδισμός as their very messiah afterwards was to endure.
He thus faced what the writer, from his own standpoint, does
not hesitate to call τὸν ὀνειδισμὸν τοῦ Χριστοῦ. Whether he had
in mind anything further, *e.g.* the idea that ὁ Χριστός here

[1] It recurs in an edict of Caracalla (215 A.D.), quoted by Mitteis-Wilcken,
i. 2. 39.

means the pre-incarnate Logos, as though a mystical sense
like that of 1 Co 10⁴ underlay the words, is uncertain and
rather unlikely, though the idea that Christ was suffering in the
person of the Israelites, or that they represented him, might be
regarded as justified by the language, *e.g.*, of Ps 89⁵¹ (τοῦ ὀνει-
δισμοῦ τῶν δούλων σου . . . οὗ ὠνείδισαν τὸ ἀντάλλαγμα τοῦ Χριστοῦ
σου). The experiences of ingratitude and insulting treatment
which Moses suffered at the hands of Israel illustrate Chrysostom's definition of τὸν ὀνειδισμὸν τοῦ Χριστοῦ : τὸ μέχρι τέλους
καὶ ἐσχάτης ἀναπνοῆς πάσχειν κακῶς . . . τοῦτό ἐστιν ὀνειδισμὸς
τοῦ Χριστοῦ, ὅταν τις παρ᾽ ὧν εὐεργετεῖ ὀνειδίζηται (citing Mt 27⁴⁰).
The basis of this estimate of life is now given : ἀπέβλεπεν γὰρ εἰς
τὴν μισθαποδοσίαν, as the writer desired his readers to do (10³⁵
11⁶). Ἀποβλέπειν εἰς is a common phrase for keeping one's eye
upon, having regard to, *e.g.* Theophrastus, ii. 10, καὶ εἰς ἐκεῖνον
ἀποβλέπων : Josephus, *Bell. Jud.* ii. 15. 1, ὁ μὲν . . . εἰς μόνον τὸ
λυσιτελὲς τὸ ἐκ τῶν ἁρπαγῶν ἀποβλέπων, παρήκουσεν. Mr. Starkie,
in his note on Arist. *Acharn.* 32, suggests that ἀποβλέπειν, which
is common in the comic poets and is also a philosophical term
(*e.g.* Plato's *Phaedo*, 115 C; *Phaedrus*, 234 D), "was used like
'to prescind' in English," *i.e.* to fix one's gaze on a single
object by withdrawing it from everything else.

The third act of faith in his life (v.²⁷) is his withdrawal from
Egypt to Midian (Ex 2¹⁴ᶠ·= Ac 7²⁹). In μὴ φοβηθεὶς τὸν θυμὸν
τοῦ βασιλέως the author ignores the statement of the OT that
Moses did fly from Egypt, in terror of being punished by the
king for having murdered the Egyptian (ὄργην ἀμείλικτον βασιλέως
ἀποδιδράσκων, Philo, *de vit. Mos.* i. 9). Josephus in his own
way also (*Ant.* ii. 10. 1) eliminates the motive of fear. Our
author declares that if Moses did retreat from Egypt, it was
from no fear of Pharaoh, but in the faith that God had a future
and a mission for him still; he had as little fear of Pharaoh as
his parents had had, τὸν γὰρ ἀόρατον (*sc.* βασιλέα) ὡς ὁρῶν ἐκαρτέ-
ρησεν (cp. Sir 2² εὔθυνον τὴν καρδίαν σου καὶ καρτέρησον). "The
courage to abandon work on which one's heart is set, and accept
inaction cheerfully as the will of God, is of the rarest and highest
kind, and can be created and sustained only by the clearest
spiritual vision" (Peake). The language and thought are illustrated by Epict. ii. 16. 45–46: ἐκ τῆς διανοίας ἔκβαλε . . . λύπην,
φόβον, ἐπιθυμίαν, φθόνον, ἐπιχαιρεκακίαν, φιλαργυρίαν, μαλακίαν,
ἀκρασίαν. Ταῦτα δ᾽ οὐκ ἔστιν ἄλλως ἐκβαλεῖν, εἰ μὴ πρὸς μόνον τὸν
θεὸν ἀποβλέποντα, ἐκείνῳ μόνῳ προσπεπονθότα, τοῖς ἐκείνου προστ-
άγμασι καθωσιωμένον. The phrase ὡς ὁρῶν means the inward
vision where, as Marcus Aurelius observes (x. 26), ὁρῶμεν, οὐχὶ
τοῖς ὀφθαλμοῖς, ἀλλ᾽ οὐχ ἧττον ἐναργῶς. In the *de Mundo*, 399a,
God is described as ἀόρατος ὢν ἄλλῳ πλὴν λογισμῷ. Philo had

already singled out this trait in Moses, e.g. *de mutat. nomin.* 2 : Μωυσῆς ὁ τῆς ἀειδοῦς φύσεως θεατὴς καὶ θεόπτης—εἰς γὰρ τὸν γνόφον φασὶν αὐτὸν οἱ θεῖοι χρησμοὶ εἰσελθεῖν (Ex 20²¹), τὴν ἀόρατον καὶ ἀσώματον οὐσίαν αἰνιττόμενοι. In *vit. Mos.* i. 15 he declares that the Pharaoh had no notion of any invisible God (μηδένα τὸ παράπαν νοητὸν θεὸν ἔξω τῶν ὁρατῶν νομίζων), and later on, commenting on Ex 20²¹ (i. 28), he adds that Moses entered the darkness, τουτέστιν εἰς τὴν ἀειδῆ καὶ ἀόρατον καὶ ἀσώματον τῶν ὄντων παραδειγματικὴν οὐσίαν, τὰ ἀθέατα φύσει θνητῇ κατανοῶν.

On μὴ φοβηθεὶς τὸν θυμὸν τοῦ βασιλέως, it may be noted that the Stoics took the prudential line of arguing that one ought not needlessly to provoke a tyrant : " sapiens nunquam potentium iras provocabit, immo declinabit, non aliter quam in navigando procellam " (Seneca, *Ep.* xiv. 7). Various attempts have been made to explain away the contradiction between this statement and that of Ex 2¹⁴. (*a*) Some think they are not irreconcilable ; " so far as his life was concerned, he feared, but in a higher region he had no fear " (A. B. Davidson), *i.e.* he was certain God would ultimately intervene to thwart Pharaoh, and so took precautions to save his own life in the interest of the cause. This is rather artificial, however, though maintained by some good critics like Lünemann. (*b*) Or, the θυμός may be not anger at the murder of the Egyptian, but the resentment of Moses' action in refusing a court position and withdrawing from Egypt (Vaughan, Dods, Delitzsch, etc.). (*c*) A more favourite method is to deny that the writer is alluding to Ex 2¹⁴·¹⁵ at all, and to refer the passage to the real Exodus later (so Calvin, Bleek, Westcott, Seeberg, and many other edd.) ; but this is to anticipate v.²⁸, and the Israelites were ordered out of Egypt by Pharaoh, not exposed to any anger of his.

The fourth act of faith (v.²⁸) is his obedience to the divine orders of Ex 12¹²⁻⁴⁸ (cp. Wis 18⁵⁻⁹), which proved that he believed, in spite of appearances, that God had protection and a future for the People. Πεποίηκεν is another aoristic perfect ; πρόσχυσις is not a LXX term, and θίγγανω (θίγῃ) only occurs in LXX in Ex 19¹³ (= Heb 12²⁰). As θίγγανω may take a genitive (12²⁰) as well as an accusative, ὀλοθρεύων might go with πρωτότοκα (*i.e.* of the Egyptians) and θίγῃ with αὐτῶν (the Israelites). Note the alliteration in πίστει πεπ. πάσχα . . . πρόσχυσιν The ἵνα μή clause explains τὴν πρόσχυσιν τοῦ αἵματος.

By one Old Latin, or at any rate a non-Vulgate, text of this passage, in Codex Harleianus (ed. E. S. Buchanan, *Sacred Latin Texts*, i., 1912), a gloss is inserted at this point : "fide praedaverunt Aegyptios exeuntes" (Ex 12³⁵·³⁶), which was evidently known to Sedulius Scotus (Migne, ciii. 268 C), who quotes it as "fide praedaverunt Aegyptios, quia crediderunt se iterum in Aegyptum non reversuros."

The fifth act of faith (v.²⁹) is the crossing of the Red Sea (Ex 14¹⁶ᶠ·). Strictly speaking, this is an act of faith on the part of the Israelites; the διέβησαν depends on, for its subject, the αὐτῶν of v.²⁸. But those who crossed were οἱ ἐξελθόντες ἐξ Αἰγύπτου διὰ Μωϋσέως (3¹⁶), and the action is the direct sequel to that of v.²⁸, though Moses is now included in the People. διὰ ξηρᾶς γῆς is from Ex 14²⁹; διαβαίνειν goes with the genitive as well as with the accusative. The Israelites took a risk, in obedience to God's order, and so proved their πίστις. But there are some things which are possible only to faith. Ἧς (*i.e.* ἐρυθρὰ θάλασσῃ) πεῖραν λαβόντες οἱ Αἰγύπτιοι κατεπόθησαν (from Ex 15⁴ κατεπόθησαν ἐν ἐρυθρᾷ θαλάσσῃ, B), *i.e.* the Egyptians tried it and were swallowed up in the sea. Here πεῖραν λαμβάνειν is a classical phrase for (*a*) making an attempt, almost in the sense of testing or risking. They "ventured on" (cp. Dt 28⁵⁶ ἡ τρυφερά, ἧς οὐχὶ πεῖραν ἔλαβεν ὁ πούς αὐτῆς βαίνειν ἐπὶ τῆς γῆς), or tried it (cp. Jos. *Ant.* 8. 6. 5, σοφίας βουλομένη λαβεῖν πεῖραν, etc.). The other meaning is that (*b*) of getting experience (so in v.³⁶), which is often the sad result of (*a*); so, *e.g.*, Demosth. *in Aristocratem*, 131, λαβὼν ἔργῳ τῆς ἐκείνου φιλίας πεῖραν. The writer ignores the legendary embroidery of Philo (*vit. Mos.* iii. 34, ὡς ἐπὶ ξηρᾶς ἀτραποῦ καὶ λιθώδους ἐδάφους—ἐκραυρώθη γὰρ ἡ ψάμμος καὶ ἡ σποράς αὐτῆς οὐσία συμφῦσα ἡνώθη).

Two more instances of faith are specially cited, both in connexion with the fall of Jericho (vv.³⁰· ³¹). During the interval between the Exodus and the entrance into Canaan the writer, we are not surprised to find (3¹⁶ᶠ·), notes not a single example of πίστις, but it is remarkable that neither here nor below (v.³²ᶠ·) is there any allusion to Joshua.

³⁰ *It was by faith that the walls of Jericho collapsed, after being surrounded for only seven days.* ³¹ *It was by faith that Rahab the harlot did not perish along with those who were disobedient, as she had welcomed the scouts peaceably.*

The faith that had enabled Israel to cross the Red Sea in safety enabled them years later to bring the walls of a city crashing to the ground (v.³⁰). There was no siege of Jericho; Israel simply marched round it for a week, and that act of faith in God's promise, against all probabilities, brought about the marvel. So the writer summarizes Jos 6¹⁻²⁰. Judas Maccabaeus and his men also appealed, in besieging a town, to τὸν μέγαν τοῦ κόσμου δυνάστην, τὸν ἄτερ κριῶν καὶ μηχανῶν ὀργανικῶν κατακρημνίσαντα τὴν Ἰεριχὼ κατὰ τοὺς Ἰησοῦ χρόνους (2 Mac 12¹⁵), and one Egyptian fanatic (for whom Paul was once mistaken, Acts 21³⁸) promised his adherents, in rebelling against the Romans, that the walls of Jerusalem would collapse at his word of command (Josephus, *Ant.* xx. 8. 6).

The faith of a community is now followed by the faith of an individual. The last name on the special list is that of a foreigner, an unmarried woman, and a woman of loose morals (v.³¹), in striking contrast to Sara and the mother of Moses The story is told in Jos 2¹⁻²¹ 6²⁵. For ἡ πόρνη (" Ratio haec cur R. solita sit peregrinos excipere," Bengel) see below on 13². A tendency to whitewash her character appears in the addition of ἐπιλεγομένη (א syrʰᵏˡ Ephr.), which is also inserted by some codices in the text of Clem. Rom. 12¹. Her practical faith (Ja 2²⁵ ; Clem. Rom. 1¹² διὰ πίστιν καὶ φιλοξενίαν ἐσώθη), shown by her friendly (μετ' εἰρήνης) welcome to the spies, which sprang from her conviction that the God of Israel was to be feared, saved (συναπώλετο, cp. Sir 8¹⁵) her from the fate of her fellow-citizens (τοῖς ἀπειθήσασιν) who declined to submit to the claims of Israel's God. They are described by the same word as are the recalcitrant Israelites themselves (3¹⁸). Even Jewish priests were proud to trace their descent from Rahab ; her reputation stood high in later tradition, owing to the life which followed this initial act of faith (cp. Mt 1⁵).

For lack of space and time the writer now passes to a mere summary of subsequent examples of faith (vv.³²ᶠ·). Roughly speaking, we may say that vv.³³· ³⁴ describe what the folk of old did by faith, vv.³⁵ᶠ· what they did for faith.

³² *And what more shall I say? Time would fail me to tell of Gideon, of Barak and Samson and Jephthah, of David and Samuel and the prophets—* ³³ *men who by faith* (διὰ πίστεως) *conquered kingdoms, administered justice, obtained promises, shut the mouth of lions,* ³⁴ *quenched the power of fire, escaped the edge of the sword, from weakness won to strength, proved valiant in warfare, and routed hosts of foreigners.*

Καὶ τί ἔτι (om. D*) λέγω (deliberative conjunctive) does not necessarily imply that Πρὸς Ἑβραίους was originally a sermon or address ; it was a literary as well as an oratorical phrase. Thus Josephus uses a similar phrase in *Ant.* xx. 11. 1 (καὶ τὶ δεῖ πλείω λέγειν ;). Faith did not die out, at the entry into Palestine. On the contrary, the proofs of faith are so rich in the later story of the People that the writer has no time for anything except a glowing abstract. Ἐπιλείψει γάρ με διηγούμενον ὁ χρόνος is one form of a common rhetorical phrase, though ἡ ἡμέρα is generally used instead of ὁ χρόνος. Three instances may be cited : Dion. Hal. *De Compositione Verb.* 4 (after running over the names of a number of authors) καὶ ἄλλους μυρίους, ὧν ἁπάντων τὰ ὀνόματα εἰ βουλοίμην λέγειν, ἐπιλείψει με ὁ τῆς ἡμέρας χρόνος : Demosth. *de Corona*, 324, ἐπιλείψει με λέγονθ' ἡ ἡμέρα τὰ τῶν προδότων ὀνόματα, and (out of several instances) Philo, *de Sacrif. Abelis et Caini*, 5, ἐπιλείψει μὲ ἡ ἡμέρα λέγοντα τὰ τῶν κατ' εἶδος ἀρετῶν ὀνόματα.

Διηγούμενον . . . περί, as, *e.g.*, in Plato's *Euth.* 6 C, πολλὰ
περὶ τῶν θείων διηγήσομαι, and Philo's *de Abrah.* 44, ὧν ὀλίγῳ
πρότερον ἔνια διεξῆλθον (= "gone over"). For με γάρ (אֹ A D*
33. 547), γάρ με is rightly read by p¹³ Dᶜ K L P W Clem. Chrys.
etc. (cp. Blass, § 475. 2), though γάρ is omitted altogether by
Ψ 216*. Six names are specially mentioned, to begin with.
Gideon's crushing victory over the Ammonites echoes down later
history (*e.g.* Is 9³ 10²⁶, Ps 83¹¹). The singling out of Barak is
in line with the later Jewish tradition, which declined to think of
him as a mere ally of Deborah; he was the real hero of the
exploit. For example, some rabbis (cp. Targ. on Jg 5²³, Yalkut
on Jg 42) gave him the high name of Michael, and praised this
brave leader for his modesty in allowing Deborah to occupy so
prominent a place. Later tradition also magnified Samson's
piety and divine characteristics (*e.g.* Sotah 9*b*, 10*a*). Of all the
four "judges" selected, Jephthah has the poorest reputation in
Jewish tradition; he is censured for rashness, and his rank is
comparatively insignificant. Augustine, however (*Quaest.* VII.
xlix.), points out that the "spirit" came both on Jephthah (Jg
11²⁹· ³⁰) and on Gideon (8²⁷). Why these four names are put in
this unchronological order (instead of Barak, Gideon, Jephthah,
and Samson), it is impossible to guess; in 1 S 12¹¹ it is Gideon,
Barak, Jephthah, and Samson, followed by Samuel. David here
(Δαυείδ τε) belongs to the foregoing group, the only one of
Israel's kings mentioned in the list. In Jewish tradition (*e.g.*
Josephus, *Ant.* vi. 2, 2–3) Samuel's career was interpreted with
quite martial fervour; he was credited with several victories over
the Philistines. Hence he forms a transition between the
previous heroes and the prophets, of which he was commonly
regarded as the great leader (cp. Ac 3²⁴). Ἄλλων (+τῶν?) is
superfluously inserted before προφητῶν by syrʰᵏˡ ᵖᵉˢʰ arm eth sah
boh 69. 1288 Theod. Dam. In οἳ διὰ πίστεως (v.³³) the οἵ covers
vv.³³· ³⁴, but διὰ πίστεως includes vv.³⁵⁻³⁸ as well, and is reiterated
in v.³⁹. The following nine terse clauses, devoid of a single καί,
begin by noting military and civil achievements. In κατηγωνί-
σαντο βασιλείας, καταγωνίζομαι (not a LXX term) is the verb
applied by Josephus to David's conquests (in *Ant.* vii. 2. 2, αὐτῷ
σῶσαι καταγωνισαμένῳ Παλαιστινοὺς δέδωκεν ὁ θεός); its later
metaphorical use may be illustrated from *Mart. Pol.* 19² (διὰ
τῆς ὑπομονῆς καταγωνισάμενος τὸν ἄδικον ἄρχοντα). Ἠργάσαντο
δικαιοσύνην in the sense of 2 S 8¹⁵ (καὶ ἐβασίλευσεν Δαυεὶδ ἐπὶ
Ἰσραήλ· καὶ ἦν ποιῶν κρίμα καὶ δικαιοσύνην ἐπὶ πάντα τὸν λαὸν
αὐτοῦ) etc., the writer applying to this specific activity, for which
πίστις was essential, a phrase elsewhere (cp. Ac 10³⁵) used for a
general moral life. Such was their faith, too, that they had promises of God's help realized in their experience; this (cp. 6¹⁵) is

the force of ἐπέτυχον ἐπαγγελιῶν. Furthermore, ἔφραξαν στόματα
λεόντων, as in the case of Daniel (Dn 6¹⁸· ²³ ὁ θεός μου ἐνέφραξεν
τὰ στόματα τῶν λεόντων, Theod.), ἔσβεσαν δύναμιν πυρός, as in the
case of Daniel's three friends (Dn 3¹⁹⁻²⁸, 1 Mac 2⁵⁹, 3 Mac 6⁶).
In ἔφυγον στόματα μαχαίρης, the unusual plural of στόμα (cp.
Lk 21²⁴ πεσοῦνται στόματι μαχαίρης) may be due to the preceding
στόματα rhetorically; it means repeated cases of escape from
imminent peril of murder rather than double-edged swords (4¹²),
escapes, *e.g.*, like those of Elijah (1 K 19¹ᶠ·) and Elisha (2 K
6¹⁴ᶠ· ³¹ᶠ·).   In ἐδυναμώθησαν (p¹³ א* A D* 1831; the *v.l.* ἐνεδυνα-
μώθησαν was probably due to the influence of Ro 4²⁰) ἀπὸ
ἀσθενείας, the reference is quite general; Hezekiah's recovery
from illness is too narrow an instance.[1]   The last three clauses
are best illustrated by the story of the Maccabean struggle,
where ἀλλότριοι is the term used for the persecutors (1 Mac 2⁷
etc.), and παρεμβολή for their hosts (1 Mac 3¹⁵ etc.).   In παρεμ-
βολὰς ἔκλιναν ἀλλοτρίων, παρεμβολή, a word which Phrynichus
calls δεινῶς Μακεδονικόν, means a host in array (so often in 1 Mac
and Polybius); κλίνω (cp. Jos. *Ant.* xiv. 15. 4, κλίνεται τὸ . . .
κέρας τῆς φάλαγγος) is never used in this sense in the LXX.

What the heroes and heroines of πίστις had to endure is now
summarized (vv.³⁵⁻³⁸): the passive rather than the active aspect
of faith is emphasized.

³⁵ *Some were given back to their womankind, raised from the very dead ;
others were broken on the wheel, refusing to accept release, that they might
obtain a better resurrection ;* ³⁶ *others, again, had to experience scoffs and
scourging, aye, chains and imprisonment—*³⁷ *they were stoned . . . sawn in
two, and cut to pieces ; they had to roam about in sheepskins and goatskins,
forlorn, oppressed, ill-treated* ³⁸ *(men of whom the world was not worthy),
wanderers in the desert and among hills, in caves and gullies.*

Ἔλαβον γυναῖκες ² κτλ. (³⁵) recalls such stories as 1 K 17¹⁷ᶠ·
and 2 K 4⁸⁻³⁷ (καὶ ἡ γυνὴ . . . ἔλαβεν τὸν υἱὸν αὐτῆς καὶ ἐξῆλθεν) ;
it was a real ἀνάστασις, though not the real one, for some
other male beings became literally and finally νεκροί, relying by
faith on a κρείσσων ἀνάστασις.   Ἄλλοι δέ (like Sokrates in Athens :
cp. Epict. iv. 1. 164–165, Σωκράτης δ' αἰσχρῶς οὐ σῴζεται . . .
τοῦτον οὐκ ἔστι σῶσαι αἰσχρῶς, ἀλλ' ἀποθνήσκων σῴζεται) could
only have saved their lives by dishonourably giving up their

---

[1] A more apt example is the nerving of Judith for her act of religious
patriotism (cp. Rendel Harris, *Sidelights on NT Research*, 170 f.), though
there is a verbal parallel in the case of Samson (Jg 16¹⁸ ἀπόστησει ἀπ' ἐμοῦ ἡ
ἰσχύς μου καὶ ἀσθενήσω).

[2] The odd *v.l.* γυναικᾶς (p¹³ א* A D* 33. 1912) may be another case (cp.
Thackeray, 149, for LXX parallels) of -ας for -ες as a nominative form ; as an
accusative, it could only have the senseless meaning of "marrying"
(λαμβάνειν γυναῖκας).   Strong, early groups of textual authorities now and
then preserve errors.

convictions, and therefore chose to suffer.   This is a plain reference to the Maccabean martyrs. Ἐτυμπανίσθησαν (Blass prefers
the more classical form in D* ἀπετυμπανίσθησαν), a punishment
probably corresponding to the mediaeval penalty of being broken
on the wheel.   " This dreadful punishment consists," says Scott
in a note to the thirtieth chapter of *The Betrothed*, " in the
executioner, with a bar of iron, breaking the shoulder-bones,
arms, thigh-bones and legs of the criminal, taking his alternate
sides. The punishment is concluded by a blow across the
breast, called the *coup de grâce*, because it removes the sufferer
from his agony."   The victim was first stretched on a frame or
block, the τύμπανον[1] (so schol. on Aristoph. *Plut.* 476, τύμπανα
ξύλα ἐφ᾽ οἷς ἐτυμπάνιζον· ἐχρῶντο γὰρ ταύτῃ τῇ τιμωρίᾳ), and
beaten to death, for which the verb was ἀποτυμπανίζεσθαι (*e.g.*
Josephus, *c. Apionem*, i. 148, quoting Berossus, Λαβοροσοάρχοδος
. . . ὑπὸ τῶν φίλων ἀπετυμπανίσθη : Arist. *Rhet.* ii. 5. 14, ὥσπερ οἱ
ἀποτυμπανιζόμενοι, etc.).   So Eleazar was put to death, because
he refused to save his life by eating swine's flesh (2 Mac 6[19]
ὁ δὲ τὸν μετ᾽ εὐκλείας θάνατον μᾶλλον ἢ τὸν μετὰ μύσους βίον
ἀναδεξάμενος αὐθαιρέτως ἐπὶ τὸ τύμπανον προσῆγεν).   It is this
punishment of the Maccabean martyrs which the writer has in
mind, as Theodoret already saw. The sufferers were " distracti
quemadmodum corium in tympano distenditur " (Calvin); but
the essence of the punishment was beating to death, as both
Hesychius (πλήσσεται, ἐκδέρεται, ἰσχυρῶς τύπτεται) and Suidas
(ξύλῳ πλήσσεται, ἐκδέρεται, καὶ κρέμαται) recognize in their definition of τυμπανίζεται.   The hope of the resurrection, which
sustained such martyrs οὐ προσδεξάμενοι (cp. 10[34]) τὴν ἀπολύτρωσιν,
is illustrated by the tales of Maccabean martyrs, *e.g.* of Eleazar
the scribe (2 Mac 6[21f.]), urged to eat some pork ἵνα τοῦτο πράξας
ἀπολυθῇ τοῦ θανάτου, and declining in a fine stubbornness; but
specially of the heroic mother and her seven sons (*ibid.* 7[1f.]),
who perished confessing αἱρετὸν μεταλλάσσοντας ἀπὸ ἀνθρώπων
τὰς ὑπὸ τοῦ θεοῦ προσδοκᾶν ἐλπίδας πάλιν ἀναστήσεσθαι ὑπ᾽ αὐτοῦ
. . . οἱ μὲν γὰρ νῦν ἡμέτεροι ἀδελφοὶ βραχὺν ἐπενέγκαντες πόνον
ἀενάου ζωῆς ὑπὸ διαθήκην θεοῦ πεπτώκασιν.

In v.[36] ἕτεροι δὲ (after οἱ μέν . . . ἄλλοι δέ in Matt 16[14])
πεῖραν ἔλαβον (see on v.[29]) ἐμπαιγμῶν (cp. Sir 27[28] ἐμπαιγμὸς καὶ
ὀνειδισμός) καὶ μαστίγων—a hendiadys; the writer has in mind
shameful tortures like those inflicted on the seven Maccabean
brothers, as described in 2 Mac 7[1] (μάστιξιν καὶ νευραῖς αἰκιζο-

---

[1] Another word for the frame was τροχός, as in 4 Mac 9[20], where the
eldest of the seven famous Jewish brothers is beaten to death. Hence
the verb used by Philo (*in Flaccum*, 10) to describe the punishment inflicted
on the Alexandrian Jews (Ἰουδαῖοι μαστιγούμενοι, κρεμάμενοι, τροχιζόμενοι,
καταικιζόμενοι).

μένους . . . ⁷ ἦγον ἐπὶ τὸν ἐμπαιγμόν), although in this case the
beating is not at once fatal, as the next words prove (ἔτι δὲ
δεσμῶν καὶ φυλακῆς). The passage would be more clear and
consecutive, however, if ἕτεροι δέ preceded περιῆλθον (in v.³⁷),
introducing the case of those who had not to suffer the martyrs'
death. This would leave ἐμπαιγμῶν κτλ. as a reiteration or
expansion of ἐτυμπανίσθησαν. Before δεσμῶν καὶ φυλακῆς, ἔτι δέ
probably (cp. Lk 14²⁶) heightens the tone—not merely passing
blows, but long durance vile : though the sense might be simply,
"and further." In v.³⁷ ἐλιθάσθησαν (as in the case of Zechariah,
2 Ch 24²⁰⁻²², Mt 23³⁵) was the traditional punishment which
ended Jeremiah's life in Egypt (Tertull. *Scorp.* 8) ; possibly the
writer also had in mind the fate of Stephen (Acts 7⁵⁸).
Ἐπρίσθησαν (Am 1⁸ ἔπριζον πρίοσιν σιδηροῖς κτλ.) alludes to the
tradition of Isaiah having being sawn in two with a wooden saw
during the reign of Manasseh, a tradition echoed in the contemporary *Ascensio Isaiae* 5¹⁻¹⁴ (Justin's *Dial.* cxx. ; Tertull. *de
Patientia*, xiv. etc.) ; cp. R. H. Charles, *The Ascension of Isaiah*
(1900), pp. xlv–xlix.

After ἐλιθάσθησαν there is a primitive corruption in the text.   Four
readings are to be noted.

ἐπειράσθησαν, ἐπρίσθησαν : א L P 33. 326 syrʰᵏˡ.
ἐπρίσθησαν, ἐπειράσθησαν : p¹³ A D Ψ 6. 104. 1611. 1739 lat boh arm.
ἐπειράσθησαν : fuld, Clem. Thdt.
ἐπρίσθησαν : 2. 327 syrᵛᵍ Eus. etc.

Origen apparently did not read ἐπειράσθησαν, if we were to judge from
Hom. Jerem. xv. 2 (ἄλλον ἐλιθοβόλησαν, ἄλλον ἔπρισαν, ἄλλον ἀπέκτειναν
μεταξὺ τοῦ ναοῦ καὶ τοῦ θυσιαστηρίου), but shortly before (xiv. 12) he quotes
the passage verbally as follows : ἐλιθάσθησαν, ἐπρίσθησαν, ἐπειράσθησαν, ἐν
φόνῳ μαχαίρας ἀπέθανον, though ἐπειράσθησαν is omitted here by H.   In
c. Cels. vii. 7 it is doubtful whether ἐπειράθησαν or ἐπειράσθησαν was the
original reading.   Eusebius omits the word in *Præp. Evang.* xii. 10 (583*d*),
reading ἐλιθασθησαν, ἐπρίσθησαν, ἐν φόνῳ κτλ., and sah reads "they were
sawn, they were stoned, they died under the sword."   It is evident that
ἐπειράσθησαν (written in some MSS as ἐπιρ.) as "were tempted" is impossible
here ; the word either was due to dittography with ἐπρίσθησαν or represents a
corruption of some term for torture.   Various suggestions have been made,
e.g. ἐπηρώθησαν (mutilated) by Tanaquil Faber, ἐπράθησαν (sold for slaves)
by D. Heinsius, ἐσπειράσθησαν (strangled) by J. Alberti, or ἐπέρθησαν
(impaled) by Knatchbull.   But some word like ἐπυρώ(άσ)θησαν (Beza, F.
Junius, etc.) or ἐπρήσθησαν (Gataker)[1] is more likely, since one of the seven
Maccabean brothers was fried to death (2 Mac 7⁴), and burning was a
punishment otherwise for the Maccabeans (2 Mac 6¹¹).   It is at any rate
probable that the writer put three aorists ending in -σθησαν together.

Death ἐν φόνῳ μαχαίρης (a LXX phrase) was not an uncommon fate for unpopular prophets (1 K 19¹⁰, Jer 26²³) ; but
the writer now passes, in περιῆλθον κτλ. (³⁷ᵇ·³⁸), to the sufferings

[1] Or ἐνεπρήσθησαν, which is used by Philo in describing the woes of the
Alexandrian Jews (*in Flaccum*, 20, ζῶντες οἱ μὲν ἐνεπρήσθησαν).

of the living, harried and hunted over the country. Not all the loyal were killed, yet the survivors had a miserable life of it, like Mattathias and his sons (1 Mac 2²⁸ ἔφυγον . . . εἰς τὰ ὄρη), or Judas Maccabaeus and his men, who had to take to the hills (2 Mac 5²⁷ ἐν τοῖς ὄρεσιν θηρίων τρόπον διέζη σὺν τοῖς μετ᾽ αὐτοῦ, καὶ τὴν χορτώδη τροφὴν σιτούμενοι διετέλουν), or others during the persecution (2 Mac 6¹¹ ἕτεροι δὲ πλησίον συνδραμόντες εἰς τὰ σπήλαια). When the storm blew over, the Maccabeans recollected ὡς τὴν τῶν σκηνῶν ἑορτὴν ἐν τοῖς ὄρεσιν καὶ ἐν τοῖς σπηλαίοις θηρίων τρόπον ἦσαν νεμόμενοι (2 Mac 10⁶). They roamed, the writer adds, dressed ἐν μηλωταῖς (the rough garb of prophets, like Elijah, 1 K 19¹³· ¹⁹), ἐν αἰγείοις δέρμασιν (still rougher pelts). According to the *Ascensio Isaiae* (2⁷ᶠ·) the pious Jews who adhered to Isaiah when he withdrew from Manasseh's idolatry in Jerusalem and sought the hills, were "all clothed in garments of hair, and were all prophets." Clement (17¹) extends the reference too widely: οἵτινες ἐν δέρμασιν αἰγείοις καὶ μηλωταῖς περιπάτησαν κηρύσσοντες τὴν ἔλευσιν τοῦ Χριστοῦ· λέγομεν δὲ Ἡλείαν καὶ Ἐλισαιέ, ἔτι δὲ καὶ Ἰεζεκιήλ, τοὺς προφήτας· πρὸς τούτοις καὶ τοὺς μεμαρτυρημένους.

A vivid modern description of people clad in goatskins occurs in Balzac's *Les Chouans* (ch. i.): "Ayant pour tout vêtement une grande peau de chèvre qui les couvrait depuis le col jusqu'aux genoux. . . . Les mèches plates de leurs longs cheveux s'unissaient si habituellement aux poils de la peau de chèvre et cachaient si complétement leurs visages baissés vers la terre, qu'on pouvait facilement prendre cette peau pour la leur, et confondre, à la première vue, les malheureux avec ces animaux dont les dépouilles leur servaient de vêtement. Mais à travers les cheveux l'on voyait bientôt briller les yeux comme des gouttes de rosée dans une épaisse verdure ; et leurs regards, tout en annonçant l'intelligence humaine, causaient certainement plus de terreur que de plaisir."

Their general plight is described in three participles, ὑστερούμενοι, θλιβόμενοι (2 Co 4⁸), κακουχούμενοι (cp. 13³, and Plut. *Consol. ad Apoll.* 26, ὥστε πρὶν ἀπώσασθαι τὰ πένθη κακουχουμένους τελευτῆσαι τὸν βίον). Κακοῦχεῖν only occurs twice in the LXX (1 K 2²⁶ 11³⁹ A), but is common in the papyri (e.g. *Tebt. Pap.* 104²², B.C. 92). This ill-treatment at the hands of men, as if they were not considered fit to live (cp. Ac 22²²), elicits a splendid aside—ὧν οὐκ ἦν ἄξιος ὁ κόσμος. Compare Mechilta, 5*a* (on Ex 12⁶): "Israel possessed four commandments, of which the whole world was not worthy," and the story of the bath qol in Sanhedr. 11. 1, which said, "One is here present who is worthy to have the Shekinah dwelling in him, but the world is not worthy of such." Κόσμος as in v.⁷; Philo's list of the various meanings of κόσμος (in *de aetern. mundi*, 2) does not include this semi-religious sense. Of the righteous, Wis 3⁵ remarks : ὁ θεὸς ἐπείρασεν αὐτοὺς καὶ εὗρεν αὐτοὺς ἀξίους ἑαυτοῦ.

"There is a class of whom the world is always worthy and more than worthy : it is worthy of those who watch for, reproduce, exaggerate its foibles, who make themselves the very embodiment of its ruling passions, who shriek its catchwords, encourage its illusions, and flatter its fanaticisms.   But it is a poor *rôle* to play, and it never has been played by the men whose names stand for epochs in the march of history" (H. L. Stewart, *Questions of the Day in Philosophy and Psychology*, 1912, p. 133).

In ³⁸ᵇ it was the not infrequent (cf. Mk 1⁴⁵) confusion of ЄN and ЄΠΙ in ancient texts which probably accounted for ἐν being replaced by ἐπί (ἐφ᾽) in p¹³ ℵ A P 33. 88, etc. ; ἐπί does not suit σπηλαίοις . . . ὀπαῖς, and the writer would have avoided the hiatus in ἐπὶ ἐρημίαις.   Still, πλανώμενοι suits only ἐρημίαις καὶ ὄρεσιν, and ἐπί may have been the original word, used loosely like πλανώμενοι with σπηλαίοις κτλ.   In Ps.-Sol 17¹⁹ the pious ἐπλανῶντο ἐν ἐρήμοις, σωθῆναι ψυχὰς αὐτῶν ἀπὸ κακοῦ.   For ὀπαῖς, cp. Ob ³ ἐν ταῖς ὀπαῖς τῶν πετρῶν.   Σπηλαῖον, like the Latin *spelunca* or *specus*, eventually became equivalent to a "temple," perhaps on account of the prominence of caves or grottoes in the worship of some cults.

Now for an estimate of this πίστις and its heroic representatives (vv.³⁹. ⁴⁰) !   The epilogue seems to justify God by arguing that the apparent denial of any adequate reward to them is part of a larger divine purpose, which could only satisfy them after death.

³⁹ *They all won their record* (μαρτυρηθέντες = ἐμαρτυρήθησαν in v.²) *for faith, but the Promise they did not obtain.* ⁴⁰ *God had something better in store for us* (ἡμῶν *emphatic*); *he would not have them perfected apart from us.*

Some of these heroes and heroines of faith had had God's special promises fulfilled even in this life (*e.g.* vv.¹¹. ³³), but *the* Promise, in the sense of the messianic bliss with its eternal life (10³⁶. ³⁷, cf. 6¹⁷ᶠ.), they could not win.   Why?   Not owing to any defect in their faith, nor to any fault in God, but on account of his far-reaching purpose in history ; οὗτοι πάντες (again as in v.¹³, but this time summing up the whole list, vv.⁴⁻³⁸) οὐκ ἐκομίσαντο (in the sense of v.¹³ μὴ κομισάμενοι ; not a voluntary renunciation, as Wetstein proposes to interpret it—"non acceperunt felicitatem promissam huius vitae, imo deliberato consilio huic beneficio renunciaverunt et maluerunt affligi morique propter deum") τὴν ἐπαγγελίαν (in v.¹³ *the* Promise was loosely called αἱ ἐπαγγελίαι, and the plural τὰς ἐπαγγελίας is therefore read here by A W 436. 1611).   The reason for this is now given (v.⁴⁰) in a genitive absolute clause, τοῦ θεοῦ περὶ ἡμῶν κρεῖττόν τι προβλεψαμένου (the middle for the active).   Προβλέπειν only occurs once in the LXX (Ps 37¹³ ὁ δὲ κύριος . . . προβλέπει ὅτι ἥξει ἡ ἡμέρα αὐτοῦ), and only here in the NT, where the religious idea makes it practically a Greek equivalent for *providere.*

Κρεῖττόν τι is explained by ἵνα μὴ χωρὶς ἡμῶν τελειωθῶσιν, which
does not mean that "our experience was necessary to complete
their reward," but that God in his good providence reserved the
messianic τελείωσις of Jesus Christ until we could share it. This
τελείωσις is now theirs (9^{15} 12^{23}), as it is ours—if only we will show
a like strenuous faith during the brief interval before the end.
This is the thought of $12^{1f.}$, catching up that of $10^{36f.}$. God
deferred the coming of Christ, in order to let us share it (cp. 1 P
$1^{10. 20}$), his plan being to make room for us as well. The
τελείωσις has been realized in Jesus; till he reappears (9^{28} $10^{12. 37}$)
to complete the purpose of God for us, we must hold on in faith,
heartened by the example of these earlier saints. Their faith
was only granted a far-off vision of the hoped-for end. We have
seen that end realized in Jesus; therefore, with so many more
resources and with so short a time of strain, we ought to be
nerved for our endurance by the sense of our noble predecessors.
It is not that we experience κρεῖττόν τι by our immediate experience of Christ (10^{14}), who fulfils to us what these former folk
could not receive before his coming. This is true, but it is not
exactly the point here. The κρεῖττόν τι is our inclusion in this
People of God for whom the τελείωσις of Christ was destined,
the privilege of the κρείττων διαθήκη. The writer does not go
the length of saying that Christ suffered in the persons of these
saints and heroes (as, *e.g.*, Paulinus of Nola, *Epist.* xxxviii. 3:
"ab initio saeculorum Christus in omnibus suis patitur . . . in
Abel occisus a fratre, in Noe irrisus a filio, in Abraham peregrin-
atus, in Isaac oblatus, in Jacob famulatus, in Joseph venditus,
in Moyse expositus et fugatus, in prophetis lapidatus et sectus,
in apostolis terra marique iactatus, et multis ac uariis beatorum
martyrum crucibus frequenter occisus"), and this consideration
tells against the theory of a "mystical" sense in v.^{26}. The conclusion of the whole matter rather is (vv.$^{39. 40}$) that the reward of
their faith had to be deferred till Christ arrived in our day. The
τελείωσις is entirely wrought out through Christ, and wrought
out for all. It covers all God's People (cp. 12^{23}), for now the
Promise has been fulfilled to these earlier saints. But the writer
significantly ignores any idea of their co-operation in our faith;
we neither pray to them, nor they for us. Josephus interpreted
the sacrifice of Isaac, as if Abraham reconciled himself to it by
reflecting that his son would be a heavenly support to him (*Ant.*
i. 13. 3, ἐκείνου, *i.e.* τοῦ θεοῦ, τὴν ψυχὴν τὴν σὴν προσδεχομένου
καὶ παρ᾽ αὑτῷ καθέξοντος· ἔσει τε μοι εἰς κηδεμόνα καὶ γηροκόμον
. . . τὸν θεὸν ἀντὶ σαυτοῦ παρεσχημένος). Such ideas lie outside
the range of our epistle, and there is significance in the fact that
the writer never touches them.

In Clement of Alexandria's comment (*Strom.* iv. 16) on this passage, he quotes 10³²⁻³⁹ (reading δεσμοῖς μου: ἑαυτούς: χρονιεῖ: δικαιός μου), then hurries on to 11³⁶–12² (reading ἐλιθάσθησαν, ἐπειράσθησαν, ἐν φόνῳ μ. ἀπέθανον: ἐν ἐρημίαις: τὴν ἐπαγγελίαν τοῦ θεοῦ), and adds: ἀπολείπεται νοεῖν τὸ κατὰ παρασιώπησιν εἰρημένον μόνοι. ἐπιφέρει γοῦν· περὶ ἡμῶν κρεῖττόν τι προειδομένου τοῦ θεοῦ (ἀγαθὸς γὰρ ἦν), ἵνα μὴ χωρὶς ἡμῶν τελειωθῶσι. The collocation of τὴν ἐπαγγελίαν with τοῦ θεοῦ is a mistake.

From the ἡμῶν . . . ἡμῶν of the epilogue the writer now passes into a moving appeal to his readers (12¹ᶠ·).

¹ *Therefore* (Τοιγαροῦν, as in 1 Th 4⁸), *with all this host of witnesses encircling us, we* (καὶ ἡμεῖς, emphatic) *must strip off sin with its clinging folds, to run our appointed course steadily* (δι' ὑπομονῆς), ² *our eyes fixed upon Jesus as the pioneer and the perfection of faith—upon Jesus who, in order to reach his own appointed joy, steadily endured* (ὑπέμεινεν) *the cross, thinking nothing of its shame, and is now " seated at the right hand" of the throne of God.*

The writer now returns to the duty of ὑπομονή as the immediate exercise of πίστις (10³⁶ᶠ·), the supreme inspiration being the example of Jesus (12¹⁻³) as the great Believer, who shows us what true πίστις means, from beginning to end, in its heroic course (τὸν προκείμενον ἡμῖν ἀγῶνα).

The general phraseology and idea of life as a strenuous ἀγών, in the Hellenic sense (see on 5¹⁴), may be seen in many passages, *e.g.* Eurip. *Orest.* 846 f. :

πρὸς δ' Ἀργεῖον οἴχεται λεών,
ψυχῆς ἀγῶνα τὸν προκείμενον πέρι
δώσων, ἐν ᾧ ζῆν ἢ θανεῖν ὑμᾶς χρεών,

Herod. viii. 102 (πολλοὺς πολλάκις ἀγῶνας δραμέονται οἱ Ἕλληνες) and ix. 60 (ἀγῶνος μεγίστου προκειμένου ἐλευθέρην εἶναι ἢ δεδουλωμένην τὴν Ἑλλάδα), and especially in 4 Mac 14⁵ πάντες (the seven martyrs), ὥσπερ ἐπ' ἀθανασίας ὁδὸν τρέχοντες, ἐπὶ τὸν διὰ τῶν βασάνων θάνατον ἔσπευδον, and Philo's *de migrat.* *Abrah.* 24, καὶ γὰρ Ἀβραὰμ πιστεύσας " ἐγγίζειν θεῷ" (Gn 18²³, cp. He 11⁶) λέγεται. ἐὰν μέντοι πορευόμενος μήτε κάμῃ (cp. He 12³) μήτε ῥαθυμήσῃ, ὡς παρ' ἑκάτερα ἐκτραπόμενος (cp. He 12¹³) πλανᾶσθαι τῆς μέσης καὶ εὐθυτενοῦς διαμαρτὼν ὁδοῦ, μιμησάμενος δὲ τοὺς ἀγαθοὺς δρομεῖς τὸ στάδιον ἀπταίστως ἀνύσῃ τοῦ βίου, στεφάνων καὶ ἄθλων ἐπαξίων τεύξεται πρὸς τὸ τέλος ἐλθών. The figure is elaborately worked out in 4 Mac 17¹¹⁻¹⁴ (ἀληθῶς γὰρ ἦν ἀγὼν θεῖος ὁ δι' αὐτῶν γεγενημένος. ἠθλοθέτει γὰρ τότε ἀρετὴ δι' ὑπομονῆς δοκιμάζουσα· τὸ νῖκος ἐν ἀφθαρσίᾳ ἐν ζωῇ πολυχρονίῳ. Ἐλεαζὰρ δὲ προηγωνίζετο· ἡ δὲ μήτηρ τῶν ἑπτὰ παίδων ἐνήθλει· οἱ δὲ ἀδελφοὶ ἠγωνίζοντο· ὁ τύραννος ἀντηγωνίζετο· ὁ δὲ κόσμος καὶ ὁ τῶν ἀνθρώπων βίος ἐθεώρει), where the Maccabean martyrs are athletes of the true Law ; but the imagery is more rhetorical and detailed than in Πρὸς Ἐβραίους, where the author, with a passing touch of metaphor, suggests more simply and suggestively the same idea.

Ἔχοντες . . . ἀποθέμενοι . . . ἀφορῶντες, three participles with the verb after the second, as in Jude ²⁰· ²¹ ; but here the first, not the second, denotes the motive. Τοσοῦτον ¹ (thrown forward, for emphasis) ἔχοντες περικείμενον ἡμῖν νέφος μαρτύρων. Μάρτυρες here, in the light of 11²· ⁴· ⁵· ³⁹, denotes those who have borne

¹ Τηλικοῦτον, א* W.

personal testimony to the faith. Heaven is now crowded with these (12²³), and the record of their evidence and its reward enters into our experience. Such πνεύματα δικαίων τετελειωμένων speak to us (11⁴) still; we are, or ought to be, conscious of their record, which is an encouragement to us (καὶ ἡμεῖς) ἐπ᾽ ἐσχάτου τῶν ἡμερῶν τούτων (1²). It is what we see in them, not what they see in us, that is the writer's main point; περικείμενον suggests that the idea of them as witnesses of our struggle (see the quot. from 4 Mac, above) is not to be excluded, but this is merely suggested, not developed. Μάρτυς is already, as in Rev 2¹³ etc., beginning to shade off into the red sense of "martyr" (cp. Kattenbusch in *Zeitsch. für neutest. Wissenschaft*, 1903, pp. 111 f. ; G. Krüger, *ibid.*, 1916, pp. 264 f. ; Reitzenstein in *Hermes*, 1917, pp. 442 f., and H. Delehaye in *Analecta Bollandiana*, 1921, pp. 20 f.), though the writer uses the word with a special application here, not as usually of the Christian apostles nor of the prophets, but of the heroes and heroines of the People in pre-Christian ages. He does not even call Jesus Christ μάρτυς (as does the author of the Johannine apocalypse).

The meaning of "witnesses of our ordeal" (*i.e.* spectators) is supported by passages like Epict. iv. 4. 31, οὐδεὶς ἀγὼν¹ δίχα θορύβου γίνεται· πολλοὺς δεῖ προγυμναστὰς εἶναι, πολλοὺς [τοὺς] ἐπικραυγάζοντας, πολλοὺς ἐπιστάτας, πολλοὺς θεατάς, and particularly Longinus, *de sublim.* xiv. 2, who, in arguing that many people catch their inspiration from others, notes : τῷ γὰρ ὄντι μέγα τὸ ἀγώνισμα, τοιοῦτον ὑποτίθεσθαι τῶν ἰδίων λόγων δικαστήριον καὶ θέατρον, καὶ ἐν τηλικούτοις ἥρωσι κριταῖς τε καὶ μάρτυσιν ὑπέχειν τῶν γραφομένων εὐθύνας πεπαῖχθαι. In *Educational Aims and Methods* (p. 28), Sir Joshua Fitch writes : "There is a remarkable chapter in the Epistle to the Hebrews, in which the writer unfolds to his countrymen what is in fact a National Portrait Gallery, as he enumerates, one by one, the heroes and saints of the Jewish history, and adds to his catalogue these inspiring words . . . [He 11³²⁻³⁴]. And, finally, he draws this conclusion from his long retrospect . . . [He 12¹]. How much of the philosophy of history is condensed into that single sentence ! It is suggestive to us of the ethical purpose which should dominate all our historical teaching. To what end do we live in a country whose annals are enriched by the story of great talents, high endeavours and noble sacrifices, if we do not become more conscious of the possibilities of our own life, and more anxious to live worthily of the inheritance which has come down to us ?"

Νέφος (never in this sense in LXX) has its usual Greek meaning of "host" (Latin nimbus or nubes), as, *e.g.*, in Herod. viii. 109, νέφος τοσοῦτο ἀνθρώπων. In ὄγκον ἀποθέμενοι πάντα καὶ τὴν εὐπερίστατον ἁμαρτίαν, ὄγκον is thrown first for the sake of emphasis : "any encumbrance that handicaps us." The conjec-

---

¹ The broader conception of the moral life as an athletic contest recurs in Epict. iii. 25. 1–3, σκέψαι, ὧν προέθου ἀρχόμενος, τίνων μὲν ἐκράτησας, τίνων δ᾽ οὔ . . . οὐ γὰρ ἀποκνητέον τὸν ἀγῶνα τὸν μέγιστον ἀγωνιζομένοις, ἀλλὰ καὶ πληγὰς ληπτέον· οὐ γὰρ ὑπὲρ πάλης καὶ παγκρατίου ὁ ἀγὼν πρόκειται . . . ἀλλ᾽ ὑπὲρ αὐτῆς εὐτυχίας καὶ εὐδαιμονίας.

ture ὄκνον (P. Junius) is relevant, but superfluous; sloth is a
hindrance, but the general sense of ὄγκος in this connexion is
quite suitable.   Compare Apul. *Apologia*, 19 ("etenim in
omnibus ad vitae munia utendis quicquid aptam moderationem
supergreditur, oneri potius quam usui exuberat"), and the evening
prayer of the Therapeutae (Philo, *vit. Contempl* 3) to have their
souls lightened from τοῦ τῶν αἰσθήσεων καὶ αἰσθητῶν ὄγκου.
Ὄγκος had acquired in Greek literature the sense of pride, both
bad and good, and it has been taken here (so sah = "having
forsaken all pride") as an equivalent for pride in the sense of
conceit (fastus), as, *e.g.*, by Bengel and Seeberg.   But what the
readers seem to have been in danger of was not arrogance so
much as a tendency to grow disheartened.   The metaphor is not
"reducing our weight," though ὄγκος had sometimes this association with fleshiness; it refers to the weight of superfluous things,
like clothes, which would hinder and handicap the runner.   Let
us strip for the race, says the writer.   Put unmetaphorically,
the thought is that no high end like πίστις is possible apart
from a steady, unflinching resolve to do without certain things.
What these encumbrances are the writer does not say (cp.
11¹⁵. ²⁵. ²⁶); he implies that if people will set themselves to the
course of faith in this difficult world, they will soon discover
what hampers them.   In καὶ τὴν εὐπερίστατον ἁμαρτίαν, the article
does not imply any specific sin like that of apostasy (v.²⁵); it is
ἁμαρτία in general, any sin that might lead to apostasy (*e.g.* v.¹⁶).
The sense of εὐπερίστατος can only be inferred from the context
and from the analogy of similar compounds, for it appears to have
been a verbal adjective coined by the writer; at any rate no instance of its use in earlier writers or in the papyri has been as
yet discovered.   As the phrase goes with ἀποθέμενοι, the introductory καί linking τὴν . . . ἁμαρτίαν with ὄγκον, εὐπερίστατος
probably denotes something like "circumstans nos" (vg), from
περιΐστάναι (= cingere).   The εὐ is in any case intensive.   Theophylact suggested "endangering" (δι' ἣν εὐκόλως τις εἰς περι-
στάσεις ἐμπίπτει· οὐδὲν γὰρ οὕτω κινδυνῶδες ὡς ἁμαρτία), as though
it were formed from περίστασις (distress or misery).   Taken
passively, it might mean (*a*) "popular," or (*b*) "easily avoided,"
or (*c*) "easily contracted."   (*a*) περίστατος may mean what
people gather round (περιστατέω) to admire, as, *e.g.*, in Isokrates,
de Permut. 135 E, θαυματοποιΐαις ταῖς . . . ὑπὸ τῶν ἀνοήτων
περιστάτοις γενομέναις, and εὐπερίστατον would then = "right
popular."   This is at any rate more relevant and pointed than
(*b*), from περιΐσταμαι, which Chrysostom once suggested (τὴν
εὐκόλως περισταμένην ἡμᾶς ἢ τὴν εὐκόλως περίστασιν δυναμένην
παθεῖν: μᾶλλον δὲ τοῦτο, ῥάδιον γὰρ ἐὰν θέλωμεν περιγενέσθαι τῆς
ἁμαρτίας), though περίστατος does mean "admired," and ἀπερί-

στατος is sometimes, by way of contrast, "unsupported." On the other hand, ἀπερίστατος may mean "unencumbered," as in the contrast drawn by Maximus of Tyre (*Diss.* xx.) between the simple life (ἁπλοῦν βίον καὶ ἀπερίστατον καὶ ἐλευθερίας ἐπήβολον) and a life τῷ οὐχ ἁπλῷ ἀλλ' ἀναγκαίῳ καὶ περιστάσεων γέμοντι. The former life he declares was that of the golden age, before men worried themselves with the encumbrances of civilization. In the light of this, εὐπερίστατος might mean "which sorely hinders" (*i.e.* active), a sense not very different from (vg) "circumstans nos," or "which at all times is prepared for us" (syr).

(*c*) is suggested by Theodoret, who rightly takes ἡ ἁμαρτία as generic, and defines εὐπερίστατον as εὐκόλως συνισταμένην τε καὶ γινομένην. καὶ γὰρ ὀφθαλμὸς δελεάζεται, ἀκοὴ καταθέλγεται, ἀφὴ γαργαρίζεται, καὶ γλῶσσα ῥᾷστα διολισθαίνει, καὶ ὁ λογισμὸς περὶ τὸ χεῖρον ὀξύρροπος. But "easily caught" is hardly tense enough for the context. Wetstein, harking back to περίστατος and περίστασις, connects the adjective with the idea of the heroic onlookers. "Peccatum uestrum seu defectio a doctrina Christi non in occulto potest committi et latere ; non magis quam lapsus cursoris, sed conspicietur ab omnibus. Cogitate iterum, spectatores adesse omnes illos heroas, quorum constantiam laudaui, quo animo uidebunt lapsum uestrum? qua fronte ante oculos ipsorum audebitis tale facinus committere?" But "open" or "conspicuous" is, again, too slight and light a sense. If any conjecture had to be accepted, εὐπερίσταλτον would be the best. Cp. the schol. on *Iliad*, ii. 183 (ἀπὸ δὲ χλαῖναν βάλε), χλαῖνα τετράγωνος χλαμὺς ἡ εἰς ὀξὺ λήγουσα· ἀπέβαλε δὲ αὐτὴν διὰ τό εὐπερίσταλτον. Hence Bentley's note : "Lego τὴν ὑπὲρ ἱκανὸν ἀπαρτίαν . . . immo potius εὐπερίσταλτον ἀπαρτίαν." In Soph. *Ajax*, 821, the hero says of the sword on which he is about to fall, "I have fixed it in the ground, εὖ περιστείλας, right carefully." The verbal adjective would therefore mean, in this connexion, "close-clinging," while ἀπαρτίαν (= burden) would be practically a synonym for ὄγκον.

Τρέχωμεν . . . ἀφορῶντες, for the motive-power in life comes from inward convictions. What inspires Christians to hold out and to endure is their vision of the unseen (cp. Herodian, v. 6. 7, ὁ δ' Ἀντωνῖνος ἔθεε . . . ἔς τε τὸν θεὸν ἀποβλέπων καὶ τοὺς χαλινοὺς ἀντέχων τῶν ἵππων· πᾶσάν τε τὴν ὁδὸν ἤνυε τρέχων ἔμπαλιν ἑαυτοῦ ἀφορῶν τε εἰς τὸ πρόσθεν τοῦ θεοῦ), as the writer has already shown (11^{1f.}). Τὸν προκείμενον ἡμῖν ἀγῶνα is built on the regular (p. 193) phrase for a course being set or assigned ; *e.g.* Lucian in *de Mercede Conduct.* 11, σοὶ δὲ ὁ ὑπὲρ τῆς ψυχῆς ἀγὼν καὶ ὑπὲρ ἅπαντος τοῦ βίου τότε προκεῖσθαι δοκεῖ : Plato's *Laches*, 182a, οὗ γὰρ ἀγῶνος ἀθληταί ἐσμεν καὶ ἐν οἷς ἡμῖν ὁ ἀγὼν πρόκειται κτλ., and Josephus, *Ant.* viii. 12. 3, οἳ προκειμένων αὐτοῖς ἄθλων, ἐπὰν περί τι σπουδάσωσιν, οὐ διαλείπουσι περὶ τοῦτ᾽ ἐνεργοῦντες. For ἀφορῶντες εἰς (v.[2]), see Epictetus, ii. 19, where the philosopher says he wishes to make his disciples free and happy, εἰς τὸν θεὸν ἀφορῶντας ἐν παντὶ καὶ μικρῷ καὶ μεγάλῳ. An almost exact parallel occurs in the epitaph proposed by the author of 4 Mac (17[10]) for the Maccabean martyrs, οἳ καὶ ἐξεδίκησαν τὸ ἔθνος εἰς θεὸν ἀφορῶντες καὶ μέχρι θανάτου τὰς βασάνους ὑπομείναντες. ᾽Αφορᾶν implies the same concentrated[1] attention as ἀποβλέπειν (see on 11[26]): "with no eyes for any one or anything except Jesus." ᾽Ιησοῦν comes at the end of the phrase, as in 2[9], and especially 3[1]; the terms τὸν τῆς πίστεως ἀρχηγὸν καὶ τελειωτήν describe him as the perfect exemplar of πίστις in his earthly life (cp. 2[13]), as the supreme pioneer (ἀρχηγός as in 2[10], though here as the pioneer of personal faith, not as the author of our faith) and the perfect embodiment of faith (τελειωτής, a term apparently coined by the writer). He has realized faith to the full, from start to finish. Τελειωτής does not refer to τελειωθῶσιν in 11[40]; it does not imply that Jesus "perfects" our faith by fulfilling the divine promises.

In ὃς ἀντὶ τῆς προκειμένης αὐτῷ χαρᾶς, the χαρά is the unselfish joy implied in 2[8, 9], "that fruit of his self-sacrifice which must be presupposed in order that the self-sacrifice should be a reasonable transaction. Self-sacrificing love does not sacrifice itself but for an end of gain to its object; otherwise it would be folly. Does its esteeming as a reward that gain to those for whom it suffers, destroy its claim to being self-sacrifice? Nay, that which seals its character as self-sacrificing love is, that this to it is a satisfying reward" (M'Leod Campbell, *The Nature of the Atonement*, p. 23). As Epictetus bluntly put it, ἐὰν μὴ ἐν τῷ αὐτῷ ᾖ τὸ εὐσεβὲς καὶ συμφέρον, οὐ δύναται σωθῆναι τὸ εὐσεβὲς ἔν τινι (i. 27. 14). So, in the Odes of Solomon 31[8-12], Christ says:

"They condemned me when I stood up . . .
But I endured and held my peace,
    that I might not be moved by them.
But I stood unshaken like a firm rock,
    that is beaten by the waves and endures.
And I bore their bitterness for humility's sake;
    that I might redeem my people and inherit it."

Hence ἀντί (as in v.[16] ἀντὶ βρώσεως: cp. Plato's *Menex.* 237 A, ἄνδρας ἀγαθοὺς ἐπαινοῦντες, οἳ . . . τὴν τελευτὴν ἀντὶ τῆς τῶν ζώντων σωτηρίας ἠλλάξαντο) means, "to secure." The sense of

---

[1] Epictetus, in his praise of Herakles (iii. 24), declares that his hero lived and worked with a firm faith in Zeus the Father. "He considered that Zeus was his own father; he called Zeus father, and did everything with his eyes fixed on Zeus (πρὸς ἐκεῖνον ἀφορῶν ἔπραττεν ἃ ἔπραττεν)."

προκειμένης (cp. v.[1]) tells against the rendering of ἀντὶ . . . χαρᾶς
as "instead of the joy which had been set before him," as though
the idea were that of 11[25-26], either the renunciation of his pre-
incarnate bliss (so Wetstein, von Soden, Windisch, Goodspeed,
etc., recently), or the renunciation of joy in the incarnate life (so
Chrysostom, Calvin), *i.e.* the natural pleasure of avoiding the way
of the cross.   This is a Pauline idea (2 Co 8[9], Phil 2[6, 7]), which
the writer might have entertained; but (p. l) he never hints at it
elsewhere, and the other interpretation tallies with the idea of
2[8. 9]. Inspired by this, Jesus ὑπέμεινε (+ τόν, p[13] D*) σταυρόν—
as we might say in English "a cross." Aristotle (*Nik. Eth.* ix.
1, 2) declares that courage is praiseworthy just because it involves
pain, χαλεπώτερον γὰρ τὰ λυπηρὰ ὑπομένειν ἢ τὰ ἡδέων ἀπέχεσθαι:
no doubt the end in view is pleasant (τὸ κατὰ τὴν ἀνδρείαν τέλος
ἡδύ, cp. He 12[11]), but the end is not always visible.   In αἰσχύνης
καταφρονήσας it is not the horrible torture of the crucifixion, but
its stinging indignity (cp. Gal 3[13] for an even darker view), which
is noted as a hard thing; it was a punishment for slaves and
criminals, for men of whom the world felt it was well rid (cp.
11[38a]).   But Jesus did not allow either the dread or the experience
of this to daunt him.   He rose above "indignity and contumely,
that is to say, all that would most touch that life which man has
in the favour of man, and which strikes more deeply than
physical infliction, because it goes deeper than the body—wound-
ing the spirit" (M'Leod Campbell, *The Nature of the Atonement*,
pp. 229, 230).   Musonius (ed. Hense, x.) defined ὕβρις or αἰσχύνη
as οἷον λοιδορηθῆναι ἢ πληγῆναι ἢ ἐμπτυσθῆναι, ὧν τὸ χαλεπώτατον
πληγαί.   But the special αἰσχύνη here is that of crucifixion.
This, says the writer, Jesus did not allow to stand between him
and loyalty to the will of God.   It is one thing to be sensitive to
disgrace and disparagement, another thing to let these hinder us
from doing our duty.   Jesus was sensitive to such emotions; he
felt disgrace keenly.   But instead of allowing these feelings to
cling to his mind, he rose above them.   This is the force of καταφρονήσας here, as in the last clause of St. Philip of Neri's well-
known maxim, "Spernere mundum, spernere te ipsum, spernere
te sperni."   It is the only place in the NT where καταφρονεῖν is
used in a good sense (true and false shame are noted in
Sir 4[20. 21] περὶ τῆς ψυχῆς σου μὴ αἰσχυνθῇς· ἔστιν γὰρ αἰσχύνη ἐπά-
γουσα ἁμαρτίαν, καὶ ἔστιν αἰσχύνη δόξα καὶ χάρις).   The climax is
put in one of the writer's favourite quotations from the psalter;
only this time he uses κεκάθικεν (perfect here alone for the more
usual aorist, 1[3] 8[1] 10[12]) = and so has entered on his χαρά.

Jesus thus had to suffer worse than anything you have had to
bear; this is the thought of vv.[3. 4], which round off the first
movement of the appeal in 12[1f.] :—

³ *Compare him who steadily endured* (ὑπομεμενηκότα) *all that hostility from sinful men, so as to keep your own hearts from fainting and failing.*
⁴ *You have not had to shed blood yet in the struggle against sin.*

The writer assumes, as in 5⁷ᶠ·, a close knowledge of the Passion story. Before proceeding to argue that suffering is a fruitful discipline, with which God honours them (v.⁵ᶠ·), he reminds them that as yet they have not had to face the worst (v.⁴). The metaphor of the race-course dies away into the general military metaphor of v.⁴, where ἁμαρτία is half-personified as in 3¹³. Ἀναλογίσασθε ¹ (the γάρ is corroborative: "yes, ἀναλογίσασθε " κτλ.) is more than κατανοήσατε (3¹): "consider him and compare his treatment at the hands of these sinners (ἁμαρτωλῶν as in Mk 14⁴¹) with what you are called to suffer." Τοιαύτην echoes σταυρόν and αἰσχύνης, and is explained by μέχρις αἵματος in the next verse, while ὑπομεμενηκότα is another aoristic perfect like κεκάθικεν.

Ἀντιλογίαν is used here of active opposition, as in Ps 17⁴⁴ (ῥῦσαί με ἐξ ἀντιλογιῶν λαοῦ), where אᶜᵃ R read ἀντιλογίας, and in the papyri (e.g. *Tebt. P.* 138 [ii B.C.] ἀντιλογιάς μάχην). Like the verb (cp. Jn 19¹², Ro 10²¹), the noun covers more than verbal opposition, as in Nu 20¹³ and Jude ¹¹ τῇ ἀντιλογίᾳ τοῦ Κορέ. The words εἰς αὐτόν (or ἑαυτόν, A P syrʰᵏˡ etc. : in semetipsum, vg.) have no special emphasis; all the writer means to say is that Jesus himself, Jesus in his own person, had to encounter malevolent opposition.

This is one of the places at which textual corruption began early. The curious *v.l.* ἑαυτούς finds early support in א* D* (αὐτούς, p¹³ אᶜ 33. 256. 1288. 1319*. 1739. 2127 Lat syrᵛᵍ boh Orig.); p¹³ א* and D* go wrong here as in 11³⁵, D* and Lat as at 11²³ (insertion). It is extremely unlikely that the reading arose from a recollection of passages like Nu 16³⁷ (Korah, Dathan, and Abiram) ἡγίασαν τὰ πυρεῖα τῶν ἁμαρτωλῶν τούτων ἐν (*i.e.* at the cost of) ταῖς ψυχαῖς αὐτῶν, or Pr 8³⁶ οἱ δὲ εἰς ἐμὲ ἁμαρτάνοντες ἀσεβοῦσιν εἰς τὰς ἑαυτῶν ψυχάς. The notion that an evil-doer really injured himself was a commonplace (*e.g.* M. Aurel. 9⁴ ὁ ἁμαρτάνων ἑαυτῷ ἁμαρτάνει· ὁ ἀδικῶν ἑαυτὸν ἀδικεῖ, the remark of Chrysippus quoted by Plutarch in *de Stoic. repugn.* xvi., ἀδικεῖσθαι ὑφ' ἑαυτοῦ τὸν ἀδικοῦντα καὶ αὐτὸν ἀδικεῖν, ὅταν ἄλλον ἀδικῇ, Aristotle in *Magn. Moral.* 1196a, ὁ ἄρα ταῦτα μὴ πράττων ἀδικεῖ αὐτόν, and Xen. *Hellen.* i. 7. 19, ἡμαρτηκότας τὰ μέγιστα εἰς θεούς τε καὶ ὑμᾶς αὐτούς); Philo works it out in *quod deter.* 15, 16. But there is no point in suggesting here, as this reading does, that the ἁμαρτωλοί were acting against their better selves, unconsciously injuring their own souls, as they maltreated Jesus. The writer deals with sin in a more straightforward and direct way, and, in spite of all arguments to the contrary (*e.g.* by Westcott, von Soden, Seeberg, Peake, Wickham), this seems a far-fetched idea here. It is like the similar interpretation of ἑαυτούς in 10³⁴, a piece of irrelevant embroidery; it "looks like the conceit which some reader wrote upon his margin" (A. B. Davidson). Theodoret took εἰς ἑαυτούς with ἀναλογίσασθε = "think to yourselves." Which is not natural, though the Ethiopic version follows this interpretation. In some early versions (*e.g.* sah arm) neither εἰς ἑαυτόν nor εἰς ἑαυτούς seems to be implied.

¹ Ἀναλογίζομαι, though not a LXX term, begins to be used in Hellenistic Judaism (*e.g.* Ps.-Sol 8⁷ ἀνελογισάμην τὰ κρίματα τοῦ θεοῦ) in a religious sense.

In ἵνα . . . ἐκλυόμενοι, ἐκλυόμενοι (ἐκλελυμένοι p¹³ D*) might
go with ταῖς ψυχαῖς ὑμῶν (cp. Polybius, xx. 4. 7, οὐ μόνον τοῖς
σώμασιν ἐξελύθησαν, ἀλλὰ καὶ ταῖς ψυχαῖς), as readily as κάμητε
(cp. Job 10¹ κάμνω δὲ τῇ ψυχῇ μου). Both verbs connect with
it, to express the general sense of inward exhaustion and faint-
heartedness; indeed, Aristotle uses both to describe runners
relaxing and collapsing, once the goal has been passed: ἐπὶ τοῖς
καμπτῆρσιν (at the goal of the race, not till then) ἐκπνέουσι καὶ
ἐκλύονται· προορῶντες γὰρ τὸ πέρας οὐ κάμνουσι πρότερον (*Rhet.*
iii. 9. 2). In v.⁴ οὔπω (γάρ is superfluously added by D L 440.
491. 823 arm sah boh) κτλ. does not necessarily imply that they
would be called upon to shed their blood in loyalty to their
faith, as if martyrdom was the inevitable result of tenacity. Nor
is the writer blaming them; he does not mean to suggest that if
they had been truly decided for God against the world, they
would by this time have suffered μέχρις αἵματος. He is shaming
them, not blaming them. "Your sufferings have been serious and
sharp (10³²ᶠ·), but nothing to what others before you, and especially Jesus, have had to bear. Will you give way under a lesser
strain than theirs?" The coming of the messiah was to be
heralded by birth-pangs of trouble for his adherents on earth,
and it might be supposed that the writer implies here: "The
Coming One (10³⁷) is near (12²⁶), as is evident from your woes;
do not fail, but be ready for him." But this line of thought is
not worked out elsewhere by the writer, and is not necessary to
his argument at this point. To fight μέχρις αἵματος is to resist
to the death; cp. the cry of Judas Maccabaeus to his troops
(2 Mac 13¹⁴), ἀγωνίσασθαι μέχρι θανάτου. Μέχρις αἵματος has the
same meaning of a mortal combat, *e.g.* in Heliod. vii. 8, τῆς
μέχρις αἵματος στάσεως.

Note another case of rhetorical alliteration in αἵμ. ἀντικ. . . . . ἁμαρτ.
ἀνταγωνιζόμενοι (cp. *Clem. Hom.* iv. 5, πρὸς τοσαύτην δύναμιν ἀνταγωνί-
σασθαι), and the use of ἀνταγωνιζέσθαι above (v.¹) in the quot. from 4 Mac.

The connexion of thought in vv.⁵ᶠ· is: God has not yet asked
from you the supreme sacrifice (v.⁴), and, besides (vv.⁵ᶠ·), any
demand he makes upon your courage is in your highest
interests.

⁵ *And have you forgotten the word of appeal that reasons with you as
sons?—*

"*My son, never make light of the Lord's discipline,
　never faint (ἐκλύου) under his reproofs;*
⁶ *for the Lord disciplines the man he loves,
　and scourges every son he receives.*"

⁷ *It is for discipline that you have to endure. God is treating you as sons;
for where is the son who is not disciplined by his father?* ⁸ *Discipline is the
portion (μέτοχοι γεγόνασι, as 3¹⁴) of all; if you get no discipline, then you are
not sons, but bastards.* ⁹ *Why, we had fathers of our flesh to discipline us,*

and we yielded to them! Shall we not far more submit to the Father of our spirits, and so live? [10] *For while their discipline was only for a time, and inflicted at their pleasure, he disciplines us for our good, that we may share in his own holiness.* [11] *Discipline always seems for the time to be a thing of pain, not of joy; but those who are trained by it reap the fruit of it afterwards in the peace of an upright life.*

With the interrogative καὶ ἐκλέλησθε κτλ. (v.⁵) the writer opens his next argument and appeal. All such ὑπομονή means a divine παιδεία or moral training, which we have the honour of receiving from God. Instead of adducing the example of Jesus, however (see on 5⁷·⁸), he quotes from the book of Proverbs (vv.⁵·⁶), and then applies the general idea (vv.⁷⁻¹¹). Ἐκλανθάνεσθαι (not a LXX term) in v.⁵ is slightly stronger than the more common ἐπιλανθάνεσθαι, though it may be rhetorically chosen for the sake of assonance after ἐκλυόμενοι. The παράκλησις is personified rhetorically; Ἥτις (2³) ὑμῖν (for the scripture applies to all believers) ὡς υἱοῖς διαλέγεται. It is the παράκλησις of God, who speaks as a father to his son (υἱέ μου), though in the original "son" is merely the pupil of the sage (personifying the divine wisdom). Παράκλησις in Alexandrian Judaism "is the regular term for 'an appeal' to an individual to rise to the higher life of philosophy" (Conybeare's ed. of Philo's *de vit. Contempl.*, p. 201). The quotation is from Pr 3¹¹·¹² (A):

> υἱέ, μὴ ὀλιγώρει παιδείας Κυρίου,
> μηδὲ ἐκλύου ὑπ᾽ αὐτοῦ ἐλεγχόμενος·
> ὃν γὰρ ἀγαπᾷ Κύριος παιδεύει (ἐλέγχει, B)
> μαστιγοῖ δὲ πάντα υἱὸν ὃν παραδέχεται.

After υἱέ, μου is added (except by D* 31 Old Latin, Clem.), but otherwise the citation is word for word. Philo (*De Congressu. Erud.* 31) quotes the same passage to prove that discipline and hardship are profitable for the soul (οὕτως ἄρα ἡ ἐπίπληξις καὶ νουθεσία καλὸν νενόμισται, ὥστε δι᾽ αὐτῆς ἡ πρὸς θεὸν ὁμολογία συγγένεια γίνεται. τί γὰρ οἰκειότερον υἱῷ πατρὸς ἢ υἱοῦ πατρί;). The LXX contains a double mistranslation. (*a*) It is at least doubtful if the Hebrew text of the second line means "be not weary of"; the alternative is a parallel to the first line, "scorn not." (*b*) It is certain that the second line of v.⁶ originally ran, "he afflicts the man in whom he delights," or "and delights in him as a father in his son." Our writer, following the free LXX version, notes the twofold attitude of men under hardship. They may determine to get through it and get over it, as if it had no relation to God, seeing nothing of him in it. Stronger natures take this line; they summon up a stoical courage, which dares the world to do its worst to them. This is ὀλιγωρεῖν παιδείας Κυρίου. It ignores any divine meaning in the rough experience. Other natures collapse weakly (ἐκλύειν); they see God in the trial, but he seems too hard upon them, and they break down in self-pity, as if they were victims of an unkind providence. Ἐλεγχόμενος . . . παιδεύει is used, as in Rev 3¹⁹ (ὅσους ἐὰν φιλῶ ἐλέγχω καὶ παιδεύω), of pointing out and correcting faults; μαστιγοῖ, as in Judith 8²⁷ (εἰς νουθέτησιν μαστιγοῖ Κύριος τοὺς ἐγγίζοντας αὐτῷ) and often elsewhere; παραδέχεται, in the sense of Lk 15². In fact, the temper inculcated in this passage resembles that of Ps.-Sol 16¹¹ᶠ·, where the writer prays:

γογγυσμὸν καὶ ὀλιγοψυχίαν ἐν θλίψει μάκρυνον ἀπ᾽ ἐμοῦ,
ἐὰν ἁμαρτήσω ἐν τῷ σε παιδεύειν εἰς ἐπιστροφήν . . .
ἐν τῷ ἐλέγχεσθαι ψυχὴν ἐν χειρὶ σαπρίας αὐτῆς . . .
ἐν τῷ ὑπομεῖναι δίκαιον ἐν τούτοις ἐλεηθήσεται ὑπὸ κυρίου.

In εἰς παιδείαν ὑπομένετε (v.⁷), with which the writer begins his application of the text, the vigour is lost by the change of εἰς into εἰ (in a group of late cursives, including 5. 35. 203. 226ᶜ. 241. 242. 257. 337. 378. 383. 487. 506. 547. 623. 794. 917. 1319. 1831. 1891. 1898. 2127. 2143 + Theophyl.), and ὑπομένετε is indicative, not imperative.[1] To endure rightly, one must endure intelligently; there is a reason for it in God's relations with us (ὡς υἱοῖς ὑμῖν προσφέρεται). Προσφέρεται (cp. *Syll.* 371¹³, i A.D.) is a non-biblical Greek term for "treating" or "handling" ("tractare, agere cum"); cp. *Syll.* 371¹³, i A.D., and Latyschev's *Inscript. Antiq. Orae Septentrionalis*, i. 22²⁸ τοῖς μὲν ἡλικιώταις προσφερόμενος ὡς ἀδελφός . . . τοῖς δὲ παισὶν ὡς πατήρ); τίς goes with υἱός, as in Mt 7⁹ (τίς ἐστιν ἐξ ὑμῶν ἄνθρωπος) etc., and ἐστιν after υἱός is rightly omitted by ℵ* A P W 104. 256 vg sah Origen.

A mood of bitter scepticism about the discipline of providence recurs in some contemporary Roman writers; both Lucan (*Pharsalia*, iv. 807 f., "Felix Roma quidem, civesque habitura beatos, | si libertatis superis tam cura placeret | quam uindicta placet") and Tacitus (*Hist.* i. 3, "nec enim umquam atrocioribus populi Romani cladibus magisve iustis indiciis adprobatum est non esse curae deis securitatem nostram, esse ultionem") speak as if the gods showed an unpaternal vindictiveness. But the idea of a fatherly providence was far-spread, both within and without Judaism. When our author argues: "You think that if God were fatherly, he would spare you these hardships? On the contrary, they are the proof of his wise affection"—he is not far from Seneca's position (in the *de Providentia*, iv. 7): "hos itaque deus quos probat, quos amat, indurat recognoscit, exercet." And in 2 Mac 6¹² the author bids his readers re-

---

[1] D takes εἰς παιδείαν with the foregoing παραδέχεται, as Hofmann does with μαστιγοῖ. This leaves ὑπομένετε (ὑπομείνατε D) in quite an effective opening position for the next sentence; but it is not the writer's habit to end a quotation with some outside phrase.

member τὰς τιμωρίας μὴ πρὸς ὄλεθρον, ἀλλὰ πρὸς παιδίαν τοῦ γένους ἡμῶν εἶναι. According to Sanhedr. 101a (cp. Sifre, Deut. 32), Rabbi Akiba comforted R. Eliezer on his sick-bed by explaining to him that "chastisements are precious," whereas the other three rabbis who accompanied him had only praised the sick man for his piety. There is a fine passage in Philo's *quod deter. potiori insid. soleat*, 39–40, where he argues that discipline at God's hands is better than being left to oneself in sin and folly; εὐτυχέστεροι δὲ καὶ κρείττους τῶν ἀνεπιτροπεύτων νέων οἱ μάλιστα μὲν ἐπιστασίας καὶ ἀρχῆς ἀξιωθέντες φυσικῆς, ἣν οἱ γεννή-σαντες ἐπὶ τέκνοις κεκλήρωνται . . . ἱκετεύωμεν οὖν τὸν θεὸν οἱ συνειδήσει τῶν οἰκείων ἀδικημάτων ἐλεγχόμενοι, κολάσαι ἡμᾶς μᾶλλον ἢ παρεῖναι. Similarly, in *de sacrificantibus*, 11, he writes of parental care, human and divine, apropos of Deut 14[1] (υἱοί ἐστε κυρίῳ τῷ θεῷ ὑμῶν) δηλονότι προνοίας καὶ κηδεμονίας ἀξιωθη-σόμενοι τῆς ὡς ἐκ πατρός· ἡ δὲ ἐπιμέλεια τοσοῦτον διοίσει τῆς ἀπ' ἀνθρώπων ὅσονπερ, οἶμαι, καὶ ὁ ἐπιμελούμενος διαφέρει. Compare M. Aur. i. 17, τῷ ἄρχοντι καὶ πατρὶ ὑποταχθῆναι, ὃς ἔμελλε πάντα τὸν τῦφον ἀφαιρήσειν μου (cp. v. 31). When the king asks, in the *Epist. Arist.* 248, what is the supreme instance of neglect (ἀμέλεια), the Jew answers, εἰ τέκνων ἄφροντίς τις εἴη, καὶ μὴ κατὰ πάντα τρόπον ἀγαγεῖν σπεύδοι . . . τὸ δὲ ἐπιδεῖσθαι παιδείαν σωφροσύνης μετασχεῖν, θεοῦ δυνάμει τοῦτο γίνεται.

Jerome writes in his letter (*Epist.* xxii. 39) to Eustochium : "haec est sola retributio, cum sanguis sanguine conpensatur et redempti cruore Christi pro redemptore libenter occumbimus. quis sanctorum sine certamine corona-tus est? Abel justus occiditur; Abraham uxorem periclitatur amittere, et, ne in inmensum uolumen extendam, quaere et invenies singulos diuersa per-pessos. solus in deliciis Salomon fuit et forsitan ideo corruit. quem enim diligit dominus, corripit ; castigat autem omnem filium, quem recipit." He often quotes this verse ([6]) in his letters of counsel and warning. Thus in lxviii. I he prefixes it with the remark, "magna ira est, quando peccantibus non irascitur deus." The modern parallel would be Browning's hero in *Christmas-Eve and Easter-Day* (pt. 2, xxxiii.), who is

"happy that I can
Be crossed and thwarted as a man,
Not left in God's contempt apart,
With ghastly smooth life."

In v.[8] πάντες (*sc.* υἱοὶ γνήσιοι) recalls πάντα υἱόν (v.[6]). Νόθοι are children born out of wedlock, who are left to themselves ; the father is not sufficiently interested in them to inflict on them the discipline that fits his legitimate children for their place in the home. Νόθος (not a LXX term) seems to mean born of mixed marriages, in Wis 4[8] (cp. Aristoph. *Birds*, 1650–1652, νόθος γὰρ εἶ κοὐ γνήσιος . . . ὤν γε ξένης γυναικός). So Philo compares polytheists and lovers of material pleasure to τῶν ἐκ πόρνης ἀποκυηθέντων (*de Confus. ling.* 28), as distinguished from the sons of God. The double ἔστε (not ἦτε) makes the sentence more vivid ; the writer supposes an actual case. In vv.⁹· ¹⁰ the writer simply develops this idea of παιδεία, comparing the human and the divine methods. Hence εἶτα cannot mean here "further" (deinde) ; it is "besides," in the sense that it brings out another element in the conception.

Εἶτα might be taken interrogatively (=itane or siccine), to introduce an animated question (as often in Plato, *e.g. Leges*, 964*b*, *Theat.* 207*d*, *Sophist.* 222*b*), though we should expect a δέ in the second clause here or a καί before οὐ πολὺ μᾶλλον. Kypke suggests that εἶτα=εἰ δέ (quodsi) as, *e.g.*, in Jos. *B.J.* iii. 8. 5, εἶτ᾽ ἂν μὲν ἀφανίσῃ τις ἀνθρώπου παρακαταθήκην, ἢ διάθηται κακῶς.

Παιδευτής only occurs once in the LXX, and there as a description of God (Hos 5² ἐγὼ δὲ παιδευτὴς ὑμῶν) ; in 4 Mac 9⁶ (ὁ παιδευτὴς γέρων) it is applied to a man, as in Ro 2²⁰. Καὶ ἐνετρεπόμεθα ("reverebamur," vg), we submitted respectfully to them (the object of the verb being πατέρας), as in Mt 21³⁷, not, we amended our ways (as in LXX, *e.g.* 2 Ch 7¹⁴ and Philo's *quaest. in Gen.* 4⁹ τὸ μὴ ἁμαρτάνειν μηδὲν τὸ παραμέγιστον ἀγαθόν· τὸ ἁμαρτάνοντα ἐντραπῆναι συγγενές ἐκείνου). In οὐ πολὺ μᾶλλον, the more common πολλῷ is read by Dᶜ K L, and after πολύ a few authorities (p¹³ אᶜ D* 1739 Origen) supply the δέ which is strictly required after the preceding μέν. The description of God as τῷ πατρὶ τῶν πνευμάτων is unexpected. In the vocabulary of Hellenistic Judaism God is called ὁ τῶν πνευμάτων καὶ πάσης ἐξουσίας δυνάστης (2 Mac 3²⁴), and "Lord of spirits" is a favourite Enochic title ; but "spirits" here cannot mean angels (cp. Nu 16²²). The contrast between τοὺς τῆς σαρκὸς πατέρας and τῷ πατρὶ τῶν πνευμάτων denotes God as the author of man's spiritual being ; the expression is quite intelligible as a statement of practical religion, and is only rendered ambiguous when we read into it later ideas about traducianism and creationism, which were not in the writer's mind. Shall we not submit to Him, the writer asks, καὶ ζήσομεν (cp. 10³⁸ ζήσεται)? "Monemur hoc verbo nihil esse nobis magis exitiale quam si nos in Dei obsequium tradere recusemus" (Calvin). In v.¹⁰ the assumption that the readers were mature men (εἴχομεν, v.⁹) is made explicit by πρὸς ὀλίγας ἡμέρας (till we became men). Πρός here, as in Wis 16⁶ (εἰς νουθεσίαν δὲ πρὸς ὀλίγον ἐταράχθησαν) etc., means duration ; it is not final, as if the parental discipline were with a view to the short, earthly life alone. Κατὰ τὸ δοκοῦν αὐτοῖς (as they chose) refers to the arbitrariness of the *patria potestas*. "Parents may err, but he is wise," as the Scottish metrical paraphrase puts it.

The writer has in mind the familiar *patria potestas* of the Romans, as in Terence's *Heauton Timoroumenos* (100: "vi et via pervolgata patrum";

204-207 : "parentum iniuriae unius modi sunt ferme . . . atque haec sunt
tamen ad virtutem omnia"), where one father is confessing to another how he
had mishandled his boy (99 f. : "ubi rem rescivi, coepi non humanitus neque
ut animum decuit aegrotum adulescentuli tractare"). Compare the remark
of the Persian officer in Xenophon's *Cyropaedia* (ii. 2. 14), who argued that a
man who set himself to make people laugh did less for them than a man who
made them weep, and instanced fathers—κλαύμασι μέν γε καὶ πατέρες υἱοῖς
σωφροσύνην μηχανῶνται. This is wholesome correction. But it was not
always so. "Qur postremo filio suscenseam, patres ut faciunt ceteri?" old
Demaenetus asks, in the *Asinaria* (49) of Plautus. Ovid's "durus pater"
(*Amores*, i. 15. 17) was more than a tradition of literature. Pliny tells us,
for example, that he had once to remonstrate with a man who was thrashing
his son for wasting money on horses and dogs (*Epp.* ix. 12): "haec tibi
admonitus immodicae seueritatis exemplo pro amore mutuo scripsi, ne
quando tu quoque filium tuum acerbius duriusque tractares." There is also
the story told by Aelian (*Var. Hist.* ix. 33) about the youth who, when asked
by his father what he had learned from Zeno, was thrashed for failing to
show anything definite, and then calmly replied that he had learned stoically
to put up with a father's bad temper (ἔφη μεμαθηκέναι φέρειν ὀργὴν πατέρων
καὶ μὴ ἀγανακτεῖν). Sons, says Dio Chrysostom (xv. 240 M), τρέφονται
πάντες ὑπὸ τῶν πατέρων καὶ παίονται πόλλακις ὑπ' αὐτῶν. The general point
of view is put by Epictetus (*Enchiridion*, 30, πατήρ ἐστιν· ὑπαγορεύεται
ἐπιμελεῖσθαι, παραχωρεῖν ἀπάντων, ἀνέχεσθαι λοιδορούντος, παίοντος), and the
connexion of "life" with παιδεία in Pr 4¹³ ἐπιλαβοῦ ἐμῆς παιδείας, μὴ ἀφῆς,
ἀλλὰ φύλαξον αὐτὴν σεαυτῷ εἰς ζωήν σου : Pr 6²³ λύχνος ἐντολή νόμου καὶ φῶς,
καὶ ὁδὸς ζωῆς καὶ ἔλεγχος καὶ παιδεία, and Sir 4¹⁷ᶠ·.

Now for the contrast. ʽΟ δὲ (God; *sc.* παιδεύει ἡμᾶς) ἐπὶ τὸ
συμφέρον (cp. 1 Co 12⁷; *Ep. Arist.* 125, συμβουλευόντων πρὸς
τὸ συμφέρον τῶν φίλων), which is explained in εἰς τὸ μεταλαβεῖν
(cp. 6⁷) τῆς ἁγιότητος αὐτοῦ. ʽΑγιότης is a rare term, which
begins to appear late in Hellenistic Judaism (*e.g.* 2 Mac 15² τοῦ
πάντα ἐφορῶντος μεθ᾽ ἁγιότητος: *Test. Levi* 3⁴ ὑπεράνω πάσης
ἁγιότητος), and, except as a *v.l.* in 2 Co 1¹², occurs nowhere else
in the NT. Here it denotes the divine life, to share in which is
the outcome of ὁ ἁγιασμὸς οὗ χωρὶς οὐδεὶς ὄψεται (*i.e.* have a
direct experience of) τὸν κύριον (v.¹⁴). The writer, in this contrast,
is simply arguing that the divine education, which involves some
suffering, as all παιδεία does, is more worthy of obedience from
mature people than even the parental discipline to which, for all
its faults ot temper, they submitted during childhood. The say-
ings of Isokrates, that while the roots of παιδεία were bitter, its
fruits were sweet, was a commonplace of ancient morals; the
writer is going to develop it in a moment. Meantime he alludes
to the equally well-known truth that παιδεία might involve severe
physical treatment.

Two examples may be added of this doctrine that education involves a
discipline which sometimes requires the infliction of pain. Maximus of Tyre
(*Diss.* iv. 7), in arguing that the desire to give pleasure is by no means an in-
variable proof of true affection, asks : φιλοῦσιν δὲ που καὶ παῖδας πατέρες καὶ
διδάσκαλοι μαθητάς· καὶ τί ἂν εἴη ἀνιαρότερον ἢ παιδὶ πατὴρ καὶ μαθητῇ διδάσκαλος; so Philo argues in *de Migrat. Abrah.* 20, σωφρονιστῶν ὡς ἔοικε τουτὶ

ἐστι τὸ ἔθος, παιδαγωγῶν, διδασκάλων, γονέων, πρεσβυτέρων, ἀρχόντων, νόμων·
ὀνειδίζοντες γάρ, ἔστι δ᾽ ὅπου καὶ κολάζοντες ἕκαστοι τούτων ἀμείνους τὰς ψυχὰς
ἀπεργάζονται τῶν παιδευομένων. καὶ ἐχθρὸς μὲν οὐδεὶς οὐδενί, φίλοι δὲ πᾶσι
πάντες. In de parent. col. 4, he explains, διὰ τοῦτ᾽ ἔξεστι τοῖς πατράσι καὶ
κατηγορεῖν πρὸς τοὺς παῖδας καὶ ἐμβριθέστερον νουθετεῖν καὶ, εἰ μὴ ταῖς δι᾽ ἀκοῶν
ἀπειλαῖς ὑπείκουσι, τύπτειν καὶ προπηλακίζειν καὶ καταδεῖν.

In v.[11] the writer sums up what he has been saying since v.[5].
Discipline or παιδεία πρὸς τὸ παρόν (a classical Greek phrase = for
the moment, e.g. Thuc. ii. 22, ὁρῶν αὐτοὺς πρὸς τὸ παρὸν χαλεπαί-
νοντας) οὐ (πᾶς . . . οὐ = absolute negative, not any) δοκεῖ (to
human feelings and judgment) χαρᾶς εἶναι ἀλλὰ λύπης (to be a
matter of, εἶναι with gen. as in 10[39]).

Πᾶσα μέν (א* P 33. 93) and πᾶσα δέ (p[13] א᷎ A D᷎ H K L Ψ 6. 326. 929.
1288. 1836 vg syr boh Chrys. etc.) practically mean the same thing, for the
μέν is concessive ("of course") and δέ is metabatic.   But probably it was the
awkwardness of the double μέν that led to the alteration of this one.   The other
readings, πᾶσα γάρ (Cosm. (221 C) Jer. Aug.) and πᾶσα (D* 104. 460. 917 arm
eth Orig. Cosm. (376 D)) are obviously inferior attempts to clear up the passage.

῾Ύστερον δέ (cp. Pr 5[3. 4] (of the harlot) ἢ πρὸς καιρὸν λιπαίνει
σὸν φάρυγγα· ὕστερον μέντοι πικρότερον χολῆς εὑρήσεις), but later
on discipline yields fruit ; it is not a stone flung down arbitrarily
on human life, but a seed.   By καρπὸν εἰρηνικὸν δικαιοσύνης the
writer means fruit (καρπός as often = result or outcome), which
consists in (genit. of apposition) δικαιοσύνη (as in 11[7] a generic
term for the good life as a religious relationship to God).   But
why εἰρηνικόν ?   Possibly in contrast to the restiveness and pain
(λύπης) of the period of discipline, when people are being trained
(γεγυμνασμένοις) ; when the discipline does its perfect work,
there is no friction between the soul and God.   But there is also
the suggestion of "saving" or "blissful."   Philo quotes Pr
3[11. 12] (see above on v.[5]) as a saying of Solomon the peaceful
(εἰρηνικός) ; the significance of this he finds in the thought that
subjection and obedience are really a wholesome state for people
who are inclined to be self-assertive, uncontrolled, and quarrelsome.   He thinks that Noah is rightly called by a name denoting
rest, since μετίασιν ἠρεμαῖον δὲ καὶ ἡσυχάζοντα καὶ σταθερὸν ἔτι τε
καὶ εἰρηνικὸν βίον οἱ καλοκἀγαθίαν τετιμηκότες (Abrah. 5).   To
take εἰρηνικόν in some such sense (salutaris) would yield a good
interpretation ; and this is confirmed by the similar use of εἰρήνη
in v.[14] and of the adjective in 3 Mac 6[32], where the Jews, in the
ecstasy of their relief, χοροὺς συνίσταντο εὐφροσύνης εἰρηνικῆς
σημεῖον.   Those who stand their training reap a safe, sound life
at last.   In its social aspect, εἰρηνικόν could only refer to the
brotherly love of the community ; the writer might be throwing
out a hint to his readers, that suffering was apt to render people
irritable, impatient with one another's faults.   The later record
even of the martyrs, for example, shows that the very prospect of

death did not always prevent Christians from quarrelling in
prison.   This may be the meaning of εἰρηνικόν in Ja 3¹⁸, but it is
out of keeping with the present context.

A close parallel to v.¹¹ is the saying of Aristotle (see above, for the similar
remark of Isokrates), quoted by Diog. Laertius (v. 1. 18): τῆς παιδείας ἔφη
τὰς μὲν ῥίζας εἶναι πικράς, γλυκεῖς δὲ τοὺς καρπούς. In *Epist. Arist.* 232,
τοὺς γὰρ ἀπ᾽ αὐτῆς (*i.e.* δικαιοσύνης) ἀλυπίαν κατασκευάζειν, though the ἀλυπία
here is freedom from misfortune. Clem. Alex. (*Strom.* vii. 10. 56), after
speaking of the time when we are delivered from the chastisements and
punishments ἃς ἐκ τῶν ἁμαρτημάτων εἰς παιδείαν ὑπομένομεν σωτήριον [He
12⁷], adds : μεθ᾽ ἣν ἀπολύτρωσιν τὸ γέρας καὶ αἱ τιμαὶ τελειωθεῖσιν ἀποδίδονται
. . . καὶ θεοὶ τὴν προσηγορίαν κέκληνται οἱ σύνθρονοι τῶν ἄλλων θεῶν, τῶν ὑπὸ
τῷ σωτῆρι πρώτων τεταγμένων, γενησόμενοι.

The writer now resumes the imperative tone (vv.¹²ᶠ·), with a
blend of counsel and warning.   The discipline of trouble is
viewed under an active aspect ; men must co-operate with God,
exerting themselves to avoid sin (v.¹) by the exercise of personal
zeal and church-discipline.   Otherwise, the results may be fatal.
The exhortation broadens out here, resuming the tone and range
of 10²⁵ᶠ·.

¹² *So* (διό as in 6¹) *" up with your listless hands!   Strengthen your weak
knees!"*   ¹³ *And "make straight paths for your feet" to walk in.   You must
not let the lame get dislocated, but rather make them whole.*   ¹⁴ *Aim at peace
with all—at that consecration without which no one will ever see the Lord ;*   ¹⁵ *see
to it that no one misses the grace of God, "that no root of bitterness grows up
to be a trouble" by contaminating all the rest of you ;*   ¹⁶ *that no one turns to
sexual vice or to a profane life as Esau did—Esau who for a single meal
"parted with his birthright."*   ¹⁷ *You know how later on, when he wanted to
obtain his inheritance of blessing, he was set aside ; he got no chance to repent,
though he tried for it with tears.*

For the first time, since the hints in 3¹² 4¹ and 6¹¹, the writer
alludes to differences of attainment in the little community.
Hitherto he has treated them as a solid whole.   But the possibility of individual members giving way has been voiced in 10²⁹,
and now the writer (¹³ᵇ) widens his appeal ; his readers are to
maintain their faith not only for their own sakes but for the sake
of those who at their side are in special danger of collapsing.
The courage of their ὑπομονή is more than a personal duty ; they
are responsible for their fellow-members, and this involves the
duty of inspiriting others by their own unswerving, unflagging
faith.   The admonition, as in 13¹ᶠ·, is addressed to the whole
community, not to their leaders.   The general aim of vv.¹²· ¹³ is
to produce the character praised by Matthew Arnold in his lines
on Rugby Chapel :

> "Ye move through the ranks, recall
> The stragglers, refresh the out-worn . . .
> Ye fill up the gaps in our files,
> Strengthen the wavering line,

> Stablish, continue our march,
> On, to the bound of the waste,
> On, to the City of God."

He begins in v.[12] by using scriptural language borrowed freely from Is 35³ (ἰσχύσατε, χεῖρες ἀνειμέναι καὶ γόνατα παραλελυμένα), but in a form already current in Sir 25³² (χεῖρες παρειμέναι καὶ γόνατα παραλελυμένα), and also from Pr 4²⁶ (ὀρθὰς τροχιὰς ποίει τοῖς ποσίν). This metaphorical language for collapsing in listless despair is common, e.g., in Sir 2¹² where χεῖρες παρειμέναι is bracketed with " cowardly hearts," in Philo's description of the Israelites who longed to return to Egypt, οἱ μὲν γὰρ προκαμόντες ἀνέπεσον, βαρὺν ἀντίπαλον ἡγησάμενοι τὸν πόνον, καὶ τὰς χεῖρας ὑπ' ἀσθενείας ὥσπερ ἀπειρηκότες ἀθληταὶ καθῆκαν (de Congressu Erud. 29, cp. He 11¹⁵), and especially in the description of moral encouragement in Job 4³. ⁴ εἰ γὰρ σὺ ἐνουθέτησας πολλούς, καὶ χεῖρας ἀσθενοῦς παρεκάλεσας, ἀσθενοῦντάς τε ἐξανέστησας ῥήμασιν, γόνασίν τε ἀδυνατοῦσιν θάρσος περιέθηκας. In Dt 32³⁶ παραλελυμένους is parallel to παρειμένους, and in Zeph 3¹⁶ the appeal is θάρσει . . . μὴ παρείσθωσαν αἱ χεῖρές σου.[1] Ἀνορθώσατε (literally = straighten, renew) goes with γόνατα better than with χεῖρας, but the sense is plain. In v.[13], if ποιήσατε is read in the first clause, καὶ τροχιὰς ὀρθὰς ποιήσατε τοῖς ποσὶν ὑμῶν is a hexameter (p. lvii). By τὸ χωλόν the writer means "those who are lame," these crippled souls in your company.

Probably the ποιεῖτε of ℵ* P 33. 917. 1831 (Orig.) has been conformed, in ποιήσατε (ℵᶜ A D H K L, etc., Chrys.), to the preceding ἀνορθώσατε (so, e.g., B. Weiss, in Texte u. Untersuch. xiv. 3. 4, 9, who declares that the older codices never yield any case of an original aor. being changed into a present), though some edd. (e.g. von Soden) regard ποιήσατε as the original text and ποιεῖτε as having been conformed to LXX (cp. Mt 3³).

As ἰαθῇ δὲ μᾶλλον shows, ἐκτραπῇ here has its medical sense (e.g. Hippol. de offic. med. 14, ὡς μήτε ἀνακλᾶται μήτε ἐκτρέπηται), not the common sense of being "turned aside" (as, e.g., in Philo, Quaest. in Exod. 23²⁰ οἱ ἀφυλάκτως ὁδοιποροῦντες διαμαρτάνουσιν τῆς ὀρθῆς καὶ λεωφόρου ὡς πολλάκις εἰς ἀνοδίας καὶ δυσβάτους καὶ τραχείας ἀτραποὺς ἐκτρέπεσθαι· τὸ παραπλήσιόν ἐστιν ὅτε καὶ αἱ ψυχαὶ τῶν νέων παιδείας ἀμοιροῦσιν, and in M. Aurel. i. 7, καὶ τὸ μὴ ἐκτραπῆναι εἰς ζῆλον σοφιστικόν). In Od. Sol 6¹⁴ᶠ· the ministers of the divine grace are praised in similar terms for their service to weaker Christians :

> "They have assuaged the dry lips,
> And the will that had fainted they have raised up : . . .
> And limbs that had fallen
> They have straightened and set up."

[1] Clem. Hom. xii. 18, αἱ χεῖρες ὑπὸ δηγμάτων παρείθησαν.

But here it is the members as a whole who are addressed, and
τροχ. ὀρθας π. τ. ποσὶν ὑμῶν means " keep straight " (ποσίν, dative =
" for your feet ")—it is the only way to help your fellow-members
who have weakened themselves.   Keep up the tone of your
community, move in the right direction, to prevent any of your
number from wavering and wandering.   The straight path is the
smooth path, it is implied ; if any limping soul is allowed to
stray from the straight course, under the influence of a bad
example, he will be made worse instead of better.   The admonition in *Test. Sim.* 5[2. 3] is interesting, as it suggests the train of
thought here between vv.[12f.] and [16f.] :

> ἀγαθύνατε τὰς καρδίας ὑμῶν ἐνώπιον Κυρίου
> καὶ εὐθύνατε τὰς ὁδοὺς ὑμῶν ἐνώπιον τῶν ἀνθρώπων
> καὶ ἔσεσθε εὑρίσκοντες χάριν ἐνώπιον Κυρίου καὶ ἀνθρώπων.
> φυλάξασθε οὖν ἀπὸ τῆς πορνείας,
> ὅτι ἡ πορνεία μήτηρ ἐστὶ τῶν κακῶν,
> χωρίζουσα ἀπὸ τοῦ θεοῦ καὶ προσεγγίζουσα τῷ Βελίαρ.

The author of Πρὸς Ἑβραίους knows that the difficulties in the way
of faith are more than mere despair.   In 12[1-11] he has been
dealing with the need of cheerful courage under the strain of
life ; this leads to the appeal of v.[12].   But while there is nothing
so infectious as cowardice or despair, he rapidly passes on,
in vv.[13f.] (καί κτλ.), to warn his readers against some specific
temptations in the moral life.   He continues, in a third imperative (v.[14]), εἰρήνην διώκετε (an OT phrase, 1 P 3[11]) μετὰ πάντων.
Here μετά goes with διώκετε in the sense of "along with" (as in
11[9] 13[23], for our author avoids σύν), and πάντων means " all the
(other) ἅγιοι " (as in 13[24]).   The call is to make common cause
with all the rest of the Christians in the quest for God's εἰρήνη,
i.e. (see above on v.[11]) the bliss and security of a life under God's
control.   It is εἰρήνη in a sense corresponding to the older sense
of felicity and prosperity on the ground of some (messianic)
victory of God, practically as in Lk 1[79] 19[38] the Christian
salvation ; only this comprehensive sense does justice to the
term here and in 13[20].   Hence the following καί is almost =
" even."

Εἰρήνη in a similar sense occurs repeatedly in the context of the passage
already quoted from Proverbs : *e.g.* 3[1. 2] υἱέ, ἐμῶν νομίμων μὴ ἐπιλανθάνου,
τὰ δὲ ῥήματα μου τηρείτω σὴ καρδία· μῆκος γὰρ βίου καὶ ἔτη ζωῆς καὶ εἰρήνην
προσθήσουσίν σοι . . . 3[9] ἀπάρχου αὐτῷ ἀπὸ σῶν καρπῶν δικαιοσύνης . . .
3[16. 17] ἐκ τοῦ στόματος αὐτῆς ἐκπορεύεται δικαιοσύνη καὶ πάντες οἱ τρίβοι αὐτῆς
ἐν εἰράνῃ . . . 3[23] ἵνα πορεύῃ πεποιθὼς ἐν εἰρήνῃ πάσας τὰς ὁδούς σου.   After
Pr 4[26] (as quoted above) there follows the promise, αὐτὸς δὲ τὰς ὀρθὰς ποιήσει
τὰς τροχίας σου, τὰς δὲ πορείας σου ἐν εἰρηνῃ προάξει.

The conventional interpretation takes εἰρήνην with μετὰ πάντων (*i.e.* all your members). This yields a fair sense, for a quarrelsome church is a real hindrance to effective faith ; the quarrelsomeness here would be due to the presence of faulty persons, whose lapses were apt to be irritating, and what would break εἰρήνη (*i.e.* mutual harmony) in such cases is the spirit of harshness in dealing with faults, censoriousness, or aloofness, just as what makes for εἰρήνη is a concern for purity and goodness inspired by forbearance and patience. But all this is read into the text. There is no hint of such dangers elsewhere in Πρὸς Ἑβραίους as there is in 1 P 3⁸ᶠ· and Ro 12¹⁶ᶠ·. Our author is characteristically putting a new edge on an old phrase like διώκετε εἰρήνην.

What εἰρήνη specially involved is shown in καὶ τὸν ἁγιασμόν κτλ. Here ἁγιασμός is not to be identified with σωφροσύνη in the special sense of 13⁴; it is the larger "consecration" to God which all ἅγιοι must maintain. In fact, διώκετε τὸν ἁγιασμόν κτλ. is simply another description of the experience called "sharing in God's ἁγιότης" (v.¹⁰). Χωρίς generally precedes, here it follows, the word it governs (οὗ), either for the sake of the rhythm or to avoid a hiatus (οὗ οὐδείς). "To see the Lord," is an expression common in Philo for that vision of the Divine being which is the rare reward of those who can purify themselves from the sensuous (cp. H. A. A. Kennedy's *Philo's Contribution to Religion*, pp. 192 f.). Κύριος is God in vv.⁵ and ⁶; here, in view of 9²⁸, it might be Jesus (as 2³), though "to see God" (vg "deum") as a term for intimate personal fellowship is more adequate to the context. People must be on the alert against tendencies to infringe this ἁγιασμός (v.¹⁵) ; ἐπισκοποῦντες, one form and function of παρακαλοῦντες (10²⁵), introduces three clauses, beginning each with μή τις, though it is not clear whether the third (v.¹⁶) is intended as an example of μιανθῶσιν or as a further definition of the second μή τις (ῥίζα κτλ.). The first clause, μή τις ὑστερῶν (*sc.* ᾖ) ἀπὸ τῆς χάριτος τοῦ θεοῦ, shows ὑστερεῖν (4¹) with ἀπό as in Eccles 6² ὑστερῶν . . . ἀπὸ πάντος οὗ ἐπιθυμήσει (Sir 7³⁴ μὴ ὑστέρει ἀπὸ κλαιόντων has a different sense). In writing ἀπὸ τῆς χάριτος τοῦ θεοῦ the writer may have had already in mind the words of Dt 29¹⁸ (μὴ τίς ἐστιν ἐν ὑμῖν . . . τίνος ἡ διάνοια ἐξέκλινεν ἀπὸ κυρίου τοῦ θεοῦ ἡμῶν), which he is about to quote in the next clause.

The rhetorical tone comes out in the two iambic trimeters οὗ χωρὶς οὐδεὶς ὄψεται τὸν κύριον and ἐπισκοποῦντες μή τις ὑστερῶν ἀπό.

The next clause, μή τις ῥίζα πικρίας ἄνω φύουσα ἐνοχλῇ, is a reminiscence of the warning against idolatry and apostasy in Dt 29¹⁸, which A (as well as F*) preserves in this form, μή τίς ἐστιν ἐν ὑμῖν ῥίζα πικρίας ἄνω φύουσα ἐνοχλῇ (so B* : ἐν χολῇ B) καὶ πικρίᾳ (B* : καὶ πικρία B). The form is ungrammatical, for ἐστιν is superfluous, as is καὶ πικρίᾳ. On the other hand, the text of B yields no good sense, for a root can hardly be said to grow up ἐν χολῇ, and καὶ πικρία is left stranded ; the alteration of πικρία in B* does not help matters, for it is not preceded by ἐν χολῇ.

14

Plainly the writer found something like the words of A in his
text of the LXX; he may have omitted ἐστιν and καὶ πικρίᾳ.
The confusion between -οχλη and χολη is intelligible, as ὄχλος
and χόλος are confused elsewhere (Blass reads ἐν χολῇ here,
which requires ᾖ or ἐστιν to be supplied). Ἐνοχλῇ is the present
subjunctive of ἐνοχλεῖν, which is used in 1 Es 2¹⁹ (ἐνοχλοῦσα)
and 2²⁴ (ἐνοχλῆσαι) of rebellion disturbing and troubling the
realm.   As a general term for "troubling" or "vexing," it is
common both in classical Greek and in the papyri, either
absolutely or with an accusative, as, e.g., Polystr. Epicur. (ed.
C. Wilke) 8b. 4, οὐδ᾽ ὑφ᾽ ἑνὸς τούτων ἐνοχλησαμένους ἡμᾶς, the
edict of M. Sempronius Liberalis (Aug. 29, 154 A.D.): ἐν τῇ
οἰκείᾳ τῇ γεω[ργ]ίᾳ προσκαρτεροῦσι μὴ ἐνοχλεῖν (BGU. ii. 372),
and Aristoph. Frogs, 709 f., οὐ πολὺν οὐδ᾽ ὁ πίθηκος οὗτος ὁ νῦν
ἐνοχλῶν.   As for ῥίζα (of a person, as, e.g., in 1 Mac 1¹⁰ καὶ
ἐξῆλθεν ἐξ αὐτῶν ῥίζα ἁμαρτωλὸς Ἀντίοχος Ἐπιφανής) πικρίας
(genitive of quality), the meaning is a poisonous character and
influence (cp. Ac 8²³).   The warning in Deuteronomy is against
any pernicious creature in the community, who by cool insolence
and infidelity draws down the divine sentence of extermination
upon himself and his fellows.   Here the writer thinks of people
who consider that immediate gratification of their wishes is
worth more than any higher end in life; they value their spiritual
position as sons (vv.⁵ᶠ·) so little, that they let it go in order to
relapse on some material relief at the moment.   Such a nature
is essentially βέβηλος, devoid of any appreciation of God's
privileges, and regarding these as of no more importance than
sensuous pleasures of the hour.   Under the bad influence of this
(διὰ ταύτης, ℵ D K L Ψ 326, etc., as in 13²: διὰ αὐτῆς, A H P 33.
424* syrʰᵏˡ boh Clem. etc., as in 11⁴ 12¹¹), all the rest (οἱ πολλοί,
after one has been mentioned, as in Ro 5¹⁵ etc.) may be tainted
(μιανθῶσι), and so (cp. on 10²²) rendered incapable of ὄψεσθαι τὸν
Κύριον.

The third clause (v.¹⁶) is μή τις (sc. ᾖ) πόρνος ἢ βέβηλος (for
the collocation see Philo, de Sacerdot. 8, πόρνῃ καὶ βεβήλῳ σῶμα
καὶ ψυχήν, and for this transferred sense of β. (= Lat. profanus)
see Jebb-Pearson's Fragments of Soph. ii. 208); βέβηλος is
only once applied to a person in the LXX, viz. in Ezk 21²⁵ σὺ
βέβηλε ἄνομε (= חלל), then to people like Antiochus (3 Mac
2². ¹⁴) or (3 Mac 7¹⁵ τοὺς βεβήλους χειρωσάμενοι) recreant Jews.
In adding ὡς Ἡσαῦ κτλ. the writer chooses the story of Esau, in
Gn 25²⁸⁻³⁴ 27¹⁻³⁹, to illustrate the disastrous results of yielding
to the ἁμαρτία of which he had spoken in v.¹.   There can be no
ὑπομονή, he implies, without a resolute determination to resist
the immediate pleasures and passions of the hour.   As Cicero
puts it in the De Finibus, i. 14, "plerique, quod tenere atque

servare id quod ipsi statuerunt non possunt, victi et debilitati
objecta specie voluptatis tradunt se libidinibus constringendos
nec quid eventurum sit provident, ob eamque causam propter
voluptatem et parvam et non necessariam et quae vel aliter
pararetur et qua etiam carere possent sine dolore, tum in morbos
graves, tum in damna, tum in dedecora incurrunt." But why
choose Esau? Probably owing to rabbinic tradition, in which
Esau is the typical instance of the godless who grow up among
good people (Isaac and Rebekah) and yet do not follow their
deeds, as Obadiah is of the good who grow up among the wicked
(Ahab and Jezebel) and do not follow *their* deeds (Sifre 133 on
Nu 27[1]). The rabbinic tradition[1] that Esau was sensual, is
voiced as early as Philo, in the *de Nobilitate*, 4 (ὁ δὲ μείζων
ἀπειθὴς ἐκ τῶν γαστρὸς καὶ τῶν μετὰ γαστέρα ἡδονῶν ἀκρατῶς ἔχων,
ὑφ' ὧν ἀνεπείσθη καὶ πρεσβείων ἐξίστασθαι τῷ μετ' αὐτοῦ καὶ
μετανοεῖν εὐθὺς ἐφ' οἷς ἐξέστη καὶ φονᾶν κατὰ τοῦ ἀδελφοῦ καὶ μηδὲν
ἕτερον ἢ δι' ὧν λυπήσει τοὺς γονεῖς πραγματεύεσθαι), where Philo
interprets the μετάνοια of Esau as simply regret for a bad bargain.
Our author may have considered Esau a πόρνος literally—and in
any case the word is to be taken literally (as in 13[4]), not in its
OT metaphorical sense[2] of "unfaithful"—but the weight of the
warning falls on βέβηλος, as is clear from the phrase ἀντὶ βρώσεως
μιᾶς (cp. Gn 25[28] ἡ θήρα αὐτοῦ βρῶσις αὐτῷ). T. H. Green
(*Prolegomena to Ethics*, § 96) points out that hunger was not the
motive. "If the action were determined directly by the hunger,
it would have no moral character, any more than have actions
done in sleep, or strictly under compulsion, or from accident, or
(so far as we know) the action of animals. Since, however, it is
not the hunger as a natural force, but his own conception of
himself, as finding for the time his greatest good in the satisfaction of hunger, that determines the act, Esau recognizes
himself as the author of the act. . . . If evil follows from it,
whether in the shape of punishment inflicted by a superior, or
of calamity ensuing in the course of nature to himself or those in
whom he is interested, he is aware that he himself has brought
it on himself." The μιᾶς is emphatic: "id culpam auget, non
misericordiam meretur" (Bengel).

In the quotation from Gn 25[33] (ἀπέδοτο δὲ Ἡσαῦ τὰ πρωτοτοκεῖα τῷ
Ἰακώβ), ἀπέδετο (A C 623), as if from a form ἀποδίδω (cp. Helbing, 105), is
preferred by Lachmann, B. Weiss, WH.

The warning is now (v.[17]) driven home. Ἴστε, indicative here
(a literary Atticism, though Blass insists that it is chosen for the

---

[1] Jub 25[1, 8] (Esau tempting Jacob to take one of his own two sensual
wives).

[2] Πορνεία has this sense, and so has the verb (*e.g.* Ps 73[27] ἐξωλέθρευσας
πάντα τὸν πορνεύοντα ἀπὸ σοῦ).

sake of the rhythm, to assimilate ἴστε γὰρ ὅτι καὶ με(τέπειτα) to the closing words of the preceding sentence), recalls to the readers the scripture story with which they were so familiar. Ἴστε ὅτι καὶ (another item in his story) μετέπειτα θέλων κληρονομῆσαι (1 P 3⁹) τὴν εὐλογίαν (=πρωτοτόκια as in 1 Ch 5¹·²) ἀπεδοκιμάσθη (Jer 6³⁰ ἀπεδοκίμασεν αὐτοὺς Κύριος: Ign. *Rom.* 8³ ἐὰν ἀποδοκιμασθῶ). Ἀποδοκιμάζεσθαι is common in the Greek orators for officials being disqualified, but the rejection here is an act of God; Esau is a tragic instance of those who cannot get a second chance of μετάνοια (6⁶). The writer has again the sombre, serious outlook which characterizes a passage like 6⁴⁻⁸. The very metaphor of plant-growth occurs here as there, and ἀπεδοκιμάσθη recalls ἀδόκιμος. Μετάνοια is impossible for certain wilful sins; certain acts of deliberate choice are irrevocable and fatal. Why this was so, in Esau's case, is now explained; μετανοίας γὰρ τόπον οὐχ εὗρε (εὑρίσκω = obtain, with ἐκζητεῖν as often in LXX, *e.g.* Dt 4²⁹), καίπερ μετὰ δακρύων (emphatic by position) ἐκζητήσας αὐτήν (*i.e.* μετανοίαν. "Μετανοίας τόπος is, in fact, μετάνοια. . . . When μετ. τόπον is taken up again, the mere secondary τόπος disappears, and it is αὐτήν, not αὐτόν, agreeing with the great thing really sought," Alford). If the writer used his usual A text of the LXX, he would not have found any allusion to the tears of Esau in Gn 27³⁸, but the tears were retained, from the Hebrew, in Jub 26³³, in other texts of the LXX, and in Josephus (*Ant.* i. 18. 7, πένθος ἦγεν ἐπὶ τῇ διαμαρτίᾳ. Καὶ αὐτοῦ τοῖς δάκρυσιν ἀχθόμενος ὁ πατὴρ κτλ.).[1] "Those tears of Esau, the sensuous, wild, impulsive man, almost like the cry of some 'trapped creature,' are among the most pathetic in the Bible" (A. B. Davidson). Αὐτήν refers to μετανοίας, not to εὐλογίας (which would require μετανοίας . . . εὗρεν to be taken as a parenthesis, a construction which is wrecked on the antithesis between εὗρεν and ἐκζητήσας). The μετάνοια is not a change in the mind of Isaac, which would require some additional words like τοῦ πατρός. Besides, Esau does not beseech Isaac to alter his mind. Nor can it refer to a change in God's mind. It is "a change of mind" on Esau's part, "undoing the effects of a former state of mind" (A. B. Davidson). Bitterly as Esau regretted his hasty action, he was denied any chance of having its consequences reversed by a subsequent μετάνοια; this is the writer's meaning. Ἀδύνατον πάλιν ἀνακαινίζειν εἰς μετάνοιαν is the law of God for such wilful offenders, and to try for a second μετάνοια is vain. Such is the warning that our author deduces from the tale of Esau.

[1] There is a striking parallel in *De Mercede Conductis*, 42, where Lucian describes an old man being met by ἡ μετάνοια δακρύουσα ἐς οὐδὲν ὄφελος.

This inexorable view agrees with Philo's idea (*Leg. Alleg.* iii. 75, πολλαῖς γὰρ ψυχαῖς μετανοίᾳ χρῆσθαι βουληθείσαις οὐκ ἐπέτρεψεν ὁ θεός) that some, like Cain[1] (*quod deter. pot.* 26, τῷ δὲ μὴ δεχομένῳ μετάνοιαν Καὶν δι᾽ ὑπερβολὴν ἄγους), are too bad to repent, though Philo illustrates it here not from Esau, but from Lot's wife. In *de Spec. Leg.* ii. 5 he declares that luxurious spendthrifts are δυσκάθαρτοι καὶ δυσίατοι, ὡς μηδὲ θεῷ τῷ τὴν φύσιν ἵλεῳ συγγνώμης ἀξιοῦσθαι. In Jub 35¹⁴ Isaac tells Rebekah that "neither Esau nor his seed is to be saved." But the idea of Πρὸς Ἑβραίους is made still more clear by the use of **μετανοίας τόπον** as an expression for opportunity or chance to repent. This is a contemporary Jewish phrase; cp. Apoc. Bar 85¹² ("For when the Most High will bring to pass all these things, there will not then be an opportunity for returning . . . nor place of repentance"), 4 Es 9¹² ("while a place of repentance was still open to them, they paid no heed"), which goes back to Wis 12¹⁰ κρίνων δὲ κατὰ βραχὺ ἐδίδους τόπον μετανοίας (of God punishing the Canaanites). It is linguistically a Latinism,[2] which recurs in Clem. Rom. 7⁵ (ἐν γενεᾷ καὶ γενεᾷ μετανοίας τόπον ἔδωκεν ὁ δεσπότης τοῖς βουλομένοις ἐπιστραφῆναι ἐπ᾽ αὐτόν) and Tatian (*Orat. ad Graecos*, 15, διὰ τοῦτο γοῦν ἡ τῶν δαιμόνων ὑπόστασις οὐκ ἔχει μετανοίας τόπον). But a special significance attaches to it in 4 Esdras, for example, where the writer (*e.g.* in 7¹⁰²ᶠ·) rules out any intercession of the saints for the ungodly after death, in his desire to show that "the eternal destiny of the soul is fixed by the course of the earthly life" (G. H. Box, *The Ezra-Apocalypse*, pp. 154, 155). Here, as in the Slavonic Enoch (53¹), which also repudiates such intercession, "we may detect the influence of Alexandrine theology, which tended to lay all stress upon the present life as determining the eternal fate of every man." The author of Πρὸς Ἑβραίους shared this belief (cp. 9²⁷); for him the present life of man contains possibilities which are tragic and decisive. He ignores deliberately any intercession of saints or angels for the living or for the dead. But he goes still further, with Philo and others, in holding that, for some, certain actions fix their fate beyond any remedy. He regards their case as hopeless; characters like Esau, by an act of profane contempt for God, are rejected for ever, a second μετάνοια being beyond their reach.

The connexion (**γάρ**) between the finale (vv.¹⁸⁻²⁹) and what precedes lies in the thought that the higher the privilege, the higher the responsibility. In *Leg. Alleg.* iii. 1, Philo quotes Gn 25²⁷ to prove that virtue's divine city is not meant for human passions; οὐ γὰρ πέφυκεν ἡ τῶν παθῶν θηρευτικὴ κακία τὴν ἀρετῆς πόλιν, wickedness banishing men from the presence and sight of God. But this line of thought is not in the writer's mind. It is more relevant to recall that Esau typifies exclusion from God in Jub 15³⁰ ("Ishmael and his sons and his brothers and Esau, the Lord did not cause to approach Him"); yet even this is not needful to explain the turn of thought. The writer is continuing his grave warning. As vv.¹⁴⁻¹⁷ recall the first warning of 6⁴⁻⁸, so he now proceeds to reiterate the second warning of 10²⁶⁻³¹, reminding his readers that they stand in a critical position,

---

[1] Philo read μείζων ἡ αἰτία μου τοῦ ἀφεθῆναι in Gn 4¹³.

[2] Livy, xliv. 10, "poenitentiae relinquens locum" (cp. xxiv. 26, "locus poenitendis"); cp. Pliny's *Epp.* x. 97, "ex quo facile est opinari, quae turba hominum emendari possit, si sit poenitentiae locus," where the phrase is used in quite a different sense, of a chance to give up Christianity.

in which any indifferences or disobedience to God will prove
fatal.   This is the note of vv.$^{25\text{-}29}$ in particular.   But he leads up
to the appeal by describing in a vivid passage the actual position
of his readers before God (vv.$^{18\text{-}24}$); their new status and environment appeals even more powerfully and searchingly for an
unworldly obedience to God than the old status of the People.

^{18} *You have not come* (προσεληλύθατε) *to what you can touch, to "flames
of fire," to "mist" and "gloom" and "stormy blasts,* ^{19} *to the blare of a
trumpet and to a Voice" whose words made those who heard it refuse to hear
another syllable* ^{20} *(for they could not bear the command, "If even a beast
touches the mountain, it must be stoned")—*^{21} *indeed, so awful was the sight
that Moses said, "I am terrified and aghast."* ^{22} *You have come* (προσεληλύθατε) *to mount Sion, the city of the living God, the heavenly Jerusalem, to
myriads of angels in festal gathering,* ^{23} *to the assembly of the first-born
registered in heaven, to the God of all as judge, to the spirits of just men made
perfect,* ^{24} *to Jesus who mediates* (8^{6} 9^{15}) *the new covenant, and to the sprinkled
blood whose message is nobler than Abel's.*

The passage moves through two phases (vv.$^{18\text{-}21}$ and $^{22\text{-}24}$),
contrasting the revelation at mount Sinai (2^2 10^{28}) with the new
διαθήκη, the one sensuous, the other spiritual; the one striking
terror with its outward circumstances of physical horror, the
other charged with grace and welcome as well as with awe.   The
meditation and appeal are woven on material drawn from the
LXX descriptions of the plague of darkness on Egypt (Ex 10$^{21f.}$
ψηλαφητὸν σκότος . . . ἐγένετο σκότος γνόφος θύελλα) and the
theophany at Sinai (Dt 4^{11} προσήλθετε καὶ ἔστητε ὑπὸ τὸ ὄρος·
καὶ τὸ ὄρος ἐκαίετο πυρὶ ἕως τοῦ οὐρανοῦ, σκότος, γνόφος, θύελλα,
φωνὴ μεγάλη, and Ex 19$^{12f.}$ προσέχετε ἑαυτοῖς τοῦ ἀναβῆναι εἰς τὸ
ὄρος καὶ θιγεῖν τι αὐτοῦ· πᾶς ὁ ἁψάμενος τοῦ ὄρους θανάτῳ τελευτήσει
. . . ἐν λίθοις λιθοβοληθήσεται ἢ βολίδι κατατοξευθήσεται· ἐάν τε
κτῆνος ἐάν τε ἄνθρωπος, οὐ ζήσεται . . . καὶ ἐγίνοντο φωναὶ καὶ
ἀστραπαὶ καὶ νεφέλη γνοφώδης ἐπ' ὄρους Σεινά, φωνὴ τῆς σάλπιγγος
ἤχει μέγα· καὶ ἐπτοήθη πᾶς ὁ λαὸς ὁ ἐν τῇ παρεμβολῇ).   In v.^{18}
the text is difficult and perhaps corrupt.   Ψηλαφωμένῳ ὄρει
would be equivalent to ψηλαφητῷ ὄρει, a tangible, material
mountain; but as ὄρει is a gloss (added, from v.^{22}, by D K L
255 syr^{hkl} arm Athan. Cosm. etc., either before or after ψηλ.),
though a correct gloss, ψ. may be taken (*a*) either with πυρί,
(*b*) or independently.   In the former case, (*a*) two constructions
are possible.   (i) One, as in vg ("ad tractabilem et accensi-
bilem ignem"), renders "to a fire that was material (or palpable)
and ablaze"; (ii) "to what was palpable and ablaze with fire"
(πυρί in an ablative sense).   (i) is a daring expression, and the
implied contrast (with v.^{29}) is too remote.   The objection to (ii)
is that πυρί here, as in the OT, goes with the following datives.
It is on the whole preferable (*b*) to take ψηλαφωμένῳ by itself

(*sc. τινι*).   The mountain could not be touched indeed (v.²⁰), but
it was a tangible object which appealed to the senses.   This is
the point of contrast between it and the Σιὼν ὄρος, the present
participle being equivalent to the verbal adjective ψηλαφητός.
Kypke connects ψ. with πυρί in the sense of "touched by
lightning" ("igne tactum et adustum"), comparing the Latin
phrase "fulmine tactum."   But the Greek term is θίγγανειν, and
in any case this interpretation really requires ὄρει, the mountain
"sundering" under the lightning touch of God (Ps 144⁵ etc.).

Two conjectures have been proposed, ὕψει νενεφωμένῳ by G. N. Bennett
(*Classical Review*, vi. 263), who argues that this "would fit in exactly with
the OT accounts, which represent the summit of the mountain as burnt with
fire, while lower down it was enveloped in a dense cloud"; and πεφεψαλω-
μένω (ὄρει) by E. C. Selwyn (*Journal of Theological Studies*, ix. 133, 134)=
"calcined" (a calcined volcano).   Others (*e.g.* P. Junius) less aptly insert
οὐ or μή before ψηλαφωμένῳ, to harmonize the phrase with v.²⁰.

In the rest of the description, ζόφῳ is a poetical word (cp.
de Mundo, 400a, heaven πάντος ζόφου καὶ ἀτάκτου κινήματος κεχω-
ρισμένον), which the writer prefers to σκότος.   Καὶ θυέλλῃ—
θύελλη, a hurricane, is defined by Hesychius as ἀνέμου συστροφὴ
καὶ ὁρμὴ, ἢ καταιγίς (cp. Hom. *Od.* 5. 317), and in *de Mundo*, 395a,
as πνεῦμα βίαιον καὶ ἄφνω προσαλλόμενον.   In v.¹⁹ ἤχῳ (ἤχη
᾿Αττικοί· ἦχος Ἕλληνες, Moeris) is a synonym for the LXX φωνῇ,
which the writer intends to use immediately.   Philo had already
used ἦχος in *de Decalogo*, 11 : πάντα δ᾽ ὡς εἰκὸς τὰ περὶ τὸν τόπον
ἐθαυματουργεῖτο, κτύποις βροντῶν μειζόνων ἢ ὥστε χωρεῖν ἀκοάς,
ἀστραπῶν λάμψεσιν αὐγοειδεστάταις, ἀοράτου σάλπιγγος ἤχῃ πρὸς
μήκιστον ἀποτεινούσῃ . . . πυρὸς οὐρανίου φορᾷ καπνῷ βαθεῖ τὰ ἐν
κύκλῳ συσκιάζοντος.   In *de Spec. Leg.* ii. 22 he explains that the
φωνὴ σάλπιγγος announced to all the world the significance of
the event.   Finally, καὶ φωνῇ ῥημάτων (the decalogue in Dt 4¹²),
ἧς (*i.e.* the φωνή) οἱ ἀκούσαντες παρῃτήσαντο μὴ (pleonastic negative as in Gal 5⁷; hence omitted by ℵ* P 467) προστεθῆναι (the
active προσθεῖναι, in A, is less apt) αὐτοῖς (*i.e.* the hearers) λόγον
(accus. and infinitive construction after μή, cp. Blass, § 429).
The reference in v.²⁰ is to the scene described in Dt 5²³ᶠ·, where it
is the leaders of the nation who appeal in terror to Moses to take
God's messages and orders for them : καὶ νῦν μὴ ἀποθάνωμεν, ὅτι
ἐξαναλώσει ἡμᾶς τὸ πῦρ τὸ μέγα τοῦτο, ἐὰν προσθώμεθα ἡμεῖς
ἀκοῦσαι τὴν φωνὴν Κυρίου τοῦ θεοῦ ἡμῶν ἔτι, καὶ ἀποθανούμεθα.
But in Ex 20¹⁹ it is the people, as here, who appeal to Moses,
μὴ λαλείτω πρὸς ἡμᾶς ὁ θεός, μὴ ἀποθάνωμεν.   Τὸ διαστελλόμενον
(in Ex 19¹³, see above) is passive.   Διαστέλλομαι is said by Anz
(*Subsidia*, 326 f.) not to occur earlier than Plato ; here, as in
Jth 11¹² (ὅσα διεστείλατο αὐτοῖς ὁ θεός), of a divine injunction.
In v.²¹ φανταζόμενον is not a LXX term (for the sense, cp. Zec 10¹

κύριος ἐποίησεν φαντασίας, of natural phenomena like rain); it is used here for the sake of alliteration (φοβ. φαντ.). To prove that even Moses was affected by the terrors of Sinai, the writer quotes from Dt 9¹⁹ ἔκφοβός εἰμι, adding rhetorically καὶ ἔντρομος. He forgets that Moses uttered this cry of horror, not over the fearful spectacle of Sinai but at a later stage, over the worship of the golden calf.   For ἔντρομος, cp. 1 Mac 13² ἔντρομος καὶ ἔκφοβος (v.l. ἔμφοβος).   The phrase ἔντρομος γενόμενος is applied by Luke to the terror of Moses at the φωνὴ Κυρίου out of the burning bush (Ac 7³²).

Assonance led to ἔκτρομος (א D*) or ἔμφοβος (M 241. 255. 489. 547. 1739 Thdt.).   Ἔντρομος was read by Clem. Alex. (Protrept. ix. 2).

The true position of Christians is now sketched (vv.²²⁻²⁴). Ἀλλὰ προσεληλύθατε Σιὼν ὄρει καὶ πόλει (11¹⁰· ¹⁶) θεοῦ ζῶντος, the author adding Ἰερουσαλὴμ ἐπουρανίῳ (11¹⁶) in apposition to πόλει, and using thus the archaic metaphors of Is 18⁷, Am 1², Mic 4¹ᶠ· etc., in his picture of the true fellowship.   Paul had contrasted mount Sinai (= the present Jerusalem) with ἡ ἄνω Ἰερουσαλήμ.   Our author's contrast is between mount Sion (= Ἰερουσαλὴμ ἐπουράνιος) and mount Sinai, though he does not name the latter.   From the πόλις he now passes to the πολῖται.

In Chagiga, 12b, i. 33, Resh Lakish deduces from 1 K 8¹³ and Is 63¹⁵ that zebul, the fourth of the seven heavens, contains "the heavenly Jerusalem and the temple," i.e. as the residence of deity; while Ma'on, the fifth heaven, holds the "companies of ministering angels."

The second object of προσεληλύθατε is καὶ μυριάσιν (so En 40¹: "I saw thousands of thousands and ten thousand times ten thousand before the Lord of spirits") ἀγγέλων, with which πανηγύρει must be taken, leaving the following καί to introduce the third object (v.²³).   The conception of the angels as μυριάδες goes back to traditions like those voiced in Ps 68¹⁷ (τὸ ἅρμα τοῦ θεοῦ μυριοπλάσιον, χιλιάδες εὐθηνούντων· ὁ κύριος ἐν αὐτοῖς ἐν Σινά) and Dan 7¹⁰ (μύριαι μυριάδες).   Πανήγυρις was a term charged with Greek religious associations (cp. R. van der Loeff, De Ludis Eleusiniis, pp. 85 f.), but it had already been adopted by Greek Jews like the translators of the LXX and Josephus for religious festivals.   Πανηγύρει describes the angelic hosts thronging with glad worship round the living God.   Their relation to God is noted here, as in 1¹⁴ their relation to human beings.   Ἔνθα πανήγυρις ἐκεῖ χαρά, as Theophylact observes (ἱλαρᾶς εὐθυμίας, ἣν πανήγυρις ἐπιζητεῖ, Philo, in Flacc. 14); but the joy of Lk 15¹⁰ is not specially mentioned.   Chrysostom's suggestion is that the writer ἐνταῦθα τὴν χαρὰν δείκνυσι καὶ τὴν εὐφροσύνην ἀντὶ τοῦ γνόφου καὶ τοῦ σκότους καὶ τῆς θυέλλης.   Augustine (Quaest. i. 168: "accessistis ad montem Sion et ad ciuitatem dei Hier-

usalem et ad milia angelorum exultantium ") seems to imply not
only that πανηγύρει goes with ἀγγέλων, but that he knew a text
with some word like πανηγυριζόντων (Blass), as is further proved
by boh ("keeping festival"), Orig[lat] (laetantium, collaudantium),
and Ambrose. There is a hint of this in Clem. Alex. *Protrept.*
ix. 6, 7, αὕτη γὰρ ἡ πρωτότοκος ἐκκλησία ἡ ἐκ πολλῶν ἀγαθῶν
συγκειμένη παιδίων· ταῦτ᾽ ἔστι τὰ πρωτότοκα τὰ ἐναπογεγραμμένα
ἐν οὐρανοῖς καὶ τοσαύταις μυριάσιν ἀγγέλων συμπανηγυρίζοντα.

The human πολῖται are next (v.[23]) described as ἐκκλησίᾳ
πρωτοτόκων ἀπογεγραμμένων ἐν οὐρανοῖς. (For the collocation of
angels and men, see En 39[5] "Mine eyes saw their [*i.e.* the
saints'] dwellings with His righteous angels, and their resting-
places with the holy "; the Enoch apocalypse proceeding to the
intercession of the angels ("and they petitioned, and interceded,
and prayed for the children of men ") which the Christian writer
deliberately omits.) The phrase describes what the author elsewhere calls ὁ λαός (τοῦ θεοῦ), but in two archaic expressions,
chosen to emphasize what Paul would have called their election.
They are πρωτότοκοι (as Israel had been πρωτότοκος, Ex 4[22] etc.),
with a title to God's blessing (v.[16] πρωτοτόκια). The choice of
the plural instead of the collective singular was due to the
previous plural in μυριάσιν ἀγγέλων. In ἀπογεγραμμένων ἐν
οὐρανοῖς there is a passing allusion to the idea of the celestial
archives or register—a favourite poetical figure in which the
Oriental expressed his assurance of salvation.[1] As in Lk 10[20]
so here, the phrase refers to men on earth, to the church militant,
not to the church triumphant; otherwise ἐν οὐρανοῖς would be
meaningless.

This interpretation, which groups πανηγύρει with what precedes, is current
in nearly all the early versions and Greek fathers, who generally assume it
without question. The real alternative is to take μυριάσιν as further defined
by ἀγγέλων πανηγύρει καὶ ἐκκλησίᾳ πρωτοτόκων ἀπογεγραμμένων ἐν οὐρανοῖς.
This introduces and leaves μυριάσιν rather abruptly, and implies that angels
alone are referred to (so recently Dods, von Soden, Peake, Seeberg), called
πρωτότοκοι as created before men. But, while a later writer like Hermas
(*Vis.* iii. 4) could speak of angels as οἱ πρῶτοι κτισθέντες, ἀπογεγραμμένων
cannot naturally be applied to them. Hermas himself (*Vis.* i. 3) applies that
term to men (ἐγγραφήσονται εἰς τὰς βίβλους τῆς ζωῆς μετὰ τῶν ἁγίων).

A fresh sweep of thought now begins (23[b-24]). The writer
is composing a lyrical sketch, not a law-paper; he reiterates the
idea of the fellowship by speaking of God, men, and him by whom
this tie between God and men has been welded, the allusion
to Jesus being thrown to the end, as it is to form the starting-
point for his next appeal (vv.[25f.]). In καὶ κριτῇ θεῷ πάντων it is
not possible, in view of 9[27] (μετὰ δὲ τοῦτο κρίσις) and of the
punitive sense of κρίνω in 10[30], to understand κριτής as defender

---

[1] *Clem. Hom.* ix. 22, τὰ ὀνόματα ἐν οὐρανῷ ὡς ἀεὶ ζώντων ἀναγραφῆναι.

or vindicator (so, *e.g.*, Hofmann, Delitzsch, Riggenbach). The words mean "to the God of all (angels and men, the living and the dead, Ac 10⁴²), and to him as κριτής, to whom you must account for your life." It is implied that he is no easy-going God. The contrast is not between the mere terrors of Sinai and the gracious relationship of Sion, but between the outward, sensuous terror of the former and the inward intimacy of the latter—an intimacy which still involves awe. In the next phrase, πνεύματα δικαίων means the departed who have in this life been δίκαιοι in the sense of 10³⁸ᶠ·; τετελειωμένων is added, not in the mere sense of "departed" (τελευτᾶν = τελειοῦσθαι, τελειοῦν), but to suggest the work of Christ which includes the δίκαιοι, who had to await the sacrifice of Christ before they were "perfected" (11⁴⁰). If this involves the idea of a descent of Christ to the under-world, as Loofs (*e.g.* in *ERE.* iv. 662) argues, it implies the group of ideas mentioned in 2¹⁴, which may have lain in the background of the writer's thought. At any rate the "perfecting" of these δίκαιοι, their τελείωσις, was due to Jesus; hence (v.²⁴) the writer adds, καὶ διαθήκης νέας μεσίτη Ἰησοῦ (again at the end, for emphasis), where νέας is simply a synonym for καινῆς (8⁸ etc.). The classical distinction between the two terms was being dropped in the κοινή. Τῆς νέας Ἱερουσαλήμ occurs in *Test. Dan* 5¹², and the two words are synonymous, *e.g.*, in *Test. Levi* 8¹⁴ (ἐπικληθήσεται αὐτῷ ὄνομα καίνον, ὅτι βασιλεὺς . . . ποιήσει ἱερατείαν νέαν). Indeed Blass thinks that the unexampled διαθήκης νεάς was due to a sense of rhythm; the author felt a desire to reproduce the — ◡◡ — — ◡ — of the preceding ων τετελειωμένων.

In Cambodia (cp. *ERE.* iii. 164) those who are present at a death-bed all "repeat in a loud voice, the patient joining in as long as he has the strength, '*Arahan! Arahan!*' 'the saint! the just one!' (Pāli *araham* = 'the saint,' 'one who has attained final sanctification ')." Bleek is so perplexed by καὶ πνευμ. δικ. τελ. coming between θεῷ and Ἰησοῦ that he wonders whether the author did not originally write the phrase on the margin, intending it to go with πανηγύρει or ἐκκλησίᾳ. The curious misreading of D d, τεθεμελιω-μένων, underlies Hilary's quotation (*tract. in Ps.* 124: "ecclesia angelorum multitudinis frequentium—ecclesia primitivorum, ecclesia spirituum in domino fundatorum "). Another odd error, πνεύματι for πνεύμασι, appears in D (boh?) d and some Latin fathers (*e.g.* Primasius)—a trinitarian emendation (= 10²⁹).

In διαθήκης νέας, as in 13²⁰, the writer recalls the conception with which he had been working in the middle part of his argument (chs. 7–10); now he proceeds to expand and explain the allusion in καὶ αἵματι ῥαντισμοῦ (9¹⁹ᶠ·) κρεῖττον (adverbial as in 1 Co 7³⁸) λαλοῦντι παρὰ (as in 1⁴ etc.) τὸν Ἅβελ (= τὸ¹ τοῦ Ἅβελ, cp. Jn 5³⁶). Reconciliation, not exclusion, is the note of the νέα διαθήκη. The blood of the murdered Abel (11⁴) called out to

¹ τὸ Ἅβελ (genitive) was actually read by L and is still preferred by Blass.

God in En 22[6f.] (where the seer has a vision of Abel's spirit
appealing to God) for the extinction of Cain and his descendants.
The κρεῖττον in Jesus here is that, instead of being vindictive
and seeking to exclude the guilty, he draws men into fellowship
with God (see p. xlii). The contrast is therefore not between the
Voice of the blood of Jesus (λαλοῦντι) and the Voice of the
decalogue (v.[19]), but between Jesus and Abel; the former opens
up the way to the presence of God, the latter sought to shut it
against evil men. The blood of martyrs was assigned an atoning
efficacy in 4 Mac 6[28f.] 17[21f.]; but Abel's blood is never viewed in
this light, and the attempt to explain this passage as though the
blood of Jesus were superior in redeeming value to that of Abel
as the first martyr (so, *e.g.*, Seeberg), breaks down upon the fact
that the writer never takes Abel's blood as in any sense typical
of Christ's.

The application of vv.[18-24] now follows. Though we have a far
better relationship to God, the faults of the older generation may
still be committed by us, and committed to our undoing (vv.[25-29]).

[25] *See (βλέπετε as 3[12]) that you do not refuse to listen to his voice. For if
they failed to escape, who refused to listen to their instructor upon earth, much
less shall we, if we discard him who speaks from heaven.* [26] *Then his voice
shook the earth, but now the assurance is, "once again I will make heaven as
well as earth to quake."* [27] *That phrase (τὸ δέ as Eph 4[9]), "once again," denotes (δηλοῖ, as in 9[8]) the removal of what is shaken (as no more than created),
to leave only what stands unshaken.* [28] *Therefore let us render thanks that we
get an unshaken realm; and in this way let us worship God acceptably—* [29] *but
with godly fear and awe, for our God is indeed "a consuming fire."*

The divine revelation in the sacrifice of Jesus (λαλοῦντι)
suggests the start of the next appeal and warning. From the
celestial order, just sketched, the divine revelation (τὸν λαλοῦντα
. . . τὸν ἀπ᾽ οὐρανῶν) is made to us; instead of rejecting it, which
would be tragic, let us hold to it. The argument is: God's
revelation (v.[25]) implies a lasting relationship to himself (v.[28]);
and although the present order of things in the universe is
doomed to a speedy fall (v.[26]), this catastrophe will only bring
out the unchanging realm in which God and we stand together
(v.[27]). The abruptness of the asyndeton in (v.[25]) βλέπετε μή κτλ.
adds to its force. Παραιτήσησθε . . . παραιτησάμενοι are only a
verbal echo of παρῃτήσαντο κτλ. in v.[19]; for the refusal of the
people to hear God except through Moses is not blamed but
praised by God (Dt 5[28]). The writer, of course, may have
ignored this, and read an ominous significance into the instinctive
terror of the people, as if their refusal meant a radical rejection
of God. But this is unlikely. By παραιτησάμενοι τὸν χρηματίζοντα
he means any obstinate rejection of what Moses laid down for

them as the will of God. Εἰ . . . οὐκ (as was the fact) ἐξέφυγον
(referring to the doom mentioned in 2² 3⁷ᶠ· 10²⁹). As in 2³ (πῶς
ἡμεῖς ἐκφευξόμεθα), ἐκφεύγω is used absolutely ; the weaker ἔφυγον
is read only by אᶜ D K L M Ψ 104, etc. In the following words
there are three possible readings. The original text ran : (a) ἐπὶ
γῆς παραιτησάμενοι τὸν χρηματίζοντα (א* A C D M d boh Cyr.),
ἐπὶ γῆς being as often thrown to the front for the sake of
emphasis. But the hyperbaton seemed awkward. Hence (b)
τὸν ἐπὶ γῆς παραιτησάμενοι χ. (אᶜ K L P Chrys. Thdt. etc.)
and (c) παραιτησάμενοι τὸν ἐπὶ γῆς χ. (69. 256. 263. 436. 462.
467. 1837. 2005 vg) are attempts to make it clear that ἐπὶ γῆς
goes with τὸν χρηματίζοντα, not with παραιτησάμενοι. The latter
interpretation misses the point of the contrast, which is not
between a rejection on earth and a rejection in heaven (!), but
between a human oracle of God and the divine Voice ἀπ᾽
οὐρανῶν to us. The allusion in τὸν χρηματίζοντα¹ is to Moses,
as Chrysostom was the first to see. To refuse to listen to him is
what has been already called ἀθετεῖν νόμον Μωϋσέως (10²⁸). As
the Sinai-revelation is carefully described in 2² as ὁ δι᾽ ἀγγέλων
λαληθεὶς λόγος, so here Moses is ὁ χρηματίζων, or, as Luke puts
it, ὃς ἐδέξατο λόγια ζῶντα δοῦναι (Ac 7³⁸) ; he was the divine
instructor of the λαός on earth. It is repeatedly said (Ex 20²²,
Dt 4³⁶) that God spoke to the people at Sinai ἐκ τοῦ οὐρανοῦ, so
that to take τὸν χρηματίζοντα here as God, would be out of
keeping with ἐπὶ τῆς γῆς. The writer uses the verb in a wider
sense than in that of 8⁵ and 11⁷ ; it means "the man who had
divine authority to issue orders," just as in Jer 26² (τοὺς λόγους
οὓς συνέταξά σοι αὐτοῖς χρηματίσαι), etc. He deliberately writes
τὸν χρηματίζοντα of Moses, keeping τὸν λαλοῦντα as usual for
God. Then, he concludes, πολὺ (altered, as in v.⁹, to πολλῷ by
Dᶜ K L M P Ψ 226, or to πόσῳ, as in 9¹⁴, by 255) μᾶλλον (sc. οὐκ
ἐκφευξόμεθα) ἡμεῖς οἱ τὸν (sc. χρηματίζοντα) ἀπ᾽ οὐρανῶν ἀποστρεφό-
μενοι (with accus. as 3 Mac 3²³ ἀπεστρέψαντο τὴν ἀτίμητον
πολιτείαν, and 2 Ti 1¹⁵ ἀπεστράφησάν με πάντες).

It is surprising that οὐρανοῦ (א M 216. 424**. 489. 547. 623. 642. 920.
1518. 1872 Chrys.) has not wider support, though, as 9²³· ²⁴ shows, there is
no difference in sense.

In v.²⁶ οὗ ἡ φωνὴ τὴν γῆν ἐσάλευσε τότε is another (cp. vv.¹³· ¹⁴)
unintentional rhythm, this time a pentameter. Τότε, i.e. at
Sinai. But in the LXX of Ex 19¹⁸, which the writer used, the
shaking of the hill is altered into the quaking of the people, and
Jg 5⁴ᶠ· does not refer to the Sinai episode. Probably the writer
inferred an earthquake from the poetical allusions in Ps 114⁷

¹ Cp. Jos. Ant. iii. 8. 8, Μωϋσης . . . ἐχρηματίζετο περὶ ὧν ἐδεῖτο παρὰ
τοῦ θεοῦ.

(ἐσαλεύθη ἡ γῆ), Ps 68⁸ᶠ· 77¹⁸, when these were associated with the special theophany at Sinai. Νῦν δὲ ἐπήγγελται (passive in middle sense, as Ro 4²¹) λέγων, introducing a loose reminiscence and adaptation of Hag 2⁶ (ἔτι ἅπαξ ἐγὼ σείσω τὸν οὐρανὸν καὶ τὴν γῆν κτλ.), where the prediction of a speedy convulsion of nature and the nations has been altered¹ in the LXX, by the introduction of ἔτι, into a mere prediction of some ultimate crisis, with reference to some preceding σεῖσις, *i.e.* for our writer the Sinai-revelation. The second and final σεῖσις is to be at the return of Jesus (9²⁸).

The anticipation of such a cosmic collapse entered apocalyptic. Thus the author of Apoc. Baruch tells his readers, "if you prepare your hearts, so as to sow in them the fruits of the law, it shall protect you when the Mighty One is to shake the whole creation" (32¹).

In v.²⁷ the Haggai prediction is made to mean the removal (μετάθεσιν, stronger sense than even in 7¹²) τῶν σαλευομένων (by the σεῖσις). There is a divine purpose in the cosmic catastrophe, however; it is ἵνα μείνῃ τὰ μὴ σαλευόμενα, *i.e.* the βασιλεία ἀσάλευτος of the Christian order. For ἀσάλευτος, compare Philo, *de vit. Mosis*, ii. 3, τὰ δὲ τούτου μόνου βέβαια, ἀσάλευτα, ἀκράδαντα . . . μένει παγίως ἀφ᾽ ἧς ἡμέρας ἐγράφη μέχρι νῦν καὶ πρὸς τὸν ἔπειτα πάντα διαμενεῖν ἐλπὶς αὐτὰ αἰῶνα ὥσπερ ἀθάνατα. Σείω and σαλεύω are cognate terms (cp. *e.g.* Sir 16¹⁸· ¹⁹ ὁ οὐρανος . . . καὶ γῆ σαλευθήσονται . . . ἅμα τὰ ὄρη καὶ τὰ θεμέλια τῆς γῆς συσσείονται). Here σείσω is changed into σείω by D K L P d arm and some cursives, probably to conform with the form of the promise in Hag 2²¹ (ἐγὼ σείω τὸν οὐρ. καὶ τὴν γῆν). The hint is more reticent, and therefore more impressive than the elaborate prediction of the Jewish apocalyptist in Apoc. Bar 59⁸ᶠ·: "but also the heavens were shaken at that time from their place, and those who were under the throne of the Mighty One were perturbed, when He was taking Moses unto Himself. For He showed him . . . the pattern of Zion and its measures, in the pattern of which was to be made the sanctuary of the present time" (cp. He 8⁵). There is a premonition of the last judgment in En 60¹, as a convulsion which shook not only heaven, but the nerves of the myriads of angels.

"There have been two notable transitions of life," says Gregory of Nazianzus (*Orat.* v. 25), in the history of the world, *i.e.* the two covenants, "which are also called earthquakes on account of their arresting character" (διὰ τὸ τοῦ πράγματος περιβόητον) ; the first from idols to the Law, the second from the Law to the gospel. We bring the good news of yet a third earthquake, the transition from the present order to the future (τὴν ἐντεῦθεν ἐπὶ τὰ ἐκεῖσε μετάστασιν, τὰ μηκέτι κινούμενα, μηδὲ σαλευόμενα).²

---

¹ *i.e.* while Haggai predicts "it will be very soon," the LXX says "once again."

² Probably a reference to He 12²⁶.

Changes and crises may only serve to render a state or an individual more stable. Thus Plutarch says of Rome, in the disturbed days of Numa, καθάπερ τὰ καταπηγνύμενα τῷ σείεσθαι μᾶλλον ἑδράζεται, ῥώννυσθαι δοκοῦσα διὰ τῶν κινδύνων (*Vit. Num.* 8). But the writer's point in v.[27] is that there is an ἀσάλευτος βασιλεία [1] already present, in the fellowship of the new διαθήκη, and that the result of the cosmic catastrophe will simply be to leave this unimpaired, to let it stand out in its supreme reality and permanence. The passage is a counterpart to 1^{10-12}, where skies and earth vanish, though they are God's own ἔργα. So here, the writer puts in, by way of parenthesis, ὡς πεποιημένων. Kypke took πεποιημένων, "pro πεποιημένην, *sc.* μετάθεσιν," comparing Mt 5^{19} where he regarded ἐλαχίστων as similarly equivalent to ἐλαχίστην. The word would then be a genitive absolute, connecting with what follows : "all this being done so that," etc. Even when πεποιημένων is taken in its ordinary sense, it is sometimes connected with ἵνα κτλ. (so, *e.g.*, Bengel and Delitzsch) ; the aim of creation was to replace the provisional by the permanent, the temporal by the eternal. A far-fetched interpretation. Even the conjecture (Valckenaer) πεπονήμενων (labouring with decay) is needless, though ingenious. In vv.[28, 29] the final word upon this prospect and its responsibilities is said. Διό (as in v.[12]), in view of this outlook (in v.[27]), βασιλείαν ἀσάλευτον (metaphorical, as, *e.g.*, Diod. Sic. xii. 29, σπονδαὶ ἀσάλευται) παραλαμβάνοντες (cp. 2 Mac 10^{11} and *Epist. Arist.* 36, καὶ ἡμεῖς δὲ παραλαβόντες τὴν βασιλείαν κτλ., for this common phrase) ἔχωμεν χάριν (διό with pres. subjunctive as in 6^1). The unique and sudden reference to the primitive idea of βασιλεία (see Introd., p. xxxiii) may be a reminiscence of the scripture from which he has just quoted ; the prediction about the shaking of heaven and earth is followed, in Hag 2^{22}, by the further assertion, καὶ καταστρέψω θρόνους βασιλέων, καὶ ἐξολεθρεύσω δύναμιν βασιλέων τῶν ἐθνῶν. Possibly our author regarded the prediction in Dn 7^{18} (καὶ παραλήψονται τὴν βασιλείαν ἅγιοι ὑψίστου καὶ καθέξουσιν αὐτὴν ἕως αἰῶνος τῶν αἰώνων) as fulfilled already in the Christian church, though he does not mean by βασιλείαν παραλαμβάνοντες that Christians enter on their reign.

Why thankfulness (for this common phrase, see Epict. i. 2. 23, ἔχω χάριν, ὅτι μου φείδῃ, and *OP.* 1381[78] (2nd century) διὰ θυσιῶν τῷ σώσαντι ἀπεδίδομεν χάριτας) should be the standing order for them, the writer explains in δι' ἧς κτλ. ; it is the one acceptable λατρεύειν (9^{14}), or, as he puts it afterwards (13^{15}), the real sacrifice of Christians. Δι' ἧς λατρεύωμεν (subj. cohortative in relative clause, like στῆτε in 1 P 5^{12}) εὐαρεστῶς (not in LXX ;

---

[1] Cp. Wis $5^{15, 16}$ δίκαιοι δὲ εἰς τὸν αἰῶνα ζῶσιν . . . λήμψονται τὸ βασίλειον τῆς εὐπρεπείας . . . ἐκ χειρὸς Κυρίου, ὅτι τῇ δεξιᾷ σκεπάσει αὐτούς.

an adverb from the verb in the sense of 11^{5. 6}) τῷ θεῷ. The *v.l.*
ἔχομεν (אּ K P Lat syr^{hkl} eth etc.) is the usual (see Ro 5¹)
phonetic blunder, though λατρεύομεν (אּ M P syr^{hkl} arm) would
yield as fair a sense as λατρεύωμεν (A C D L 33. 104 Lat sah
etc.). In μετὰ . . . δέους he puts in a characteristic warning
against presumption. There are three readings. (*a*) εὐλαβείας
καὶ δέους, אּ* A C D 256. 263. 436. 1912 sah boh syr^{vg} arm.
(*b*) εὐλαβείας καὶ αἰδοῦς, אּ^c M P Ψ 6. 104. 326. 1739 lat Orig.
(*c*) αἰδοῦς καὶ εὐλαβείας, K L 462 syr^{hkl} Chrys. Thdt. The accidental doubling of αι (from καί) led to (*b*), especially as αἰδοῦς
and εὐλαβεία were often bracketed together, and as δέος was a
rare word (first popularized in Hellenistic Judaism by 2 Maccabees). Εὐλαβεία here as in 5⁷ (cp. 11⁷) of reverent awe. Καὶ
γὰρ ὁ θεὸς ἡμῶν πῦρ καταναλίσκον (v.²⁹). Not "for our God too
is a πῦρ ἀν.," for the writer believed that the same God was God
of the old διαθήκη and of the new; besides, this rendering would
require καὶ γὰρ ἡμῶν ὁ θεός. The phrase is from Dt 4²⁴ (Moses
at Sinai to the Israelites) ὅτι Κύριος ὁ θεός σου πῦρ καταναλίσκον
ἐστίν, θεὸς ζηλωτής (cp. 9³), referring to his intense resentment of
anything like idolatry, which meant a neglect of the διαθήκη.
There is no allusion to fire as purifying; the author of Wisdom
(16¹⁶) describes the Egyptians as πυρὶ καταναλισκόμενοι, and it is
this punitive aspect of God which is emphasized here, the divine
ζῆλος (see p. xxxvi).

This is one of Tertullian's points (*adv. Marc.* i. 26–27) against the
Marcionite conception of a God who is good-natured and nothing more :
"tacite permissum est, quod sine ultione prohibetur . . . nihil Deo tam
indignum quam non exsequi quod noluit et prohibuit admitti . . . malo
parcere Deum indignius sit quam animadvertere. . . . Plane nec pater tuus
est, in quem competat et amor propter pietatem, et timor propter potestatem ?
nec legitimus dominus, ut diligas propter humanitatem et timeas propter
disciplinam." In Πρὸς Ἑβραίους there is no softening of the conception, as in
Philo's argument (*de Sacrificantibus*, 8) that God's requirement is simply
ἀγαπᾶν αὐτὸν ὡς εὐεργέτην, εἰ δὲ μή, φοβεῖσθαι γοῦν ὡς ἄρχοντα καὶ κύριον, καὶ
διὰ πασῶν ἰέναι τῶν εἰς ἀρέσκειαν ὁδῶν καὶ λατρεύειν αὐτῷ μὴ παρέργως ἀλλὰ
ὅλῃ τῇ ψυχῇ πεπληρωμένῃ γνώμης φιλοθέου καὶ τῶν ἐντολῶν αὐτοῦ περιέχεσθαι
καὶ τὰ δίκαια τιμᾶν. In *de Decalogo*, 11, he spiritualizes the fire at Sinai thus :
τοῦ πυρὸς τὸ μὲν φωτίζειν τὸ δὲ καίειν πέφυκεν (those who obey the divine laws
being inwardly enlightened, those who disobey being inflamed and consumed
by their vices), and closes the treatise (33) by enunciating his favourite doctrine that God never punishes directly but only indirectly (here by Δίκη, whose
appropriate task is to punish those who disobey her liege Lord). Indeed he
allegorizes the OT comparison of God to a flame (*Quaest. in Exod.* 24¹⁷
ὥσπερ δὲ ἡ φλὸξ πᾶσαν τὴν παραβληθεῖσαν ὕλην ἀναλίσκει, οὕτως, ὅταν ἐπι-
φοιτήσῃ εἰλικρινὴς τοῦ θεοῦ ἔννοια τῇ ψυχῇ πάντας τοὺς ἑτεροδόξους ἀσεβείας
λογισμοὺς διαφθείρει, καθοσιοῦσα τὴν ὅλην διάνοιαν). The closest parallel to
our passage lies in Ps.–Sol 15⁵ᵗ· where the author declares that praise to God
is the one security for man. Ψαλμὸν καὶ αἶνον μετ' ᾠδῆς ἐν εὐφροσύνῃ καρδίας,
καρπὸν χειλέων . . . ἀπαρχὴν χειλέων ἀπὸ καρδίας ὁσίας καὶ δικαίας, ὁ ποιῶν
ταῦτα οὐ σαλευθήσεται εἰς τὸν αἰῶνα ἀπὸ (*i.e.* ὑπὸ) κακοῦ, φλὸξ πυρὸς καὶ

ὀργὴ ἀδίκων οὐχ ἅψεται αὐτοῦ, ὅταν ἐξέλθῃ ἐπὶ ἁμαρτωλοὺς ἀπὸ προσώπου κυρίου.

With this impressive sentence Πρὸς Ἑβραίους really closes. But the writer appends (see Introd., pp. xxviii f.) a more or less informal postscript, with some personal messages to the community. A handful of moral counsels (vv.¹⁻⁷) is followed by a longer paragraph (vv.⁸⁻¹⁶), and the closing personal messages are interrupted by a farewell benediction (v.²⁰).

¹ *Let your brotherly love continue.* ² *Never forget to be hospitable, for by hospitality* (διὰ ταύτης, as 12¹⁵) *some have entertained angels unawares.* ³ *Remember prisoners as if you were in prison yourselves; remember those who are being ill-treated* (11³⁷), *since you too are in the body.*

Neither φιλαδελφία nor φιλοξενία is a LXX term, though the broader sense of the former begins in 4 Mac 13²³·²⁶ 14¹. Μενέτω (cp. 6¹⁰ 10²⁴·³²ᶠ·), though its demands might be severe at times (cp. Ro 12¹⁰, 1 P 1²²; Clem. Ro 1²; Herm. *Mand.* 8¹⁰); the duty is laid as usual on members of the church, not specially on officials. In v.² a particular expression of this φιλαδελφία is called for. Φιλοξενία was practically an article of religion in the ancient world. The primary reference here in τινες is to Abraham and Sara (Gn 18¹ᶠ·), possibly to Manoah (Jg 13³ᶠ·), and even to Tobit (Tob 12¹⁵); but the point of the counsel would be caught readily by readers familiar with the Greek and Roman legends of divine visitants being entertained unawares by hospitable people, *e.g.* Hom. *Odyss.* xvii. 485 f. (καί τε θεοὶ ξείνοισιν ἐοικότες ἀλλοδαποῖσι | παντοῖοι τελέθοντες, ἐπιστρωφῶσι πόληας, cp. Plat. *Soph.* 216 B); *Sil. Ital.* vii. 173 f. ("laetus nec senserat hospes | advenisse deum"), and the story of Philemon and Baucis (Ovid, *Met.* viii. 626 f.) alluded to in Ac 14¹¹. In the Hellenic world the worship of Zeus Xenios (*e.g.* Musonius Rufus, xv. *a*, ὁ περὶ ξένους ἄδικος εἰς τὸν ξένιον ἁμαρτάνει Δία) fortified this kindly custom. According to Resh Lakish (Sota, 10*a*), Abraham planted the tree at Beersheba (Gn 21³³) for the refreshment of wayfarers, and φιλοξενία was always honoured in Jewish tradition (*e.g.* Sabbath, 127. 1, "there are six things, the fruit of which a man eats in this world and by which his horn is raised in the world to come: they are, hospitality to strangers, the visiting of the sick," etc.). But there were pressing local reasons for this kindly virtue in the primitive church. Christians travelling abroad on business might be too poor to afford a local inn. Extortionate charges were frequent; indeed the bad repute which innkeepers enjoyed in the Greek world (cp. Plato's *Laws*, 918 D) was due partly to this and partly also to a "general feeling against taking money for hospitality" (cp. Jebb's *Theophrastus*, p. 94). But, in addition, the moral repute of inns stood low (Theophrastus, *Char.* 6⁵

δεινὸς δὲ πανδοκεῦσαι καὶ πορνοβοσκῆσαι κτλ.) ; there is significance
in the Jewish tradition preserved by Josephus (*Ant.* v. i. i)
that Rahab ἡ πόρνη (11[81]) kept an inn. For a Christian
to frequent such inns might be to endanger his character,
and this consideration favoured the practice of hospitality on
the part of the local church, apart altogether from the discomforts
of an inn. ("In the better parts of the empire and in the larger
places of resort there were houses corresponding in some
measure to the old coaching inns of the eighteenth century ; in
the East there were the well-known caravanserais ; but for the most
part the ancient hostelries must have afforded but undesirable
quarters. They were neither select nor clean," T. G. Tucker,
Life in the Roman World, p. 20.) Some of these travellers
would be itinerant evangelists (cp. 3 Jn [5-8]).

According to Philo the three wayfarers seen by Abraham did
not at first appear divine (οἱ δὲ θειοτέρας ὄντες φύσεως ἐλελήθεσαν),
though later on he suspected they were either prophets or angels
when they had promised him the birth of a son in return for his
splendid hospitality (*Abrah.* 22–23). "In a wise man's house,"
Philo observes, "no one is slow to practise hospitality : women
and men, slaves and freedmen alike, are most eager to do
service to strangers" ; at the same time such hospitality was
only an incident (πάρεργον) and instance (δεῖγμα σαφέστατον)
of Abraham's larger virtue, *i.e.* of his piety. Josephus also
(*Ant.* i. 11. 2) makes Abraham suppose the three visitors
were human strangers, until at last they revealed themselves
as divine angels (θεασάμενος τρεῖς ἀγγέλους καὶ νομίσας εἶναι
ξένους ἠσπασατό τ' ἀναστὰς καὶ παρ' αὐτῷ καταχθέντας παρεκάλει
ξενίων μεταλαβεῖν). It was ignorance of the classical idiom (cp.
Herod. i. 44, ὑποδεξάμενος τὸν ξεῖνον φονέα τοῦ παιδὸς ἐλάνθανε
βόσκων) in ἔλαθον ξενίσαντες, which led to the corruptions of
ἔλαθον in some Latin versions into "latuerunt," "didicerunt,"
and "placuerunt." Note the paronomasia ἐπιλανθάνεσθε . . .
ἔλαθον, and the emphatic position of ἀγγέλους. "You never know
whom you may be entertaining," the writer means. "Some
humble visitor may turn out to be for you a very ἄγγελος θεοῦ"
(cp. Gal 4[14]).

Μιμνήσκεσθε (bear in mind, and act on your thought of) τῶν
δεσμίων. Strangers come within sight ; prisoners (v.[3]) have to
be sought out or—if at a distance—borne in mind. Christian
kindness to the latter, *i.e.* to fellow-Christians arrested for some
reason or other, took the form either of personally visiting them
to alleviate their sufferings by sympathy and gifts (cp. Mt 25[36],
2 Ti 1[16]), or of subscribing money (to pay their debts or, in the
case of prisoners of war, to purchase their release), or of praying
for them (Col 4[18] and 4[3]). All this formed a prominent feature

of early Christian social ethics.   The literature is full of tales
about the general practice: *e.g.* Aristid. *Apol.* 15; Tertull. *ad
Mart.* 1 f. and *Apol.* 39, with the vivid account of Lucian in the
de Morte Peregr. 12, 13.   This subject is discussed by Harnack
in the *Expansion of Early Christianity* (bk. ii. ch. 3, section 5).
Our author urges, "remember the imprisoned" ὡς συνδεδεμένοι.
If ὡς is taken in the same sense as the following ὡς, the meaning
is: (*a*) "as prisoners yourselves," *i.e.* in the literal sense, "since
you know what it means to be in prison"; or (*b*) "as imprisoned," in the metaphorical sense of Diognet. 6, Χριστιανοὶ
κατέχονται ὡς ἐν φρουρᾷ τῷ κόσμῳ.   A third alternative sense is
suggested by LXX of 1 S 18¹ (ἡ ψυχὴ Ἰωνάθαν συνεδέθη τῇ ψυχῇ
Δαυίδ), but the absence of a dative after συνδεδεμένοι and the
parallel phrase ὡς ἐν σώματι rule it out.   Probably ὡς is no more
than an equivalent for ὡσεί.   Christians are to regard themselves
as one with their imprisoned fellows, in the sense of 1 Co 12²⁶
εἴτε πάσχει ἓν μέλος, συμπάσχει πάντα τὰ μέλη.   This interpretation tallies with 10³⁴ above (cp. Neh 1³·⁴).   It does not, however,
imply that ἐν σώματι, in the next clause, means "in the Body (of
which you and your suffering fellows are alike members"); for
ἐν σώματι refers to the physical condition of liability to similar
ill-usage.   See Orig. *c. Cels.* ii. 23, τῶν τοῖς ἐν σώμασι (Bouhéreau
conj. σώματι) συμβαινόντων, and especially Philo's words describing some spectators of the cruelties inflicted by a revenue officer
on his victims, as suffering acute pain, ὡς ἐν τοῖς ἑτέρων σώμασιν
αὐτοὶ κακούμενοι (*de Spec. Leg.* iii. 30).   So in *de Confus. Ling.* 35,
καὶ τῷ συμφορῶν ἀνηνύτων τῶν κακουχομένων (*i.e.* by exile, famine,
and plague; cp. He 11³⁷) οὐκ ἐνδεθεῖσαι χωρίῳ, σώματι.

Seneca (*Ep.* ix. 8) illustrates the disinterestedness of friendship by
observing that the wise man does not make friends for the reason suggested
by Epicurus, viz., to "have someone who will sit beside him when he is ill,
someone to assist him when he is thrown into chains or in poverty," but
"that he may have someone beside whom, in sickness, he may himself sit,
someone whom he may set free from captivity in the hands of the enemy."
The former kind of friendship he dismisses as inadequate : "a man has made
a friend who is to assist him in the event of bondage ('adversum vincula'),
but such a friend will forsake him as soon as the chains rattle ('cum primum
crepuerit catena')."   In *Ep. Arist.* 241, 242, when the king asks what is the
use of kinship, the Jew replies, ἐὰν τοῖς συμβαίνουσι νομίζωμεν ἀτυχοῦσι μὲν
ἐλαττοῦσθαι καὶ κακοπαθῶμεν ὡς αὐτοί, φαίνεται τὸ συγγενὲς ὅσον ἰσχύόν ἐστι.
Cicero specially praises generosity to prisoners, and charity in general, as
being serviceable not only to individuals but to the State (*de Offic.* ii. 18,
"haec benignitas etiam rei publicae est utilis, redimi e servitute captos, locu-
pletari tenuiores").

⁴ *Let marriage be held in honour by all, and keep the marriage-bed unstained.   God will punish the vicious and adulterous.*
⁵ *Keep your life free from the love of money; be content with what you
have, for He* (αὐτός) *has said,*

"*Never will I fail you, never will I forsake you.*"

⁶ *So that we can say confidently,*

"*The Lord is my helper* (βοηθός, cp. 2¹⁸ 4¹⁶), *I will not be afraid. What can men do to me?*"

As vv.^{1. 2} echo 10^{24. 32. 33}, v.⁴ drives home the πόρνος of 12¹⁶, and vv.^{5. 6} echo the reminder of 10³⁴. Evidently (v.⁴), as among the Macedonian Christians (1 Th 4³⁻⁹), φιλαδελφία could be taken for granted more readily than sexual purity. Τίμιος (*sc.* ἔστω as in v.⁵, Ro 12⁹, the asyndeton being forcible) ὁ γάμος ἐν πᾶσιν, *i.e.* primarily by all who are married, as the following clause explains. There may be an inclusive reference to others who are warned against lax views of sexual morality, but there is no clear evidence that the writer means to protest against an ascetic disparagement of marriage. Κοίτη is, like the classical λέχος, a euphemistic term for sexual intercourse, here between the married; ἀμίαντος is used of incest, specially in *Test. Reub.* i. 6, ἐμίανα κοίτην τοῦ πατρός μου: Plutarch, *de Fluviis*, 18, μὴ θέλων μιαίνειν τὴν κοίτην τοῦ γεννήσαντος, etc.; but here in a general sense, as, *e.g.*, in Wisdom :

μακαρία ἡ στεῖρα ἡ ἀμίαντος,
ἥτις οὐκ ἔγνω κοίτην ἐν παραπτώματι,
ἕξει καρπὸν ἐν ἐπισκοπῇ ψυχῶν (3¹³),

and οὔτε βίους οὔτε γάμους καθαροὺς ἔτι φυλάσσουσιν,
ἕτερος δ' ἕτερον ἢ λοχῶν ἀναιρεῖ ἢ νοθεύων ὀδύνᾳ (14²⁴).

In πόρνους γὰρ καὶ μοιχούς κτλ., the writer distinguishes between μοιχοί, *i.e.* married persons who have illicit relations with other married persons, and πόρνοι of the sexually vicious in general, *i.e.* married persons guilty of incest or sodomy as well as of fornication. In the former case the main reference is to the breach of another person's marriage; in the latter, the predominating idea is treachery to one's own marriage vows. The possibility of πορνεία in marriage is admitted in Tob 8⁷ (οὐ διὰ πορνείαν ἐγὼ λαμβάνω τὴν ἀδελφήν μου ταύτην), *i.e.* of mere sexual gratification¹ as distinct from the desire and duty of having children, which Jewish and strict Greek ethics held to be the paramount aim of marriage (along with mutual fellowship); but this is only one form of πορνεία. In the threat κρινεῖ (as in 10³⁰) ὁ θεός, the emphasis is on ὁ θεός. "Longe plurima pars scortatorum et adulterorum est sine dubio, quae effugit notitiam iudicum mortalium . . . magna pars, etiamsi innotescat, tamen poenam civilem et disciplinam ecclesiasticam vel effugit vel leuissime persentiscit" (Bengel).

This is another social duty (cp. Philo, *de Decalogo*, 24). In view of the Epicurean rejection of marriage (*e.g.* Epict. iii. 7. 19), which is finely

---

¹ μὴ ἐν πάθει ἐπιθυμίας, as Paul would say (1 Th 4⁵).

answered by Antipater of Tarsus (Stob. *Florileg.* lxvii. 25 : ὁ εὐγενὴς καὶ
εὔψυχος νέος . . . θεωρῶν διότι τέλειος οἶκος καὶ βίος οὐκ ἄλλως δύναται
γενέσθαι, ἢ μετὰ. γυναικὸς καὶ τέκνων κτλ.), as well as of current ascetic
tendencies (*e.g.*, 1 Ti 4³), there may have been a need of vindicating marriage,
but the words here simply maintain the duty of keeping marriage vows
unbroken. The writer is urging chastity, not the right and duty of any
Christian to marry. Prejudices born of the later passion for celibacy led to
the suppression of the inconvenient ἐν πᾶσι (om. 38. 460. 623. 1836. 1912*
Didymus, Cyril Jerus., Eus., Athan., Epiphanius, Thdt.). The sense is
hardly affected, whether γάρ (ℵ A D* M P lat sah boh) or δέ (C Dᶜ Ψ 6 syr
arm eth Clem., Eus., Didymus, Chrys.) is read, although the latter would
give better support to the interpretation of the previous clause as an anti-
ascetic maxim.

A warning against greed of gain (vv.⁵·⁶) follows the warning
against sexual impurity. There may be a link of thought between
them. For the collocation of sensuality and the love of money,
see *Epict.* iii. 7. 21, σοὶ καλὴν γυναῖκα φαίνεσθαι μηδεμίαν ἢ τὴν
σήν, καλὸν παῖδα μηδένα, καλὸν ἀργύρωμα μηθέν, χρύσωμα μηθέν:
Test. Jud. 18, φυλάξασθε ἀπὸ τῆς πορνείας καὶ τῆς φιλαργυρίας . . .
ὅτι ταῦτα . . . οὐκ ἀφίει ἄνδρα ἐλεῆσαι τὸν πλησίον αὐτοῦ, and
Philo's (*de Post. Caini*, 34) remark, that all the worst quarrels,
public and private, are due to greedy craving for ἢ εὐμορφίας
γυναικὸς ἢ χρημάτων κτλ. In *de Abrah.* 26, he attributes the
sensuality of Sodom to its material prosperity. Lucian notes the
same connexion in *Nigrin.* 16 (συνεισέρχεται γὰρ μοιχεία καὶ
φιλαργυρία κτλ., the love of money having been already set as
the source of such vices). In 1 Co 5¹⁰ᶠ· Paul brackets οἱ πόρνοι
with οἱ πλεονέκται, and πλεονεξία (cp. 1 Th 4⁶) as selfishness
covers adultery as well as grasping covetousness. But the
deeper tie between the two sins is that the love of luxury and
the desire for wealth open up opportunities of sensual indulgence.
In injuries to other people, Cicero observes (*de Offic.* i. 7. 24),
"latissime patet avaritia." When Longinus describes the deterior-
ating effects of this passion or vice in character (*de Sublim.* 44),
he begins by distinguishing it from mere love of pleasure ;
φιλαργυρία μὲν νόσημα μικροποιόν, φιληδονία δ᾽ ἀγεννέστατον.
Then he proceeds to analyse the working of φιλαργυρία in life,
its issue in ὕβρις, παρανομία, and ἀναισχυντία.

Ἀφιλάργυρος (the rebel Appianus tells Marcus Aurelius, in
OP. xxxiii. 10, 11, that his father τὸ μὲν πρῶτον ἦν φιλόσοφος, τὸ
δεύτερον ἀφιλάργυρος, τὸ τρίτον φιλάγαθος) ὁ τρόπος (in sense of
"mores," as often, *e.g.*, M. Aurelius, i. 16, καὶ πᾶς ὁ τοιοῦτος
τρόπος). Ἀρκούμενοι is the plur. ptc. after a noun (as in 2 Co 1⁷,
Ro 12⁹), and with τοῖς παροῦσιν reproduces a common Greek
phrase for contentment, e.g. *Teles*, vii. 7, ἀλλ᾽ ἡμεῖς οὐ δυνάμεθα
ἀρκεῖσθαι τοῖς παροῦσιν, ὅταν καὶ τρυφῇ πολὺ διδῶμεν, and xxviii. 31,
καὶ μὴ ἔχων οὐκ ἐπιποθήσεις ἀλλὰ βιώσῃ ἀρκούμενος τοῖς παροῦσιν.
The feature here is the religious motive adduced in αὐτὸς γὰρ

εἴρηκεν (of God as usual, e.g., 1¹³), a phrase which (cp. Ac 20³⁵ αὐτὸς εἶπεν) recalls the Pythagorean αὐτὸς ἔφα ("thus said the Master "). The quotation οὐ μή σε ἀνῶ οὐδ᾿ οὐ μή σε ἐγκαταλίπω is a popular paraphrase of Jos 1⁵ or Gn 28¹⁵ (cp. Dt 31⁸, 1 Ch 28²⁰) which the writer owes to Philo (de Confus. Ling. 32), who quotes it exactly in this form as a λόγιον τοῦ ἵλεω θεοῦ μεστὸν ἡμερότητος, but simply as a promise that God will never leave the human soul to its own unrestrained passions. The combination of the aor. subj. with the first οὐ μή and the reduplication of the negative (for οὐδ᾿ οὐ μή, cp. Mt 24²¹) amount to a strong asseveration. Note that the writer does not appeal, as Josephus does, to the merits of the fathers (Antiq. xi. 5. 7, τὸν μὲν θεὸν ἴστε μνήμῃ τῶν πατέρων ᾿Αβράμου καὶ ᾿Ισάκου καὶ ᾿Ιακώβου παραμένοντα καὶ διὰ τῆς ἐκείνων δικαιοσύνης οὐκ ἐγκαταλείποντα τὴν ὑπὲρ ἡμῶν πρόνοιαν) in assuring his readers that they will not be left forlorn by God.

᾿Εγκαταλείπω (so all the uncials except D) may be simply an orthographical variant of the true reading ἐγκαταλίπω (aorist subj.). In Dt 31⁶ the A text runs οὐ μή σε ἀνῇ οὐδ᾿ οὐ σε ἐγκαταλείπῃ, in Jos 1⁵ οὐκ ἐγκαταλείπω σε οὐδὲ ὑπερόψομαί σε, and in Gn 28¹⁵ οὐ μή σε ἐγκαταλείπω. The promise originally was of a martial character. But, as Keble puts it (Christian Year, "The Accession "):

> "Not upon kings or priests alone
>   the power of that dear word is spent;
> it chants to all in softest tone
>   the lowly lesson of content."

῞Ωστε (v.⁶) θαρροῦντας (on the evidence for this form, which Plutarch prefers to the Ionic variant θαρσεῖν, cp. Crönert's Memoria Graeca Herculanensis, 133²) ἡμᾶς (om. M, accidentally) λέγειν. What God says to us moves us to say something to ourselves. This quotation from Ps 118⁶ is exact, except that the writer, for the sake of terseness, omits the καί (= so) before οὐ φοβηθήσομαι, which is reinserted by ℵᶜ A D K L M syrʰᵏˡ etc. For the phrase θαρροῦντας λέγειν, see Pr 1²¹ (Wisdom) ἐπὶ δὲ πύλαις πόλεως θαρροῦσα λέγει: and for βοηθός and θαρρεῖν in conjunction, see Xen. Cyr. v. i. 25, 26, ἐπειδὴ δ᾿ ἐκ Περσῶν βοηθὸς ἡμῖν ὡρμήθης . . . νῦν δ᾿ αὖ οὕτως ἔχομεν ὡς σὺν μὲν σοὶ ὅμως καὶ ἐν τῇ πολεμίᾳ ὄντες θαρροῦμεν. Epictetus tells a man who is tempted (ii. 18. 29), τοῦ θεοῦ μέμνησο, ἐκεῖνον ἐπικαλοῦ βοηθὸν καὶ παραστάτην. This is the idea of the psalm-quotation here. Courage is described in Galen (de H. et Plat. decr. vii. 2) as the knowledge ὧν χρὴ θαρρεῖν ἢ μὴ θαρρεῖν, a genuinely Stoic definition; and Alkibiades tells, in the Symposium (221 A), how he came upon Sokrates and Laches retreating during the Athenian defeat at Delium καὶ ἰδὼν εὐθὺς παρακελεύομαί τε αὐτοῖν θαρρεῖν, καὶ ἔλεγον ὅτι οὐκ ἀπολείψω αὐτώ. In the touching prayer preserved in the Acta Pauli (xlii.), Thekla cries, ὁ θεός μου καὶ τοῦ οἴκου τούτου, Χριστὲ Ἰησοῦ ὁ υἱὸς τοῦ θεοῦ, ὁ ἐμοὶ βοηθὸς ἐν φυλακῇ, βοηθὸς ἐπὶ ἡγεμόνων, βοηθὸς ἐν πυρί, βοηθὸς ἐν θηρίοις.

According to Pliny (*Epp.* ix. 30: "primum est autem suo esse contentum, deinde, quos praecipue scias indigere sustentantem fouentemque orbe quodam societatis ambire") a man's first duty is to be content with what he has; his second, to go round and help all in his circle who are most in need. Epictetus quotes a saying of Musonius Rufus: οὐ θέλεις μελετᾶν ἀρκεῖσθαι τῷ δεδομένῳ; (i. 1. 27); but this refers to life in general, not to money or property in particular. The argument of our author is that instead of clinging to their possessions and setting their hearts on goods (10³⁴), which might still be taken from them by rapacious pagans, they must realize that having God they have enough. He will never allow them to be utterly stripped of the necessaries of life. Instead of trying to refund themselves for what they had lost, let them be content with what is left to them and rely on God to preserve their modest all; he will neither drop nor desert them.

Hitherto the community has been mainly (see on 12¹⁴ᶠ·) addressed as a whole. Now the writer reminds them of the example of their founders, dead and gone, adding this to the previous list of memories (12¹ᶠ·).

> ⁷ *Remember your leaders, the men who spoke the word of God to you; look back upon the close of their career, and copy their faith.*

Μνημονεύετε τῶν ἡγουμένων ὑμῶν οἵτινες (since they were the men who) ἐλάλησαν ὑμῖν τὸν λόγον τοῦ θεοῦ. The special function of these primitive apostles and prophets was to preach the gospel (cp. 1 Co 1¹⁷) with the supernatural powers of the Spirit. Then the writer adds a further title to remembrance, their consistent and heroic life; they had sealed their testimony with their (ὧν κτλ.) blood. Ἡγούμενος, like ἄρχων, was a substantival formation which had a wide range of meaning; here it is equivalent to "president" or "leader" (cp. *Epp. Apollon.* ii. 69, ἄνδρας τοὺς ἡγουμένους ὑμῶν = your leading citizens, or prominent men, and Ac 15²²).[1] It was they who had founded the church by their authoritative preaching; ἐλάλησαν ὑμῖν τὸν λόγον τοῦ θεοῦ recalls the allusion to the σωτηρία which ὑπὸ τῶν ἀκουσάντων (*i.e.* Jesus) εἰς ἡμᾶς ἐβεβαιώθη (2³). The phrase denotes, in primitive Christianity (*e.g.* Did. 4¹ where the church-member is bidden remember with honour τοῦ λαλοῦντός σοι τὸν λόγον τοῦ θεοῦ), the central function of the apostolic ministry as the declaration and interpretation of the divine λόγος. These men had died for their faith; ἔκβασις here, as in Wis 2¹⁷ (τὰ ἐν ἐκβάσει αὐτοῦ), is, like ἔξοδος, a metaphor for death as the close of life, evidently a death remarkable for its witness to faith. They had laid down their lives as martyrs. This proves that the allusion in 12⁴ does not exclude some martyrdoms in the past history of the community, unless the reference here is supposed to mean

---

[1] In *Ep. Arist.* 310, of the headmen of the Jewish community at Alexandria.

no more than that they died as they had lived κατὰ πίστιν (11¹³), without giving up their faith.

In Egypt, during the Roman period, "a liturgical college of πρεσβύτεροι or ἡγούμενοι was at the head of each temple" (*GCP.* i. 127), the latter term being probably taken from its military sense of "officers" (*e.g.* ἡγεμόνες τῶν ἔξω τάξεων).

'Αναθεωροῦντες is "scanning closely, looking back (ἀνα-) on"; and ἀναστροφή is used in this sense even prior to Polybius; *e.g.* Magn. 46³⁵·⁴⁴ (iii B.C.) and Magn. 165⁵ (i A.D.) διὰ τὴν τοῦ ἤθους κόσμιον ἀναστροφήν. As for μιμεῖσθε, the verb never occurs in the LXX except as a *v.l.* (B*) for ἐμίσησας in Ps 31⁶, and there in a bad sense. The good sense begins in Wis 4² (παροῦσάν τε μιμοῦνται αὐτήν), so far as Hellenistic Judaism goes, and in 4 Mac 9²³ (μιμήσασθε με) 13⁹ (μιμησώμεθα τοὺς τρεῖς τοὺς ἐπὶ τῆς Συρίας νεανίσκους) it is used of imitating a personal example, as here. In the *de Congressu Erudit.* 13, Philo argues that the learner listens to what his teacher says, whereas a man who acquires true wisdom by practice and meditation (ὁ δὲ ἀσκήσει τὸ καλὸν ἀλλὰ μὴ διδασκαλίᾳ κτώμενος) attends οὐ τοῖς λεγομένοις ἀλλὰ τοῖς λέγουσι, μιμούμενος τὸν ἐκείνων βίον ἐν ταῖς κατὰ μέρος ἀνεπιλήπτοις πράξεσι. He is referring to living examples of goodness, but, as in *de Vita Mos.* i. 28, he points out that Moses made his personal character a παράδειγμα τοῖς ἐθέλουσι μιμεῖσθαι. This stimulus of heroic memories belonging to one's own group is noted by Quintilian (*Instit. Orat.* xii. 2. 31) as essential to the true orator: "quae sunt antiquitus dicta ac facta praeclare et nosse et animo semper agitare conveniet. Quae profecto nusquam plura maioraque quam in nostrae civitatis monumentis reperientur. . . . Quantum enim Graeci praeceptis valent, tantum Romani, quod est maius, exemplis." Marcus Aurelius recollects the same counsel: ἐν τοῖς τῶν Ἐπικουρείων γράμμασι παράγγελμα ἔκειτο συνεχῶς ὑπομιμνήσκεσθαι τῶν παλαιῶν τινος τῶν ἀρετῇ χρησαμένων (xi. 26).

Human leaders may pass away, but Jesus Christ, the supreme object and subject of their faithful preaching, remains, and remains the same; no novel additions to his truth are required, least of all innovations which mix up his spiritual religion with what is sensuous and material.

⁸ *Jesus Christ is always the same, yesterday, to-day, and for ever.* ⁹ *Never let yourselves be carried away with a variety of novel doctrines; for the right thing is to have one's heart strengthened by grace, not by the eating of food—that has never been any use to those who have had recourse to it.* ¹⁰ *Our* (ἔχομεν as 4¹⁵) *altar is one of which the worshippers have no right to eat.* ¹¹ *For the bodies of the animals whose "blood is taken into the holy Place" by the highpriest as a "sin-offering, are burned outside the camp";* ¹² *and so Jesus also suffered outside the gate, in order to sanctify the people* (cp. 10²ᵗ·) *by his own blood* (9¹²). ¹³ *Let us go to him "outside the camp," then, bearing*

his obloquy [14] (*for we have no lasting city here below, we seek the City to come*). [15] *And by him " let us" constantly "offer praise to God" as our "sacrifice," that is, "the fruit of lips" that celebrate his Name.* [16] *Do not forget* (μὴ ἐπιλανθάνεσθε, *as in* v.[2]) *beneficence and charity either ; these are the kind of sacrifices that are acceptable to God.*

V.[8] connects with what precedes and introduces what follows. Ἔχθες [1] refers to his life on earth (2[3] 5[7]) and includes the service of the original ἡγούμενοι; it does not necessarily imply a long retrospect. Σήμερον as in 3[15], and ὁ αὐτός as in 1[12]. The finality of the revelation in Jesus, sounded at the opening of the homily (1[1f.]), resounds again here. He is never to be superseded; he never needs to be supplemented. Hence (v.[9]) the warning against some new theology about the media of forgiveness and fellowship, which, it is implied, infringes the all-sufficient efficacy of Jesus Christ. Διδαχαῖς (6[2]) ποικίλαις (2[4] in good sense) καὶ ξέναις μὴ παραφέρεσθε. Παραφέρεσθαι (cp. Jude [12]) is never used in this metaphorical sense (swayed, swerved) in the LXX, where it is always literal, and the best illustration of ξέναις in the sense of "foreign to" (the apostolic faith) is furnished by the author of the epistle to Diognetus (11[1]), who protests, οὐ ξένα ὁμιλῶ . . . ἀλλὰ ἀποστόλων γενόμενος μαθητὴς γίνομαι διδάσκαλος ἐθνῶν. Such notions he curtly pronounces useless, ἐν οἷς οὐκ ὠφελήθησαν οἱ περιπατοῦντες, where ἐν οἷς goes with περιπατοῦντες; they have never been of any use in mediating fellowship with God for those who have had recourse to them. It is exactly the tone of Jesus in Mk 7[18].

Παραφέρεσθε was altered (under the influence of Eph 4[14]) into περιφέρεσθε (K L Ψ 2. 5. 88. 330. 378. 440. 491. 547. 642. 919. 920. 1867. 1872. 1908. arm sah). Περιπατήσαντες (א° C D° K L M P syr[hkl] arm Orig. Chrys. etc.) and περιπατοῦντες (א* A D* 1912 lat) are variants which are substantially the same in meaning, περιπατεῖν ἐν being used in its common sense = living in the sphere of (Eph 2[10] etc.), having recourse to.

The positive position is affirmed in καλόν κτλ. (καλόν, as in 1 Co 7[1], Ro 14[21] etc.). "Καλός . . . denotes that kind of goodness which is at once seen to be good" (Hort on 1 P 2[12]), *i.e.* by those who have a right instinct. The really right and good course is χάριτι βεβαιοῦσθαι τὴν καρδίαν, *i.e.* either to have one's heart strengthened, or to be strengthened in heart (καρδίαν, accus. of reference). Bread sustains our physical life (ἄρτος καρδίαν ἀνθρώπου στηρίζει, Ps 104[15]), but καρδία here means more than vitality ; it is the inner life of the human soul, which God's χάρις alone can sustain, and God's χάρις in Jesus Christ is everything (2[9] etc.). But what does this contrast mean? The explanation is suggested in the next passage (vv.[10-16]), which flows out of

---

[1] The forms vary ; but this, the Attic spelling, has the best repute upon the whole (see W. G. Rutherford's *New Phrynichus*, pp. 370 f.), and strong support here in א A C* D* M.

what has just been said. The various novel doctrines were
connected in some way with βρώματα. So much is clear. The
difficulty is to infer what the βρώματα were. There is a touch of
scorn for such a motley, unheard of, set of διδαχαί. The writer
does not trouble to characterize them, but his words imply that
they were many-sided, and that their main characteristic was a
preoccupation with βρώματα. There is no reference to the
ancient regulations of the Hebrew ritual mentioned in 9¹⁰; this
would only be tenable on the hypothesis, for which there is no
evidence, that the readers were Jewish Christians apt to be
fascinated by the ritual of their ancestral faith, and, in any case,
such notions could not naturally be described as ποικίλαι καὶ
ξέναι. We must look in other directions for the meaning of this
enigmatic reference. (a) The new διδαχαί may have included
ascetic regulations about diet as aids to the higher life, like the
ἐντάλματα καὶ διδασκαλίαι τῶν ἀνθρώπων which disturbed the
Christians at Colossê. Partly owing to Gnostic syncretism,
prohibitions of certain foods (ἀπέχεσθαι βρωμάτων, 1 Ti 4³) were
becoming common in some circles, in the supposed interests of
spiritual religion. "We may assume," says Pfleiderer, one of
the representatives of this view (pp. 278 f.), "a similar Gnostic
spiritualism, which placed the historical Saviour in an inferior
position as compared with angels or spiritual powers who do not
take upon them flesh and blood, and whose service consists in
mystical purifications and ascetic abstinences." (b) They may
also have included such religious sacraments as were popularized
in some of the mystery-cults, where worshippers ate the flesh of
a sacrificial victim or consecrated elements which represented the
deity. Participation in these festivals was not unknown among
some ultra-liberal Christians of the age. It is denounced by
Paul in 1 Co 10, and may underlie what the writer has already
said in 10²⁵. Why our author did not speak outright of εἰδωλόθυτα,
we cannot tell; but some such reference is more suitable to the
context than (a), since it is sacrificial meals which are in question.
He is primarily drawing a contrast between the various cult-feasts
of paganism, which the readers feel they might indulge in, not
only with immunity, but even with spiritual profit, and the
Christian religion, which dispensed with any such participation.
(c) Is there also a reference to the Lord's supper, or to the
realistic sense in which it was being interpreted, as though
participation in it implied an actual eating of the sacrificial body
of the Lord? This reference is urged by some critics, especially
by F. Spitta (*Zur Geschichte u. Litteratur des Urchristentums*,
i. pp. 325 f.) and O. Holtzmann (in *Zeitschrift für die neutest.
Wissenschaft*, x. pp. 251–260). Spitta goes wrong by misinterpret-
ing v.¹⁰ as though the σῶμα of Christ implied a sacrificial meal

from which Jewish priests were excluded. Holtzmann rightly
sees that the contrast between χάρις and βρώματα implies, for
the latter, the only βρῶμα possible for Christians, viz. the Lord's
body as a food. What the writer protests against is the rising
conception of the Lord's supper as a φαγεῖν τὸ σῶμα τοῦ Χριστοῦ.
On the day of Atonement in the OT ritual, to which he refers,
there was no participation in the flesh of the sacrificial victim ;
there could not be, in the nature of the case (v.[11]). So, he
argues, the σῶμα Χριστοῦ of our sacrifice cannot be literally eaten,
as these neo-sacramentarians allege ; any such notion is, to him,
a relapse upon the sensuous, which as a spiritual idealist he
despises as " a vain thing, fondly invented." A true insight into
the significance of Jesus, such as he has been trying to bring out
in what he has written, such as their earlier leaders themselves
had conveyed in their own way, would reveal the superfluousness
and irrelevance of these διδαχαί. As the writer is alluding to
what is familiar, he does not enter into details, so that we have
to guess at his references. But the trend of thought in vv.[10f.] is
plain. In real Christian worship there is no sacrificial meal ;
the Christian sacrifice is not one of which the worshippers
partake by eating. This is the point of v.[10]. The writer
characteristically illustrates it from the OT ritual of atonement-
day, by showing how the very death of Jesus outside the city of
Jerusalem fulfilled the proviso in that ritual (vv.[11. 12]) that the
sacrifice must not be eaten. Then he finds in this fact about
the death of Jesus a further illustration of the need for unworldliness (vv.[13. 14]). Finally, in reply to the question, "Then have
Christians no sacrifices to offer at all ?" he mentions the two
standing sacrifices of thanksgiving and charity (vv.[15. 16]), both
owing their efficacy to Christ. Inwardness is the dominating
thought of the entire paragraph. God's grace in Jesus Christ
works upon the soul ; no external medium like food is required
to bring us into fellowship with him ; it is vain to imagine that
by eating anything one can enjoy communion with God. Our
Lord stands wholly outside the material world of sense, outside
things touched and tasted ; in relationship to him and him
alone, we can worship God. The writer has a mystical or
idealistic bent, to which the sacramental idea is foreign. He
never alludes to the eucharist ; the one sacrament he notices is
baptism. A ritual meal as the means of strengthening communion
with God through Christ does not appeal to him in the slightest
degree. It is not thus that God's χάρις is experienced.

The clue to v.[10] lies in the obvious fact that the θυσιαστήριον
and the σκηνή belong to the same figurative order. In our
spiritual or heavenly σκηνή, the real σκηνή of the soul, there is
indeed a θυσιαστήριον ἐξ οὗ (partitive ; cp. τὰ εἰς τοῦ ἱεροῦ ἐσθίου-

σιν, 1 Co 9¹³) φαγεῖν (emphatic by position) οὐκ ἔχουσιν ἐξουσίαν [1]
(1 Co 9⁴) οἱ τῇ σκηνῇ λατρεύοντες (λατρεύειν with dative as in 8⁵).
It makes no difference to the sense whether οἱ . . . λατρεύοντες
means worshippers (9⁹ 10²) or priests (8⁵), and the writer does not
allegorize θυσιαστήριον as Philo does (e.g. in de Leg. Alleg. i. 15, τῆς
καθαρᾶς καὶ ἀμιάντου φύσεως τῆς ἀναφερούσης τὰ ἄμωμα τῷ θεῷ,
αὕτη δὲ ἐστι τὸ θυσιαστήριον). His point is simply this, that the
Christian sacrifice, on which all our relationship to God depends,
is not one that involves or allows any connexion with a meal. To
prove how impossible such a notion is, he (v.¹¹) cites the ritual
regulation in Lv 16²⁷ for the disposal of the carcases of the two
animals sacrificed περὶ τῆς ἁμαρτίας (ὧν τὸ αἷμα εἰσηνέχθη ἐξιλάσ-
ασθαι ἐν τῷ ἁγίῳ ἐξοίσουσιν αὐτὰ ἔξω τῆς παρεμβολῆς καὶ κατακαύσου-
σιν αὐτὰ ἐν πυρί). For a moment the writer recalls his main argument
in chs. 7–10; in v.¹⁰ Christ is regarded as the victim or sacrifice
(cp. προσενεχθείς in 9²⁸), but here the necessities of the case
involve the activity of the Victim. Διὸ καὶ Ἰησοῦς κτλ. (v.¹²).
The parallel breaks down at one point, of course; his body was
not burned up.[2] But the real comparison lies in ἔξω τῆς πύλης
(sc. τῆς παρεμβολῆς, as Ex 32²⁶· ²⁷). The Peshitto and 436 make
the reference explicit by reading πόλεως, which seems to have
been known to Tertullian (adv. Jud. 14, "extra civitatem"). The
fact that Jesus was crucified outside Jerusalem influenced the
synoptic transcripts of the parable in Mk 12⁸ = Mt 21³⁹ = Lk 20¹⁵.
Mark's version, ἀπέκτειναν αὐτὸν καὶ ἐξέβαλον αὐτὸν ἔξω τοῦ ἀμπελῶνος, was altered into (ἐξέβαλον) ἐκβαλόντες αὐτὸν ἔξω τοῦ ἀμπελῶνος
(καὶ) ἀπέκτειναν. Crucifixion, like other capital punishments, in
the ancient world was inflicted outside a city. To the writer this
fact seems intensely significant, rich in symbolism. So much so
that his mind hurries on to use it, no longer as a mere confirmation of the negative in v.¹⁰, but as a positive, fresh call to unworldliness. All such sensuous ideas as those implied in sacrificial
meals mix up our religion with the very world from which we
ought, after Jesus, to be withdrawing. We meet Jesus outside
all this, not inside it. In highly figurative language (v.¹³), he
therefore makes a broad appeal for an unworldly religious fellowship, such as is alone in keeping with the χάρις of God in Jesus
our Lord.

Τοίνυν (beginning a sentence as in Lk 20²⁸ τοίνυν ἀπόδοτε κτλ.,
instead of coming second in its classical position), let us join
Jesus ἔξω τῆς παρεμβολῆς, for he is living. The thought of the

---

[1] The omission of ἐξουσίαν by D* M and the Old Latin does not affect the
sense; ἔχειν then has the same meaning as in 6¹³.

[2] The blood, not the body, of the victim mattered in the atonement ritual.
Hence, in our writer's scheme of thought, as Peake observes, "while he fully
recognises the fact of the Resurrection of Christ, he can assign it no place in
his argument or attach to it any theological significance."

metaphor is that of Paul's admonition μὴ συνσχηματίζεσθε τῷ αἰῶνι τούτῳ (Ro 12²), and the words τὸν ὀνειδισμὸν αὐτοῦ φέροντες recall the warnings against false shame (11²⁶ 12²), just as the following (v.¹⁴) reason, οὐ γὰρ ἔχομεν ὧδε (in the present outward order of things) μένουσαν ¹ πόλιν ἀλλὰ τὴν μέλλουσαν ἐπιζητοῦμεν recalls the ideas of 11¹⁰· ¹⁴⁻¹⁶. The appeal echoes that of 4¹¹ σπουδάσωμεν οὖν εἰσελθεῖν εἰς ἐκείνην τὴν κατάπαυσιν. It is through the experiences of an unsettled and insulted life that Christians must pass, if they are to be loyal to their Lord. That is, the writer interprets ἔξω τῆς παρεμβολῆς figuratively ("Egrediamur et nos a commercio mundi huius," Erasmus). Philo had already done so (cp. specially *quod. det. pot.* 44), in a mystical sense : μακρὰν διοικίζει τοῦ σωματικοῦ στρατοπέδου, μόνως ἂν οὕτως ἐλπίσας ἱκέτης καὶ θεραπευτὴς ἔσεσθαι τέλειος θεοῦ. Similarly in *de Ebrietate*, 25, commenting on Ex 33⁷, he explains that by ἐν τῷ στρατοπέδῳ (= ἐν τῇ παρεμβολῇ) Moses meant allegorically ἐν τῷ μετὰ σώματος βίῳ, the material interests of the worldly life which must be forsaken if the soul is to enjoy the inward vision of God. Such is the renunciation which the writer here has in view. It is the thought in 2 Clem. 5¹ (ὅθεν, ἀδελφοί, καταλείψαντες τὴν παροικίαν τοῦ κόσμου τούτου ποιήσωμεν τὸ θέλημα τοῦ καλέσαντος ἡμᾶς, καὶ μὴ φοβηθῶμεν ἐξελθεῖν ἐκ τοῦ κόσμου τούτου) and 6⁵ (οὐ δυνάμεθα τῶν δύο φίλοι εἶναι· δεῖ δὲ ἡμᾶς τούτῳ ἀποταξαμένους ἐκείνῳ χρᾶσθαι). Only, our author weaves in the characteristic idea of the shame which has to be endured in such an unworldly renunciation.

The next exhortation in v.¹⁵ (ἀναφέρωμεν) catches up ἐξερχώμεθα, as δι' αὐτοῦ carries on πρὸς αὐτόν. For once applying sacrificial language to the Christian life, he reminds his readers again of the sacrifice of thanksgiving. The phrase καρπὸν χειλέων explains (τοῦτ' ἔστιν) the sense in which θυσία αἰνέσεως is to be taken ; it is from the LXX mistranslation (καρπὸν χειλέων) of Hos 14³ where the true text has פָּרִים (bullocks) instead of פְּרִי (fruit). In ὁμολογούντων τῷ ὀνόματι αὐτοῦ, ὁμολογεῖν is used in the sense of ἐξομολογεῖσθαι by an unusual ² turn of expression. The ὄνομα means, as usual, the revealed personality. Probably there is an unconscious recollection of Ps 54⁸ (ἐξομολογήσομαι τῷ ὀνόματί σου); θυσία αἰνέσεως ³ is also from the psalter (*e.g.* 50¹⁴· ²³). Ἀναφέρειν elsewhere in the NT is only used of spiritual sacrifices in the parallel passage 1 P 2⁵ ἀνενέγκαι πνευματικὰς θυσίας εὐπροσδέκτους θεῷ διὰ Ἰησοῦ Χριστοῦ. We have no sacri-

---

¹ In the sense of Aeneas (Verg. *Aen.* iii. 85, 86, "da moenia fessis | et genus et mansuram urbem "). Note the assonance μένουσαν . . . μέλλουσαν.

² But ὁμολογεῖν τινι occurs in 3 Es 4⁶⁰ 5⁵⁸ (A).

³ In the LXX ἐξομολόγησις is generally preferred to αἴνεσις as an equiva-lent for תּוֹדָה.

ficial meals, the writer implies ; we do not need them. Nor have
we any sacrifices—except spiritual ones. (The οὖν after δι' αὐτοῦ,
which אᶜ A C Dᶜ M vg syrʰᵏˡ boh arm eth Orig. Chrys. etc. retain, is omitted by א* D* P Ψ vt syrᵛᵍ; but א* D* om. οὖν also
1 Co 6⁷, as D in Ro 7²⁵). The thought of 12²⁸ is thus expanded,
with the additional touch that thankfulness to God is inspired
by our experience of Jesus (δι' αὐτοῦ, as Col 3¹⁷ εὐχαριστοῦντες τῷ
θεῷ πατρὶ δι' αὐτοῦ); the phrase is a counterpart of διὰ τοῦ
ἀρχιερέως in v.¹¹. This thank-offering is to be made διὰ παντὸς
(sc. χρόνου), instead of at stated times, for, whatever befalls us, we
owe God thanks and praise (cp. 1 Th 5¹⁶). The Mishna (cp.
Berachoth 5⁴) declares that he must be silenced who only calls
upon God's name with thankfulness in the enjoyment of good
(Berachoth 5⁸ הָאוֹמֵר . . . עַל טוֹב יִזָּכֵר שְׁמֶךָ מוֹדִים מוֹדִים מְשַׁתְּקִין אוֹתוֹ).

The religious idea of thanksgiving was prominent in several quarters.
According to Fronto (Loeb ed. i. p. 22) thank-offerings were more acceptable
to the gods than sin-offerings, as being more disinterested : μάντεων δὲ παῖδές
φασιν καὶ τοῖς θεοῖς ἡδίους εἶναι θυσιῶν τὰς χαριστηρίους ἢ τὰς μειλιχίους.
Philo had taught (de Plant. 30) that εὐχαριστία is exceptionally sacred, and
that towards God it must be an inward sacrifice : θεῷ δὲ οὐκ ἔνεστι γνησίως
εὐχαριστῆσαι δι' ὧν νομίζουσιν οἱ πολλοὶ κατασκευῶν ἀναθημάτων θυσιῶν—οὐδὲ
γὰρ σύμπας ὁ κόσμος ἱερὸν ἀξιόχρεων ἂν γένοιτο πρὸς τὴν τούτου τιμήν—ἀλλὰ δι'
ἐπαίνων καὶ ὕμνων, οὐχ οὓς ἡ γεγωνὸς ᾄσεται φωνή, ἀλλὰ οὓς ὁ ἀειδὴς καὶ
καθαρώτατος νοῦς ἐπηχήσει καὶ ἀναμέλψει. He proceeds (ibid. 33) to dwell
on the meaning of the name Judah, ὃς ἑρμηνεύεται κυρίῳ ἐξομολόγησις. Judah
was the last (Gn 29³⁵) son of Leah, for nothing could be added to praise of
God, nothing excels ὁ εὐλογῶν τὸν θεὸν νοῦς. This tallies with the well-known
rabbinic saying, quoted in Tanchuma, 55. 2 : "in the time of messiah all
sacrifices will cease, but the sacrifice of thanksgiving will not cease ; all
prayers will cease, but praises will not cease" (on basis of Jer 33¹ and Ps
56¹³). The praise of God as the real sacrifice of the pious is frequently noted
in the later Judaism (e.g. 2 Mac 10⁷).

In v.¹⁶ the writer notes the second Christian sacrifice of
charity. Εὐποιΐα, though not a LXX term, is common in
Hellenistic Greek, especially in Epictetus, e.g. Fragm. 15 (ed.
Schenk), ἐπὶ χρηστότητι καὶ εὐποιΐᾳ; Fragm. 45, οὐδὲν κρεῖσσον
. . . εὐποιΐας (where the context suggests "beneficence").
Κοινωνία in the sense of charity or contributions had been
already used by Paul (2 Co 9¹³ etc.). To share with others,
to impart to them what we possess, is one way of worshipping
God. The three great definitions of worship or religious service
in the NT (here, Ro 12¹·² and Ja 1²⁷) are all inward and
ethical; what lies behind this one is the fact that part of the
food used in ancient OT sacrifices went to the support of the
priests, and part was used to provide meals for the poor.
Charitable relief was bound up with the sacrificial system, for such
parts of the animals as were not burnt were devoted to these
beneficent purposes. An equivalent must be provided in our

spiritual religion, the writer suggests; if we have no longer any
animal sacrifices, we must carry on at any rate the charitable
element in that ritual. This is the force of μὴ ἐπιλανθάνεσθε.
Contributions, e.g., for the support of ἡγούμενοι, who were not
priests, were unknown in the ancient world, and had to be
explicitly urged as a duty (cp. 1 Co 9⁶⁻¹⁴). Similarly the needs
of the poor had to be met by voluntary sacrifices, by which
alone, in a spiritual religion, God could be satisfied—τοιαύταις
(perhaps including the sacrifice of praise as well as εὐποιία and
κοινωνία) θυσίαις εὐαρεστεῖται (cp. 11⁵·⁶ 12²⁸) ὁ θεός. This counsel
agrees with some rabbinic opinions (e.g. T. B. Sukkah, 59b : "he
who offers alms is greater than all sacrifices"). The special duty
of supporting the priesthood is urged in Sir 7³⁰ᶠ·, but our author
shows no trace of the theory that almsgiving in general was not
only superior to sacrifices but possessed atoning merit before
God (Sir 3¹⁴ ἐλεημοσύνη γὰρ πατρὸς οὐκ ἐπιλησθήσεται, καὶ ἀντὶ
ἁμαρτιῶν προσανοικοδομηθήσεταί σοι). In the later rabbinic
theology, prayer, penitence, the study of the Torah, hospitality,
charity, and the like were regarded as sacrifices equivalent to
those which had been offered when the temple was standing.
Thus Rabbi Jochanan b. Zakkai (cp. Schlatter's *Jochanan ben
Zakkai*, pp. 39 f.) consoled himself and his friends with the
thought, derived from Hos 6⁶, that in the practice of charity
they still possessed a valid sacrifice for sins; he voiced the
conviction also (e.g. b. baba bathra 10ᵇ) that charity (צדקה) won
forgiveness for pagans as the sin-offering did for Israel. In the
Ep. Barnabas (2⁷ᶠ·) the writer quotes Jer 7²²·²³ (Zec 8¹⁷) as a
warning to Christians against Jewish sacrifices (αἰσθάνεσθαι οὖν
ὀφείλομεν τὴν γνώμην τῆς ἀγαθωσύνης τοῦ πατρὸς ἡμῶν ὅτ' ἡμῖν
λέγει, θέλων ἡμᾶς μὴ ὁμοίως πλανωμένους ἐκείνοις ζητεῖν, πῶς
προσάγωμεν αὐτῷ), but he quotes Ps 51¹⁹ as the description of
the ideal sacrifice.

The tendency in some circles of the later Judaism to spiritualize sacrifice
in general and to insist on its motive and spirit is voiced in a passage like
Jth 16¹⁵ᶠ·:

> ὅρη γὰρ ἐκ θεμελίων σὺν ὕδασιν σαλευθήσεται,
> πέτραι δ' ἀπὸ προσώπου σου ὡς κηρὸς τακήσονται·
> ἔτι δὲ τοῖς φοβουμένοις σε σὺ εὐιλατεύεις αὐτοῖς·
> ὅτι μικρὸν πᾶσα θυσία εἰς ὀσμὴν εὐωδίας,
> καὶ ἐλάχιστον πᾶν στέαρ εἰς ὁλοκαύτωμά σοι·
> ὁ δὲ φοβούμενος τὸν κύριον μέγας διὰ παντός.

Also in a number of statements from various sources, of which that in *Ep.
Arist.* 234 (τὶ μέγιστόν ἐστι δόξης; ὁ δὲ εἶπε· τὸ τιμᾶν τὸν θεόν· τοῦτο δ' ἐστὶν
οὐ δώροις οὐδὲ θυσίαις, ἀλλὰ ψυχῆς καθαρότητι καὶ διαλήψεως ὁσίας) may be
cited as a fair specimen. The congruous idea of bloodless sacrifices was
common in subsequent Christianity. Thus the martyr Apollonius (*Acta
Apollonii*, 44; Conybeare's *Monuments of Early Christianity*, pp. 47-48)
tells the magistrate, "I expected . . . that thy heart would bear fruit, and

that thou wouldst worship God, the Creator of all, and unto Him continually offer thy prayers by means of compassion ; for compassion shown to men by men is a bloodless sacrifice and holy unto God." So Jerome's comment runs on Ps 15⁴ οὐ μὴ συναγάγω τὰς συναγωγὰς αὐτῶν ἐξ αἱμάτων. Συνάγων, φησὶν, συναγωγὰς ἐκ τῶν ἐθνῶν, οὐ δι' αἱμάτων ταύτας συνάξω· τοῦτ' ἔστιν, οὐ παρασκευάσω διὰ τῆς νομικῆς μοι προσέρχεσθαι λατρείας, δι' αἰνέσεως δὲ μᾶλλον καὶ τῆς ἀναμάκτου θυσίας (*Anecdota Maredsolana*, iii. 3. 123). Both in the Didache (14¹ κλάσατε ἄρτον καὶ εὐχαριστήσατε προσεξομολογησάμενοι τὰ παραπτώματα ὑμῶν, ὅπως καθαρὰ ἡ θυσία ὑμῶν ᾖ) and in Justin Martyr (*Dial.* 117, πάντας οὖν οἱ διὰ τοῦ ὀνόματος τούτου θυσίας, ἃς παρέδωκεν Ἰησοῦς ὁ Χριστὸς γίνεσθαι, τουτέστιν ἐπὶ τῇ εὐχαριστίᾳ τοῦ ἄρτου καὶ τοῦ ποτηρίου, τὰς ἐν παντὶ τόπῳ τῆς γῆς γινομένας ὑπὸ τῶν Χριστιανῶν, προλαβὼν ὁ θεὸς μαρτυρεῖ εὐαρέστους ὑπάρχειν αὐτῷ), the very prayers at the eucharist are called θυσίαι, but this belongs to a later stage, when the eucharist or love-feast became the rite round which collections for the poor, the sick, prisoners, and travelling visitors (vv.¹⁶·) gathered, and into which sacrificial language began to be poured (cp. Justin's *Apol.* i. 66, 67). In Πρὸς Ἑβραίους we find a simpler and different line of practical Christianity.

Now for a word on the living ἡγούμενοι of the community (v.¹⁷), including himself (vv.¹⁸· ¹⁹).

¹⁷ *Obey your leaders, submit to them ; for they* (αὐτοί) *are alive to the interests of your souls, as men who will have to account for their trust. Let their work be a joy to them and not a grief—which would be a loss to yourselves.*
¹⁸ *Pray for me, for I am sure I have a clean conscience ; my desire is in every way to lead an honest life.* ¹⁹ *I urge you to this* (*i.e.* to prayer) *all the more, that I may get back to you the sooner.*

The connexion of vv.¹⁷ᶠ· is not only with v.⁷, but with vv.⁸⁻¹⁶. It would be indeed a grief to your true leaders if you gave way to these ποικίλαι καὶ ξέναι doctrines, instead of following men who are really (this is the force of αὐτοί) concerned for your highest interests. Πείθεσθε (cp. Epict. Fragm. 27, τὸν προσομιλοῦντα . . . διασκοποῦ . . . εἰ μὲν ἀμείνονα, ἀκούειν χρὴ καὶ πείθεσθαι αὐτῷ) καὶ ὑπείκετε (ὑπείκω is not a LXX term); strong words but justified, for the λόγος τοῦ θεοῦ which Christian leaders preached meant authoritative standards of life for the community (cp. 1 Co 4¹⁷· ²¹ 14³⁷ etc.), inspired by the Spirit. Insubordination was the temptation at one pole, an overbearing temper (1 P 5³) the temptation at the other. Our author knows that, in the case of his friends, the former alone is to be feared. He does not threaten penalties for disobedience, however, as Josephus does (*c. Apionem*, ii. 194) for insubordination on the part of the Jewish laity towards a priest : ὁ δέ γε τούτῳ μὴ πειθόμενος ὑφέξει δίκην ὡς εἰς τὸν θεὸν αὐτὸν ἀσεβῶν. Rather, he singles out the highminded devotion of these leaders as an inducement to the rank and file to be submissive. Αὐτοὶ γὰρ ἀγρυπνοῦσιν ὑπὲρ τῶν ψυχῶν ὑμῶν, almost as Epictetus says of the true Cynic who zealously concerns himself with the moral welfare of men, ὑπερηγρύπνηκεν ὑπὲρ ἀνθρώπων (iii. 22. 95 ; he uses the verb once in its literal sense of a soldier having to keep watch through the night, iii. 24. 32).

The force of the phrase is flattened by the transference of ὑπὲρ τῶν ψυχῶν ὑμῶν to a position after ὡς λόγον ἀποδώσοντες (as A vg). The latter expression, ὡς (conscious that) λόγον ἀποδώσοντες (ὡς with fut. ptc. here only in NT), is used by Chrysostom, *de Sacerdotio*, iii. 18 (cp. vi. 1), to enforce a sense of ministerial responsibility (εἰ γὰρ τῶν οἰκείων πλημμελημάτων εὐθύνας ὑπέχοντες φρίττομεν, ὡς οὐ δυνησόμενοι τὸ πῦρ ἐκφυγεῖν ἐκεῖνο, τί χρὴ πείσεσθαι προσδοκᾶν τὸν ὑπὲρ τοσούτων ἀπολογεῖσθαι μέλλοντα;), but in Πρὸς Ἑβραίους the writer assumes that the ἡγούμενοι are doing and will do their duty. Any sadness which they may feel is due, not to a sense of their own shortcomings, but to their experience of wilfulness and error among their charges. Λόγον ἀποδιδόναι is more common in the NT than the equivalent λόγον διδόναι, which recurs often in Greek literature, *e.g.* in Plato's *Sympos.* 189b, πρόσεχε τὸν νοῦν καὶ οὕτως λέγε ὡς δώσων λόγον, or in the complaint of the Fayyum peasants (A.D. 207), who petition the local centurion that the disturbers of their work may be called to account: ἀξιοῦντες, ἐάν σοι δόξῃ, κελεῦσαι αὐτοὺς ἀχθῆναι ἐπὶ σε λόγον ἀποδώσοντας περὶ τούτου (*GCP.* i. 354[25. 26]). In Clem. Alex. *Quis div. salv.* 42, John says to the captain of the robbers, ἐγὼ Χριστῷ λόγον δώσω ὑπὲρ σοῦ.

The ἵνα clause (ἵνα μετὰ χαρᾶς τοῦτο ποιῶσιν καὶ μὴ στενάζοντες) goes back to πείθεσθε . . . ὑπείκετε. The members have it in their power to thwart and disappoint their ἡγούμενοι. Τοῦτο π. refers to ἀγρυπνοῦσιν, and the best comment on καὶ μὴ στενάζοντες is in Denny's hymn :

"O give us hearts to love like Thee,
  Like Thee, O Lord, to grieve
Far more for others' sins than all
  The wrongs that we receive."

The last four words, ἀλυσιτελὲς γὰρ ὑμῖν τοῦτο, form a rhetorical litotes, as when Pindar (*Olymp.* i. 53) remarks, ἀκέρδεια λέλογχεν θαμινὰ κακαγόρος. It would be a "sore loss" to them if their lives failed to answer the hopes and efforts of their ἡγούμενοι, hopes like those implied in 6[9] and 10[39]. Ἀλυσιτελές ("no profit") is probably used after λόγον ἀποδώσοντες with its sense of "reckoning." Compare the use of the adverb in Theophrastus, viii. 11 (οὐ γὰρ μόνον ψεύδονται ἀλλὰ καὶ ἀλυσιτελῶς ἀπαλλάττονσι), and the dry remark of Philo (*in Flaccum*, 6), speaking about the attempt of the Alexandrian anti-Semites to erect images in Jewish places of worship, when he says that Flaccus might have known ὡς οὐ λυσιτελὲς ἔθη πάτρια κινεῖν! The term lent itself to such effective under-statements, as in Philo's aphorism (*Fragments of Philo*, ed. J. Rendel Harris, p. 70) τὸ ἐπιορκεῖν ἀνόσιον καὶ ἀλυσιτελέστατον.

The next word (v.¹⁸) is about himself. Προσεύχεσθε (continue praying) περὶ (cp. 2 Mac 1⁶ καὶ νῦν ὧδε ἔσμεν προσευχόμενοι περὶ ὑμῶν) ἡμῶν (plural of authorship), πειθόμεθα (a modest confidence: "whatever some of you may think, I believe") γὰρ ὅτι καλὴν συνείδησιν ἔχομεν. He is conscious of a keen desire (θέλοντες as in 12¹⁷) to act in a straightforward, honest way; hence he can ask their prayers. Hence also they may feel confident and eager about praying for him. The writer chooses καλήν (cp. on v.⁹) instead of ἀγαθήν as his adjective for συνείδησιν, probably for the sake of assonance with the following καλῶς, perhaps also to avoid the hiatus after ὅτι. When he adds, ἐν πᾶσιν (here neuter) καλῶς θέλοντες ἀναστρέφεσθαι (a phrase which occurs in the Pergamos inscript. 459⁵ καλῶς καὶ ἐνδόξως ἀναστραφῆναι, in the 1st century B.C. inscription (Priene, 115⁵) ἀναστρεφόμενος ἐν πᾶσιν φιλ[ανθρώπως], and in Epict. iv. 4. 46, ἑορτὴν ἄγειν δύνασαι καθ' ἡμέραν, ὅτι καλῶς ἀνεστράφης ἐν τῷδε τῷ ἔργῳ, etc.), the language recalls that of 2 Co 1¹¹· ¹² where Paul appeals for the help of his readers' prayers and pleads his honesty of conscience (τὸ μαρτύριον τῆς συνειδήσεως ἡμῶν, ὅτι . . . ἀνεστράφημεν κτλ.). Perhaps the writer is conscious that his readers have been blaming him, attributing (say) his absence from them to unworthy motives, as in the case of Paul (e.g. 1 Th 2¹⁸, 2 Co 1¹⁷ᶠ·). This may be the feeling which prompts the protest here and the assurances in vv.¹⁹· ²³. "I am still deeply interested in you; my absence is involuntary; believe that."

Καί is inserted before περί by D vt Chrys. (possibly as a reminiscence of 1 Th 5²⁵), i.e. pray as well as obey ("et orate pro nobis," d); this would emphasize the fact that the writer belonged to the ἡγούμενοι. But the plural in v.¹⁸ is not used to show that the writer is one of the ἡγούμενοι mentioned in v.¹⁷, for whom the prayers of the community are asked. He was one of them; ἡμῶν here is the literary plural already used in 5¹¹ 6⁹· ¹¹. There are apt parallels in Cicero's de Officiis, ii. 24 ("Quem nos . . . e Graeco in Latinum convertimus. Sed toto hoc de genere, de quaerenda, de collocanda pecunia vellens etiam de utenda"), and OP. x. 1296 (the letter of a boy to his father), ποιῶ . . . φιλοπονοῦμεν καὶ ἀναψυχόμεν. Πειθόμεθα (πείθομαι 256. 1319. 2127) has been changed into πεποίθαμεν by κᶜ Cᶜ D Ψ W 6. 104. 263. 326 (Blass), probably because the latter ("we are confident") is stronger than πειθόμεθα, which (cp. Ac 26²⁶) only amounts to "we believe" (though implying "we are sure"). Retaining πειθόμεθα, A. Bischoff (Zeits. für die neut. Wiss. ix. 171 f.) evades the difficulty by altering the order of the words: προσεύχ. περὶ ἡμῶν· καλὴν γὰρ συν. ἔχομεν, ὅτι πειθόμεθα ἐν πᾶσιν κ. θ. ἀναστρέφεσθαι, i.e. taking ὅτι as "because."

As in Philem ²², the writer's return is dependent on his friends' prayers (v.¹⁹); specially (see p. 17) let them intercede with God for his speedy restoration to them, ἵνα τάχιον ἀποκατασταθῶ ὑμῖν (cp. OP. 1⁸¹ (A.D. 49–50) ἀποκατεστάθη μοι ὁ υἱός). Τάχιον may mean "the sooner" (i.e. than if you did not pray) or simply "soon" (as in v.²³, where, as in Hellenistic Greek, it has lost its comparative meaning). What detained the writer, we cannot tell. Apparently (v.[23]) it was not imprisonment.

A closing prayer and doxology, such as was not uncommon in epistles of the primitive church (e.g. 1 Th 5[23], 1 P 5[11]), now follows. Having asked his readers to pray for him, he now prays for them.

[20] *May the God of peace "who brought up" from the dead our Lord* (7[14]) *Jesus* (see p. lxiii), *"the" great "Shepherd of the sheep, with the blood of the eternal covenant,"* [21] *furnish you with everything that is good for the doing of his will, creating in your lives by Jesus Christ what is acceptable in his own sight! To him* (i.e. God) *be* (sc. εἴη) *glory for ever and ever. Amen.*

Ὁ θεὸς τῆς εἰρήνης means the God of saving bliss (see on 12[11]), εἰρήνη being taken in a sense like the full OT sense of the secure prosperity won by the messianic triumph over the hostile powers of evil (cp. 2[14] 7[2]). There is no special allusion here, as in Paul's use of the phrase (Ro 15[33], 2 Co 13[11] etc.), to friction in the community; the conflict is one in which God secures εἰρήνη for his People, a conflict with evil, not strife between members of the church. The method of this triumph is described in some OT phrases, which the writer uses quite apart from their original setting. The first quotation is from Is 63[11] ποῦ ὁ ἀναβιβάσας ἐκ τῆς γῆς τὸν ποιμένα τῶν προβάτων, which the writer applies to Jesus—his only reference to the resurrection (cp. on vv.[11. 12]). But there is no need (with Blass) to follow Chrysostom in reading τῆς γῆς here for νεκρῶν. With ἀναγεῖν in this sense, ἐκ νεκρῶν (so Ro 10[7]) or some equivalent (ἐξ ᾅδου, Ps 30[4], Wis 16[13], Joseph. *Ant.* vi. 14. 2) is much more natural. In τὸν ποιμένα τῶν προβάτων τὸν μέγαν, ὁ μέγας is applied to him as in 4[14] 10[21]. The figure of the ποιμήν, which never occurs in Paul, plays no rôle in our author's argument as it does in 1 Peter (2[25] 5[4]); he prefers ἱερεύς or ἀρχηγός, and even here he at once passes to the more congenial idea of the διαθήκη. Jesus is the great Shepherd, as he has made himself responsible for the People, identifying himself with them at all costs, and sacrificing his life in order to save them for God. But as death never occurs in the OT description of the divine shepherd, not even in the 23rd Psalm, the writer blends with his quotation from Isaiah another—ἐν αἵματι διαθήκης αἰωνίου, a LXX phrase from Zech 9[11] (ἐν αἵματι διαθήκης σου ἐξαπέστειλας δεσμίους σου), Is 55[3] (διαθήσομαι ὑμῖν διαθήκην αἰώνιον), etc. Ἐν αἵματι διαθήκης αἰωνίου goes with ἀναγαγών, not with τὸν ποιμένα, in which case τόν would need to be prefixed to the phrase. Jesus was raised to present his blood as the atoning sacrifice which mediated the διαθήκη (9[11. 24f.]). To the resurrection (cp. on v.[12]) is thus ascribed what elsewhere in the epistle is ascribed to the εἰσελθεῖν εἰς τὰ ἅγια. But as the stress falls on αἰωνίου, then more is implied than that apart from the αἷμα no διαθήκη could have been instituted. In reality the thought resembles that of 9¹⁴ (ὃς διὰ πνεύματος αἰωνίου ἑαυτὸν προσήνεγκεν . . . καθαριεῖ τὴν συνείδησιν ἡμῶν . . . εἰς τὸ λατρεύειν θεῷ ζῶντι), where εἰς τὸ λατρεύειν θεῷ corresponds to εἰς τὸ ποιῆσαι τὸ θέλημα αὐτοῦ below ; ἔν κτλ. is "equipped with," not "in virtue of." This interpretation is in line with the author's argument in chs. 7–10. "Videtur mihi apostolus hoc belle, Christum ita resurrexisse a mortuis, ut mors tamen eius non sit abolita, sed aeternum vigorem retineat, ac si dixisset: Deus filium suum excitavit, sed ita ut sanguis, quem semel in morte fudit, ad sanctionem foederis aeterni post resurrectionem vigeat fructumque suum proferat perinde ac si semper flueret" (Calvin). In καταρτίσαι (the aor. optative)[1] κτλ., there is a parallel to the thought of Ph 2¹³. Εἰς τὸ ποιῆσαι τὸ θέλημα αὐτοῦ recalls the language of 10³⁶, and διὰ Ἰησοῦ Χριστοῦ goes with ποιῶν : the power of God in our lives as for our lives (v.²⁰) works through the person of Jesus Christ. To take διὰ Ἰ. Χ. with τὸ εὐάρεστον ἐνώπιον αὐτοῦ yields an unobjectionable sense, corresponding to the thought of v.¹⁵. But τὸ . . . αὐτοῦ stands quite well by itself (cf. 1 Jn 3²²).

The writer makes no such use of the shepherd and flock metaphor as, *e.g.*, Philo had done. The Jewish thinker (*Vit. Mos.* i. 11) argues that the calling of a shepherd is the best preparation for anyone who is to rule over men ; hence "kings are called *shepherds of their people*" as a title of honour. He also interprets the sheep as the symbol of a nature which is capable of improvement (*de sacrif. Abel.* 34, προκοπῆς δὲ πρόβατον, ὡς καὶ αὐτὸ δηλοῖ τοὔνομα, σύμβολον). The classical habit of describing kings as shepherds of their people would help to make the metaphor quite intelligible to readers of non-Jewish origin. Compare, *e.g.*, the saying of Cyrus (Xenophon, *Cyropaedia*, viii. 2. 14), that a good shepherd resembled a good king, τὸν τε γὰρ νομέα χρῆναι ἔφη εὐδαίμονα τὰ κτήνη ποιοῦντα χρῆσθαι αὐτοῖς, ἡ δὴ προβάτων εὐδαιμονία, τόν τε βασιλέα ὡσαύτως εὐδαίμονας πόλεις καὶ ἀνθρώπους ποιοῦντα χρῆσθαι αὐτοῖς.

Παντί was soon furnished with the homiletic addition of ἔργῳ (C K M P syr sah arm eth Chrys. Thdt. etc.), or even ἔργῳ καὶ λόγῳ (A, from 2 Th 2¹⁷). Ποιῶν has either αὐτῷ (א* A C* 33* 1288 boh) or ἑαυτῷ (Greg. Nyss.) or αὐτός (d 1912) prefixed. Hort, admitting that "it is impossible to make sense of αὐτῷ" (B. Weiss, Blass=ἑαυτῷ), maintains that αὐτός is original. It is a homiletic insertion, out of which αὐτῷ arose by corruption. Ἡμῖν (א D M Ψ 33. 104. 181. 326. 917. 927. 1288. 1739. 1912, etc. syrᵛᵍ sah boh arm) is merely an error for ὑμῖν, due to the preceding ἡμῶν.

A personal postscript (vv.²²⁻²⁴) is now added, as 1 P 5¹²⁻¹⁴ after 5¹⁰. ¹¹.

²² *I appeal to you, brothers* (3¹. ¹² 10¹⁹), *to bear with this appeal of mine. It is but a short letter.*

---

[1] This lonely occurrence of the optative points to its tendency after the LXX to disappear ; thus, apart from μὴ γένοιτο, it only occurs once in a writer like Epictetus (iii. 5. 11).

[23] *You must understand that our brother Timotheus is now free. If he comes soon, he and I will see you together.* [24] *Salute all your leaders and all the saints. The Italians salute you.* [25] *Grace be with you all. Amen.*

The Timotheus referred to (in v.[23]) is probably the Timotheus who had been a colleague of Paul. The other allusions have nothing to correspond with them in the data of the NT. But there is no ground for supposing that vv.[22-25] were added, either by the writer himself (Wrede) or by those who drew up the canon, in order to give a Pauline appearance to the document (see Introd., pp. xxviii f.). Seeberg's reasons for regarding vv.[22-25] as a fragment of some other note by the same writer are that 23[b] implies not a church but a small group of Christians, and that vv.[18, 23] presuppose different situations; neither reason is valid. The style and contents are equally unfavourable to Perdelwitz's theory, that vv.[22-25] were added *brevi manu* by some one who wrote out a copy of the original λόγος παρακλήσεως and forwarded it to an Italian church.

In v.[22] ἀνέχεσθε, for which ἀντέχεσθε (J. Pricaeus apud Tit 1[9]) is a needless conjecture, takes a genitive (as in 2 Ti 4[3] τῆς ὑγιαινούσης διδασκαλίας οὐκ ἀνέξονται, and in Philo, *quod omnis probus*, 6, καὶ πῶς πατρὸς μὲν ἢ μητρὸς ἐπιταγμάτων παῖδες ἀνέχονται, γνώριμοι δὲ ὧν ἂν ὑφηγηταὶ διακελεύωνται). It has been flattened into ἀνέχεσθαι (infinitive as in 1 P 2[11]) by D* Ψ vg arm 181. 436. 1288. 1311. 1873, etc. (Blass). A written homily may be like a speech (Ac 13[15]), a λόγος τῆς παρακλήσεως (cp. on 12[5]); παράκλησις echoes παρακαλέω He is not the only early Christian writer who mildly suggested that he had not written at undue length (cp. *e.g.* 1 P 5[12] δι᾿ ὀλίγων ἔγραψα, παρακαλῶν κτλ.; Barn 1[5, 8]) Καὶ γὰρ ("etenim" as 4[2]) διὰ βραχέων (*sc.* λόγων) ἐπέστειλα[1] (epistolary aorist) ὑμῖν. Διὰ βραχέων was a common phrase in this connexion; *e.g.* Lucian's *Toxaris*, 56 (πειστέον καὶ ταῦτά σοι νομοθετοῦντι καὶ διὰ βραχέων λεκτέον, μὴ καὶ κάμῃς ἡμῖν τῇ ἀκοῇ συμπερινοστῶν). Πρὸς Ἑβραίους may be read aloud easily in one hour. The writer has had a good deal to say (πολύς, 5[11]), and he has now said it. Not I hope, he adds pleasantly, at too great length ! As for the δυσερμήνευτος λέγειν, that is another question which he does not raise here. He is not pleading for a patient reading, because he has had to compress his argument into a short space, which makes it hard to follow, owing to its highly condensed character. What he does appear to anticipate is the possibility of his readers resenting the length at which he has

---

[1] For ἐπέστειλα (here as in Ac 15[20] 21[25]; Theophr. 24[18] ἐπιστέλλων μὴ γράφειν κτλ. = "write," "send a letter"), see Laqueur's *Quaest. Epigraph. et Papyr. Selectae*, 16 f. (ἐπιστέλλειν = "communicare aliquid cum aliquo sive per hominem sive per epistolam").

written. When the younger Pliny returned a book to Tacitus, with some criticisms upon its style and matter, he said he was not afraid to do so, since it was those most deserving praise whc accepted criticism patiently ("neque enim ulli patientius reprehunduntur quam qui maxime laudari merentur," *Epp.* vii. 20). The author of Πρὸς Ἑβραίους might have taken this line, for he has done justice to the good qualities of his friends (*e.g.* 6⁹ᶠ· 10³⁹ 13¹ᶠ·), even in reproving them for backwardness and slowness. But he prefers to plead that his words have not been long; his readers surely cannot complain of being wearied by the length of his remarks. Not long before, Seneca had made the same kind of observation to Lucilius (*Ep.* xxxviii. 1) about short letters being more effective than lengthy discussions. "Merito exigis ut hoc inter nos epistularum commercium frequentemus, plurimum proficit sermo, quia minutatim inrepit animo . . . aliquando utendum est et illis, ut ita dicam, concionibus, ubi qui dubitat inpellendus est: ubi vero non hoc agendum est ut velit discere sed ut discat, ad haec submissiora uerba ueniendum est. facilius intrant et haerent: nec enim multis opus est, sed efficacibus." But Seneca's practice was not always up to his theory in this respect. His Stoic contemporary Musonius Rufus gave examples as well as precepts of brevity, which were more telling (*e.g.* ὅστις δὲ πανταχοῦ δεῖται ἀποδείξεως καὶ ὅπου σαφῆ τὰ πράγματά ἐστιν, ἢ διὰ πολλῶν ἀποδείκνυσθαι βούλεται αὐτῷ τὰ δι᾽ ὀλίγων δυνάμενα, παντάπασιν ἄτοπος καὶ δυσμαθής, ed. Hense, pp. 1, 2). The literary critic Demetrius considered that the length of a letter should be carefully regulated (τὸ δὲ μέγεθος συνεστάλθω τῆς ἐπιστολῆς, *De Elocut.* 228); letters that were too long and stilted in expression became mere treatises, συγγράμματα, as in the case of many of Plato's, whereas the true ἐπιστολή, according to Demetrius (*ibid.* 231), should be φιλοφρόνησις in a brief compass (σύντομος). Which would apply to Πρὸς Ἑβραίους. Erasmus comments: "Scripsi paucis, ut ipse vos brevi visurus." He may have, but he does not say so.

In v.²³ γινώσκετε is imperative; he is conveying a piece of information. See, *e.g.*, *Tebt. P.* 37² (73 B.C.) γίνωσκε Κεφαλᾶν . . . προσεληλυθέναι Δημητρίῳ: *ibid.* 12² (118 B.C.) 36² 56⁵. The construction with the participle is common (*e.g.* Lk 8⁴⁶); you must understand τὸν ἀδελφὸν ἡμῶν (omitted by ℵᶜ Dᵇ· ᶜ K P Ψ 6 Chrys. etc.) Τιμόθεον ἀπολελυμένον, *i.e.* "is (set) free," not necessarily from prison. The general sense, ranging from "is free" to "has started," may be illustrated, *e.g.*, from the application of a woman to leave Alexandria via Pharos (*OP.* 1271⁴· ⁵, iii A.D. : ἀξιῶ γράψαι σε τῷ ἐπιτρόπῳ τῆς Φάρου ἀπολῦσαι με κατὰ τὸ ἔθος), or from *BGU.* i. 27¹²⁻¹⁵ (καθ᾽ ἡμέραν προσδεχόμ[ε]θα διμισσωρίαν ὥστε ἕως σήμερον μηδέναν ἀπολελύσθαι τῶν μετὰ σίτου),

where ἀ. = "has set out," as in Ac 28²⁵ (ἀπελύοντο). The interpretation of the next words μεθ᾽ οὗ ἐὰν τάχιον ἔρχηται ὄψομαι ὑμᾶς
depends upon whether Timotheus is supposed to join the writer
or to journey straight to the community addressed. In the
latter case, the writer, who hopes to be coming soon (v.¹⁹)
himself, looks forward to meeting him there. In the former
case, they will travel together. It is natural to assume that when
the writer sent this message, Timotheus was somewhere else, and
that he was expected ere long to reach the writer. For ὄψομαι =
visit, see 3 Jn ¹⁴ ἐλπίζω δὲ εὐθέως ἰδεῖν σε, etc. Ἐὰν τάχιον
ἔρχηται may mean either, "as soon as he comes," or "if he
comes soon." The latter suits the situation implied in v.¹⁹
better. The writer (in v.¹⁹) asks the prayers of his readers, that
some obstacle to his speedy return may be removed. If this
obstacle were the hindrance that kept Timotheus from joining
him on a journey which they had already planned to the church
(Riggenbach), he would have said, "Pray for Timotheus, I
cannot leave for you till he rejoins me." But the idea is : as
the writer is rejoining his friends soon (he hopes), he will be
accompanied by Timotheus, should the latter arrive before he
has to start. Written advice is all very well, but he hopes soon
to follow up this λόγος παρακλήσεως with personal intercourse,
like Seneca in *Ep.* vi. 5 ("plus tamen tibi et uiua vox et conuictus
quam oratio proderit. in rem praesentem uenias oportet, primum
quia homines amplius oculis quam auribus credunt, deinde quia
longum iter est per praecepta, breue et efficax per exempla").

The greeting comes as usual last (v.²⁴). Ἀσπάσασθε κτλ. is
an unusual turn, however ; the homily was evidently sent to the
community, who are told to greet all their ἡγούμενοι. This finds
its nearest parallel in Paul's similar injunction (Ro 16³ᶠ·) to the
Ephesian Christians to salute this and that eminent member of
their circle. Still, no other NT church is bidden to salute its
leaders ; and though the writer plainly wishes to reinforce his
counsel in v.¹⁷, the πάντας suggests that the persons addressed
were "part of the whole church of a large city . . . a congregation attached to some household" (Zahn) ; they are to convey
the writer's greetings to all the leaders of the larger local church—
and to all their fellow-members (καὶ πάντας τοὺς ἁγίους being more
intelligible, in the light of a passage like Ph 4²¹ ἀσπάσασθε πάντα
ἅγιον). To his personal greetings he now adds greetings from some
Italians. In οἱ ἀπὸ τῆς Ἰταλίας, ἀπό may have its usual sense of
"domiciled at" (practically = ἐν), as, *e.g.*, in *OP.* i. 81 (A.D. 49–50),
where τῶν ἀπ᾽ Ὀξυρύγχων means "the inhabitants of Oxyrhynchus," or in Πλήνι . . . ἀπὸ Φμαῦ, *i.e.* at Phmau (ostracon of
A.D. 192, quoted in Deissmann's *Light from the East*, p. 186).
If it thus means residents in Italy, the writer is in Italy

himself. But οἱ ἀπὸ τῆς Ἰταλίας, on the analogy of Ac 21²⁷ (οἱ ἀπὸ τῆς Ἀσίας Ἰουδαῖοι), might equally well mean Italians resident for the time being outside Italy; in this case the writer, who is also abroad, is addressing some Italian community, to which their countrymen forward greetings. Grammatically, either rendering is possible, and there is no tradition to decide the question. Perhaps οἱ ἀπὸ τῆς Ἰταλίας is more natural, however, as a description of some Italian Christians abroad who chanced to be in the same locality as the writer and who take this opportunity of sending their greetings by him to an Italian community. If the writer was in Italy, we should have expected πάντες οἱ ἀπὸ τῆς Ἰταλίας, considering the size of Italy and the scattered Christian communities there at this period.

The final benediction, ἡ χάρις (*sc.* ἔστω or εἴη) μετὰ πάντων ὑμῶν (Tit 3¹⁵, 2 Ti 4²²) has a liturgical ἀμήν, which is omitted by ℵ* W fuld sah 33; the homily was, of course, intended to be read aloud at worship.

INDEXES.

I. INDEX GRAECITATIS.

Words marked * are peculiar in NT to Hebrews.

,,   ,,   † occur only in quotations from LXX.

,,   ,,   ‡ are peculiar in NT to Luke (gospel, Acts) and Hebrews.

,,   ,,   [Paul] [T] [P] are only used elsewhere in NT by Paul, or in the Pastoral Epistles, or in 1 Peter.

‡ Ἀαρών, 5^4, 7^{11}, 9^4.

Ἄβελ, 11^4, 12^{24}.

Ἀβραάμ, 2^{16}, 6^{13}, $7^{1. 2. 4. 5. 6. 9}$, $11^{8. 17}$.

ἀγαθός, 13^{21} : τὰ ἀγαθά, 9^{11}, 10^1.

† ἀγαλλίασις, 1^9.

† ἀγαπάω, 1^9, 12^6.

ἀγάπη, 6^{10}, 10^{24}.

ἀγαπητός (ἀγαπητοί), 6^9.

ἄγγελος, $1^{4. 5. 6.}$ (LXX) $7.$ (LXX) 13, $2^{2. 5. 7.}$ (LXX) $9. 16$, 12^{22}, 13^2.

* ἀγενεαλόγητος, 7^3.

ἀγιάζω, 2^{11}, 9^{13}, $10^{10. 14. 29}$, 13^{12}.

ἀγιασμός, 12^{14}.

ἅγιος, 3^1 (Christians) : οἱ ἅγιοι, 6^{10}, 13^{24} : (τὰ) ἅγια, 8^2, $9^{2. 3. 8. 12. 24. 25}$, 10^{19} 13^{11} : πνεῦμα ἅγιον, 2^4, 3^7, 6^4, 9^8, 10^{15} : τὸ ἅγιον, 9^1.

ἀγιότης, 12^{10} [Paul ?].

‡ ἄγκυρα, 6^{19}.

ἀγνοέω, 5^2.

* ἀγνόημα, 9^7.

ἀγρυπνέω (ὑπέρ), 13^{17}.

ἄγω, 2^{10}.

ἀγών, 12^1 [Paul].

ἀδελφός, $2^{11. 12.}$ (LXX) 17, $3^{1. 12}$, 7^5, 8^{11} (LXX), 10^{19}, $13^{22. 23}$.

† ἀδικία (1^9?), 8^{12}.

ἄδικος, 6^{10}.

ἀδόκιμος, 6^8 [Paul].

ἀδύνατος (ἀδύνατον), $6^{4. 18}$, 10^4, 11^6.

† ἀεί, 3^{10}.

ἀθετέω, 10^{28}.

* ἀθέτησις, 7^{18}, 9^{26}.

* ἄθλησις, 10^{32}.

* αἴγειος, 11^{37}.

‡ Αἰγύπτιος, 11^{29}.

Αἴγυπτος, 3^{16}, 8^9, $11^{26. 27}$.

αἰδώς, 12^{28} (s.v.l) [T].

αἷμα, 2^{14}, $9^{7. 12. 13. 14. 18. 19. 20}$ (LXX) $21. 22. 25$, $10^{4. 19. 29}$, 11^{28}, $12^{4. 24}$, $13^{11. 12. 20}$ (LXX).

* αἱματεκχυσία, 9^{22}.

*† αἴνεσις, 13^{15}.

αἱρεῖσθαι (ἑλόμενος), 11^{25} [Paul].

* αἰσθητήριον, 5^{14}.

αἰσχύνη, 12^2.

αἰτία, 2^{11}.

‡ αἴτιος, 5^9.

αἰών, 1^8 (LXX), 5^6 (LXX), $6^{5. 20}$, $7^{17.}$ (LXX) 21 (LXX), $7^{24. 28}$: οἱ αἰῶνες, 1^2, 9^{26}, 11^3, $13^{8. 21}$.

αἰώνιος, 13^{20} (διαθήκη), 9^{15} (κληρονομία), 6^2 (κρῖμα), 9^{12} (λύτρωσις), 9^{14} (πνεῦμα), 5^9 (σωτηρία).

ἄκακος, 7^{26} [Paul].

ἄκανθα, 6^8.

* ἀκατάλυτος, 7^{16}.

* ἀκλινής, 10^{23}.

ἀκοή, 4^2, 5^{11}.

ἀκούω, $2^{1. 3}$, $3^{7.}$ (LXX) $15. 16$, $4^{2. 7}$ (LXX), 12^{19}.

* ἀκροθίνιον, 7^4.

† ἄκρος, 11^{21} (τὸ ἄκρον, LXX).

ἀλήθεια, 10^{26}.

ἀληθινός, 8^2, 9^{24}, 10^{22}.

250 INDEXES

ἀσπάζομαι, 11^13, 13^24.
†‡ ἀστεῖος, 11^23.
‡ ἄστρον, 11^12.
ἀσφαλής, 6^19.
αὐτά, 2^10, 9^23.
αὐτή, 4^6, 6^7, 7^11. 18, 9^5, 11^4. 11, 12^11. 17.
αὐτός (αὐτά, αὐτοῖς, αὐτοῦ, αὐτῷ, αὐτῶν), 1^3. 4. 6. 7. 8. 11. 12 (LXX), 2^6. (LXX) 7. (LXX) 11, 3^2. 3. 10 (LXX), 4^6. 8, 5^5. 7, 8^8. 9. (LXX) 10, 9^23, 10^16, 11^5. 6. 11. 16. 19, 12^5. (LXX) 10. 17, 13^3. 13. 17.
αὐτός, 1^5. (LXX)^12, 2^14. 18, 4^10, 5^2, 10^12, 13^5. 8 : αὐτοί, 1^11 (LXX), 3^10(LXX), 8^9. (LXX) 10 (LXX), 13^3. 17 : αὐτόν, 2^6. (LXX) 7 (LXX), 3^2. 3, 5^5. 7, 7^1. 21. 24, 9^24. 26. 28, 11^5. 6. 19, 13^13 : αὐτούς, 1^4. 12 (LXX), 2^11, 4^8, 8^9. (LXX) 10 (LXX), 10^16 (LXX), 11^16 : αὐτά, 9^23 : αὐτάς, 10^11, 11^13 : αὐτή, 11^11 ; αὐτήν, 4^6, 5^11, 10^1, 12^17 : αὐτῆς, 6^7, 7^18, 9^5, 11^4. 9, 12^11 : αὐτοῦ, 1^3, 2^6. (LXX) 8 (LXX), 3^2. (LXX) 5. 6. 7. (LXX) 15 (LXX), 4^1. 7. (LXX) 10. 13, 6^10, 7^25, 10^13 (LXX), 11^4. 5, 12^5. (LXX) 10, 13^13. 15. 21 : αὐτῶν (2^10, 7^5. 6. 25, 11^16. 28. 35 : LXX=8^9. 10. 11. 12, 10^16. 17) : αὐτῷ, 1^5. (LXX) 6 (LXX), 2^8. 10. 13 (LXX), 4^11, 5^9, 7^10, 10^38 (LXX), 12^2 : αὐτοῖς, 6^16, 8^8. 10 (LXX), 11^16, 12^10. 19 : αὐτῇ, 7^11 : αὐταῖς, 10^13 : αὐτό, 9^19.
ἀφαιρέω, 10^4.
* ἀφανής, 4^13.
* ἀφανισμός, 8^13.
ἄφεσις, 9^22, 10^18.
ἀφίημι, 2^8, 6^1.
ἀφιλάργυρος, 13^5 [T].
ἀφίστημι, 3^12.
* ἀφομοιόω, 7^3.
ἀφοράω, 12^2 [Paul].
ἄχρι, 4^12, 6^11, 3^13 (ἄχρις οὗ).

βαπτισμός, 6^2, 9^10.
* Βαράκ, 11^32.
βασιλεία, 1^8 (LXX), 11^33, 12^28.
βασιλεύς, 7^1. 2 (LXX), 11^23. 27.
βέβαιος, 2^2, 3^6. 14, 6^19, 9^17.
βεβαιόω, 2^3, 13^9.
βεβαίωσις, 6^16 [Paul].
βέβηλος, 12^16 [T].
† βιβλίον, 9^19, 10^7 (LXX).
βλαστάνω, 9^4.
βλέπω, 2^9, 3^12. 19, 10^25, 11^1. 37, 12^25.

‡ βοήθεια, 4^16.
βοηθέω, 2^18.
*† βοηθός, 13^6.
*† βολίς (s.v.l.), 12^20.
* βοτάνη, 6^7.
βουλή, 6^17.
βούλομαι, 6^17.
βραχύς, 2^7. (LXX) 19, 13^22.
βρῶμα, 9^10, 13^9.
βρῶσις, 12^16.

γάλα, 5^12. 13.
γάμος, 13^4.
γάρ (90 times).
* Γεδεών, 11^32.
† γενεά, 3^10.
* γενεαλογέω, 7^6.
γεννάω, 1^5 (LXX), 5^5 (LXX), 11^12 (?). 23.
γεύω, 2^9, 6^4. 5.
* γεωργέω, 6^7.
γῆ, 1^10 (LXX), 6^7, 8^4. 9 (LXX), 11^9. 13. 29. 38, 12^25. 26 (LXX).
γηράσκω, 8^13.
γίνομαι (30 times).
γινώσκω, 3^10 (LXX), 8^11 (LXX), 10^34, 13^23.
*† γνόφος, 12^18.
† γόνυ, 12^12.
† γράφω, 10^7.
γυμνάζω, 5^14, 12^11.
γυμνός, 4^13.
γυνή, 11^35.

δάκρυ, 5^7, 12^17.
* δάμαλις, 9^13.
Δανείδ, 4^7, 11^32.
δέ (67 times).
δέησις, 5^7.
δεῖ, 2^1, 9^26, 11^6.
† δεικνύω, 8^5.
* δεκάτη, 7^2. 4. 8. 9.
* δεκατόω, 7^6. 9.
δεξιός (ἐκ δεξιῶν), 1^13 (LXX), (ἐν δεξιᾷ), 1^3, 8^1, 10^12, 12^2.
* δέος (s.v.l.), 12^28.
* δέρμα, 11^37.
δέσμιος, 10^34, 13^3.
δεσμός, 11^36.
δεύτερος, 8^7, 9^3. 7. 28, 10^9.
δέχομαι, 11^31.
δηλόω, 9^8, 12^27 (of the Spirit [P]).
* δημιουργός, 11^10.
* δήπου, 2^16.
διά, with accusative (17 times).
with genitive (38 times).
διαβαίνω, 11^29

II. SUBJECTS AND AUTHORS.

III. QUOTATIONS OR REMINISCENCES OF THE OLD TESTAMENT.